HOSPITAL
INTERIOR
ARCHITECTURE

HOSPITAL INTERIOR ARCHITECTURE

CREATING HEALING ENVIRONMENTS FOR SPECIAL PATIENT POPULATIONS

JAIN MALKIN

VNR VAN NOSTRAND REINHOLD
New York

Copyright © 1992 by Van Nostrand Reinhold

Library of Congress Catalog Card Number 91-13803
ISBN 0-442-31897-9

Printed in Hong Kong by Excel Graphic Arts Company

Van Nostrand Reinhold
115 Fifth Avenue
New York, New York 10003

Chapman and Hall
2–6 Boundary Row
London, SE1 8HN, England

Thomas Nelson Australia
102 Dodds Street
South Melbourne 3205
Victoria, Australia

Nelson Canada
1120 Birchmount Road
Scarborough, Ontario MIK 5G4, Canada

16 15 14 13 12 11 10 9 8 7 6 5 4 3 2 1

Library of Congress Cataloging-in-Publication Data

Malkin, Jain
    Hospital interior architecture: creating healing environments for special patient
populations/Jain Malkin.
        p.   cm.
    Includes bibliographical references and index.
    ISBN 0-442-31897-9
    1. Hospitals—Design and construction.   I. Title.
RA967.M3   1991
725'.51—dc20   91-13803

I dedicate this book to the
memory of my mother,
whose energy and passion
in the brief time I shared with her
set the course of my life . . .
and to my father,
whose humor and commonsense
philosophy made the most
challenging things seem possible.

Contents

PREFACE

The purpose of this book is to gather together the finest examples of health care design across the nation to create a much-needed reference for design professionals and health care senior management. I am convinced that the quality of health care environments can be improved by sharing ideas, learning from one another, and having an opportunity to survey a vast number of projects that transcend mere competence to achieve excellence.

Each of us sees, apart from our own work, a handful of projects we happen to visit or those few that are published in professional periodicals. I suspect that lack of exposure to a wide variety of outstanding projects is the reason that excellence is not achieved more often. To my surprise, many prominent architects I interviewed candidly used the word *mediocrity* to describe their feelings about the current state of health care design. I was touched by their sincere desire to change this situation, and I hope they will regard this book as a stepping-stone toward achieving this goal. I am truly indebted to the many professionals who shared their observations and perceptions with me and who put their trust in me.

Initially I wondered if I could count on the support of other health care design professionals. Would they be willing to share their work? Would the giants of this industry whose work is frequently published and often honored with awards care to participate or see a benefit in it? Using the AHA *Directory of Design Professionals for Health Facilities*, the NASLI (National Association of Senior Living Industries) membership directory, and my own extensive file of clippings on projects and topics, I wrote to nearly 300 professional design firms. I explained the purpose of the book, enclosed a table of contents, and solicited projects that met two criteria: true integration between architecture and interior design, and successful response to the needs of a special patient population. I cautioned respondents to overlook projects that could be described as "merely competent" in favor of those that are innovative or that exceed standard expectations.

For weeks I felt like a nervous hostess who sends out party invitations and wonders if anybody is going to come. My fears were unfounded. I received many letters of encouragement and support from principals of some of the most prominent firms. There was widespread acknowledgment of the book's value as a tool in meeting with hospital administrators, for example, to illustrate that it is indeed possible to create truly great architecture and still respond to functional and regulatory agency requirements. Shortly thereafter, submittals began to arrive. Every day was like Christmas. I was elated by the number and quality of submittals. In all I had gathered close to a thousand projects that had to be catalogued and filed.

The next challenge was corresponding with about 500 people. Each project had an architect, interior designer, and photographer who each had to be contacted either for comments about the project or for permission to publish the photos. During the two years I spent assembling this material, principals changed, marketing directors changed, and I sometimes had to start all over again to negotiate use of the photos. Generally, I received anywhere from 2 to 20 projects from a firm. I had to review each of them, decide which met my criteria, and return the remainder.

My perception of excellence became more sharply focused as I neared the end of the selection process, and I then reevaluated certain earlier projects. I was surprised to see how much my idea of excellence had evolved and was shaped by exposure to an increasingly larger number of projects.

I realized that some of my initial responses to submittals were based on a superficial—largely cosmetic—analysis of their merits. In time, after reviewing a great deal of research and reading everything I could find on the subject of healing environments, I was able to peer beneath the surface and really understand which projects had substance. I am not saying that aesthetic qualities are unimportant; however, they are but one measure of a project's success. Seeing a thousand projects gave me a unique perspective that complemented my 20 years of experience as a health care designer.

The final step was requesting photos that I could keep in excess of a year until the book had been produced. With the best of intentions, deadlines for receipt of photos were often not met, resulting in more correspondence and phone calls. In all, this monumental task took much longer than I had anticipated.

Toward the end I felt both satisfied and frustrated—satisfied every time I discovered one more project that showed great imagination and frustrated that I could not read, interview, or include every significant book, person, or study I encountered. Always I had a sense of missing that one great project that was just around the corner, but ultimately I had to set a cutoff date.

I offer my humble apologies to those whose work I did not discover. I extend my sincere thanks to those who chose to participate and to share their ideas, and to the many talented photographers who allowed me to publish their work. To Wayne Ruga, I offer my gratitude for his insightful comments during preparation of the manuscript. I also salute the physicians, nurses, administrators, and academicians who took time out of their busy schedules to critique my work.

I also wish to acknowledge and thank Mary Anne Jones, my executive assistant, who typed more than 800 letters associated with this book, plus the manuscript, in addition to fulfilling her role as office administrator. She never lost her composure or good humor, even under the most stressful deadlines. I applaud my design staff for carrying some of my burden while I worked on the book and for sharing my passion about the importance of excellence in health care design.

INTRODUCTION

All excellent things are as
difficult as they are rare.
Spinoza

The relationship between architecture and interior design is not easy to articulate. In one sense it can be thought of as analogous to that of plastic surgery and cosmetics: without altering the bone structure of the face, cosmetics can only camouflage a structural defect. The interior designer, in the context of a hospital, cannot rescue and make beautiful a building suffering from poor architecture. Some may take offense at this characterization of interior design, but an interior designer cannot independently change the hospital building shell. Spatial volumes, scale, relationship between indoor and outdoor spaces, form, and composition of principal structural elements are entirely the province of the architect. In the most successful projects interior design and architecture reinforce each other: one cannot tell where architecture stops and interior design begins. The effort is totally integrated. Admittedly this collaboration happens too rarely, but this book is dedicated to those projects that successfully meet this challenge.

The overall goal of this book is to improve the quality of the health care environment. Nevertheless, readers should not expect to find a comprehensive set of design guidelines or an ABC primer on how to meet the needs of special patient populations. The subject is far too complex to be dealt with in this fashion. Those who like easy answers may find themselves having to draw their own conclusions. Prominent clinicians differ in their philosophical approaches to patient care because no one right way to do things exists, and the perfect project will never exist because the criteria for judging depend on the eyes of the viewer.

The book will have been a success if it stimulates intellectual thought about alternative solutions to problems, introduces controversial issues heretofore unexplored, provides access

to resources and "great minds," and inspires the sharing of ideas. Once again, this project could not have been possible without the willingness of hundreds of design professionals to share their knowledge for the greater good of the profession.

HOW TO USE THIS BOOK

Photos of individual projects might appear in different chapters of the book because photos are grouped by room type (e.g., patient rooms, nurse stations, and lobbies) or by patient population (e.g., cancer centers, mental health facilities, and ambulatory surgical centers). Indexes allow the reader to look up a specific facility by name (e.g., Cleveland Clinic) or to look up projects of a particular type (e.g., ambulatory surgical centers). The subject index also lists the many topics and individuals, and the research mentioned in the text.

A number of chapters begin with lists of essential concepts in order to guide readers through the text. The lists are divided into three types: psychological factors, activities, and issues. In some chapters, a summary paragraph explains the psychological factors, making that list unnecessary. Those who have a penchant for order and consistency may view the varied chapter introductions as an imperfection; however, the nature of the material varied considerably from one chapter to another, making a consistent format too cumbersome.

In anticipation that some readers may turn immediately to one of the chapters dealing with a special patient population, I strongly encourage reading the preface, the introduction, and chapters 2 and 3 first to lay the foundation for reading other chapters.

PROJECT SELECTION

The initial goal was to present a comprehensive review of projects and research for each special patient population, but too much material is available to cover in any single volume. My intention was also to provide geographic and stylistic diversity, but certain anomalies were noted. Few projects were received from the Great Plains states, for example, and very few from Chicago, a city noted for outstanding architecture. Projects submitted were heavily concentrated in Sunbelt states and the East

1

Coast. Cities such as Cleveland, Minneapolis, Seattle, St. Louis, and Atlanta were adequately represented, but states such as Wisconsin and Illinois were not.

Representative projects from different sectors of the health care market are included: the military, teaching hospitals, venerable institutions (Mayo, Johns Hopkins, Cleveland Clinic, Menninger), community hospitals, low-income and federally funded facilities, and proprietary hospitals (for profit), plus several international projects.

As things turned out, many of the military projects that were submitted showed a remarkable similarity. They were austere, straightforward, and, although probably successful by a number of parameters, failed to meet the selection criteria. However, a few outstanding military projects have been included in the book. The low-income projects, with the exception of the two clinics that appear in the book, were bleak. Several proprietary health care organizations known for supporting good design were contacted; however, they did not have photo materials available. In spite of these disappointments, the projects included represent a fairly wide cross-section of health care architecture, and they do explore how the needs of diverse patient populations are being met.

In addition to work submitted by established health care design firms, the author sought projects by prominent architects and designers who are not normally recognized for work in health care, with the hopes that they might offer a new perspective on design sensitivities. Such projects include the Comprehensive Cancer Center at Cedars Sinai by Morphosis, the Cleveland Clinic by Cesar Pelli, the Menninger Foundation by SOM, and the Corinne Dolan Alzheimer Center by Taliesin Associated Architects.

A number of projects found their way into the book simply because they were technologically fascinating (Gamma Knife suite, Jarvik 7 heart transplant unit). The book also includes congregate care projects that address issues of design for the elderly, even though they are not, strictly speaking, health care facilities. Medical and dental offices have not been included in this book because they are the subject of my previous volume, *Medical and Dental Space Planning for the 1990s* (Van Nostrand Reinhold 1990).

DESIGNING FOR SPECIAL PATIENT POPULATIONS

Ten years ago health care designers were, for the most part, generalists. It became increasingly evident, however, that specialized knowledge was required to meet the needs of special patient populations (e.g., psychiatric, neonatal, Alzheimer's, cancer, rehabilitation, critical care, and labor and delivery). I am not saying that all cancer patients, as an example, have the same needs, but certain commonalities result from the side effects of the treatment, and various stages of emotional trauma may be shared.

Chapters outline the needs of each patient population and refer readers to selected writings and research or, in some cases, to notable individuals engaged in studying a particular topic.

THE TYRANNY OF INTERPRETING REGULATORY CODES

Examining projects for this book provided an interesting perspective about regulatory codes, especially those pertaining to interior finishes. Wide discrepancies exist between what is allowable in one state versus another, so the regulations sometimes seem capricious. Originally developed to protect the public health and safety by setting minimum standards for such concerns as flammability and asepsis (infection control), codes sometimes seem irrational. They occasionally place so much emphasis on what appear to be trivial issues, and sometimes scientific research has not substantiated the need for the level of protection that is mandated.

In some states, codes pertaining to asepsis have become so restrictive as to place a stranglehold on designers trying to create a nonclinical, healing environment. Some jurisdictions do not allow the use of wood (even if fire treated) in hospital patient care areas unless it is a functional item such as a handrail. Wood as a decorative material for molding or trim or for embellishing a nurse station is not allowed, although here and there an individual project has occasionally made its way through the approval process with wood detailing intact. If wood constitutes such a threat to infection control, then why do some states have no such restrictions?

A higher rate of hospital-acquired infection would by this reasoning be expected in facilities using decorative wood trim; but has this difference ever been documented?

In reviewing submittals for this book, I noted many examples of interior finish materials that might constitute a breach of asepsis or make routine maintenance difficult. When questioned, the respective architects replied that those materials were within their state regulatory codes. Examples include the use of brick walls in lobbies and dining rooms (cafeterias), extensive use of wood in high-profile patient care areas, wood ceilings, fabric-upholstered walls in elevator lobbies, and an impressive open stair in a hospital lobby, reminiscent of the staircase at Tara in *Gone with the Wind*—a grand, spiral marvel of woodworkers' art.

The point to be made here is that some consistency should develop among state regulatory agencies as to what does and does not constitute a threat to infection control. Certainly a designer could play it safe by using only smooth, nonporous materials that could be hosed down for ease of maintenance, but this tactic would not address the emotional and psychological needs of patients or the aesthetic demands of an increasingly competitive industry.

THE CHALLENGE OF EXCELLENCE

The projects selected for this book represent imaginative and sometimes even innovative solutions to designing for special patient populations. They are benchmarks by which to measure the quality of our own work. Repeated exposure to excellence results in a heightened awareness of what constitutes a high-quality environment and makes the possibility of achieving design excellence that much more attainable. I hope that this book will result in improving the design of health care facilities throughout this country and abroad.

chapter 1

THE RESEARCH QUANDARY

No one disputes the need for research to provide designers with scientific evidence to support their selections of color, layout of space, lighting design, or any number of other issues. In reality, not enough research presently exists testing these issues in specific patient care settings, and the practicality of doing so makes this work especially challenging. Setting up different conditions of lighting in patient rooms, for example, may be difficult or expensive, plus variables such as the patient's type of illness, stage of recovery, prognosis for recovery, number of family visits, and the attitude of nursing staff are numerous and difficult to control. Setting out to test whether indirect lighting or overhead fluorescents caused patients to recover sooner requires knowing what role family support and encouragement played, the prognosis for recovery, and a host of other factors before the effect of the lighting can be assessed. Even age could make a difference. Older patients might be more sensitive to glare and react more favorably to indirect lighting than young adults, who might find bright light stimulating. Moreover, experimenting on patients is difficult. Sick people have little interest in participating in environmental research.

Psychologists and other behavioral scientists for years have been studying how people respond to color, light, sizes of rooms, seating arrangements, and other issues that might conceivably have application to architecture or interior design. Performed under controlled laboratory conditions, the findings collected in basic research have been hard to apply with confidence to real-life situations. In fact, the form and style of basic research studies make the data almost incomprehensible to anyone except advanced students in these disciplines (Sommer 1983). The studies are written by scholars for other scholars.

SCIENCE VERSUS EXPERIENCE

Science involves testing theories according to certain rules of evidence. The scientist does not question whether something is true but whether it can be proven according to specific criteria. This approach may not be valid when dealing with architecture. How is "experiencing" a work of architecture factored into the equation? Patterns of light and shadow, reflections of color, and expansive or constricted spaces create in the best of buildings a poetry that can be experienced but not measured quantitatively. Scientists might respond by saying this "experience" is not considered significant; the behavioral outcome of experiencing the space is significant.

The gap between architects and researchers is vast. The former are largely practical humanists who were attracted to their fields of endeavor because they believed the built environment could influence behavior; the latter are scientists who, understandably, believe only what can be tested in a controlled environment. The attitude of the two disciplines might be represented by whether the glass is seen as half empty (researchers) or half full (architects). Designers want to believe; scientists want to challenge.

The principal hallmarks of scientific experimentation are that studies can be replicated and that variables can be controlled. Such experimentation is very difficult with architectural research. Sommer (1983) observes,

> There has been a tendency for practitioners to question the value of academic evaluations because they are so costly, time consuming, cumbersome, and seemingly unrelated to the realities of practice. On the other hand, there is a tendency for academics to dismiss the informal assessment procedures used by architectural firms. Some degree of mutual tolerance is required so that the field can profit both from an academic evaluation, the goal of which is to advance theory, and brief evaluations, the goal of which is to advance practice.

Architects and designers have always followed their own theories about what might work in a given situation. Combining bits and pieces of theory, a smattering of research, and some empirical observations of how people seem to use space, with enthusiasm they charge ahead to create new environments. Afterward, they note from casual interviews with patients and staff what works and what does not. This informal anecdotal research or experience (as opposed to a rigorous postoccupancy evaluation study) is carried forward to other projects.

Noting the difficulty of documenting behavioral outcomes in the field because of the problem of controlling variables, Sommer (1969, 166) states,

> A designer would profit more from training in the techniques of systematic observation than in empty rituals included under the category of experimental design. It is extremely difficult if not impossible to execute a rigorous experiment that deals with important relationships under natural conditions.

Yet researchers are intolerant of design professionals who build or create without scientific data to back them up. When asked what colors should be used in an environment for Alzheimer's disease patients, one prominent researcher admitted that, in the absence of any scientific studies on the topic, she would paint all the walls white and focus more on programming issues.

In discussing what vehicle is best for gathering environmental research data, Sommer (1969, 168) believes "there is no single best method—questionnaire, interview, simulation, or experiment—for studying man's adaptations to his [sic] environment. One chooses methods to suit the problem and the people and not vice versa."

THE VALIDITY OF ANECDOTAL RESEARCH

Truth is, much can be said for years of collecting comments about what works from nursing staff, environmental services staff, administrators, and patients and their families. Certainly scientific studies would be welcomed by any design professional, but they are often not available, and building on experience seems valid.

In collecting data for this book, I noted a curious anomaly. A number of prominent architectural firms known for their research and articulate discourse on design criteria for specific patient populations submitted projects that ap-

peared lifeless and ordinary. As motivational speakers and often-published authors, these practitioners have contributed much to the field of health care design and increased others' awareness of the most significant issues in the field. In contrast were the imaginative, sensitively designed projects that addressed magnificently the needs of various patient groups. These firms seemed to have an innate sense of what was suitable, yet many of them are firms whose principals are not public speakers, writers, or even particularly fluent about how they arrived at their design approach for that project. This observation is neither an affirmation of the value of empirical wisdom nor an attempt to diminish the value of scientific research. It was an unexpected occurrence worthy of mention.

BEGINNING A PROJECT

Every project must start with intensive programming and interviewing sessions with key staff who will be using the facility. The quality of this aspect of the project, combined with a sensitive design team who can empathetically imagine themselves in the roles of patient, family member, and staff, is directly proportional to the success of the outcome. Beyond that, success derives from the design team's ability to conceive a physical structure that is functional, meets codes, and is spiritually uplifting. An aesthetically beautiful project can be created without a rigorous programming effort, but can such a project be viewed as successful if it fails to meet the users' immediate and long-range clinical objectives?

DESIGN LOG METHOD

The Design Log[1] is a systematic method of gathering information about how people use or behave in a particular environment. It is a formal method of recording observations (Fig. 1-1) to augment the architectural program, incorporating performance specifications (behavioral objectives for the room) and general specifications (such as color, HVAC, size of room, and acoustic requirements), and ending with an evaluation (after the new facility has been in use for some time) of whether the stated objectives have been met. The format of the Design Log lends itself to postoccupancy evaluation by turning

OBSERVATION #

18

TIME BEGUN 8:50 am
TIME ENDED 9:00 am

TYPE OF ACTIVITY
1st Floor Nursing Unit
SPACE UTILIZATION

WEATHER
getting hot,
no breeze

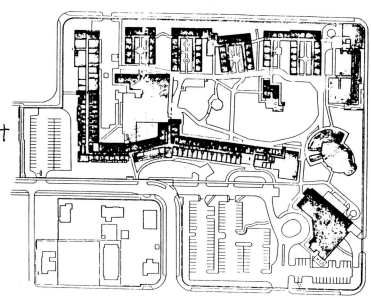

MJHHA

- Everybody is up... most beds have been made ... less wheelchair users but a number of emptees. (70-80% have wheelchair or walker)
- 8-10 residents in activity room watching TV ... one nurse also watching TV!
- one man wheels himself around the floor pulling on grab bar/handrail to get started and then races down hallway pushing wheels.
- smell of cleaning fluids... floors look wet and shiny
- very active area (by comparison to other nursing units) ...more verbalization... "look out"... "sorry"... "can I get by"... "hello"
- very congested at nurse's station ... two residents watch TV through doorway of activity room
- half a dozen or so sleeping on top of made bed (many have afghans) ... most doors are ajar... security? (for resident or staff?)
- Mrs B. (alert and clear) says she feels trapped because they put the siderails on her bed up, so she can't get in or out by herself.
- no one seems to hear the music on the PA system, very annoying to me.
- nurse's seem hidden from view behind the high front of the nurse's station.

the initial suppositions into questions by which to gauge the project's success.

In creating the Design Log, the design team may actually live with residents of the facility for a number of days to be able to experience it through their eyes. An observer uses a separate sheet of paper for recording each observation. A typical field note might read, ''10:30 P.M., 2 West Nurse Station, nurses conversing loudly; patient in wheelchair approaches desk but cannot be seen by seated staff as countertop is too high.'' The design team may actually ''live'' in a wheelchair for a day, rub petroleum jelly on their eyeglasses to simulate the visual distortion caused by cataracts, or wear yellow-tinted lenses to be able to view colors as the elderly do. Role-playing and behavioral modeling are other techniques used to help designers understand the users' viewpoint.

The Design Log is an effective tool for long-term documentation of a project. In booklet form, it provides a verbal snapshot of each room in the facility and outlines observations, design intentions, approaches or solutions, and postoccupancy evaluation. Initially, it allows the client to review and collaborate on assumptions, and it enables new design team members to enter the project midstream and understand its history. Staff may use the document as a handbook to explain the basis for the design and how rooms were intended to function; it can provide a bridge between the caregiver and the architect. Long term, it provides a data base that reduces the firm's learning curve on similar projects.

BEWARE OF SYLLOGISTIC CONCLUSIONS

I visited a facility for the mentally retarded to see a color system devised by a European color consultant that is intended to curb vandalism and enhance the residents' environment. The consultant, having juxtaposed the strangest of colors, claimed that the children's behavior was positively influenced by that specific color palette because little vandalism had been noted. This syllogism is questionable. The facility, prior to redecorating, was colorless and grim, and residents tended to abuse the walls. The question is whether any palette of colors would have reduced vandalism because it would have been a deviation from the prior lack of color. Perhaps the interest shown in the residents by embark-

ing upon redecorating was equally significant in modifying their behavior, a variant of the Hawthorne effect[2]; sometimes any attention, even negative changes, boosts productivity. Unless other variables are screened out, the claim cannot be made that a specific palette of colors caused that group of mentally retarded children to be less abusive. That kind of syllogism enrages researchers and reaffirms their prejudices about architects and designers who base design decisions on anecdotal research.

Environmental Research

Some of the most relevant research for health care design has been done by Janet Carpman, Myron Grant, and Deborah Simmons. Their *Design That Cares* is a milestone for its wealth of practical information, its bibliography of relevant research, and its reporting of the Patient and Visitor Participation Project of the University of Michigan Hospitals.

Mayer Spivack's *Institutional Settings* is required reading for anyone who sets out to design institutional environments. A superb blend of theory, research, personal insight, and practical information, it ties together the interests of architects, psychologists, geriatric specialists, environmental psychologists, sociologists, interior designers, art therapists, and psychiatrists. Words and phrases create vivid images of institutional life. Originator of the Design Log method of gathering data, Spivack advocates participant observation—living in the setting under study as a nonstaff person—to experience firsthand what being a patient there means.

Child Health Care Facilities by Anita Olds and Patricia Daniel offers scholarly and practical information in a highly readable outline format. Quoting from dozens of research studies, books, and articles, the text briefly covers every conceivable topic of design from acoustics to playroom design to suitable types of animals for inpatient pet therapy. Occasional photos illustrate various concepts, including imaginative play units designed by Dr. Olds.

The Environmental Design Research Association (EDRA),[3] founded in 1968, is an international, interdisciplinary organization dedicated to advancing the art and science of environmental design research and to improving the understanding of the interrelationships between people and the built environment. Membership in this organization gains access to newsletters and information about conferences and publications.

The Health Facilities Research Program (HFRP) is a nonprofit, centrally coordinated, architecturally driven research program established in 1986 to provide long-term collaboration, joint research funding, and pooled resources among the various organizations and agencies having an interest and involvement in health facilities. It is operated and supported by the American Institute of Architects (AIA) and the Association of Collegiate Schools of Architecture (ACSA). The overall goal of the HFRP is to bridge academia and the pragmatics of practice to generate research results that directly benefit health care facility design and operation. It funded and published *Environments for People with Dementia: annotated bibliography* by Uriel Cohen and Gerald Weisman.

Environmental Psychology

A relatively new field, environmental psychology offers the promise of bridging the gap between researchers and designers. A hybrid of both disciplines, environmental psychology and architectural psychology both focus on human behavior in the built environment. The increase in postoccupancy evaluation (POE) studies is due to the influence of these practitioners.

Mardelle McCuskey Shepley holds a doctorate in architecture and a master's in psychology and is affiliated with The Design Partnership in San Francisco. Her research for a children's psychiatric facility at Camarillo State Hospital in California is an example of the type of data so desperately needed by architects and designers. Her unpublished 1989 study is discussed in greater detail in chapter 5 and accompanied by photos of the facility.

Gerald Weisman, a psychologist at the University of Wisconsin at Milwaukee, has contributed many valuable studies on wayfinding and architectural legibility. His student Margaret Calkins wrote *Design for Dementia: Planning Environments for the Elderly and the Confused*, the first book to deal with the design of prosthetic environments for Alzheimer's disease victims.

A discussion of behavioral research would be incomplete without paying tribute to the field's progenitors, anthropologist Edward T. Hall (*The Hidden Dimension, The Silent Language*),

psychologist Robert Sommer (*Personal Space, Tight Spaces, Social Design*), and sociologist Erving Goffman (*Behavior in Public Spaces, The Presentation of Self in Everyday Life, Asylums: Essays on the Social Situation of Mental Patients and Other Inmates*). These books are classics in the behavioral sciences and should be read by anyone engaged in shaping residential environments for patients.

Tangentially related to the current discussion is a provocative book by industrial designer Victor Papanek, *Design for the Real World*, an intellectually stimulating treatise on a designer's social and moral responsibilities.

Leaps of Faith

The next ten years will no doubt increase the quantity of environmental research, although the elusive qualities of architectural space will remain difficult to measure. To paraphrase Robert Sommer (1983), perhaps a leap of faith is required to be able to overlook hard evidence in order to concentrate on experiences and behavior and know that they have some causal relationship to performance, however difficult it is to measure. Rudolf Arnheim (as reported in Sommer, 1983) comments:

> The qualities that carry value can be described with considerable precision. But many of these descriptions cannot be quantitatively confirmed by the measuring or counting of data. They share this trait with many other facts of mind and nature, and it does not prevent them from existing or being important. Nor does a lack of numerical proof exclude them from objective discussion. The "extensive" method of arguing with the index finger by pointing to perceivable facts, making comparisons, and drawing attention to relevant relations is a legitimate way of furthering understanding by common effort.

NOTES

1. The Design Log Method is attributed to Mayer Spivack. For more information, refer to Chapter 16 in *Institutional Settings*.

2. The Hawthorne effect refers to worker productivity studies conducted in the 1930s by Western Electric Co. When environmental conditions were improved, morale and productivity increased. When the changes were removed,

productivity remained high, causing researchers to wonder whether the physical changes caused the increased productivity or if it was attributable to the workers feeling that management was interested in their welfare.

   3. P.O. Box 24083, Oklahoma City, OK 73124; (405) 848-9762.

REFERENCES

Calkins, Margaret. 1988. *Design for Dementia: Planning Environments for the Elderly and the Confused*. Owings Mills, MD. National Health Publishing.

Carpman, Janet, Myron Grant, and Deborah Simmons. 1986. *Design That Cares*. Chicago: American Hospital Publishing.

Cohen, Uriel, and Gerald Weisman. 1987. *Environments for People with Dementia: Annotated Bibliography*. Milwaukee, WI: Health Facilities Research Program.

Cousins, Norman. 1979. *Anatomy of an Illness*. New York: W. W. Norton & Co.

————. 1983. *The Healing Heart*. New York: W. W. Norton & Co.

Goffman, Erving. 1959. *The Presentation of Self in Everyday Life*. New York: Anchor Books.

————. 1961. *Asylums: Essays on the Social Situation of Mental Patients and Other Inmates*. New York: Anchor Books.

————. 1963. *Behavior in Public Spaces*. New York: The Free Press (Macmillan Publishing).

Hall, Edward T. 1969. *The Hidden Dimension*. New York: Anchor Books.

————. 1973. *The Silent Language*. New York: Anchor Books.

Olds, Anita, and Patricia Daniels. 1987. *Child Health Care Facilities: Design Guidelines & Literature Outline*. Bethesda, MD: Association for the Care of Children's Health.

Papanek, Victor. 1973. *Design for the Real World*. New York: Bantam Books, Inc.

Shuchman, Miriam, and Michael Wilkes, 1990. Acts of Faith. *Los Angeles Times Magazine*, August 26: 34, 37.

Siegel, Bernie. 1986. *Love, Medicine and Miracles*. New York: Harper & Row.

————. 1989. *Peace, Love & Healing*. New York: Harper & Row.

Sommer, Robert. 1969. *Personal Space*. New Jersey: Prentice-Hall, p. 168.

————. 1974. *Tight Spaces*. New Jersey: Prentice-Hall.

————. 1983. *Social Design*: Creating Buildings with People in Mind. New Jersey: Prentice-Hall, pp. 72, 66, 134.

Spivack, Mayer. 1984. *Institutional Settings*. New York: Human Sciences Press.

chapter 2

CREATING A HEALING ENVIRONMENT

This chapter acquaints the reader with historical and recent approaches to healing, examines the relationship between stress and illness, explores the therapeutic potential of the built environment, and looks at research documenting the role of nature as healer.

Defining a healing environment is not easy, although the basic components include air quality, thermal comfort, noise control, privacy, light, views of nature (Figs. 2-1 and 2-2), visual serenity for those who are very ill, and visual stimulation for those who are recuperating.

ANCIENT PHILOSOPHIES OF HEALING

European and Asian cultures have historically been receptive to holistic healing. Their treatments have incorporated at various times spa therapy, music, nutrition, herbs, vibrational medicine, and colored light. The five-element theory (fire, wood, earth, water, and metal) is the basis for Chinese medicine. Each organ of the body is related to one of the five elements; the internal organs are thought to mirror cycles of generation and destruction between the five earthly elements in the universe.

Historians report that healing was a highly developed art in Atlantis (9500 B.C.) with three different schools of thought on the treatment of illness. Some healers used spiritual methods (flower essences, crystals, and color therapies); priests used homeopathy, an integration of spiritual and scientific methods; and the allopathic healers used herbs, drugs, and surgical treatments similar to practices used by today's orthodox physicians (Gerber 1988).

INTEGRATION OF MIND AND BODY

As new views evolve about the relationship between stress and illness and about the influence of positive attitudes on healing, more emphasis will be placed on design of the patient care environment. The physical environment, or setting, is often viewed as a stressor and linked with disease processes; the potential of the environment to enhance therapeutic goals has been grossly underemphasized.

Formal prescriptions for creating a healing environment are not likely in the near future, but general agreement exists on a broad number of factors known to cause measurable physiological reactions in the body. These factors have to do with noise level, lighting, color, privacy, access to nature, communication with caregivers, and accommodation for family members. Beyond them, numerous studies have explored various theories and variables. Although many of these studies have produced interesting findings, sometimes other researchers have not been able to replicate the results, or flaws in the design of the study have caused doubt about its validity. The state of research today is one reason why this field does not have, and probably never will have, a fixed formula for creating a healing environment. Another reason is that each hospital's operational protocols, staffing, types of patients, and a host of other variables, including the physical design of the building itself, demand a highly specific application of a particular theory or group of theories. Nevertheless, clearly a large amount of research information already exists that is not widely being incorporated into patient care.

An example of a well-known study that could not be replicated was one designed by Rogers (as reported in Williams 1988), whose hypothesis was that human beings and their environments are comprised of electrical and magnetic energy fields, with change in the patterning of the energy waves of either giving rise to simultaneous change in the other. Various studies based on that conceptualization have included investigation of differing wavelengths of light on heart rate, judgment about loudness of sound, and attention behavior in hyperactive and non-hyperactive children (the more hyperactive a child, the more preference for hues associated

2-1 *Atrium garden, London Bridge Hospital (London, England)*

Architect: Llewelyn-Davies Sahni, Inc.; Photographer: Jo Reid and John Peck

with short-wavelength light, the blue-green spectrum, and the more ability to identify numbers illuminated with that wavelength). Results of these studies, however, have shown no support or debatable support for Rogers's hypothesis, although it is certainly an interesting one (Williams 1988).

The New Frontier

The new frontier for health care design will be the creation of healing environments. Presently most hospitals seem to be competently designed, if *competently* means reasonably functional, appropriate for the community and patient populations served, and responsive to the hospital's mission statement. In my opinion, ten years from now hospital administrators will demand that their design consultants know how to design healing environments. Whether each environment created will succeed in achieving this goal may be subject to debate, but at least the inherent potential of the physical setting to complement and enhance the healing effects of drugs and medical technology will be widely acknowledged.

In recent years, a more holistic approach to healing has gained favor and been popularized in best-selling books such as those by Bernie Siegel and Norman Cousins. Increasing numbers of these articles have been written by physicians and appeared in fairly respectable periodicals, if not in scientific journals. The general tenor of these articles is that alternative and conventional medicine need not be mutually exclusive. Historically, a certain amount of mistrust between unlicensed healers and physicians has sometimes forced patients to choose between them. People seek alternative methods of treatment because they offer hope and restore feelings of control. Faith healing, diet and vitamin therapies, life-style management, and visualization techniques are popular alternative adjuncts to conventional medicine.

The new age of medicine seems likely to be a holistic paradigm uniting body and mind with modern technology. To quote Norman Cousins

---

2-2 *Serene courtyard offers opportunity for private contemplation. Aga Khan University Hospital and Medical College (Karachi, Pakistan)*
Architect: Payette Associates, Inc.; Mozhan Khadem, design consultant; Photographer: Paul Warchol

(Shuchman and Wilkes 1990, 34), "Currently in medicine, everything is technology, testing, and procedures. Instead of listening with their ears, doctors spend too much time with their stethoscopes."

STRESS AND ILLNESS

In 1936, Austrian physician and scientist Hans Selye pioneered a new frontier with his revolutionary discoveries about stress. His research demonstrated that hormones released during stress participate in the development of many nonendocrine degenerative diseases, including brain hemorrhage, hardening of the arteries, coronary thrombosis, certain types of high blood pressure, kidney failure, arthritis, peptic ulcers, and cancer. He gave new definition to the word *stress*, which had been thought of as an external force. His definition refers to wear and tear on the body from its attempts to cope with environmental stressors; it was a new concept of mental and physical illness. In fact, for years Selye's name has been synonymous with the word *stress*. He meticulously documented the effects of stress on the structure and chemical composition of the body by charting the paths of chemicals as they made their way from one organ to another and noting interactions between specific and nonspecific events.

Although popular literature often reduces the effects of stress on the human body to a few simplistic, easy-to-understand concepts, a reading of Selye's classic *The Stress of Life* (1956) reveals the enormously complex series of interactions among almost all systems of the body as a reaction to stress. Irrefutably, measurable and highly predictable physiological changes take place in the body as a reaction to psychological and environmental stress.

MECHANISMS OF STRESS

Many articles written for design professionals contain an overly simplified explanation of the effects of stress on the body. The following is an attempt to explain the mechanisms of stress more accurately, according to Selye's research (1956).

The Three Stages of Response

After exposure to a stressor, the general adaptation syndrome involves three stages:

1. An alarm *reaction* is the initial response, a marshaling of the body's defense mechanisms.

2. A stage of resistance or adaptation follows, because no living organism can continuously maintain itself in a state of alarm.

3. After prolonged exposure to the stressor, the organism's adaptation eventually fails and a third phase, the stage of exhaustion, ensues. Symptoms at this stage are similar to those in the initial alarm reaction phase.

At the end of a life under stress, this syndrome causes a kind of premature aging or wear and tear on the body.

PATTERN OF STRESS REACTIONS

Regardless of where the stressor initially acts, it eventually produces a generalized stress reaction in the entire body. This generalized response is accomplished by the two master coordinating systems, the endocrine and the nervous. An alarm signal reaches the pituitary gland, which is located in the floor of the brain; the pituitary initiates hormonal responses. At the same time, the alarm stimulates the nerves, which influence virtually all organs in the body without having to engage the endocrine system. The nerves, as a response to stress, produce the hormones adrenaline and acetylcholine. In response to stress, an excess of adrenaline is secreted.

The pituitary orders the secretion of adrenocorticotropic hormone (ACTH), which stimulates the adrenal cortex to produce substances that, in turn, destroy white blood cells, which are necessary for immunity and for controlling allergic, hypersensitivity reactions. In this way stress debilitates the immune system. Suppressive effects on immune functioning cause susceptibility to disease and can potentially impede recovery.

An increased demand on an organism, such as a response to stress, requires additional energy. In mammals the source of energy is blood sugar; repeated demands exhaust the supply, and the animal goes into shock (Hall 1969, 34).

Definitions

Hormones are chemical messengers produced by the endocrine glands and released into the blood. Interestingly, each hormone is coded to

target specific organs. The *pituitary* is a small endocrine gland embedded in the bones at the base of the skull, underneath the brain. *Adrenal glands* are endocrines lying above the kidneys, on each side. The release of ACTH enlarges the adrenal glands and causes them to produce a great excess of adrenal hormones. The adrenal glands play an important role in controlling the body's defense mechanisms. The size and weight of these glands are not fixed; they respond to stress.

Conditioning Factors

Conditioning factors such as heredity, diet, previous exposures, and attitude can predispose or enhance vulnerability to stress. Figure 2-3 shows the principal regulators of the stress syndrome: brain, nerves, pituitary, thyroid, adrenals, liver, kidney, blood vessels, and, at the bottom, connective tissue cells and white blood

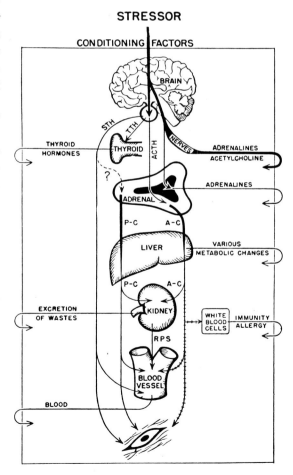

2-3 *Synoptic view of the whole stress mechanism. Photo courtesy McGraw-Hill, from* The Stress of Life *by Hans Selye, M.D.*

cells. The concept of selective conditioning explains how individuals react differently to stress because of inherited and acquired traits.

In summary, stress causes a number of significant physiological responses including the release of numerous hormones, elevated blood pressure and heart rate, increased muscle tension, constriction of blood vessels, gastric disturbances, and suppression of the immune system.

ENVIRONMENTAL STRESS

The six qualities of the environment most likely to contribute to stress are these (Saegert 1970):

1. *Physical threat:* filth; heat or cold, exposure to elements.
2. *Stimulus information overload:* negative only when it is unpredictable or uncontrollable. This would include on-the-job stress associated with high-performance careers: too many decisions to make, too much to do, too little time, pushing oneself too hard. This type of stress is rarely the result of the environment, but usually a characteristic of the individual's relationship to the environment, based on personality type, cultural expectations or conditioning, and personal goals.
3. *Suitability of environment:* the ability of the environment to support or frustrate people's goals. As an example, buildings with wayfinding problems create this type of stress.
4. *Psychological and social:* environments are coded with messages that convey feelings of social worth, security, identity, and self-esteem, as well as indications of status.
5. *Demandingness of the environment:* amount of effort, energy, or resources required to interact with it. This can mean physical effort, time, or money. An example might be stress associated with the cost of hospitalization.
6. *Stimulus or information deprivation:* occurs in isolated environments; to function normally, people need tension and challenge.

The design of the environment causes stress by affecting "person-environment fit" (Zimring 1981). The designed environment and its relationship to stress are complex issues that have been the focus of numerous studies, some of which pertain to health care settings. Clearly design can directly support or thwart the user's goals. An example might be a lighting level that is improper for adequately performing a given task. An example of an indirect method of affecting person-environment fit would be a design that either facilitates or hinders social interaction. A misfit forces the individual to adopt a coping mechanism based on past experience and the parameters of the current situation. Denial, for example, is a coping mechanism.

HOSPITAL STRESS FACTORS

The experience of hospitalization itself is a source of psychological stress for most patients, regardless of the nature of the illness (Volicer and Isenberg 1977). A designer can better understand the sources of stress by viewing the facility through the patient's eyes (Table 2-1): isolation from family and friends, lack of familiarity with the environment, medical jargon, fear of procedures, loss of control, lack of privacy, worries about job or finances, and inaccessibility to information.

In a survey of hospital-induced stress, newly admitted patients exhibited increased urinary corticosteroid levels and elevated urine potassium, which decreased to normal levels several days after admission (Mason, as reported in Volicer and Isenberg 1977). Numerous controlled studies by nurse researchers have relied upon nursing intervention techniques, such as preoperative instructions and patient education, to reduce stress. Indicators of reduced psychological stress were deemed to be reduced length of stay and reduced use of postoperative narcotics (Volicer and Isenberg 1977).

A hospital stress rating scale was developed listing 49 events relevant to the experience of hospitalization (Table 2-1). Researchers analyzed and controlled variables such as gender, age, marital status, education, previous hospitalization, and severity of illness in making comparisons. The study set out to analyze differences between medical and surgical patients' reactions to the experience of hospital-

Table 2-1. Hospital Stress Factors

Factor	Stress Scale Events	Assigned Rank	Mean Rank Score
1. Unfamiliarity of surroundings	Having strangers sleep in the same room with you	01	13.9
	Having to sleep in a strange bed	03	15.9
	Having strange machines around	05	16.8
	Being awakened in the night by the nurse	06	16.9
	Being aware of unusual smells around you	11	19.4
	Being in a room that is too cold or too hot	16	21.7
	Having to eat cold or tasteless food	21	23.2
	Being cared for by an unfamiliar doctor	23	23.4
2. Loss of independence	Having to eat at different times than you usually do	02	15.4
	Having to wear a hospital gown	04	16.0
	Having to be assisted with bathing	07	17.0
	Not being able to get newspapers, radio or TV when you want them	08	17.7
	Having a roommate who has too many visitors	09	18.1
	Having to stay in bed or the same room all day	10	19.1
	Having to be assisted with a bedpan	13	21.5
	Not having your call light answered	35	27.3
	Being fed through tubes	39	29.2
	Thinking you may lose your sight	49	40.6
3. Separation from spouse	Worrying about your spouse being away from you	20	22.7
	Missing your spouse	38	28.4
4. Financial problems	Thinking about losing income because of your illness	27	25.9
	Not having enough insurance to pay for your hospitalization	36	27.4
5. Isolation from other people	Having a roommate who is seriously ill or cannot talk with you	12	21.2
	Having a roommate who is unfriendly	14	21.6
	Not having friends visit you	15	21.7
	Not being able to call family or friends on the phone	22	23.3
	Having the staff be in too much of a hurry	26	24.5
	Thinking you might lose your hearing	45	34.5
6. Lack of information	Thinking you might have pain because of surgery or test procedures	19	22.4
	Not knowing when to expect things will be done to you	25	24.2
	Having nurses or doctors talk too fast or use words you can't understand	29	26.4
	Not having your questions answered by the staff	37	27.6
	Not knowing the results or reasons for your treatments	41	31.9
	Not knowing for sure what illnesses you have	43	34.0
	Not being told what your diagnosis is	44	34.1
7. Threat of severe illness	Thinking your appearance might be changed after your hospitalization	17	22.1
	Being put in the hospital because of an accident	24	26.9
	Knowing you have to have an operation	32	26.9
	Having a sudden hospitalization you weren't planning to have	34	27.2
	Knowing you have a serious illness	46	34.6
	Thinking you might lose a kidney or some other organ	47	35.6
	Thinking you might have cancer	48	39.2
8. Separation from family	Being in the hospital during holidays or special family occasions	18	22.3
	Not having family visit you	31	26.5
	Being hospitalized faraway from home	33	27.1
9. Problems with medications	Having medications cause you discomfort	28	26.0
	Feeling you are getting dependent on medications	30	26.4
	Not getting relief from pain medications	40	31.2
	Not getting pain medication when you need it	42	32.4

Source: From Volicer, Isenberg, and Burns. 1977. Medical-surgical differences in hospital stress factors. Journal of Human Stress

ization. The results showed that surgical patients had higher stress scores relevant to unfamiliar surroundings, loss of independence, and threat of severe illness; medical patients scored higher on financial problems (worried if insurance would cover a long stay) and on lack of information. The implication is that medical patients often do not have a well-defined understanding of their illnesses and the probable outcomes; obviously, these issues are more clearcut for surgical patients.

MALADAPTION

Given the body's physiological reactions to stress, the patient's maladaption to the hospital environment can be expected to produce altered cardiovascular and endocrine responses associated with this anxiety, which can negatively affect the course of an illness or impede recovery. The hospitalized patient must, of course, accept the environment as a given, whereas healthy people can generally leave or change it to suit their needs. A number of special conditions unique to hospitalization are responsible for considerable stress. They include unfamiliar diagnostic tests, such as the ECG, and setting up an intravenous line, which can be a frightening experience.

With respect to privacy, territorial intrusions were found to produce anxiety, but intrusions of personal space were not. In other words, being touched and prodded by caregivers at close range was not stressful, but the presence of strangers and intrusions in the room itself were a cause of stress. Finally, being hospitalized and surrounded by illness is stressful because it forces the patient to think about death and mortality, topics rarely contemplated under normal conditions.

PSYCHONEUROIMMUNOLOGY

Psychoneuroimmunology (PNI) is a term coined by Robert Ader to refer to the role that emotions play in the pathogenesis of physical diseases that are associated with immunological dysfunctions, especially autoimmune diseases thought to be associated with states of relative immunological incompetence, as well as cancer, infections, and allergic diseases (Solomon and Amkraut in press). This emerging field holds great promise for unlocking the mysteries of

how the emotions can influence the onset and progress of diseases such as cancer.

Central to this theory is the notion that the failure of psychological defenses is largely responsible for the onset and course of disease. The PNI research deals with neuroendocrine effects on immune function and the role of the central nervous system in modulation of the immune response. Because both the central nervous system and the immune system perform functions of defense and adaptation, illness ensues from inappropriate defenses in either system, according to George Solomon, a physician and leading researcher in this field. This effect appears to be an extension of Selye's research, which also points to the critical role of hormones under central nervous system control with respect to immune response. Solomon has noted that most hormones are secreted in a pulsatile, episodic fashion; many have 24-hour secretion rhythms, and mechanisms of immunity also tend to show a 24-hour periodicity, which relates to some of the latest research in the field of chronobiology, discussed later in this chapter.

FOCUS ON THE SENSES

An interesting aspect of PNI is its focus on the senses (hearing, sight, smell, touch, and taste) and their ability to influence emotions. If emotional factors predispose people to illness, then through the senses people can learn to channel their energies into creative outlets that might allow them to view the world differently or develop feelings of self-worth and self-esteem. Emotional conflicts, feelings of powerlessness, and inability to respect and love oneself can, over time, alter body chemistry and lead to physiological damage of any organ system of the body.

IMMUNOLOGIC COMPETENCY

Until recently, in spite of Freud's evidence to the contrary, the orthodox medical community has had difficulty accepting the idea that the mind can contribute to the causation of illness. Throughout most of this century physicians viewed body and mind as separate and distinct components; however, an increasing number of physicians now recognize that treating the whole person, not just the diseased organ system, is important. Much has been written about immunologic competency, especially with respect to understanding cancer, and physiological and psychological stresses both play a role in the body's ability to resist disease, which is also termed *host resistance*.

Significant research by a number of physicians supports the link between emotional attitudes and the onset of disease. Edward Bach in England was a pioneer in this research. In the early twentieth century he was an orthodox physician and a bacteriologist, prior to becoming a homeopathic physician. He discovered that fear and negative attitudes were the most significant emotional attributes leading to illness (Gerber 1988). His work was a precursor to PNI research being done today.

PERSONALITY TRAITS LINKED TO SPECIFIC DISEASES

Thomas and Duszynski's landmark study (1973) on personality traits and emotional attitudes indicates that family relationships and psychological factors can be helpful in predicting the onset of diseases such as cancer and heart disease. The sample population consisted of 1,300 Johns Hopkins Medical School students who graduated between 1948 and 1964 and whose medical histories she continued to update over the years. Having gathered detailed information about each person's family history and having administered a variety of physical and psychological tests, they were able to refer back to the data as the older physicians began to succumb to various illnesses to determine whether common psychological factors could be linked to particular types of diseases.

They studied five diseases specifically: suicide, mental illness, malignant tumors, hypertension, and coronary heart disease. They discovered common psychological factors among students who succumbed to cancer in that they were emotionally detached from parents and in general described negative early family relationships (Gerber 1988). Another study, by psychologist Lawrence LeShan (as reported in Gerber 1988) suggested that cancer patients tend to withhold their emotions especially negative ones.

ATTITUDE AND SURVIVAL

Carl Simonton (1975), a radiation oncologist who has worked with cancer patients in an effort to change negative self-images and attitudes, found that aggressive attitudes toward survival and a strong will to live can have a positive effect on survival from advanced malignancies (Gerber 1988, 473). A study reported in the June 13, 1985, *New England Journal of Medicine* claimed to have found no relationship between emotional attitudes and survival in patients with advanced high-risk cancers; however, the authors did feel that emotional attitudes had a positive effect upon quality of life and that these attitudes may be significant in deterring less advanced cancers (Gerber 1988, 474).

NOISE REDUCTION

Any attempt to reduce stress on a hospitalized patient must include noise reduction. Clearly noise is one of the most noxious of environmental stressors; it produces a generalized stress reaction that can increase blood cholesterol levels, increase the need for pain medications by lowering an individual's pain threshold, and keep the brain stimulated so that the patient cannot rest or sleep, which impedes healing. One study found that noise levels in the recovery room can be exceedingly high because of the density of patients and conversations among staff and that noise may have adverse effects on patients taking certain antibiotics, could be disruptive of sleep, and enhances the perception of pain (Falk and Woods as reported in Olds and Daniel 1987).

HOLISTIC THERAPIES

One of the best books to explain the vast number of alternative therapies and to put them in perspective as adjuncts to conventional medical treatments is *Vibrational Medicine* by physician Richard Gerber (1988). Many books dealing with holistic[1] therapies suffer from weak scientific underpinnings; by contrast, this book is well researched, scholarly enough to be respected by physicians and scientists, yet reasonably accessible to a well-educated lay reader. It spans a vast period of civilization to explain methods of healing, the scientific basis of Western medicine, and significant milestones in research, and then integrates this data with topics as diverse as planetary evolution, new-age energetic medicine, homeopathic healing, and metaphysical consciousness.

Holistic therapies include many possibilities to help integrate and balance the mind, body, and spirit. If emotional stress or maladaption to the environment causes illness, then therapies that provide an outlet for expressing negative feelings can be therapeutic. Although the benefits of these therapies are still viewed with skepticism by orthodox physicians, considerable historical precedent supports this viewpoint.

ART AS THERAPY

The arts are expressions of humanity that carry the legacy of a culture and can touch and stir individuals in their times of deepest need to help them transcend their pain. As an example, during World War II a decision was made to close the theaters in Paris and turn them into hospitals. After the German occupation, authorities recognized the importance of the theater for healing the emotional wounds of the populace, who were stressed by battles and personal losses. Theaters were subsequently reopened to the performing arts, paintings were hung, and people naturally gravitated back to these spiritually nurturing environments.

Nazi prisoners of war in concentration camps serve as another example of how art was able to sustain people through the most horrendous atrocities. Numerous books have been published on art that was created by these prisoners during their incarceration. Many stated that their lives were made bearable by those few moments of beauty and by the ability to express, in a positive way, their incredible anguish and sorrow. Painters through the ages have continued to paint when they were almost blind or in great pain from arthritis. They sometimes had to tie paintbrushes to their fingers, but the pleasure of painting overcame the pain.

In the hospital setting, music and art therapy can help to distract people from their pain, enable them to see the beauty around them, and encourage them to feel that life is worth fighting for. This state of mind positively influences healing and enhances immunologic competency.

MUSIC THERAPY

Music has been used to help treat depression, to reach autistic children, and to relax agitated psychiatric patients. Music is thought to affect the limbic system, deep areas of brain tissue that produce sensations of extreme pleasure. Some researchers theorize that this area of the brain is responsible for the sensations of pleasure and bliss experienced by those who meditate regularly: "Repetitive stimulation of certain limbic structures is known to cause bursts of electrical activity along special paths within the limbic system" (Gerber 1988). Through a number of very complex interactions, the limbic portion of the brain, when stimulated by the sensory cortex, affects the functioning of the autonomic nervous system, which controls processes such as breathing, heart rate, and other unconscious bodily processes.

Music can also have an analgesic or painkilling effect when pleasure centers of the brain stimulate the pituitary gland to release endorphins, the body's natural opiates. Those who suffer from chronic pain sometimes use biofeedback techniques to learn to stimulate the portion of the brain that causes the release of endorphins. In fact, the release of endorphins is a measurable event in acupuncture pathways (Gerber 1988). Soothing music has been known to lower the level of catecholamines, such as adrenaline, and to lower blood pressure, heart rate, and the amount of free fatty acids in the blood, potentially reducing the risks of hypertension, stroke, and coronary heart disease.

Kaiser Permanente Medical Center, Los Angeles, offers patients music therapy by providing a portable tape deck and recordings of soothing harp music or guided relaxation techniques. Physicians sometimes prescribe music therapy instead of tranquilizers or analgesic medications, and they also use it prior to cardiac catheterization, during chemotherapy, and for patients suffering the pain of spinal injuries. In their outpatient stress management clinic, tapes are recommended for people suffering high blood pressure, migraine headaches, and ulcers. Memorial Sloan-Kettering, New York, has a full-time music therapist who visits patients' rooms with her guitar and other instruments to enable patients to discharge feelings of anxiety or fear and to offer hope. Physicians, nurses, and social workers refer patients to the music therapist.

Certain types of new age music are extremely relaxing because they are based on natural body rhythms. Biological sounds, such as an adult heartbeat, have been thought to diminish stress in infants. Babies are said to respond positively to classical music, and some believe it helps them develop motor coordination; classical music played in an operating room has been known to reduce anxiety, and some claim it can actually reduce anesthesia requirements.

CHAKRAS AND COLOR THERAPY

The *chakras* are specialized energy centers, each of which is associated with a major nerve and glandular center in the body. They act as transformers to step down subtle energies and translate them into hormonal, nerve, and cellular activity in the physical body. The major chakras, especially the crown, brow, and throat chakras, are also subtle organs of perception and are associated with the psychic abilities of higher intuition, clairvoyance, and clairaudience (the ability to hear things at a subtle energetic level), respectively. Energetic threads, known as *nadis*, connect the chakras to each other and to various aspects of the physical body, forming the chakra-nadi network (Gerber 1988).

Each major visible color has particular qualities that are linked to the chakra with which it resonates. An understanding of the chakras and their higher energetic links to body physiology helps to explain why certain colors are used to heal specific illnesses. The following is a list of colors and their respective associations with specific diseases (Gerber 1988):

Violet: nervous and mental disorders
Indigo: disorders of the eye
Blue: thyroid and laryngeal diseases
Green: heart disease and hypertension
Yellow: disorders of stomach, pancreas, and
          liver
Orange: disorders of lungs and kidneys
Red: blood disorders and anemias

The interrelationships between the chakras, the physiology of the body, and color cannot be explained within the confines of this chapter. A more thorough discourse is provided by Gerber (1988, 278), who explains, "There are intricate

systems and approaches to color healing that are utilized by various practitioners. The selective use of color vibrations to treat human illness is a complex . . . art." Sometimes colors are applied alone or in therapeutic combinations in order to enhance the potential of healing through synergistic effects. Color may be applied as light (which has passed through colored filters), ingested as color-solarized water, or inhaled as air that has been charged with the energies of a particular color.

To understand how color applied in this manner can effect healing, remember that certain color frequencies resonate strongly with particular chakras. The color frequencies energize and rebalance dysfunctional chakras that may have become blocked by the disease process.

AROMATHERAPY

The olfactory sense is often underestimated both as a cause of stress and, when positive, as therapy. Some claim that smells are retained more acutely in memory than are visual images or sounds. Remember how vividly Marcel Proust, one of France's leading twentieth-century writers, described odors and fragrances. When he walked down the street and smelled the aroma of freshly baked *madeleines* (a type of French cookie), it immediately conjured up memories of his grandmother's kitchen when he was a small boy. This memory, in turn, triggered many related emotions.

In the hospital, the negative corollary would be medicinal smells that produce anxiety. Unpleasant odors are known to increase heart rate and respiration, whereas pleasant fragrances actually lower blood pressure and heart rate. Some research has shown that olfactory messages reach the brain faster than auditory or visual ones.

The field of aromatherapy is a recognized aspect of a holistic approach to healing. Research at Yale and Duke has demonstrated that sniffing specific floral and fruit fragrances slowed respiration, lowered blood pressure and heart rate, and relaxed muscles; fragrances were also found to reduce pain. If fragrances are able to relax people, then they can enable them to concentrate or focus their attention on other matters.

To summarize, the senses are important to PNI research because through these receptors the environment is experienced. Much more could be written about ongoing studies, both scientific and anecdotal (clinical observation) with respect to the healing potential of music, art, aromatherapy, and pet therapy, but further discussion of these topics would be outside the scope of this book.

CHRONOBIOLOGY

As physicians probe increasingly subtle approaches to treatment and therapy, they reach that rarefied domain where human biology and metaphysics meet, as in the emerging field of chronobiology. According to Charles Czeisler, director of the Laboratory for Circadian Rhythms at Harvard's Brigham and Women's Hospital, "Doctors are becoming increasingly sensitive to time effects in their evaluations and treatment" (Rosenthal 1990). (*Circadian* refers to behavioral or physiological rhythms in humans associated with the 24-hour cycles of the earth's rotation.) Studies have shown there is a best and worst time to administer every drug.

The medical world's interest in rhythms has been stimulated by observations that some diseases occur more frequently at certain times of day and during certain seasons. Heart attacks, for example, are twice as likely to occur shortly after waking. Levels of adrenaline, which makes the heart pump faster, are highest then, and other factors, like the tendency of platelets to clump in the blood, are also at their extremes. Researchers are discovering previously unrecognized internal rhythms: the viscosity of blood rises and falls on a 24-hour cycle; the number of T-cells, which fight infections and tumors, peaks in winter and falls to an annual low in June (Rosenthal 1990).

Research has revealed a number of internal body cycles that govern a person's susceptibility to disease and response to treatment. For example, hormones that rise and fall in the menstrual cycle have been linked to breast cancer. In one small study, women who underwent mastectomies at the middle of the cycle were more likely to survive without a recurrence of cancer (*Lancet* as reported in Rosenthal 1990). What makes this all so fascinating is that, after years of focusing on medical technology, physicians are just now starting to explore and appreciate the human body's responses to metaphysical forces, theories hinted at by healers centuries ago.

HOSPITAL DESIGN AND HUMAN BEHAVIOR

A sizable body of research suggests that the design of the physical setting has an impact on both patients and caregivers. Obviously space planning greatly impacts function and ease of circulation, but more subtle are the psychological messages encoded in the environment. This comment evokes the power inherent in the physical setting:

> I began to realize that the sensation [I was feeling] was linked with the experience of beauty. It was a sense of dignity that I felt in this place. . . . For the first time, I saw clearly the incredible effect and impact of environment. In that moment . . . I understood that people can be made to feel degenerate or divine by the mere fact of their physical environment. I saw everything around me as a reflection, and understood that we feel ourselves to be what our mirrors tell us we are. (Ismael as reported in Venolia 1988)

Influence of Florence Nightingale

One of the earliest environmentalists, and certainly ahead of her time, Florence Nightingale combined perspectives from environment, health, and environmental psychology in her best-known works, *Notes on Nursing* and *Notes on Hospitals*, both published in 1859. She emphasized the importance of adequate ventilation, sanitation, noise control, and light and advocated a social environment free of "chattering hopes and advices"; she also provided instructions for designing wards to enhance recuperation. *Notes on Hospitals* was an enormous influence on hospital architecture throughout the world (Williams 1988).

Walking through many hospitals brings to mind Norman Cousins's observation that "a hospital is no place for a person who is seriously ill" (1979, 29). In a similar vein, more than a century earlier, Florence Nightingale explained that the first requisite of a hospital should be that it does the patients no harm. Clearly Nightingale was referring to central issues of sanitation (prior to the germ theory of disease) and to heating, fresh air, and diet. Cousins was referring to the many things he has criticized over the years that make our major medical centers so unyielding to the needs and comforts of individual patients.

Reizenstein's Analysis

One of the most thought-provoking articles on environmental research was written by Janet Reizenstein (now Carpman) in *Advances in Environmental Psychology* (Baum and Singer 1982, 137–69). In it, she reviews the literature between 1969 and 1979 that deals specifically with the topic of hospital design and human behavior. She analyzes characteristics of the literature, notes the country of origin, and provides insights about the nature of the studies, some of which follow.

Interdisciplinary Collaboration Lacking

Reizenstein ponders why the same design concepts are used over and over in hospitals, regardless of their often negative effects on users, and she laments that interdisciplinary transfer of information contained in studies often fails. Research does exist, but it does not seem to be applied by architects and designers. She speculates that one problem may be that architects are not always the decision makers. Observing how buildings are used or altered over time might reveal clues that others are often responsible for making design decisions over the life span of a building. Some of these individuals may be administrators and nurses who may have difficulty accessing some of the literature in environmental design journals. Relevant studies are scattered in books and journals in the architectural, hospital, and medical fields; retrieving the information is not easy.

Moreover, the form of research data is such that decision makers often do not know how to apply it. Some who work in the field of knowledge utilization speculate that an intermediary, or linking agent, may be needed to translate and prepare research results for specific applications.

Empirical versus Nonempirical Studies

Empirical research is conducted according to scientific principles; nonempirical work is purely descriptive and based on anecdotal observations, and it may include design guidelines based on some measure of research. Reizenstein noted that during this ten-year period not much empirical research was published in the area of hospital design and behavior. She criticized the "fashion show" type of descriptive article often found in design periodicals in which concepts deemed "successful" are endorsed

for application to other settings. The implication is that it worked in one facility and therefore would work for others. In reality, a concept may be a dismal failure in another setting where the givens are quite different.

Reizenstein praised a number of nonempirically based design guidelines that tend to give performance criteria; that is, they specify a desired result and allow the designer and decision maker to figure out how to achieve it. By comparison, prescriptive criteria specify a formula that, if executed, will achieve the desired results. Some design guidelines incorporate individual observations with others' research. An example is *Child Health Care Facilities, Design Guidelines and Literature Outline* (Olds and Daniel 1987).

User Participation

Much of the literature stressed the need for involving users in the design and planning of a facility. User participation has several benefits, including enhancing their awareness of the environment, ensuring their commitment to the final product, and making certain that all clinical needs have been adequately reviewed and factored into the design.

Role of Research in Decision Making

Much of the literature reviewed indicated that "although the inclusion of research-based data in the design decision-making processes would be desirable, it is rarely if ever done" (Reizenstein 1982, 160). Unfortunately, not a lot of systematic research done in acute care settings has examined the effects of physical design on patient care, patient or staff satisfaction, or the organization and functioning of the hospital itself. "There is generally a resistant attitude regarding the use of information in decision-making and problem solving, as well as limited awareness of the information available (Heath and Green as reported in Reizenstein 1982, 163). They found that commonly used sources of information were personal contacts, the experience of colleagues, and information gathered at seminars.

PLANETREE MODEL HOSPITAL PROJECT

A remarkably commonsense approach to patient care was pioneered by Angelica Thieriot in 1978 with the Planetree[2] Model Hospital Project, which was developed for a medical-surgical unit at Pacific Presbyterian Medical Center, San Francisco. Initially, physicians and nursing staff were hesitant about deviating from traditional patient care protocols. Over a period of time, however, comments from patients and staff who worked in the unit transformed skeptics into believers. The Planetree vision has since achieved national prominence, and few doubt the significance of the Planetree philosophy, although it may not be easy to implement on a large scale in major medical centers. Historically, many hospitals have had their roots in the hierarchical and authoritarian organizational structures of religious orders and military institutions. The Planetree philosophy is based on offering patients choices and individual control over most aspects of their care, which runs counter to the strict timetables and treatment protocols that enable hospitals to function efficiently.

Patient-Centered Care

At the root of the Planetree model is a respect for the patient as an individual with unique emo-

tional and medical needs. The patient is allowed to choose various types of nurturing care, active involvement, family support, or privacy to satisfy personal needs. In the traditional acute care setting, the patient must fit in with the system by suppressing personal needs and preferences. The empowered patient becomes actively engaged in the process of healing. Instead of expending energy coping with a hospital's inflexible regulations, the patient can rally strength toward fighting the disease. In the Planetree model (Fig. 2-4) the patient is the center of the care paradigm.

Access to Information

A Planetree unit has no secrets. Patients have access to their own medical charts, to nurse stations, and to a resource library of tapes and books informing them of medical options and encouraging them to become informed participants in their own care.

2-4 *Conceptual model of Planetree. Illustration courtesy Laura Gilpin © 1986, Program Planetree*

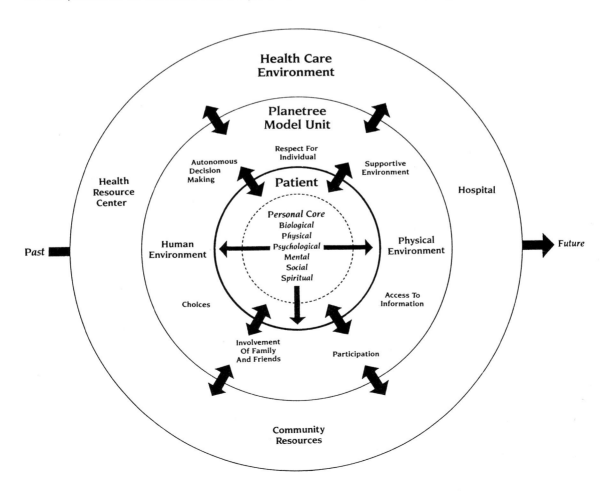

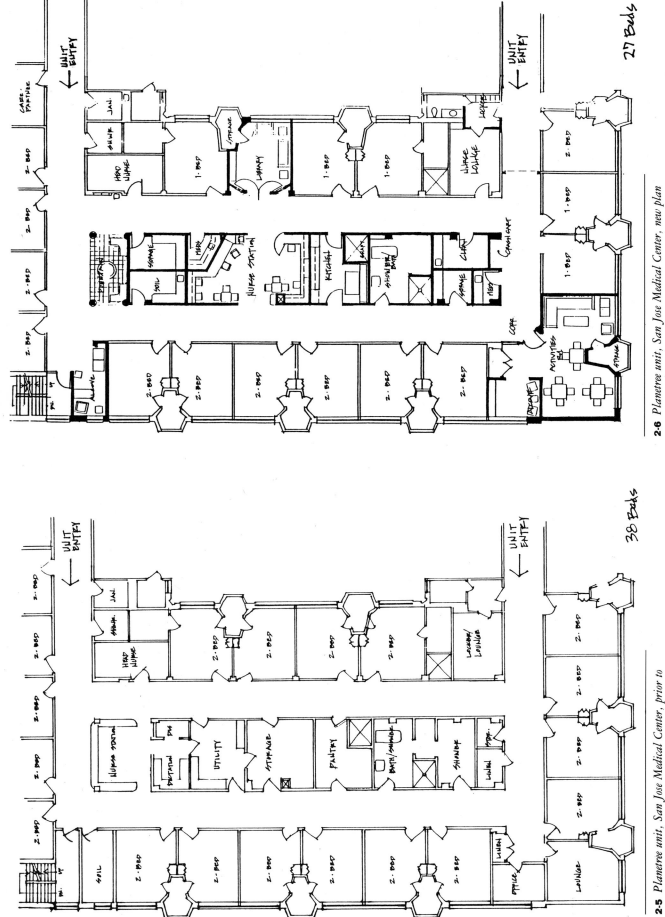

2-6 Planetree unit, San Jose Medical Center, new plan after remodeling. Courtesy Mark Schweitzer, architect

2-5 Planetree unit, San Jose Medical Center, prior to remodeling. Courtesy Mark Schweitzer, architect

24

Choice and Personal Control

Patients are encouraged to be as independent as they wish, and the design of the unit must support this intention by allowing patients to control room lighting, the amount of privacy they desire, and the involvement of the patient's family as caregiving partners. The Planetree philosophy involves innovative changes in all aspects of patient care (nursing, doctor-patient relationship, nutrition, patient education, unrestricted visiting hours, care partner rooms). The focus of this discussion, however, is the interior architecture of a Planetree unit. Figures 2-5 and 2-6 illustrate the conversion of a medical-surgical nursing wing to a Planetree unit. Nurses' stations (Figs. 2-7 and 2-8) do not project the "we're in here and you're out there" mentality that is typical of hospital nursing units. Low counters, small conference tables, and wide-open access encourage patients and families to enter. The patients' lounge (Fig. 2-9) is cozy and offers a retreat for those with insomnia. A nearby kitchen allows patients to prepare any type of food, including popcorn, and encourages family members to bake cookies or special treats. Imagine the aroma of chocolate chip cookies wafting down a hospital corridor. Oak trim, carpet, pleasant artwork, and track lighting (Fig. 2-10) create a nonthreatening environment. Patients' reading rooms in each unit provide periodicals, books, and other educational materials.

Patients' rooms include shelves for plants, greeting cards, and personal mementos from home where the patient can view them. Daybeds or sleeper chairs in some rooms allow patients to invite a family member to stay overnight. In many nursing units visitors feel as if they are in the way because they do not have a chair to sit in, a lounge for relaxing, or the opportunity to share in caring for the patient. At Planetree, visitors have places that support their needs during a stressful situation. Equally important are the needs of staff for privacy, comfort, and an attractive environment so that they can express well-being when caring for

2-7 *Open nurse station, Planetree unit, San Jose Medical Center (San Jose, CA)*

Architectural consultant: Mark Schweitzer; Architect of record: Kaplan McLaughlin Diaz; Interior design: Victoria Fay; Photographer: Donna Kempner

2-8 *Open nurse station, Planetree unit, Pacific Presbyterian Medical Center (San Francisco, CA)*
  Architects: Roslyn Lindheim and Mark Schweitzer; Interior design: Victoria Fay; Photographer: Christopher Irion

patients. Nursing is often characterized as a low-control, high-responsibility job, which underscores the importance of opportunities to escape and relax, even briefly.

A Totally Supportive Environment

In essence, a Planetree unit provides opportunities for personal choice, nurturing, and support, rather than constraints. Patients' recovery is enhanced by music, film, literature, and laughter, all available to them as part of their therapy. The activities room is equipped with large-screen TV and a VCR; patients can enjoy a night at the movies. Occasionally entertainers do live performances in the unit. By introducing patients to the therapeutic properties of the arts and nature, Planetree arms them with resources to help them cope with their illness. As an outreach to the community, every Planetree hospital unit has a Health Resource Center to provide consumer-oriented literature in a

2-9 *Patient lounge, Planetree unit, San Jose Medical Center (San Jose, CA)*
  Architectural consultant: Mark Schweitzer; Architect of record: Kaplan McLaughlin Diaz; Interior design: Victoria Fay; Photographer: Donna Kempner

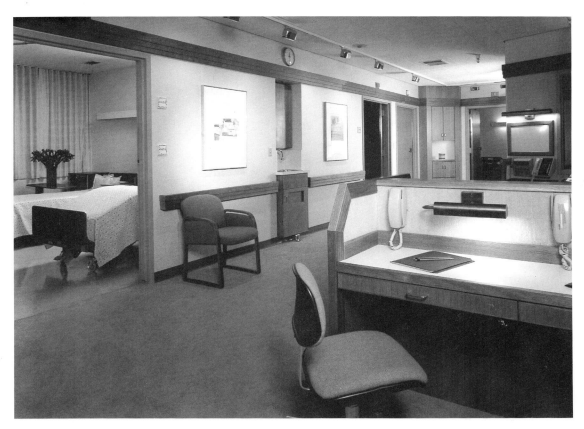

2-10 *Corridor view, Planetree unit, Pacific Presbyterian Medical Center (San Francisco, CA)*
Architects: Roslyn Lindheim and Mark Schweitzer; Interior design: Victoria Fay; Photographer: Christopher Irion

friendly, nonthreatening atmosphere (Figs. 2-11 and 2-12) that is more accessible than most medical libraries.

Additional Planetree units have been established at San Jose Medical Center in California and at Beth Israel Hospital in New York City. Units are being planned for other hospitals as well.

VIDARKLINIKEN

A number of my colleagues visited and were impressed by the 74-bed Vidarkliniken hospital in Järna, Sweden. Designed by architect Erik Asmussen and based on Rudolf Steiner's theory of anthroposophy (science of the spirit), the building's use of organic shapes, color, texture of materials, lighting, and views of nature is said to enhance healing (Fig. 2-13). Along with architecture as therapy, baths, massage, music (created by Steiner), and sculpture and painting assignments help to restore harmony and equi-

librium to the patient. *Interiors* magazine (Tetlow 1989, 94) features this facility and some color photos of it.

Rudolf Steiner (1861–1925) was an Austrian-born scholar, scientist, and artist. He saw the practice of anthroposophic medicine as an extension of Western scientific medicine, rather than an alternative to it. His goal was to engage the patient in the conscious process of self-healing and spiritual growth. "It is designed to be a nurturing and therapeutic environment which, through its spaces, forms, colors and materials, helps patients regain health by bringing into balance their faculties of thinking, feeling, and willing" (Coates and Siepl-Coates 1990).[3] Much can be learned about the life-enhancing possibilities of architecture by careful analysis of this project.

Opened in 1985, it is part of a larger community including a mill and bakery, several biodynamic farms, and a number of curative homes for children and adults in need of special care. Vidarkliniken employs a holistic approach to healing. Anthroposophical medicine conceives of illness as a gift and an opportunity to gain new insight into the purpose of life and to become renewed at a higher level of consciousness.

2-11

2-12

2-13

PROGRESSIVE STAGES OF HEALING

Central to the Vidarkliniken philosophy is the concept that different diseases, as well as different stages of healing, demand specific, rather than general, environmental support.

Stage One

A sick organism often attempts to conserve energy by narrowing its focus and avoiding stimuli; it turns inward and seeks isolation. A patient room that is varied and interesting, with good views, is recommended. The interior of these rooms is painted by the "lazur" method in which paint is applied in several thin, transparent layers to achieve soft luminosity. The paint itself consists of vegetable dyes in a casein and beeswax medium (Fig. 2-14). Corridors, in a warm yellow-ochre color, use paints with mineral dyes (Fig. 2-15). Some patient rooms have a blue or blue-violet palette; others are warm rose. "Health, according to anthroposophy, is a dialectical process of balancing tendencies toward 'sclerosis' (excessive hardening or building up—cold—illnesses) and inflammation or breaking down—warm—illnesses" (Coates and Siepl-Coates 1990). Consequently, doctors prescribe warm- or cool-colored rooms based on the type of illness and stage of healing. Color is never merely symbolic or decorative at Vidarkliniken; it is always carefully selected to aid the process of healing.

Second Stage

Patients on their way to recovery tend to move out to socialize in corridors that are broken into

2-14 *Typical patient room, Vidarkliniken (Järna, Sweden)*

Photo courtesy Gary Coates and Susanne Siepl-Coates

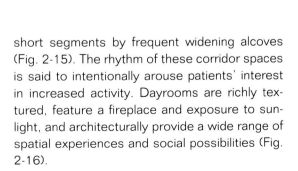

2-11 *Planetree Health Resource Center, San Jose Hospital (San Jose, CA)*

Architectural consultant: Mark Schweitzer; Architect of record: Kaplan McLaughlin Diaz; Interior design: Victoria Fay; Photographer: Mark Schweitzer

2-12 *Planetree Health Resource Center, San Jose Hospital (San Jose, CA)*

Architectural consultant: Mark Schweitzer; Architect of record: Kaplan McLaughlin Diaz; Interior design: Victoria Fay; Photographer: Mark Schweitzer

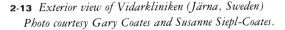

2-13 *Exterior view of Vidarkliniken (Järna, Sweden)*
Photo courtesy Gary Coates and Susanne Siepl-Coates.

short segments by frequent widening alcoves (Fig. 2-15). The rhythm of these corridor spaces is said to intentionally arouse patients' interest in increased activity. Dayrooms are richly textured, feature a fireplace and exposure to sunlight, and architecturally provide a wide range of spatial experiences and social possibilities (Fig. 2-16).

Third Stage

At this stage patients have the impulse to explore the world outside the patient wing. The gallery, courtyard, kitchen, dining rooms, and cafe encourage patients to venture forth and renew their zest for living. These spaces ex-

2-15 *Typical patient corridor. Vidarkliniken (Järna, Sweden)*
Photo courtesy Gary Coates and Susanne Siepl-Coates

2-16 *Patient dayroom, Vidarkliniken (Järna, Sweden)*
Photo courtesy Gary Coates and Susanne Siepl-Coates

2-17 *Patient dining room, Vidarkliniken (Järna, Sweden)*
Photo courtesy Gary Coates and Susanne Siepl-Coates

pose patients to nature, music, and social discourse.

A UNITY OF OPPOSITES

The architecture at Vidarkliniken was carefully and meticulously planned to express a unity of opposites. An example would be the polarities of a cultivated garden on one side and wild, untamed landscape on the other. Different floors of the facility offer the same type of contrasts. The basement contains spa rooms for mineral and herbal baths, a contrast to the light-filled and social character of the first floor. The spa is clearly the realm of earth and water, filled with strong scents of oils and ointments made from healing plants. It affords a protected, secure feeling.

The second-floor assembly hall, used for musical and dramatic performances, is an exuberant, soaring space. In this room, upper and lower windows are separated so that patients can choose to view the sky or the earth and can consider the natural polarities of up and down,

or heaven and earth. The second floor contains rooms for sculpture and painting therapy. Here the mood is less buoyant and spaces more constricted, mirroring the intense concentration associated with therapeutic activity. Each of these rooms has been shaped to express and support one specific activity. In the dining room, which is shared by patients and staff, yellow pine floors add texture and warmth (Fig. 2-17).

NATURE AS HEALER

Urban life-styles and pressure to produce more work in less time do not encourage an appreciation of nature. Whether homemaker or businessperson, rushing through the day's tasks does not leave much time for awareness of trees, flowers, cloud patterns, or the flicker of early morning light. Yet many make pilgrimages on weekends or vacations to commune with nature by camping out, traveling to a cabin in the country, or vacationing in Hawaii. According to Anita Olds (1985, 106), many people hold ''subconscious images of nature as a primal source of nourishment and rejuvenation." In her workshop "Spaces Can Heal," designed for health care professionals (designers, therapists, nurses, architects), she asked participants to visualize conditions of woundedness and healing. When asked to draw pictures of their healing spaces, 75 percent of these spaces had common elements: outdoor scenes, growing things, and nature as healer. People saw themselves as being alone, perhaps with a pet, but able to experience connectedness with the universe, causing Olds to speculate about the universal significance, or collective unconscious, of nature as healer; people seem to have an intuitive awareness of what constitutes a healing environment. "However disillusioned, modern man has clearly not wiped out his primal connections to the earth, sky, water, and all living matters" (Olds 1985, 107).

EVOLUTIONARY THEORY

In trying to understand why human beings feel so drawn to nature, some have espoused an evolutionary theory in which at the most visceral level people respond to elements that have been important to humans throughout millions of years: water, sunlight, trees, animals, and plants. Recent research by Roger Ulrich (1984) at Texas A&M investigated the stress-reducing effects of viewing water by measuring levels of stress hormones released into the blood, with the implication that immune functioning can be enhanced by frequent or prolonged visual exposure to nature.

The following is Roger Ulrich's (1990) summary of recent research. In testing various images, for example, views of nature versus urban scenes, psychophysiologists at Texas A&M found urban scenes to be less effective than nature in holding people's attention. They noted that relaxation occurred in only three to six minutes when people viewed nature scenes, according to measurements of muscle tension, galvanic skin response, systolic blood pressure, brain electrical activity, and stress hormones (catecholamines), which are tied to suppression of the immune system.

Abstract Art Not Appropriate
In 1985 Ulrich and his colleagues studied psychiatric patients in an "open" ward in a hospital in Sweden. Even though these patients were not very ill or violent, abstract art was so disturbing to them that they attacked these paintings, whereas no attacks were made on art images of nature. The implication is that abstract art portrays disorder and, for patients who already have trouble in ordering their environment, abstract art can upset that fragile framework. Art can be very powerful and not always healing. Other studies have shown that abstract art can be very damaging to highly stressed people after surgery and to those under the influence of certain drugs. Another of Ulrich's studies in Sweden examined the beneficial effects of visual exposure to nature on patients recovering from open heart surgery. The results showed that visual stimulation can facilitate recovery from the ischemic brain injury associated with surgery involving a heart pump.

Visual Stimulation
A well-publicized study of patients recovering from gallbladder surgery found that patients assigned to rooms with views of trees were able to be discharged earlier, had fewer negative evaluations from nurses, and required fewer painkilling medications than did patients assigned to rooms that faced a brick wall (Ulrich 1984). Other studies reported by Ulrich had similar implications. For example, cats or other animals with brain lesions that are placed in a white, unembellished box do not recover. They do recover, however, if visual stimulation is added. With intensive-care patients after open heart surgery, effects of visual stimulation and views of nature were tested by placing photos of nature in a frame mounted at the foot of the bed. The control group had only a white partition. Findings revealed gross differences in levels of anxiety. Patients who viewed nature showed less anxiety; moreover, when abstract art was substituted, even if colored like nature, anxiety increased.

Symbolism in Nature
Although human beings have many reasons for finding comfort and solace in nature, some of these feelings may result from the symbolism inherent in nature itself. Water, for example, is associated with baptism and rebirth or purification; flowers express the fragility of life; autumn leaves symbolize the onset of winter or advancing age; stones and rocks express strength, permanence, and ability to withstand stress; a

rainbow may symbolize hope and unexpected good fortune that may be just around the corner.

Perhaps the most appealing aspect of nature is the fact that it is always changing slightly and never static. The movement of leaves, the ever-changing angle and color of a sunset, wind currents on the ocean, the direction of waves, sway of a palm tree, movement of clouds, and shimmering of sunlight on leaves provide just enough stimulation to prevent boredom. The pattern of water is always stimulating, yet relaxing, as it swirls around stones, bubbling and gurgling as it flows downstream. "Rhythmic patterns of predictable sameness, combined with moderate diversity, allow the senses to maintain optimal levels of response and experience comfort" (Olds 1985). The flicker of a fire or the sensation of a warm or cool breeze can periodically reawaken the nervous system and provide an antidote to the monotonous character of most institutional environments.

Pet Therapy
Contact with animals offers similar benefits. One study showed that petting a dog or cat lowered people's blood pressure and stimulated the release of endorphins. Pets have been shown to be a significant deterrent to depression in the elderly and have helped victims of heart attacks recover more rapidly. Many people are starved for contact with living things, and watching a spider weave a web, petting a dog, or tending a cage of songbirds seems to combat feelings of isolation and alienation.

Appropriateness of Images
Given that views of nature effect measurable physiological changes, are static views of nature, as in photo murals or art, as effective as the real thing? If one of the benefits of nature is that it is always changing, then the static nature of a photograph might make it less effective in eliciting desired responses. I was unable to find any studies testing this hypothesis; however, Yvonne Clearwater (Facilities Planning News 1990), senior research psychologist and human factors specialist at NASA Ames Research Center, has conducted a number of studies with simulated views of nature (artwork). She offers these guidelines based on her research into the connection between visual images and physiology:

- Urban views are not perceived as positively as landscapes.
- Close-up views are not as pleasing as views with greater perspective.
- Landscapes having a short focal distance are less appropriate than those with a greater focal distance.
- A scene that includes an animal, building, person, or any kind of technology rated lower on the criterion "appropriateness for the setting." The introduction of these items stimulated an increase in physiological arousal over a serene landscape.

According to Clearwater, "the biological relevance of water is very clear." Dry landscapes are not as successful as wet, and scenes of the sun shining on water can predictably elicit positive responses.

Infinite Variety of Nature Themes
For a hospital art program a nature theme might seem too limiting and lack variety. However, the designer could take a number of directions. To supplement the more traditional views of trees, flowers, and ocean, the designer could present a series of photographs of Japanese gardens with raked sand, lily ponds with brightly colored *koi* fish, sand dunes, or desert scenes at daybreak, noon, and twilight, each time of day reflecting a dramatic change in colors and shadows; scenes of the Grand Canyon, glaciers, and tropical rain forests; or a rippling wheat field under a hot sun or an orchard in full fruit. In patient care areas where increased stimulation or arousal is desirable, these images might include animals: a scene of Antarctica with penguins, a stream with beavers building a dam, the African veldt with a cluster of zebras turning their heads to look at the viewer. Other dynamic nature scenes might include water sports such as surfing or sailing; these express the power and wonder of nature as well as zest for life.

THERAPEUTIC POTENTIAL OF THE ENVIRONMENT

Does the physical environment of health care facilities have a therapeutic potential? The answer is yes. Conventional hospital architecture often conveys negative messages, but architects do not willfully set out to send them. The problem stems from the fact that most of what architects deal with is well defined and concrete: the client's program, local or state codes, minimum-size spaces recommended for pieces of equipment, size of site, and zoning restrictions; and the list goes on. They become so bogged down with the many layers of specific requirements that have to be met that they rarely have time or energy available to explore the very amorphous and imprecise elements that define a therapeutic environment. Specific guidelines, like a book of codes, do not exist. Nevertheless, many architects believe that people should not have to adapt themselves to buildings that, in theory at least, have been designed for their comfort and to support clinical programs.

The setting can have therapeutic potential; architects and designers have to think about how to develop it.

- ''Spaces can act as sociopetal vectors to bring people together, or sociofugal ones, to keep them apart'' (Spivack 1984. Refer to chapter 11 for further discussion of this concept).
- The environment can be thought of as a stage richly encoded with cues that define the actors'

roles in terms of their own behavior and interaction with others.
- Has the building's design fully exploited the potential for providing natural light and views for patients, visitors, and staff (Figs. 2-18 and 2-19)?
- Look at ways to design corridors to prevent them from becoming tunnel-like and monotonous, which causes problems in perception: optical illusions, errors in size and distance relationships, and visual distortions due to reflections and glare. Mayer Spivack's classic study on sensory distortions in tunnels and corridors (1967), although focusing on the psychiatric setting, offers architects

2-18 *Main lobby, University of Chicago Hospitals, Bernard Mitchell Hospital (Chicago, IL)*
   Architecture and interior design: Perkins & Will; Photographer: Hedrich Blessing

2-19 *Foodservice and dining pavilion, Walter C. Mackenzie Health Sciences Centre (Edmonton, Alberta)*
   Architects (joint venture): Zeidler Roberts Partnership, Groves Palenstein Barton Irvine Architects Ltd., Wood and Gardener Architects Ltd.; Interior design: Neish Gantly; Photographer: Balthazar Korab Ltd.

much information that can be applied to nonpsychiatric settings as well.

• If the budget for high-quality design details is modest, keep the building simple, but allow a disproportionately large amount of the budget for lighting. The benefits of full-spectrum lighting in patient care areas and elsewhere are indisputable. People working "graveyard" shifts, which are always difficult to staff, have shown marked improvement in mood, less depression, and less stress when lighting was changed to full spectrum. Lighting upgrades should not be limited to full-spectrum lamps, however. Most areas would benefit enormously by the use of indirect lighting rather than overhead luminaires.

SETTING AND PERCEPTION

Abraham Maslow, one of the fathers of humanistic psychology, did one of the first experiments to demonstrate the effects of beautiful surroundings on an individual's perception. He created a "beautiful" room, an "average" one, and an "ugly" one. The beautiful room had large windows, a soft armchair, a mahogany desk, and nice artwork; the average room was neat and orderly but plain and undistinguished; the ugly room was full of clutter, had torn window shades, and looked like a storage closet. Volunteers were assigned to these rooms ostensibly to view photographs of people and decide whether their faces showed energy and well-being. Those who worked in the beautiful room ascribed positive attributes to the faces, but those who worked in the ugly room saw sickness and fatigue in those same faces: the setting had a definite impact on their judgment. Interestingly, those working in the ugly room tended to rush through their work and to complain of fatigue, headaches, irritability, and discontent (Maslow and Mintz 1956).

In summary, the major benefit of a therapeutic, supportive environment is its immune-enhancing effects, which are complementary to the effects of drugs and medical technology. Supplemental patient benefits are reduced length of stay, reduced health care costs, and more positive feelings about the hospital experience. With respect to staff, the benefits include fewer sick days, less turnover, and a competitive edge in recruiting staff and physicians.

DEVELOPING A HEALING ENVIRONMENT

Many factors have to be considered in the creation of a healing environment.

1. Noise control

   • Sound of footsteps in corridor
   • Slamming doors, clanking latches
   • Loudspeaker paging system
   • Staff conversations from nurse stations or staff lounge
   • Other patients' televisions and radios
   • Clanking of dishes on food carts

2. Air quality

   • Need for fresh air, solarium, or roof garden
   • Avoidance of noxious off-gassing from synthetic materials, including certain types of paint
   • Avoidance of odiferous cleaning agents
   • Adequate number of air changes

3. Thermal comfort

   • Ability to control room temperature, humidity, and air circulation to suit personal needs

4. Privacy

   • Ability to control view of the outdoors
   • Ability to control social interaction and view of patient in adjacent bed
   • Secure place for personal belongings
   • Place to display personal mementos (family photos, get-well cards, flowers)

5. Light

   • Nonglare lighting in patient room
   • Ability to control intensity of light
   • Good reading light
   • Window should be low enough for patient to see outdoors while lying in bed
   • Patient room lighting should be full spectrum

6. Communication

   • Ability to contact staff when needed
   • Comfortable places to visit with family
   • Television, radio, and telephone available as needed

7. Views of nature

   • Views of trees, flowers, mountains, or

ocean from patient rooms and lounges
- Indoor landscaping

8. Color

- Careful use of color to create mood, lift spirit, and make rooms cheerful
- Use in bed linens, bedspreads, gowns, personal hygiene kits, accessories, food trays

9. Texture

- Introduce textural variety in wall surfaces, floors, ceilings, furniture, fabrics, and artwork

10. Accommodation for families

- Provide place for family members to make them feel welcome, rather than intrusive
- Provide visitor lounges and access to vending machines, telephones, and cafeteria

Noteworthy Examples

The administrators and clinical staff of Wausau Hospital Center in Wisconsin have a remarkable respect for the healing benefits of nature. Half the patient rooms face a man-made lake with a geyser (Fig. 2-20) and half face a garden court (Fig. 2-21). The low windowsills permit outstanding views from beds. For ambulatory patients, visitors, or staff, a stroll through the garden reveals that it is not merely a haphazard collection of flowers; it is an English-style garden where color, line, and form are carefully considered as plants are placed next to each other. Walking through it, they can feel the love and dedication that have been lavished on it.

Inside the hospital, two large gardens have been created in patient care areas, one with tropical plants (Fig. 2-22) and the other with desert plants. The tropical garden includes a small fountain and cherub statuary; the lush foliage exudes good health—not a dusty or brown leaf anywhere. A hundred-year-old brick path winds its way through the atrium space; each plant species is labeled. This garden is situated so that family members in the surgical waiting room face it, as do staff in the hospital business office. In fact, throughout the hospital, practically every corridor and room has views of nature. The architect has framed it magnificently. Specimen trees on the site were protected and preserved during construction.

This progressive institution is located in a rural, agricultural region, where designers might least expect to find an awareness of the potential of the environment in enhancing healing. Nevertheless, people with vision—bold, courageous risk takers—can make it happen, wherever they find themselves. The aesthetics

2-20 *View from patient rooms, Wausau Hospital Center (Wausau, WI)*   *Architect: Skidmore Owings & Merrill; Photographer: Jain Malkin*

2-21 *Garden courtyard, Wausau Hospital Center (Wausau, WI)*
   Architect: Skidmore Owings & Merrill; Photographer: Jain Malkin

2-22 *Tropical garden with atrium enclosure, Wausau Hospital Center (Wausau, WI)*
   Architect: Skidmore Owings & Merrill; Photographer: Jain Malkin

committee of the board of directors has overseen the environment of the hospital since its construction in 1976. A color brochure, distributed in the lobby, explains the importance of the hospital's permanent art collection and underscores the value of atria and courtyards to help people heal faster and feel better. Interestingly, this hospital successfully uses sounds of the surf, generated by an electronic device, to calm agitated pediatric patients and to mask corridor traffic noise for ICU patients.

The Walter C. Mackenzie Health Sciences Center in Edmonton (University of Alberta) is a gigantic 2-million-square-foot, 943-bed medical center serving vast, remote regions of the country. Architecturally it is unique because it expresses high technology without sacrificing those elements so important to human beings: access to nature, natural light, visual stimulation, contact with water, and opportunities to socialize. Enormous exposed ducts are at first intimidating, but after repeated exposure they become an interesting part of the overall tapestry of line, form, and pattern. One writer likens the clusters of air-handling pipes to huge stalactites that spill down the walls (Freeman 1987).

Although the exterior is, as Freeman describes it, "unremarkable," the interior is a spectacular environment of multilevel pedestrian streets, walkways daringly crisscrossing the atrium (supported by a filigree of white pipe trusses), and everywhere exuberant plants and

vines spilling from window boxes and bridges (Figs. 2-19 and 2-23). Furnished as an outdoor streetscape, the atrium features "symbolic" umbrellas that have been fancifully created out of white pipe rail, awnings and enclosures with the same skeletal structure, and globe-shaped street lamps that line walkways and terraces

2-23 *Waterfall in tiered dining area of atrium lobby, Walter C. Mackenzie Health Sciences Centre (Edmonton, Alberta)*

Architects (joint venture): Zeidler Roberts Partnership; Groves Palenstein Barton Irvine Architects Ltd.; Wood and Gardener Architects Ltd.; Interior design: Neish Gantly; Photographer: Balthazar Korab Ltd.

2-24 *Pedestrian street and lobby, Walter C. Mackenzie Health Sciences Centre (Edmonton, Alberta) Architects (joint venture): Zeidler Roberts Partnership,* *Groves Palenstein Barton Irvine Architects Ltd., Woo, and Gardener Architects Ltd.; Interior design: Neish Gantly; Photographer: Balthazar Korab Ltd.*

(Fig. 2-24); reddish brick pavers in radial patterns contribute to the outdoor ambience, as does colorful patio furniture.

Tiered dining terraces (Fig. 2-23) invite conversation, and patient lounges perching over the atrium provide stimulating views of diners and other activity below.

Aesthetics are not the only measure of excellence in this facility. Interstitial spaces, 7¾ feet high, between floors accommodate all mechanical and electrical equipment and facilitate access for routine maintenance and for upgrading equipment during the 100-year life of the building. Highly sophisticated computer systems monitor fire and security, as well as heating, cooling, water, and piped gases.

This facility succeeds magnificently as a building devoted to both medicine and people. In a harsh climate, an inviting, nonclinical environment has been created to provide contact with nature, a variety of spaces in which to chat with friends, and a large dose of good cheer. Waterfalls cascade from one level to another (Fig. 2-23), and the nighttime lighting is as dramatic as the daytime lighting is spirited.

The hospital's nursing education and research department has been studying the effects of the building on staff and patient attitudes, patients' length of stay, use of postoperative painkillers, levels of anxiety, and amount of ambulation (walking). To date, their informal analysis of patient charts has revealed very favorable findings.

SUMMARY

The new frontier in health care design will be the creation of environments that support and enhance healing. In order to evaluate these environments, however, demonstrating that enhanced therapeutic outcomes have occurred will be imperative. This proof involves a two-part process of identifying, during the programming phase of the project, the desired therapeutic outcomes and then documenting and comparing these outcomes to others during the postoccupancy evaluation phase. Outcomes should be compared to historical precedents, the before-and-after conditions for that particular institution, as well as to a control group. Through this rigorous method of documentation, a solid body of data can be developed to help shape health care environments of the future.

NOTES

1. Holistic medicine addresses the balance between the body and mind and the multidimensional forces of the spirit. It regards humans as beings of energy and light, whose physical body is only one component of a larger dynamic system.

2. The planetree or sycamore is the tree that Hippocrates sat beneath when he began teaching in Greece centuries ago. Robin Orr and Marc Schweitzer are to be thanked for the information provided on Planetree.

3. I wish to thank professors Gary Coates and Suzanne Siepl-Coates of Kansas State University for the information and photos provided on Vidarkliniken.

REFERENCES

Baum, Andrew, and Jerome Singer, editors. 1982. *Advances in Environmental Psychology,* vol. 4, Environment and Health. Hillsdale, NJ: Lawrence Erlbaum Associates.

Beck, William, and Ralph Meyer, editors. 1982. *The Health Care Environment: The User's Viewpoint.* Boca Raton, FL: CRC Press.

Berlyne, D. 1971. *Aesthetics and Psychobiology.* New York: Appleton-Century-Crofts.

Canter, D., and S. Canter, editors. 1979. *Designing Therapeutic Environments: A Review of Research.* New York: John Wiley & Sons.

Coates, Gary, and Suzanne Siepl-Coates. 1990. Vidarkliniken: A study of the anthroposophical healing center in Jarna, Sweden. Unpublished paper by professors in the Dept. of Architecture at Kansas State University.

Facilities Planning News. 1990. Light, windows, art provide a ''psychic escape'' from confined settings. 9(9) Sept.: 5, 6; a Tradeline Publication.

Flynn, J., A. Segil, and G. Steffy. 1988. *Architectural Interior Systems: Lighting/Acoustics/Air Conditioning,* ed. 2. New York: Van Nostrand Reinhold.

Freeman, A. 1987. Evaluation: Therapeutic environment. *Architecture,* January, pp. 52–57.

Gerber, Richard. 1988. *Vibrational Medicine.* Santa Fe: Bear & Co.

Hall, Edward. 1969. *The Hidden Dimension.* New York: Anchor Books.

Jacobs, K., and F. Hustmyer. 1974. Effects of four psychological primary colors on GSR, heart rate, and respiration rate. *Perceptual and Motor Skills* 38:763–66.

Kornfeld, D. S. 1972. The hospital environment: Its impact on the patient. In *Advances in Psychosomatic Medicine: Psychosocial Aspects of Physical Illness*, ed. Z. J. Lipowski, pp. 252–70.

LeShan, L. 1959. Psychological states as factors in the development of malignant disease: A critical review. *Journal of the National Cancer Institute* 22: 1–18.

Lyons, Albert, and R. Joseph Petrucelli. 1987. *Medicine: An Illustrated History*. New York: Harry Abrams, Abradale Press.

Maslow, A., and N. Mintz. 1956. Effects of esthetic surroundings: Initial short-term effects of 3 esthetic conditions upon perceiving ''energy'' and ''well-being'' in faces. *Journal of Psychology* 41: 247–54.

Mehrabian, A., and S. Diamond. 1971. Effects of furniture arrangement, props, and personality on social interaction. *Journal of Personality and Social Psychology* 20(1):18–30.

Nightingale, Florence. 1859. *Notes on Hospitals*.

———. 1859. *Notes on Nursing*.

Nourse, J., and R. Welch. 1971. Emotional attributes of color: A comparison of violet and green. *Perceptual and Motor Skills* 32:403–406.

Olds, Anita. 1985. Nature as healer. In *Readings in Psychosynthesis: Theory, Process & Practice*, ed. John Weiser and Thomas Yeomans. Ontario Institute for Studies in Education, Toronto, pp. 97–110.

Olds, Anita, and Patricia Daniel. 1987. *Child Health Care Facilities: Design Guidelines & Literature Outline*. Bethesda, MD: Association for the Care of Children's Health.

Pierman, Brian. 1978. Color in the health care environment. Proceedings of a special workshop held 16 November 1976 at the National Bureau of Standards, Gaithersburg, MD. Issued by U.S. Dept. of Commerce.

Porter, R., and P. Watson. 1985. Environment: The healing difference. *Nursing Management* 16(6): 19–24.

Potter, C. 1983. Alberta's brave, new glass-domed world. *Health and Social Service Journal* 1: 1438–39.

Reizenstein, Janet. 1982. Chap. 6. Hospital design and human behavior: A review of the recent literature. In *Advances in Environmental Psychology* vol. 4, Environment and Health, ed. Andrew Baum and Jerome Singer, pp. 137–169. Hillsdale, NJ: Lawrence Earlbaum Associates.

Rosenthal, E. 1990. Timing the medical punch. *San Diego Union*, October 8.

Saegert, S. 1970. Stress-inducing and reducing qualities of environments. In *Environmental Psychology: People and their Physical Settings*, ed. W. H. Proshansky, W. H. Ittleson, and L. G. Rivlin, ed. 2. New York: Holt, Rinehart & Winston, pp. 218–23.

Selye, Hans. 1956. *The Stress of Life*. New York: McGraw-Hill.

Simonton, O. and S. Simonton. 1975. Belief systems and management of the emotional aspects of malignancy. *Journal of Transpersonal Psychology* 7(1):29–47.

Smolan, Rick, Phillip Moffitt, and Matthew Naythons. 1990. *The Power to Heal: Ancient Arts and Modern Medicine*. New York: Prentice-Hall.

Solomon, G. F., and A. A. Amkraut. In press. Emotions, immunity and disease. In *Emotions, Health and Illness: Foundations of Clinical Practice*, ed. Leonard Zegans. Academic Press.

Spivack, M. 1967. Sensory distortions in tunnels and corridors. *Hospital & Community Psychiatry* 18(1): 24–30.

———. 1984. *Institutional Settings*. New York: Human Sciences Press.

Srivastava, R., and T. Peel. 1968. Human movement as a function of color stimulation. Topeka: Environmental Research Foundation.

Starr, Paul. 1982. *The Social Transformation of American Medicine*. New York: Basic Books.

Thomas, C., and D. Duszynski. 1973. Closeness to parents and the family constellation in a prospective study of five disease states: Suicide, mental illness, malignant tumor, hypertension, and coronary heart disease. *The Johns Hopkins Medical Journal* 134:251–70.

Ulrich, Roger. 1984. View through a window may influence recovery from surgery. *Science* 224:420–21.

———. 1990. Effects of Interior Design on Physiological Well-Being and Health-Related Indicators. Paper read at National Symposium on Health Care Interior Design, November, in San Francisco.

Venolia, Carol. 1988. *Healing Environments*. Berkeley: Celestial Arts.

Volicer, B., and M. Isenberg. 1977. Medical-surgical differences in hospital stress factors. *Journal of Human Stress* June:3–13.

Williams, M. 1988. The physical environment and patient care. *Annual Review of Nursing Research* 6:61–84.

Zimring, C. 1981. Stress and the designed environment. *Journal of Social Issues* 37(1): 145–71.

chapter 3

THE QUEST FOR EXCELLENCE

*We are shaping the future
with every project we create today*

The enormity of the economic and ethical issues burdening today's health care system, in one sense, makes the quest for excellence in architecture seem as irrelevant as a prisoner on death row planning his next vacation. Idealists would argue that doing things well should not cost any more than doing things poorly. As human nature and the laws of physics tend toward decline and disintegration, however, countering those forces, bucking the system, and doing things right take tremendous energy. Reading the newspaper or examining any aspect of contemporary urban life demonstrates that those citizens who resist greed and their own self-interests to dedicate themselves to a higher goal are not the norm. Whether schoolteacher in an inner-city school, dedicated police officer, priest who creates a shelter for AIDS patients, or Mother Teresa, against all odds these people struggle to pursue a dream of excellence. When they succeed, society celebrates them because they are indeed rare.

No less rare is the possibility of achieving excellence in hospital architecture and design. No project will ever be "perfect" because excellence is to some degree a subjective evaluation and therefore dependent upon the experience and viewpoint of the observer. Nevertheless, the rigorous pursuit of excellence must guide every responsible, dedicated health care design professional.

OBSTACLES TO CREATING EXCELLENCE

Hospitals are perhaps the most complex building type, not only because of obvious life safety issues and complex engineering systems but also because of the lengthy planning process, regulatory agency review, and construction time, all of which typically dictate a five-year turnaround from initial start to occupancy. During this period reimbursement policies may change, populations may shift, competition might indicate a need for new services, or new alliances may be formed with other providers, and the architectural plans may have to change practically until the date of occupancy. Once constructed, few building types undergo the ravages of change as often as hospitals, which means that buildings that were once architecturally legible may become a maze of twisted corridors that pose serious wayfinding challenges.

Other obstacles to achieving excellence concern facility size and budget. An architect faced with squeezing three pounds of program into a two-pound bag will be forced to cut amenities such as a spacious patient lounge, courtyards, and corridors wider than the eight-foot minimum, and reduce the size of the lobby in order to accommodate a few more procedure rooms or a new department. The budget may have been developed for a 400,000-square-foot facility, which has grown to 450,000 square feet by the time the preliminary planning process has been completed, yet no additional funds are available. The "frills" or discretionary items such as skylights, high-quality lighting, ceiling treatments, architectural detailing, and interior finishes are cut; landscaping is downgraded. At this point no money is left for artwork, and simply meeting the program and the budget supersedes attempts at creating a healing environment. Constant alterations to the scope of the project sometimes wear out the planning consultants and diminish the sparks of creativity and excitement that characterized their initial responses to the project's potential.

Perhaps less obvious than the foregoing reasons but clearly an obstacle to creating excellence is the simple lack of exposure to a wide variety of excellent projects. Each year a few projects are published in architectural journals, others are exhibited at health care design conferences, and a designer may tour an occasional project when visiting another city. This lack of professional communication makes it difficult to share ideas, to learn from one another, and to survey a vast number of projects that transcend the expected to achieve excellence.

When I collected material for this book, the willingness to share information was evident. Highly competitive firms felt so impassioned about their mission to create better-quality health care environments, both for caregivers and for patients, that they were actually enthusiastic about pooling and sharing ideas for the overall good of the profession. Clearly health care architects and designers were, by and large, imbued with an incredible passion about their work and a sincere desire to create high-quality healing environments, although many expressed frustration about the mediocrity that characterizes most health care facilities today.

COMPETENCE VERSUS EXCELLENCE

Heath care design as an industry has matured to the point of having produced a vast amount of competently executed work. *Competent* work is sufficient to meet the facility's requirements for a reasonably functional building. Aesthetically, the architecture and interior design could be described as adequate and ''pleasant,'' but spaces lack variety, visual interest, and imagination. Certainly some clients or individual projects will always demand this type of treatment because of limited resources or because of the short anticipated life of that facility. Unfortunately, ''merely competent'' projects happen all too often because of lack of time to do a more thorough job, because of a low fee that does not allow for going beyond the program requirements, or because so much energy is required to challenge the accepted way of doing things. To create excellence means taking risks, confronting regulatory agencies to apply for waivers, and challenging boards of governance at hospitals who, more often than not, like what they know, that which is safe and familiar. It requires working with hospital administrators and key clinical staff to explain the ways that excellence in architecture and design can benefit them.

BENEFITS OF EXCELLENCE

Environmental quality can enhance patient care and staff satisfaction while supporting the hospital's efforts in strengthening strategic market position. Although a number of highly specific individual parameters can measure success, several benefits are more general in nature. The first has to do with image and marketing. Although some hospitals still enjoy a relatively captive population, with little competition from other providers, most hospitals today find themselves engaged almost in combat with neighboring hospitals. When consumers have a choice among health care providers, image becomes increasingly important. Patients can rarely assess the quality of the clinical care they receive, but they make a judgment, nevertheless, based on interactions with staff and an evaluation of the physical environment. Image is also important for attracting and keeping top clinical staff. Although an attractive environment will not compensate for low pay or poor benefits in fending off the nursing shortage, it does foster pride in the workplace and enhances self-esteem, and this sense of well-being is reflected in interactions with patients and their families.

Enhanced recovery and healing are certainly additional measures of success, as numerous studies have proven. If presented with scientific research to support specific design objectives, hospital administrators and clinical staff are likely to become allies in trying to accomplish these goals.

Other, more specific, measurements of success include improved nurse-physician relationships, reduced length of stay, fewer patient falls, reduced nurse absenteeism or turnover, patient and physician satisfaction, and fewer negative comments about nursing care. Somewhat more difficult to document, but certainly important, are issues such as reduced eyestrain and improved morale.

Costs of Inadequate Research

Mistakes resulting from lack of adequate research can be very specific, such as failure to meet a licensing code requirement, or less tangible, such as a design that is incompatible with the hospital's mission statement. The results of these types of mistakes include additional costs, short-term facility obsolescence, patient or staff discomfort. and patient or staff inconvenience. Following are a number of common mistakes resulting from lack of adequate research in the planning process (Heath and Green as reported in Baum and Singer 1982):

1. Design inappropriate for function
2. Maintenance problems

3. Duplication of work already done
4. Inadequate services provided
5. Regulations ignored
6. Overly lavish facilities
7. Lack of appreciation of environmental effects

Intuitive Nature of Design

The quantity of information that a health care architect or interior designer has to have at his or her command is vast. In fact, information overload afflicts every dedicated professional today who struggles to keep abreast of relevant information. Because so much data are available now to inform any and every design decision, designers sometimes feel overwhelmed and, instead of following a systematic process for discovering and analyzing information relevant to their projects, may resort to a somewhat haphazard approach. They may scan whatever information happens to be on file in the office, use a consultant occasionally when confronted by a specific design problem, and rely on intuition to fill in the blanks. Bits and pieces of randomly selected information may be twisted into new forms that defy analysis. Designers appear to have a certain amount of resistance toward employing a systematic process of approaching a design problem, as if it might deaden their powers of intuition. Design must always be in some part an intuitive endeavor, but this aspect of the work does not negate the need for an exhaustive process of due diligence.

> The modern designer relies more and more in his position as an "artist" on catch words, personal idiom, and intuition—for all these relieve him of some of the burden of decision, and make his cognitive problems manageable. Driven on his own resources, unable to cope with the complicated information he is supposed to organize, he hides his incompetence in a frenzy of artistic individuality. As his capacity to invent clearly conceived, well-fitting forms is exhausted further, the emphasis on intuition and individuality only grows wilder. (Alexander 1964, 10–11)

Critical Analysis

The field of architecture has benefited greatly from the writings of architectural critics like Ada Louise Huxtable, Charles Jencks, and Paul Goldberger. This type of critical writing does not exist in the field of interior design. In fact one of the failings of mainstream interior design magazines is that they do not write critical articles; instead, they describe projects as if narrating a fashion show. This approach does not foster critical analysis. Their rationale is that critical writing may offend advertisers.

Architectural journals, by contrast, provide less narration; they attempt to relate the project under discussion to historical antecedents, compare it with other buildings of that type by contemporary colleagues, and perhaps analyze the sociological significance of the project. Controversy about the design, if it exists, is stated in a straightforward manner. The writers typically have some critical comments or questions even about projects for which they have, in general, high praise. No project is perfect and shortcomings, however slight or few, may be instructive to others The field of interior design is a relative newcomer when compared with the venerable history of architecture, and perhaps it is presently in a developmental stage awaiting its rites of passage to maturity

THE NEEDS OF SPECIAL PATIENT POPULATIONS

Being a generalist in health care design used to be sufficient. Understanding the general needs of patients, staff, and family members was adequate and all that health care clients demanded. This level is no longer acceptable. After 20 years of generalist doctrine, the need is great for specialists who understand the unique requirements of special patient populations. This is the next step for health care architects and interior designers who have spent the past 10 years finely honing their skills in understanding hospitals as a building type, including the many options for patient room design, options for nursing unit layout, efficiencies in delivering support services to patient care areas, HVAC engineering strategies, the design of lobbies with atria to introduce natural lighting and views of the outdoors, designing for flexibility, and incorporating expansion without disrupting existing operations.

While this vast body of general knowledge was accumulating, the prevailing notion was that the physical environment or setting represented a passive background for human behavior, with little recognition of its dynamic power to actually shape behavior. Early studies in man-environment research dealt with large issues such as crowding proxemics (cultural use of space), and territoriality. Within the past 10 years, however, the emerging fields of architectural psychology and environmental psychology have directed attention to the impact of the interior environment—sizes of rooms, acoustics, lighting, and color—on human behavior.

Although the body of research on these topics is not vast, it is steadily increasing and in coming years should provide a good deal of general information about the microenvironment of the hospital. In order to fine-tune the physical setting for *specific* patient populations, however, the focus of research will have to shift to studying, for example, cancer patients, neonates, psychiatric patients, and those requiring critical care. The elderly, as a group, have been studied extensively, although those who specialize in this field might feel that such research is still in its infancy. If that is so, then research on other patient populations, by volume comparison, is almost nonexistent.

Environmental Docility Hypothesis

To appreciate the importance of meeting the needs of special patient populations, two concepts borrowed from research on aging help to provide a framework of understanding. The *environmental docility hypothesis*, developed by M. Powell Lawton (1980), states that "the less competent the individual, the greater the impact of environmental factors on that individual." The impact of the environment is greatest on patient populations who are most vulnerable and who can exert limited control over changing it, such as the mentally ill, neonates, the frail elderly, and critical care patients. Because of the extreme vulnerability of these patient groups, a small positive or negative change in the environment may produce a disproportionate amount of improvement or disability in an individual patient.

Competence and Environmental Press

The second concept that gives theoretical structure to understanding the importance of person-environment fit is Lawton's concept of competence and environmental press. *Competence* is a measure of an individual's biological health, sensorimotor functioning, cognitive skill, and ego strength; it is "an entity of definable

reality independent of the way the person perceives himself" (Lawton 1980, 14). These characteristics of competence can be measured by specific behaviors, such as biological health (e.g., respiratory difficulty, high blood pressure), sensorimotor functioning (e.g., failure to hear conversation), cognitive skill (e.g., forgetting names or dates), and ego strength (e.g., feeling depressed or angry).

Lawton and Nahemow (as reported in Lawton 1980) classified environments on the basis of their "demand character": some environments make behavioral demands on people and others do not. This quality is known as *environmental press*. No matter how high an individual's level of competence, a point of high press, where adaptation fails and behavior deteriorates, always occurs. Even persons of very low competence, however, if presented with a low-press environment, are capable of adaptive behavior and positive affect; the higher a person's competence, the wider the range of press the person is able to cope with in a positive manner (Lawton 1980). In this sense, behavior is viewed as the outcome of interaction between personal competence and environmental press.

Unfortunately, no formula or recipe provides a design response that is equally applicable to all patients in a specific population. Cancer patients, as an example, have individual levels of competence that, depending upon the press of the environment, either enhance or weaken their abilities to function. In spite of this lack of a formula, I hope that the present discussion will increase the design professional's awareness of these issues so that the right questions can be asked to create a framework for the design program. Each facility has its unique combination of givens, such as budget, staffing patterns, mission statement, design of existing facility, and individual personalities, that affect the application of any set of theories.

UNIVERSAL DESIGN

The concept of barrier-free design is not new. However, the passage of the Americans with Disabilities Act, which states that all disabled persons should be covered by the same civil rights protection as other Americans, makes the understanding of universal design imperative. The concept of universal design is that the environment should address the needs of all age groups—young, old, disabled, or able-bodied—without appearing different or special. These features should be incorporated into all interior environments as a normal course of events so that each environment is appropriate for individuals during their entire life spans. Any person, at some point in life, may be temporarily disabled, at which time he or she often becomes painfully aware of the inconvenience, loss of independence, and humiliation suffered needlessly by disabled persons who have to interact with unresponsive environments.

According to Susan Behar (a consultant on the Morton Plant Project featured in several places in this book), accessibility, adaptability, aesthetics, and affordability constitute the four A's that characterize universal design.

Cynthia Leibrock's new book, *Beautiful Barrier-free Design: A Visual Guide* (Van Nostrand Reinhold 1991), is an outstanding reference on this topic. A designer can meet the code and not meet the need. For example, the five-foot turning radius assumed for wheelchairs might be fine for people with good upper body strength, but it is certainly not adequate for frail individuals. Grab bars installed according to code are at the wrong location and height to be useful to many who need them.

Universal design affects everything from selection of hardware to clearances under countertops, color, and furniture selection. Contrast between floor and wall, and other surfaces, make the environment more suitable for those who are visually impaired. Lowering a section of the reception desk makes it accessible to children or those in wheelchairs. A reception counter with a deeper and higher than standard, recessed toe-kick accommodates footplates on wheelchairs. Seating with arms and firm upholstery makes chairs easier to get out of for orthopedic patients, pregnant women, and the elderly.

I hope that greater interest in universal design will prompt manufacturers of hardware and other items to focus more on aesthetics. Too often these products are grossly unattractive and serve to widen the gap of consciousness between the disabled and able-bodied populations.

POSTOCCUPANCY EVALUATION

Postoccupancy evaluations (POEs) offer the greatest hope for measuring the success of in-

dividual design responses for various environments. They are the only way to measure failures and successes methodically and scientifically. Most architects and interior designers do not have the background or experience to know how to develop or pursue this type of research, and those who created the design might be ill suited to evaluate it due to their bias, whether conscious or subconscious. Preiser, Rabinowitz, and White's *Post-Occupancy Evaluation*, an excellent guide to understanding the historical and theoretical background of performance-based evaluation, outlines the steps, activities, and resources required to carry out such evaluations in the field. A designer wishing to engage a researcher to conduct this sort of investigation should contact a university offering a program in architecture, environmental design, or environmental psychology.

The postoccupancy evaluation of Quincy Mental Health Center (Welch and Epp 1988) is an example of a comprehensive study of a state-owned community mental health center. Under Massachusetts law, the Office of Programming within the Division of Capital Planning and Operations is required to undertake postoccupancy evaluations of state facilities. The scope of this POE makes it a good reference not only for data relating to design of mental health facilities but also for format of other POEs.

ARCHITECTURAL EXPRESSION OF EXCELLENCE

Architecture, when it is well executed, can express the spirit of an institution more powerfully than words. Design is never created in a void; it must be appropriate for that individual institution, based on its mission statement or values, the community it serves, geographic location, and strategic planning objectives. In formulating the design for a new facility, the personality and vision of the hospital administrator often set the aesthetic goals and objectives. In fact, sometimes an individual administrator leaves such a strong imprint on a facility that several generations of administrators who followed have pointed with pride to various aesthetic features of the hospital and attributed them to their predecessor's dedication to architectural quality. This sort of awareness and pride fosters great architecture and allows it to step forth from mere competence to achieve excellence.

INTEGRATION OF ARCHITECTURE AND INTERIOR DESIGN

Unity between architecture and interior design is essential to any excellent project. For years architects and interior designers have viewed each other with skepticism and a certain amount of mistrust. Conservative architects have held fast to the notion that the architect should be responsible for the entire building. Central to this concept is the idea that interior design cannot possibly be separated from the architecture itself. There are master architects like Louis Sullivan and Frank Lloyd Wright, whose handling of interior spaces and details was so masterful that collaboration with another design professional is hard to imagine, and a few contemporary architects also demonstrate such impressive abilities, but wunderkinder aside, the practitioners who are the mainstream of architectural practice sometimes find themselves less adept at dealing with the intricacies of interior spaces than they would like. Some of these individuals have relied upon interior designers to develop color palettes, select and specify furniture, and propose interior finishes; others rely on interior designers to collaborate with them on shaping interior spaces, which includes space planning, lighting design, casework design, and detailing of ceilings and structural elements.

Arthur Gensler has been credited with introducing the specialty of space planning as a separate entity from architecture some 20 years ago, when architecture was in a slump economically and he was trying to carve out a niche for himself, and the rest is, as the saying goes, history. Actually, the bridge between architects and interior designers was created by interior architects, many of whom were architects who devoted their practices specifically to the interior environment. Today, many of the top commercial or contract interior designers are architects who do not practice in the traditional sense but rather dedicate their work entirely to interior design. For some reason, few of these prominent interior architects have devoted themselves to health care; most are associated with high-profile corporate design.

Fortunately, in recent years, a growing respect between architects and interior designers has led to a desirable collaboration between the two professions on health care projects. However, a great deal more effort needs to be made to truly integrate the two disciplines. The single reason many projects submitted for this book were disqualified was because of a total lack of integration between architecture and interior design. I do not wish to focus on negatives, but the problem was so widespread that the point needs to be made emphatically.

Furniture layouts often seemed totally inappropriate for the shape of the space, as if the furniture had been arbitrarily plunked down into the room with little regard for scale or circulation. The architecture sometimes had very little detailing or interest: the ceiling of a main lobby might have had a two- by four-foot suspended ceiling with fluorescent luminaires; the information or reception desk might have been stuck in the middle of the lobby and dwarfed by the space around it, having no soffit or ceiling treatment overhead to call attention to it and make it more prominent.

Corridors were often totally devoid of interest: they were eight- by eight-foot tunnels with suspended ceilings and two- by four-foot luminaires running across the width of the corridor, walls were painted or had vinyl wallcovering, and floors had carpet or tile. Miles of these undistinguished corridors characterized hundreds of facilities submitted for consideration. Lobbies or lounges were often an extension of these corridors, with no changes in ceiling height, no changes in lighting (either lighting level or type of fixtures), and little change in ambience. Nurse stations and even reception desks in lobbies were sometimes handled in the most perfunctory way, with a 42-inch-high plastic laminate countertop and nothing special in the way of detailing.

Sometimes the shape of a major room, such as a lobby or dining room, was so odd and irregular that it seemed to have been forced by the coming together of external forces, like the geological theory of plate tectonics. Some special care areas that were submitted purported to meet the needs of a special patient group, but had the most trivial of cosmetic treatments as the method of accomplishing this goal. As an example, a pediatric patient room might have been no different than an adult patient room except for its clown posters and a small shelf for stuffed animals; accommodation for a parent to sleep in the room and child-height plumbing fixtures were not considered. The most sobering thought about all of this is not that health care design professionals created these projects, but that they believed them to be excellent. I hope that the projects in this book will serve as examples of excellent integration between architecture and interior design.

Architectural Features

Central to the architectural expression of excellence is functional space planning that supports the goals of clinical programs and enables caregivers to execute their tasks efficiently. Over and above that are the following issues, some of which are less tangible and harder to measure.

- Scale: volume, ceiling heights, massing of horizontal or vertical elements
- Relationship between indoor and outdoor space
- Use of materials: texture, form, color
- Acoustics
- Lighting
- Ease of wayfinding: architectural legibility
- Variety

As you review projects in this chapter and elsewhere in the book, evaluate them in terms of the above criteria. Variety is one of the elements most noticeable both between one area of the hospital and another and within an individual room itself. In lieu of an institutional sameness, successful projects offer a variety of settings, some uncluttered and soothing and others highly stimulating. Variety in individual rooms may be expressed with layers of elements or detailing, reading against each other. A rich variety of textures stimulates the senses. The designs show an appreciation of form and its ability to lead the eye around the room in a prescribed manner.

ENVIRONMENTAL FACTORS

Several environmental factors affect the senses and, in turn, impact stress levels. Sound can be negative if it is perceived as noise and cannot be controlled; in fact, noise is one of the most significantly detrimental environmental factors known to cause physiological changes in the body and affect healing. Then again, sound perceived as music can be positive and therapeutic (see chapter 2). Acoustics are largely under the control of the design team, and every effort should be made during the design process to anticipate sources of noise and find ways to mitigate them.

BIOLOGICAL IMPORTANCE OF LIGHT

Light is another highly significant environmental factor, whether natural or artificial. A large body of research documents the biological effects of light on animals and humans, some of which is summarized in chapter 2 and elsewhere in this book. Lighting is known to affect hormonal and metabolic balance and entrainment of circadian rhythms. In fact, neuroscientist Richard Wurtman believes that ''light is the most important environmental input, after food, in controlling bodily function'' (Olds and Daniel 1987). The physiological impact of light is dependent upon full-spectrum light striking the retina, which influences the production of several neurotransmitters that are thought to affect the entire nervous system. One of these, melatonin, ''which appears to be the pineal gland's main secretory product, is influenced strongly by frequency, duration, and intensity of environmental light'' (Feierman 1982, 463). The pineal gland is the photoneuroendocrine transducer responsible for reproduction, light and dark (day-night) differentiation, sleep, and appetite.

Light is so important to the biological and physiological health of human beings that Canada and Japan have enacted sunshine laws that require city planners, when designing new buildings, to assure each individual's entitlement to a minimum number of hours of sunshine per day. A Tokyo court, when announcing the new regulation, stated: ''Sunshine is essential to comfortable life, and, therefore, a citizen's right to enjoy sunshine at his home should be duly protected by law'' (*New York Times*, July 17, 1975, as reported in Olds and Daniel 1987).

In the clinical setting, lighting has been used as therapy. Most notably, phototherapy has replaced blood transfusions in treating neonatal jaundice; ultraviolet light is commonly used to treat a dermatological condition, psoriasis; and full-spectrum light is used to treat seasonal affective disorder (SAD), which is thought to result from suppression of melatonin production during winter months, during which time people are exposed to artificial lighting that is often deficient in certain wavelengths. This lack of light causes depression, moodiness, and even a craving for carbohydrates. Nurses at Fresno Community Hospital in California found they had more energy, higher productivity, and a greater ability to solve complex problems when

Environmental Factors **51**

lighting was changed to Sylvania Designer 50 and GE Compax fluorescent lamps, following research done at the National Institute of Mental Health (conversation with Sue Simms, Assistant Administrator of Nursing, January 12, 1991).

Benefits of Full-Spectrum Lighting

Traditionally, lighting engineers and those in the design professions have been concerned with lighting in terms of either vision or aesthetics. What has been overlooked is the biological significance of light. Many studies prove the benefits of full-spectrum lighting, especially in patient care areas, but this comment from Mayer Spivak and Joanna Tamer (reported in Olds and Daniel 1987, 12) presents an evolutionary perspective:

> The human psychological system and the behavior which is linked to it evolved over millions of years. The whole of that evolution took place under the influence of the sunlight spectrum, to which particular light-sensitive and light-modulated organ systems are specifically adapted. . . . We have all been participating in a nearly century-long and completely undocumented and unmeasured experiment on the effects of electrical lighting with deficient spectra.

One of the most interesting studies was performed by Harold Wohlfarth in Germany. He documented the impact of full-spectrum lighting on blood pressure and respiration rates of both blind and sighted children. When lighting was changed to full spectrum, the children's mean systolic blood pressure dropped 17 percent, and their behavior showed less aggression and restlessness. When lighting was returned to the original design, the children's blood pressure increased to former levels, as did their restlessness. The researcher hypothesized that light striking the retina influenced the pineal gland's synthesis of melatonin, which in turn affected the body's output of the neurotransmitter serotonin (Gruson as reported in Olds and Daniel 1987). Serotonin levels control feelings of depression.

Numerous studies have shown other benefits of full-spectrum lighting such as shorter reaction times, better visual acuity, improved fine motor skills, less physiological fatigue, overall improved task performance, and vitamin D synthesis. The importance of full-spectrum light, whether natural sunlight or from an electrical source, is even more important in environments for hospitalized children because children are accustomed to playing outdoors for lengthy periods each day.

TECHNICAL DATA

Full-spectrum lighting refers to a source that closely resembles the spectral distribution of sunlight; it includes radiation in the near-ultraviolet band. Unfortunately, full-spectrum fluorescent lamps are not always readily available from electrical wholesalers, and they are considerably more expensive than the Cool White and Warm White fluorescents that are commonly used in hospitals. Fluorescent lamps are selected on the basis of lumen output, color temperature, color rendition, and energy consumption. The color temperature is expressed in degrees Kelvin. The higher the color temperature, the bluer the appearance and the closer to daylight; the lower the color temperature, the redder the appearance. The color rendering index (CRI) describes the ability of a lamp to render objects as they would be seen in outdoor sunlight, which has a CRI of 100. Thus a lamp with a CRI of 80 renders the object 80 percent as accurately as outdoor sunlight. Lamps with a high CRI produce less lumens per watt, which has to be factored into the calculation when trying to achieve a desired footcandle level.

In patient care areas, rendering the skin as realistically as possible is important. The least expensive lamp that has a high enough CRI to accomplish this goal is *Cool White Deluxe*. Although it is not totally full spectrum, it would be the fluorescent lamp of choice in patient care areas if full-spectrum lamps are beyond budget considerations.

Types of Fluorescent Lamps

Here is a list of the most commonly used fluorescent lamps, plus a few unique ones.

Cool White lamps are approximately 4100° K with a CRI of 68. They intensify white, gray, blue, and green and do not blend well with incandescent.

Cool White Deluxe lamps are 4100° K with a CRI of 89. Their color rendition is a big improvement over Cool White lamps, but the lumens per watt are reduced considerably; more of them are needed to achieve the same level of illumination as Cool White. They produce a very light pink-white color.

Warm White lamps are approximately 3000° K with a CRI of 56. They slightly distort all colors and have a pink glow, but mix well with incandescent.

Warm White Deluxe lamps are 3000° K with a CRI of 71. They greatly intensify warm colors, are not as pink as standard Warm White, and blend well with incandescent.

Daylight lamps are 6500° K and usually have a CRI of 75, but Duro-Test makes one with a CRI of 92. This lamp produces a cold blue-white light, not enhancing to warm colors and incandescent light, but useful in a room where a large quantity of natural light is present.

Standard White lamps are 3500° K with a CRI of 64. These lamps fall between Cool White and Warm White, so they are a good middle-of-the-road choice for a budget that does not permit a higher-quality lamp. The one with the highest CRI number is best. These lamps blend adequately with incandescent light.

Vita-Lite lamps are 5500° K with a CRI of 91. This high-quality lamp is made only by Duro-Test. It is a bright white lamp that simulates the full color and ultraviolet spectrum of sunlight.

Ultralume 3000 lamps are 3000° K with a CRI of 85. Made by Phillips, this lamp enhances warm colors and has better color rendition than Warm White Deluxe.

Optima 32 lamps are 3200° K with a CRI of 82. Manufactured by Duro-Test, this general purpose lamp has the warmth of incandescent but better color rendition.

Optima 50 lamps are 5000° K with a CRI of 91. Made by Duro-Test, it is recommended where visual acuity is required and where color matching is performed.

Chroma 50 lamps are 5000° K with a CRI of 90. Made by General Electric, it is close to a full-spectrum lamp.

SP35 lamps are 3500° K with a CRI of 73. Made by General Electric, this lamp renders skin tones very well, making it ideal for medical offices. It has the good color rendering properties of Cool White Deluxe and Warm White Deluxe, but has considerably higher lumen output. Cool White Deluxe has 56 lumens per watt; SP35 offers 83 lumens per watt. The SP35 complements both cool and warm color palettes and produces a crisp light midway between Cool White and Warm White.

SPX35 is 3500° K with a CRI of 82. Manufactured by General Electric, it is an enhanced version of the SP35; it is more expensive, but makes colors appear more vivid.

Compact fluorescent lamps are available from 2700° K to 3500° K with a CRI of 82. Manufactured by many lamp companies, this new type of fluorescent is a small twin tube in a U shape, available in 7-watt, 9-watt, and 13-watt lamps. The color rendition is very similar to incandescent, but tends to be pinker and less yellow. The 7-watt lamp is equivalent to a 40-watt incandescent; the 9-watt lamp, to a 60-watt incandescent; and the 13-watt, to a 75-watt incandescent. These lamps are very popular because they combine the high efficiency and long life of fluorescent lamps with good color rendition. Their size allows them to be used in downlights, wall sconces, and other types of fixtures that previously required incandescent bulbs.

Low-voltage lamps are of many types, the most common of which is the MR-16. These 12-volt quartz halogen lamps average 3000° K and render colors vividly. The beam can be precisely focused to enhance textures or an art object or to add drama to a room. Low-voltage lamps accomplish a desired level of illumination with fewer watts than required by incandescent lamps, which makes them energy efficient. Additionally, the miniature size of the lamp allows it to be used in fixtures much smaller than those that accommodate incandescent bulbs. MR-16s give a clean, white light that enhances all colors.

For comparison, an incandescent lamp is 2800° K, and daylight (although it does vary with the time of day, the time of the year, and whether the sky is sunny or cloudy) is arbitrarily established at 6500° K. The reader is encouraged to write to the Duro-Test Corporation in North Bergen, New Jersey, and to Westinghouse in Bloomington, New Jersey. Both manufacturers have excellent technical literature on their lamps. The General Electric Company in Nela Park, Ohio, also publishes a number of interesting booklets.

Energy Conservation

Energy conservation, although well intentioned, has had a devastating effect on the aesthetics of lighting in health care facilities. Corridors that were carefully and properly designed to the appropriate footcandle level might now be operating at 50 percent of that intended level. Curtailing energy usage can also result in impaired visual acuity that affects nursing tasks, such as reading the label on medication or searching for supplies in an emergency.

Many states require lamps to be wired for dual switching, which enables the hospital maintenance engineer to switch off half of the lamps in order to save energy. The result is that light levels are unreasonably low, colors are dulled, and considerable contrast appears between upper and lower portions of a wall; the upper two feet of a corridor wall, close to the ceiling, may actually appear to be a medium shade of gray (due to shadow), even though the wall is white. To make matters worse, sometimes the color of the lamp is changed from what was originally installed to one that is less expensive, such as Cool White, which might have a devastating effect on the perception of certain colors. These changes are the nemesis of architects and interior designers. The most effective way to control them is through operational protocols established by the administrator.

Worse than not enough light is too much light. More is not better. A high level of general illumination tends to wash out textures and colors. Much more interesting, as well as energy efficient, is an interplay of high and low levels of illumination. In areas where visual tasks of medium or high contrast must be performed, the task, not the entire room, should receive light, although achieving this is certainly not as simple as stated. Glare, veiling reflections, ratio of overall brightness to task illumination, and age of the worker must be taken into account. (Chapter 14 discusses age-related vision changes and appropriate design guidelines.) Lighting, skillfully handled, can set up a rhythm of patterns, light, and shadow that can transform an otherwise commonplace interior environment into something quite spectacular. Lighting in health care facilities is probably one of the most underappreciated and underexploited aesthetic components of the interior environment.

Illumination Requirements

An in-depth discussion of lighting design and technical data is not within the scope of this chapter, but several publications are highly recommended sources of additional information. For hospital illumination requirements, specifically detailed for each type of room and taking into consideration the types of tasks to be performed and the ages of occupants or workers, consult *Lighting for Health Care Facilities* (1985) and chapter 14 in William Beck and Ralph Meyer's *The Health Care Environment: The User's Viewpoint*. Beck is a physician, president of the Donald Guthrie Foundation for Medical Research in Sayre, Pennsylvania, and the author of numerous highly respected studies on health care lighting, especially that of the operating room. Readers interested in a review of the literature and research on lighting should see Olds and Daniel (1987).

Asking the Right Questions

In programming various areas of the hospital, the designer has to be able to ask the right questions about tasks so that lighting can be designed appropriately. The following list of questions has been taken from *Lighting for Health Care Facilities* (1985):

1. What are the tasks and their background reflectance?
2. How much time is spent on each task?
3. What percentage of time is spent on each task?
4. How important is each task?
5. How important is speed?
6. How important is accuracy?
7. Which tasks are most visually difficult?
8. Which tasks are most fatiguing?
9. What are the ages of the personnel performing the tasks?

Evaluation of Lighting Systems

An evaluation of lighting systems for various areas of the hospital should be based on these criteria (*Lighting for Health Care Facilities* 1985):

1. Visual comfort
2. Compatibility with architectural design
3. Compatibility with mounted equipment, such as x-ray
4. Flexibility of arrangement

5. Compatibility with air conditioning design
6. Compatibility with acoustical requirements
7. Performance
8. Ease of cleaning and decontamination
9. Aesthetics
10. Economics of selected systems with regard to maintained illuminance level

   a. Initial installed cost
   b. Maintenance and other annual costs
   c. Cost of rearrangement
   d. Depreciation and replacement costs

The Collaborative Approach

Lighting design is a vast topic of enormous complexity best handled in a collaborative effort between architect, interior designer, electrical engineer, and perhaps a lighting design consultant. Planning for natural lighting can more easily be controlled by the architect who can design into the project, wherever possible, courtyards, atria, greenhouses, solaria, clerestories, skylights, window wells, and balconies. The beauty of natural light is that it changes continually, cuing the passage of time and giving variety and form to the perception of objects and architecture. The luminosity of natural light, of course, can never be matched by an artificial source.

HEAT AND VENTILATION

In a hospital, heating and ventilation are very complex issues that require careful consideration. Needs vary, depending upon an individual department and the patient population served. In the operating room, for example, a delicate balance must be maintained between relative humidity and room temperature in order to avoid problems of condensation or static electricity. Similarly, air pressure must be carefully regulated in laboratories to control the spread of viruses and in patient isolation rooms to protect from infection patients who have compromised immune systems.

Patient populations especially vulnerable to thermal conditions are patients under anesthesia, those with spinal cord injuries, infants, patients with cardiac conditions or burns, and the elderly; temperature and humidity are known to affect wound healing (Williams 1988). Special consideration should be given to the elimination of drafts by making sure doors and windows close tightly and by the use of Thermopane insulated glass. Temperature control is especially important in the zone close to the floor in any area serving children. A number of suggestions for dealing with this issue are discussed in Olds and Daniel (1987).

The most significant problem in contemporary buildings, including hospitals, is tight building syndrome, which is caused by sealed buildings and a total dependence on mechanical systems for heating, ventilation, and air conditioning; windows cannot be opened. The National Institute for Occupational Safety and Health (Olds and Daniel 1984, 35) did research that revealed a correlation between poor ventilation and a number of illnesses including headaches, fatigue, sinus congestion, eye irritation, chest tightness, nausea, dizziness, and dermatitis. Many nosocomial (originating in a hospital) diseases were traced to this condition. These problems are common in large buildings with nonoperable windows and ventilation systems that filter only about 85 percent of the air (Olds and Daniel 1987). A variety of pollutants such as smoke, hair spray, perfume, body odors, airborne bacteria, and formaldehyde resulting from the off-gassing of synthetic building materials are recirculated and inhaled by the building's inhabitants.

COLOR

The intensity and passion of the debate about the possibility of predicting and measuring physiological responses to color bear witness to the power of color and its ability to arouse emotion. Centuries ago, healers associated color with symbolism and magic. Even today, every culture has taboos about certain colors, and others are favored; certain colors are reserved for royalty. Throughout all periods of history color has engendered debate and discussion in fashion, art, and decorating. The psychedelic movement of the sixties was characterized by an explosion of color.

Biological Importance of Color

In the biological world, since the dawn of civilization, color has been a necessity for locating food and observing predators. It is nature's survival kit for plants and animals in that it attracts, camouflages, and protects them; color has a biological cue function in certain organisms. In humans, studies have documented the effects of specific colors on individuals having certain diseases. For example, epileptics and others with certain types of neurological diseases lost their equilibrium or were more subject to seizures when wearing red. Goldstein noted a large variety of differential motor reactions displayed by patients under the respective effects of red and green light. Movements executed with the same intention were performed much more exactly in green than in red light; handwriting, for example, was nearer to normal with green ink than with red. Moreover, estimates of length, weight, and time were better under green light than red (Goldstein as reported in Sharpe 1974).

Arousal Value of Certain Colors

Other investigators have noted that blood pressure and respiration increased during exposure to red light but decreased in blue illumination. Red light has been said to reduce the pain of rheumatism and arthritis. It dilates the blood vessels and produces heat in the tissues. Birren (1969) postulates that the red color of Mercurochrome may be effective in the healing of wounds because of its absorption of blue light. Blue light relieves headaches and lowers blood pressure, and its tranquilizing effect is said to aid insomniacs.

Tests of galvanic skin response (GSR) have demonstrated significant relationships between GSR and colors that have been rated high in arousal value, mainly reds and yellows. Gerard (as reported in Jacobs and Hustmyer 1974) reported that the autonomic nervous system and the visual cortex were significantly less aroused during blue than during red or white illumination. Jacobs and Hustmyer (1974) found that the most arousing color was red, followed by green and yellow, with blue the least arousing, based on GSR, but they noted a lack of significant effect with respect to heart rate. Such inconsistencies in similar studies were thought to be due to differences in the color stimuli themselves (the same specifications were not used).

The correlation between color and emotion has been further demonstrated by the Rorschach inkblot test, which, although not uncontested, has been used for years to measure the emotional state of neurotics and schizophrenics who are assumed to suffer color shock when presented with the chromatic cards.

Controversy in Color Research

Despite many attempts to document the effects of color on human behavior and on physiological systems of the body, investigators remain skeptical. Margaret Williams (1988, 73), a nurse researcher, states: "Color . . . has aesthetic and symbolic meaning . . . however there is no evidence that certain hues actually affect health; studies of patient behavior under different color conditions are lacking." Richard Wurtman (Gruson 1982, C6), a nutritionist at the Massachusetts Institute of Technology, states: "Several experiments have shown that different colors affect blood pressure, pulse and respiration rates, as well as brain activity and biorhythms. As a result, colors are now used in the treatment of a variety of diseases."

William Beck (1983, 43), physician and prominent researcher in lighting, suggests that "there is very little hard evidence that visual responses to colored light evoke specific physiologic responses. The data suggesting a color response on blood pressure, heart rate, and respiration, are, in my opinion, inconclusive. My own studies have been completely equivocal. We do realize that there are emotional responses to certain colors, so we should let these guide us rather than anticipate a therapeutic effect."

Alexander Schauss (Gruson 1982, C6), director of The American Institute for Biosocial Research, believes that color has a direct physiological impact: "The electromagnetic energy of color interacts in some still unknown way with the pituitary and pineal glands in the hypothalamus. These organs regulate the endocrine system, which controls many basic body functions and emotional responses, such as aggression." Harold Wohlfarth, president of The German Academy of Color Science (whose study of the effects of full-spectrum lighting on a group of blind and sighted children was discussed earlier), asserts that "minute amounts of electromagnetic energy that compose light affect one or more of the brain's neurotransmitters, chemicals that carry messages from nerve to nerve and from nerve to muscle" (Gruson 1982, C6).

The controversy, for the most part, deals with what portion of the electromagnetic spectrum has an effect on health. Some doubt that the visible spectrum (color) elicits anything more than an emotional response based on past experience, cultural conditioning, or association with trends and what is fashionable. However, the effects of the nonvisible portion of the spectrum (light) are incontrovertible.

Occasionally a practical application of a particular color causes interest and controversy. For example, the San Bernardino County Probation Department in California found that if they put aggressive children into a small cell painted "bubble gum pink," the children tended to relax immediately, ceased yelling and banging, and often fell asleep within ten minutes (Gruson 1982). Previously, brute force had been required to calm highly agitated juveniles. Based on these results, many correctional facilities across America employed "passive pink" in at least one room. Yet some psychologists have doubted the effect claimed because it is too simple a solution to a complex problem. Research has shown that the effects of color are not constant; after a short time, people adapt, which accounts for some of the mixed reviews about the efficacy of passive pink. Studies of this type and others mentioned previously come under the heading of photobiology.

One investigator hypothesized that a change in the color of an environment will bring a change in the pattern of movement within that space. In an experiment done with museum visitors rather than hospital patients, subjects in a dark brown room took more footsteps, covered more area, and spent less time in the room than subjects in a light beige room. The conclusion was that color does, in fact, affect human movement (Srivastava and Peel 1968).

Intuitive Bias about Color
Color and pattern are so integral to an interior designer's life that intuitive bias might influence the selection of colors for a particular project. In residential design such a bias would pose no problem, but in restaurants, offices, retail spaces, and particularly in health care, color must be used to make food appear more attractive, draw people into a store, reduce eyestrain in offices, and, in a hospital, enhance visual acuity in surgery or soothe anxious patients. A designer's personal preference should have little to do with the proper selection of color in nonresidential spaces and particularly in hospitals. The fact that a patient is captive and cannot easily leave the treatment environment puts a

great responsibility on the designer to select a color that will not be detrimental to the patient's feeling of well-being, or worse, negatively alter blood pressure, respiration, or endocrine activity.

Given this responsibility, erring on the side of blandness might be preferable to creating an overly stimulating color palette. However, such caution would be incorrect. Evidence suggests that bland, monotonous environments cause sensory deprivation and are detrimental to healing. The brain needs constant change and stimulation in order to maintain homeostasis (stabilization of physiological functions). In addition, white walls cause considerable glare, which in turn causes the pupil to constrict. White walls have a clinical appearance that is unfamiliar and strange to most people; the absence of color is eerie. The combination of white walls, white ceiling, and white floor create strange perceptual conditions that can be very upsetting to patients trying to stabilize their balance or orient themselves.

Unfortunately, substantive guidelines for selection of color in health care facilities do not exist. Nevertheless, enough concrete information is available to enable an intelligent, motivated designer to develop color palettes that are reasonably appropriate and not detrimental.

An Approach to Color
Of the many possible ways of dealing with color in interior design, the following approach is suggested.

1. *Consider the needs of each specific patient population that might affect the selection of color.* In elderly populations, understand how vision changes as the eye ages. People need more contrast and more saturated color; pastel tones are sometimes not visible. With neonates, vigilance for cyanosis and jaundice is always necessary; use of blue or yellow would make observing these conditions difficult.

2. *Understand the laws of perception:* simultaneous contrast, successive contrast and afterimage, metameric color pairs, reflectance, Purkinje effect, color constancy, advancing and receding colors, figure-ground reversal. (Recommended source: *The Theory and Practice of Color* by Frans Gerritsen [1974]).

3. *Consider religious or symbolic associations with color, including cultural taboos, bias, and*

nationality, that may be relevant to that particular community. (Recommended sources: Edward T. Hall, *The Silent Language* [1973], and other books on social or cultural anthropology.)

4. *Read as many studies as you can find about the physiological effects of color.* (See references at the end of chapters 2 and 3.)

5. *Consider functional factors:*

- Effect of lighting on color
- Ages of people who will use the space
- Is the space for patients, staff, or visitors, and what is the typical length of time these people will be exposed to these colors?
- The nature and severity of the illness
- Suitability of color palette for women, men, and children
- Types of tasks: amount of contrast desired, level of visual acuity required
- Is the goal to emphasize differences or to camouflage?
- Is the goal to organize spaces?
- How much contrast is desirable?
- Interaction of texture can cause the same color to look different on two surfaces
- Use as cueing device in wayfinding
- Use to denote hazards or warn of danger
- Color blindness of some individuals
- Geographic bias: in northern climates with long, harsh winters, warm colors might be more appropriate than cool; in the West, the quality of light is a warmer and more intense color than in the East; in tropical areas, strong saturated colors (hot pink, orange, peacock, purple, lime) are often favored

6. *Understand how color affects the perception of space.*

7. *Think about practical applications of color psychology.*

8. *Consider aesthetics:* Although studies may indicate that a blue accent wall is desirable for a coronary care patient, for example, the specific hue and its saturation or value, coupled with the way the color is used, are entirely dependent on the designer's skill and talent. Therefore, even though the initial development of color palettes may not have been based on intuition or personal taste, the final product still bears the stamp of the individual designer's unique talent.

Color and Its Effect on the Perception of Space

The laws of perception can be translated into the following guidelines for interior design and architecture:

1. To prepare people for the color of a room they are about to enter, the entry should be painted a complementary color.

2. Color modifies architectural form. It can expand, shorten, widen, lengthen, and give the illusion of lowering or raising a ceiling. Color can change the appearance of the environment so markedly that it can alter the individual's mood.

3. Bright colors appear to be lighter in weight. Ordered from "heavy" to "light" they are: red, blue, purple, orange, green, yellow.

4. Bright objects are overestimated in size. Yellow appears the largest, followed by white, red, green, blue, and black, in descending order.

5. A light object appears larger against a dark background. A dark object appears smaller against a light background.

6. The wall opposite a window should generally be kept light, or it will absorb much of the daylight. (However, in a patient room, this approach might create glare if appropriate window treatment is not provided.)

7. A window wall and frame should be light so as not to contrast too much with daylight sky. High contrast can result in headaches and eyestrain.

8. If a red wall is placed next to a yellow wall, the yellow wall will appear greener than it actually is due to the afterimage of red: cyan. The blue afterimage of the yellow will cause the red to appear more purple.

9. Warm colors advance; cool colors recede. (Warm colors are long wavelength colors; cool colors are short wavelength.)

10. Light colors and small patterns visually enlarge a space. Dark colors and large patterns make it appear smaller.

11. The absence of variety in the visual environment causes sensory deprivation. Those who are confined to nursing homes, hospitals, and institutions need changes in lighting, accent walls, and artwork for their nervous systems to function properly. A variety of colors is essential because the individual quickly adapts to the effects of any one color, no matter how predominant, and it becomes monotonous.

12. According to Kruithof's principle, in low levels of light (under 30 footcandles) the color of objects and surfaces will appear normal when the light source is slightly tinted with pink, orange, or yellow; at higher levels of lighting, objects and surfaces will appear normal when the light source is cooler. Therefore, a "warm" light source is best with low levels of illumination, and a "cooler" light source is best with high levels of illumination (Birren 1969).

Practical Applications of Color Psychology

Although the systematic investigation of the effects of color upon human behavior is in its infancy, and some studies have been viewed with skepticism, certain practical applications of this research may be warranted.

1. Red and yellows, for example, should be used in settings where creative activity is desired and socialization encouraged; greens and blues in areas that require more quiet and extended concentration and high visual acuity.

2. Cool colors may be appropriate in environments for agitated, hypertensive, or anxious individuals; red may be appropriate in the depressed person's environment. Highly saturated colors should be avoided with autistic schizophrenics; red should be avoided for those afflicted with epilepsy and other neurological diseases.

3. Rousing, bright colors are more appropriate in environments for the aged than pastels, which are barely visible to those with failing eyesight.

4. Strongly contrasting figure-ground patterns and extremely bright colors should be avoided in rooms of psychotic patients because these patterns—when not worn by the patients but impinging upon them from their environment—are thought to have an overwhelming, even intimidating, threatening effect.

5. Under warm colors, time is overestimated, weights seem heavier, objects seem larger, and rooms appear smaller. Under cool colors, time is underestimated, weights seem lighter, objects seem smaller, and rooms appear larger. Thus, cool colors should be used where monotonous tasks are performed to make the time seem to pass more quickly, and red, for example, should be used in an employees' restroom to reduce the amount of time spent there. Red and orange are commonly used in fast food restaurants, where quick turnover of tables is desired.

6. Warm colors with high illumination encourage increased alertness and outward orientation; they are good where muscular effort or action are required, such as a physical therapy gym. Cool colors and low illumination encourage less distraction and more opportunity to concentrate on difficult tasks; an inward orientation is fostered. Noise induces increased sensitivity to cool colors, probably because the tranquillity of these colors compensates for increased aural stimulation. People become less sensitive to warm colors under noise because they offer additional stimulation rather than less.

7. In patient rooms as well as staff areas, patterns should always be accompanied by a neutral wall to provide relief.

8. Looking at a specific color produces an afterimage of its complement. A practical application of this principle is the surgical operating room, where walls and garments are usually blue-green because the eye is concentrated on a red spot (blood); when surgeons look up from their work, they see afterimages of cyan or blue-green because red and cyan are opposite each other on the color wheel. If walls and garments were white, surgeons would see blue-green spots before their eyes every time they looked away from the operative site. Thus blue-green walls and apparel act as a background to neutralize afterimages.

Another example of afterimage can be experienced by walking through a corridor that has yellow walls, a warm-toned floor, and incandescent (warm) light—essentially a yellow-hued environment. Leaving the corridor to enter a lobby produces afterimages of blue, the complement of yellow. This concept is very important for interior design. An understanding of it can prevent a designer from creating undesirable color relationships.

9. In patient rooms, use colors that are flattering to skin tones near the patient's head; in patient bathrooms, use a light tint of rose or peach, in a shade that is flattering to skin tones, especially if fluorescent lighting is used around the mirror. Self-appraisal is important to a patient's morale; if lighting is poor and colors are unflattering to skin tones, patients may be shocked at their appearance.

Summary

Color no longer carries the mystical symbolism of ancient times, yet a precise understanding of color and its effect on human behavior remains beyond our reach. However, investigations over the past 20 years provide enough of a framework for interior designers to be able to develop an appropriate strategy for health care facilities. Using color requires a basic understanding of lighting as well because the appearance of color depends entirely on the spectral distribution of the light source and on the level of illumination. Other chapters contain specific guidelines on color for special patient populations, especially chapters 5, 11, and 14.

SPECIAL PLACES

"When a physically defined space becomes the focus or locus, on whatever level of man's [sic] behavior, a space becomes a place."
Mayer Spivack

Having just explored the features that characterize excellence in health care architecture and having examined the qualities of healing environments, here are a number of projects illustrating these concepts. The following rooms or areas can be thought of as special places because they are the principal spaces that influence patients' and visitors' evaluations of the hospital. In these rooms the hospital is experienced most vividly. Except for renal dialysis units, these rooms are generic sorts of spaces; the needs of specific patient populations are dealt with in individual chapters. Lobbies of children's hospitals, for example, are in chapter 5; patient rooms in a mental health unit are in chapter 11; critical care units are discussed in chapter 8.

The best way to read this section of the book would be in tandem with a copy of *Design That Cares* (Carpman, Grant, and Simmons 1986). Every possible functional consideration for each of these spaces has been taken into account, culminating in a series of checklists at the end of each section. Duplicating that information here would be counterproductive when *Design That Cares* should be part of every health care architect and designer's professional library. The focus of the present discussion, then, is to explain how the following projects exemplify the issues discussed thus far.

LOBBY

The lobby is the patient's or visitor's introduction to the hospital, and the design of this space sets expectations for the quality of clinical care. Sometimes just getting from the parking structure to the lobby can be such a circuitous task, involving a series of elevators, bridges, tunnels, and ramps, that the patient is worn-out upon arrival at the destination. On arrival in the lobby, the information desk and admitting department should be visible. The lobby and the hospital's main artery corridors must be architecturally legible and readily navigated by a wide variety of visitors, including local residents who have some familiarity with the hospital, first-time visitors, out-of-town travelers, disabled people, children, the illiterate, and those who cannot read English. Lobby visitors may include companions who are waiting for a patient being treated in the emergency room, family members awaiting news of a loved one in surgery, a friend waiting for a patient undergoing an outpatient test or procedure, or a family member taking a break while visiting an inpatient.

The most important features of a lobby are seating grouped to provide privacy (Figs. 3-1 and 3-2), access to nature and sunlight (Figs. 3-3 and 3-4), clearly defined admitting and cashier functions (Figs. 3-3 and 3-5), accommodation for children (Fig. 3-6), elevators that are easy to locate (Fig. 3-7), and interesting works of art (Figs. 3-8 and 3-9). A vestibule or wind lock is important because staff sitting at the information desk are often in a draft. A multilevel lobby provides a variety of spaces to explore (Fig. 3-10). A variety of seating options allows visitors to select one that satisfies individual comfort requirements (Figs. 3-11 and 3-12). A variety of light sources, both natural and artificial, accentuate architectural forms (Figs. 3-3 and 3-13). A clearly defined entry, with a directory and information desk that are easy to locate, eases wayfinding anxiety upon arrival at the facility (Figs. 3-14 and 3-15).

According to Anita Olds (1985, 105), "The entrance to every healing space should have a *torre* or Japanese arch, signalling the transition from profane to sacred territory, from that which is spontaneous and ordinary to that which is spiritually and aesthetically integrated." The lobby entry in Figure 3-16 has these qualities. Architectural elements are harmonious and balanced; in the total integration between architecture and interior design, each surface has been carefully and meticulously detailed, lighting has been precisely planned to achieve specific effects, and a dense thicket of plants introduces nature.

Some lobbies express grandeur with a glass galleria ceiling spanning a majestic lobby, not unlike what the visitor might find in a fine hotel

3-2

3-1 *Atrium lobby admits natural light and features hanging gardens cascading from corridor railing; The Christ Hospital Courtyard Atrium, Cancer Treatment Ambulatory Care Facility (Cincinnati, OH)*

Architecture and interior design: Hansen Lind Meyer; Photographer: Don DuBroff, The Sadin Group, Chicago

3-2 *Main lobby of the Mayo Building, Mayo Clinic (Rochester, MN); mural on rear wall by English artist John Piper is from the 1953 original building construction and depicts the city of the future in the cycle of urban growth; all patients pass through this lobby on their initial visit to the clinic*

Architecture and interior design: Payette Associates, Inc.; Photographer: Paul Ferrino

3-3 *Main lobby features natural light and lush landscaping, University Hospital Atrium Pavilion (Boston, MA)*

Architect: Hoskins Scott Taylor and Partners Inc., in association with Hansen Lind Meyer; Interior design: Hoskins Scott Taylor and Partners Inc., in conjunction with University Hospital Design Services; Photographer: © 1987 Paul Gobeil

3-3

3-4 *Main lobby, Pali Momi Medical Center (Aiea, HI)*
Architecture and interior design: Media Five Limited;
Photographer: Ron Starr

3-5 *Lobby registration area, Mayo Clinic (Rochester, MN)*

Architecture and interior design: Payette Associates, Inc.; Photographer: Paul Ferrino

3-6 *Waiting room/lounge, Detroit Receiving Hospital & Wayne State University Health Care Institute (Detroit, MI)*

Architecture and interior design: William Kessler & Associates Inc., Zeidler Roberts Partnership, and Giffels Associates Inc. (associated architects); Photographer: Balthazar Korab Ltd.

3-7 *The ambience of a fine hotel characterizes this hospital lobby that anchors one end of a comprehensive medical and health care mall complex, Elmwood Hospital (Metairie, LA)*

Architecture and interior design: Gresham, Smith and Partners; Photographer: © Alan Karchmer

3-6

3-7

3-8 *Main lobby, Pali Momi Medical Center (Aiea, HI) Architecture and interior design: Media Five Limited; Photographer: Ron Starr*

(Fig. 3-17). Granite floors, large-scale sculpture, fountains, and carefully planned lighting contribute to the ambience of the medical center in Figure 3-18. The lobby in Figure 3-7 was designed to convey an image of old southern hospitality for a new freestanding hospital with operations focused toward outpatient services. The architect notes that the interior ambience contrasts with the contemporary design of the exterior in order to meet the expectations of both affluent patients, who expect southern hospitality, and physicians, who desire the image of a modern medical center.

Impressive art collections can increasingly be found at major medical centers, indicating an appreciation of the benefits of art both as an investment and as a component of a healing environment. Detroit Receiving Hospital, part of the Wayne State University Health Center, has one of the largest and most comprehensive health facility art collections in the United States. Major works of public art were commis-

sioned, including the Anne Healy diagonal fabric sculpture in the seven-story courtyard (Fig. 3-19) and the George Sugarman metal sculpture in one of the courtyards accessible for outdoor dining (Fig. 3-20). Other large-scale works include a 14- x 17-foot bas-relief of gray and white shaded mosaic tiles and silver castings, installed in ten sections on steel frames above the reception desk. Another piece of environmental art called "Help" consists of two figures, one extending a hand to the other, fabricated from one-inch-thick aluminum; the figures rise 32 feet high in a third-floor courtyard space. A large, richly textured wool tapestry from Bogota, Colombia, has been executed in the style of a *mola* and hangs in the entrance lobby of the University Health Center.

Hundreds of additional original works of art were purchased from local artists, and other pieces by internationally prominent artists are on extended loan from the Wayne State University collection. The architecture of the hospital, designed by William Kessler & Associates in collaboration with Zeidler Roberts Partnership and Giffels Associates, reads from the exterior like a contemporary sculpture. Bold swathes of primary color accent building forms. The interior

3-9 *Main lobby features weaving by Urban Jupena, Detroit Riverview Hospital (Detroit, MI)*

Architecture and interior design: Harley Ellington Pierce Yee Associates, Inc.; Photographer: Daniel Bartush

3-10

3-11

3-10 *New interior courtyard atrium provides additional public circulation to unburden traffic through various departments, Lakewood Hospital (Lakewood, OH)*
   Architecture and interior design: Braun & Spice; Photographer: William E. Schuemann

3-11 *Family waiting, surgery, features natural light, plants, and seating grouped to offer families privacy, Scripps Memorial Hospital (La Jolla, CA)*
   Architect: Brown Gimber Rodriguez Park; Interior design: Jain Malkin Inc.; Photographer: Steve McClelland

3-12 *Hospital lobby with ambience of fine hotel, Scripps Memorial Hospital (Encinitas, CA)*
   Architect: Brown Gimber Rodriguez Park; Interior design: Jain Malkin Inc.; Photographer: Sandra Williams

3-12

3-13 *Admitting area and lobby benefit from natural light and interior plantscaping, Scripps Memorial Hospital (Encinitas, CA)*

Architect: Brown Gimber Rodriguez Park; Interior design: Jain Malkin, Inc.; Photographer: Sandra Williams

3-14

3-15

3-16 *Main lobby uses texture and form to create image of quality, St. Paul Ramsey Medical Center (St. Paul, MN)*

Architect: Alpha Architects, Inc.; Interior design: Wheeler Hildebrandt & Associates, Inc.; Photographer: Jerry Swanson

3-14 *Entry canopy carries exterior stucco into lobby (also see Figure 3-15), Scripps Memorial Hospital (Encinitas, CA)*

Architect: Brown Gimber Rodriguez Park; Interior design: Jain Malkin, Inc.; Photographer: Sandra Williams

3-15 *Entry foyer has hospitality ambience, Scripps Memorial Hospital (Encinitas, CA)*

Architect: Brown Gimber Rodriguez Park; Interior design: Jain Malkin Inc.; Photographer: Sandra Williams

3-17 (on following page) *Spacious lobby with glass-enclosed atrium garden features tropical plants and sculpture fountain, The Methodist Hospital, Dunn Tower (Houston, TX)*

Architect: Morris Architects; Interior design: Janita Lo & Associates; Photographer: Rick Gardner

3-18

3-18 (on following page) *Fountain with sculpture is focal point of lobby, The Methodist Hospital, Dunn Tower (Houston, TX)*
    Architect: Morris Architects; Interior design: Janita Lo & Associates; Photographer: Rick Gardner

3-19 Color Cross Section, *panels of vinyl sail cloth diagonally laced through the seven-story courtyard, by Anne Healy, Detroit Receiving Hospital (Detroit, MI)*
    Architect: William Kessler & Associates, Inc., Zeidler Roberts Partnership, and Giffels Associates, Inc. (associated architects); Photographer: Balthazar Korab Ltd.

3-19

3-20 *Public art displayed in courtyard accessible for outdoor dining; created by George Sugarman,* Field Sculpture *is an environmental piece that provides seating and shade and invites direct interaction; Detroit Receiving Hospital (Detroit, MI)*
Photographer: Balthazar Korab Ltd.

design, also executed by the architects, uses bold colors and geometric shapes (Fig. 3-6). Note the angled partitions that provide a degree of privacy without causing isolation.

A close look at Figure 3-19 reveals what a patient or visitor would see of the brightly colored fabric strips lacing the courtyard in counterpoint to the sensuous shapes and colors of the lobby furniture on each floor. To enhance appreciation and awareness of the Medical Center's art program, a color brochure available for visitors describes each of the major pieces and locates them on a reduced scale floorplan. Figures 13-12 and 16-3 also show this facility.

DINING FACILITIES FOR VISITORS AND PHYSICIANS

Eating is one of life's great pleasures. Meals or snacks shared with friends in an attractive cafeteria or dining room can be a bright spot in an employee's busy day. The cafeteria may pro-

vide respite for family members attending sick patients around the clock, or it may relieve boredom for ambulatory patients who wish to have a cup of coffee with visitors. Unfortunately, too many hospital cafeterias are buried (no pun intended) in basements and have limited access to natural light and garden views. Often a cafeteria has no design at all in terms of "ambience." It has a vinyl composition tile floor, a large room with tables and chairs, and a conventional stainless-steel foodservice line with quarry tile floor; spanning the entire space is a two- by four-foot suspended ceiling with lay-in fluorescent luminaires. The ambience varies little from morning to night; it has a uniformly high level of illumination with considerable glare, as well as a good deal of noise. Sometimes this ambience is compounded by poor air handling, and noxious cooking odors from the grill surround diners. Such a cafeteria or dining room does not adequately fulfill the vital role of providing an outlet for relaxation and social cama-

3-21 La Cocina Roja *is a cafeteria with upbeat decor featuring large paintings by artist Richard Phipps; adjacent patio offers views of flowers, trees, and a sculpture fountain; Saint Agnes Medical Center (Fresno, CA)*

Architect: Rochlin Baran & Balbona Inc.; Interior design: Struble-Chambers Design Associates; Photographer: © Kasparowitz Architectural Photography

raderie, in addition to offering nutritional sustenance.

Table sizes or shapes should accommodate groups of different sizes, from individuals dining alone to a table of eight housekeeping staff who may enjoy dining together (Fig. 3-21) If the hospital permits smoking indoors, a separate area for smokers should be set aside where the odor will not affect other diners. Natural light (Fig. 3-22) and a view of gardens are desirable; an outdoor feeling can be enhanced by the use of Italian market umbrellas and by carrying exterior materials, such as brick, into the space (Fig. 3-23). Note in Figure 3-23 the attention to detail in the design of built-in banquettes and recessed uplights that illuminate umbrellas. The handsome color palette of this dining room consists of the russet-colored brick complemented by green tabletops and upholstery fabric, oak trim on tables and chairs, and beige umbrellas. Carpeting on the floor and articulations in ceilings and walls provide solutions to the problem of noise in Figure 3-24. Low partitions, capped by panels of sandblasted glass, divide a large dining room into quieter, intimate spaces in Figure 3-25. Food tray lines should be wide enough to prevent traffic congestion and should clearly note the types of food that may be picked up at each station (Fig. 3-26).

3-22 *Cafeteria offers natural light and access to nature, Bethesda Memorial Hospital (Boynton Beach, FL)*

Architecture and interior design: Henningson, Durham, & Richardson, Inc.; Photographer: HDR

3-23 *Brick walls, built-in planters, and Italian market umbrellas make this cafeteria especially appealing, Methodist Hospitals of Memphis (Memphis, TN)*

Architecture and interior design: Stone Marraccini Patterson; Photographer: Abby Sadin, Sadin Photo Group, Ltd.

3-24 *Cafeteria, Saint Joseph Hospital (Bellingham, WA)*

Architect: Kaplan McLaughlin Diaz; Interior design: Balzhiser Group; Photographer: Stephen Cridland

3-25 *Cafeteria, California Medical Center (Los Angeles, CA)*

Architect: Kaplan McLaughlin Diaz; Interior design: Tardy and Associates; Photographer: John Sutton Photography

3-26 *Foodservice area features colorful partitions, Mercywood Mental Health Facility, Catherine McAuley Health Center (Ann Arbor, MI)*

Architecture and interior design: Harley Ellington Pierce Yee Associates, Inc.; Photographer: Beth Singer

3-27 *Cafe Med coffee shop, South County Hospital (Wakefield, RI)*

Architect: TRO/The Ritchie Organization; Interior design: IDS/Interior Design Systems, a division of TRO; Photographer: R. Mikrut

Some hospitals have coffee shops as well as large dining rooms. Cafe Med is reminiscent of a 1950s neighborhood diner (Fig. 3-27); the Nob Hill Grille features a more contemporary treatment (Fig. 3-28).

Physicians' dining rooms are generally designed like a private club (Figs. 3-29 and 3-30). Seating should be comfortable, lighting subdued, and acoustics good.

VISITOR AND PATIENT LOUNGES

Many inpatient nursing units have a lounge on each floor to attract ambulatory patients and to provide a place, other than the patient room, for visiting with family and friends. The location of the lounge and its size depend on the number of beds it serves and the layout of the nursing unit. A lounge is also a refuge for patients who cannot sleep and wish to watch television or view a video movie without disturbing their roommates.

Patient lounges should offer a variety of seating, a television viewing area, perhaps a small kitchen and bathroom, and a variety of lighting to accommodate reading, conversation, or playing games (Fig. 3-31). A solarium is a good place to be warmed by afternoon sun, watch

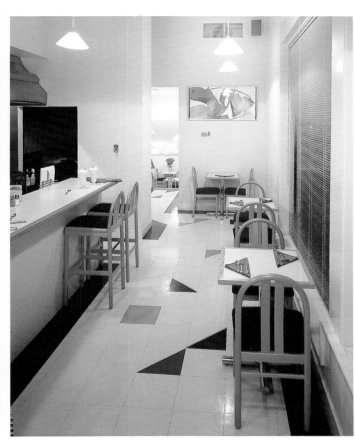

3-28 *The Nob Hill Grille, St. Francis Memorial Hospital (San Francisco, CA)*
  Architect: Kaplan McLaughlin Diaz; Interior design: Michael E. Stinetorf; Photographer: Sally Painter

3-29 *Physicians' dining room, Herrick Hospital and Health Center (Berkeley, CA)*
  Architect: Kaplan McLaughlin Diaz; Interior design: James A. Davis and Genevra Gilcrest; Photographer: Russell Abraham

3-30 *Physicians' dining room, London Bridge Hospital (London, England)*
   Architect: Llewelyn-Davies Sahni, Inc.; Photographer: Jo Reid and John Peck

3-31 *Patient dayroom, St. Vincent Stress Center, St. Vincent Hospital (Indianapolis, IN)*
   Architecture and interior design: Howard Needles Tammen & Bergendoff; Photographer: Wilbur Montgomery

the city skyline by night, or visit with friends (Fig. 3-32). Photos of other patient and visitor lounges are scattered throughout various chapters.

An interesting experiment was carried out a number of years ago by Richard Olsen, who at that time was director of environmental design at Bellevue Hospital in New York City. He noted that patient lounges, even though they had a view of the Manhattan skyline or the East River, were underused. He introduced large-scale photo murals accompanied by short audiotapes of sounds appropriate for each image. One lounge had a mural of aerial photographs of the East River, the Statue of Liberty, and New York Harbor. A tape with sounds of sea gulls, foghorns, tugboats, and the splashing of water could be activated by patients.

3-32 *Patient solarium, California Medical Center (Los Angeles, CA)*

Architect: Kaplan McLaughlin Diaz; Interior design: Tardy and Associates; Photographer: John Sutton Photography

The other lounge had a Central Park theme with trees, the Manhattan skyline, and an ornamental bridge. The accompanying sound track had horses' hooves on cobblestone paths, vendors hawking wares, sounds of oars plying the lake, and music from a merry-go-round. Plants were also added to the lounges. Patients who used the lounges had very positive comments, but many patients did not know of their existence. For patients to enjoy the lounge, they must know it exists. Patients who used the lounges suggested that they would be even more appealing if areas for playing games and watching television were offered, and if comfortable seating could be provided for reading. The conclusion was that, even though the lounge was highly successful for the purposes of improving morale and for experiencing the sights and sounds of the harbor or of Central Park, a single-purpose lounge is less appealing overall than one offering a number of activities.

PATIENT ROOMS

The design of the acute care inpatient room is important because for many it is the only room they see during their period of hospitalization. The room must be designed for privacy, comfort, and easy interface with both visitors and caregivers. To make this environment enhance healing, the patient should have views of nature (from the bed), be able to control lighting levels, have control over room temperature and privacy, not have to suffer noise of carts or conversation in corridors, and be surrounded by a moderately stimulating palette of colors and texture. The components of healing environments are discussed more thoroughly in chapter 2. The goal, overall, is to reduce a patient's stress levels so that healing can take place.

Privacy and Isolation

Many issues beyond environmental ones cause stress for hospitalized patients. Table 2-1 (chapter 2) presents the results of a survey indicating the chief causes of stress for both medical and surgical patients. As lack of privacy usually rates high as a source of stress, hospitals have been addressing it by providing a large number of private rooms. In fact, some newer hospitals offer all private rooms. Interestingly, a study at the University of Michigan Hospitals found that even if cost were no object, 45 percent of patients would choose a private room, 48 percent would choose a semiprivate room, and 7 percent would prefer a multiple-bed room (Carpman, Grant, and Simmons 1986). Many

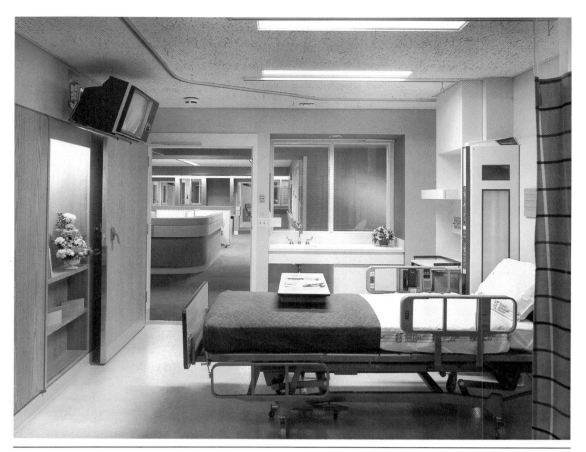

3-33 *Patient room with window to corridor, Beth Israel Hospital, The Reisman Building (Boston, MA)*

Architect: Rothman Rothman Heineman Architects Inc.; Interior design: Crissman & Solomon Architects Inc.; Photographer: Steve Rosenthal

people seem to prefer having someone to talk to.

Another study, in which patients were randomly assigned to single and semiprivate rooms, revealed more disturbances among patients in private rooms, which were attributed to reduced sensory stimulation and social isolation (Wood as reported in Williams 1988). Thus the issue of privacy is a complex one and perhaps should be interpreted as a need for control rather than the desire to be alone.

With respect to visual privacy, the essential point is always the trade-off between the patient being able to see into the corridor and yet not be seen by passersby. An interior window (Fig. 3-33) provides an opportunity to people-watch and allows nursing staff to monitor the patient without having to walk into the room. The window must have a drape to provide privacy when needed or else use glass such as Varilite Vision panels by Taliq that turn opaque at the flick of a switch that is controlled at the patient's bedside.

Layout of Room

Each of the alternatives for patient room layouts accomplishes one or more objectives. The location of the bathroom on the corridor wall maximizes exterior views but, depending on the layout, can block the view of the patient's head and force the nurse to walk inside the room to observe the patient. A toilet on the corridor wall generally precludes an observation window. Beds placed toe to toe on opposite headwalls give both patients equal window access and make maneuvering equipment easier. This layout enhances patient privacy because outlining territories is easier. The downside is that patients may be forced to stare at each other unless they pull the privacy curtain. Beds placed side by side (Fig. 3-34) do not afford equal access to the window, and visitors to the window bed are forced to intrude upon the privacy of the other patient. Newer approaches to the design of semiprivate patient rooms include trapezoid or diamond-shaped rooms that allow beds to be positioned at 90 degrees to one another.

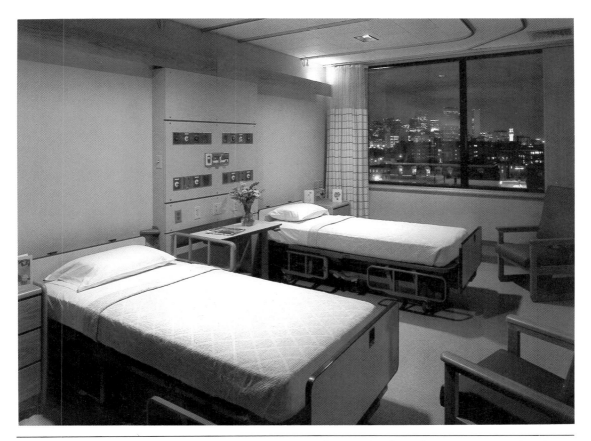

3-34 *Patient room, University Hospital Atrium Pavilion (Boston, MA)*
Architect: Hoskins Scott Taylor and Partners Inc. in association with Hansen Lind Meyer; Interior design:
Hoskins Scott Taylor and Partners Inc. in conjunction with University Hospital Design Services; Photographer:
© 1987 Paul Gobeil

3-35 *Patient rooms with shared sitting area, University Hospital Atrium Pavilion (Boston, MA)*
Architect: Hoskins Scott Taylor and Partners Inc. in association with Hansen Lind Meyer; Interior design: Hoskins Scott Taylor and Partners Inc. in conjunction with University Hospital Design Services; Photographer: © 1987 Paul Gobeil

The semiprivate corner rooms in Figure 3-35 share a small lounge.

Amenities

Aesthetic amenities that make the room look less clinical are a plastic laminate, oak-trimmed headboard permanently affixed to the wall (note that the bed itself has a short headboard that abuts the one on the wall) and a cover for medical gas outlets (Fig. 3-36). Often the medical gas cover consists of a framed piece of artwork that lifts up on a hinge to expose gas outlets. Storage of patients' belongings is important, along with shelves for plants and gifts, and a tackable surface for get-well cards. These needs are particularly well addressed in Figure 3-37. Designed of oak and recessed into the wall, the built-in storage gives the room a residential appearance that is further enhanced by the seating niche. A private room might include a desk, small dining table, and lounge chair and ottoman as in Figure 3-38.

Although patient comfort is very important, occasionally it may conflict with efficient circulation of supplies and services to the patient. The same is true for visitor access. The need for quick staff access to patients (generally from the patient's right side for examination and treatment) takes precedence over the patient's need for control and privacy. In a medical emergency, people and equipment must have unobstructed easy access to the patient's head.

3-36 *Patient room, FHP Fountain Valley Hospital (Fountain Valley, CA)*
  Architect: Dan Rowland and Associates; Interior design: Formerly Conant Associates, Doug Smith, project director, currently of Life Designs, Salt Lake City; Photographer: Michael Shoenfeld

---

3-37 *Patient room features attractive wood built-in storage and seating niche, Beth Israel Hospital, The Reisman Building (Boston, MA)*
  Architect: Rothman Rothman Heineman Architects Inc.; Interior design: Crissman & Solomon Architects Inc.; Photographer: Steve Rosenthal

---

3-38 *Patient room, St. Mary's Hospital (Reno, NV)*
  Architecture and interior design: Anshen + Allen; Photographer: Craig Buchanan

3-36

3-37

NURSING UNIT DESIGN

Just as alternative patient room layouts exist, several nursing unit layouts are possible. Architects have hotly debated this topic for years and continually struggled to refine their solutions. Overall, the goal of good nursing unit design is to maximize both nursing efficiency and patient-centered care. According to Margaret Williams (1988, 61), the design of the unit can influence nursing staff behaviors, including "frequency of interaction with patients and families, travel time, staffing requirements, infection control practices, satisfaction with the ability to carry out treatment, surveillance, communication, and satisfaction with the work setting." Travel time and ability to observe patients have become increasingly important with the nursing shortage and the pressure to reduce costs.

One nurse may care for many more patients now than ten years ago, and the patients are generally much sicker. If travel distances are short and supplies are handy, then nurses are able to spend more time with patients. However, as space planning is not the focus of this book, the discussion will move to other issues.

Nurses' stations need to be large enough for a number of nurses to work side by side and for physicians to do charting. Design should be such that the nurses' station does not appear to be a barrier between staff and patient. In fact,

3-39 *Colorful nursing corridor presents nonclinical ambience, Beth Israel Hospital, The Reisman Building (Boston, MA)*

Architect: Rothman Rothman Heineman Architects Inc.; Interior design: Crissman & Solomon Architects Inc.; Photographer: Steve Rosenthal

3-40 *Modular nurse station, University Hospital Atrium Pavilion (Boston, MA)*

Architect: Hoskins Scott Taylor and Partners Inc. in association with Hansen Lind Meyer; Interior design: Hoskins Scott Taylor; Photographer: © 1987 Paul Gobeil

the Planetree philosophy (see chapter 2) promotes removal of the barrier entirely, opening the nurse station to patients and their families. If the nurse station is an island design, as many are, then building in video display terminals (VDTs) becomes difficult without increasing the height of the transaction counter in excess of 42 inches. If they are not built in, then the exposed backs of the VDTs present a rather unattractive view from the corridor.

Use of strong color characterizes the nursing unit in Figure 3-39 and totally alleviates a clinical appearance. The inclusion of both warm and cool colors, offset by white, is stimulating without being overpowering. Note the interior windows between the patient rooms and corridor. The modular nurse station in Figure 3-40 features an enclosed nursing conference room; wall slot perimeter lighting eliminates glare, and angled accent walls frame patient room doors.

Neutral floors and walls with one bold accent wall provide a refreshing color palette for redecorating an existing, older facility when interesting architectural features do not exist (Fig. 3-41).

Renovation of existing hospital corridors offers a continual challenge. Often they are nothing more than cosmetic changes, but the results can be dramatic as evidenced in the "before" photo in Figure 3-42 and the successful outcome in Figure 3-43. An extra layer of gypsum board has been applied to walls to create a design feature, and a new acoustic tile ceiling has been installed. Wall sconce lighting, new carpeting, complete redesign of the nurse station, and a dramatic color palette have transformed this into an uplifting, hospitality environment. Note that existing doors and hardware have not been changed; they just look better with the new design treatment.

Nursing units sometimes have decentralized nurse stations outside each patient room where charts and supplies may be kept, and sometimes a computer terminal is located there (Fig. 3-44). Also note in this photo the color band that continues around the perimeter of the entire nursing unit, each floor having its own distinctive color that is repeated in the carpet border and constitutes the dominant palette for that floor. Most walls are neutral. The same type of detailing is repeated on nurse stations (Fig. 3-45).

Sometimes a nursing corridor can be very simply handled with a disciplined use of color and pattern (Fig. 3-46). Soft pastels, vinyl composition tile patterns, and radiused walls create a soothing and very appealing interior environment.

3-41 *Colorful accent wall brightens nursing core, St. Joseph Hospital (Bellingham, WA)*

3-42 *"Before" photo of drab nursing corridor, Wilson Memorial Hospital (Wilson, NC)*
     Photo courtesy BLM Group

3-43 *"After" photo of renovated nursing corridor, Wilson Memorial Hospital (Wilson, NC)*

Architecture and interior design: BLM Group; Photographer: Tom Crane Photography © Maureen C. Wikiera

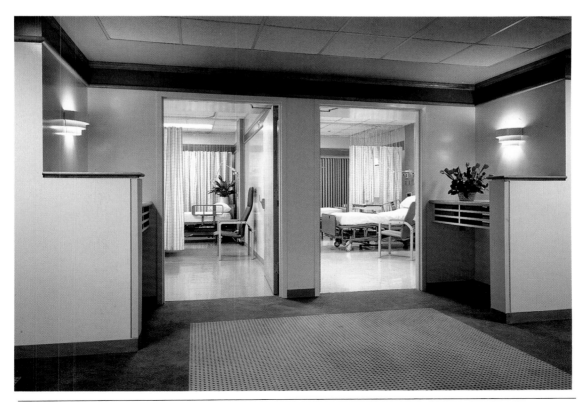

3-44 *View of patient rooms, California Medical Center (Los Angeles, CA)*

Architect: Kaplan McLaughlin Diaz; Interior design: Tardy and Associates; Photographer: John Sutton Photography

3-45 *Nurse station, California Medical Center (Los Angeles, CA)*
   Architect: Kaplan McLaughlin Diaz; Interior design: Tardy and Associates; Photographer: John Sutton Photography

3-46 *Good use of color and flooring patterns brightens nursing corridor, California Veterans' Home, Holderman Hospital Acute Care Addition (Yountville, CA)*
   Architecture and interior design: The Ratcliff Architects; Photographer: Andrew McKinney

VIP SUITES

VIP suites—deluxe patient rooms—have become rather popular in the past ten years. Increased revenue from private-pay patients helps hospitals offset their losses in other areas. Typically they are designed to include the amenities of a fine hotel suite. The Palmetto Pavilion at the University of South Carolina is a 32,000-square-foot facility consisting of deluxe patient rooms, suites, and ancillary spaces. Patient rooms (Fig. 3-47) are tastefully furnished, and the adjoining sitting room (Fig. 3-48) allows a family member to spend the night or watch television without disturbing the patient. The residential character of these rooms is enhanced by wood crown moldings and wainscots, formal drapery treatments, and traditional style furnishings. Visitor (Fig. 3-49) and patient (Fig. 3-50) lounges are appealing destinations for patients who need to exercise. These rooms also accommodate informal conferences of hospitalized executives and their staffs.

3-47 *Typical patient bedroom, The Palmetto Pavilion, Medical University of South Carolina (Charleston, SC) Architect: Wilkins & Wood; Interior design: Lucas Stubbs Pascullis Powell & Penney, Ltd.; Photographer: Rick Alexander, Inc.*

3-48

3-50 *TV and game room, The Palmetto Pavilion, Medical University of South Carolina (Charleston, SC) Architect: Wilkins & Wood; Interior design: Lucas Stubbs Pascullis Powell & Penney, Ltd.; Photographer: Rick Alexander, Inc.*

3-48 *Sitting room, patient suite, The Palmetto Pavilion, Medical University of South Carolina (Charleston, SC) Architect: Wilkins & Wood; Interior design: Lucas Stubbs Pascullis Powell & Penney, Ltd.; Photographer: Rick Alexander, Inc.*

3-49 *Reading room, The Palmetto Pavilion, Medical University of South Carolina (Charleston, SC) Architect: Wilkins & Wood; Interior design: Lucas Stubbs Pascullis Powell & Penney, Ltd.; Photographer: Rick Alexander, Inc.*

EMERGENCY ROOM

The approach to the emergency room should be clearly marked and visible for vehicles traveling from any direction. Being confronted by confusing traffic patterns on the hospital campus upon arrival can be overly taxing and dramatically add to the stress experienced by driver and patient. Ambulances and passenger vehicles may share the road leading to the emergency entrance, but the ambulance entrance should be visually screened from the passenger vehicle entrance. Neither of the emergency drop-off entries should be visible from the main lobby. Many people become uncomfortable and extremely nervous watching an ambulance unload patients.

Individuals requiring emergency care are under tremendous stress. The nature of these injuries is that they are sudden and unexpected; the life-and-death aspect causes their companions to experience tremendous stress. In fact, driving a critically ill person to the emergency room in the middle of the night can make a ten-minute trip seem like an eternity. Therefore, clearly marked emergency entrance roads and drop-off points are very important.

Upon entering the emergency department, the patient or the companion has to register. Here vital information is obtained as to the cause of the injury, insurance eligibility is validated or arrangements made for payment, and the patient is triaged. *Triage* is the assessment or evaluation of the patient's condition to help prioritize those needing treatment. The registration desk should provide privacy and visual separation between patients. Each carrel should be large enough for a patient (perhaps in a wheelchair) and one or two companions.

The waiting room will be used by patients and their companions; therefore, a carpeted floor may be a problem. Although many would agree that carpet and fabric upholstery on seating would make the room appear more comfortable, in reality the furniture and finishes take high abuse and must be easy to clean. Of course, much of this depends on the community the hospital serves. An inner-city hospital that receives many victims of gunshot wounds and stabbings or a hospital that receives many industrial accidents would have more stringent requirements in this regard than a hospital serving a suburban residential community.

The period of time spent in the waiting room may be extensive, requiring comfortable chairs, a television, calming colors (blues and greens are particularly effective), natural light, telephones, rest rooms, and vending machines or other access to food. The television should be located where it will not disturb those who wish to avoid it. Lighting is critically important here; if at all possible, it should be indirect and of a color temperature that is flattering to skin tones. A play area for children may be provided, but it should encourage quiet activity rather than climbing or jumping, which might irritate nervous adults in the room. The aquarium in Figure 5-35 offers a calming diversion for children.

In treatment areas, good visibility of treatment bays from the nurse station and easy access to patients are critical. Enclosures, whether glass (Fig. 3-51) or drapery (Fig. 3-52), must open wide for quick access by people and equipment. Finishes must be smooth and easily cleaned.

A separate patient waiting area may be provided near treatment bays, allowing good visibility from the nurse station. A rest room should be immediately available. Natural light, views of nature, artwork, or any other diversion that may help to calm frightened patients would be beneficial. Seating must have vinyl upholstery, and flooring should be sheet vinyl because nausea and bleeding are common. Recliner chairs or an upholstered bench might be more comfortable for patients who wish to lie down.

Much has been written about the benefits of trauma care and the ''golden hour'' in terms of saving lives that might otherwise be lost with more traditional emergency care protocols. Designated trauma centers are part of a county-wide system designed to provide coordinated care by highly skilled teams of physicians and nurses to critically injured individuals or to treat victims of large-scale disasters. A trauma team is trained to assess the multiple injuries of the victim quickly, stabilize the patient, and then

3-51 *Emergency room trauma unit, Mercy Hospital (Port Huron, MI)*

Architecture and interior design: Harley Ellington Pierce Yee Associates, Inc.; Photographer: © Gary Quesada, Balthazar Korab Ltd.

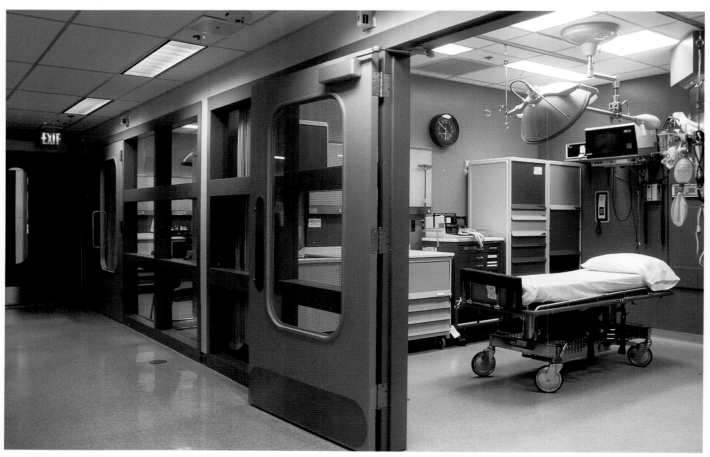

work simultaneously both medically and surgically to treat the wounds or injuries. Although the design of the trauma unit is not the focus of this discussion, the room needs to be large, as ten or twelve people may be attending the patient.

CHAPEL

A hospital chapel may be used by an individual or a family group. Staff may also use it for quiet meditation during stressful events, such as the death of a patient. Occasionally weddings or religious ceremonies may take place in the chapel. A low level of lighting is appropriate and it should not be from overhead fluorescent luminaires. Colors and textures should be soothing and foster inward concentration and reflection. Stained-glass and wood detailing add warmth and spiritual beauty to a chapel (Fig. 3-53), as do brick and weavings or tapestries (Fig. 3-54). A more contemporary treatment, with glass block, interesting lighting, and a restful palette of various shades of blue, is equally appealing (Fig. 3-55).

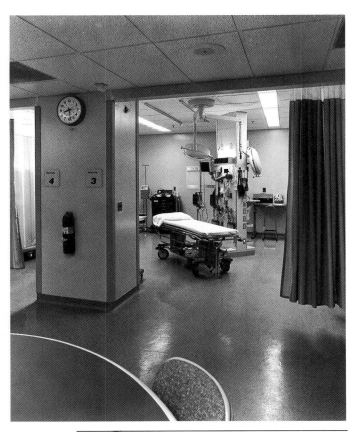

3-52 *Trauma bay, University Hospital, University of Michigan Medical Center (Ann Arbor, MI)*
Architect: Albert Kahn Associates, Inc., Architects and Engineers; Interior design: Anne Schallhorn Parker; University of Michigan Hospitals Design Group; Photographer: Balthazar Korab Ltd.

3-53 *Chapel, St. Mary's Hospital (Grand Rapids, MI)*
Architecture and interior design: Harley Ellington Pierce Yee Associates, Inc.; Photographer: Balthazar Korab Ltd.

3-54 *Chapel, Evans U.S. Army Community Hospital (Fort Carson, CO)*
Architecture and interior design: Smith, Hinchman, & Grylls Associates, Inc.; Photographer: Balthazar Korab Ltd.

3-55 *Chapel, St. John's Mercy skilled nursing facility (St. Louis, MO)*
Architecture and interior design: The Hoffmann Partnership, Inc.; Photographer: Alise O'Brien

RENAL DIALYSIS

Patients needing renal dialysis are not a homogeneous group with respect to treatment setting. Patients may be classified as home training, self-care, outpatient chronic, alert inpatient, and distressed acute inpatient, progressing in descending order from well to sickest. Those who require home training are generally treated in a totally separate area, away from the chronic unit. The self-care patient also requires a separate area for treatment. Both the stable and unstable chronic will be treated in the outpatient chronic unit, but in separate areas. The alert inpatient may be treated

in the patient's room or in a designated area of the chronic unit. Within the confines of the present discussion, the many important environmental factors that should be considered in designing a dialysis unit cannot be adequately reviewed; therefore, the following is a brief summary of the most important issues. It is based on Richard Olsen (1979) and Norman Rosenfeld's study.

Home Training Unit
Home training units are differentiated from other renal dialysis areas.

▪ They should have entry, waiting, and treatment areas distinctly separate from the chronic unit; the rationale is that home training patients see themselves as elite and do not want to mix with sicker patients. Furthermore, different relationships exist between the home training nurse and patients. "Chronic" nurses guard patients, whereas home training nurses teach them. The home training unit can offer patients more flexibility with respect to running late or smoking, for example, which would create havoc in the chronic unit.
▪ Each patient area should have a distinct territory that allows patients complete visual and auditory access to each other and to staff.

▪ The unit should look residential in character (Fig. 3-56). Individual modules should include a homey recliner chair, a table or desk, plants, natural light, and artwork. Wood louver shutters add a nice residential touch and allow as much or as little privacy as desired. Chair comfort is very important; its arms must be wide, and the cushions must not cause discomfort during treatment.
▪ Patients like to talk to each other for mutual support and learning, but they must also be able to see the nurse for security. Nurses, when stationed at a central location, can address or instruct all patients at the same time.
▪ A high-intensity task light is important to help patients put in their own needles.
▪ Each module needs a supply storage cabinet that the patient and his or her partner can organize. This task enables them to learn how to rotate stock, when to order supplies, and how to do inventory on their own.
▪ Artwork that can be rotated is desirable; anything too strong, like wall graphics, is inadvisable because patients would be forced to stare at it for four hours per day.

3-56 *Home training treatment area, study for Monmouth Medical Center (Long Branch, NJ)*
Courtesy Norman Rosenfeld, AIA, Architects

3-57 *Kidney dialysis center, Froedtert Memorial Lutheran Hospital Kidney Dialysis Center, Milwaukee Regional Medical Center Campus (Milwaukee, WI)*
  Architecture and interior design: The Zimmerman Design Group; Photographer: Mark Heffron/Zimmerman Design

- Televisions may be mounted overhead, above the nurse station (Fig. 3-57), or in the treatment module. Earphones should be provided.
- Patients are fed as soon as they arrive; if they do not wish to eat, they may save the food for later. Patients may also bring in their own food and share it with others; therefore, a small kitchen area with a refrigerator is advisable.
- Temperature control is important; dialysis patients get cold. Individual heaters, which perhaps are not practical in a hospital setting, would be desirable.
- Certain plumbing issues are pertinent: floor drains are required at each dialysis machine to accommodate overflow; good water pressure is essential; if each machine has the same waste line, they can empty simultaneously.

Self-Care Patients

Self-care patients should be treated in a separate area, which may be part of the chronic unit. These patients are more independent than chronic patients, but less so than home training patients. They need constant observation.

Outpatient Chronic Unit

The outpatient chronic person is less independent than self-care and home training patients.

- The optimal location would be a separate wing of the hospital with direct entry from outdoors so that patients need not feel they are entering a hospital for treatment.
- Patients and staff generally preferred a number of small treatment modules to one large space, provided that patients could be separated according to severity of illness and that the nurse station allowed good observation of all patients.
- Individual modules should contain three or six patients as the patient-to-staff ratio tends to be 3:1.
- Chronic patients should not be exposed to sick acute patients in either treatment or waiting areas because the depressing sight of patients who are

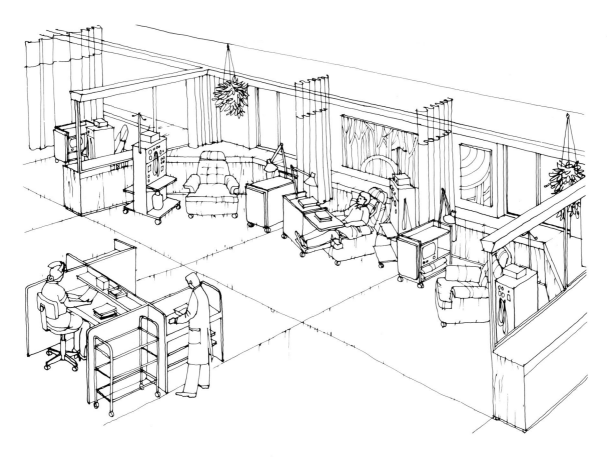

3-58 *Outpatient chronic treatment area, study for Monmouth Medical Center (Long Branch, NJ) Courtesy Norman Rosenfeld, AIA, Architects*

sicker can trigger negative reactions such as vomiting or drops in blood pressure.

■ Patients prefer as much independence as possible with respect to listening to audio tapes, watching television, or controlling module lighting. Lighting must be indirect so that it does not shine in patients' eyes.

■ Each treatment module needs storage, a hook for a handbag or umbrella, and a flat surface or overchair tray table for working puzzles, eating, or doing paperwork (Fig. 3-58).

■ Patients should be able to see dialysis machine panels and blood lines.

■ The patient's chair should have the same characteristics as those described for home training.

■ As with any outpatient area, the less clinical it appears, the more pleasing it is to patients, especially those who have to visit the facility as frequently as dialysis patients do.

■ A quantity of bathrooms is important in waiting and in treatment areas because large numbers of patients come off the machine at one time and urgently need to access rest rooms.

■ Patients must be able to see a clock so that they know when to come off the machine.

■ A chronic unit is a busy place, and noise can sometimes be a problem. Acoustic treatments that do not compromise sanitation should be considered.

■ A properly sized staff lounge, as well as male and female staff locker areas and bathrooms, should be provided.

Alert Inpatient

A survey indicated that alert inpatients sometimes prefer to be treated in the chronic unit rather than at their bedsides because getting away from their hospital rooms boosts their morale. Patients in acute renal failure (distressed acute inpatient) cannot be transported for dialysis.

Summary

Dialysis patients become quite territorial and often prefer to have the same machine and chair. Upsetting aspects include lack of privacy, waiting to get on the machine, getting hooked up to the machine, viewing a sick patient, and seeing a lot of blood. According to Olsen (1979), patients feel secure and relaxed when they are able to see the nurse, after needles are inserted, and when their attention can be diverted by entertainment, chatting with a companion, or reading.

SPECIAL SUPPORT SYSTEMS

The efficient delivery of materials to patient care areas and expedient removal of soiled items is a fascinating aspect of hospital design. Although many hospitals still handle these tasks manually, others have pioneered high-technology robotic systems or monorail conveyances to accomplish these tasks. Etobicoke General Hospital in Toronto, designed 20 years ago, remarkably seems as innovative today as it did then. When it opened, it was one of the most aesthetically beautiful hospital environments for both patients and staff. Every area benefited from the most exquisite attention to detail, incorporating indirect lighting, unique ceiling designs, and a bold palette of colors used with wild abandon: bright magenta, yellow, pink, red-orange, and nectarine.

Every room and area of the hospital basked in color, whether an accent wall in a supply corridor (Fig. 3-59) or a wall or equipment in the decontamination area. No area was considered too unimportant for the careful and deliberate consideration of color. Whether conference room, nurse station, or children's playroom, each space was unique and original in design. Furnishings had a timeless quality and, in general, a Scandinavian appearance. The signage and graphic system, designed by the architects, is one of the most successful, as well as aesthetically appealing, to be found in any medical center. One example can be seen in Figure 3-60, although it took the guise of many formats as needed to accomplish its goals in directing visitors.

Perhaps the most interesting aspect of this hospital is the overhead monorail system that carries electronically controlled conveyances for medical and linen supplies, waste, and soiled goods to and from all points in the hospital (Figs. 3-59 and 3-61). On the first floor, a monorail circulates through decontamination, processing, linen, and supply areas, conveying trucks to and from elevators that are operated by remote control. Central surveillance of cart locations and outlets in all areas of the hospital allows the system to supply either on urgent demand or according to a regular routine.

Although not on a monorail system, battery-powered robocarriers at the University of Mich-

3-59 *Electronically controlled cart transport system on overhead monorail, Etobicoke General Hospital (Toronto, Ontario)*

Architecture and interior design: NORR Partnership Limited; Photographer: Panda Associates

3-60 *Administrative Communication Centre, Etobicoke General Hospital (Toronto, Ontario)*

Architecture and interior design: NORR Partnership Limited; Photographer: Panda Associates

3-61 *Electronically controlled cart transport system on overhead monorail, Etobicoke General Hospital (Toronto, Ontario)*

Architecture and interior design: NORR Partnership Limited; Photographer: Panda Associates

3-62 *Electronically controlled material handling conveyances in main distribution corridor, University Hospital, The University of Michigan (Ann Arbor, MI) Architect: Albert Kahn Associates, Architects & Engineers; Photographer: Balthazar Korab Ltd.*

3-63 *Administrative office features partition with glass and built-in planter, MacNeal Hospital (Berwyn, IL) Architecture and interior design: Stone Marraccini Patterson; Photographer: Abby Sadin, Sadin Photo Group, Ltd.*

igan's University Hospital can move as much as 800-pound loads in all nonpublic areas of the hospital; when low on charge, they plug themselves into a charging station (Fig. 3-62). This material transport system has been designed to make scheduled deliveries automatically to all general hospital floors, as well as other locations, via an automated floor guidance system and a computer-based network of automated vehicles.

ADMINISTRATION OFFICES AND BOARDROOMS

Administrative offices and boardrooms in hospitals do not differ from their counterparts in corporate America. They are included in this book because the following projects are so well executed that they demanded publication. Offices in the administrative suite at MacNeal Hospital feature glass and planter walls to provide privacy without isolation (Fig. 3-63). Note the indirect light flowing from a light cove.

Executive offices of Brigham Medical Corporation occupy three floors of the historic Peter Bent Brigham administration building. A two-story atrium was created in what was formerly the interns' on-call rooms, which included showers, toilets, and locker room (Figs. 3-64

3-64 Executive offices of Brigham Medical Corporation house corporate offices for Brigham & Women's Hospital (Boston, MA); two-story atrium was created in what was formerly interns' on-call rooms

Architecture and interior design: Tsoi/Kobus & Associates; Photographer: Steve Rosenthal

3-65 *Executive offices of Brigham Medical Corporation, located in historic Peter Bent Brigham Administration Building (Boston, MA)*
Architecture and interior design: Tsoi/Kobus & Associates; Photographer: Steve Rosenthal

and 3-65). Interesting spaces have been created, natural light has been introduced, and richly varied textures have been combined. Interior offices have glass walls with dark wood mullions and base.

Located in the Countway Library Building, Harvard Medical School's new boardroom accommodates small luncheon meetings (Fig. 3-66) as well as large board meetings. The custom-designed armoire acts as a room divider and also functions as coat and storage closet (Fig. 3-67). The anteroom of Christ Hospital boardroom introduces finishes and detailing used in the boardroom (Fig. 3-68). Although

fairly neutral in color, the anteroom is dramatic because of the composition of line and pattern and the juxtaposition of materials. The interior of the boardroom features indirect lighting, walls wrapped with acoustic panels, granite and cherrywood tables, and leather chairs. The room is uncluttered and simple, with exquisite attention to composition and detail (Fig. 3-69).

3-66 *Harvard Medical School Boardroom, located in the Countway Library building, comfortably accommodates both small luncheon meetings and large board meetings in a single room; the armoire divides the space and also functions as a coat closet*
Architecture and interior design: Tsoi/Kobus & Associates; Photographer: Steve Rosenthal

3-67 *Harvard Medical School Boardroom (Boston, MA)*
Architecture and interior design: Tsoi/Kobus & Associates; Photographer: Steve Rosenthal

3-66

3-67

3-68 *Anteroom to boardroom introduces the same type of detailing used within boardroom; The Christ Hospital Courtyard Atrium (Cincinnati, OH)*
Architecture and interior design: Hansen Lind Meyer; Photographer: Don DuBroff, The Sadin Group, Chicago

3-69 *Boardroom expresses elegance and exquisite attention to detail; The Christ Hospital Courtyard Atrium (Cincinnati, OH)*
Architecture and interior design: Hansen Lind Meyer; Photographer: Don DuBroff, The Sadin Group, Chicago

NEW DIRECTIONS

Occasionally articles appear about the hospital of the future. At the start of a new decade, forecasts about trends are especially prevalent, and the available material on the topic is too extensive to cover here.

Instead, readers are referred to books by the health care futurist Russell Coile, and to the November/December 1990 issue of *Healthcare Forum Journal* that features a number of articles on the future of health care. One of the

most provocative, about design in the next century, was written by Jeff Goldsmith and Richard Miller (1990). It begins with criticism of the custodial mind-set of the twentieth-century hospital and also takes punches at hospital architecture and design by calling to attention the prodigious lack of human scale that tends to dwarf and intimidate users.

The subject of new directions in health care tends to bring to mind future technology and delivery systems. In the larger sense, however, new directions also refers to bringing health care to remote populations. One of the most fascinating projects is the 95,000-square-foot Yukon-Kuskokwim Delta Regional Hospital in Bethel, Alaska. This is a 50-bed hospital, completed in 1980, located in the tundra 60 miles from the Bering Sea (Fig. 3-70). The architecture incorporated forms and concepts of the Eskimos such as triple-glazed, 12-inch perimeter windows that reduce glare, derived from the slit-bone, glare-reducing glasses worn by Eskimos. As in igloo construction, the entrance is oriented to the south to eliminate snowdrifts. The central concourse includes public areas and serves as an active social gathering place for the community of Bethel (Fig. 3-71). This portion of the facility has the ability to expand in four directions with minimum disruption of activities. Pediatric patient rooms are as compact as space capsules, taking advantage of every means to reduce heat loss (Fig. 3-72).

Lightweight, prefabricated building elements were dictated by climate and the spring thaw of the Kuskokwim River, which prevented overland access to Bethel. Steel thermopiles extract heat from the ground through convection to prevent the permafrost from melting. A light steel frame connects to the thermopiles to provide a stable structure. The building is elevated to permit free air movement across the site to keep the permafrost frozen. The architect, Paul Kennon, refers to the building's image as "pioneer futurism." This term also refers to the way the catchment area is served. Each small regional village has paraprofessionals with two-way radios linked to the hospital. When a patient needs treatment, a bush pilot is alerted. Remote diagnosis is made possible by a geostationary satellite over Hawaii that connects the hospital to a tertiary medical center in Fairbanks.

This building is a remarkable piece of high-technology engineering. Not only did architects have to learn about Eskimo culture, they had to deal with a very short construction season and virtually no local construction labor force—quite a challenge and an accomplishment.

3-70 *Yukon-Kuskokwim Delta Regional Hospital (Bethel, AL), a fifty-bed hospital located in southwestern Alaska, sixty miles from the Bering Sea*
Architecture and interior design: CRSS Commercial Group, Inc.; Photographer: Balthazar Korab Ltd.

3-71 *Central waiting and lounge area also serves as a community center; Yukon-Kuskokwim Delta Regional Hospital (Bethel, AL)*

Architecture and interior design: CRSS Commercial Group, Inc.; Photographer: Balthazar Korab Ltd.

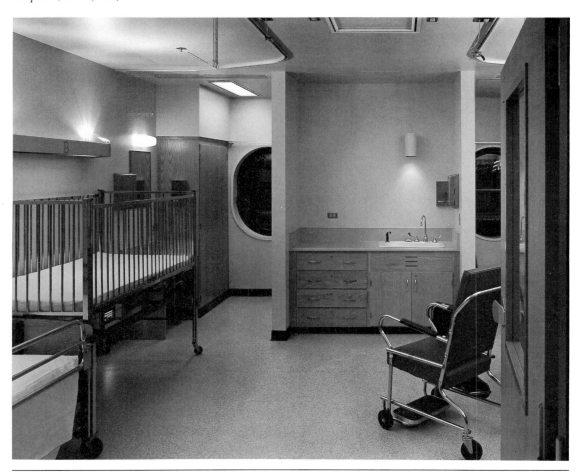

3-72 *Pediatric bay is compact and has the feeling of a space capsule; Yukon-Kuskokwim Delta Regional Hospital (Bethel, AL)*

Architecture and interior design: CRSS Commercial Group, Inc.; Photographer: Balthazar Korab Ltd.

ADAPTIVE REUSE

The highly imaginative projects submitted under this category ranged from warehouses that were converted to hospitals (see Fig. 2-1) to a steam mill that was converted to congregate care apartments. Unfortunately, space did not permit the inclusion of many of these fine projects; the two that follow are indicative of the many. The Fairmount Health Center is a neighborhood health care facility that also meets the social needs of the area's Hispanic residents by

3-73 *The Fairmount Health Center (Philadelphia, PA) was created in a building that formerly housed an auto parts dealership*
    Architect: Dagit-Saylor Architects; Photographer: Matt Wargo

3-74 *Clinic reception area is upbeat and festive, and also serves as a community center for the neighborhood; The Fairmount Health Center (Philadelphia, PA)*
    Architecture and interior design: Dagit-Saylor Architects; Photographer: Matt Wargo

3-73

3-74

3-75

serving as a contemporary community center where neighbors can meet and spend time together. Located in a former auto parts dealership, the exterior was enhanced with colorful flags and a fanciful canopy (Fig. 3-73). Inside, an urban piazza was created with a two-story skylit waiting area and indoor garden (Fig. 3-74). Exam rooms, waiting, and support areas occupy the remainder of the ground floor. Administrative offices and a conference room are located on the upper floor.

A freestanding bank gave birth to the Ingalls Memorial Hospital Family Care Center. At night, the clinic draws attention because of its striking

3-75 *Outpatient clinic created in former bank building, Family Care Center, Ingalls Memorial Hospital (Matteson, IL)*
   Architecture and interior design: Perkins & Will; Photographer: HNK Architectural Photography

3-76 *Clinic waiting area, Family Care Center, Ingalls Memorial Hospital (Matteson, IL)*
   Architecture and interior design: Perkins & Will; Photographer: HNK Architectural Photography

3-76

color palette and design details (Fig. 3-75). Inside, a series of posts and lintels helps to define spaces (Fig. 3-76). Colors are soft and calming.

DONOR RECOGNITION

Without the generosity of donors, hospitals would lack funding for important research programs, expensive pieces of equipment, and important but discretionary items such as fountains, sculpture, and commissioned works of art. Therefore, recognizing donors in a prominent location and in a manner that pays tribute to benefactors' philanthropy is important. The selection of materials and design of individual plaques runs the gamut from the traditional engraved bronze to highly imaginative treatments such as a fountain with dancing colored jets of water that leap from one donor tile to another. The trend is moving away from brass or bronze ''trees of life'' (each leaf of the sprawling tree carries a donor's name) toward more creative treatments. One of the most visually interesting is shown in Figure 3-77, created by the architect's in-house graphics team. Glass plaques carry ''etched'' pressure-sensitive vinyl letters applied to the back of the glass. The colorful frame and pegs are aluminum; the pegs are secured into position with set screws. It is located in a main corridor leading away from the lobby.

The donor wall in Figure 3-78 is an understated design of quiet elegance. Beveled glass plaques with engraved names have been placed

3-77 *Innovative donor recognition display, Arnold Palmer Hospital for Children & Women, Orlando Regional Medical Center (Orlando, FL)*

Architecture and graphic design: Hansen Lind Meyer, Barbara J. Martin, SEGD, designer; Photographer: George Cott

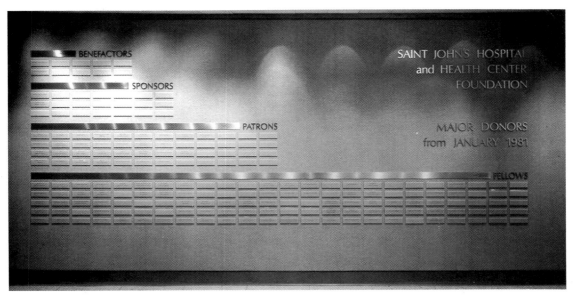

3-78 *Donor recognition wall, Saint John's Hospital and Health Center (Santa Monica, CA)*

Graphic design: Sanchez Kamps Associates; Photographer: Paul Bielenburg

on a natural linen wall. Raised brass letters are a beautiful counterpoint to the rough linen texture and transparent green glass.

ACHIEVING EXCELLENCE

The nature of excellence is somewhat elusive because it depends in large part upon the experience and viewpoint of the observer. A design professional who has visited or worked with 300 hospitals will have a very different view of excellence than an individual who has knowledge of ten hospitals. Patients and staff similarly have their own agendas and criteria for evaluating excellence. In view of these differences, do any general characteristics or principles have a timeless or universal application? Do standards for excellence exist that do not change and are not subject to fashion? How do we recognize excellence when we see it? Questions of this magnitude are worthy of debate by scholars and philosophers. With trepidation and humility, I undertake the burden of response.

Certainly excellence in the design of a building may be characterized by many things, including integration between architecture and interior design, functional space planning, access to nature, handicapped accessibility, appropriateness of materials, creation of environments that support or enhance healing, appropriateness for special patient populations, and aesthetic issues of scale, form, composition, and sensitivity to the site.

The list of parameters for evaluating excellence is extensive, but all of these qualities, in the end, may be distilled to a few simple truths expressed so well by the Roman architect, Vitruvius, in the first century B.C. To define what makes a good building, he recognized three qualities: commodity (function and the ability to create social order), firmness (structural adequacy), and delight (the joy of experiencing it).[1] Vitruvius (Morgan 1960) further states that structures must be built with reference to durability, convenience, and beauty. Add to this the three basic fundamentals of architecture—appropriateness to time, place, and technology—and a timeless and universal definition of excellence emerges.

Some may argue that aesthetics cannot be considered in a universal view of excellence because composition, form, scale, style, and use of materials are often an expression of a specific culture or a response to indigenous environmental factors, but that does not invalidate aesthetics as a parameter of excellence. Consider timeless works of architecture such as the Parthenon or Frank Lloyd Wright's Johnson Wax Administration Building, Fallingwater, or Guggenheim Museum. Innovation is certainly a feature of excellence in the three Wright projects just mentioned. People can visit a great work of architecture dozens of times and continually make new discoveries. In fact, one of the hallmarks of excellence is that a person never sees it totally the first time. A person may initially be affected deeply by one or more features of the structure, but repeated exposure to it reveals a myriad of pleasures, and appreciation of the structure deepens with greater familiarity and the passage of time.

NOTES

1. Vitruvius, in his work *The Ten Books on Architecture* (ed. Morris 1960), recognized these qualities as *utilitas, firmitas,* and *venustas.* Henry Wotton, Elizabeth I's ambassador to Venice, translated this into the familiar "Fine building hath three qualities: commodity, firmness, and delight." (Foster 1982)

REFERENCES

Alexander, Christopher. 1964. *Notes on the Synthesis of Form.* Cambridge: Harvard University Press.

Baum, Andrew, and Jerome Singer, editors. 1982. *Advances in Environmental Psychology*, vol. 4 Environment and Health. Hillsdale, NJ: Lawrence Erlbaum Associates.

Beck, William, and Ralph Meyer, editors. 1982. *The Health Care Environment: The User's Viewpoint.* Boca Raton, FL: CRC Press.

Beck, William. 1983. Reflections II. Color and illumination. *Guthrie Bulletin* 53:43–45.

———. 1985. *Operating Room Lighting.* Erie, PA: Education Division, AMSCO.

———. 1986. The patient in the light of the hospital. *Hospital Topics* March-April: 34–35, 39–41.

Birren, Faber. 1969. *Light, Color and Environment.* New York: Van Nostrand Reinhold Co. Inc.

Carpman, Janet, Myron Grant, and Deborah Simmons. 1986. *Design That Cares*. Chicago: American Hospital Publishing.

Feierman, J. 1982. Nocturnalism: an ethological theory of schizophrenia. *Medical Hypotheses* 9(5):455–79.

Flynn, J., A. Segil, and G. Steffy. 1988. *Architectural Interior Systems: Lighting/Acoustics/Air Conditioning*, ed. 2. New York: Van Nostrand Reinhold.

Foster, Michael, editor. 1982. *Architecture Style, Structure and Design*. New York: Excalibur Books (Simon & Schuster).

Gerritsen, Frans. 1974. *The Theory and Practice of Color*. New York: Van Nostrand Reinhold Co. Inc.

Goldsmith, Jeff, and Richard Miller. 1990. Restoring the human scale. *Healthcare Forum Journal* November-December: 22–27.

Gruson, L. 1982. Color has powerful effect on behavior, researchers assert. *New York Times*, October 19.

Hall, Edward T. *The Silent Language*.

Healthcare Forum Journal. November-December 1990. Entire issue.

Jacobs, K., and F. Hustmyer. 1974. Effects of four psychological primary colors on GSR, heart rate, and respiration rate. *Perceptual and Motor Skills* 38:763–66.

James, W. Paul, and William Tatton-Brown. 1986. *Hospitals: Design and Development*. New York: Van Nostrand Reinhold Co. Inc.

Journal of Health Care Interior Design. 1990, 1991. Vols. 2 and 3 (published by National Symposium on Health Care Interior Design, 4550 Alhambra Way, Martinez, CA 94553).

Lawton, M. Powell. 1980. *Environment and Aging*. Monterey, CA: Brooks/Cole Publishing Co.

Leibrock, Cynthia. 1991. *Beautiful Barrier-Free Design: A Visual Guide*.

Lighting for Health Care Facilities. 1985. Illuminating Engineering Society of North America, New York.

Malkin, Jain. 1990. *Medical and Dental Space Planning for the 1990s*. New York: Van Nostrand Reinhold.

Morgan, Morris. 1960. *Vitruvius: The Ten Books on Architecture*. New York: Dover Publications.

Olds, A. 1985. Nature as healer. In *Readings in Psychosynthesis: Theory, Process and Practice*, ed. John Weiser and Thomas Yeomans, Ontario Institute for Studies in Education. Toronto, pp. 97–110.

Olds, Anita, and Patricia Daniel. 1987. *Child Health Care Facilities*. Bethesda: Association for the Care of Children's Health.

Olsen, Richard. 1979. *Environmental Considerations for the Design of the New Dialysis Service for Monmouth Medical Center*. Study prepared for Norman Rosenfeld, AIA Architects.

National Institute of Occupational Safety and Health. 1984.

Preiser, Wolfgang, Harvey Rabinowitz, and Edward White. 1988. *Post-Occupancy Evaluation*. New York: Van Nostrand Reinhold Co. Inc.

Sharpe, Deborah. 1974. *The Psychology of Color and Design*. Chicago: Nelson Hall Co.

Spivack, Mayer. 1984. *Institutional Settings*. New York: Human Sciences Press.

Srivastava, R., and T. Peel. 1968. *Human Movement as a Function of Color Stimulation*. Topeka, KS: Environmental Research Foundation.

Welch and Epp Associates. 1988. *Post Occupancy Evaluation of the Quincy Mental Health Center*. (This study may be ordered from Welch and Epp, 7 Greenough Avenue, Boston, MA 02130.)

Williams, M. 1988. The physical environment and patient care. *Annual Review of Nursing Research* 6:61–84.

chapter 4

DIAGNOSTIC IMAGING CENTERS

psychological factors

- vulnerability
- information
- privacy
- security
- comfort

activities

- waiting
- undressing/dressing
- examination/treatment
- consultation

issues

- fear of the unknown
- intimidating equipment
- forced intimacy with strangers
- expectation of pain or discomfort

PSYCHOLOGICAL FACTORS

Diagnostic imaging and ambulatory surgery both seem to elicit terror in many people. Perhaps it starts with the psychological significance of giving up street clothes and surrendering to the role of patient. Without the protection of clothing, people feel immediately vulnerable. Lack of familiarity with equipment and little or no information about the radiologic examination generate anxiety because diagnostic tests are rarely routine to the patient; they are often unfamiliar and frightening.

Something about the way radiologic technologists robotically perform the movements associated with setting up each procedure makes the patient feel like an outsider, an alien unable to decode what is going on. Silently moving about the room, replacing cassettes, twisting dials, adjusting equipment, the technologist *unintentionally* creates an aura of mystery that intensifies patients' fears. The equipment itself can be terrifying and intimidating (Figs. 4-1 and 4-2). Softening and humanizing such equipment-dominated rooms can be virtually impossible.

Some of the psychological stress associated with imaging procedures has to do with lack of information. Radiology staff sometimes take too much for granted in interacting with patients by not explaining in advance why the patient has to come prepared in a certain way (fasting, enemas, or full bladder), how long the tests or examination will take, and how the patient may feel afterward. Just the act of having to hold perfectly still while pressing against cold steel in a chilly room can be stressful. Patients experience a sense of required submissiveness; they cannot behave ''normally'' under these conditions.

Most people are accustomed to general radiographic procedures such as chest x-rays and films of extremities. However, invasive procedures such as those performed in a radiography and fluoroscopy (R/F) room may be experienced as an acute invasion of privacy. Barium studies of the lower gastrointestinal tract are a prime example. In order to feel secure, the patient would want to know the sequence of events and be assured that a bathroom is immediately accessible. Even though fluoroscopy is performed in a semidark room, the patient's first impression of the room is formed when the lights are on. Although the floor of this room cannot be carpeted, an attractive design in hard-surface flooring and patterned wallcovering in a warm-color palette (to counteract the cool room temperature) may make the equipment appear less foreboding.

Respect and concern for patients' needs during the stress of diagnostic imaging examinations will help them feel comfortable in what otherwise might be experienced as a hostile environment. Amenities include comfortable waiting areas; private, well-appointed dressing rooms; ready access to rest rooms, drinking fountains, and telephones; and a concerted effort to shield patients from sights and sounds that do not concern them.

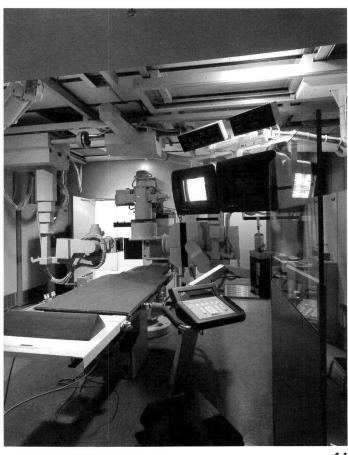

4-1

4-1 *Digital radiology room, University Hospital, University of Michigan Hospitals (Ann Arbor, MI)*
    Architect: Albert Kahn Associates, Architects & Engineers; Photographer: Balthazar Korab Ltd.

4-2 *Lithotripter, University Hospital, University of Michigan Hospitals (Ann Arbor, MI)*
    Architect: Albert Kahn Associates, Architects & Engineers; Photographer: Balthazar Korab Ltd.

The principal activities in a diagnostic imaging center are waiting, undressing and dressing, examination and treatment, and consultation. These are either self-explanatory or described more fully below.

SPACE PLANNING

Of prime importance to the financial health of a radiology department is the amount of throughput or the number of patient examinations that can be completed each day. The capital outlay for equipment is great, and operating efficiency is a major concern. Therefore, dressing rooms are positioned close to examination rooms even though patients, while undressing, may hear the

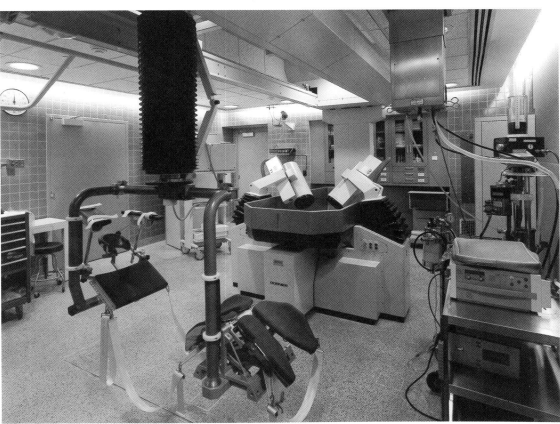

4-2

sounds of equipment being positioned for other patients and possibly overhear instructions meant for others. Under the best of conditions, the radiology department will be planned so that patients cannot overhear staff discussing another patient's diagnosis or see another patient's films displayed on a viewbox illuminator. Processing, film reading, and the staff lounge should be accessed from a discrete staff corridor.

Despite the level of anxiety most patients experience, many facilities pay little attention to patient privacy in the design of the dressing room itself, in the location of dressing rooms with respect to examination areas, and in the logical sequence of rooms. In many radiology departments, mazelike corridors create confusion and patients do not know whether they are trespassing in a "staff only" area or if they are where they are supposed to be.

Dressing Area

A patient's comfort level can be enhanced by providing a secure place for belongings and by making the dressing room a pleasant and attractive space. Patients may be asked to undress and wait in the dressing room until they are called for the examination, which provides a certain degree of privacy for gowned patients and protects them from forced intimacy with strangers. The room must then be large enough not to be claustrophobic, however, and it must provide a comfortable place to sit, a magazine rack, a place to hang or secure clothing, and attractive finishes on the floor and walls. A mirror for patients to check their appearance prior to leaving is also a requirement.

If patients are expected to gown, place their belongings in lockers, and proceed to a second or subwaiting area until they are called, an additional layer of stress is imposed. Gowns are often skimpy; even if a robe is provided, some individuals feel uncomfortable having to wait with strangers of the opposite sex under these conditions. Line of sight is also important. Patients in the primary waiting room should not be able to view gowned patients every time the door opens.

Gurney Holding Area

This department sees both inpatients and outpatients who may be sick or well. Inpatients should be separated from outpatients, and those waiting on gurneys should never come into view of ambulatory patients; however, the gurney holding area must be under direct observation of staff so that patients do not feel isolated or forgotten. Gurney patients must have some way to communicate with staff, just as ambulatory patients in a dressing room or bathroom have to be able to summon staff by an emergency call button.

LIGHTING

Lighting is especially important in imaging rooms and in the gurney holding area. A patient lying on a gurney would be uncomfortable to have to look up into the lens of a fluorescent fixture. The same holds true for a patient during a procedure in an imaging room. Generally a high level of illumination is needed only when equipment is being serviced or when some type of invasive procedure is being performed. Most of the time, however, indirect perimeter lighting creates a pleasant ambience for the patient. Overhead lights would be turned on only when needed.

INTERIOR DESIGN

Despite the widespread acknowledgment that patients experience psychological stress and discomfort in a radiology clinic, interior design often stops at the waiting room. Few facilities address radiologic examination rooms at all in terms of providing color, distractions, or attractive finish materials, and few address internal patient corridors. All too often, once the patient leaves the waiting room, walls have neutral semigloss enamel and a nondescript hard-surface flooring or an equally unattractive level-loop carpet. Artwork on walls is rare. Perhaps the cost of equipment is so great that money is not available to be spent for discretionary design features. A more likely explanation is that radiologists truly do not understand the terror felt by most patients because the equipment in those rooms is beautiful to them and represents state-of-the-art technology; they are not intimidated by it.

The skillful use of color and texture in selected finishes, artwork, and accessories throughout the space can do much to relax patients (Fig. 4-3). As many distractions as possible should be provided to keep patients

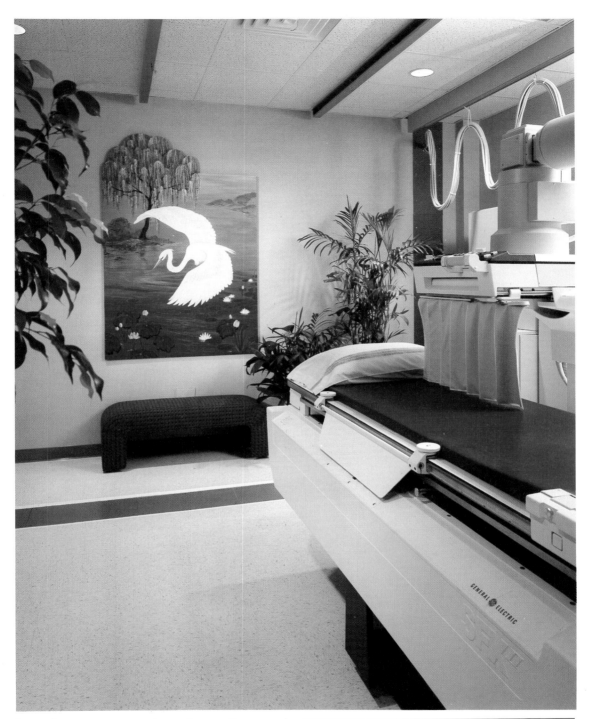

from focusing on equipment, monitors, and viewboxes in what is very much a technology-dominated environment.

MAMMOGRAPHY

Mammography has become a commonplace screening technique for determining the presence of breast tumors. Mammography rooms can be found in primary care clinics or in diagnostic imaging centers. Wherever they occur,

4-3 *Radiograph room with nonclinical ambience, Morton Plant Hospital (Palm Harbor, FL)*

Architect: Pauline Obrentz Interiors, Inc., Kathryn Stephens, ASID, IBD, designer; Photographer: George Cott

they should be designed to appeal to women. Even if patients register at a central desk, they should be directed to a dedicated mammography changing area (Fig. 4-4) or to a second or subwaiting area (Fig. 4-5). The mammography procedure room itself may be carpeted and have attractive wallcovering, wood moldings, or any type of decorative treatment without regard for the type of sanitation requirements imposed by certain other types of imaging procedures. Indirect lighting is recommended. Sometimes a suite includes a separate education room where patients may view a videotape explaining how to do a breast self-examination. This room would usually have a table or built-in bench that allows the patient to lie down.

4-4 *Women's dressing area, radiology suite, Morton Plant Hospital (Palm Harbor, FL)*
Architect: Pauline Obrentz Interiors, Inc., Kathryn Stephens, ASID, IBD, designer; Photographer: George Cott

4-5 *Mammography waiting area, Morton Plant Hospital (Palm Harbor, FL)*

Architect: Pauline Obrentz Interiors, Inc., Kathryn Stephens, ASID, IBD, designer; Photographer: George Cott

CT SCANNER

Computed tomography has been around long enough that the equipment probably is not regarded as intimidating. In fact, the design has not changed much since its introduction; it resembles a large machine with a "doughnut hole" in the center. Compared with other types of imaging equipment, it is rather clean looking and free of tubestands, cords, and monitors. Because very little is mounted to walls in a CT room, it has ample space for decorative treatments such as murals, wall graphics, or art. Flooring should be hard surface. The room in Figure 4-6 cleverly uses large-scale film transparencies of underwater images to distract patients.

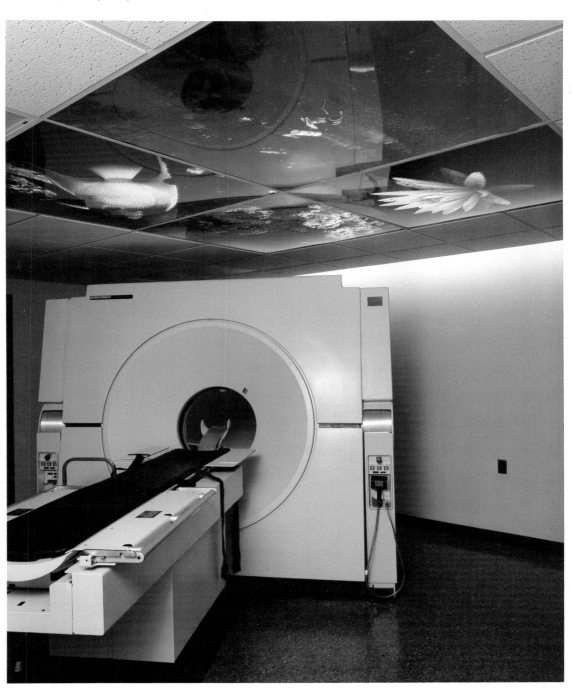

4-6 *CT scanning suite features underwater photography overhead; St. Mary's Hospital (Grand Rapids, MI)*
Architecture and interior design: Harley Ellington Pierce Yee Associates, Inc.; Photographer: The Image Center

GAMMA KNIFE SUITE

The Gamma Knife uses precisely focused beams of radiation to destroy otherwise inoperable lesions deep within the brain. Called *stereotactic radiosurgery*, it has the advantage over conventional radiation therapy in that it does not risk damaging healthy areas of the brain; it allows neurosurgeons to reach previously inaccessible brain tumors without opening the patient's skull. Because it relies on precise aim, the area being treated must be kept completely still, necessitating that a frame be attached to the skull with needle-thin screws in order to immobilize the head (Fig. 4-7). At present only a handful of American institutions are using stereotactic radiosurgery, although worldwide interest in the technique is growing (Montgomery 1990).

MAGNETIC RESONANCE IMAGING (MRI)

Magnetic resonance imaging is considered by many to be the most revolutionary imaging technology of the century. Manufacturers of radiology equipment have committed large sums of money to engineering, research, and product development in continually expanding the capabilities of MRI. For example, advances in magnet technology have reduced the area of magnetic field influence (the Gauss field) surrounding the equipment to allow it to be more easily integrated into existing structures. Many environmental issues must be considered when planning an MRI facility. These and other issues such as shielding requirements, HVAC, floor loading, and cryogenic replenishment are discussed in detail in chapter 5 of my book *Medical and Dental Space Planning for the 1990s*. The present discussion will cover interior design issues.

When MRI was first introduced, any ferrous substance was thought to negatively affect image quality. Very expensive construction techniques using totally nonferrous materials were standard procedure. Wood beams, glued connections, stainless-steel nails, Fiberglas, copper, and aluminum were considered appro-

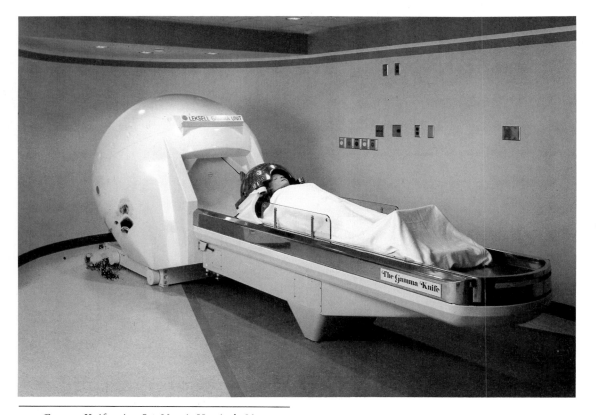

4-7 *Gamma Knife suite, St. Mary's Hospital, Mayo Medical Center (Rochester, MN)*
Architect: Hammel Green and Abrahamson, Inc.;
Photographer: Shin Koyama

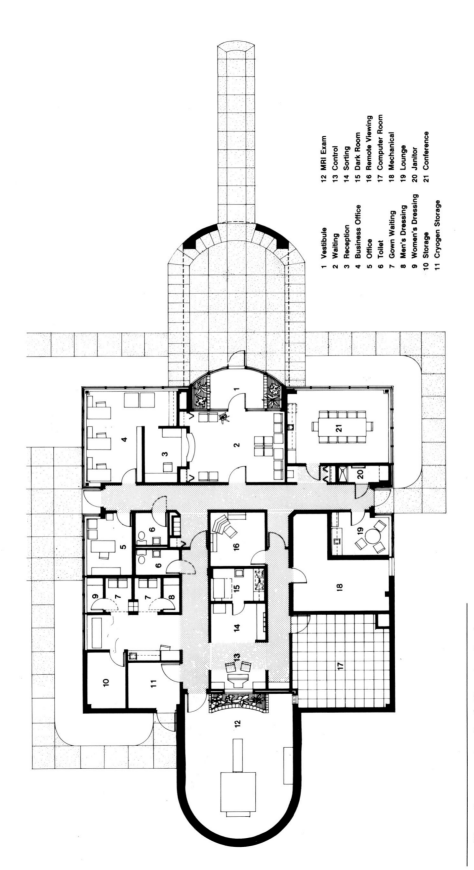

1 Vestibule
2 Waiting
3 Reception
4 Business Office
5 Office
6 Toilet
7 Gown Waiting
8 Men's Dressing
9 Women's Dressing
10 Storage
11 Cryogen Storage
12 MRI Exam
13 Control
14 Sorting
15 Dark Room
16 Remote Viewing
17 Computer Room
18 Mechanical
19 Lounge
20 Janitor
21 Conference

4-8 *Magnetic resonance imaging facility, Associated Imaging Center (Grand Chute, WI)*
Courtesy Flad & Associates Architects

priate construction materials. Now, however, manufacturers generally agree that shimming of the magnet is able to compensate for static ferrous building materials. The use of conventional construction techniques and materials greatly reduces the expense of constructing an MRI facility. A typical layout of an MRI facility is shown in Figure 4-8.

The facility in Figure 4-9 benefits from natural light from clerestory windows spilling into waiting areas below. Note that all lighting is indirect, either from wall sconces or from light-coved

4-9 *Magnetic resonance imaging suite, waiting area/ reception, The Good Samaritan Hospital of Santa Clara Valley (San Jose, CA)*

Architecture and interior design: Kaplan McLaughlin Diaz; Photographer: John Sutton

coffers overhead. Walls have a double layer of gypsum board to create "cut-out" designs. Built-in planters act as room dividers and afford privacy for small pods of seating.

Noise generated by equipment can be frightening and irritating to patients; acoustical treatment is recommended for a successful MRI procedure room. Carpeting and acoustic-wrapped panels will absorb sound and soften the appearance of the room (Fig. 4-10). Some brands of equipment lend themselves to being built-in so that the huge magnet is barely visible from the patient's side of the room (Fig. 4-11). In this illustration, fabric-wrapped acoustic panels absorb noise. A view of the outdoors can be simulated with a *trompe l'oeil* mural painted on the wall or by using an acrylic material that looks like glass block installed either as a full wall or as an upper window. Behind it might be artificial plant material and a computer-operated system of colored lights that simulate sunrise, daylight, and sunset (Fig. 4-11). Care must be taken in the selection of both interior finish materials and construction techniques to avoid interfering with radio frequency shielding or disturbing the magnetic field. Shimmed and self-shielded units, an advancement over earlier models, permit a companion to remain in the room and also allow adjacent foot traffic without ghosting of images. Note that the cryogen replenishment pipe has been concealed in Figure 4-10 by a windowlike structure with photos simulating a view of the outdoors. One of the most beautiful MRI rooms features backlit stained-glass panels in the wall and ceiling to distract patients (Fig. 4-12).

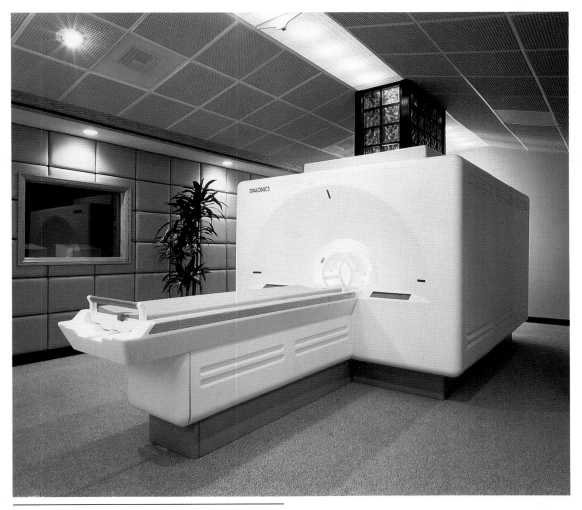

4-10 *Magnetic resonance imaging room, product demonstration suite, Toshiba America MRI Inc. Interior architecture: Donald Gardner, IBD, GardnerDominick; Photographer: Gary Laufman*

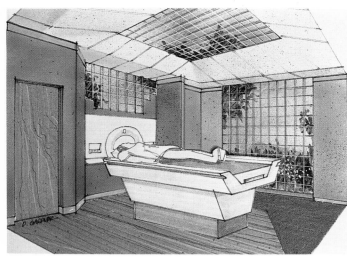

4-11 *Conceptual design for MRI suite, Holston Valley Medical Center*
Designer: Donald Gardner, IBD, Gardner Dominick; Photo courtesy Donald Gardner

4-12 *Magnetic resonance imaging room, Tuttleman Center, Graduate Hospital (Philadelphia, PA)*
Architecture and interior design: Medifac; Stained glass: Sigstedt Studio; Photographer: Tom Crane

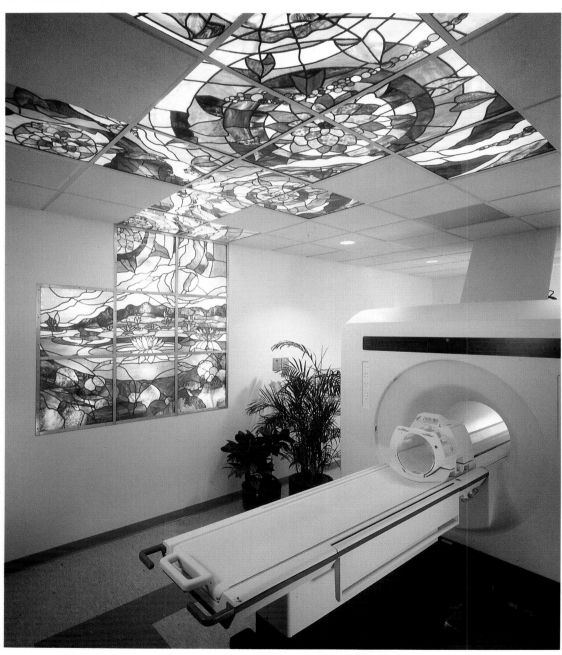

CARDIAC CATHETERIZATION LABORATORY

The "cath lab" is vital to the diagnosis and treatment of coronary disease. It may be located adjacent to the radiology department or in the surgical suite. Cardiac catheterization is the insertion of a catheter (a long, narrow, flexible tube) through a blood vessel into the heart. It allows examination of the heart and coronary arteries. The procedure may be either diagnostic or therapeutic. Therapeutic catheterizations are performed only in hospitals having a backup open heart surgery program. Coronary angiography (injection of contrast media) is a diagnostic procedure that causes arteries to become visible on x-rays (Fig. 4-13). Therapeutic procedures include the installation of pacemakers and angioplasty (balloon catheter), which can clear an occlusion in the artery.

4-13 *Angiography Lab features backlit photo of soothing image of trees and waterfall; Grace Hospital (Detroit, MI)*

Photo art treatment: Quartus Photo Design Systems; Photographer: Bob Stewart

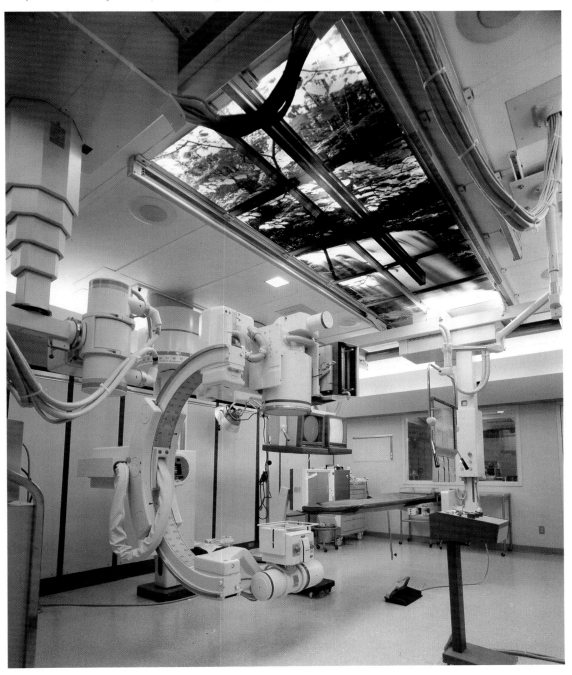

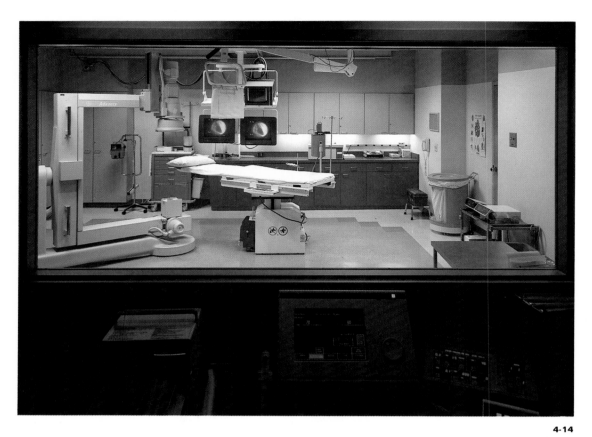

4-14

COMPONENTS OF CATHETERIZATION SUITE

The rooms that comprise this suite are the procedure room, a patient holding area, darkroom, film viewing area, chemistry support lab, and a clerical area. The cath lab is a clean procedure room with a sterile field that includes the patient, angiographer (cardiologist), assistant, and supply cart. The cardiologist inserts the catheter. This procedure can be terrifying for the patient, who is transported to the room on a gurney and no doubt is apprehensive and anxious. During the procedure the patient is typically sedated with an IV of Valium; however, he or she is conscious and able to notice the surroundings. Therefore, the gurney holding area should be as attractive as possible, and in the procedure room itself the wall and ceiling in view of the patient should be treated in a manner that is positively engaging. However, interior design enhancements must not reflect on equipment monitors.

INTERIOR DESIGN FEATURES

In most hospitals the cath lab procedure room is totally devoid of color, and the room is packed with large equipment, monitors, cables,

4-15

4-16 *Exam room corridor, Cardiac Catheterization Suite, Heartland Health Systems (St. Joseph, MO) Architecture and interior design: Henningson, Durham, & Richardson Inc.; Photo courtesy HDR*

tubes, and other paraphernalia. Imagine how much less threatening the experience might be if the room looked like that in Figure 4-14. Cibachrome film images used in the lenses of fluorescent light fixtures divert the patient's attention to scenes of nature or perhaps a harbor view, which may recall pleasant memories rather than force the patient to focus on the procedure (Figs. 4-13 and 4-15). Corridors can also be attractive and nonclinical, as exemplified by the examination corridor in Figure 4-16.

REFERENCES

Fischer, Harry. 1982. *Radiology Departments: Planning, Operation, and Management.* Ann Arbor: Edwards Brothers, Inc.

Goldberg, Alan, and R. DeNoble (eds.). 1986. *Hospital Departmental Profiles.* Chicago: American Hospital Publishing.

Malkin, Jain. 1990. *Medical and Dental Space Planning for the 1990s. New York: Van Nostrand Reinhold.*

Montgomery, S. 1990. Precision radiology. *Los Angeles Times* December 10:B5.

4-14 *Cardiac Catheterization Lab, Rex Hospital (Raleigh, NC)*
Architecture and interior design: BLM Group; Photographer: © Jim Sink, Archtech, Inc.

4-15 *Cardiac Catheterization Lab with backlit photo of seaport, Grace Hospital (Detroit, MI)*
Photo art treatment: Quartus Photo Design Systems; Photographer: Balthazar Korab Ltd.

chapter **5**

CHILDREN'S HOSPITALS

psychological factors

- family support
- social interaction
- security
- territorial privacy
- harmony
- movement
- comfort
- competency
- control
- independence
- access to outdoors
- fantasy

activities

- play
- rest/sleep
- therapy
- eating
- study
- surgery/treatment
- examination
- parent/staff conferences
- peer interaction
- parent caregiving
- visiting

issues

- acoustics
- lighting
- privacy
- visibility of patients
- views of nature
- opportunities to personalize space
- infection control
- accommodation for parents
- normalization
- visual stimulation
- crowding
- stress
- scale

Unlike many special patient populations, much has been written on design of health care facilities for children. In fact, two books (Olds and Daniel 1987; Lindheim, Glaser, and Coffin 1972) outline practically every aspect of design of these facilities, starting with the planning process and philosophy and including explanations of a child's social, emotional, and developmental needs translated into design guidelines. Instead of trying to cover the same topics, this chapter summarizes current philosophy about the design of children's hospitals, acquaints the reader with significant literature in the field, highlights key design issues, presents an approach to incorporating fantasy into a children's hospital, and then presents a variety of projects that respect and honor children.

For many years hospitalized children were treated in environments that differed little in terms of design from those of adult populations, with the exception of colorful graphics or cartoons that might be applied to the walls. Adapting the environment to children was often handled in a superficial or cosmetic manner. Accommodation for families who wanted to be with their children during hospitalization was either nonexistent or handled so poorly that parents felt unwelcome. As an example, the interior designer might have been directed to specify only individual chairs for a parent's lounge to discourage sleeping there. The unspoken message was that parents would be in the way and interfere with hospital efficiencies.

In the early 1970s, a survey of hospitals caring for children in the Boston area documented little consistency in parental access or in accommodation for parents to stay with their children, to be with them during tests and procedures, and in availability of overnight facilities (Lambert 1990). Since then advocacy groups across the nation have worked with hospitals to effect changes in philosophy and policy to bring about family-centered care. Parent advisory groups have become a part of the planning process for many recently designed children's hospitals, and the consensus is that a multidisciplinary approach—a participatory effort of design team, nurses, social workers, psychologists, child-life specialists, physicians, administrators, therapists, parents, and even a committee of school-age children and adolescents—is essential to the success of any new children's hospital.

A CHANGE IN PHILOSOPHY

The enlightened children's hospital meets not just the child's basic medical needs but also the physical, social, developmental, and emotional needs of children and their families. These changes cannot be effected by the design team unless they are based on administrative policy decisions to set guidelines for involving the family in the child's care, protect from budget cuts certain aesthetic elements that might be regarded as luxuries, and be open to new ways of doing things that support children's psychosocial needs, even if they slightly compromise hospital protocols for organization or efficiency.

In contrast to the adult patient, when a child is hospitalized the entire family becomes the patient. Parents suffer because their role as providers and protectors is threatened; brothers and sisters suffer because their parents' attention is diverted. Today children's hospitals recognize that they must provide support to the entire family to see them through the unending demands and periodic crises of illness and occasionally the final stages of life.

RESOURCES

Child Health Care Facilities (Olds and Daniel 1987) is published by the Association for the Care of Children's Health, a national advocacy organization coordinating, under the direction of Jill Hall, literature on the relationship between children's health and environmental design issues. The book is divided into design guidelines, literature outlines, and references. The format makes finding either literature or design guidelines on a particular topic easy. It is an impressive work of scholarship and an invaluable guide for the health care designer. The book incorporates occasional black and white photos of design concepts successfully implemented at various facilities.

Changing Hospital Environments for Children (Lindheim, Glaser, and Coffin 1972) deals thoughtfully with the medical, psychological, social, and developmental needs of the hospitalized child; it is organized according to age groupings of infants, toddlers and preschoolers, grade school children, and adolescents. Principles of child development are applied to concepts of hospital planning. A comprehensive review of literature on the hospitalized child is presented in support of various planning concepts. Two especially interesting features are the chapter on design of nursing units and the appendix, containing design log observations of hospitalized children in various settings over a period of time. The authors present options for nursing unit layouts that place priority on the patients' sense of security and well-being, which they achieve by decentralizing nurse stations to allow enhanced visibility and interaction with patients.

Design That Cares (Carpman, Grant, and Simmons 1986) presents valuable information of a more general nature for all major areas of a hospital. Design guidelines are based on recent environmental research; however, children are not the specific focus of the book.

Children's Hospital (Anderson 1985) is a compassionate firsthand account of the day-to-day hospital experiences of six children ranging in age from 9 days to 15 years who suffer from serious illnesses or injuries. Written in the style of a novel, the author gives the reader a carefully detailed portrayal of the hospital from the perspectives of physicians, nursing staff, social workers, therapists, patients, and parents.

Perspectives in Perinatal and Pediatric Design (Ross Planning Associates 1988) is the latest edition of a planning guide for obstetric, neonatal, and pediatric units in hospitals. Summarizing 30 years of experience in planning these types of facilities, the book provides a wealth of information on space planning, critical dimensions, programming, philosophical issues, and interior design. Best of all, the book's format makes the data easily accessible and enjoyable to read. Ross Planning Associates is a division of Ross Laboratories, publisher of a number of other excellent resources such as the journal *Frontline Planning, Perspectives in NICU Planning,* and environmental research papers.

Hospital Care of Children and Youth (Committee on Hospital Care 1986) covers a broad range of topics, including design. Written by physicians, the book provides an excellent discussion of contemporary issues encompassing community planning, quality assurance, administration of surgical services, health care financing, air and ground transport, pediatric intensive care units, the dying child, and a plethora of other topics. Although not specifically a planning book for architects and designers, this resource contributes to an understanding of the big picture from the physician's perspective.

PSYCHOLOGICAL FACTORS
IMPORTANCE OF FAMILY

Authorities in the field of child development note that the ability of one or both parents to be with the young child is the most significant factor in helping both child and parents cope with the trauma of hospitalization. The presence of the parent also helps to normalize unfamiliar hospital routines.

Parents experience tremendous frustration and anguish as they watch their children struggle against formidable illnesses. Being a parent of a very ill child tests the limits of human endurance. To help parents deal with feelings of helplessness, fear, and anger, they need as much information as possible about their child's

5-1 *Interior of Ronald McDonald House (Charleston, SC)*
Architecture and interior design: Lucas Stubbs Pascullis
Powell & Penney, Ltd.; Photographer: Rick Alexander, Inc.

illness and need to share in caregiving. For parents to feel welcome, they need to have a comfortable chair to sit on, sleeping accommodations, designated lounges, and meditation rooms to which they can withdraw and rest from the demands of caregiving. A family lounge should have a relaxed, homelike atmosphere and offer some degree of privacy. At the same time, it offers social interaction with other parents and opportunities for mutual support (Fig. 5-1). A playroom for siblings is much appreciated (Fig. 5-2). A chair that opens out into a bed (Fig. 5-3) allows a parent to be with the child at all times. Guest suites (Fig. 5-4) offer parents privacy; a quiet area for making phone calls, doing office work, or taking a nap; and a place to visit with relatives. They can make coffee, enjoy a snack, and have a personal space or refuge from the maelstrom of hospital activity (Fig. 5-5). These facilities are especially important for out-of-town parents who have traveled with their child to a regional children's hospital.

5-2 *Playroom, Ronald McDonald House (Charleston, SC)*

Architecture and interior design: Lucas Stubbs Pascullis Powell & Penney, Ltd.; Photographer: Rick Alexander, Inc.

5-3 *Patient room permits view of corridors and incorporates a place for parent to sleep; Mercy Memorial Medical Center, Pediatric Unit (St. Joseph, MI)*

Architecture and interior design: Hansen Lind Meyer; Photographer: Elizabeth Ernst

5-4 *Guest bedroom suites for families of hospitalized children, Schneider Children's Hospital, Long Island Jewish–Hillside Medical Center (New Hyde Park, NY)*

Architecture and interior design: The Architects Collaborative; Photographer: © Peter Aaron/Esto

5-5 *Family dining area in pediatric unit, St. Francis Regional Medical Center (Wichita, KS)*

Architecture and interior design: Howard Needles Tammen & Bergendoff; Photographer: Mike Sinclair, Sinclair Reinsch

SOCIAL INTERACTION

Interaction with peers is a normal part of a child's daily activities. Specially designed playrooms (Fig. 5-6), lounges, classrooms, and corridors (if they are designed properly) facilitate socialization.

5-6 *Children's playroom, Etobicoke General Hospital (Toronto, Ontario)*
Architecture and interior design: NORR Partnership Limited; Photographer: Panda Associates

SECURITY

A sense of security can be fostered by laying out rooms or orienting furniture so that the child's back is against the wall or perpendicular to it, rather than toward the center of the room. When people enter the room, they are facing the child rather than approaching from behind. Playrooms in particular should take this factor into account.

TERRITORIAL PRIVACY

Much has been written about the basic human need to stake out an area and claim it. It is a means of establishing a sense of personal identity, and it implies that a person may exert control over the area within those boundaries. In a hospital, people surrender the protective armor of their own clothing and relinquish control over many routine aspects of daily living. Therefore, the patient room must be arranged in such a fashion that the patient can define a territorial boundary and enjoy a measure of personal space. The "best" layout of semiprivate rooms has been hotly debated for decades. Unless economics and available space allow the room to be larger than that required by code, compromises will always have to be made between maximum view of the outdoors, patient privacy, nurses' visibility into the room, and adequate access around the bed to deliver care. In recent years, the trend toward single-bed rooms makes issues of territoriality and privacy easier to address.

HARMONY

An environment is harmonious when all components fit together and are balanced so that no single element overpowers the others. Thus the patient does not have to adapt to the environment or fight it. That energy can be turned inward to allow the patient to focus on healing. This issue is complex, however, because what is perceived as harmonious might differ from one individual to another depending upon their personalities, cultural background, and the environment they are accustomed to at home.

In addition to environmental harmony, psychological harmony can be enhanced by addressing four principal patient needs in the design of the facility (Olds and Daniel 1987): the need for movement, the need to feel comfortable, the need to feel competent, and the need to feel in control.

Movement

Movement is an essential part of well-being. For children, the need to run and move about freely does not diminish because they are hospitalized. If suitable opportunities are not provided, disruptive behaviors may result. Playrooms, therapy rooms, and corridors give opportunities for use of large muscle groups; quiet play in bed or at tables exercises small muscle groups.

Comfort

Comfort can be achieved by having basic needs met (food, sleep, and medical care) and by an aesthetically harmonious environment. When people are comfortable, they can relax, which provides an opportunity for healing.

Competency

The child has a need to master the environment and not be overwhelmed or intimidated by it.

Freedom to explore, to try skills, to be defeated, or to win are necessary aspects of child development that foster feelings of competency. Making the environment legible to children with color cues, understandable signage, and clear wayfinding devices helps them to master their surroundings.

Control

Control is expressed by being able to set limits on privacy, being able to predict events, having a place to be alone, and being able to see the approach of visitors or strangers.

Olds and Daniel (1987) advocate balancing these four key factors in order to maintain harmony. When one of these elements is limited (e.g., restricted movement due to a body cast), the value of the other factors must be increased. Illness sometimes produces multiple limitations such as restricted movement, restricted opportunities for interesting activities, and diminished control, making the comfort element exceedingly important and more deserving of attention than might be required in an environment for a healthy person. Limitations such as these sometimes allow more time to focus on small details. A noise that may hardly be noticeable during normal levels of activity might become irritating when activity is restricted.

INDEPENDENCE

Being hospitalized often means becoming dependent on others to satisfy basic needs. To the extent possible, allow children to do things for themselves. Sinks, toilets, mirrors, and wardrobes should be scaled for children to give them a measure of control over the environment and enhance their feelings of self-worth.

ACCESS TO OUTDOORS

Access to a patio, deck, or enclosed solarium enables patients to enjoy the benefits of sunshine, watch activities outside the hospital, and observe nature (Fig. 5-7). Playing outdoors is such a normal part of a child's day that not

5-7 *Conceptual design for atrium lobby, The Hospital for Sick Children (Toronto, Ontario)*
Architect: Zeidler Roberts Partnership/Architects; Renderer: Michael McCann Associates Ltd.

being able to do it for an extended period may cause stress.

FANTASY

Bruno Bettelheim (1976) tells us that fantasy is an important part of a child's life. It offers an opportunity to escape and to appear powerful against adults or adversaries, and in fantasy children can battle monsters and win at great odds. A children's hospital should contain elements of fantasy to provide an outlet for children to resolve their fears and to encourage them to dream of conquering their illnesses.

TYPES OF HEALTH CARE SETTINGS

Children's health care services may be provided on an ambulatory basis, in a pediatric unit of a community hospital, in a specialized children's hospital that may be a regional facility drawing patients from a wide area, in a psychi-

atric hospital, or in a long-term care facility. Each imposes a unique set of challenges and opportunities for the designer.

Children stricken with the normal, transient illnesses of childhood are often treated at a local community hospital. Children with more severe injuries, trauma, and complicated illnesses are often transported to a children's hospital where clinicians as well as the diagnostic and treatment equipment are highly specialized to meet the needs of children. Children born with deformities or stricken with life-threatening illnesses such as cystic fibrosis or cancer and those requiring radical reconstructive surgery look to a children's hospital for hope that is simply unavailable elsewhere.

SPECIAL NEEDS

Children's needs vary depending on their ages as well as on their illnesses or disabilities. The following discussion outlines a number of general needs of children at various developmental stages and then focuses on the special needs of children in long-term care facilities, rehabilitation units, and psychiatric settings.

DEVELOPMENTAL STAGES

Infants (0–12 Months)
Babies at this stage do well if their basic needs for food, warmth, safety, and hygiene are met and if they are provided with stimulating sensory experiences. Their well-being depends on familiar activities, and they seem to do well even if these activities are provided by unfamiliar people. Rocking meets an infant's needs for warmth, sensory contact, rhythmic motion, and possibly even auditory stimulation if the parent or caregiver sings or talks to the infant. Infants in a neonatal intensive care unit, however, have very special needs, which are detailed in chapter 10.

Toddlers and Preschoolers (1–6 Years)
The needs of toddlers and preschoolers are different from those of infants. They need

- Direct visual supervision by nursing staff
- A safe environment
- Opportunities for safe climbing
- Appropriate scale: variations in ceiling heights and changes in levels (if possible) to allow a child to feel big and an adult to appear small by contrast
- Low sinks, toilets, and clothes hooks
- Provisions for self-care
- Raised play areas for children in wheelchairs and on gurneys
- Adequate stimulation in the environment
- Glazed doors (glass panel) at toddlers' height to avoid hitting an unseen child on blind side of door when it is opened

Grade School Children (6–12 Years)
School-age children need

- Opportunities to acquire and exercise cognitive and motor skills
- A hospital classroom with space for gurneys and wheelchairs
- A soundproofed music practice room
- Outdoor play areas
- A group dining area
- Shared bedrooms for up to four children with space near each bed for school projects
- Opportunities for self-care
- Opportunities for socialization with peers
- A kitchenette to enable parents to prepare snacks and treats
- Special features such as a library from which to select books, a greenhouse where a child may select a live plant to care for, or a place to select a small, "nonallergenic" animal (e.g., turtle, fish, gerbil, ant farm) to take back to the child's room and care for.

Adolescents (12–18 Years)
In a hospital adolescents need

- A choice of room accommodations
- Privacy in their room, when desired
- Vanity areas for grooming
- A telephone near their bed
- Space for personal possessions and visitors; an opportunity to decorate the room with posters and express their own identities
- A teen sanctuary for activities unsupervised by adults
- A dayroom for studying, with a nearby kitchenette for preparing snacks
- Classrooms with an electronic learning environment

CHILDREN WITH SPECIAL NEEDS

Children, normal children, experience the world differently than adults. They have a more visceral, immediate reaction to color, texture, and auditory stimulation. Adults see something magical in a child's ability to fantasize and to create make-believe worlds at will. In the child's imagination, a cardboard carton becomes a castle and a dog becomes a monster threatening the inhabitants of a village. If adults have trouble understanding how normal children experience the world, then understanding how special children—those with cognitive impairments or physical disabilities or perhaps victims of child abuse—experience their environments is especially difficult.

Children born with handicaps live in special worlds that are often inaccessible to the observer. In order to help these vulnerable children adapt, understanding how they perceive their environments is important. Often these children are in frail health and cannot live independently; their deficits are a constant source of pain and frustration. However, a child in an institutional setting may actually be showing the effects of sensory deprivation. Children who have been hospitalized for long periods in sensorially and behaviorally barren environments may have tuned out the meaninglessness of such places so that they may not notice or appear to notice changes in them. They have an incredibly restricted range of behavior and sometimes seem to display hardly any behavior at all (Spivack 1984).

In order to study these children effectively, first enriching their environments may be necessary to restore their stimulation and behavioral opportunities to the levels available to healthy people in ordinary settings. "Locked within the perceptual, physical, and emotional handicaps that these children may have, we must assume there are capacities and needs to love, aesthetic sensibilities, social needs, the desire to be as much a free, full human as is possible within the limitation with which the child was born" (Spivack 1984, 72).

Spivack talks about the possibility of creating "prosthetic environments" where exceptional children can develop and flourish to the limits of their individual abilities. Chapter 5 of Spivack's book *Institutional Settings* contains a number of poignant personal observations of exceptional children that will interest all health care designers.

Long-Term Care

Children needing long-term care have physical, mental, or emotional disabilities that may cause them to be hospitalized for months or years, or perhaps they may require custodial care for a lifetime. Little has been written about the specialized needs of these children. The needs of hospitalized normal children, as previously outlined, would perhaps apply, provided they are supplemented by design guidelines for specific patient populations such as rehabilitation, cancer, mental health, or critical care.

Children who require long-term care may be confined to bed and suffer sensory deprivation, loss of independence, limited mobility, boredom, and loneliness. These children would benefit from an occasional change in the look of the room that can be made by introducing different colors and artwork that may be slipped into a wall-mounted frame and changed every so often. A selection of posters or actual color photographs called an *art cart* may be circulated by a volunteer who slips the image into a frame fastened to the wall and locks it with a key.

Play environments for beds (Fig. 5-8) may be custom designed. Delores Pacileo has dedicated her career to creating prosthetic environments for hospitalized and handicapped children. Illness does not stop the child from being a child and wanting to play. Play environments that do not require much body movement or energy can be designed for the bed, such as a dart board mounted to the end of a bed with "darts" that are Velcro balls attached to a string, a crib wall consisting of a fabric panel with pockets for dolls and other toys, a puppet theater that slips over the bed and can be used by a child without sitting up; and a long, narrow Plexiglas fish tank that slips across the bed frame and can be used for turtles as well (the child can lie in bed and look up at it). All the items have Velcro attachments. A Velcro wall specifically for cerebral palsy patients disguises as a play experience repetitive exercises to develop and strengthen designated muscle groups.

5-8 *Entertaining diversions for children confined to bed*
Illustration courtesy Delores Pacileo

NEW YORK FOUNDLING HOSPITAL

Long-term care and skilled nursing are provided for disabled infants, toddlers, and young children on four floors of a 179,000-square-foot building that houses seven different programs for children with seven different licensing agencies, codes, and standards (Fig. 5-9). Other floors provide residential programs such as group homes and diagnostic centers for troubled boys and girls, an island of safety for abused children, and administrative headquarters for managing the institution's foster care program for a network encompassing five boroughs and two counties. An education and training center for parents and staff is also included. A unique feature of this hospital is a special elementary school licensed by the New York Board of Education. A playground and inner courtyard for nonambulatory children are also provided.

5-9 *New York Foundling Hospital (New York City) Illustration courtesy Perkins Geddis Eastman Architects*

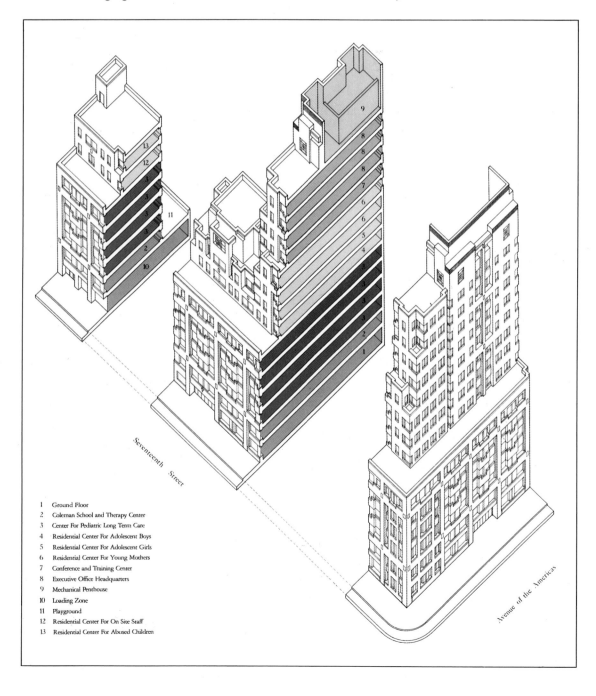

1   Ground Floor
2   Coleman School and Therapy Center
3   Center For Pediatric Long Term Care
4   Residential Center For Adolescent Boys
5   Residential Center For Adolescent Girls
6   Residential Center For Young Mothers
7   Conference and Training Center
8   Executive Office Headquarters
9   Mechanical Penthouse
10 Loading Zone
11 Playground
12 Residential Center For On Site Staff
13 Residential Center For Abused Children

5-10 *Main lobby and visiting area, New York Foundling Hospital (New York City)*
Architecture and interior design: Perkins Geddis Eastman Architects; Photographer: Norman McGrath

5-11 *Interior of elevator cab incorporates fine detailing and richly textured materials; New York Foundling Hospital*
Architecture and interior design: Perkins Geddis Eastman Architects; Photographer: Norman McGrath

Exceptional Attention to Detail

In spite of the complexity of programs and codes, the attention to detail throughout this building is exceptional. Starting with the terracotta medallions of allegorical imagery inserted into the masonry skin of the building, to the toddler's-height mirror and tack wall detail in corridors, residents' needs have been anticipated and met. The music room has a wood floor so that deaf children can feel the vibration of the music when they lie on the floor. Lobbies are visually connected by a wood wainscot of cherry veneer with mahogany inlay and a continuous floor pattern of multicolored terrazzo based on a quilt theme (Fig. 5-10). Cherry wood is used in detailing throughout, including elevators and chapel (Fig. 5-11). Nurse stations include "stairs" for children to sit on in front and an alcove for visiting behind.

Child's Scale Important

A special feature of this facility is that, wherever appropriate, things are scaled to the eye level of a toddler, generally 24 inches off the floor. Figure 5-12 shows panes of glass in a door that allow a toddler to look into the room. Narrow horizontal slots of mirror in corridors enable children to see themselves, and windows in patient bedrooms, activity rooms, and classrooms start a few inches off the floor to allow infants and toddlers the visual stimulation of looking out the window at people and automobiles several stories below. A deep sill provides a place for toddlers to stow toys and dolls (Fig. 5-13). The architect relates that staff were initially quite worried about children's safety at the low window, but experience has proven the worry to be unfounded. Realizing that the windows would be an attraction for young children, the designer incorporated a radiant heating panel into the ceiling across the width of the windows (Fig. 5-14).

Accommodation for Bathing

An interesting item in patient bedrooms is the custom-designed bathing countertop made in Sweden (Fig. 5-15). Typically these units are designed for infants and are not appropriate for bathing or diapering developmentally disabled children who may be quite large and heavy. A specially designed mixing valve allows automatic temperature control that prevents accidentally burning the child.

5-12 *Alcove entrance of quad room, Pediatric Long-term Care, New York Foundling Hospital (New York City)*

Architecture and interior design: Perkins Geddis Eastman Architects; Photographer: Norman McGrath

5-13 *Coleman Elementary School classroom (second floor), New York Foundling Hospital (New York City)*

Architecture and interior design: Perkins Geddis Eastman Architects; Photographer: Norman McGrath

Small details such as the custom design silk-screened onto ceramic accent tiles in residents' bathrooms may not be appreciated by young children, but they establish an image of quality that makes the staff feel good about caring for these children.

Patient Room Lighting

Lighting in four-bed rooms is especially interesting. Understanding that some children may be receiving phototropic drugs (making patients sensitive to light) and that some children need attention during the night (without disturbing others) caused the architects to develop a flexible lighting system incorporating indirect lighting, examination lighting, and a task light over the bathing area. Window shades control exterior light.

Achieving a Residential Ambiance

This building is remarkable because it does not look like a hospital. Even though a children's hospital makes the most challenging demands on furniture and finishes, institutional materials have been avoided. All walls of public areas have a polyolefin-woven fabric (Tek-Wall™) wallcovering (including corridors of nursing floors), and most floors have carpet tile. Cherrywood handrails, doors to residents' rooms, and trim on nurse stations (Fig. 5-16) add a residential warmth, as do wall sconces and indirect lighting (Fig. 5-17). Corridors have frequent alcoves that soften their linearity, and hard-surface floors have beautiful quiltlike patterns (Fig. 5-17). A carpet tile accent is used to mark the parking lane for strollers outside activity rooms (Fig. 5-18).

Color Activity Levels

Because this hospital is a long-term care residential environment, color was used to provide variety and also to cue activity levels. Color is bright and stimulating in classrooms and activity rooms, but soothing in patient bedrooms. On upper floors soft pastel colors are used in living quarters for older children who may have come from violent home environments and who need a calm setting in order to stabilize themselves.

REHABILITATION

Children faced with a long course of rehabilitation, like adults, need tremendous encourage-

5-14 *Four-bed patient room features window starting low to the floor and radiant heating panel in ceiling, near windows; New York Foundling Hospital (New York City)*

Architecture and interior design: Perkins Geddis Eastman Architects; Photo courtesy Perkins Geddis Eastman

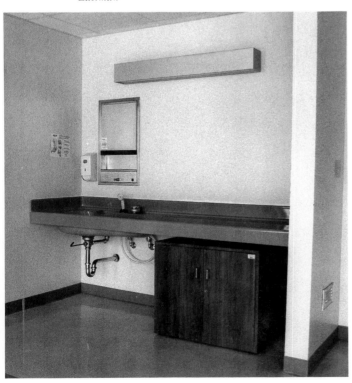

5-15 *Custom bathing countertop unit typical in patient rooms, New York Foundling Hospital (New York City)*
Architecture and interior design: Perkins Geddis Eastman Architects; Photo courtesy Perkins Geddis Eastman

5-16 *Climbable nurse station, Pediatric Long-term Care, New York Foundling Hospital (New York City)*

Architecture and interior design: Perkins Geddis Eastman Architects; Photographer: Fred George

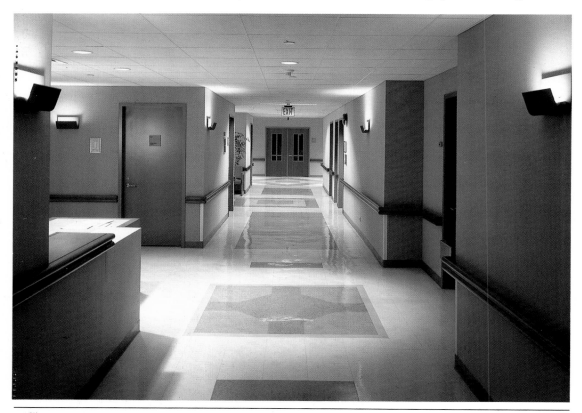

5-17 *Third-floor patient corridor features vinyl composition tile designs and indirect lighting; Pediatric Long-term Care, New York Foundling Hospital (New York City)*

Architecture and interior design: Perkins Geddis Eastman Architects; Photographer: Norman McGrath

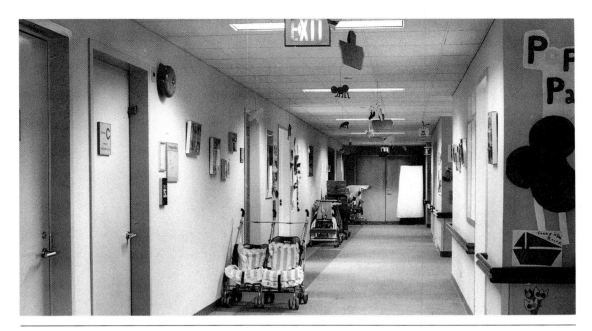

5-18 *Parking lane for strollers, adjacent to activity rooms and classrooms, is designated by inset carpet design: New York Foundling Hospital (New York City)*

Architecture and interior design: Perkins Geddis Eastman Architects; Photo courtesy Perkins Geddis Eastman

ment and support. Environmental design can actually motivate children with physical disabilities to exercise and look forward to occupational therapy. Strong color contrasts, inset designs, or patterns in hard-surface flooring or carpeting can make ambulation more of a game than a chore. Colorful wall graphics and art mounted at the proper height to be appreciated by children also enhance the environment and bolster morale.

Fantasy and Motivation

Children in a rehab facility may use crutches, braces, prostheses, and wheelchairs. Often they are viewed as negative because they remind children of limitations. The fanciful wheelchair cover in Figure 5-19 imparts special status to the child who gets to ride in it, and the ride now becomes an adventure. The child is seen as experiencing something special. For a disabled child the wheelchair cover removes the stigma from the wheelchair and allows a more positive interchange between disabled and able-bodied children in social situations. Non-handicapped children love to ride in it and gather around the wheelchair to admire it and pet the soft sculpture.

Wheelchair covers may be the slip-on type that can be removed when they might prove a distraction in a learning or therapy situation, or they may be permanent and made of durable

5-19 *Soft-sculpture wheelchair cover*
Created by Delores Pacileo; Photo courtesy Delores Pacileo

hard and soft materials. The wheelchair can be transformed into another kind of vehicle—a train, boat, or seahorse. Incidentally, fabrication of wheelchair covers can be tied into a volunteer program through the women's auxiliary. The designer provides the patterns and volunteers sew them at home. This activity involves the community with the hospital and provides a handmade item that represents the care and love of an individual.

Crutch covers (Fig. 5-20) encourage children to smile and put one foot in front of the next. Each leg is a different image to teach right from left. The dog barks and the cat meows when the crutch touches the floor, a response that delights young children.

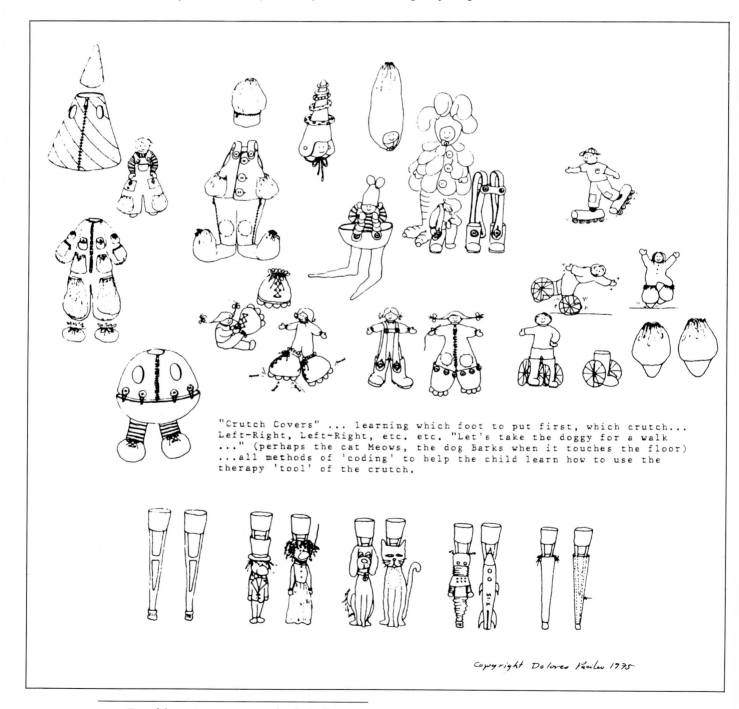

"Crutch Covers" ... learning which foot to put first, which crutch...
Left-Right, Left-Right, etc. etc. "Let's take the doggy for a walk
..." (perhaps the cat Meows, the dog Barks when it touches the floor)
...all methods of 'coding' to help the child learn how to use the
therapy 'tool' of the crutch.

Copyright Dolores Pacileo 1975

5-20 *Fanciful creations to encourage the physically and mentally disabled child*
Illustration courtesy Delores Pacileo

Therapeutic Environments

Other therapeutic environments designed by Pacileo include, for a blind infant, a multisensory playpad that has different tactile properties combined with a number of auditory signals (Fig. 5-21). The blind child can lose his fear of falling and explore new territories. A Knob Ball with protuberances starting out narrow at the base and widening at the top allows children who lack fine motor control to grasp and throw the ball. Multisensory infant and toddler playpads encourage the child to lift his or her head and to reach for the colorful, appealing forms, all the while strengthening weakened muscles.

One of the most innovative motivational therapy environments converts the rehab gym into a giant game board incorporating all pediatric therapy disciplines (Fig. 5-22). Called Easy 1, 2, 3™, it uses the same basic principles its designer, David Guynes, developed for Easy Street Environments for adult rehabilitation. It redirects patients' mind-sets toward their abilities rather than their disabilities.

Based on a human-scale game board, Easy 1, 2, 3™ provides a visual and physical context in which the pediatric patient will encounter and sequence standard gym activities. The game board format is activated by a master control panel known as Mr. PIPES (Pediatric Interactive Pneumatic Education System) that is controlled by a series of pneumatic (air-powered) switching devices that initiate a wide variety of outcomes. This unit is intended to provide an area for upper body strengthening and fine motor skill activities, along with an integrated cognitive and perceptual training program (Fig. 5-23).

The control center, in turn, activates devices throughout the game board that indicate the next step in the sequence of events that will lead the patient through the course of the game. For example, after sequencing a series of commands, a series of appropriately spaced cylinders rise from the floor (like stepping-stones) for the patient to use in crossing the graphic ''river'' painted on the floor. Another variation allows the patient to open the door to the ''fort.''

The entire environment is freestanding and modular. Pneumatic lines connect to a centralized compressor by running lines under a raised modular floor system. All standard clinical modalities are represented, transforming a clinical gym into an environmental tool that therapists can tailor to meet the specific needs of a broad range of patients.

5-21 *Sensory playpad for blind infant*
   Created by Delores Pacileo; Photo courtesy Delores Pacileo

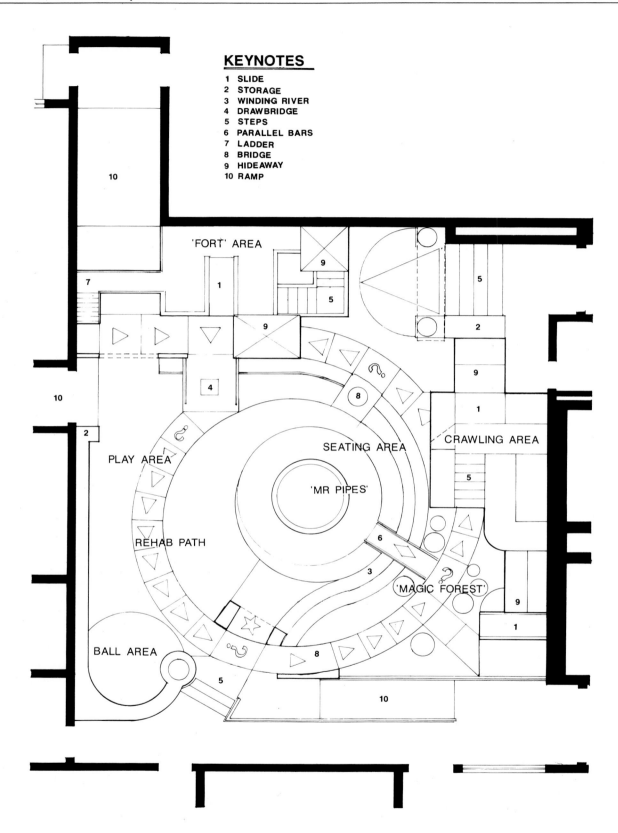

KEYNOTES
1 SLIDE
2 STORAGE
3 WINDING RIVER
4 DRAWBRIDGE
5 STEPS
6 PARALLEL BARS
7 LADDER
8 BRIDGE
9 HIDEAWAY
10 RAMP

5-22 *Easy 1, 2, 3 is a giant game board incorporating all rehabilitation therapy disciplines in an environment designed to motivate pediatric patients*
    Designer: David Guynes, Guynes Design Incorporated

5-23 *Perspective view of Easy 1, 2, 3*
Designer: David Guynes, Guynes Design Incorporated

PSYCHIATRIC FACILITIES FOR CHILDREN AND ADOLESCENTS

Writing a prescription for a therapeutic environment for emotionally disturbed children is difficult. The variety of individual disorders coupled with each child's emotional and physical disabilities makes one thing certain: what works for one patient population, in one specific institution, may be a dismal failure for even the same type of patient population located in a different community, where variables such as ethnic background, program protocols, or even building architecture differ. Only by the most painstaking process of dialogue and observation by an interdisciplinary team of architects, designers, staff, and even patients can clinical treatment practices and the idiosyncrasies of an individual institution be translated into a meaningful architectural program.

The discussion here focuses on three things: providing a description of the many and varied behavioral problems that cause these children to require treatment, acquainting the reader with the most significant research in this area, and presenting design guidelines that may be general enough to be applicable to most settings. Meeting the needs of emotionally disturbed children is a subject so complex that even the manipulation of one subtle environmental variable can make a significant differ-

ence to an individual child. I hope that the present discussion will give the designer a rudimentary background sufficient to stimulate further study and to facilitate participation in a team design effort.

Behavioral Problems Requiring Treatment

Children in a treatment program may be autistic, schizophrenic, self-destructive, or even suicidal. Behavior problems that caused them to be referred for treatment might have resulted from stressful family situations (divorce, death of a parent, child abuse, chemical or alcohol dependency of a parent) or chronic problems that have become impossible for parents to deal with such as running away, setting fires, stealing, acting out at school, lying, bullying other children, cruelty to animals, or problems with drug or alcohol abuse. Children with emotional problems can sometimes be treated on an outpatient basis, but when these measures fail or the severity of the problem demands more immediate intervention, the child may be admitted to an inpatient treatment unit.

Available Research

Creating therapeutic environments for psychiatric treatment has always been one of the greatest challenges for architects and designers. The task is especially frustrating because little research is available on which to base a design strategy. Mardelle Shepley grappled with this problem when designing a children's psychiatric facility for the state of California.

After reviewing existing research, she had two goals in mind when she decided to undertake her own study: that the results be applicable both to this particular project and to the design of psychiatric facilities in general, and that all data be directly translatable to the design of buildings. In her study (Shepley 1989) she summarizes nine presumptions that are supported by available research:

1. *The environment does have an impact on behavior in psychiatric settings.* Few people doubt this statement, but specific correlations between architectural design and the users' experience are hard to document owing to the complexity of buildings (both structurally and in terms of social implications) and to the individual personalities of inhabitants. The variables are so numerous.

2. *Residential aesthetics are preferred over institutional.* The use of residential materials such as carpeting was perceived positively by patients, indicating that a more familiar environment is preferred to one that emphasizes the separation from home.

3. *Some numbers and densities of patients are more appropriate than others for inducing specific behaviors in psychiatric treatment settings.* Total population and density are known to influence behavior. The smallest unit size possible is desirable to enhance the perception of the group as a family.

4. *Certain unit size, dining, and sleeping density preferences are expressed by patients.* Children retreated less frequently to two-bed rooms than to other size bedrooms. A preponderance of two-bed rooms was recommended if the staff's goal is to keep children involved in group activities.

5. *Security, surveillance, and privacy are important factors to hospital patients in the evaluation of their wards.* Security requires surveillance by staff, which makes privacy difficult. The designer must balance these two issues in the design of the facility.

6. *An orienting environment is useful in making mental health patients or other handicapped people comfortable.* A confusing environment makes wayfinding difficult for the mentally or emotionally disabled, but just how uncluttered the

5-24 *Patient lounge, Camarillo State Psychiatric Hospital, Children's Unit (Camarillo, CA)*

Architecture and interior design: The Design Partnership, Architects and Planners; Photographer: © Peter Malinowski/Insite

Direct View From Nurses' Station

Enclosure reduces senses of vulnerability, increases sense of privacy

5-25 *Conceptual sketch. Camarillo State Psychiatric Hospital. Children's Unit (Camarillo, CA)*
 Architecture and interior design: The Design Partnership. Architects and Planners

environment must be before it becomes uninteresting and lacking in stimulation is not clear.

7. *The involvement of staff in the programming and design process is important to the appropriate utilization of the completed project.* Staff involvement assures that the design of the project will be compatible with the operations of the facility and that staff will feel part of the creative process, which will enhance their acceptance of it in the end.

8. *Certain colors have specific physiological impacts on those experiencing them and can be supportive in achieving desired behaviors in child treatment facilities.* Studies have documented physiological responses to color as well as to color preference, although sometimes with conflicting results.

9. *Operational and clinical concepts can be effectively translated into building design.* The methodologies for extracting programming information from users include note-taking systems

and gaming (using color-coded chips of paper to represent spaces and establish adjacencies).

Based on these assumptions, Shepley incorporated the following concepts into the project design: when concrete block was exposed on the interior, it was covered with gypsum topping compound to give the appearance of drywall; fluorescent fixtures were avoided, and incandescents and downlights were used as much as possible; the motif of a peaked entrance (Fig. 5-24) was used to suggest the feeling of a house; carpet was used wherever permitted by code; each unit consisted of eleven children; the majority of patient rooms had two beds; from the nurse station all shared spaces are visible (Fig. 5-25); to enhance orientation, numerous windows provide views of the outdoors from all rooms; color was used to differentiate floor, wall, and ceiling planes, and architectural elements were used to highlight entrances (Fig. 5-26).

Hallways integrated with dayrooms for clear territorial definition

Ceiling height defines transition

Color defines transition

5-26 *Conceptual sketch. Camarillo State Psychiatric Hospital. Children's Unit (Camarillo, CA)*
 Architecture and interior design: The Design Partnership. Architects and Planners

Use of Color

Color served to establish an identity for each unit and also to define transition between areas (Fig. 5-26). Territorial boundaries were defined by changes in finishes. Seclusion and quiet rooms used a saturated pink color known to have an immediate calming effect on agitated children (see chapter 3).

Research Results

Shepley (1989) drew the following conclusions:

1. Accidents, aggressive acts, and being away without leave (AWOLs) were the most common types of incidents. Most incidents occurred as children passed from one space to another in transitional zones without territorial definition. Corridors had the most significant occurrence of incidents.

2. The majority of AWOLs occurred from school, dining, and the grounds.

3. A significant number of occurrences of aggression to peers occurred in dormitories, corridors, and courtyards.

4. A significant number of accidents occurred at the front door, at the unit entry, in the courtyard, and on the grounds.

5. More than the expected number of acts of aggression to staff occurred in corridors and seclusion rooms.

6. To prevent acts of aggression when a resident is using the telephone, in the new facility public telephones were located adjacent to the nurse station and given partial acoustical protection (Fig. 5-25). This arrangement also allows staff to monitor phone call activity.

The hypothesis that certain spaces create a climate conducive to undesirable behavior was confirmed by the research, which demonstrated a correlation between behavioral incidents and the locations where they occur.

Architecture as Therapeutic Tool

Much was written in the 1950s and 1960s by observers such as Erving Goffman, Robert Sommer, and Edward Hall about the effects of interior architecture on the behavior of patients in mental hospitals. They documented how the arrangement and shape of rooms, as well as furniture layouts, encouraged antisocial and destructive behaviors. Today few people doubt the therapeutic potential of the treatment environment, yet architecture and interior design decisions are often based on intuition and speculation rather than on rigorous study of how treatment goals and philosophy can be translated into design criteria. Such a process is outlined by Cotton and Geraty (1984), in which Mayer Spivack's Design Log technique was the basis for gathering clinical data and for facilitating a dialogue between design consultants and clinicians.

Design Log. Typically each type of room would be analyzed in a Design Log, starting with observation and progressing to diagnosis, prescription, and treatment, in this sequence (Spivack, as reported in Cotton and Geraty 1984):

1. *Observation (diagnosis):* Observations made about the existing unit combined with information from other field experiences and expert knowledge.
2. *Performance requirements (prescription):* Behaviorally related objectives that will remedy and improve the observed environment.
3. *Generic specifications (treatment):* Design specifications at a general level that allow the architect or designer a full but relevant range of design options.
4. *Material specifications:* Exact design and choice of materials.

Milieu Treatment. The mood that emanates from a particular setting carries with it nonverbal messages about expectations for behavior. Bruno Bettelheim's Orthogenic School for Autistic Children pioneered the use of nonverbal communication to reach the autistic child (Bettelheim 1972). For example, a dining room was beautifully decorated and elegant table settings were used. Bathrooms were decorated with beautiful tile and plumbing fixtures to convey that elimination is an important activity about which a person should not feel ashamed. "Milieu treatment is a modality that attempts to structure therapeutically all dimensions of daily life from human interaction on all levels down to the very smallest detail of our physical setting. Children, in particular, are susceptible to the messages of physical space" (Cotton and Geraty 1984, 625). Based on this concept, clinicians can describe the kinds of behavior that usually occur in a particular room or area, detail the treatment protocols that would be appropriate, and specify the behavioral incidents that should be discouraged. Design consultants can then mold this information into an architectural program that also takes into account various local, state, and federal code requirements, as well as specific limitations of the site and budget.

Environmental Details

The study by Cotton and Geraty for a 12-bed inpatient psychiatric unit at New England Memorial Hospital, Stoneham, Massachusetts, illustrates how design features were used to articulate treatment goals. They concluded that the physical environment either supports or hinders other milieu factors used to reinforce treatment goals.

Goal 1: *to provide patients and their families with a friendly, warm, adaptive setting that would convey a willingness to tolerate psychological troubles without judgment, despair, or avoidance.*

The institutional feeling of the ward was diminished by keeping the unit small. Family-style dining occurred at small groups of tables, and weekly community suppers were prepared by staff and children. Various textures were used on seating and in fabric wall hangings, and most floors were carpeted to create a residential ambience. Wherever appropriate, wood furniture was chosen over metal. Walls had few decorations to allow for large marker board surfaces, bulletin boards, and tackboards, which children could use to express their feelings. Artwork, school papers, and star charts (acknowledging successful management of a behavioral problem) were also displayed.

Color was used to convey positive messages. Pastel colors were avoided as were muddy greens, grays, and browns. A deep red color was used on door frames, as an accent wall in the living room, and in children's bathrooms. Ceilings of bedrooms were painted lighter shades of the wall color, several colors were used in a room, and contrasting colors outlined living spaces. Quiet rooms (seclusion rooms) had warm colors.

Cloth wall hangings conveyed messages of hope for change. As an example, one quiet room had an image of weather patterns. Sun, rain, clouds, and lightning were pointed out to children to validate different affective (mood) states. All finish materials and upholsteries were selected for their ease of maintenance.

Goal 2: *to provide spaces that represent a continuum of external controls and can be adapted to the needs of individual patients and groups of patients as they fluctuate in their capacity to use internal controls.*

The polarity between safety and freedom in the environment creates a design dilemma. Locks and bars are not in keeping with a residential ambience, although these highly visible protective devices may be comforting to children who are out of control. Which rooms must have doors is decided on an individual basis, but within rooms all drawers must be lockable so that supplies, scissors, knives, and tools cannot be used as weapons. Certain cabinets having paper goods, pots, and pans were locked only when the milieu was out of control. "Our design articulated our treatment philosophy to close down when out of control behavior dominated and open up when patients regained their control" (Cotton and Geraty 1984, 360). Quiet rooms were used for dealing with extremely disturbed children without having to resort to mechanical restraints or psychotropic drugs (see the section on quiet rooms in this chapter).

Furniture was selected carefully so that it could not be used either as weapons or for self-destructive purposes. Mattresses with vinyl covers that cannot be ripped even when punctured prevent patients from using mattress springs for self-destruction. Closets with air vents allow children to hide in them without worries about smothering. Clothing hooks are used instead of poles, and magnetic catches assure that children cannot lock themselves in. Toy chests were designed with divided compartments too small to hold a child. In bathrooms and bedrooms no wiring or plumbing is visible.

Goal 3: *to support all levels of integration in the patient at all developmental levels.*

Spaces must be adaptable to lower-level and higher-level functioning. Overwhelmed patients require a predictable and consistent controlled environment with well-organized stimuli. As patients become healthier, they need more complex, enriched environments with less predictability and more opportunities to make choices and statements about their identities.

Patterns and colors were selected to meet the needs of the overwhelmed child. Paint was used effectively to emphasize boundaries, mark entrances, to suggest excitement, convey warmth, and to outline individuality. Rooms that were off-limits to children had door frames painted to match the adjacent wall. Large rooms for communal activities were painted neutral colors. Scheduling boards, calendars, and clocks were used to orient children. The living room contained a bookcase with books and toy boxes filled with toys; the kitchen and dining area had supply cabinets to support a variety of therapeutic activities, such as crafts, games, puppets, and books.

Corridor walls were viewed as opportunities for patients to "finish" the environment. The quality and nature of bulletin board decorations were assumed to express the tenor of the community. During constructive phases of treatment, children created busy, full, attractive displays. Bulletin boards that contained out-of-date material or ripped papers or were empty were taken to indicate an angry, depressed, or uninvested group of patients or staff. The boards became a challenge and opportunity for children to commit themselves to the treatment process.

Goal 4:   *to provide opportunities for constructive peer relations and private times.*

Living, dining, and kitchen areas were continuous small rooms separated by curves and nooks rather than doors and walls to encourage social interaction. Long corridors were eliminated because of the impersonal messages they convey. Furniture in dayrooms was arranged to create circles of interaction rather than lined against the walls because circular arrangements have been documented to facilitate conversation and encourage discussion of more intimate topics (Hall 1969). Because of the observation that children use furniture in unconventional ways and that they also use interior space as furniture, spaces between existing air conditioning units were lined with built-in toy boxes for children to sit in or climb on.

For dining, three-foot-square sturdy oak tables with plastic laminate tops were used. Tables could be grouped together in various configurations for banquet settings or other activities.

Opportunities for privacy are hard to achieve because of the constant threat of violence or self-destructive behavior among acutely disturbed patients. In this facility children were allowed to escape to the quiet room, bathroom, their bedrooms, or a closet, crawl under the bed, sit on a windowsill behind a curtain, or curl up in a fantasy box covered with a blanket in order to feel safe.

Goal 5:   *to redirect pathological, maladaptive behavior (e.g., assaults or destruction of property) and substitute more adaptive behavior.*

The design strategy anticipated and planned for destructiveness by selecting durable furnishings and materials and by avoiding fragile or easily broken items. Tamper-proof screws were used throughout the unit to reduce minor acts of vandalism. Wood baseboards were attached by screws. Theft was discouraged by adequate lockable storage for staff members' personal property. Velcro tabs were used to fasten draperies onto rods. An interesting color strategy was employed by painting indestructible surfaces stimulating colors and using neutral colors for easy-to-destroy equipment or items such as window treatments.

Short, interrupted corridors minimize assaultive behavior. In the living room and dayroom any items that are loose and able to be thrown are soft (pillows, stuffed animals, papers); furniture was selected for its weight (too heavy to be thrown) and is constructed so that it cannot be torn apart, with its pieces used as weapons. A wall in each room is allowed to be used for a "swearing board" where children may write swear words on a sheet of paper covered by another paper. In the quiet room children have the option of saying whatever they want either into the air or into a tape recorder. The paint finish on walls must be such that marker pens can be washed off it.

A successful treatment environment contains flexible spaces with opportunities for quiet reflection, quiet play, group activities, and roughhouse play to encourage the expression of a wide variety of impulses and feelings.

Quiet Room.   A quiet room, also called a *seclusion room* or *time-out room*, is used to decrease stimulation and prevent further escalation of aggressive acts. Typically the two elements emphasized in a quiet room are safety (prevention of self-destructive acts) and minimal sensory stimulation. The design of these rooms has no formula beyond those two elements, although several features seem to be commonly found. The room needs to be simple and uncluttered, have soft surfaces, and be as resistant as possible to aiding a suicide attempt. Carpeting is the flooring of choice, although it may have to be replaced every six months. Walls of this room may also be carpeted. If the room is small and cozy and the color appropriate, it will not be viewed as punishment but as a refuge or place to escape sensory overload. The design of this room deserves careful thought because it can too easily become cold and barren, owing to the fact that it is very sparsely furnished and devoid of visual stimulation.

Spivack (1984) points out that staff are often dissatisfied with the option of isolating an emotionally disturbed child in a room that may be viewed as punitive; he advocates, instead, that isolation be done in the "best room in the house." In fact, the quiet room in the aforementioned inpatient unit at New England Memorial Hospital was located adjacent to the director's office where the child can be directly supervised by the person with the most responsibility to assure that the room is not misused as a punitive measure. In the new facility, a door adjoins the quiet room and the director's office; at the child's option, the door may be left open so the child may watch the director at work.

Furniture usually consists of a built-in bench upholstered with carpet pad and carpeting. It must be upholstered in such a way that it cannot be loosened, which could allow children to swallow the staples. A number of loose pillows should be provided with Velcro-fastened covers that can be removed for washing. A locked storage cabinet can be used for storing books, pillows, or other items. The built-in bench should be large enough for a staff member to sit alongside the child. Rheostatically controlled recessed downlights (provided ceiling height is such that the child cannot stand on the bench and reach fixtures) is appropriate for lighting. The door of the room should be solid core, open inward, and have low-height torque handles on both sides and no lock (Spivack 1984). Needless to say, this room should have a window.

Martin Teicher (director of the Developmental Biopsychiatry Research Program at Hall Mercer Center for Children and Adolescents, McLean Hospital, Belmont, Massachusetts) has applied for a grant to study and document the therapeutic effect of a quiet room equipped with a computerized Window of Nature (see chapter 7). He proposes that the calming natural images be supplemented by complementary natural sounds with the hypothesis that children will regain their composure and behavioral control more quickly than in a more traditionally designed quiet room. The overall goal is to design an environmentally sound quiet room that can enhance the therapeutic efficacy of this important intervention. Children assigned to these rooms are expected to require fewer major interventions such as physical restraints or psychotropic drugs.

Design Guidelines

Design issues that relate specifically to psychiatric facilities for children and adolescents have been mentioned; the reader may also wish to refer to chapter 11 for general guidelines applicable to all psychiatric facilities.

DESIGN ISSUES

Several design issues relate specifically to children. All too often they are overlooked or treated in a superficial manner. Unfortunately, painted wall graphics are not enough (and at times are not even appropriate) to establish a comfortable environment for children. Research indicates that children remember places and the way they felt about them more than they remember people; they may be even more sensitive to their surroundings than adults and may be able to recall details vividly for a long time (Prescott and David as reported in Olds and Daniel 1987). Children live in the present and are initially more responsive to the stimulation of color, music, texture, and form than adults because they are unfettered by inhibitions about expressing their zeal. Therefore, a child's first impression of the hospital is critically important in setting his or her expectations of what is to follow (Figs. 5-7, 5-27, 5-28, and 5-29).

SCALE

Scale is an important issue that is sometimes hard to address in hospitals because codes specify minimum heights for ceilings, handrails, and certain other items. From a practical standpoint, mounting artwork, mirrors, bulletin boards, and other items of interest at a child's height in the corridor may be difficult because equipment and carts are sure to damage it. Nevertheless, every attempt should be made to

5-27 *Colorful lobby reception desk, Texas Scottish Rite Hospital for Crippled Children (Dallas, TX)*

Architecture and interior design: HKS Inc.; Photographer: Rick Grunbaum

5-28

5-29

5-30

A theme of "transportation" is carried throughout the building in two- and three-dimensional artwork; in this photo note the hot-air balloon and, beyond it, the airplane; this is a satellite pediatric surgery center and medical clinic, Children's Outpatient North, Children's Hospital Medical Center (Cincinnati, OH)

Architecture and interior design: KZF Incorporated; Photographer: Artog/D. G. Olshavsky

5-29 *Main lobby, Kosair Children's Hospital and The Norton Hospital (Alliant Health System, Louisville, KY)*

Architecture and interior design: The Falick/Klein Partnership, Inc.; Photographer: R. Greg Hursley

5-30 *Fanciful pediatric nursing wing creates a streetscape between patient rooms and nurse station; Mercy Memorial Medical Center, Pediatric Unit (St. Joseph, MI)*

Architecture and interior design: Hansen Lind Meyer; Photographer: Elizabeth Ernst

address the child's line of sight so that he or she does not feel dwarfed by the surroundings. Patient room doors with panes of glass at child's height (Figs. 5-3 and 5-30) and child's-height room identification are easy to accomplish. Being able to identify their rooms gives children confidence in mastering the environment.

Young children spend a great deal of time on the floor; therefore, it should be aesthetically interesting, incorporating inset carpet designs or vinyl composition tile patterns (Figs: 5-12 and 5-17). Safety must also be considered; HVAC registers, electrical outlets, and exposed plumbing must not be accessible to crawling infants or toddlers. The fanciful design of nursing unit corridors (Figs. 5-30 and 5-31) transforms a clinical area into a child's scale playscape. Multi-lite windows, lighting, and detailing around doors create a setting that appears residential.

5-31

5-31 *Toy room, one of several vignette rooms designed to entertain hospitalized children, St. John's Child Health Center (St. Louis, MO)*
  Architecture and interior design: The Hoffmann Partnership Inc.; Photographer: Alise O'Brien

5-32 *Pediatric Intensive Care Unit, St. Luke's Methodist Hospital (Cedar Rapids, IA)*
  Architecture and interior design: Ellerbe Becket; Photographer: © Peter Aaron/Esto

Patient rooms benefit from corridor windows that give children an opportunity to watch passersby and offer the security of knowing they can be seen by nurses if they need assistance (Fig. 5-32). A built-in bench (Fig. 5-3) provides a bed for a parent.

To really understand how children perceive the setting, give them a camera and have them photograph what they see and what attracts them. This exercise is excellent for understanding scale. Many wall graphics, decorations, and detailing provided for the benefit of children are simply not visible to them unless they are being carried or are viewing from bed or from a gurney. Some elements can be at that height as

long as other objects can be appreciated when the child is walking or crawling. As an example, the children's photos show the inappropriateness of the standard 42-inch-high nurse station, which makes nurses look like giants behind a barricade. A lowered section of casework (Fig. 5-33) reduces the barrier and enhances the child's mastery over the setting.

VARIETY

Variety can be provided both programmatically and in terms of architecture and interior design (Fig. 5-34). The shapes and sizes of rooms should vary, as should ceiling heights, lighting levels, and color. Rooms dedicated to certain activities may have unique identities (class-

rooms, playrooms, therapy, activity rooms, dining). Studies have shown that patients may benefit from a variety of environments, depending upon their stages of healing. When patients are very ill, a more subdued, uncluttered setting is best; as they recover, additional stimulation is appropriate (Fig. 5-35).

The varied personalities, energy levels, moods, and abilities of children of different ages need to be accommodated. Imagine a child's delight in using the learning center in Figures 5-36 and 5-37. The design is creative and colorful. For children who need more physical activity, the playroom in Figure 5-38 features carpeted platforms and cubbyholes. Figures 5-39 and 5-40 feature a variety of play settings for children and therapists.

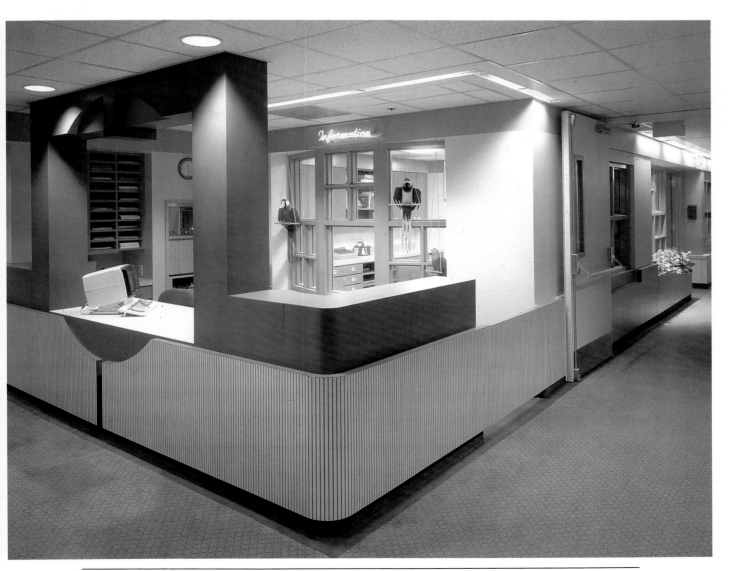

5-33 *Information desk, St. John's Child Health Center (St. Louis, MO)*   *Architecture and interior design: The Hoffman Partnership Inc.; Photographer: Alise O'Brien*

5-34

5-35

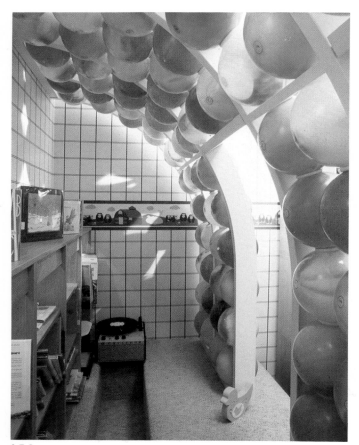

5-34 *Pediatric tub room, Baystate Medical Center (Springfield, MA)*
  Architecture and interior design: Henningson, Durham, & Richardson Inc.; Photo courtesy HDR

5-35 *Emergency room waiting area with saltwater aquarium, Primary Children's Medical Center (Salt Lake City, UT)*
  Architect: Karlsberger Architects; Interior designer: Life Designs; Photographer: Michael Schoenfeld

5-36 *Frito-Lay Children's Learning Center, HCA Medical Center (Plano, TX)*
  Project created and funded by Frito-Lay, Inc.; Designed and fabricated by Peter Wolf Concepts Dallas, TX; Photo courtesy Peter Wolf

5-36

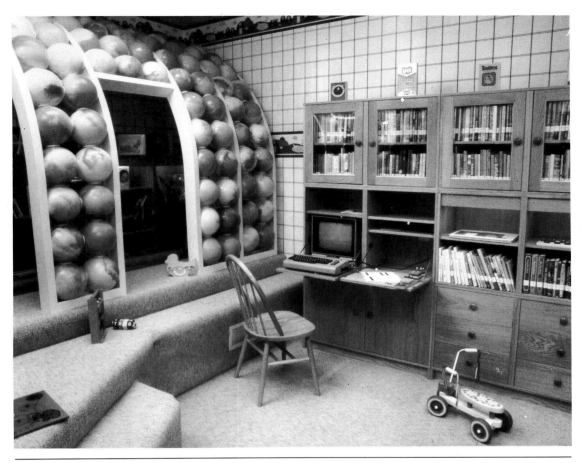

5-37 *Frito-Lay Children's Learning Center, HCA Medical Center (Plano, TX)*

Project created and funded by Frito-Lay, Inc.; Designed and fabricated by Peter Wolf Concepts, Dallas, TX; Photo courtesy Peter Wolf

5-38 *Children's playroom offers opportunities for physical activity; Lutheran Medical Center (Brooklyn, NY)*

Architecture and interior design: Rogers, Burgun, Shahine & Deschler, Inc.; Photographer: Robert Perron

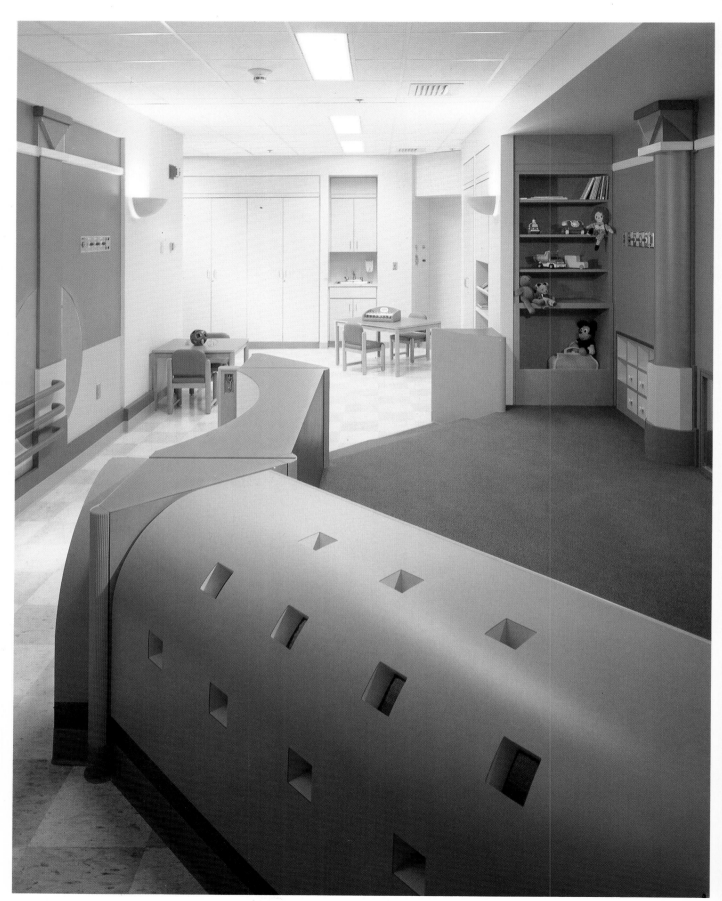

5-40

5-39 *Pediatric playroom, Ellison Building, Massachusetts General Hospital (Boston, MA)*
Interior architecture: Hancock & Hancock;
Photographer: Warren Jagger Photography Inc.

5-40 *Pediatric playroom offers opportunities for independent play as well as for working with therapists; Ellison Building, Massachusetts General Hospital (Boston, MA)*
Interior architecture: Hancock & Hancock;
Photographer: Warren Jagger Photography Inc.

Parker Lane

A trip down Parker Lane at Arkansas Children's Hospital reveals an imaginative, interactive play environment for children and adults. It presents an opportunity to explore, experiment, and examine a number of thought-provoking phenomena. Designed collaboratively by hospital staff designer Harry Loucks (whose background is museum exhibit design) and outpatient child life specialist Dawna Breuer, the environment invites people to investigate it and to think logically, critically, and creatively. It provides a balance of active and passive activities, and the beauty of it is that it requires little or no maintenance, needs no instruction, and is safe for use without supervision. The designers state ''it appeals to the child in all of us.'' According to the designers, evidence abounds supporting the stress-relieving benefits of patient play opportunities in pediatric health care settings. They recognize that parent stress can also affect the child, and therefore they desired to serve both children and adults. The success of Parker Lane is that it encourages relaxed, natural interactions and is neither too mentally challenging for children nor too boring for adults. The exhibit crosses age, education, and socioeconomic barriers. Figure 5-41 shows the entire corridor and locates each of the para-

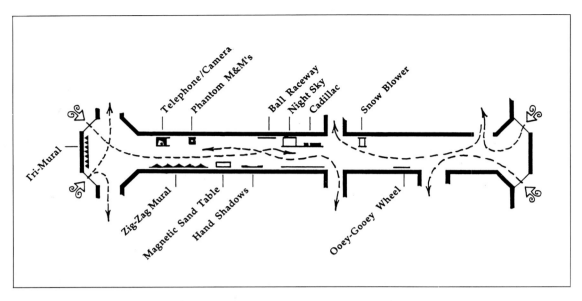

5-41 *Floor plan of Parker Lane, Sturgis Clinic, Arkansas Children's Hospital (Little Rock, AK)*
     Designer: Harry Loucks

5-42 *Cutaway of Cadillac, with mirror on opposite wall, allows children to see themselves as if riding in the car; Parker Lane, Arkansas Children's Hospital (Little Rock, AK)*
     Designer: Harry Loucks

doxes, puzzles, and devices. The ''Cadillac'' in Figure 5-42 is a cutaway of an automobile that children can sit behind and see themselves in a mirror. The Ooey-Gooey Wheel (Fig. 5-43), Tri-Mural (Fig. 5-44), Magnetic Sand Table (Fig. 5-45a), and Telephone Camera (Fig. 5-45b) represent four of the imaginative events that have been created. This project won an award of excellence at the National Symposium for Health Care Interior Design in 1990. Hats off to Arkansas Children's for a highly imaginative creation rarely seen within the hospital setting.

5-43 *Ooey-Gooey Wheel in Parker Lane, Arkansas Children's Hospital (Little Rock, AK)*
    Designer: Harry Loucks

5-45 *A, Magnetic sand table delights toddlers; B, telephone camera, Parker Lane, Arkansas Children's Hospital (Little Rock, AK)*
    Designer: Harry Loucks

5-44 *Tri-Mural interactive display in Parker Lane, Arkansas Children's Hospital (Little Rock, AK)*
    Designer: Harry Loucks

5-45

The Frustrations of Waiting

Children are easily frustrated by waiting because it usually means being forced to sit in a chair and restricted from moving freely about the space. Lobbies and corridors such as those in Figures 5-46 and 5-47 feature large-scale murals that immediately command a child's interest. The mural in Figure 5-48 is particularly captivating; it extends floor to ceiling and seems to wrap around the viewer. It is highly textured and has a number of objects attached to it, including a ladder. Created by artist De-

Loss McGraw, it illustrates a delightful poem titled "John J. Plenty and Fiddler Dan," about an ant (John J. Plenty) and a grasshopper (Fiddler Dan).

The lobby in Figure 5-49 features a life-size dollhouse through which all children pass as they are admitted to the hospital. Figure 5-50 features a roller coaster that appears to emerge from inside the wall. It was actually designed to distance children from the glass balustrade overlooking the atrium space.

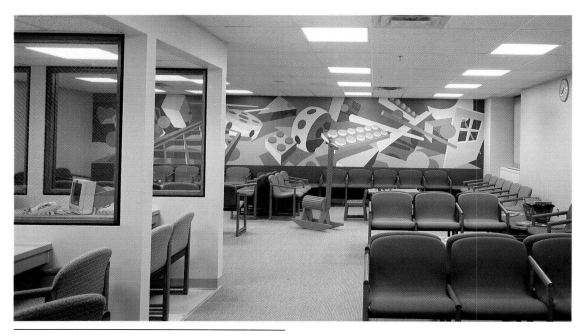

5-46 *Outpatient admitting features playful mural by Richard Taylor; Children's Hospital of Wisconsin (Milwaukee, WI)*

Architecture and interior design: Henningson, Durham, and Richardson, Inc.; Photographer: HDR Inc.

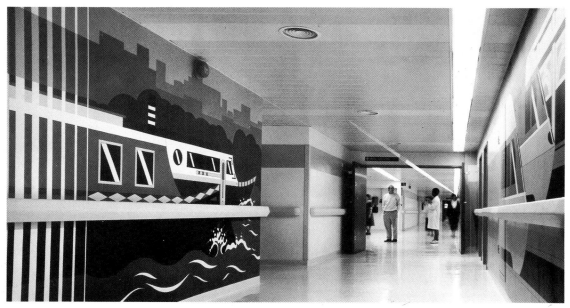

5-47 *Pediatric floor with large-scale murals representing transportation: canals, railway, roads (a canal basin runs alongside the hospital); St. Mary's Hospital, Queen Elizabeth the Queen Mother Wing (Paddington, London, England)*
  Architect: Llewelyn-Davies Sahni; Mural: Llewelyn-Davies Weeks; Photographer: Crispin Boyle Photography & Assoc.

5-48 *Three-dimensional mural created by artist DeLoss McGraw, Whittier Institute, Scripps Memorial Hospital (La Jolla, CA)*
  Architecture and interior design: The Austin Hansen Group; Photographer: The Austin Hansen Group

5-49 *Patients are admitted on the "porch" of this Victorian house in the main lobby; access to elevators is through the house; Children's Hospital of Wisconsin (Milwaukee, WI)*
  Architecture and interior design: Henningson, Durham, and Richardson, Inc.; Photographer: HDR Inc.

5-48

5-50 *Roller coaster has hand-carved animals and Plexiglas base, one element of a lively atrium space overlooking historic Charleston; Medical University of South Carolina, Children's Pavilion (Charleston, SC)*
  Architect: Ellerbe Becket; Interior design: Bohm-NBBJ; Photographer: Michael Houghton/STUDIOHIO

COLOR

A child's use of color is an indicator of his or her emotional maturity and provides clues to personality organization and internal conflicts. Apart from a child's individual expression of color, a child's developmental age and cultural background bias color preferences.

Color-Form Dominance

Most preschool children are color dominant. This stage evolves into a color-and-form transitional period between the ages of seven and nine with form dominance increasing over color from approximately the age of nine into adulthood. As the child gets older, the representational nature of the image becomes more important. However, all children do not follow this pattern. As an example, approximately 10

percent of preschool children show pure form dominance (Sharpe 1974). Form-dominant children are thought to be intellectually brighter than those who are color dominant or color-form oriented; some theorists attribute greater creativity to color-dominant personalities (Sharpe 1974).

Brain-damaged adults sometimes regress to a manner of information processing associated with an earlier developmental age—color preference—in tests requiring subjects to sort stimulus materials on the basis of form or color (Goldstein and Oakley 1986).

Color and Subject Preferences

Studies documenting children's responses to paintings showed that orange, followed by pink and red, were the favorite colors of children ages three to six. Animals tended to be favorite subjects. Children show sensitivity to color harmony at the age of four, although it does not become an element of artistic analysis until sometime between the ages of eight and twelve with full development occurring by adulthood (Sharpe 1974).

With regard to subject matter, "Most of the studies on children's preferences among paintings consistently show that younger children prefer paintings based on subject matter and color without regard to the degree of realism apparent; older children select paintings based on realistic representation, often with some attention focused on harmony and contrast" (Sharpe 1974, 13).

In evaluating color as an insight into the child's emotional life, Alschuler and Hattwick (as reported in Sharpe 1974, 16) concluded that red is the color of preference for preschool children who function naturally on an impulsive level; preference for red decreases and interest in cool colors increases as children move from the impulsive stage into the age where reasoning and greater emotional control are evident. The researchers found red to be associated with two extremes: feelings of affection and love or feelings of aggression and hate. As red is associated with strong emotion, blue is associated with drives toward control. They found that green was also used by children who function at a relatively controlled level, although they noted that "children who emphasize blue may give evidence of very strong underlying emotions which they have redirected or sublimated, whereas those who emphasize green often lack all evidences of a strong underlying core."

Researchers have found evidence of color preferences biased by sex. Children between the ages of six and seventeen show a female preference for warm colors and a male preference for cool colors. As age increases, hue is more important than saturation and brightness (Sharpe 1974).

Such data could be applied to the selection of the artwork and color palette for children's health facilities, but the body's physiological responses to certain colors and their appropriateness for patients with various illnesses must be taken into consideration (see chapters 2 and 3). Over and above that, however, adults select subject matter according to what they think children may like, which even though well intentioned may be at odds with research. A study of students' (in the first six grades) responses to color and realism based on evaluations of photographs and illustrations revealed the following:

> (a) In looking at a picture, a child apparently seeks first to recognize its content; (b) any picture (assuming a certain content) proves satisfying to the child in proportion to its success in making that content appear real or lifelike—whether it is colored or uncolored is less important than the appearance of realism; and (c) a perfect visual representation of realism includes color, and color in pictures proves satisfying to the child in proportion to its success in increasing the impression of realism or lifelikeness. (Sharpe 1974, 20)

Color and Culture
Perhaps no area of color research has received quite as much attention as the relationship between color preference and culture. A review of the literature suggests that every conceivable group has been sampled, from differences between rural Zambian children and urban Zambian children to a study comparing color preferences of college students from the United States, Iran, Lebanon, and Kuwait. Color preferences in many cultures are the result of climatic factors as well as political and religious beliefs. Colors associated with mourning, those in the national flag, or colors associated with certain superstitions are generally not favored.

In the United States, however, red and blue are the most highly favored colors, and they are associated with the American flag.

Because color preferences of adults are so much a result of learning, many researchers have preferred to work with children to minimize the effects of learning and experience. A researcher in this field, T. R. Garth, conducted tests among children of six different cultural groups—white, black, American Indian, Filipino, Japanese, and Mexican—and found that preference differences were minimal among them; he concluded that the differences that do appear in adulthood are due to factors related in nurturing. Eysenck, in a critical review of numerous color preference studies conducted all over the world and also in his own experiments, concluded that studies show a high degree of agreement among investigators and that the general order of preference is blue, red, green, violet, orange, and yellow. He found no sex differences apart from a slight preference among girls for yellow over orange and among boys for orange over yellow.

Studies of color preferences among different cultures are so numerous and the conclusions so highly specific to the groups being studied that summarizing them within the scope of the present discussion is impossible. However, strong cultural and national differences do exist in the way people look at and react to various colors. A designer embarking upon a foreign project should spend considerable time researching that culture's use of space and color preferences and taboos. Even certain figures that might innocently be proposed in artwork or a mural might be highly offensive due to their symbolic content. As an example, pictures of cows and monkeys are acceptable in India but disapproved of by Arabs (Sharpe 1974). Chapter 3 of Sharpe (1974) contains an excellent discussion of the cultural significance of color, and books by Edward T. Hall are full of fascinating information such as this tidbit: in discussing the superstitions associated with numbers in various cultures he notes that the Japanese "have numbers that mean good luck, wealth, bankruptcy, and death. This fact complicates the Japanese telephone system. Good numbers bring a high price, unlucky ones are palmed off on foreigners" (Hall 1973, 112).

For a more thorough discussion of color and its impact on the medical environment, see chapter 11 of my book *Medical and Dental Space Planning for the 1990s* (Malkin 1990).

PLAY AREAS

The importance of play in the life of a child cannot be overemphasized. It is not an activity for a portion of a day; it is what children do during most waking hours. Although sick children may have more trouble paying attention and perhaps have lower thresholds for frustration, a variety of play opportunities should be available to them in the hospital (Fig. 5-51). Because "many things [in the hospital] are unfamiliar and frightening to children [there is a need for] a total play environment or playroom that is a comfortable, secure retreat from the scary aspects of medical treatment and the loneliness of bedrooms" (Olds 1978, 124). The playroom in Figure 5-31 allows children to role-play in vignette settings scaled for a child. The playroom in Figure 5-52 supplies props to stimulate a child's imagination. The raft may provide a therapeutic outlet for thoughts of escaping the hospital or may remind the child of nice experiences shared with family. The playroom in Figure 5-6 is a fantasy environment that provides a variety of play experiences for children of different ages. The design is imaginative with an excellent use of color.

Child development specialist Anita Olds has designed a number of interesting play units suitable for children of various ages and with various disabilities. Her Play Frame (Fig. 5-53) unit is a versatile work surface that provides as many as 20 different activities in a four-foot-square space: easel, puppet theater, busy board, house, dart games, and play kitchen. Play panels (which can be stored in the upper portion of the frame) provide opportunities to manipulate dials and spin and twist knobs.

A Potpourri of Ideas

Anita Olds presented this potpourri of interesting ideas and thoughts at the National Symposium for Health Care Design (1990).

1. Consider all elements of a room as interactive surfaces. Anything can be a seat, a toy, and a place to lie down. Think of activities children enjoy.

5-51 *Pediatric playroom, Emanuel Hospital & Health Center, Pediatrics Unit (Portland, OR)*   *Architect: Kaplan McLaughlin Diaz; Interior design: Karol Niemi Associates; Photographer: Stephen Cridland*

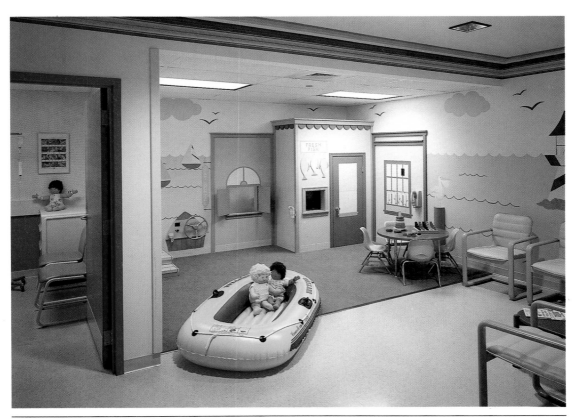

5-52 *Pediatric playroom, continuation of "transportation" theme (see Figure 5-28); this is a satellite pediatric surgery center and medical clinic, Children's Outpatient North,*

Children's Hospital Medical Center (Cincinnati, OH) Architecture and interior design: KZF Incorporated; Photographer: Artog/D. G. Olshavsky

5-53 *The Play Frame, a freestanding unit with interchangeable panels, provides activities for children of various ages*
   Designer: Anita Olds; Illustration courtesy Anita Olds

Make lowering or raising all surfaces possible.

2. Infants love to be up high; consider a raised crib structure, akin to a treehouse, so that adults are at the same eye level. Toddlers need an open corral where they can move around yet be secure. Teens like to cook, eat, and play games. Every age group needs at least six different types of activities.

3. Premature babies develop better on water mattresses. Consider providing, in a playroom, a waterbed on the floor with a five-inch-high carpeted platform around it. A tape player built into the platform allows kids to listen to stories.

4. In a playroom, water should be controlled from underneath the counter or play area.

5. If children must face a wall, put a mirror there.

6. Provide a wall with a series of little mirrors, knobs, handles, and a curved "funny" mirror. Include magnification or multiplication lenses.

7. Small barrel-like structures, carpeted, provide a protected cocoon in a playroom for children who want to be alone, yet peek out at activity in the room.

8. Plan a series of three-inch-high carpeted risers in the playroom to stimulate movement.

9. Consider a low partition with a little door or window hatch that opens on a hinge to allow a child to poke her or his head through (the door lid should be padded).

10. Provide soft fabric slipcovers for furniture that can be easily laundered if a child vomits.

11. For children who are very sick, locate on the wall "exploratorium"-type items that require very little energy to engage, for example one of those devices that moves sand or "waves" into different configurations when tilted. A large magnet under Plexiglas can "move" objects around.

12. Provide a hook in the ceiling to mount a punching bag to encourage gross motor activity.

13. Create a little box structure to resemble a car. Affix headlamps and flashing lights and dials to simulate a dashboard.

14. Create a room or area filled with large fabric-covered foam blocks of all different shapes that have Velcro strips on all sides so that they can be combined to form trains, forts, and other structures. Also affix Velcro strips to walls so that lightweight blocks can be fastened to them.

15. Create an area of high texture for infants and toddlers to step on. Imbed smooth stones, for example, in a raised bed of concrete; create oddly textured ceramic tile areas; mount plungers (with wood handles removed) as a surface to walk on.

16. Photo images might include infants at the beach exploring rocks and tide pools or close-ups of a child's foot or hand.

17. One of the most imaginative, therapeutic environments Olds has designed was created in a small rotunda space, opposite elevators, at the University of Maryland Hospital. A setting created with real tree trunks provides an opportunity for staff and children to experience nature. Children can curl up in a tree hollow, listen to sounds of birds chirping, or talk to little forest creatures tucked here and there. Skilled carpenters and craftspeople carefully selected the tree trunks and sanded and sculpted them into the miniforest environment that is reported to be enormously successful in reassuring and soothing frightened children.

A successful playroom requires careful thought and consultation with a child development specialist, plus the commitment of a designated staff monitor who continually replenishes disposable supplies and keeps materials sorted and organized. Closed cabinets may make the room appear more orderly to adults but limit the attractiveness of the room to children who are visually stimulated by looking at the toys and play materials. "A child's invitation to play really is not communicated by Lilliputian furniture and play platforms, but by the visual presence of play materials" (Olds 1978, 122). Open shelving or labeled bins encourage children to put things away (Fig. 5-39). Ideally, appropriate types of work surfaces would be located immediately adjacent to storage bins to provide cues for what materials should be used there. Hospital playrooms crammed with a profusion of toys, puzzles, and games may be frustrating to children. The chaos of such a setting sometimes encourages abuse. At the other end of the spectrum are barren playrooms with the perfunctory plastic table and chairs, a handful of inexpensive and unchallenging toys, and a few Sesame Street posters.

THE HOSPITAL AS FANTASY ENVIRONMENT

Consider the possibility of a children's hospital that integrates fantasy with clinical care to transform a frightening experience into one that has elements of surprise and pleasure. Fantasy will not take the place of loving parents or make a painful medical procedure fun, but it can help to relieve anxiety and establish a more supportive environment for healing. Certainly self-esteem, emotional strength, and courage are present in differing degrees in each child, and they color his or her experience of hospitalization. The extent to which individual personality traits, strengths, and weaknesses are recognized and respected will in large part determine the child's level of comfort in that institution.

Design professionals know that the opportunities are many to change what is typically an unpleasant experience into one that provides its own rewards, surprises, and satisfactions, independent of the clinical treatment. This responsibility anticipates an expanded role for interior designers that goes beyond the client's normal expectations of specifying finishes and furniture. What if the designer considered the patient's experience from the time he or she entered the lobby, is admitted, receives treatment, and is later discharged? The designer would be involved in decisions relating to where people should sit while waiting to be admitted, what is the first thing they see when they enter the lobby, and what printed materials and staff uniforms should look like. The difference is that between furnishing rooms and really trying to understand and being able to shape the patient's experience.

Does a child cease to be a child on becoming a patient? Of course not. Yet hospitalization often deprives from a child the fulfillment of basic needs. Being a child gets put on hold until the hospitalization ends. The child is penalized for being sick. These special needs include being entertained and having opportunities to play, socialize, fantasize, explore, experience, and be independent.

A child's need for fantasy and its beneficial effects have been well documented by Bruno Bettelheim and others. It offers an opportunity to escape, to appear powerful against adversaries, and to resolve frustrations and anxieties. From a child's point of view, the child is admitted to the hospital accompanied by a parent who must sign insurance forms, consent for surgery forms, and maybe even consent for donating an organ if the patient should die. Meanwhile the child is restless and waits in what sometimes resembles a bus station with row upon row of seating and little if anything for amusement. The hospital may in fact be the largest building that child has ever experienced, and that can be intimidating.

FIRST IMPRESSIONS

Imagine, instead, that while the parent is filling out the paperwork at admissions, the child is issued a VIP identification card with his or her photo laminated to it and, at the same time, is given an orientation packet that acquaints the child with a cast of make-believe characters who appear throughout the facility in various formats or media. Included in the orientation packet is a coloring book with the characters. Children's Hospital San Diego engaged an artist to create a group of characters for them, and these endearing tykes and anthropomorphized animals appear on a variety of items sold in the hospital's gift shop, in large-scale wayfinding orientation murals throughout the hospital, and in printed materials. Each character has a humorous name to give it personality and to allow the group to become a make-believe family away from home. In corridors these characters give the child an association with something familiar while being wheeled down to radiology, for example.

Opportunities for Personal Expression

Also included in the orientation packet would be literature for the parent explaining that the child's room may be personalized by bringing favorite items from home. It assures parents that provision has been made to accommodate personal articles so necessary to make a child feel comfortable. The child goes from a highly personalized room at home with strong color and pattern to a stark, unfamiliar hospital room. A large bulletin board that uses magnets, not tacks, can be used to display get-well cards, family photos, and favorite posters (Fig. 5-54). A swing-away shelf near the bed might hold a terrarium, fishbowl, or ant farm (for children requiring long-term care). Built-in niches for books, toys, and stuffed animals make the room seem less barren and more like home. Mobiles hung from the ceiling provide visual relief for those flat on their backs. For bedridden children, diversions such as those designed by Dr. Pacileo, mentioned previously, would relieve boredom.

Parents would be invited to participate in their children's care; policies for visiting and over-

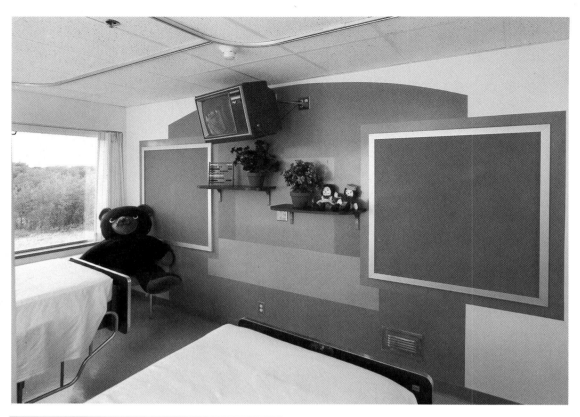

5-54 *Young adult patient room features brightly colored wall at foot of bed incorporating large tackboards; Methodist Hospital (St. Louis Park, MN)*
    Architecture and interior design: Ellerbe Becket;
Photographer: © Peter Aaron/Esto

night sleeping accommodations would be outlined. Lounges or other areas specifically dedicated to parents could be described or located on a map, as would kitchenette areas where parents can prepare a child's favorite snack. By addressing these items in the orientation packet rather than have parents find out accidentally that such accommodations are available, the hospital has created a valuable public relations tool.

Parents with children in the hospital are worried and uprooted from their daily routines. They need an environment of empathy and understanding. They should be made to feel that they belong with their hospitalized child and that their presence is, in general, welcomed by the staff.

In the admissions and orientation process, both parent and child are being reassured and developing trust and confidence in the hospital. This experience must be positive as it sets up expectations for the quality of clinical care to be

received and engenders in the parent a spirit of cooperation.

The child can be engaged in other ways during the admitting process. He or she could be issued a "driver's license" for a wheelchair, an 8 x 10" card with his or her photo, a big gold seal, and some colorful graphics. The child could post it on the bulletin board in his or her room. Easy to execute and inexpensive, the driver's license accomplishes four things: it increases the child's self-esteem (we all love to see our own photo), assures the child that some fun things might happen in the hospital after all, removes the negative status of using a wheelchair, and caters to the child's love of make-believe.

The VIP pass, mentioned previously, could be expanded in concept to be large enough to hold stamps or seals given out for good behavior. If the child takes his or her medicine, goes to physical therapy without complaining, keeps bandages on, or eats meals, nursing staff could give seals that would lead to a small reward that becomes something to work toward.

Art Cart
Before leaving the admitting area, the child could be shown a book of photos or posters of various subjects from which to select an image

to hang in his or her room. This art program could be administered by the hospital auxiliary. An art cart, a concept developed by photographer Joey Fischer, can carry 50 colored photo images, each mounted on a 24 x 30'' panel that slips into a picture frame permanently mounted in each patient's room. The photo locks into the frame with a special key and is therefore secure. Within hours of being admitted to the hospital, a hospital volunteer could visit the child's room and place the specified photo in its frame. The patient has regained some small but significant control over the immediate environment. Appropriate photo subjects might be baby animals, hot air balloons, or a bouquet of balloons for young children, and sports photos, surfing scenes, or naturescapes for adolescents.

To carry this concept a bit further, when the child has selected an art image, he or she could also receive an 8 x 10'' color print of the same photo that slips into a frame on the patient room door. Frames could be permanently mounted at two heights, a low one when young children occupy the room and a high one for teens. They help young children identify their rooms and give adolescents an opportunity to express a public identity to others.

MAKING NEGATIVE EXPERIENCES POSITIVE

A child's expectations of what a hospital should be can be changed in other ways. Imagine a transitional corridor space that children must pass through after being admitted en route to their rooms. It could be a magical corridor with special lighting effects, interesting shapes on the ceiling, and large, recessed display windows featuring an electronically controlled event that would delight children. Why not add to the hospital's team of consultants a theatrical lighting designer or a technician who engineers illusions for magicians to work with the interior designer and architect to create this corridor?

Such a corridor event could be designed just outside the physical therapy department or radiology; when children pass through it, an electric eye sensor makes something predictable happen in the tableau. An animated character might pop up, or another special effect may occur. As the child is wheeled to that department, the orderly may stop for a moment to enable the child to press a button that causes the event to take place. Imagine a display of

colored lights that simulates a rainbow overhead as the child passes under it. This type of activity has the potential to change a negative experience into a positive one.

In a holding area where children on gurneys have to look up at the ceiling, a visual event could be created immediately over the door frame that would give them something to look at. For example, an electric train on a track could follow the perimeter of the room and be timed to encircle the room four times per hour, giving the children something to look forward to.

Sometimes children are uncooperative about taking medications, pull the IV needle out of their arms, and need to be encouraged to eat. In Children's Hospital San Diego a puppet named Sockie personally addresses individual children who need special encouragement. Every evening, on closed circuit television, Sockie urges them by name to eat their food and to take their medicine. Hospitals close to a college campus can attract students from the drama or communications departments to staff this service.

What about patient gowns? Could they be designed more like costumes yet still meet the 160°F temperature requirement for laundering and be easy to fabricate? Meal trays and utensils, instead of looking so drab, could have a colorful design on them.

Upon discharge, positive aspects of the child's hospitalization can be reinforced when he or she carries home the driver's license, VIP photo certificate, perhaps a Sockie puppet, and a coloring book of hospital "characters" as a reminder that the hospital was not such a bad place after all.

Starbright Pavilion

Located in Los Angeles, part of the University of Southern California master plan, the 50,000-square-foot Starbright Pavilion is a prototype design for facilities the Starlight Foundation hopes to build around the world. Dedicated to granting last wishes to children with life-threatening illnesses, the purpose of the building is to integrate some aspects of medical care with entertainment. A communications tower is to broadcast events at the center to locations worldwide via satellite.

The imagery of the building was inspired by children's toys and uses bright colors and abstract geometric forms (Fig. 5-55). The pavilion houses a large auditorium with three levels of balconies, child care, indoor and outdoor gardens, an audiovisual library, computer education, dining, case management offices, and therapy spaces for art, music, and play. An unmanned tram rises from ground level to the third and fourth levels, which have gardens, an outdoor stage, and a petting zoo (Figs. 5-56 and 5-57). This highly imaginative, fantasy environment should delight children and adults.

Children's Medical Center of Israel
Located northeast of Tel Aviv, in Petah Tikva, Israel, this 360,000-square-foot building transcends international boundaries to serve a vast area of Asia and Africa between Athens, Bangkok, and Johannesburg. It will be the only free-

5-55 *Architectural model of Starbright Pavilion (Los Angeles, CA)*

  Architect: Kaplan McLaughlin Diaz; Courtesy Zdravco Turziev

5-56 *Conceptual design Starbright Pavilion (Los Angeles, CA)*

Architect: Kaplan McLaughlin Diaz; Rendering: Richard Lee

5-57 *Starbright Pavilion integrates medical care with entertainment for children with life-threatening illnesses (Los Angeles, CA)*
Architect: Kaplan McLaughlin Diaz; Rendering: Richard Lee

standing medical center devoted exclusively to the medical and surgical needs of children and adolescents of all races, religions, and nationalities throughout the Middle East. Programming and design of the hospital were based on the knowledge that physical environments profoundly affect attitudes, behavior, and feelings.

Cultural Issues. A great deal of cross-cultural research was required to understand how each culture uses space. Pagodas in the lobby have the feeling of little houses, as do admitting carrels. Because Bedouin families accompany their

children to the hospital, outdoor plazas have been set aside for families in which to gather and eat. The design respects Jewish religion and culture in that no symbols are used that may suggest other religions, and two separate kitchens have been provided (one for meat and one for dairy products) in accordance with Jewish dietary law.

The interior design is reminiscent of a friendly country village with patient corridors as village streets; each room appears to be an individual cottage with a front door and window overlooking a town square atrium (Fig. 5-58). From the atrium, children can watch elevators going up and down to their rooms, and they can see the suspended origami-like bird sculptures that cascade from the ceiling. Made of a space-age plastic material, the sculpture is activated by low-voltage electricity and glows. To ensure that children feel secure and confident, great attention has been paid to the scale of waiting and treatment rooms and to sizes and heights of doors, shelves, window sills, railings, fixtures, and furniture.

Accommodation of cultural norms and values of different user groups was achieved through the use of symbols, colors, and materials with positive cultural meanings. Decorative mosaic tiles, developed from pictures drawn by Israeli schoolchildren, and Jerusalem stone finishes are among the details successfully integrating local customs and tradition (Fig. 5-59). The path children follow from the street (Fig. 5-59) is flanked on one side by a fishpond and on the

5-58 *Main lobby and admitting area, Children's Medical Center of Israel (Petah Tikva, Israel)*

Architect: Cannon; Photographer: Patricia Layman Bazelon

5-59 *Entry corridor features terrarium on one side and fish pond on other; Children's Medical Center of Israel (Petah Tikva, Israel)*
Architect: Cannon

other by a terrarium. Eventually the path crosses a bridge over water to reach the lobby.

Family-Centered Care. The design encourages collaborative care between family and professionals and allows for parent rooming-in accommodations and separate overnight guest units. These facilities provide opportunities for relaxation, snacks, and storage of personal belongings. The design also enables children to amuse, feed, and groom themselves, which fosters a sense of independence and self-esteem. Windows between inpatient bedrooms and interior corridors permit children to maintain contact with general floor activity and, at the same time, offer easy visibility of patients.

Waiting areas function as pleasant environments where children and parents may learn about health matters. These spaces provide equipment for play and recognize children's needs for gross motor activity. Staff needs have also been respected. Their work areas an efficient and attractive, and ample space has been provided for lounges outside the view of

families, where staff can relax or engage in informal discussions.

Wayfinding Design. Good wayfinding was also considered. Note the ''main street'' on each level that connects all elevators (Fig. 5-60). Children gain entrance to all departments along the main street without having to navigate a maze of corridors. As an example, a child who is an oncology inpatient or outpatient can go to the doctor's office, oncology clinic, lab, or daycare area without leaving the seventh floor (Fig. 5-60). Also note courtyards on the outpatient and diagnostic side that let light into examination, treatment, and office spaces. Corner playrooms of inpatient units have child's-scale window seats to allow a view of the park side of the campus (Fig. 5-61). Each floor contains a full-height aquarium located at the corner of the conference area (Fig. 5-61).

Security against Terrorism. As I put the finishing touches to this manuscript, war has recently erupted between Iraq and the United States. Iraq is bombing Israel, and I cannot help wondering about the fate of this hospital, currently under construction. A year previously, I questioned the architects about defense measures designed into the building because few

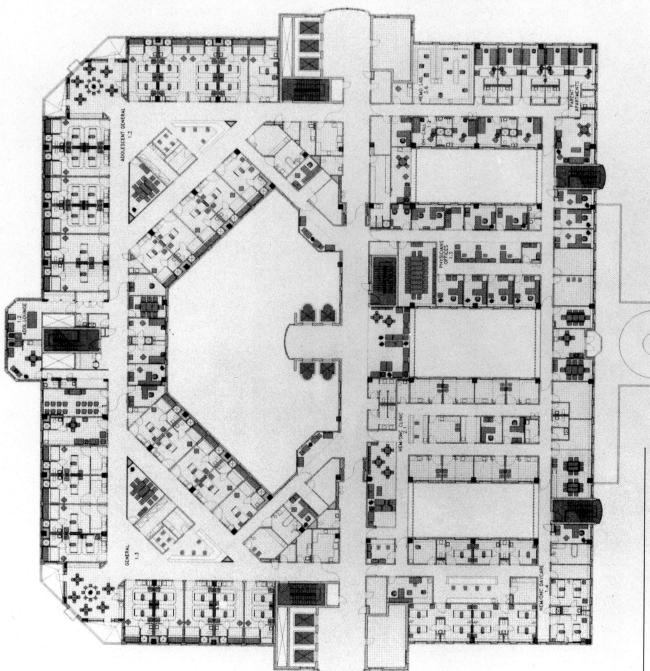

5-60 *Floor plan makes wayfinding easy: Children's Medical Center of Israel (Petah Tikva, Israel) Architect: Cannon*

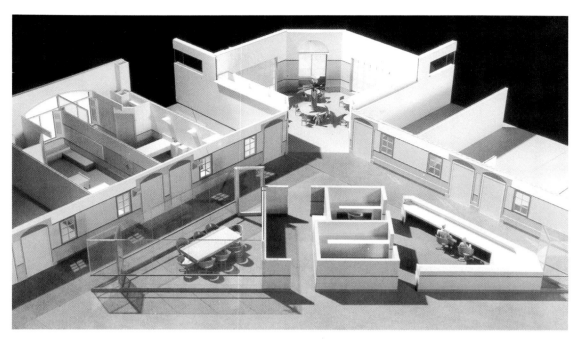

5-61 *Model of typical patient room, nurse station, nurses' conference room, and corner patient lounge, Children's Medical Center of Israel (Petah Tikva, Israel)*
Architecture and interior design: Cannon; Photographer: Patricia Layman Bazelon

architects would have to consider this issue in the United States. The response was that a defense barrier exists around the entire hospital complex. American-style security measures do not exist in terms of surveillance devices and other safeguards; however, the employee cafeteria is constructed of reinforced concrete and doubles as a bomb shelter. Special air-handling equipment guards against chemical warfare, and the Department of Defense controls lighting design.

REFERENCES

Anderson, Peggy. 1985. *Children's Hospital*. New York: Harper & Row.

Bettelheim, Bruno. 1972. *Milieu Therapy*. New York: Hoffman-LaRoche.

————. 1974. *A Home for the Heart*. New York: Alfred A. Knopf.

————. 1976. *The Uses of Enchantment*. New York: Alfred A. Knopf.

Canter, D. 1977. Children in hospital: A facet theory approach to person/place synomorphy. *Journal of Architectural Research* 6:20–32.

Canter, D., and S. Canter, editors. 1979. *Designing for Therapeutic Environments, a Review of Research*. New York: John Wiley & Sons.

Carpman, Janet, Myron Grant, and Deborah Simmons. 1986. *Design That Cares*. Chicago: American Hospital Publishing.

Committee on Hospital Care. 1986. *Hospital Care of Children and Youth*. Elk Grove, IL: American Academy of Pediatrics.

Cotton, N. S., and R. Geraty. 1984. Therapeutic space design: Planning an inpatient children's unit. *American Journal of Orthopsychiatry* 54(4):624–36.

Goldstein, L., and D. Oakley. 1986. Colour versus orientation discrimination in severely brain-damaged and normal adults. *Cortex* 22:261–66.

Hall, Edward. 1969. *The Hidden Dimension*. New York: Doubleday.

————. 1973. *The Silent Language*. New York: Anchor Books.

Lambert, Ruth. 1990. *Child Health Design*. Bethesda, MD: Association for the Care of Children's Health.

Lindheim, R., H. Glaser, and C. Coffin. 1972. *Changing Hospital Environments for Children*. Cambridge: Harvard University Press.

Malkin, Jain. 1990. _Medical and Dental Space Planning for the 1990s._ New York: Van Nostrand Reinhold.

Moltzen, S., H. Gurevitz, M. Rappaport, and others. 1986. The psychiatric health facility: An alternative for acute inpatient treatment in a nonhospital setting. _Hospital and Community Psychiatry_ 37(11):1131–35.

Olds, Anita R. 1978. Psychological considerations in humanizing the physical environment of pediatric outpatient and hospital settings. In E. Gellert, ed. _Psychosocial Aspects of Pediatric Care._ New York: Grune and Stratton.

———. 1979a. A play center for handicapped infants and toddlers. In T. M. Field, ed. _Infants Born at Risk: Behavior and Development._ New York: SP Medical and Scientific Books.

———. 1979b. Designing developmentally optimal classrooms for children with special needs. In S. Meisels, ed. _Special Education and Development: Perspectives on Young Children with Special Needs_, pp. 91–138.

———. 1982. Designing play environments for children under 3. In _Topics in Early Childhood Special Education_, Aspen Systems Corp., Rockville, MD, pp. 87–95.

———. 1990. With Children in Mind: Novel Approaches to Waiting Area and Playroom Design. Paper read at National Symposium for Health Care Design, November, in San Francisco.

Olds, Anita, and Patricia Daniel. 1987. _Child Health Care Facilities: Design Guidelines and Literature Outline._ Bethesda, MD: Association for the Care of Children's Health.

Rivlin, L., and M. Wolfe. 1979. Understanding and evaluating therapeutic environments for children. In _Designing for Therapeutic Environments, A Review of Research._ New York: John Wiley & Sons.

Ross Planning Associates. 1977, 1988. _Planning and Design for Perinatal and Pediatric Facilities._ Columbus, OH: Ross Laboratories.

Sharpe, Deborah. 1974. _The Psychology of Color and Design._ Chicago: Nelson-Hall Co.

Shepley, M. 1989. Designing a children's psychiatric facility. Unpublished research study. San Francisco: The Design Partnership.

Sommer, Robert. 1969. _Personal Space._ New Jersey: Prentice-Hall.

———. 1974. _Tight Spaces._ New Jersey: Prentice-Hall.

Spivack, Mayer. 1984. _Institutional Settings._ New York: Human Sciences Press.

Strock, R. 1987. _Tuning into Color._ The Color Research Institute.

White, M., P. Williams, and others. 1990. Sleep onset latency and distress in hospitalized children. _Nursing Research_ 39(3):138.

Willis, V. J. 1980. Design considerations for mental health facilities. _Hospital and Community Psychiatry_ 31:483–90.

chapter 6

CANCER CENTERS

psychological factors

- anticipatory grief
- depression
- uncertainty
- coping mechanisms
- isolation
- vulnerability
- loss of control
- social interaction
- privacy
- territoriality

activities

- diagnosis/evaluation
- simulation
- waiting
- chemotherapy
- radiation therapy
- examination
- counseling
- surgery
- interaction with other patients
- visiting

issues

- wayfinding
- waiting (companions)
- new patients' anxiety
- wheelchair access
- fear of radiation
- discomfort of side effects
- gurney holding area
- staff burnout

No word strikes terror in our hearts quite as much as the word *cancer*. Initially the news is perceived as a death sentence and, for some, it ultimately is. For others the disease may be permanently arrested; for some, periodic courses of treatment keep the disease at bay to extend the individual's life as long as possible. Significant progress made in cancer treatment in recent years has led to a cure rate of nearly 50 percent of all cases treated (Salick Health Care 1987; Cancer Statistics 1990). Early diagnosis and treatment provided by a multidisciplinary team of specialists is essential to success, but equally important is the patient's psychological attitude, which can be influenced positively or negatively by the environment in which treatment is provided.

ORGANIZATION OF TREATMENT AND RESEARCH PROGRAMS

The National Cancer Institute was created in 1937 as a separate organization within the National Institutes of Health in order to develop and manage a national cancer program throughout the United States. Funding from the National Cancer Institute for research and development grants has greatly impacted the current structure of research and cancer health care delivery programs. Cancer centers typically take the form of one of the following models:

- Treatment programs at community hospitals. Experimental therapies, if used there, are managed by research programs headquartered elsewhere.
- Federal basic research centers, funded by the federal government to study cellular and molecular aspects of cancer.
- Federal clinical research centers where promising new drugs and other therapies are tested.
- Comprehensive cancer centers, a designation held by (as of this writing) 24 of the premier cancer treatment centers in the nation. This designation is bestowed on the facilities by the National Cancer Institute, and they receive federal funding; most are located within major university medical centers. These institutions must have strong programs in basic research, clinical trials of new therapies, transfer of technology to community oncologists, cancer education programs, and tertiary-level patient care.

Cancer research may be directed at finding the causes of cancer, detecting it, prevention, and treatment. Treatment includes surgical techniques, radiation therapy, development of chemical agents and drugs, and rehabilitation.

The trend is toward integrating research with clinical practice, so that scientists can interact directly with physicians and their patients.

PLANNING CONSIDERATIONS

Planning considerations that are unique to cancer facilities are a response to the treatment modalities of surgery, chemotherapy, and radiation therapy. Beyond that are the special issues associated with treatment of immunosuppressed patients who are highly vulnerable to infection. The nature of the disease is such that psychological and behavioral issues factor prominently into the design of the facility. These issues are discussed in greater detail later in this chapter.

This chapter focuses on the psychosocial aspects of cancer and discusses key issues associated with principal treatment therapies. Readers are encouraged to contact Ellerbe Becket Architects to obtain a copy of their three-volume study on the design of cancer centers (Ellerbe Becket 1989). It appears to be the most comprehensive planning guide available in that it covers in-depth topics as diverse as business plans, funding, site evaluation, conceptual design issues, design prototypes, mechanical systems, and state-of-the-art technology, as well as a multitude of architectural and interior design issues. Carefully detailed floor plans for individual treatment rooms and entire departments are included. One volume deals entirely with planning radiation therapy facilities. Another volume describes the research team's site visits to six prominent comprehensive cancer centers.

PSYCHOLOGICAL IMPACT OF THE DISEASE

Certainly each cancer patient is unique, and individual personality traits to some degree determine how each person will deal with the disease. Nevertheless, certain common physical and psychological symptoms are imposed by the life-threatening nature of this illness and by the treatment protocols. Elisabeth Kubler-Ross (1969) describes the five stages of response as denial, anger (''Why me?''), depression, acceptance, and bargaining. Other psychological factors of cancer include:

Anticipatory grief: Preparation for future loss of one's life, body part, or function; anticipation of pain.
Depression: A response to onset of the disease; a coping mechanism for dealing with anxiety.
Uncertainty: The patient may not know for a period of years whether the disease has been effectively arrested; uncertainty about the future can be difficult for the victim and his or her family.
Isolation: The ''Why me?'' phenomenon causes feelings of separation and isolation at the start of the illness. Friends are reluctant to talk about the disease for fear they will say the wrong thing. For terminally ill patients, social isolation increases as friends, family, and sometimes even physicians or caregivers withdraw to protect themselves from anguish and feelings of failure.

THE BODY–MIND CONNECTION

The last ten years have produced some remarkable research in the field of psychoneuroimmunology (PNI), demonstrating that the mind can have a powerful effect on the course of a disease (see chapter 2). Most notably, Bernie Siegel's *Love, Medicine and Miracles* (1986) and *Peace, Love and Healing* (1989) made the world aware of an individual's potential for healing. His not-for-profit organization, Exceptional Cancer Patients, founded in 1978, promoted a specific form of individual and group therapy using patients' dreams, drawings, and images to facilitate personal change and healing. Norman Cousins (1979, 1983) has also challenged traditional medical wisdom by triumphing over his encounter with a rare crippling disease through unconventional therapies of laughter, high spirits, and visual imagery.

One of the alternative cancer therapies is called *visualization,* a technique pioneered by radiation oncologist Carl Simonton. Although it is controversial, when used as an adjunct to conventional medical treatment this method has brought hope and successful cures to many individuals thought to have terminal cancer (Gerber 1988).

ONCOLOGIC THERAPIES

Surgery is the primary treatment for cancer in order to arrest or retard the progress of the disease. It is followed by chemotherapeutic or radiation treatment that sometimes causes irreversible physiological changes and may require intermittent periods of hospitalization. Side effects of the therapy include nausea, vomiting, diarrhea, anorexia, difficult swallowing, soreness of the mouth, weakness, fatigue, difficult walking, bleeding, weight loss, hair loss, generalized aches and pains, and suppression of the immune system. Patients need to understand that these difficulties are normal side effects of treatment, not a progression of the disease. Biofeedback therapy and medications are often used to help relieve the side effects of treatment.

SURGERY

The objective of cancer surgery is to remove tumors before they have grown too large or have spread. The current challenge is to develop techniques that involve less disfigurement via improved reconstruction and grafting techniques, advances in prosthetic materials, and transplantation. During intraoperative surgery, the tumor is directly exposed to radiation prior to the wound being closed.

CHEMOTHERAPY

Chemotherapy is the oral or intravenous administration of chemicals targeted at cancerous tissues. This treatment modality is developing more rapidly than any other and is thought to possess the greatest potential for future development. The treatment might consist of several cycles of chemicals, each cycle lasting several days to several weeks. Treatment on an individual day might last eight to ten hours, during which time a patient may lie down, sit in a recliner chair, or walk around with an IV pole and computer-operated pump. For certain types of cancers, chemotherapy may be the patient's only hope for survival, although the treatment is very stressful and causes the significant side effects mentioned previously. Patients increasingly receive chemotherapy in an outpatient setting such as a cancer center or an oncologist's office. Patients have the security of knowing they can live at home but have access to treatment and care around the clock.

Diversions such as television (with headphones) and VCRs are important to help pass

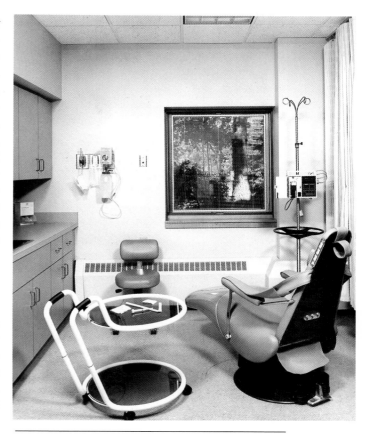

6-1 *Blood drawing room, Cancer Care Center, Framingham Union Hospital (Framingham, MA)*
Architect: TRO/The Ritchie Organization; Interior design: IDS/Interior Design Systems, a division of TRO; Photographer: R. Mikrut

the long hours during chemotherapy. Views of nature (gardens, courtyards, mountains) may help patients relax and allow them to focus on something other than the treatment. The blood-drawing room in Figure 6-1 has a tidy appearance and the patient can see views of nature while seated in the chair.

RADIATION THERAPY

Ionizing radiation is one of the common treatment modalities for cancer patients. It is often combined with other forms of therapy. Three types of machines are commonly used: cobalt unit, superficial x-ray machine, and linear accelerator. Cobalt is used for deep therapy; superficial x-ray is often used for skin cancers; the linear accelerator treats a wide range of oncologic diseases and has become the most common machine used. Sometimes the treatment plan includes implanting radioisotopes during surgery.

Treatment Protocol

Radiation therapy may be done on an inpatient or outpatient basis, although most treatments tend to be outpatient. A course of radiation treatment may run anywhere from two weeks to three months. It begins with a highly skilled radiation oncology team evaluating the patient's tumor and planning the course of treatment. A radiation oncologist, physicist, technologist, and nurse all work together to guide the course of treatment and provide emotional support and reassurance. The patient's introduction to treatment begins in the simulator room (as described later in this chapter) and is followed by daily visits to receive carefully targeted doses of radiation. On each visit the patient usually changes into a gown for the daily treatment and is weighed and examined by a physician on a regular basis. The patient may consult with a nurse or dietician for nutritional counseling to minimize weight loss or for suggestions on combating nausea, diarrhea, or mouth sores.

Waiting

Waiting becomes part of the routine for undergoing a series of treatments. The patient becomes accustomed to seeing the same patients, as visits are often scheduled for the

6-3 *Radiation therapy lobby features indirect lighting, the warmth of brick, and an overall color palette of cocoa and apricot; University Hospital, University of Michigan Medical Center (Ann Arbor, MI)*

Architect: Albert Kahn Associates, Inc., Architects and Engineers; Interior design: Anne Schallhorn Parker, University of Michigan Hospitals Design Group; Photographer: Balthazar Korab Ltd.

same time each day. Friendship and social camaraderie become a positive aspect of treatment for some patients, although those who are depressed or self-conscious about their appearance (baldness, pallor) may prefer privacy. The waiting room should provide ample space for wheelchairs to be integrated with other seating, rather than placed at the end of a row of chairs or in the middle of the room. An aquarium is a nice diversion and built-in planters can create privacy groupings (Fig. 6-2). Seating must

6-2 *Waiting area provides small groupings of seating for privacy, offers natural light, and has a graceful silk banner with the delicacy of rice paper; Radiation Therapy Building, Kaiser Permanente Outpatient Clinic and Medical Office Building (Los Angeles, CA)*

Architect: Langdon Wilson Architecture Planning; Medical Planner: The RFM Group; Interior design: Langdon Wilson Architecture Planning; Photographer: Paul Bielenberg Photography

have arms and a straight back, be stable, and have a firm, high seat (Fig. 6-3). Warm colors and texture in carpeting, wallcoverings, artwork, and wood trim may help to relieve patients' anxiety and make their companions more comfortable.

Patients are usually asked to gown prior to entering the treatment room for the sake of both privacy and efficiency. A subwaiting area allows gowned patients to wait out of view of those in the primary waiting room (see the section on gowning later in this chapter).

Patients often arrive for treatment with companions in order to have someone to talk with or because of a need for transportation. The companion often remains in the waiting room while the patient gowns for treatment. Amenities (rest room, drinking fountain, telephone, reading material) should be accessible to them. Sometimes a game table with a jigsaw puzzle is a welcome diversion, especially because patients' daily visits make continuity possible.

Companions often come with children, which necessitates a safe play area with appropriate amusements. A child who can be occupied with quiet activities is often a source of joy and diversion for adults.

Wherever possible, the waiting area should be accessible to an outdoor patio or garden. It relieves the boredom of waiting and helps to soothe anxiety, and the fresh air sometimes makes a nauseous patient feel better. Comfortable seating should be provided.

Gurney Holding Area

Inpatients are brought for therapy on a gurney, which is awkward both for the patient and for other patients who are ambulatory. The gurney holding area needs to be located where staff can continually observe and monitor the patient and where the patient will not feel isolated and forgotten. However, this area should be out of sight for outpatients who might feel uncomfortable seeing a very ill patient. The balance is difficult to achieve because the patient needs privacy for using a bedpan or perhaps when vomiting, yet if the patient is cut off from social interaction or medical observation, feelings of fear and isolation can be intensified.

If possible, some type of design or diversion on the ceiling (such as a mobile) would be appreciated by patients. Indirect lighting (avoiding fluorescents overhead) enhances patients' comfort.

Need for Social Interaction

Patients form a special bond with the clinical staff who treat them, often bringing them gifts and mementos. Friendship with other patients is also important to be able to share and discuss their feelings about the illness, which is often not possible at home where a patient may wish to protect the family from the pain. Therefore, spaces should be designed to encourage social interaction. Chairs placed at right angles foster conversation much better than chairs aligned in a row.

Privacy

The reception desk should be separated somewhat from waiting patients to afford a level of privacy where conversations with a patient cannot easily be overheard. This area should allow patients to sit comfortably while transacting business with reception staff.

Routinization

People have a tendency to repeat behaviors in order to help normalize a setting or experience (routinization). In this regard a patient may always sit in the same chair in the waiting room or perform a certain ritual each visit, such as hanging up a coat, visiting the bathroom, or using the drinking fountain. This coping mechanism reduces anxiety.

Gowning

Gowning is a significant part of the treatment protocol because it symbolizes the transfer from autonomy to committing oneself for treatment. Wearing a gown may produce anxiety for patients whose cultural backgrounds have strong taboos about nudity or for those who are disfigured by surgery. The patient's personal standard of modesty dictates the level of comfort or discomfort experienced. The dressing room should have a door that can be locked, a secure place for personal belongings, a bin for the soiled gown and robe, a bench, a shelf for clean gowns, and a mirror. A carpeted floor is desirable. Patients are normally weighed after gowning to achieve consistency. The combination of gown and bathrobe helps gowned patients feel more comfortable and not quite as vulnerable.

Sense of Control

A sense of control and independence may be fostered by offering patients choices about where to wait for treatment. Loss of control makes people feel dependent; allowing patients to do as much as possible by themselves enhances control. In this regard, a clear distinction between off-limits staff areas and pathways from the dressing area to the subwaiting room or treatment room makes it easy for patients to move about independently. Unfortunately, wayfinding is sometimes difficult, both internally and externally. The facility is often located in the basement of a hospital; just finding it can be a lengthy, circuitous route. Once there, if staff and patient areas blend together with no clear separation, the internal circulation system can seem like a maze—too taxing for a person who is seriously ill.

Territoriality

Much has been written about the natural tendency to protect a space and claim it. Sitting in a certain section of the waiting room, for example, may enhance personal comfort in a frequently visited environment. It also affords the patient some degree of control to choose who to sit next to.

Simulation

The simulator (Fig. 6-4) is a piece of x-ray equipment that is used to define the treatment area and supply measurements for treatment calculations. The machine also does fluoroscopy to enable the oncologist to watch the simulation on video. During this procedure the patient's body is marked with indelible pens to enable the technologist to target and position the equipment properly in future treatments. A carpeted floor is not recommended in this room because barium is sometimes used and patients are sometimes incontinent (or have a catheter) or may vomit. Gentian violet or other marking agents might spill and stain the floor.

The equipment and the procedure may be frightening to first-time patients; therefore, distractions such as a graphic design on the wall or artwork would be appropriate. The stained-glass art in Fig. 6-5 is reminiscent of Chagall's cathedral windows in its fluidity and use of cobalt blue.

Treatment

The radiation treatment itself takes only a few minutes, but ten minutes may be required each time to position the patient and set up the lead molds that are inserted into the machine to direct the angle of radiation to the targeted area. The technologist positions the patient by adjusting the table and rotating the machine. Foam molds or sandbags may be used to maintain the patient's body in a certain position. The technologist leaves the room during the radiation treatment to avoid the cumulative exposure to radiation but observes the patient through

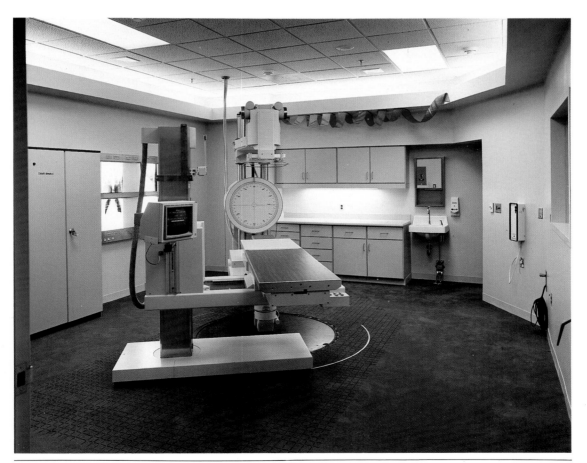

6-4 *Radiation therapy simulator room, University Hospital, University of Michigan Medical Center (Ann Arbor, MI)*

Architect: Albert Kahn Associates, Inc. Architects and

Engineers; Interior design: Anne Schallhorn Parker, University of Michigan Hospitals Design Group; Photographer: Balthazar Korab Ltd.

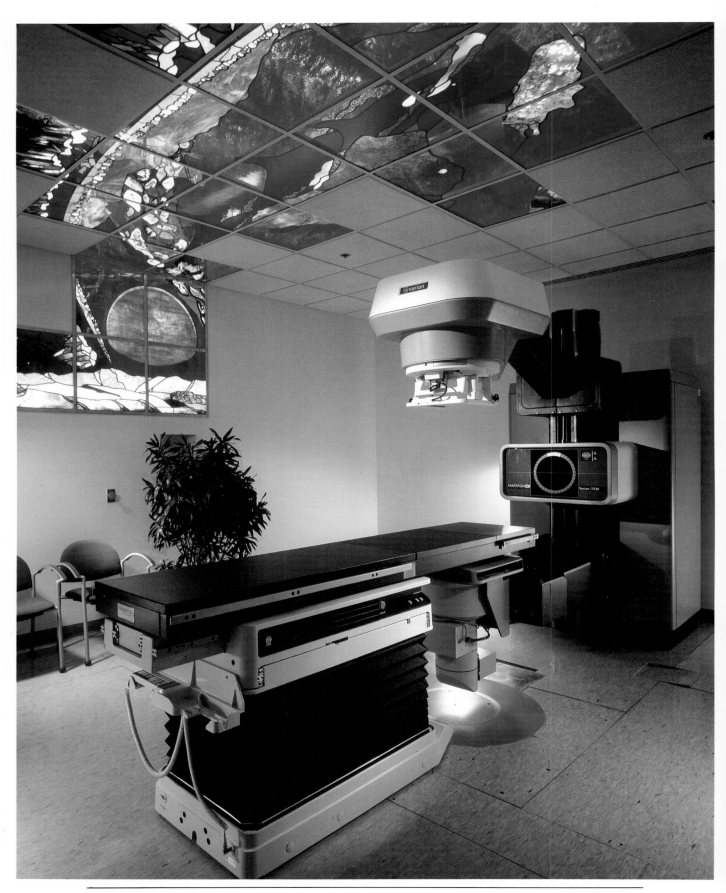

6-5 *Radiation therapy simulator room features Chagall-like stained-glass panels to relax and distract patients; Tuttleman Center, Graduate Hospital (Philadelphia, PA)*

Architecture and interior design: Medifac; Stained glass: Sigstedt Studio; Photographer: Tom Crane

6-6 *Radiation therapy linear accelerator room, Morton Plant Hospital (Largo, FL)*
Interior design: Pauline Obrentz Interiors, Inc., Kathryn Stephens, ASID, IBD, designer; Photographer: George Cott

closed-circuit television from the control station. Two-way intercom allows the patient and the technologist to talk to each other. An x-ray film may be taken after positioning the patient to compare with previous visits. Positioning is done in a dark room so that the laser light used to position patients is visible. The laser light may be recessed in the wall and cleverly concealed by a piece of artwork (Fig. 6-6) that can be removed if necessary for access or repairs. Only the aperture of the laser must be exposed; the remainder may be concealed.

Certain aspects of the treatment room may cause anxiety. The tomblike chamber typically has a maze entry somewhat resembling a chambered nautilus shell. A six- to eight-inch-thick lead door leads to a chamber of two- to three-foot-thick concrete walls and ceiling, which evokes an eerie sensation of quiet; patients can hear their own breathing. The absence of natural light or familiar points of reference may be compensated for by a trompe l'oeil mural (Fig. 6-7) to provide a psychological escape route. Photos of nature may be used (Fig. 6-8) in the lenses of light fixtures to simulate the outdoors and relieve anxiety. No doubt radiation warning signs posted outside the room contribute to a new patient's anxiety. A lifetime fear of the dangers of radiation must give way in an instant to regarding it as beneficial.

The treatment itself can be especially stressful to new patients. In the treatment room a patient is at the mercy of the machine and the technologist; autonomy is impossible. The machine can move in several planes at once, which can be disorienting. The patient's field of vision from a supine position should be considered in placement of art in the room. The activity of the technologist occurs in the patient's peripheral field of vision, which is always blurred. The macular cone of vision (the ability to focus on detail) is on the ceiling or floor. A mobile or sculpture overhead is often appreciated. Indirect lighting (Figs. 6-7 and 6-8) is ideal to prevent glare from overhead fluorescents. A high level of lighting is not needed in this room except when the physician occasionally needs to examine a patient in the treatment position. Lighting controlled by a dimmer should be considered.

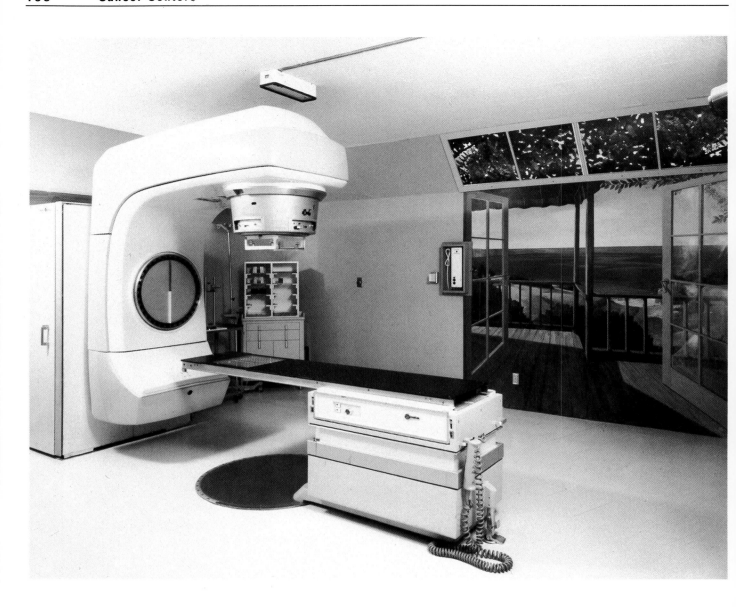

6-7 *Radiation therapy linear accelerator room features realistic trompe l'oeil mural to provide psychological escape route, and Cibachrome transparencies of bougainvillea placed in lenses of light fixtures further enhance outdoor image; Scripps Memorial Hospital (La Jolla, CA)*
Interior design: Jain Malkin Inc.; Photographer: John Christian; Cibachromes: Joey Fischer/Art Research Institute Limited

Linear accelerators produce ozone when they emit radiation, and patients may develop nausea. Carpet is not desirable in this room because some patients vomit and others may have catheters or incontinence. The hard-surface flooring needs to be extremely durable as well as resilient because sometimes lead blocks or molds drop and nick the flooring. Re-

siliency is important for the technologists who work in the room all day.

INPATIENT CARE

Elements of a general nature that make any patient room a good one have been discussed elsewhere, but issues specific to cancer patients are worthy of mention. Chemotherapy causes very severe nausea. Three or four drugs are commonly administered simultaneously to combat the nausea. These drugs can cause dizziness, blurred vision, and confusion. For this reason busy patterns in wallcovering and strong colors should not be used at the level where the patient will see them when lying in bed. A wood molding might be placed around the room at a certain height with a softly patterned wall-

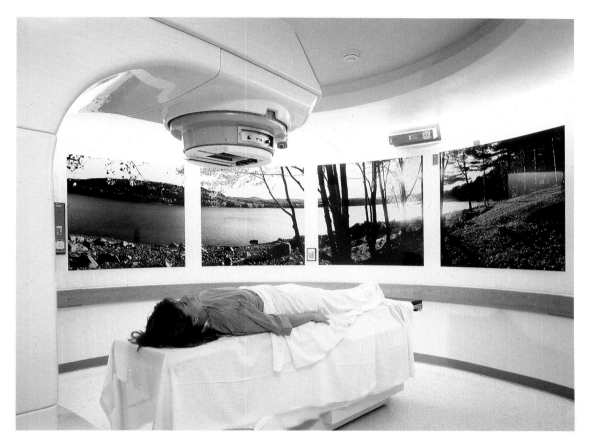

6-8 *Nature scene surrounds and relaxes patients in linear accelerator treatment room; Stanford University Medical Center (Palo Alto, CA)*
   Photo images: Joey Fischer/Art Research Institute Limited

paper above it where the patient can look at it if he or she chooses. The patient should be able to control room lighting from the bed. Large clocks and wall calendars enhance patients reality orientation.

IMMUNOSUPPRESSED PATIENTS

Occasionally serious side effects of chemotherapy may dictate special conditions for the designer. As an example, leukopenia, one of the most serious toxic effects of chemotherapy, results from suppression of bone marrow function in which a lowered white blood cell count makes the patient especially vulnerable to infection. The patient may be put in reverse isolation, in which case the designer may need to combat the effects of sensory deprivation (Marino and LeBlanc 1976). Hospitals that do bone marrow transplants also make use of reverse isolation

units for recovering patients. Imagine the psychological stress caused by this condition and the lack of visual stimuli; anything introduced into the environment is capable of introducing microorganisms.

The design of a room for an immunosuppressed patient has highly specific requirements. Sometimes patients are in this room as long as several months. The most prominent feature of the room is its sterile environment, which necessitates completely controlled access to the room by people, supplies, or services. The patient bed would be located next to an internal window or opening into the corridor which is enclosed by a Plexiglas curtain with "sleeves." Visitors or caregivers have access to the patient principally through this opening, by placing their arms in plastic sleeves. Positive air pressure in the room is required as are laminar flow ventilation systems with high efficiency particulate absorption (HEPA) filtration units. The isolation experienced by patients in this room must be monumental. Color and pattern should be introduced into the room to provide visual stimulation, but care must be taken to select materials that do not compromise infection control.

OTHER CONCERNS

Insomnia is sometimes a problem. A 24-hour patient lounge with television, VCR, small refrigerator, microwave, cozy seating, and perhaps a table with a jigsaw puzzle encourages patients' social interaction and makes the long night pass more quickly.

Accommodation for family is an important consideration in a cancer center. Family members may spend long hours at the hospital and may help in providing patient care. They need dedicated lounges where they can relax, have a snack, make phone calls, and visit with families of other patients. Chapters 2 and 3 include discussions of a more general nature relating to the creation of comfortable and supportive patient care environments.

STAFF WELL-BEING

Staff burnout is a problem in cancer facilities. The stress of working with critically ill patients is debilitating. Staff need lounges that are private but close to patient care areas, so that they can take frequent breaks to relax, chat with each other, or get a breath of fresh air. Access to nature by way of a rooftop garden or patio is desirable. The lounge should include a rest room, small kitchen, dining area, and lounge seating. Staff work areas should be carefully designed to make the tasks that must be performed there easy to do. Well-being of the staff is critically important, and every measure should be employed to make their work areas comfortable and as nurturing as patient care areas.

Nurses and physicians who work in designated subspecialty cancer units such as hematology or oncology wards suffer more stress than those who work with cancer patients who have been integrated with other types of patients on a medical-surgical floor. A study designed to examine this issue (Blanchard, Ruckdeschel, and others 1987) noted that the concentration of sick cancer patients on a designated cancer unit diminishes house staff ability to engage in supportive behaviors and to address the needs of patients during morning rounds. When these sick patients were integrated with noncancer patients on a general medicine floor, house staff were better able to offer support to those who were terminally ill.

PEDIATRIC CARE

Cancer centers that treat a large population of children must take into account all of the design considerations mentioned in chapter 5, including scale, accommodations for parents and siblings, wayfinding, and playroom diversions. Psychological issues of separation from family, fear of pain, and sense of abandonment are discussed in chapter 5.

PROJECTS
CEDARS-SINAI COMPREHENSIVE CANCER CENTER

One of the most interesting and innovative projects of this type is the Cedars-Sinai Comprehensive Cancer Center in Los Angeles. Founded by nephrologist Bernard Salick, the center's 24-hour care is a concept he pioneered in a successful group of kidney dialysis centers. When his young daughter was stricken with cancer, he was confronted with the problems of receiving care in a facility open only on weekdays, from 8 A.M. to 5 P.M. A patient needing treatment or tests after those hours would have to go to an emergency room or undergo the ordeal of checking into a hospital. This was the impetus for Salick to develop the Cedars-Sinai facility.

The design of this 53,000-square-foot building by Morphosis Architects and Gruen Associates is a radical departure from conventional health care facilities, and some might say the architecture is controversial. The building challenges the intellect with complex geometry and metaphor. It is neither high-tech clinical nor the currently popular ''hospitality'' health care design. It has a haunting beauty; the architecture goes beyond a structure to house the program. It is one of those rare health care projects that is spiritually significant.

The deconstructivist style of architecture addresses the brutality of the disease and its intrusion into the patient's life. Given a difficult site, except for the street level entry, the remainder of the structure is below grade, which is not unusual for cancer centers or at least the radiation therapy portions of them. Nevertheless, the association with a tomb or crypt develops when visitors lose the sense of horizon and descend underground. Many scenes from the theater and opera depict the underworld,

6-9 *Chemotherapy atrium has nurse stations at each end with treatment cubicles on two parallel walls; Cedars-Sinai Comprehensive Cancer Center (Los Angeles, CA) Architecture and interior design: Morphosis Architects/ Gruen Associates; Photographer: Grant Mudford Studio*

most recently the hauntingly beautiful scene in "Phantom of the Opera." George Rand (1989), psychologist and professor at UCLA, describes the psychological experience of vertical buildings as having a duality—from the "highs" associated with a test of balance or feelings of invulnerability to the weaknesses of the flesh, to a "low" feeling that comes from entering below the plane of everyday reality. Moving downward in the vertical dimension connotes yielding to the demands of the natural world.

Rand explains the ambivalence that a patient must feel when entering the building: it is a refuge from illness and, at the same time, a source of dread, shame, and guilt. Parenthetically, he makes an interesting observation about the phenomenon of entering the lobbies of many cancer centers: the patient "confronts a reception desk, is placed in a wheelchair and elevated up, down, and around corridors with little concern for his or her residual phenomenological experience. The body becomes a physical

projectile . . . to be relocated in space" (1989, 5). This building, by contrast, uses the compressed entry level to channel the patients' vision and keep them oriented.

> Vertical descent is passage to a realm of contemplation in which the reaching hands and exploring eyes appropriate to coping with the outside world are gradually surrendered in a process analogous to dark adaptation. The patients give up worldly coping skills and turn with meditative awareness to their own internal physical processes. (Rand 1989, 6)

A striking feature is the chemotherapy atrium (Fig. 6-9) with its expansive, 24-foot-high ceiling. Individual treatment cubicles flanking the atrium are equipped with telephones, pull-out toilets, and curtains that allow patients undergoing therapy to regulate the amount of privacy they desire. Light scoops above each cubicle provide natural light. Patients may, if they prefer, walk through the atrium with their IV poles. Although underground, the barrel-vaulted skylight and clerestory windows admit natural light.

One of the architects' objectives was that the architecture occupy the mind and affect the

6-10 *Waiting room with 24-foot-high steel-and-wood play structure and aquarium; the tree symbolically marks ground level (Los Angeles, CA)*

Architecture and interior design: Morphosis Architects/ Gruen Associates; Photographer: Grant Mudford Studio

spirit to keep the patient from becoming obsessively preoccupied with the illness. In this regard, the whimsical play structure (Fig. 6-10) engages children through the use of video, hand-operated parts, fragments of sculpture, and an aquarium. It continues two stories up to the entry level, where it is topped off by a fake tree cleverly marking street level.

Unwilling to follow conventional prescriptions for soothing patient environments, architect Thom Mayne decided: "If frightening things go on here, then the architecture should reflect it . . . it should be tough enough not to condescend to patients, and uplifting enough to reflect their own courage in struggling to recover from their disease'' (Viladas 1988, 70).

The neutral color palette and hard surfaces are unusual in patient care areas, but the architecture is exciting and intellectually stimulating. Noise is reported to be a problem because of the lack of sound-absorbing materials. Nevertheless, this bold experiment in architecture is a welcome challenge to traditional structures for delivering care.

H. LEE MOFFITT CANCER CENTER AND RESEARCH INSTITUTE

The H. Lee Moffitt Cancer Center and Research Institute in Tampa, Florida (part of the University of South Florida Medical Center), combines a 162-bed twin tower with a low-rise diagnostic and treatment center and a research laboratory. Funded entirely by state cigarette taxes, this tertiary-care hospital is one of a number of stand-alone specialized hospitals planned for the campus. Its architecture has a solid and reassuring quality, and the interiors exhibit a hospitality ambience that is enhanced by attention to guest relations: professional staff are trained by former Disney and Marriott employees.

The symmetry of the building helps patients and visitors to find their way. Exterior vehicular access points are clear: inpatients and visitors enter straight ahead, radiation therapy outpatients turn left, other outpatients turn right. In the interior, two axial corridors (main artery corridors running north to south and east to west) make wayfinding easy. The corridor leading away from the main lobby terminates at the other end at a covered passageway leading to the medical center; in the opposite direction, a corridor starts at radiation therapy and terminates at the outpatient department. Main artery corridors are defined by wall treatment and the dramatic curvilinear form of the ceiling (Fig. 6-11), created by stretching fabric over formed acoustical backboard (each panel is easily removed to access utilities above). The ceiling treatment is repeated on each floor and leads visitors to nurse stations.

The exterior form of the building is highly articulated (Fig. 6-12) to accommodate the 24-bed pod-type nursing wing layout. This layout permits close observation of most beds from the nurse station (rooms have interior windows

6-11 *Main artery circulation spine is delineated by stretched fabric ceiling treatment; H. Lee Moffitt Cancer Center (Tampa, FL)*

Architects: Heery Architects & Engineers in joint venture with Stuart Bentler; Interior design: Heery Interiors, Inc.; Photographer: Timothy Hursley

so that patients can see the nurse station). The solid feeling of the building derives from the beige cast stone on the exterior, which is carried into the lobby (Fig. 6-13). The raised latticework pattern provides interesting texture and contrast with the bluestone on walls of main artery spines. The main entrance (Fig. 6-13) combines many textures and materials; it has large potted palms and the ambience of Florida. Curving glass block walls in the outpatient lobby combine with granite, marble, and stone in a vocabulary of design details that looks like anything but a hospital. Neon signs in vending and dining areas are a cheerful reminder of the world outside. Patient dayrooms in each nursing wing (Fig. 6-14) resemble a corporate lounge. The cafeteria features an exterior dining court with water sculpture that contributes to the non-clinical feeling of this facility.

6-12 *Entry court, H. Lee Moffitt Cancer Center (Tampa, FL)*

Architects: Heery Architects & Engineers in joint venture with Stuart Bentler; Interior design: Heery Interiors, Inc.; Photographer: Timothy Hursley

6-13 *Main lobby, with critical care family waiting areas above, H. Lee Moffitt Cancer Center (Tampa, FL)*

Architects: Heery Architects & Engineers in joint venture with Stuart Bentler; Interior design: Heery Interiors, Inc.; Photographer: Timothy Hursley

6-14 *Typical patient dayroom, H. Lee Moffitt Cancer Center (Tampa, FL)*

Architects: Heery Architects & Engineers in joint venture with Stuart Bentler; Interior design: Heery Interiors, Inc.; Photographer: Timothy Hursley

BODINE CENTER FOR CANCER TREATMENT

The Bodine Center for Cancer Treatment at Thomas Jefferson University Hospital, Philadelphia, offers the full range of state-of-the-art cancer treatment modalities including an intraoperative suite with a fully equipped operating room adjacent to one of the 25-megavolt linear accelerators, allowing patients to be operated on and radiated immediately (Fig. 6-15).

The 51,000-square-foot facility has two levels below grade and one above. The lowest level contains all treatment areas; the middle level contains physicians' offices and a comprehensive radiobiology research lab; the upper level contains patient reception, examination, business office, and a day hospital for patients receiving chemotherapy. The entire facility was constructed under the existing hospital and designed with light wells to bring daylight to all levels (Fig. 6-16).

OTHER FACILITIES

The entrance to the Comprehensive Cancer Center at the Good Samaritan Hospital and Medical Center in Portland, Oregon, commands attention (Fig. 6-17). Its message is that cancer patients are important people. The facility is located in a densely developed hospital and medical center campus and is connected by sky bridges to existing structures. At Graduate Hospital's Tuttleman Center in Philadelphia, the outpatient oncology lobby (Fig. 6-18) is flooded with natural light and has a residential living room atmosphere and a three-tiered coral granite fountain with plants cascading into the seating area. The two-story vaulted ceiling is accented with white neon lighting. Mahogany and oak trim highlights reception desks in the lobby and in departmental suites. Colorful area rugs introduce the colors and patterns used throughout the remainder of the facility.

HOSPICE

The hospice movement evolved as an alternative to hospitals and nursing homes as places to die. Although the word *hospice* can refer to a building designed for this purpose, it generally refers to a concept of care to support terminally ill patients and their families. In medieval times

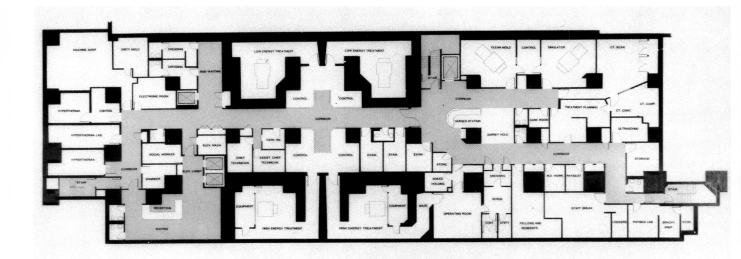

6-15 *Lower-level floor plan, accommodating two 25 MEV and two 6 MEV linear accelerators, including an intra-operative suite with a fully equipped operating room, adjacent to one of the 25 MEV machines, Bodine Center for Cancer Treatment, Thomas Jefferson University Hospital (Philadelphia, PA)*

Architect: Mirick Pearson Batcheler Architects; Medical space planner: CDP Associates, Inc.; Interior design: Merlino Interior Design Associates

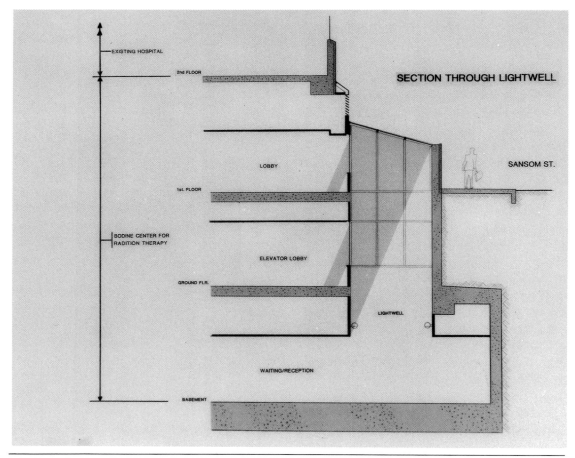

6-16 *Section through light well illustrates how natural light is brought down into radiation therapy waiting area; Bodine Center for Cancer Treatment, Thomas Jefferson University Hospital (Philadelphia, PA)*
Architect: Mirick Pearson Batcheler Architects; Medical space planner: CDP Associates, Inc.

6-17 *Impressive entry bolsters patients' confidence about treatment; Comprehensive Cancer Center, The Good Samaritan Hospital and Medical Center (Portland, OR) Architect: BOOR/A; Photographer: Michael Mathers*

a hospice was a way station for pilgrims and travelers, where they could rest and be cared for. Individuals generally are eligible for hospice care when they are thought to have six months or less to live.

The major difference between hospice care and that provided in hospitals is that hospices provide what is known as *palliative care*, which means that heroic life support systems and measures are not used to try to extend the patient's life. Instead, everything is done to make the patient feel comfortable and to reduce pain, so that the patient may die naturally. Other aspects of hospice care address psychological preparation for death, support for the family before and after death, the desire of people to die in their own homes in familiar surroundings, and a coordinated program of care that includes inpatient and home care. A hospice unit may be set up in an acute care setting, or it may be a freestanding building. In either case, the focus should be a residential environment in terms of furnishings, accessories, and other design features.

Deborah Allen Carey's *Hospice Inpatient Environments* (1986) is an excellent resource for historical background, philosophy, facility design, and a multitude of other considerations. The book integrates the writings of theologians, psychologists, and scientists and also includes floor plans and photos of numerous hospice facilities. An additional resource is the National Hospice Organization located in Arlington, Virginia.

SUMMARY

The increased incidence of cancer is recognized as a medical problem requiring highly focused, federally funded research programs and an integrated network of clinical care programs. Success at controlling or extinguishing other diseases has extended people's life spans, thus

6-18 *Tiered marble fountain, with cascading plants, surrounds patients with the soothing and healing qualities of nature; the room also benefits from natural light; note cold cathode lighting delineating second-story soffits; Tuttleman Center, Graduate Hospital (Philadelphia, PA)*

Architecture and interior design: Medifac; Photographer: Tom Crane

providing more opportunities for contracting cancer. Certainly environmental pollution, smoking, and poor dietary habits have increased the incidence of cancer. Moreover, individuals with certain personality traits seem to be more susceptible to developing cancer (see chapter 2). Few people have not been touched by the devastation of the disease, either through the loss of a loved one or a personal battle with the illness.

Cancer treatment facilities may be integrated into a large medical center, or they may be a freestanding building. In either case, the image conveyed by the architecture and design is important. Ellerbe Becket (1989) categorizes a number of public image types as follows:

- *Patient-friendly:* Careful attention to details in areas the patient first enters, such as the lobby or waiting rooms. The design should allow patients maximum control over the environment. Such environments often have a hospitality image.
- *Nonstressful:* Conveyed through the use of soft materials integrated into high-tech areas. It may incorporate art, plants, aquariums, and other elements to distract patients.
- *Contemporary:* Conveyed through simple, uncluttered spaces that clearly express their purpose as being designed for the treatment of cancer.
- *High-tech:* Although controversial, attention is focused on high-tech elements of the facility by exposing them and making them visible to the public and patients. Art, design, and color are critical elements in the integration of high-tech environments into the cancer facility.
- *Clinical:* Focuses on the function of the department or clinic specialty. The function of the diagnosis and treatment process is clearly communicated through the architectural environment and layout.
- *Homelike:* Focuses on a residential-style environment that provides a number of amenities for patients and their families, such as guest accommodations for family, dining facilities, and entertainment.

REFERENCES

Blanchard, C., J. Ruckdeschel, and others. 1987. The impact of a designated cancer unit on house staff behaviors toward patients. *Cancer* 60(9):2348–54.

Cancer Statistics 1990. *Cancer Journal for Clinicians* 40(1):26.

Carey, Deborah Allen. 1986. *Hospice Inpatient Environments.* New York: Van Nostrand Reinhold.

Conway, D., J. Zeisel, and others. 1977. *Radiation Therapy Centers: Social and Behavioral Issues for Design.* Bethesda, MD: Radiation Oncology Branch, National Institutes of Health.

Cousins, Norman. 1979. *Anatomy of an Illness.* New York: W. W. Norton & Co.

———. 1983. *The Healing Heart.* New York: Avon Books.

Dunphy, J. E. 1976. Annual discourse—caring for patients with cancer. *New England Journal of Medicine* 295(6):313–19.

Ellerbe Associates. 1987. *A Planning Guide for Radiation Therapy.* Minneapolis: Ellerbe Becket, Inc.

Ellerbe Becket. 1989. *Study of Cancer Facilities in the United States,* vols. 1 and 2. Minneapolis: Ellerbe Becket, Inc.

Gerber, Richard. 1988. *Vibrational Medicine.* Santa Fe: Bear & Co.

Goldberg, Alan, and Robert DeNoble, editors. 1985. *Hospital Departmental Profiles.* Chicago: American Hospital Association.

Kubler-Ross, Elisabeth. 1969. *On Death and Dying.* New York: Macmillan.

Kubler-Ross, E., E. Wesslar, and L. Avioli. 1972. On death and dying. *Journal of the American Medical Association.* 221:174–79.

Marino, E. G., and LeBlanc. 1976. Cancer chemotherapy. Atlanta, GA: American Cancer Society.

Moody, Raymond. 1988. *The Light Beyond.* New York: Bantam Books.

Rand, George. 1989. *Morphosis.* Unpublished monograph.

Salick Health Care. 1987. *Annual Report.* Los Angeles, CA: Salick Health Care, Inc.

Siegel, Bernie. 1986. *Love, Medicine and Miracles.* New York: Harper and Row.

———. 1989. *Peace, Love, and Healing.* New York: Harper and Row.

Viladas, P. 1988. The road to recovery. *Progressive Architecture* 7:67–75.

chapter 7

REHABILITATION

psychological factors

- motivation
- reassurance
- support
- hope
- staff well-being
- reality orientation
- acceptance

activities

- physical therapy
- hydrotherapy
- occupational therapy
- speech and hearing
- gait lab
- recreational therapy
- bracing
- prosthetics
- physiatry
- inpatient-outpatient treatment
- family counseling
- psychological counseling
- vocational counseling
- work hardening
- ADL (activities of daily living)

issues

- depression
- anger
- frustration
- loss of memory
- length of stay
- accessibility
- life safety
- storage
- visibility from wheelchair
- social participation

Rehabilitation services are one of the fastest growing hospital product lines. Painting a portrait of the typical rehab patient is difficult be-cause people require these services as a result of a broad variety of injuries ranging from motorcycle accidents to strokes to industrial accidents. The major sources of referral for rehab services are brain injury, management of chronic pain, arthritis, neurological disease, spinal cord injury, musculoskeletal injury, stroke, and postsurgical therapy. Generally patients are medically stable before they embark upon a rigorous course of rehabilitation therapy. Patients may suffer minor to multiple impairments. A trauma victim, for example, might be left with cognitive, emotional, and behavioral disabilities. Patients with neurological disease may suffer paralysis, headaches, seizures, problems with memory and learning, and confusion. Patients admitted to rehab often need chemical dependency treatment or psychiatric counseling to address the multiple nature of their afflictions.

REHABILITATION SERVICES

A comprehensive rehabilitation program offers services including physical therapy, hydrotherapy, occupational therapy, speech and hearing therapy, pain management programs, injury assessment, vocational assessment, disabled driver evaluation and training, neurodiagnostic services, high-speed video for gait and motion analysis, fitness center or gym for the disabled, hand rehabilitation program, work hardening, psychological counseling, social services, inpatient and outpatient treatment, prosthetics lab, and activities of daily living skills.

The goal of rehabilitation is to help patients gain the highest level of independence possible. It involves a multidisciplinary, coordinated team approach. Treatment begins with diagnostic evaluation, which culminates in a program of therapies aimed at rebuilding patients' bodies and lives. People with severe impairment often face overwhelming problems; giving up or becoming deeply depressed becomes easy. They must learn new ways to deal with simple everyday tasks like feeding themselves and bathing and often have to make major adjustments in life-style. Treating the whole person—body, mind, and spirit—is essential, which is why the physical environment in which these patients receive care is so important. It must promote healing and, by its uplifting design expression, motivate patients to persevere. Views of nature

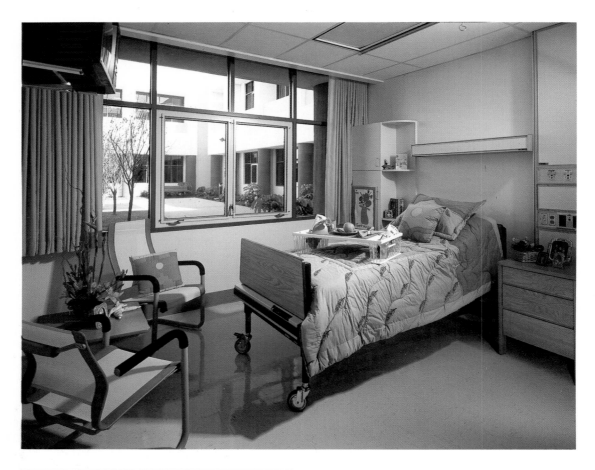

7-1 *Patient room offers view of courtyard garden; pale apricot walls are soothing and accented by teal window frames; Scripps Memorial Hospital (Encinitas, CA)*
   Architect: Brown Gimber Rodriguez Park; Interior design: Jain Malkin Inc.; Photographer: Sandra Williams

such as a landscaped courtyard (Fig. 7-1) may be helpful in reducing the effects of depression.

INTERIOR DESIGN CONSIDERATIONS
PATIENT ROOM AMENITIES

In the patient room, shelves for personal memorabilia and family photos should be provided. A tackboard for greeting cards or for posting children's artwork is a nice addition to the room. The duration of stay can be lengthy for a rehab patient, and often they bring into the room a favorite chair, quilt, or other items from home that help to personalize the room. A common problem of rehab rooms is that they are too small. Lots of room on the sides of beds is required for furniture and wheelchair access. Patients with spinal cord injuries have a particularly long stay, and beds placed foot to foot in a semiprivate room promote socialization. In these rooms, everything should be wheelchair accessible to allow patients to care for themselves as much as possible. Note that plumbing pipes must be turned sideways to enable wheelchair users to pull up to sinks.

REALITY ORIENTATION

Patients recovering from neurological impairment need reality orientation accessories such as bulletin boards for family photos, a calendar, clock, and, in the dayroom, a changeable letter board to remind patients what season it is and what day of the week.

Reality orientation is a technique used in the beginning phase of rehabilitation for individuals who have person, place, and time disorientation. The rationale for reality orientation programs is based on the assumption that relearning can take place in intact areas of cerebral function by re-educative stimulation (Ashmore 1982). The reality board, placed in a prominent location, becomes a visual cue citing place, date, the next meal, next holiday, the weather, and so forth. Typically it has slots for changeable signs that can be stored in a rack at the nurse station. Boards in two languages will be needed for bilingual patients.

COLOR AND PATTERN

Typically, calm, soothing colors are most appropriate for these patients. High contrasts in color or value, as well as certain types of patterns, can be very disturbing and even trigger seizures. By contrast, a totally bland environment lacking in stimulation would also be inappropriate. In creating patterns or designs in vinyl composition tile, sheet vinyl flooring, or carpeting (Fig. 7-2), consider the impact of various shapes not just in terms of aesthetics but also as wayfinding cueing devices. Simple shapes such as squares, diamonds, rectangles, circles, triangles, and crosses can be easily identified by many brain-injured or confused patients and may enhance their abilities to locate a therapy

room or identify their own bedrooms on the return trip; such cues help them to be independent.

Wayfinding may be difficult in a hospital where all doors are alike, and few landmarks or points of reference in public corridors trigger memory. One solution is to highlight doors patients need to find and to differentiate sections of the hospital. Each wing of the hospital in Figure 7-2 has a different geometric design and differences in the predominant field color of the flooring material so that a patient embarking down a corridor can perceive if it is correct because the overall perception would be of a darker color (or perhaps a lighter color) and the inset shapes would be different. Certainly not all patients would be aware of and able to use these cueing devices, but if even half of them benefit by them the effort is worthwhile. Some patients are color dominant and others form dominant; therefore, cueing devices must consider both issues.

7-2 *Inset carpet designs identify nurse stations and assist patients in wayfinding; each wing has a different geometric pattern; Scripps Memorial Hospital (Encinitas, CA)*

Architect: Brown Gimber Rodriguez Park; Interior design: Jain Malkin Inc.; Photographer: Sandra Williams

7-3 *Patient rooms in each wing have a different inset vinyl wallcovering design to help ambulatory rehabilitation patients with wayfinding; Scripps Memorial Hospital (Encinitas, CA)*

Architect: Brown Gimber Rodriguez Park; Interior design: Jain Malkin Inc.; Photographer: Sandra Williams

A painted or inset vinyl design around patient room doors (Fig. 7-3) may help patients identify their rooms. All patient rooms in a particular wing might have the same type of design around the doors (which has an additional benefit of downplaying other doors that patients should not enter), or three variations of a design might alternate in a particular wing. In this same facility, geometric cuing elements were incorporated into the building's signage to identify rooms in, or a path to, a specific wing or area. Note coded symbols on the nurse station sign in Figure 7-2.

PSYCHOLOGICAL FACTORS

Given the multiple disabilities and injuries suffered by many patients, designers can easily understand the need for motivating patients to persevere and for reassuring them that they can achieve a certain level of performance and independence. The first step is creating an environment that supports patients in accepting their new condition and working through their denial so that they can become socially involved in the milieu of the unit. At this point the motivational aspects of the environment begin to

7-4 *Spanish Colonial furniture, handwoven rugs, and contemporary Mexican arts and crafts create a uniquely different image for this facility, Warm Springs Rehabilitation Hospital (San Antonio, TX)*

Architect: HKS Inc.; Interior design: Life Designs; Photographer: Edward Rosenberger

influence therapeutic outcomes. Providing life-enhancing surroundings helps patients and benefits the staff, whose attitude and well-being is reflected in their ability to withstand the stress and emotional anguish of dealing with patients who are so severely impaired (Figs. 7-4 and 7-5). In rehab services progress is often measured in centimeters, a series of tiny steps with incremental advances almost imperceptible from day to day. Patience must certainly be an attribute of therapists in a rehab unit.

The patient is not the only one devastated by the injury. Families suffer terribly when, for example, a once vigorous young man, after a motorcycle accident, is paralyzed from the waist down for the rest of his life. A woman in her seventies who had relied upon her husband to manage their financial affairs, repair items around the house, and drive her to the grocery store suddenly finds herself frightened and helpless when her husband is disabled by a stroke and faces a lengthy period of rehabilita-

7-5 *Design motif is carried into patient rooms with fabric insert on headboard and wallpaper border encircling the room; Warm Springs Rehabilitation Hospital (San Antonio, TX)*

Architect: HKS Inc.; Interior design: Life Designs; Photographer: Edward Rosenberger

tion. Social workers and psychologists counsel family members and offer much needed emotional support and hope.

Reality orientation, described previously, is an important technique in challenging patients to remember meaningful information, which in turn builds confidence and enhances self-esteem. As patients progress with their recovery and approach discharge, acceptance of their disabilities or limitations is critical to building a new life.

ISSUES
DEPRESSION

Assuming that an attractive environment alone could combat depression would not be realistic. A stretch of the imagination is not required to understand how a person might feel being suddenly rendered dependent on others for feeding, bathing, and toileting and being dependent on a wheelchair, crutches, or prostheses for ambulation. Learning to hold a spoon and get it to the mouth without spilling the contents or hitting oneself in the eye with it causes extreme frustration. Many rehab patients, because of the nature of their illness or paralysis, are on a diet of unappealing soft foods. In the beginning everything encountered must seem like a barrier to freedom and independence. A multidisciplinary approach to depression includes recreational therapy, counseling, and, as time passes, learning to accept and live with disabilities. Added to this approach, and certainly not insignificant, would be the quality of the rehabilitation environment. Color, lighting, furnishings, and artwork used in living rooms and dayrooms should simulate a residential environment.

Certain types of rooms in a hospital seem to be given little attention aesthetically, yet they are the very rooms that are so important to rehab patients in terms of bolstering morale. Hydrotherapy is a normal part of a rehab patient's treatment; often these rooms are buried in the basement of the hospital and are devoid of windows or views. Floors and walls tend to be an institutional type of ceramic tile, and faucets, gauges, and plumbing hookups are closer to a Rube Goldberg contraption than to Italian product design. Few people seem to think these areas deserve something better. They could, instead, resemble the ambience of a fine health spa (Figs. 7-6 and 7-7).

7-6 *Hydrotherapy area features inset "area rug" design in mosaic ceramic tile; Scripps Memorial Hospital (Encinitas, CA)*

Architect: Brown Gimber Rodriguez Park; Interior design: Jain Malkin Inc.; Photographer: Sandra Williams

7-7 *Indoor pool is anchored at one end by attractive mosaic ceramic tile mural; note that second-story running track overlooks pool; Baptist Medical Plaza and Wellness Center, Baptist Hospital (Nashville, TN)*

Architecture and interior design: Gresham, Smith and Partners; Photographer: Bill LaFevor

A similar question comes to mind about physical therapy departments. They either have garish supergraphics, or, more typically, are totally devoid of color or architectural detailing. These units tend to be the most institutional and unappealing patient care areas of any hospital. Yet in no area are color and design so vital to motivating patients and enhancing their well-being. Most physical therapy departments have two-by four-foot fluorescent lighting in the ceiling, even though many patients have to do routines on mat tables and are forced to look up into the glare of overhead lighting. Ambient lighting is much more appropriate. Clerestory windows can admit light and a view of the sky without taking away wall space for wall-mounted equipment.

One of the most carefully detailed physical therapy and hydrotherapy units (Figs. 7-8 and 7-9) offers interesting ceilings, an exceptionally fine use of color (green is traditionally associated with growth, nature, hope, and balance), and the overall ambience of an executive health club rather than a hospital rehab department.

7-8 *Physical therapy department of new rehabilitation/ sports medicine unit, St. Mary's Hospital (Grand Rapids, MI)*

Architecture and interior design: Harley Ellington Pierce Yee; Photographer: Balthazar Korab Ltd.

7-9 *Hydrotherapy area features refreshing green accent color, natural light, and upbeat interior design; St. Mary's Hospital (Grand Rapids, MI)*
  Architecture and interior design: Harley Ellington Pierce Yee; Photographer: Balthazar Korab Ltd.

ANGER

Patients are sometimes angry and may express their frustration by running wheelchairs into walls or abusing the facility by other means. As a general note in any rehab unit, corridor floors and walls must be able to withstand the abuse of people who are learning to get around by wheelchair, walker, crutches, or prosthetic device and who may accidentally run into walls. Care should be taken to select flooring that does not offer much resistance to people in wheelchairs. Dayrooms and lounges can be carpeted, but the carpet should be dense and level-loop, with the direct glue-down method of installation.

LOSS OF MEMORY

Orientation devices such as calendars, clocks, and reminders of seasons and hospital location (city) help patients suffering from memory loss. Wayfinding cuing devices, discussed previously, may help patients find their way around the rehab unit without getting lost.

LENGTH OF STAY

Patients in a rehab unit probably have the longest length of stay of any type of hospitalized patient. It might be anywhere from three or four weeks to a year, depending upon the severity of injuries and the availability of family to continue therapy on an outpatient basis. A lengthy stay makes all the more important deinstitutionalizing the environment and creating rooms that have a residential feeling (Fig. 7-5). In this situation patients tend to accumulate more personal belongings and require proper storage for these items in their rooms. Areas should be differentiated, as would be characteristic of any residential setting, so that patients may experience a distinguishable change when proceeding from therapy, for example, to an activities room or to a television lounge (Figs. 7-10 and 7-11). Color, lighting, and patterned finish materials are vehicles for creating change.

ACCESSIBILITY

All areas of the unit should be accessible to patients in wheelchairs. Hardware (door handles, cabinet pulls, and faucets) that is easy to manipulate and drawer glides and door closers that do not offer too much resistance should be selected. Smooth transitions between flooring materials are important for accessibility and

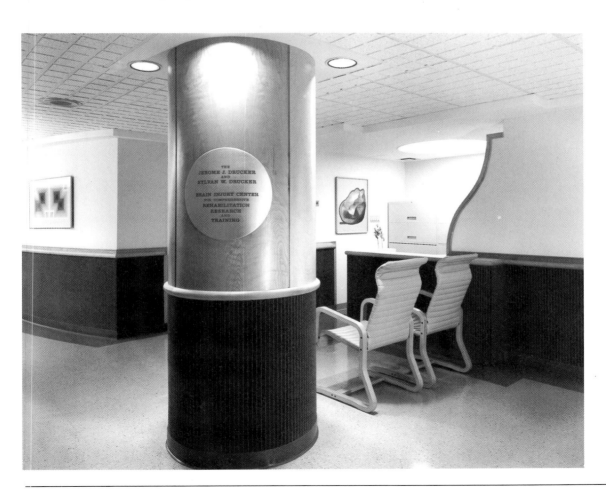

7-10 *New lobby entrance identifies the outpatient Drucker Brain Injury Center for visitors entering the floor from elevators; Moss Rehabilitation Hospital (Philadelphia)*

Architecture and interior design: Dagit-Saylor Architects; Photographer: © Tom Bernard

7-11 *Activities room features attractive built-in storage cabinets, interesting lighting, and uplifting design treatment; Drucker Brain Injury Center, Moss Rehabilitation Hospital (Philadelphia, PA)*
Architecture and interior design: Dagit-Saylor Architects; Photographer: © Tom Bernard

comfort. Corridors must have handrails on both sides because patients may have unilateral weakness.

LIFE SAFETY

Patients with certain types of trauma to the brain may become easily confused or have poor judgment about touching something that is hot; they may fall down down stairs, or otherwise injure themselves. The design of the facility should be viewed with this problem in mind, much as a parent tries to make the home safe when a toddler is underfoot. In addition, brain-injured patients may wander a lot, necessitating alarms at exit doors and stairs to assure their safety.

STORAGE

Rehab units have a number of special storage requirements. A wheelchair must be available

for virtually every bed. Battery charging for wheelchairs takes a lot of space and requires certain considerations. Storage is also needed for crutches, canes, walkers, and a multitude of devices used by therapists in each area. In activity rooms storage is needed for games and puzzles.

VISIBILITY FROM WHEELCHAIR

Designers must carefully view the facility from the sight line of the person in a wheelchair. Sections of a nurse station should be lowered from the standard 42-inch-high shelf to a height that would allow the patient to approach without being dwarfed by the barrier of a high counter. Glazed panels at eye level in doors (Fig. 7-12) allow patients to see into a room before entering it. Artwork and the placement of video recorders, televisions, phonographs, and storage cabinets should be considered from this perspective.

SOCIAL PARTICIPATION

As the patient begins to accept his or her new condition, social participation becomes increas-

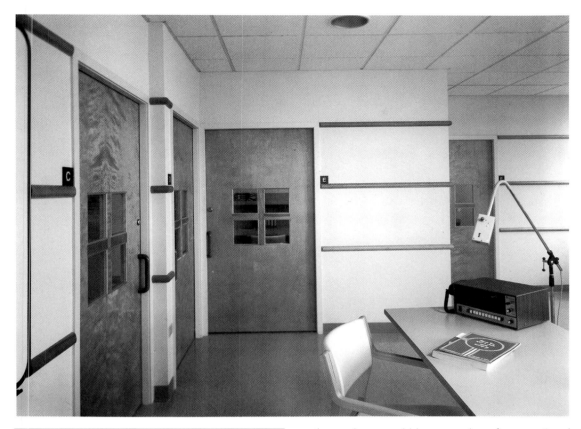

7-12 *Glazed panels in doors are low enough to accommodate wheelchair patients and also allow therapists to monitor patients within the room; triple bands of wood molding add interest to corridors; Drucker Brain Injury Center, Moss Rehabilitation Hospital (Philadelphia, PA)*

Architecture and interior design: Dagit-Saylor Architects; Photographer: © Tom Bernard

ingly important to provide support, enhance a sense of well-being, and shift the focus from preoccupation with self to interest in others.

ACTIVITIES

Physical therapy: concerned with restoring function to large muscle groups and ambulation. It involves use of arms and legs and strengthening of the spine.

Hydrotherapy: involves submersion of a limb or the entire body in water. The tank may be a portable whirlpool or a full-body tank. The heat and motion of water increase circulation and exercising a limb is often easier in water, without the force of gravity.

Occupational therapy: concerned principally with the upper body and the building of fine motor skills. Patients learning how to feed or dress

themselves would be examples of occupational therapy.

Speech and hearing: concerns cognition and perception; depending upon the location of damage to the brain, a patient may lose the ability to speak and have to relearn it. Patients may also have problems in recognizing certain shapes and being able to sort out elements that are similar from those that are different.

Gait lab: analysis and correction of the patient's gait (walk).

Recreational therapy: uses music, games, and exercise to support therapeutic objectives of physical therapy and to stimulate laughter and enhance a sense of well-being.

Bracing: the design of braces to support the body and aid ambulation.

Prosthetics: Patients may have to be fitted with prosthetic devices to help them achieve maximum independence. It requires supervised training to learn to manipulate these devices. Examples are artificial legs, arms, or hands.

Physiatry: A physiatrist is a physician who specializes in treating people with physical disabilities. He or she manages the patient's rehabilitation care and also manages the rehab team. Sometimes this role is performed by a neurologist.

INPATIENT AND OUTPATIENT TREATMENT

Rehabilitation services might be delivered as short-term therapy for general medicine or surgical patients or may be part of an intensive rehab program, including a lengthy program of follow-up visits on an outpatient basis. Outpatient reception and waiting rooms (Fig. 7-13) should be uplifting in color and visually stimulating. Ample space must be allowed for patients in wheelchairs; other seating must be stable and selected for its suitability for patients with

crutches, braces, and prosthetic devices. A high flat seat, straight back, and arms are required.

7-13 *Outpatient rehabilitation waiting room features colorful inset carpet designs; ample space is provided for patients in wheelchairs, integrated with other seating; Scripps Memorial Hospital (Encinitas, CA)*

Architect: Brown Gimber Rodriguez Park; Interior design: Jain Malkin Inc.; Photographer: Sandra Williams

COUNSELING

A variety of counseling services are offered (family, psychological, and vocational counseling) to help restore the family unit and integrate the recovering patient into the community.

WORK HARDENING

Work hardening is goal-oriented clinical treatment geared to return people to the work force in a timely manner following an injury. Real or simulated job tasks, coupled with conditioning, are included in the treatment plan for each patient. A series of work stations allows systematic clinical evaluation of a patient's functional capacity and endurance, postinjury conditioning, and rehabilitation needs. The factory or workroom training module would be designed and equipped for tasks inherent in industries representative of the hospital's service area. Module task simulators include a studwall simulator, which is an open studwall with predrilled holes at a variety of angles and heights permitting plumbing and electrical wiring simulations. A bending/range of motion simulator is fully adjustable for complete range-of-motion exer-

cises. A shelf system is designed to evaluate the ability to lift or reach, required for certain industrial tasks. Weighted containers in assorted sizes and shapes are also provided.

The work hardening environment in Figure 7-14 is particularly effective because equipment modules are placed in a simulated industrial environment where appropriate visual cues make the training experience more realistic. Work hardening is a fairly new concept that is winning great support from employers who are motivated to rehabilitate injured workers quickly. As a preventive measure, training new employees to use muscles properly for specific tasks makes sense.

ADL

An activities of daily living (ADL) unit is a part of most rehab departments. It is typically a small apartment with living room, bedroom, bathroom, and kitchen, furnished as a home to serve as a transition between the hospital and home. Patients may stay there, either with or without a spouse, one or two nights before discharge so that staff can evaluate problem areas and help the patient learn to adapt to residential

7-14 *Work-hardening laboratory allows patients to practice industrial skills under the guidance of therapist Designer: Guynes Design; Photographer: David A. Guynes*

7-15 *A prototype facility for the physically disabled, based on a village concept, with a landscaped courtyard as the focus; kitchen allows for adjustable-height work surfaces with oven and storage at wheelchair-accessible heights; Camino Alto Court (Mill Valley, CA)*

Architect: Kaplan McLaughlin Diaz; Photographer: Charles Callister

appliances, bathroom fixtures, and furniture. Patients can practice getting into and out of a standard bed and learn to maneuver the wheelchair around tight spaces. In the kitchen, a tilted mirror fastened over the cooktop allows a person in a wheelchair to see inside the pot. A reacher tool such as that used in old-fashioned grocery stores retrieves canned goods from upper cabinets. Cabinet doors are labeled on the front with their contents. A kitchen with adjustable-height countertops, sink module, and cooktop (Fig. 7-15) and a bathroom that is totally wheelchair accessible (Fig. 7-16) can be designed.

BARRIER-FREE DESIGN

Several nationally prominent consultants have written books on barrier-free design. One who specializes in adapting the home for easy access is Cynthia Leibrock, a faculty member of Colorado State University. She is the author of *Beautiful Barrier-free Design: A Visual Guide*, published by Van Nostrand Reinhold (1991).

EASY STREET

One of the most imaginative approaches to training physically disabled people in the skills

7-16 *Handicapped-accessible bathroom, Camino Alto Court (Mill Valley, CA)*

Architect: Kaplan McLaughlin Diaz; Photographer: Charles Callister

of daily living is Easy Street Environments, developed by David Guynes of Guynes Design in Phoenix. They are custom-designed architectural vignettes simulating daily experiences such as going to the post office, shopping for groceries, going to the bank, climbing onto a stool in a coffee shop (Fig. 7-17), getting on a bus, getting into an automobile, buying a newspaper from a vending machine, and stepping off a curb (Fig. 7-18). Ranging in size from 1,000 to 6,000 square feet, the individual modules can be combined to suit the needs of a particular hospital; the design is based on the indigenous character of the given locale. Intricate architectural detailing may range from Victorian to southern traditional to urban contemporary. Careful attention (Fig. 7-19) to small decorative touches and to props that would be appropriate for that setting adds realism and interest.

As an example, a life-size photo mural of a local bus stop is equipped with a three-step platform, wooden bench, newspaper vending machine, and concrete sidewalk. The laundromat consists of coin-operated washer and dryer and all appropriate accessories. The bank module features simulated marble teller counters, rope barriers, and an automatic teller machine. The bank offers a variety of opportunities for interactive role-playing between patient and therapist. The cafe-diner includes an old-fashioned lunch counter with swivel stools. Dinnerware, menus, and flatware are stored behind the counter in built-in case work. A wall-mounted menu board has movable letters to allow cognitive training. The department store setting includes clothing racks, a dressing room with swinging door, glass jewelry case, lighted makeup counter, mirrors, and mannequins. The grocery store includes a produce counter stocked with realistic-looking fruits and vegetables, along with bulk food bins, freezer case, and stocked shelf area. The checkout counter has a cash register, check-writing platform, and chrome turnstile (Fig. 7-20).

The office module contains two workstations and can be fully equipped with electronic equipment. The theater, with its sloped aisle seating, doubles as an audiovisual presentation area as well. A pediatrics module with schoolroom and playground settings is also available.

7-17 *Easy Street Environments allow rehabilitation patients to practice everyday skills in a safe, protected environment*
Designer: David A. Guynes, Guynes Design;
Photographer: David A. Guynes

7-18

7-19

7-20 *Easy Street Environments supermarket*
   Designer: David A. Guynes, Guynes Design;
Photographer: David A. Guynes

7-18 *Easy Street Environments allow rehabilitation patients to practice a variety of skills including stepping up into a bus, purchasing a newspaper, walking through a grocery store turnstile, getting into an automobile, purchasing groceries, or stepping off a curb*
   Designer: David A. Guynes, Guynes Design;
Photographer: Al Payne

7-19 *Easy Street Environments for rehabilitation patients use photo murals and props to realistically simulate restaurants, banks, supermarkets, and other environments*
   Designer: David A. Guynes, Guynes Design;
Photographer: David A. Guynes

Together these modules incorporate the common barriers, surfaces, and props that an individual recovering from stroke, arthritis, trauma, amputation, or other disabilities is likely to encounter at home or in the community. The best thing about Easy Street is that it allows patients to practice necessary functional skills without the stigma and embarrassment of being observed by the public. Patients feel comfortable practicing in the privacy of the hospital and are reassured by doing it with the therapist nearby.

Easy Street Environments are custom-designed for each hospital (Figs. 7-21 and 7-22). Most components and fixtures are completely finished prior to shipment, and only need assembly when they arrive at their destination. (Fig. 7-23). Individual modules are connected by a yellow-striped Main Street with sidewalks, curbs, ramps, and traffic signs. An interesting footnote is that these modules offer many opportunities for donor recognition. The name of the bank, street names, the grocery store, and restaurant-diner all offer vehicles for recognizing major donors. Hospital foundations and auxiliaries find this aspect appealing.

7-21 *Lighted columns accentuate elevator lobbies at entry to* Easy Street, *introducing architectural components to stimulate patients visually; other whimsical forms are used in conjunction with rich and lively colors and materials to denote spaces of importance and procession; Physical Rehabilitation Department/Easy Street, Bethesda Oak Hospital (Cincinnati, OH)*
   Architecture and interior design: KZF Incorporated; Photographer: Ron Forth Photography

7-22 *Floor plan of 22,000-square-foot physical rehabilitation department incorporating Easy Street Environments; Physical Rehabilitation Department/Easy Street, Bethesda Oak Hospital (Cincinnati, OH)*
   Architecture and interior design: KZF Incorporated; Easy Street design: David A. Guynes, Guynes Design

Bethesda Oak Hospital
5th Floor Physical Rehabilitation Services

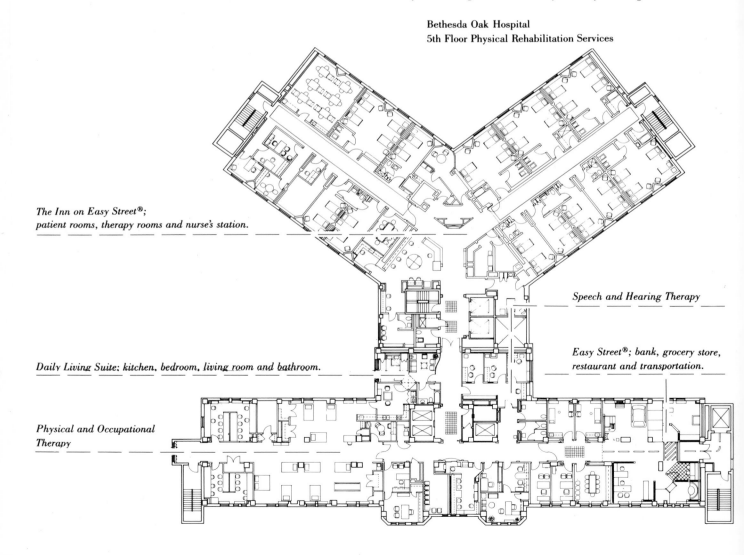

The Inn on Easy Street®;
patient rooms, therapy rooms and nurse's station.

Speech and Hearing Therapy

Daily Living Suite: kitchen, bedroom, living room and bathroom.

Easy Street®; bank, grocery store, restaurant and transportation.

Physical and Occupational Therapy

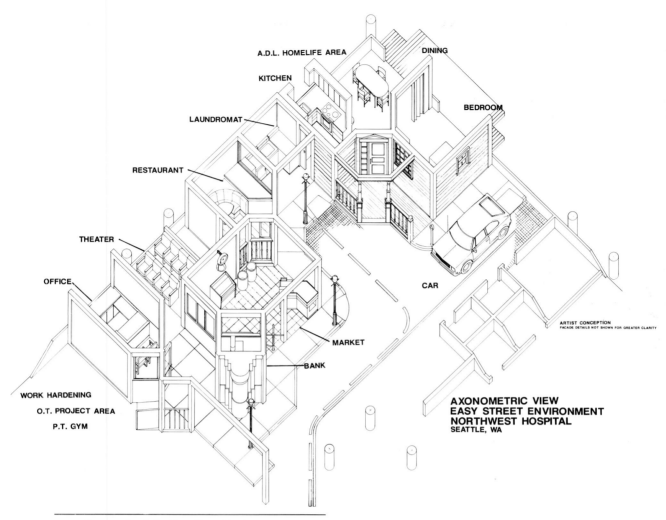

7-23 *Concept sketch for Easy Street Environment incorporating a variety of therapy modules; Northwest Hospital (Seattle, WA)*
Illustration courtesy Guynes Design

DESIGN FOR THE DISABLED IN SWEDEN

Many consider Sweden to have the most enlightened approach to design for the disabled. The government publishes a number of books and pamphlets explaining these policies, and it makes available (pays for) all kinds of devices to retrofit a home to enable an individual to function independently. An astonishing assortment of these items are displayed in the NHR national store in Stockholm[1] (*Katalog* 1989). Included are garden tools, toilets that "wipe and dry" an individual, silverware designed for arthritics, a device to allow a person with poor manual dexterity to slice a loaf of bread, all types and styles of wheelchairs, adjustable-height kitchens, and literally thousands of household, industrial, or workplace aids and appliances, many of which are aesthetically beautiful in design. Some of the best-designed items were featured in an exhibition in 1988 at the Museum of Modern Art, which has produced a brochure of the items (*Design for Independent Living* 1988).

UNIVERSAL DESIGN

The philosophy in Sweden is that individuals with disabilities should not be viewed as separate user groups who have special needs: "It is in many cases the deficiencies in the environment which create the special needs and not the unfortunate lot of the people afflicted by handicaps or lack of ability" (Beckman 1976, p. 33).

The philosophy assumes that all people at some time in their lives will be functionally disabled or unable to manage everyday routines. Overall elimination of obstacles in the environment is the goal in order to normalize living conditions for the disabled, keeping in mind that the disabled includes the visually and hearing impaired, allergy sufferers, and the confused, in addition to those who have impaired mobility. "Viewed in this perspective it is no longer relevant to speak of special needs. The needs of the handicapped form part of the needs of the entire community" (Beckman 1976, p. 33). *Building for Everyone* (Beckman 1976) is highly informative and explains the government's policies, legislation, and solutions for the built environment. It was prepared for the United Nations Conference on Human Settlements.

LOOKING AHEAD

Medical miracles have become almost commonplace, rescuing people from the jaws of death. For patients with multiple disabilities, an arduous and intimately personal struggle for rehabilitation begins. The need for rehabilitative services will grow as the elderly population expands. Seeking an enhanced quality of life and avoidance of frailty, the elderly will become an increasingly larger market for rehab services to maintain skills of daily living. Work hardening is predicted to be one of the fastest growing outpatient services including therapy for carpal tunnel syndrome [2] (one of the most common industrial claims of the 1990s) and repetitive motion syndrome (injuries associated with manufacturing tasks). Sports medicine rehabilitation techniques, which achieved great prominence n the 1980s, are likely to continue to be a strong market.

"Aging in place," as a national priority, will affect the residential design of thousands of homes in an attempt to maintain the independence of the elderly as they age, by the use of physical modifications to make the home truly barrier free.

NOTES

1. Hjälpmedels Center, Kungsgatan 32, 11135 Stockholm, Sweden. A catalog of products for the disabled is available.

2. Carpal tunnel syndrome compresses the nerves in the wrist, which results in neurological symptoms like numbness and tingling. It is a trauma that usually results from repetitive motion such as working at a computer keyboard or performing manufacturing assembly tasks.

REFERENCES

Ashmore, M. 1982. Reality orientation boards: A new design. *Dimensions in Health Service* 59(11):15–16.

Beckman, M. 1976. *Building for Everyone*. Stockholm: Ministry of Housing and Physical Planning.

Design for Independent Living. 1988. New York: Museum of Modern Art.

Hansen, Preben, and Thorkild Barre, editors. 1984. *Denmark Review/Disability Aids*. Copenhagen: Ministry of Foreign Affairs.

Katalog 1989. 1989. Stockholm: Hjälpmedels Center.

Leibrock, Cynthia. 1991. *Beautiful Barrier-free Design: A Visual Guide*. New York: Van Nostrand Reinhold.

Södereström, B., and E. Viklund. 1986. Housing, care and service for elderly and old people—the situation in Sweden. Stockholm: The Swedish Ministry of Housing and Physical Planning.

chapter 8

CRITICAL CARE

psychological factors

- privacy
- reality orientation
- visibility
- comfort/personal control over environment
- communication
- family support
- security
- reassurance

activities

- sleeping
- eating
- therapy
- bathing/grooming
- guest visitation

issues

- fear of death
- noise or sound perception
- boredom
- dependency on others for life support
- fear of abandonment
- isolation
- worries about family, job, money
- color reflection on skin tone
- staff access to patient
- ICU psychosis

The shift of emphasis to ambulatory care indicates that hospitals will increasingly become critical care units for acutely ill patients. In recent years many hospitals have increased their intensive care beds. These specialty nursing units are designed for patients facing life-threatening illnesses. Although the most common types of intensive care units are medical ICU (MICU), surgical ICU (SICU), coronary care units (CCU), pediatric ICU (PICU), and neonatal

ICU (NICU), hospitals may also have neurology, oncology, and respiratory ICUs.

An MICU may receive patients with internal bleeding problems, kidney, or respiratory ailments. An SICU would receive critically ill presurgical and postsurgical patients, including those with organ transplants. A CCU provides highly specialized care for heart transplant patients, heart attack or stroke victims, or those recovering from a cardiac catheterization procedure. A PICU serves children with medical, surgical, or other complications. The NICU cares for premature babies and high-risk newborns.

Critical care units are generally located close to the hospital emergency room and surgery suites to provide faster access for transport of patients. The most prominent features of an intensive care department are the electronic telemetry units, which monitor patients' vital functions, and life-support equipment. The ratio of nursing staff to patients is very high, usually one to one or one nurse per two patients. Typically these nurses are RNs with specialized expertise geared to the needs of each of these patient populations. The fast pace and urgent nature of an ICU make it a stressful environment for nurses.

Much has been written about the layout of critical care units with respect to nurses being able to observe both patients and monitors. Horseshoe or semicircular layouts around a central observation hub have been used effectively, as has a small cluster of rooms around a nurse station (Fig. 8-1). In older hospitals intensive care units are often large, multibed wards, but more recently hospitals have been favoring private rooms with floor-to-ceiling glass facing the nurse station (Fig. 8-2). Two of the biggest problems with ward (multibed) layouts is lack of privacy and lack of a window for each patient. Without a view of the sky, distinguishing between day and night is difficult, and the body's circadian rhythm is disturbed. Since 1977, federal law has mandated that each intensive care bed have direct access to natural light.

PSYCHOLOGICAL FACTORS

Critical care units have a tempo all their own. Strange percussive sounds from respirators and the continual beeping of monitors create an unreal kind of "Twilight Zone" atmosphere. Pa-

8-1 *Nurse station allows maximum visibility of patients and has parabolic lighting that can be separately controlled to allow staff to lower light levels at night; corridors feature indirect cove lighting and skylights to accommodate patients, who are typically transported in a horizontal position on their backs; Adult Intensive Care Unit, St. Luke's Methodist Hospital (Cedar Rapids, IA) Architecture and interior design: Ellerbe Becket; Photographer: © Peter Aaron/Esto*

8-2 *Respiratory/surgical intensive care unit provides optimum visibility of patients; The Reisman Building, Beth Israel Hospital (Boston, MA) Architect: Rothman Rothman Heineman Architects Inc.; Interior design: Crissman & Solomon Architects Inc.; Photographer: Steve Rosenthal*

tients may be comatose, sleeping, or staring up at the ceiling. The unit tends to be brightly illuminated and noisy. For a patient or a family member, the emotional stress is great. Both feel helpless. The patient has to rely on others for the most basic needs, such as toileting and turning over in bed. The family member often feels abandoned by the patient and burdened by the responsibility of having to make critical decisions about the patient's care.

PRIVACY

Even if the patient is in a private room, providing devices for total visual privacy is important so that a patient being bathed or using the commode is not exposed (Fig. 8-3). Family members should be able to visit with the patient

8-3 *Patient room features a power column with monitoring devices, wall-mounted wardrobe, and swing-out toilet; Adult Intensive Care Unit, St. Luke's Methodist Hospital (Cedar Rapids, IA)*

Architecture and interior design: Ellerbe Becket; Photographer: © Peter Aaron/Esto

without their conversations being overheard and without overhearing another patient's family.

REALITY ORIENTATION

Patients in an intensive care unit may have difficulty maintaining a sense of reality about days of the week, time of the day, or seasons. Each patient should be able to see a clock and a calendar, although placing them directly at the foot of the bed is not ideal because a patient forced to lie on his or her back all day may find continuously watching the clock rather tedious.

Perhaps the most imaginative solution to this problem was developed by California photographer Joey Fischer. Stanford Medical Center had lost the use of two ICU rooms when their windows were obstructed by new construction. Without windows the rooms had their licensed use in jeopardy. The hospital contacted Fischer, well known for his nature photography used in health care settings, to see if he could create an artificial window. Installed early in 1990, the four- by five-foot window (Fig. 8-4) simulates the passage of time from sunrise to sunset, controlled by an electronic digital timer that manages 650 separate light changes every 24 hours. The image is a blowup of a 35 mm slide, behind which is a light box recessed in the wall. To make it more realistic, the window has a sill, frame, and mullions. It gives the illusion of the sun rising on one side and setting on the other. Images can be interchanged so that they are seasonally appropriate. Geographic familiarity is important, and to achieve it landscapes of the surrounding locale are used.

Future editions of the Windows of Nature will have twinkling stars and a moon that rises and sets in the night sky. The creator also hopes to introduce a model with motion by using rear video projection to create the illusion of clouds moving or waves lapping on the shore. The Office of Statewide Health Planning and Development in California has given temporary approval for use of the window in an intensive care room in order to meet the federal requirement. Final approval will be based on studies of patient reaction to the window.

Since its invention, Fischer reports many orders from the military for use in normalizing the environment of nuclear submarines, for use in underground missile sites, and from hotel

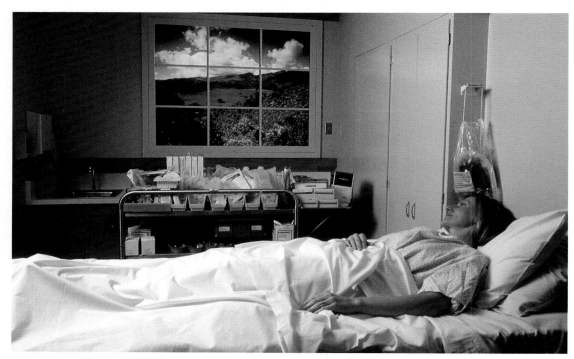

8-4 *Electronic Window of Nature simulates a twenty-four-hour night-day cycle to entertain circadian rhythms in a cardiac transplant intensive care unit, Stanford University Medical Center (Palo Alto, CA)*
Created by Joey Fischer/Art Research Institute Limited

chains who plan to use them in VIP suites. The window has also become the subject of a research grant to see whether it can be used to decrease aggression in children and adolescents placed in the quiet room of a psychiatric hospital.

VISIBILITY

Patients in a critical care unit often worry about being able to communicate their needs. Often too weak even to push the call buzzer, they are reassured by being able to see the nurse station and know that they can be seen.

COMFORT AND PERSONAL CONTROL

Comfort is a word not often associated with an intensive care unit. Bright lights and noise often characterize the unit, and undisturbed sleep may be difficult. Patients with IVs, tubes, respirators, and various other life-support equipment often cannot turn over or move without assistance. Being hooked up to this equipment can be very uncomfortable. Because patients are often unable to change position by themselves,

lighting must be located where it does not create glare for a patient lying in bed. Everything in this room should be evaluated from the viewpoint of a person lying in bed. If a television is provided, it must be viewable from a supine position. The nightstand should be placed where the patient can reach it without being a contortionist. Similarly, the telephone should be accessible with very little stretching.

For some reason critical care units seem to be very bland in decor. Although strong, stimulating colors and patterns would certainly not be appropriate for critically ill persons, the absence of color is frightening and unfamiliar and only serves to make the equipment more prominent. Colorful cubicle draperies, carpet, softly colored accent walls, a border of color around the perimeter of the room near the ceiling, or wood trim (Fig. 8-3) can do much to make the space less foreboding.

Management of lighting, temperature, and humidity could add greatly to an individual's comfort level but, unfortunately, in many facilities the patient has little individual control over these elements.

COMMUNICATION

Communication is especially important for patients who are either partially or totally paralyzed. They may be mentally alert but unable to tell anyone what they need or want. One of the most poignant accounts of this experience is related by Sue Baier in *Bed Number Ten*. Suddenly a victim of the mysterious Guillain-Barré syndrome, she spent six months in an intensive care unit intellectually totally alert but physically paralyzed. She could not swallow, eat, or even breathe on her own. Her story is a riveting account of what being a patient in an intensive care unit means, as well as an indictment of the effects of careless planning and thoughtless care. The book contains some shocking photos of what she was forced to look at every day, 24 hours a day, from her viewpoint lying in bed. Subtle details can make an enormous difference to a patient totally confined to bed.

FAMILY SUPPORT

Contact with loved ones is critically important. If a comfortable chair is provided for the family alongside the bed, the patient will feel more relaxed, knowing that the family member does not have to stand or sit on the edge of the bed. An intensive care lounge should be provided for family members, who often spend the entire day and may even sleep there. Unfortunately, in many hospitals it is a tiny room, originally used for something else, with poor ventilation, no windows, poor lighting, and a jumble of seating that forces strangers into intimate contact. Ideally this room would be large enough to allow for private groupings so that individual families can sit together. Indirect lighting on a dimmer control would be desirable. The room may be divided by attractive planter walls to achieve privacy. A small kitchen or coffee bar should be provided for snacks, and recliner chairs allow people to nap or spend the night with some degree of comfort. A storage area might be provided for pillows and blankets. Bathrooms should be nearby, with convenient public telephones that afford privacy to family members.

Family members have to be able to receive information about the patient's condition. A hospital volunteer seated at a desk in the family lounge can serve this function. If at all possible, this room should be shielded from passersby so that hospital visitors need not observe crying and grieving. In that regard a chapel, meditation room, or grieving room is a necessity. Usually designed as a nondenominational room, it is a serene place where people can grieve or pray in private. A nearby consultation room is a good place to tell bad news, and it enables grieving families to be out of the lounge.

SECURITY

A secure place must be provided for patients' personal belongings, especially in open wards where visitors come and go and patients are often not alert enough to observe thefts.

REASSURANCE

Although unfamiliar and stressful, the intensive care unit offers security to patients: they know that the most advanced life-saving equipment is close at hand.

ISSUES

Both patients and family members associate a critical care unit with death. It is often the closest they have ever come to death. Everything is unfamiliar and confusing. Patients may feel isolated and alone and, although very ill, during waking hours may have plenty of time to worry about family, job, or finances. As they start to recover, boredom sets in. An ICU does not have much to look at, and many patients leave the unit with a lifetime memory of counting holes in the acoustic tile over their heads. They wish they had had something to look at on the ceiling. Amazingly, many ICUs have a fluorescent fixture mounted precisely over each patient bed, where it imposes an uncomfortable amount of light and glare.

NOISE

In chapter 2 the stressful effects of noise were discussed. Noise is one of the most serious deterrents to healing and a major cause of psychological stress. Concern for acoustics should be part of every responsible design treatment.

COLOR REFLECTION

In this area more so than any other in the hospital, a patient's skin tone is used as an indication of the patient's condition. Jaundice, cyanosis, or a variety of other conditions would be difficult to notice if colors such as yellow or blue were used on the headwall. However, these colors in the right shades and quantity can effectively be used on walls at the foot of the bed or in a border around the room.

STAFF ACCESS TO PATIENT

Instantaneous intervention is essential in a critical care unit. Within seconds, staff must be able to access the head of the patient and move equipment up to the bed without running into furniture and obstructions. Often portable x-ray equipment is brought to the patient; the requirement of a clear path must be considered in the location of any built-in furniture.

ICU PSYCHOSIS

This condition is characterized by disorientation and hallucinations resulting from side effects of drugs, sleep deprivation (constant interruptions for medical treatment), and interruption of circadian rhythms because of 24-hour lighting. ICU psychosis can be mitigated by providing orientation to the outdoors so that day-night changes are noticeable, by separating the ceiling plane visually from the wall (through a change of color or a border), and by keeping visual surfaces uncluttered—no complicated patterns or design.

INTENSIVE CARE UNIT INITIATIVE

Readers are encouraged to review the December 1990 issue of *Interiors*, which features an ICU room designed by Orlando Diaz-Azcuy (Tetlow 1990). Sponsored by the National Symposium on HealthCare Interior Design and *Interiors*, the intention was to create a room that addressed important patient care issues by using technology that is currently available. The resultant design is aesthetically beautiful; although some of its features challenge code compliance, it provokes critical thought about the possibilities for improving what is traditionally a colorless, harshly lit, aesthetically hostile environment.

OPEN HEART SURGERY

Among the great medical accomplishments of the 1980s were advances in open heart surgery and the development of the Jarvik 7 artificial heart transplant. Specialized operating rooms such as that shown in Figure 8-6 have been

8-5 *Open heart surgery operating room, The Fairfax Hospital (Falls Church, VA)*
  Architect: Heery Architects & Engineers; Photographer: Dennis O'Kain

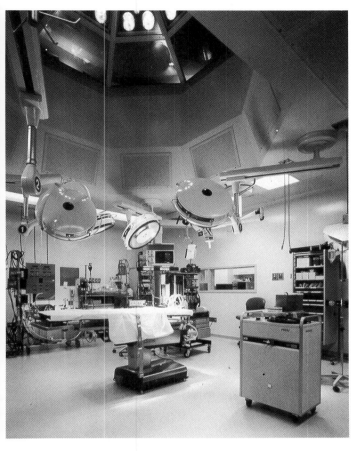

developed to accommodate the needs of open heart surgery. The observation gallery (Fig. 8-5) provides a view into the specialized operating room designed to accommodate the needs of open heart surgery (Fig. 8-6).

Designed to accommodate patients receiving the Jarvik 7 artificial heart, the room in Figure 8-7 is part of a six-room unit for heart transplant patients who require one-on-one, 24-hour nursing care. The highly technical nature of these rooms demands architectural sensitivity and carefully planned engineering systems. Each room must contain uninterrupted power sources for computer monitors, the Jarvik 7 equipment, and dialysis and cardiac equipment, as well as outlets for standard medical gasses. Note that the equipment nearest the window is the Jarvik 7 heart. Lighting has been carefully planned to provide three options: an overhead examination light for medical procedures, indirect perimeter lighting with controls for lighting

8-6 *Open heart surgery operating room, The Fairfax Hospital (Falls Church, VA)*
Architect: Heery Architects & Engineers; Photographer: Dennis O'Kain

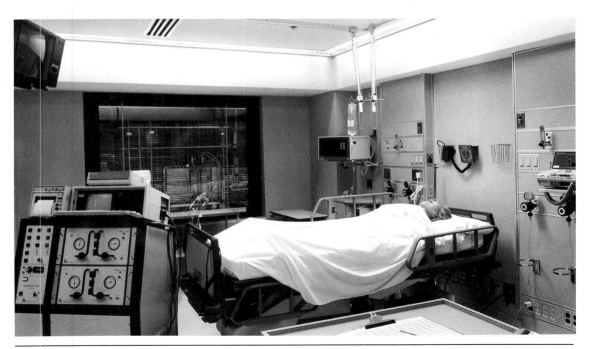

8-7 *Heart transplant unit designed to accommodate patients receiving the Jarvik 7 artificial heart (the machinery nearest the window is the Jarvik 7 heart); Abbott-Northwestern Hospital (Minneapolis, MN)*

Architect: Hammel Green and Abrahamson, Inc.; Photographer: Shin Koyama

only half the room, if desired, and indirect baseboard lighting for nighttime. Patients have the option of requesting a softly lit environment. Because heart transplant patients require round-the-clock nursing care, the architects designed a monitoring station for nurses just outside patient rooms. It allows staff to observe patients without creating any disruptive activity that might interfere with recovery and healing. Aesthetics were also considered. Color palettes of blues, pinks, and a soft gray were selected to transform a clinical environment into a more soothing one.

SUMMARY

If vulnerability is one of the criteria used to determine which patient populations are most deserving of careful planning and thoughtful design, then critical care has got to be the choice. With lives often hanging by a thread, these patients are sometimes so sick or weak that they are unable to make any changes at all in their immediate environment. Designers need to lie down in an ICU bed and understand what the patient sees from that perspective. The room should be designed accordingly, considering orientation to the outdoors, visibility of nursing staff, color palette, location of clocks, and options for room lighting.

REFERENCES

Baier, Sue, and Mary Schomaker. 1986. *Bed Number Ten*. Boca Raton, FL: CRC Press.

Beck, William, and Ralph Meyer. 1982. *Health Care Environment: The User's Viewpoint*. Boca Raton, FL: CRC Press.

Carpman, Janet, Myron Grant, and Deborah Simmons. 1987. *Design That Cares*. Chicago: American Hospital Publishing.

Goldberg, Alan, and Robert DeNoble, editors. 1985. *Hospital Departmental Profiles*. Chicago: American Hospital Publishing.

Rosner, S. 1972. Emotional aspects of intensive care: An area of confusion. *Journal of Contemporary Psychotherapy* 5(1):62–66.

Tetlow, K. 1990. Design heals. *Interiors*, December: 60–65.

chapter 9

CHEMICAL DEPENDENCY RECOVERY HOSPITALS

psychological factors

- tranquillity
- privacy
- support
- love
- trust
- friendship
- social interaction

activities

- family counseling
- group therapy
- individual therapy
- dining
- sleeping
- detoxification
- lounging, socializing
- exercise
- classrooms/learning
- personal hygiene (laundry, hair)
- entertainment
- outpatient treatment

issues

- confidentiality
- security
- intervention
- observation
- anxiety, anger, hyperactivity
- durability of furnishings

Substance abuse has reached epidemic proportions and facilities such as Beech Hill and CareUnit of Coral Springs help victims and their families put their lives back together, knowing that tomorrow holds the promise of recovery. Situated in the hills of New Hampshire and in South Florida, respectively, these facilities maximize expansive views of lush landscaping and are oriented toward nature (Fig. 9-1).

Interior courtyards and outdoor spaces can be used for meetings, therapy, and counseling sessions and for informal patient gatherings and socializing—critical ingredients of the treatment program. Large expanses of glass in visitor and patient areas provide tranquil vistas of trees and mountains in the distance. Clerestory windows flood spaces with natural light (Figs. 9-2 and 9-3).

Inside, spaces are broadly zoned as residential (patient rooms and nursing), therapy and counseling, public space, and administrative offices. More specifically, the hospital usually has numerous group and family counseling rooms, a large dining room that can be divided into smaller rooms with acoustical folding partitions, visitors' lounges, patients' lounges (Fig. 9-4), staff lounges, exercise room, laundry, hair salon, nurse stations, activity rooms, classrooms, patient bedrooms, solarium, and administrative offices with conference rooms.

The course of treatment for an individual patient will vary. An inpatient may reside in the facility for a period of six weeks followed by a rigorous program of outpatient visits. Some parts of the country have seen a gradual shift away from inpatient programs to outpatient care, due in part to a greater emphasis on developing individualized programs, changes in reimbursement benefits, and an increased awareness of chemical dependency, which has created a number of treatment opportunities in other settings. Consistent with health care delivery in general, economies of scale are increasingly emphasized; some chemical dependency recovery hospital (CDRH) administrators wish they had designed greater flexibility into their programs. One lamented that, had he been licensed as a psychiatric facility, he would have had the latitude to run separate programming tracks to accommodate a wide variety of mental health disorders, which would have enabled him to keep his beds full.

9-1 *Design of this hundred-bed chemical dependency rehabilitation hospital is residential in scale and contextual with neighboring southern Florida architecture; CareUnit of Coral Springs (Coral Springs, FL)*
Architecture and interior design: Anderson DeBartolo Pan, Inc.; Photographer: Timothy Hursley

PLANNING BASED ON TREATMENT PROTOCOLS

Six or seven years ago the protocols for treating chemical dependency patients were more consistent. More recently, in response to changes in reimbursement and greater emphasis on individual needs, treatment protocols have been somewhat in a state of flux. The response to certain issues may vary from one facility to another with respect to how detoxification is handled and whether adolescents are treated in separate facilities or integrated with adult populations. As with any medical illness, although each individual is unique, certain common characteristics and psychological factors strongly influence planning in a CDRH. Bear in mind that the following is not cast in concrete; it is intended only to acquaint the designer with mainstream treatment philosophy.

1. Patients must see themselves as equals regardless of socioeconomic level. To this end, most facilities plan all patient rooms to be identical. VIP suites, although they do exist, would undermine this goal.
2. Semiprivate rooms are more common than private because alcoholics and addicts tend to isolate themselves from people. During their period of treatment, they need the support and trust of others.

9-2 *Reception and lobby of chemical dependency recovery hospital feature architectural detailing not often found in a clinical setting; Beech Hill Hospital (Dublin, NH)*
Architecture and interior design: DeGiorgio Associates Inc.; Photographer: Robert E. Mikrut

9-3 *Reception/lobby benefits from geometry of vaulted ceiling and window grid detail; CareUnit of Coral Springs (Coral Springs, FL)*

Architecture and interior design: Anderson DeBartolo Pan, Inc.; Photographer: Timothy Hursley

9-4 *Patient lounge features variation of architectural detailing introduced in lobby, Beech Hill Hospital (Dublin, NH)*

Architecture and interior design: DeGiorgio Associates Inc.; Photographer: Robert E. Mikrut

3. Recovering alcoholics and addicts are often restless, hyperactive, and anxious. To address this, furnishings and design concepts should be simple and understated. Avoid busy patterns or stripes that vibrate; even pindots on a contrasting background can be uncomfortable to a person battling nausea or postdetox hallucinations.

4. Architecturally, CDRHs are designed around the treatment program. If detoxification rooms are to be located in a separate wing, then care should be taken to locate them so that these patients do not have to navigate elevators or stairs. If adolescent bedrooms are in a separate wing or building, a central commons area for dining, therapy, and recreational activities may be shared by both adults and adolescents. This practice avoids duplication of services and fosters maximum social interaction. Each facility, of course, has its own program, and clinical staff set the parameters for each of these patient care prerogatives.

INTERIOR DESIGN CONSIDERATIONS

Often the goal of interior design in a CDRH is to create an environment more like a hotel than a hospital. The objective is not to make it look like home but, through the use of color and texture, to provide a restful and calm background for rehabilitation.

Dining is an important social activity that can be enhanced by orientation to a landscaped garden or courtyard (Fig. 9-5) and by designing the room more like a restaurant (Fig. 9-6) than like a hospital cafeteria.

Although design theme or style of furnishings varies from one facility to another, special considerations should be noted in regard to selection of interior finishes and furniture. Durability and ease of maintenance are critical in all areas.

Color. A warm color palette (rose or apricot) seems to be preferred for adolescent areas, perhaps loosely based on the passive pink theory (discussed in chapter 3); this color has had an immediate calming effect on agitated children in correctional facilities. A blue-green color palette is often favored for adult areas because these colors are considered tranquil, they do

9-5 *Dining room offers residents serene views of nature; The McDonald Center (Chemical Dependency Recovery Hospital), Scripps Memorial Hospital (La Jolla, CA)*
Architect: Brown Leary; Interior design: Jain Malkin Inc.; Photographer: Michael Denny

9-6 *Upbeat dining facility in this chemical dependency recovery hospital resembles a bistro or cafe; Beech Hill Hospital (Dublin, NH)*
Architecture and interior design: DeGiorgio Associates Inc.; Photographer: Robert E. Mikrut

not advance toward the individual as do warm colors, and they are thought to provide a good background for reflection and concentration. CareUnit of Coral Springs, in its tropical setting, uses a refreshing cool palette of colors: peach, green, and lavender (Fig. 9-3).

Flooring. Detoxification is a medical function that is typically carried out in a room with a standard hospital bed and typical patient room lighting. Detox rooms usually have hard-surface flooring. Patient bedrooms should be carpeted.

Corridors, group therapy rooms, and other areas may be carpeted with a commercial carpet that provides little resistance to carts or unsteady feet.

Walls. Vinyl wallcovering or polyolefin fabric (Tek-Wall) is desirable in all patient or visitor areas if the budget permits. The texture of wall coverings enhances the hotel ambience and makes people forget they are in a hospital. In corridors, a heavily textured vinyl is recommended because it tends to withstand more punishment than a smooth one.

Furniture. Stress associated with treatment and the accompanying emotional turmoil cause residents to be hard on furniture. They may even be unaware of minor destructive acts such as absentmindedly picking on the seam of a chair until the fabric is worn away. In a group therapy room, men sometimes rock back on chairs and stress the rear legs and frames; chairs must be sturdy with glued and doweled or rabbeted joints. A chair with bentwood frame or laminated layers of wood holds up well under these circumstances because the frame is prestressed.

In patient lounges solid hardwood frames (usually oak) are appropriate because of their durability and resistance to carving or surface scratching. Wood frames are preferable to chrome or powder-coated paint finishes because of the ''warmth'' and homey character of wood. Patients relate well to it.

Tables in patient areas should have plastic laminate or other durable tops. Cigarette burns are a major problem in this type of facility because many people smoke: it is a way of relieving tension or substituting a lesser dependency for a fatally serious one.

Patient Rooms. Dormitory-type furniture works well here (Fig. 9-7). Solid hardwood frames with plastic laminate inset tops for casegoods, and beds with pullout storage drawers underneath, are suitable. Beds should be arranged in the room to afford each resident maximum privacy. (Refer to the semiprivate room layout at the Menninger Foundation described in chapter 11.) Bedspreads ought to be provided, and an attractive upholstered headboard is a nice detail if the budget permits. Overhead lighting is unnecessary. Table lamps on the

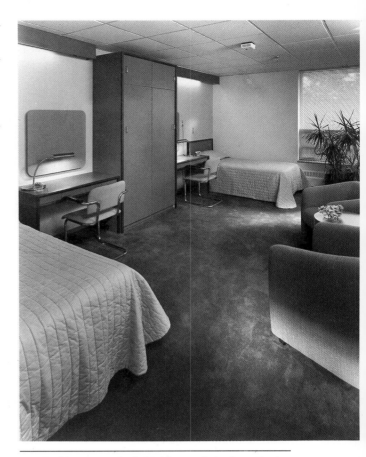

9-7 *Residents' room is divided by wardrobe closet; Beech Hill Hospital (Dublin, NH)*
Architecture and interior design: DeGiorgio Associates Inc.; Photographer: Robert E. Mikrut

nightstand and on the desk are more intimate and more residential. The room needs twin beds, nightstands, wardrobes, desks, tackboards, and possibly a bookshelf.

Upholstery. Fabric, not vinyl, should be used in all areas except in detox rooms or lounges in the detox wing.

Artwork. CDRH presents a number of interesting opportunities for ''relevant'' art based on treatment therapies. The twelve steps, for example, are familiar and meaningful to anyone undergoing treatment, and the concept lends itself well to graphic expression.

PSYCHOLOGICAL FACTORS

Tranquillity is important so that the environment does not compete with the treatment program, distract the resident from dealing with emotional issues, or prevent the type of inner reflection necessary for recovery. Although social interaction is a major focus, personal territory must be well defined in each patient room. The support of family, friends, and counselors is critical to the recovery process. Patients often suffer from low self-esteem and need to learn to love themselves and to trust others. Treatment activities may involve trust walks in which two residents are paired: one is blindfolded and has to rely on the sighted partner for direction and care.

SPECIAL ISSUES

Intervention is a technique used to encourage the substance abuser to seek treatment. Therapists assist the process as a coach would to help the family confront the person to break through the denial and, hopefully, to seek help.

Confidentiality is of prime importance in a substance abuse facility; residents might include celebrities, government officials, physicians, or others for whom public awareness of their addiction might compromise public trust, threaten job security, or embarrass family members. Security is important in an adolescent facility because the institution is legally responsible for their safety, although in many facilities adolescents are in open units that, in theory, they could leave if they wished. The idea is that people must voluntarily wish to undergo treatment. In an adult facility, residents are generally assumed to be there because they have reached the depths of despair and truly want help in recovering; therefore, participation is voluntary, and residents are free to leave if they wish. Security is important, however, *within* the facility; counselors offices, nurse stations, medical records areas, staff lounges, and any other rooms patients should not enter are kept locked whenever staff are not present.

Typically, substance abuse treatment programs are highly structured with activities changing incrementally throughout the day and evening. Patients move from group therapy to family counseling sessions, individual therapy, dining, classrooms, lectures, exercise, and lounging, and they occasionally take trips in groups off campus for various types of entertainment. Observation by counselors is important throughout the day so that residents do not avoid necessary routines or linger by themselves when they should be participating in activities. Patients undergoing this type of treatment experience a great deal of anxiety, anger, and hyperactivity. Pacing and nervous habits such as tapping or picking at a piece of wallpaper can be observed.

SUMMARY

When successful, a recovery program restores confidence, self-esteem, and a reason for living. Understandably, residents often experience a deep bonding with counselors and therapists, and their gratitude to the treatment center causes many to return as volunteers who give generously of their free time to help others. Designers who have the opportunity to work on a CDRH are indeed fortunate. The treatment program embraces concepts that reach out to all who enter. The outpouring of care and concern from the staff is sincere, and their compassion is highly personal. At many facilities, everyone who works in any capacity with patients is a recovering alcoholic or addict.

Form 20 5M

THE CORONADO HOSPITAL
CORONADO, CALIFORNIA

Date........ February 21, ...194 9

Name........ Mr. James Saunders ....

For Services Rendered........ Mrs. Rose Saunders

	Balance		
Hospital Service 3¾ Days at $ 8.50		29	75
From Feb 17, 1949 To Feb 21, 1949 Incl.			
Operating Room			
Delivery Room		28	50
Laboratory Fees			
X-Ray			
Drugs and Dressings		3	60
Physio-Therapy			
Miscellaneous Baby Days		6	00
	Total	67	85
	Credits	20	00
	Due	47	85

**Weekly Payments
In Advance
Will Be Appreciated.**

**Your Check Will Be
Your Receipt.**

10-1 *Having a baby used to be so simple, as evidenced by
this hospital bill for a birth in 1949*
Courtesy Carol Saunders Lynn

chapter 10

BIRTH CENTERS: FREESTANDING AND ACUTE CARE SETTING

psychological factors

- comfort
- choice
- respect
- reassurance
- support
- education
- bonding with infant
- patient satisfaction
- access to outdoors/views

activities

- examination/preparation
- labor
- delivery
- rest/sleep
- family visiting
- dining
- waiting
- infant care

issues

- accommodation for family
- convenience
- aesthetics
- color
- storage of equipment
- access to medical gasses
- lighting
- height of casework
- noninstitutional setting
- ability to maintain/clean finishes
- security (nursery)
- environmental hazards of special care nurseries

The 1980s heralded a dramatic shift in attitude toward the birth experience. For years hospital protocols for labor and delivery disregarded the fact that birth is not an illness but a natural phenomenon. Women entering a maternity unit to give birth often found it a terrifying experience; for many it was their first encounter with a hospital. The act of becoming a patient, laboring in what was usually an ugly, clinical room with glaring fluorescent lights overhead, and being carted off to an operating room for delivery made pregnancy seem more like a disease than a joyful family experience. The first attack on the system occurred in the 1970s with alternate birth centers (ABCs). Many hospitals put in one or more ABC rooms to accommodate those who wanted to experience natural childbirth surrounded by family in a residential setting. Many of these rooms had double beds so that the husband could more easily comfort his wife and share in the experience. Obstetricians, however, often found these rooms a nuisance, and felt that their efficiency was compromised.

The next assault on the acute care maternity center came in the mid-1980s. The women's movement (women gaining confidence about making decisions and taking control), a more informed consumer (the average age of women bearing their first child has increased), greater focus on health and well-being, and the fact that women are exerting a major influence on the marketing of health care services all combined to create a favorable climate for the germination of a new approach to birth.

Much of the impetus for hospitals to change their way of doing things resulted from the competitive atmosphere hospitals found themselves in during the 1980s. Freestanding birth centers were starting to draw off a portion of that large base of insured middle-income patients who read and want to experience the newest methods (actually the oldest, in this case) of doing things. Although acute care hospitals do sometimes call their labor and delivery units *birthing centers*, technically a birth center is a nonhospital facility organized to provide family-centered maternity care for women judged to be at low risk for obstetrical complications. In 1975 the first urban birth center was established by Maternity Center Association in New York City, which developed the risk criteria, policies, and procedures for operation. Considered an alternative to conventional hospital

10-2 *Entrance to maternity unit features cathedral ceiling and residential detailing; Cottonwood Hospital Women's Center (Murray, UT)*

Architect: Kaplan McLaughlin Diaz in association with Willard C. Nelson Associates, Inc.; Interior design: Conant Associates; Photographer: © John Sutton

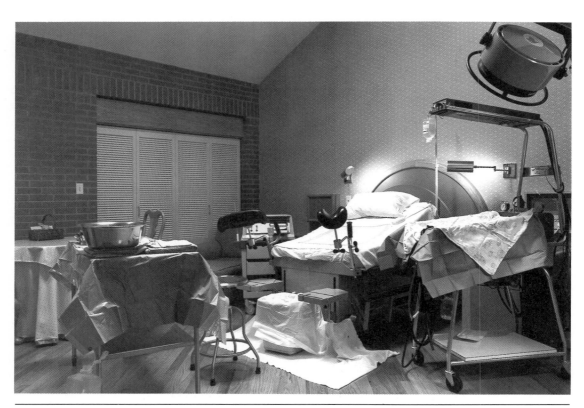

10-3 *One of the first facilities to embrace the new LDR (labor, delivery, recovery) concept of maternity care, 1984; Cottonwood Hospital Women's Center (Murray, UT)*

Architect: Kaplan McLaughlin Diaz in association with Willard C. Nelson Associates, Inc.; Interior design: Conant Associates; Photographer: © John Sutton

care, advocates of this philosophy strongly believe that achieving the same objectives within an acute care setting is difficult, if not impossible.

The first facility of this type to gain national attention for its trend-setting design was completed in 1984. Cottonwood Hospital (Intermountain Healthcare) in Murray, Utah, had patient rooms with wood floors (Fig. 10-2), nontraditional furniture for a hospital, and beautiful accessories (Fig. 10-3). This project set the theme for many that were to follow.

FREESTANDING BIRTH CENTERS

Although the purpose of this book is design, understanding the differences in philosophy between freestanding birth centers and labor and delivery units in acute care settings is important because it affects the design of these facilities. Penny Armstrong and Sheryl Feldman's *A Wise Birth: Bringing Together the Best of Natural Childbirth with Modern Medicine* (1990) explores all the issues involved: culture, psychology, technology, and economics. One of the authors is a certified nurse-midwife who worked with the Amish in Pennsylvania and delivered more than 1200 babies. Advocates of natural childbirth, they question why "women continue to be needled, tested, wired up, put on their backs, tied into stirrups, cut, and sewn" when a safer, more humane way to have babies is available.

STATISTICS

The National Birth Center Study published recently in the *New England Journal of Medicine* (Rooks, Weatherby, and Ernst 1989) studied outcomes of care in birth centers. The study was designed to respond to the recommendations of the Institute of Medicine (Committee on Assessing Alternative Birth Settings 1982) and to address the concerns of the American College of Obstetricians and Gynecologists and the American Academy of Pediatrics. The nationwide prospective descriptive study examined the labor, delivery, follow-up care, and outcomes of 11,814 women who were admitted to 84 birth centers from mid-1985 through 1987 in its first report. As a point of information, the National Association of Childbearing Centers in Perkiomenville, Pennsylvania, reports 140 free-

standing birth centers in the United States as of 1990.

- 79 percent of births in freestanding centers are attended by nurse-midwives.
- 99.4 percent of participants in the study had spontaneous vaginal deliveries; forceps were used for 0.2 percent.
- The overall rate of cesarean sections was 4.4 percent.
- No maternal deaths occurred in the study.
- Among the women 70.7 percent had no or minor complications; 7.9 percent had serious emergency complications during labor and delivery; 15.8 percent were transferred to a hospital; 2.4 percent had emergency transfers.

When compared to studies of low-risk mothers in hospitals, the study suggests that modern birth centers are safe for women who are at low risk for obstetrical complications and particularly for those who have previously had children. Benefits include lower cost and a less intimidating setting for rural patients and for certain groups of women who infrequently use health care facilities because of social or emotional barriers.

PHILOSOPHY

The professionals who establish or practice in birth centers, in or out of a hospital, believe that pregnancy and birth are natural family events. They do not accept the premise that pregnancy is an illness and birth a medical event. Therefore, the environments they create begin with the needs of women and their families. They depend on the acute care hospital obstetrics department for the high-tech medical-surgical environment required for high-risk pregnancies. A birth center is designed for primary care, whereas a hospital is designed for acute care. Hospitals, by their very nature and size, do not lend themselves to flexibility and accommodation of individual primary care needs. Patients are expected to adapt to acute care hospital protocols, not the other way around, although family-centered birth units in acute care hospitals have made considerable progress in addressing these issues.

Eunice K. M. Ernst, director of the National Association of Childbearing Centers, believes that the benefits accruing to this philosophy (fewer cesarean sections, dramatically decreased labor time, decreased use of medication during labor, increased family support, more alert babies) derive directly from the following points.

- People change the way they do things in a birth center. The mother is free to roam and find her own level of comfort. She is free to seek pain relief in a tub of warm water, take nourishment, and birth in the position most comfortable for her.
- The nurse-midwife stays close to the mother, never leaves her side during labor, and comforts and encourages her. As the time of birth approaches, the nurse-midwife calls the nurse or physician.
- After the birth, the husband and children surround the new mother and baby for family bonding. The midwife or physician hovers, always watchful and careful, but not interfering with the psychosocial dynamics. Grandparents often share in the experience to make it an extended family event.
- High-tech equipment such as electronic fetal monitoring devices are not considered appropriate or necessary for normal births (Leveno, Cunningham, and others 1986).

BENEFITS

An unpublished study by the largest freestanding birth center in the United States based on the number of births per year (985 to 1,100) has documented 7,000 admissions and noted that 37 percent of first-time mothers (who generally labor twelve to sixteen hours in a traditional setting) had significantly decreased active labor to an average of 7.5 hours due to the soothing aesthetic character of the facility, the choices offered to the laboring mother, and the total commitment and support of nursing staff to meet the mother's needs. According to Yvonne Fisher, nursing director of Mercy San Dimas Family Birth Center in Bakersfield, California, other benefits include less use of medication during labor, which tends to produce greater alertness in babies due to shorter labor time and fewer or no drugs. Families are very much part of the experience to offer comfort and support.

DESIGN CONSIDERATIONS

The use of theme rooms has been an excellent marketing tool for many birth centers. Pa-

tients understand that they may not be able to get the room of their choice when they actually go into labor, but they are encouraged to list their first, second, and third choices during a preparatory visit to the facility. Themes may include English Garden, Tropical Paradise, Gingham and Lace, and Country French (Figs. 10-4 and 10-5). Flooring, wallcoverings, window treatment, furniture, artwork, and accessories contribute to the theme of the room. An engraved brass plaque, naming the room's theme, might be affixed to the door.

Regardless of theme, wallcovering patterns must be subtle and colors soft. Primary colors are inappropriate in a birthing room because they are stimulating rather than relaxing. Yvonne Fisher attributes much of her success with reduced labor times to the use of a color she calls *French mauve*. It is a soft mauve with a hint of blue in it. She has observed it has a soothing effect on laboring women, and she carries this color into the corridors of her facility as well.

Beds used in a birthing center can be residential double beds raised to the proper height. Some nurses feel that the breakaway birthing beds commonly used in hospitals are designed to accommodate the physician, not the mother. A birthing center cares for healthy women; therefore, furniture and design can be more domestic than might be appropriate for a hospital setting and sick people.

Window treatment needs to be functional as well as decorative; darkening the room must be possible so that the mother can rest or sleep after giving birth (Fig. 10-6). Clean, simple, uncluttered design (Figs. 10-7 and 10-8) is best, but that does not mean that beautiful architectural detailing cannot be achieved (Fig. 10-9). Interesting combinations of materials might be used on the floor as in Figure 10-10, which incorporates wood with vinyl composition tile. A window seat (Fig. 10-5) can be used to store boxes of disposable diapers and other supplies, as well as the bedspread.

Theme artwork can be successfully used in a birthing center. In this facility, a carousel horse theme leads visitors from the elevators down a long corridor to the birth center. The carousel horse is used in the nursery (Fig. 10-11), silk-screened in gold on the room identification plaque (Fig. 10-12), incorporated in the hand-painted art that covers patient room medical gas panels, and used in printed materials for the center.

Some facilities like to use photographs of pregnant women, the birth experience, and new babies. As a resource, photographer Harriett Hartigan of Artemis in Stamford, Connecticut, offers for sale a selection of 10,000 photo images of pregnancy, birth, and babies catalogued on a laser disk.

10-4 *The Quilt Room is an LDRP room in a freestanding birthing center located in a medical office building, Washington Birthing Center, owned and operated by a hospital, Washington Hospital (Fremont, CA)*

Interior design: Starr Associates; Photographer: Laurie E. Dickson

10-5 *Washington Birthing Center, Washington Hospital (Fremont, CA)*

Interior design: Starr Associates; Photographer: Laurie E. Dickson

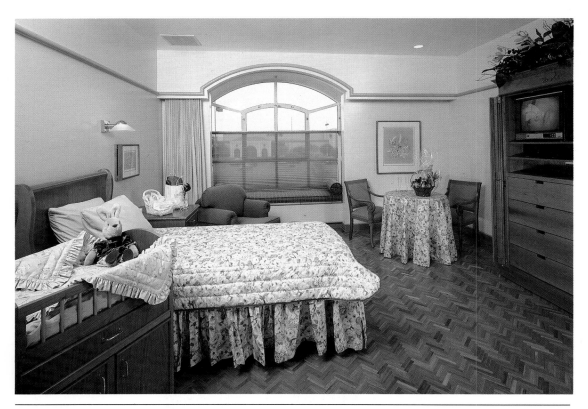

10-6 *LDRP room (labor, delivery, recovery, postpartum) features hardwood floor, built-in window seat, slot to conceal drapery header, and residential furnishings; Women's Center, Saddleback Memorial Medical Center (Laguna Hills, CA)*

Architect: The NBBJ Group in association with Benson Architectural Group; Interior design: The Design & Marketing Group (formerly Conant Associates); Photographer: Vincent Limongelli

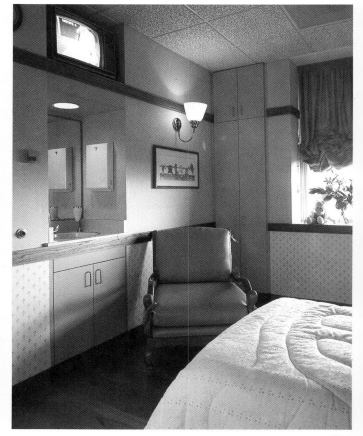

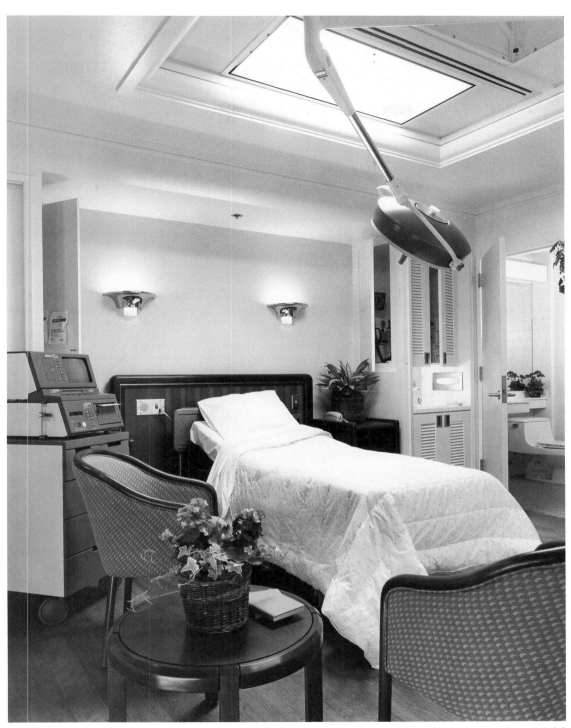

10-9

10-7 *LDR (labor, delivery, recovery) room has hotel ambience; Family Life Center, St. Vincent Hospital (Indianapolis, IN)*

Architecture and interior design: Howard Needles Tammen & Bergendoff; Photographer: Wilbur Montgomery

10-8 *LDR (labor, delivery, recovery) room, part of a 20,000-square-foot obstetrical services center, Washoe Medical Center (Reno, NV)*

Architecture and interior design: Anshen + Allen; Photographer: Christopher Irion

10-9 *Sophisticated interior design for this LDR (labor, delivery, recovery) room features oak hardwood floors, soft yellow accent wall behind headboard, crisp white woodwork and trim, and mahogany headboard and furniture; The Good Samaritan Hospital of Santa Clara Valley (San Jose, CA)*

Architecture and interior design: Kaplan McLaughlin Diaz; Photographer: © John Sutton

10-10

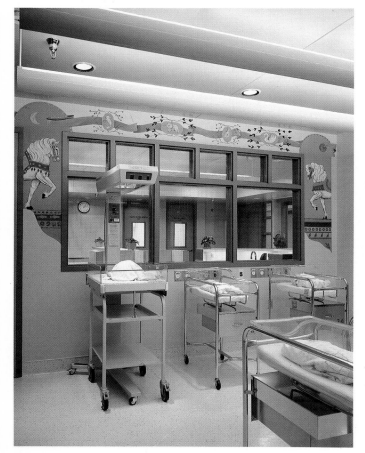

10-11

10-10 *Family waiting room features flooring design that combines Genuwood hardwood flooring and vinyl composition tile; J. M. Long Hospital's Birthing Center, University of California Medical (San Francisco, CA)*
Interior design: Blair Spangler Interior and Graphic Design; Photographer: Chas McGrath

10-11 *Level 1 normal newborn nursery features handpainted graphics with antique carousel horse theme; Mercy Hospital and Medical Center (San Diego, CA)*
Architecture: Kaplan McLaughlin Diaz; Interior design: Jain Malkin Inc.; Mural: The Aesthetics Collection; Photographer: Milroy/McAleer Photography

10-12 *Entries to postpartum patient rooms in family birth center have hospitality ambience; Mercy Hospital and Medical Center (San Diego, CA)*
Architecture: Kaplan McLaughlin Diaz; Interior design: Jain Malkin Inc.; Photographer: Milroy/McAleer Photography

HOSPITAL-BASED (ACUTE CARE) MATERNITY UNITS

For many, hospitals offer the security and reassurance they desire when giving birth. Across the nation hospitals are expanding and making labor and delivery units the centerpiece of the new building. Some create a separate entry to downplay the feeling of being admitted to a hospital. The most successful of these units (in terms of nonclinical ambience and patient satisfaction) resemble a fine hotel. From the time the elevator doors open onto the unit, expectant parents are often pleasantly surprised by what they find. Here's a typical scenario:

As the couple approaches the birth unit, they may be greeted by a smiling volunteer seated at a country French concierge desk. On the wall behind the desk is a brass plaque with a rosebud engraved in one corner and the name "The Women's Pavilion." On another wall is a graphic mural of babies' names. Opposite the mural is the nursery, which is decorated with gingham and lace. Anticipation of the big event builds.

The volunteer picks up the mother-to-be's suitcase and ushers her to a room of her choice (Fig. 10-13). Corridors have peach and gray carpeting with a rosebud design; walls have traditional wood moldings and residential wallcoverings with the texture of fabric. Wall sconces and silk plants are complemented by contemporary impressionist-style paintings.

The expectant parents enter an LDR (labor/delivery/recovery) or an LDRP (labor/delivery/recovery/postpartum) room, which is the newest thing in maternity care. Formerly a patient was moved from a labor room to an operating and delivery room, to the recovery room, and back to a patient room for postpartum care. Systems analysts came to realize that this moving took a lot of staff time each time a patient was moved and that it was potentially dangerous for some patients. In an LDRP room the patient remains in one place throughout the stay. Services and people are brought to the patient, not the other way around. Considerable costs are saved, but more important, patients receive better care. In addition, only one room, not several, needs to be cleaned. Figures 10-14, 10-15, 10-16, and 10-17 illustrate suggested room layouts.

The infant, for the most part, remains in the room with the parents so that early bonding can take place. Formerly infants were taken to a nursery where they were cared for out of view of the mother. The new way allows the nurse to care for the infant in the mother's room.

New parents enjoy a candlelight dinner served on fine china and a linen tablecloth in a special dining room (Fig. 10-18) or perhaps at a table specially set in the patient's room. An LDRP is no ordinary patient room. Typically they are large private rooms that might have hardwood floors and entire walls of functional, but elegant, built-in cabinets to house not only the patient's belongings but, more important, all of the instruments and medical equipment needed during the birth (Figs. 10-19 through 10-22). It is important psychologically that all instruments and equipment be stored out of sight so that the room does not appear threatening.

10-13 *Entry to LDR (labor, delivery, recovery) suite features wall sconce and interesting corner detail; St. Mary's Health Center (Clayton, MO)*
Architecture and interior design: The Hoffmann Partnership, Inc.; Photographer: Alise O'Brien

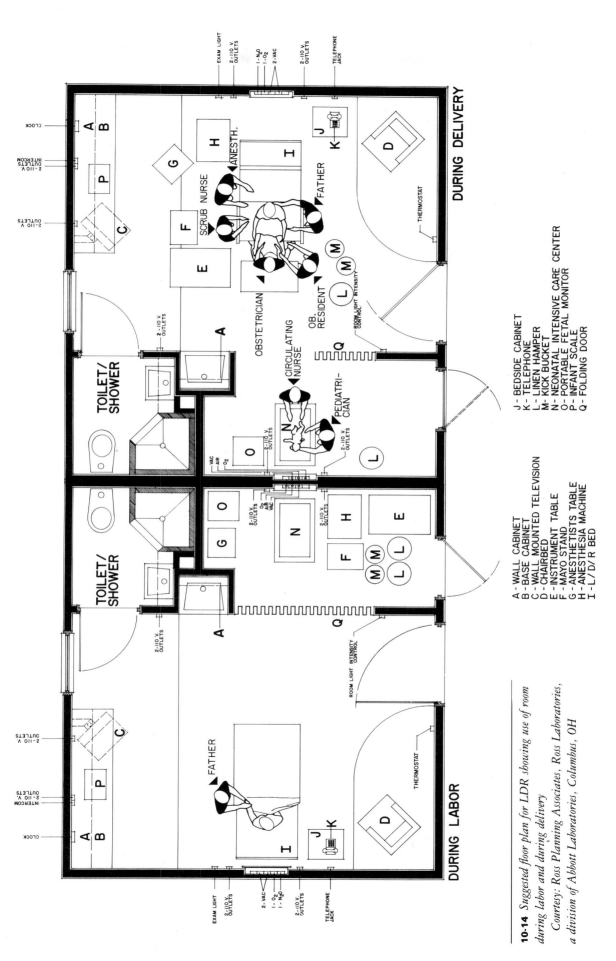

10-14 *Suggested floor plan for LDR showing use of room during labor and during delivery*

Courtesy: Ross Planning Associates, Ross Laboratories, a division of Abbott Laboratories, Columbus, OH

DURING DELIVERY

DURING LABOR

TOILET/SHOWER

TOILET/SHOWER

SCRUB NURSE

ANESTH.

FATHER

OBSTETRICIAN

OB. RESIDENT

ROOM LIGHT INTENSITY CONTROL

CIRCULATING NURSE

PEDIATRICIAN

ROOM LIGHT INTENSITY CONTROL

FATHER

A - WALL CABINET
B - BASE CABINET
C - WALL MOUNTED TELEVISION
D - CHAIRBED
E - INSTRUMENT TABLE
F - MAYO STAND
G - ANESTHETISTS TABLE
H - ANESTHESIA MACHINE
I - L/D/R BED

J - BEDSIDE CABINET
K - TELEPHONE
L - LINEN HAMPER
M - KICK BUCKET
N - NEONATAL INTENSIVE CARE CENTER
O - PORTABLE FETAL MONITOR
P - INFANT SCALE
Q - FOLDING DOOR

CLOCK
INTERCOM
2-110 V. OUTLETS
2-110 V. OUTLETS

EXAM LIGHT
2-110 V. OUTLETS
I - N₂O
I - O₂
2-VAC
2-110 V. OUTLETS
TELEPHONE JACK

THERMOSTAT

2-110 V. OUTLETS

VAC
AIR
O₂

2-110 V. OUTLETS

O₂
AIR
VAC

2-110 V. OUTLETS

CLOCK
INTERCOM
2-110 V. OUTLETS
2-110 V. OUTLETS

THERMOSTAT

EXAM LIGHT
2-VAC
I - O₂
I - N₂O
2-110 V. OUTLETS
TELEPHONE JACK

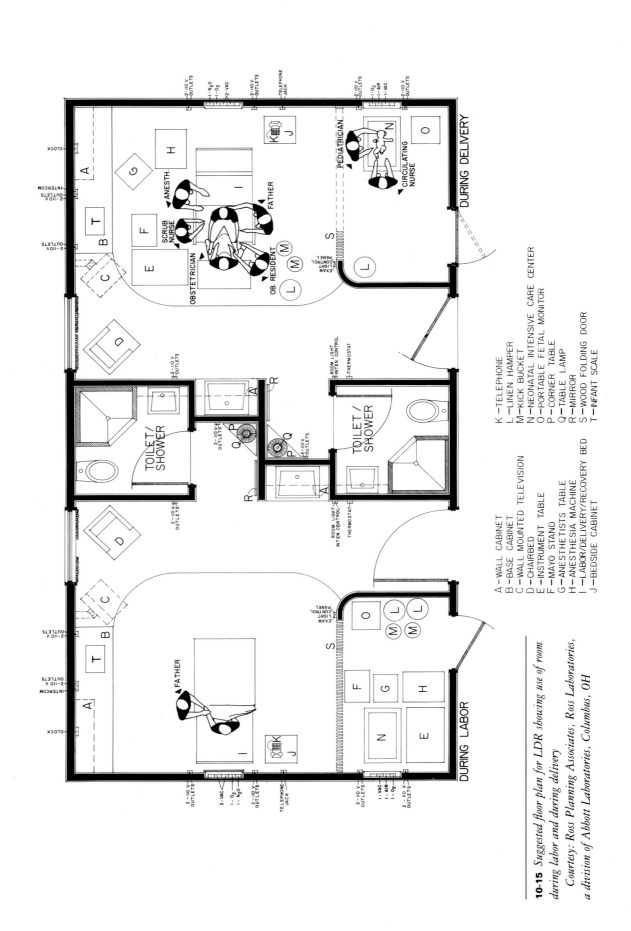

10-15 Suggested floor plan for LDR showing use of room during labor and during delivery

Courtesy: Ross Planning Associates, Ross Laboratories, a division of Abbott Laboratories, Columbus, OH

A – WALL CABINET
B – BASE CABINET
C – WALL MOUNTED TELEVISION
D – CHAIRBED
E – INSTRUMENT TABLE
F – MAYO STAND
G – ANESTHETISTS TABLE
H – ANESTHESIA MACHINE
I – LABOR/DELIVERY/RECOVERY BED
J – BEDSIDE CABINET

K – TELEPHONE
L – LINEN HAMPER
M – KICK BUCKET
N – NEONATAL INTENSIVE CARE CENTER
O – PORTABLE FETAL MONITOR
P – CORNER TABLE
Q – TABLE LAMP
R – MIRROR
S – WOOD FOLDING DOOR
T – INFANT SCALE

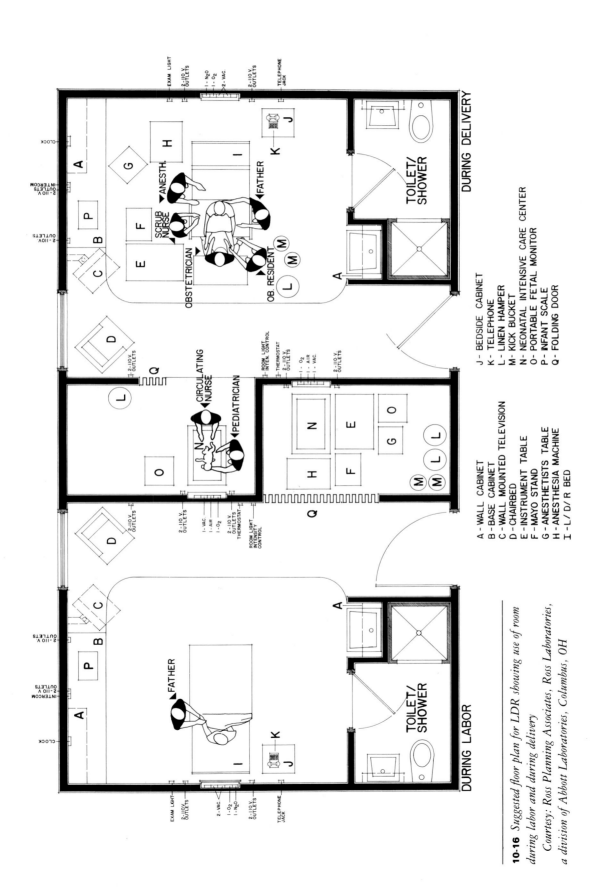

10-16 *Suggested floor plan for LDR showing use of room during labor and during delivery*

Courtesy: Ross Planning Associates, Ross Laboratories, a division of Abbott Laboratories, Columbus, OH

DURING DELIVERY

DURING LABOR

TOILET/ SHOWER

A - WALL CABINET
B - BASE CABINET
C - WALL MOUNTED TELEVISION
D - CHAIRBED
E - INSTRUMENT TABLE
F - MAYO STAND
G - ANESTHETISTS TABLE
H - ANESTHESIA MACHINE
I - L/ D/ R BED

J - BEDSIDE CABINET
K - TELEPHONE
L - LINEN HAMPER
M - KICK BUCKET
N - NEONATAL INTENSIVE CARE CENTER
O - PORTABLE FETAL MONITOR
P - INFANT SCALE
Q - FOLDING DOOR

ACCEPTABLE MINIMUM

12'-20' POST PARTUM ROOM, PLUS 6'-6' TOILET / SHOWER

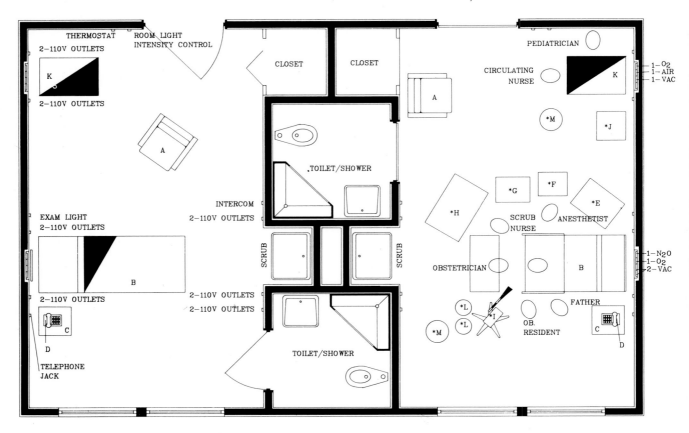

A — CHAIRBED

B — BIRTHING BED

C — NIGHTSTAND / CABINET

D — TELEPHONE

E — ANESTHESIA MACHINE

F — ANESTHETISTS TABLE

G — MAYO STAND

H — INSTRUMENT TABLE

I — PORTABLE EXAM LIGHT

J — PORTABLE FETAL MONITOR

K — INFANT WARMER

L — KICK BUCKET

M — LINEN HAMPER

* — MOVED INTO THE ROOM PRIOR TO DELIVERY

10-17 *Acceptable minimum size of postpartum room conversion to LDR room*
   Courtesy: Ross Planning Associates, Ross Laboratories, a division of Abbott Laboratories, Columbus, OH

10-19 *LDRP (labor, delivery, recovery, postpartum) features wood floor and headwall, an armoire housing a television, a table where parents can share a celebratory dinner, private balcony, and private bathroom with hydrotherapy tub; Women's Center, Grossmont District Hospital (La Mesa, CA)*
   Architect: The Design Partnership, in association with Lennon Associates; Interior design: Interspec; Photographer: Owen McGoldrick

10-18 *The Stork Club dining room for new parents,*
Washoe Medical Center (Reno, NV)

Architecture and interior design: Anshen + Allen;
Photographer: Christopher Irion

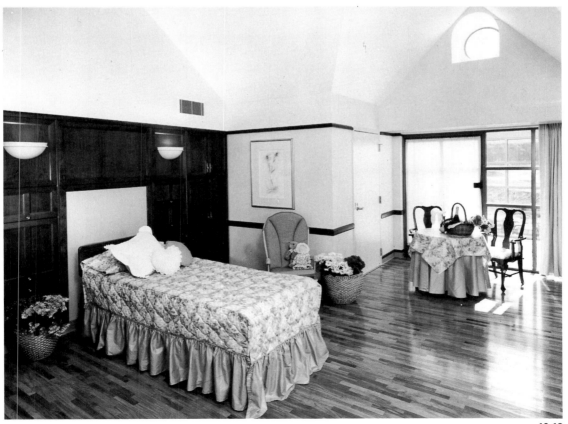

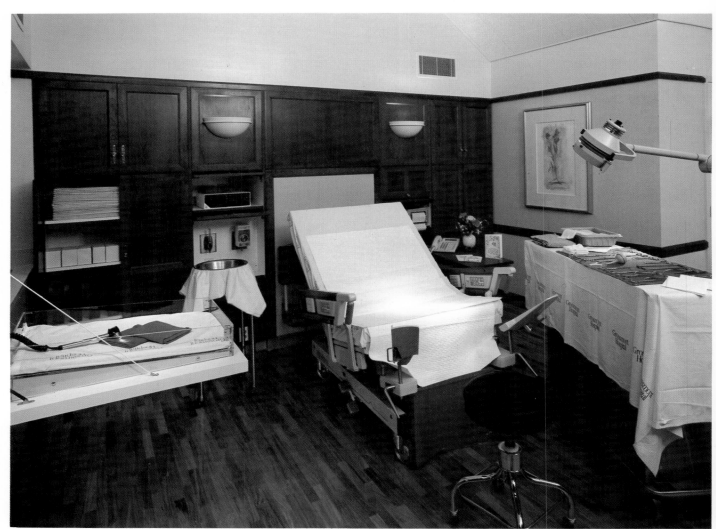

10-20

10-21

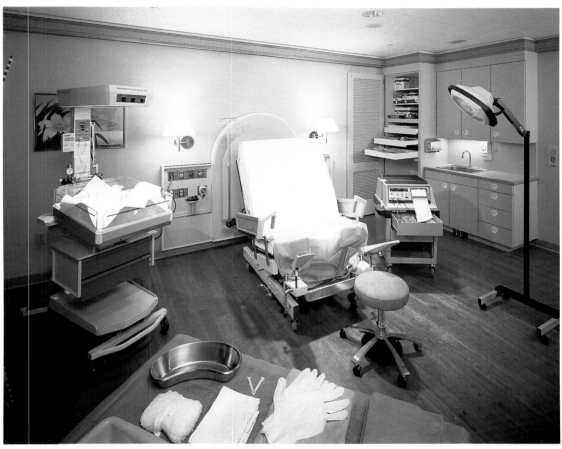

10-22

10-20 *LDRP room set up for delivery, Women's Center, Grossmont District Hospital (La Mesa, CA)*

Architect: The Design Partnership, in association with Lennon Associates; Interior design: Interspec; Photographer: Owen McGoldrick

10-21 *LDRP room is residential in character and contains a wardrobe unit with built-in entertainment center, controlled from the mother's bed; side panels of headboard slide back to access medical gasses; the birth cart and other equipment are accessed from a central storage room; Pacific Presbyterian Medical Center (San Francisco, CA)*

Architecture and interior design: Stone Marraccini and Patterson, in collaboration with architect Shirley Kiyoko Osumi (furniture and furnishings); Photographer: David Wakely

10-22 *LDRP room during delivery; Built-in case work stores fetal monitor, birth packs, and other medical supplies; Pacific Presbyterian Medical Center (San Francisco, CA)*

Architecture and interior design: Stone Marraccini and Patterson, in collaboration with architect Shirley Kiyoko Osumi (furniture and furnishings); Photographer: David Wakely

Lace curtains and valances adorn windows; wallcoverings and wood moldings (Fig. 10-8) add interest and texture. The bed is a breakaway type with a custom headboard to match the room. Upon the patient's arrival, an attractive quilted bedspread and matching pillow shams are removed from the bed and stored in the cabinet (Fig. 10-5). Color-coordinated bed linens, a terrycloth robe, and a basket of toiletries may be provided.

Admittedly, upgrading a traditional maternity unit to beautifully furnished LDRP suites is an expensive venture, but hospitals in many communities have found that couples are willing to pay a surcharge to have a "catered experience" to commemorate a very special moment in their lives. In fact today expectant parents often shop hospitals in order to select one that has the program and ambience that appeals to them. Hospitals have placed a high priority on upgrading their labor and delivery units to standards set by the high-quality providers in their community and view the patient and her family as consumers.

DESIGN CONSIDERATIONS

A number of issues must be considered when planning this type of facility.

1. Although not common, for certain physiological conditions such as toxemia and preeclampsia, the environment can actually decrease symptoms. Avoidance of external stimuli and bright light reduces symptoms, which is further validation for rooms having an uncluttered appearance, soft colors, subtle wallcoverings, and soft lighting.

2. Items of furniture in the patient room may include a rocking chair and a large mirror that stands on the floor so that the mother can watch the birth. Depending on philosophy and the infant's health, the newborn might be placed in a bassinet or wooden cradle (Figs. 10-5 and 10-6) or in a temperature-controlled neonatal intensive care center (Fig. 10-23).

3. A large window seat is practical for family members, for storing equipment (Figs. 10-5 and 10-6), and for adding a residential quality to the room.

4. Medical gasses on the headwall can be camouflaged by a number of clever devices, as seen in Figures 10-6, 10-22, and 10-23. Portions of the headboard may slide toward the center of the bed and reveal medical gas connections; a piece of art with a hinged frame (with hardware to allow it to remain in the upward position when required) is another method.

5. A great deal of equipment may be stored in an LDR or LDRP room, including fetal monitor, neonatal intensive care center, sometimes a portable surgical light, ECG monitor, anesthesia machine, and sometimes an electronic vital signs monitor tied into a computer. This equipment is what advocates of natural childbirth refer to as a "high-tech delivery." Each hospital has its preference for arrangement of equipment and configuration of custom-designed storage units. Sometimes equipment is stored in a central location outside the room. Regardless of preference, the equipment must be easy to reach and close at hand; if monitors and printouts are involved, height, in terms of eye level, is very important. The staff are princi-

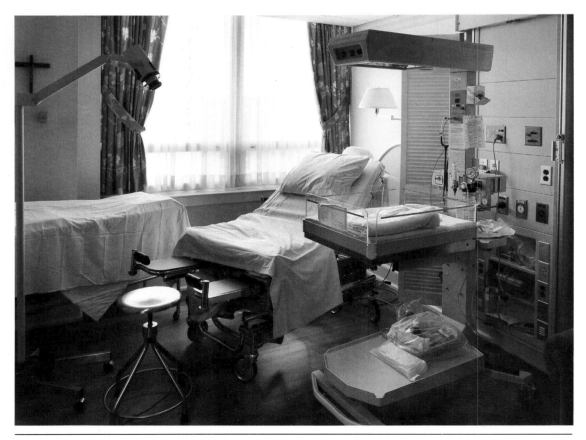

10-23 *Conversion of semiprivate room to LDRP room set up for delivery; painted wood louvered doors cover medical gasses when not in use and also enclose sink and closet; half of room is carpeted, and half has vinyl-impregnated* *hardwood flooring; Birthing Center, St. Francis Xavier Hospital (Charleston, SC)*

Architecture and interior design: Bohm-NBBJ; Photographer: Michael Houghton/STUDIOHIO

pally women, and the average height of a woman is five feet, four inches. A common complaint is that equipment, shelving, or certain pieces of case work are either above eye level or out of reach of the average woman.

6. Common planning mistakes in the LDRP room reported by a number of hospitals include:

locating the pediatrician's newborn examination area too close to the mother's bed, with all medical gas outlets on the headwall, concentrating too much activity in a small area. A better location would be on the side wall, closer to the foot of the bed.

improper location of medical gasses for newborn care. A total of three sets of gas outlets are recommended: one set on headwall and two sets on other walls for newborns (accommodates twins).

locating an armoire for the patient's wardrobe at the foot of the bed crowds the delivery team and takes up room needed for a supply cart.

failure to provide adequate lighting and ready access to examination instruments and supplies to make it easy for pediatricians to examine newborns.

7. Lighting should be varied in the patient room and nursing core (Fig. 10-24). Wall sconces flanking the bed (Figs. 10-9 and 10-21) add soft, indirect lighting and, depending upon the style, may even be adequate for reading. Ideally all lighting should be indirect with no overhead fluorescents. A surgical light for the delivery may be recessed in the ceiling over the bed (Fig. 10-9) or may be portable and stored in the closet (Fig. 10-22).

8. Aesthetic styling of the room needs to be appropriate for the community served. In rural areas a more homespun look with dark woods and patchwork quilts might be appropriate. A hospital serving a community where residents have a high level of education and income might use a sophisticated combination of architectural detailing, colors, and furnishings (Figs. 10-25, 10-26, and 10-27). The design of the bathroom is important, and some LDRP rooms include spa tubs (Figure 10-28). Knowing the average age of women bearing their first child is important. In one community it

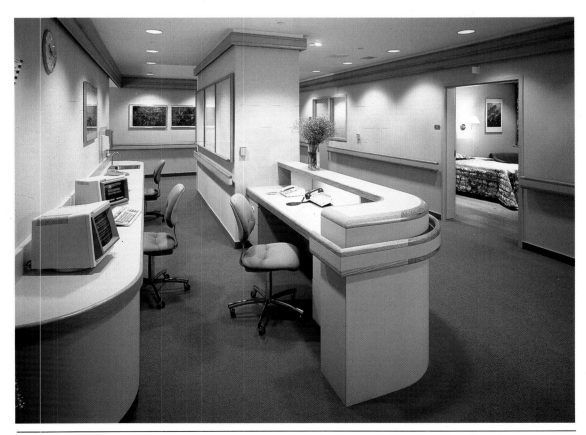

10-24 *Nurse station features oak valance and trim, warm color palette, and nonclinical ambience; Pacific Presbyterian Medical Center (San Francisco, CA)*

Architecture and interior design: Stone Marraccini and Patterson, in collaboration with architect Shirley Kiyoko Osumi (furniture and furnishings); Photographer: David Wakely

10-26 *Visitors' lobby, Solana Suites Birthing Center, The Good Samaritan Hospital of Santa Clara Valley (San Jose, CA)*

Architecture and interior design: Kaplan McLaughlin Diaz; Photographer: © John Sutton

10-25 *Expansive corridor and high ceiling give this LDRP corridor a feeling of spaciousness and elegance. Unique indirect lighting treatment creates multiple patterns of light on ceiling. Nurse station has marble tile floor and trim on desk. (LDRP rooms flank both sides of corridor.) Pale lavender and jade color palette have an ethereal feeling, both calming and restful. Women's Center, Grossmont District Hospital (La Mesa, CA).*

Architect: The Design Partnership, in association with Lennon Associates; Interior design: Interspec; Photographer: Owen McGoldrick

may be 20, whereas it may be 30 in another community where two-career households cause couples to delay starting a family until they are established in careers. Details of design and styling that might be appropriate for younger couples might not appeal to older couples. Variety is important to accommodate individual tastes.

9. Hospitals may house their birthing center in a separate building called a women's center or women's pavilion, where a full range of outpatient services are also provided. In this case the entire building might have a special ambience carried from the entry through the lobby into the outpatient clinics as well as into labor and delivery because all of the patients and many of the staff are women. In other hospitals, an entire floor might be dedicated to women's services with classrooms for prenatal counseling, a special grandparents' lounge, mammography, gift shop with specialized merchandise for newborns, and a variety of ancillary facilities so that, in terms of marketing, women come to that unit for one service and become aware of others that are available. With traditional layouts, the maternity unit is somewhat isolated from other services, and people visit it only to have a baby or to visit someone who does.

10-27 *Main lobby welcomes patients and families with architecture and interior design that resemble a fine residence or hotel; Women's Center, Grossmont District Hospital (La Mesa, CA)*

Architect: The Design Partnership, in association with Lennon Associates; Interior design: Interspec; Photographer: Owen McGoldrick

10. Birthing centers present unique opportunities for display of relevant art. As an example, a display of antique christening gowns might be recessed in a focal point wall. Hospital auxiliaries are always good resources for gathering items of this nature.

A wall graphic of babies' names may be welcomed by expectant parents.

NURSERY

Healthy neonates are kept in a normal newborn nursery (also known as a *level I* nursery) when they are not in the mother's room. Premature infants, those of low birth weight, or those who are ill are placed in a neonatal special care unit where they can be carefully observed and treated. They are referred to as a *level II* nursery for intermediate care and a *level III* nursery for intensive care.

10-28 *Tub room and spa, Women's Surgical Suite, Cottonwood Hospital Center for Women's Health (Murray, UT)*
    Interior design: Matthes Design; Photographer: Jack McManemin

NORMAL NEWBORN NURSERY

Certainly one of the most pleasant experiences is that of peering at newborn babies in the nursery. Their size, amount (or lack of) hair, and delicacy never cease to enchant and delight visitors. Placing the nursery where it is accessible to visitors is desirable, provided that window treatment, on the inside of the glass, can be controlled by nurses. A variety of vinyl-coated wallcovering borders with appropriate design motifs are available and may be used effectively in the nursery, provided they are placed at a height where color does not reflect on the newborns' skin, where they are out of the way of wall-mounted equipment and medical gas connections, and high enough not to pose sanitation problems. Handpainted murals are also appropriate (Fig. 10-11). Indirect lighting is definitely preferable to overhead fluorescents so that infants are not forced to stare at bright light. Environmental issues that need to be con-

sidered to some degree even in a normal care nursery are discussed later in this chapter.

The recent trend of mother-baby nursing (one nurse caring for both mother and baby), also known as couplet care, eliminates the need for normal newborn nurseries; only infant holding areas within the postpartum unit are needed.

NEONATAL INTENSIVE CARE UNIT (NICU)

This special care unit is for both premature and full-term newborns with a variety of medical and surgical problems requiring constant observation, care, and treatment.

Levels of Care

A maximal care (level III) nursery cares for neonates requiring constant observation, highly specialized support, and frequent medical intervention. These high-risk newborns have respiratory complications, low birth weight, or congenital disorders that require careful monitoring and care until they grow or are stabilized and moved to an intermediate or minimal care unit.

An intermediate care (level II) nursery cares for neonates whose conditions do not require intensive management but do need frequent observation or special intervention.

A minimal care (level I) nursery cares for neonates who are convalescing from medical management or intervention at the maximal or intermediate care levels (Ross Planning Associates 1977 and 1988).

Infants are hooked up to a great deal of equipment in an NICU. These monitor leads restrict their movement. Electronic monitors are diagnostic equipment to track and record variations in body functions (heart function, blood pressure, and apnea respiration). Life-support equipment principally consists of respirators and oxyhoods.

ENVIRONMENTAL HAZARDS

So much attention is focused on engineering issues (monitors, life-support systems, HVAC) and physical aspects of patient care that sometimes the psychosocial needs of infants, family, and staff are not adequately anticipated or met. That neonates sometimes must be hospitalized when vital bonding relationships with parents should be taking place is a tragedy. Coupled with the loss of parental intimacy and the serenity that most infants enjoy when they are brought home from the hospital, the infant in an NICU is subjected to a number of extremely severe environmental hazards. Numerous studies have been done to determine the infant's sensory experience in an intensive care unit with regard to possible long-term negative effects, such as hearing loss and visual impairment.

Premature infants have stages of development that are affected by the NICU environment. The first developmental task of immature infants is stabilization of their physiology—heart rate, blood pressure, respiration, temperature, gastrointestinal function. Because these infants were not yet ready to live outside the uterus, they have trouble integrating their physiological functions. Noise and interruption of circadian rhythms can impede the infants' progress (Graven 1987).

What makes this issue so critical for the 1990s is that babies of very low birth weight—700 grams—can now be saved, but they have to spend 90 days or more of important developmental time in an NICU. Neonatologists worried less about the NICU environment when infants typically spent ten days there. Judging by the number of clinical papers on this subject,

however, they are worried now. The potential problems are many.

Sensory Overload

Lack of sensory stimulation is never a problem in an NICU. Although these infants receive plenty of visual, auditory, and tactile stimulation, the problem is that it is not well coordinated or integrated, and little night-day rhythmic change occurs (Gottfried and others as reported in Olds and Daniel 1987).

Visual Distortion

Major problems in an NICU include acoustical and visual distortions that occur due to incubators and oxyhoods (Jones as reported in Olds and Daniel 1987). They are compounded by the perceptual and cognitive distortions that result from anesthesia and administration of drugs.

One researcher reports that an infant looking through the plastic angle of an isolette may see an adult as having two noses or four eyes. Babies cannot see through misted plastic and cannot bring their hands to their mouths for exploration or self-comfort. He notes that this period is the beginning of the neonate's self-image, but it is distorted (Jones as reported in Olds and Daniel 1987).

Acoustics

Noise level is probably the biggest problem in an NICU. It is as stressful to staff as it is to infants, but staff can leave the room periodically or develop coping mechanisms that infants cannot. Staff, of course, must be able to hear monitors and life-support equipment, but the constant percussive noises from respirators combined with the high-pitched beeping of monitors create quite a din.

Noise Levels

In one study noise levels were measured in infant incubators, the recovery room, and two rooms of an acute care unit. The average noise levels were:

Incubators:	57.7 dB (A) and 74.5 dB (linear)
Patients' heads:	65.6 dB (A) and 80.0 dB (linear)
Recovery room:	57.2 dB (A) and 69.8 dB (linear)
Acute care room #1:	60.1 dB (A) and 73.3 dB (linear)

Acute care room #2:   55.8 dB (A) and
                       68.1 dB (linear)

The researchers concluded that

> On the basis of present knowledge of physiologic effects of noise, the noise levels measured probably stimulate the hypophysealadrenocortical [pituitary—adrenal gland] axis of patients, exceed the noise threshold for peripheral vasoconstriction [constriction of blood vessels], pose a threat to hearing and to patients receiving aminoglycosidic [certain types of] antibiotics, and are incompatible with sleep. (Falk and Woods as reported in Olds and Daniel 1987)

One study documented that the typical NICU was as noisy as the hospital's boiler room, 24 hours a day. Another study of NICUs found sound levels averaging between 70 and 80 decibels, comparable to light auto traffic or the sound of large machinery. The acoustic environment was characterized by high intensities and low frequencies with little diurnal rhythm—a cacophony of sound. Inside the incubators, light and sound levels were high enough to be potentially hazardous (Gottfried et al., as reported in Olds and Daniel 1987).

Incubator or tent therapy modifies sound. Inside the chamber the sound level, especially certain pitches, is higher as it reverberates. Voices may be distorted. One study recorded samples of sound inside infant oxygen tents and incubators and determined that masking of outside sounds occurs when background sounds inside the incubator measured 80 dB. Additionally, the incubator accentuates certain sounds made by the infant through reverberation inside the chamber. The oxygen tent itself provides loud, random, self-generated sound (League et al., as reported in Olds and Daniel).

Noise inside the isolette is increased dramatically by sudden impact—the shutting of the door or kicking of the incubator—to levels of 140 to 150 decibels, which often causes the baby to mottle. After a while, the baby tunes out sounds, including the quiet voices of the parents; then parents worry that the baby is unresponsive or cannot hear.

Physiological Effects of Noise. Long-term studies of neonates that follow them for the first ten years of their lives might be valuable to see

if permanent impairment results from these environmental hazards. A number of researchers have noted that incubators and oxyhoods place infants at risk for hearing or language impairments, but follow-up studies on those same infants are needed to document these suppositions. One researcher has noted that the oxyhood creates a barrier between the head and body that causes acoustical distortions likened to the echoes experienced in a mosaic-tiled dome (Jones as reported in Olds and Daniel 1987).

The American Academy of Pediatrics Committee on Environmental Hazards, in reviewing literature on noise hazards in an NICU, states that incubators operate at between 50 and 86 decibels (linear) with increases up to 90 or 100 decibels from slamming of incubator doors and infant crying. Noise in incubators and recovery rooms exceeds the level at which changes in heart rate and peripheral vasoconstriction occur. Their hypothesis is that long-term exposure to incubator noise may impair speech and language development. The American Academy of Pediatrics suggests that manufacturers of incubators reduce motor noise level as much as possible, that physicians limit use of ototoxic drugs (drugs affecting hearing and balance), and that hospital staff eliminate unnecessary noise such as loud radios (Committee on Environmental Hazards, 1974, as reported in Olds and Daniel 1987). Other studies deal with the interaction of noise and drugs and the relationships between noise and sleep and between noise and blood pressure.

Suggestions for Reducing Noise. Designers should investigate the use of sound-absorbing construction materials and possibly consult an acoustics engineer to determine how surfaces of the room can be manipulated to absorb sound, reduce reverberation, isolate vibration, shield equipment to reduce noise transmission, and eliminate structural vibration (see Flynn, Segil, Steffy 1988). The level II special care nursery in Figure 10-29 uses carpet to absorb noise, although it should be noted that codes often forbid this, causing the architect to apply for a waiver to make it happen.

Lighting
Many NICUs have glaring overhead fluorescent fixtures as the sole source of light. In many fa-

10-29 *Neonatal intensive care unit incorporates special design features (lighting and acoustics) that eliminate environmental stress on neonates; Women's Center, Grossmont District Hospital (La Mesa, CA)*
  Architect: The Design Partnership, in association with Lennon Associates; Interior design: Interspec; Photographer: Owen McGoldrick

cilities it cannot be modulated by dimmers or switching, and infants lying on their backs are forced to stare at high levels of brightness. Babies under intensive light 24 hours a day do not track objects with their eyes, which can retard infant-mother bonding. Because a high level of light is needed for attending to the infants, this problem has no easy solution or quick fix, although indirect lighting (pendant or stem-mounted fluorescents that direct light at the ceiling, which in turn bounces it in a diffused manner to the room), supplemented by high-intensity examination lights at the isolette, seems feasible (Figs. 10-29 and 10-30). One researcher reports having attempted to modulate lighting in an NICU with chaotic results. He tried to dim lights in various areas but found that several minutes later they would be turned on again while the nurse cared for an infant. Rather than provide a kind of circadian patterning, infants were instead subjected to erratic, constantly fluctuating conditions (Jones as reported in Olds and Daniel 1987).

In addition to ambient lighting, babies are exposed to high levels of supplemental lighting. The intensity under a phototherapy lamp is usually 250 to 400 footcandles. Typically a baby's

10-30 *Level 2 special care nursery features cherrywood window frames and trim to coordinate with design motif of adjacent labor and delivery unit (Figure 10-37); nursery has elevated nurse station (Figure 10-36), areas of colorful wallcovering, carpet, and special lighting; Bethesda Oak Hospital (Cincinnati, OH)*

Architecture and interior design: KZF Incorporated; Photographer: Gordon Morioka

eyes are covered during treatment, but the baby in the nearby isolette is not protected; the highly intense lighting levels are also uncomfortable for nursing staff.

Lighting Levels.　Inside the nursery a minimum of 100 maintained footcandles measured 39 inches from the floor (at the mattress level of incubator) with a maximum of 150 footcandles is recommended. Deluxe Cool White lamps are suggested (Ross Planning Associates 1988).

Lighting levels in an NICU with typical overhead fluorescents vary from 60 to 195 footcandles, according to a recent study. Babies subjected to high levels of light lost their defensive eye blink. Even shining a bright flashlight in their eyes could not elicit a reflexive blink. Two weeks were required for the defensive blink to return in babies who had been in intensive care for several months.

Color of Lighting.　Although some consultants recommend Deluxe Cool White lamps, others prefer full-spectrum fluorescent lamps. In fact, few environmental features have been studied as thoroughly as lighting, and the research has produced consistent findings: full-spectrum light is essential to physiological and psychological well-being because it affects blood pressure rates, respiration, and metabolic function (Gruson 1982; Spivack and Tamer 1981; Thorington 1973; Olds, Lewis and Joroff 1985 as reported in Olds and Daniel 1987). It is especially important for infants who are hospitalized for long periods without access to natural light.

Physiological Effects of Light.　A study comparing the typical brightly illuminated NICU with one having reduced light levels showed a higher incidence of retinal damage to premature neonates with prolonged exposure to high levels of light (Glass, Avery, and others 1985).

The monotony of lighting in most NICUs is a problem. The limited variation over a 24-hour period is compounded by the fact that some NICUs have no, or few, windows to the outdoors. The constancy of bright artificial illumination disturbs circadian rhythms. Often the color of the lamp is Cool White. One study questions whether such lighting might have adverse consequences for premature infants, as has been demonstrated with other organisms (Gottfried et al. 1981).

Layout of Unit

There are a number of theories about optimum layout for an NICU. The Ross Laboratories planning guide (1988) acquaints designers with pertinent issues. Most space plans share these common goals: to store supplies as close to the patient as possible in order to cut down travel by caregivers; to provide complete access to patient's head and neck for resuscitation; and to provide sufficient space for portable equipment and for staff in order to avoid having too much equipment and too many beds close together, causing stress.

A bassinet is 18 by 30 inches and an isolation incubator is 24 by 39 inches. Mattress height is typically 39 inches; therefore, if case work nearby has countertops at 39 inches (Fig. 10-31), nurses will have a work surface at a convenient height for working in the isolette. The

stress on caregivers in an NICU is a very important consideration. If environmental factors such as lighting, noise, temperature, humidity, and color can be balanced and appropriate, then nursing staff will experience less stress and will not have to fight the environment in order to do their jobs. Burnout is a problem for NICU nurses. Anything that can be done in the design of the unit to relieve their stress or improve morale is worthwhile. Views of the outdoors (plants and trees, not just sky) would be desirable, but their placement must be carefully considered because windows can draw heat away from a baby's body.

The hexagonal pinwheel island concept (Fig. 10-32) is designed for maximal care nursing. It provides all life-support, monitoring, supplies, and individual nursing services for six infants, arranged in radiating wings around a lazy Susan supply tray. Removable exchange tray inserts are replaced on a regular basis; space below the counter level is devoted to disposal of waste and soiled materials. Headwalls have piped services, monitor stand, and pole for

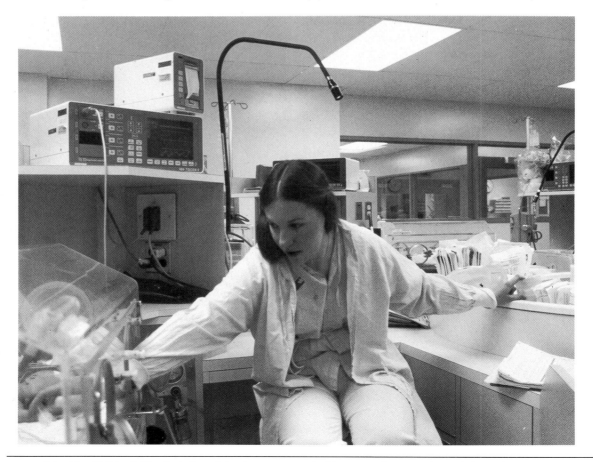

10-31 *Schneider Children's Hospital, Long Island Jewish–Hillside Medical Center (New Hyde Park, NY)*   *Architecture and interior design: The Architects Collaborative; Photographer: © Peter Aaron/Esto*

mounting IV or other equipment. Everything is within arm's reach (Fig. 10-31). Placement and visibility of physiological monitors is an important feature of this design. One nurse can see all six monitors and infants simultaneously and can respond quickly to an infant in distress without resorting to audible or illuminated warnings.

The overall benefits of this design are better organization of life-support systems to minimize clutter, a one-to-one nursing ratio, open visibility, and a reduction in stress for staff and neonates. This 6-bed unit is part of a 40-bed neonatal unit having 18 maximum care stations (three hexagonal pinwheel islands) arranged in three separate rooms for infection control and reduction of noise levels. Figures 10-33, 10-34, and 10-35 show a similar concept. Each of the island units provides care for four isolettes (Fig. 10-34) and allows for maximum visibility. The rotating centerpiece of the island is stocked with medical supplies.

Color

Color is a very important aspect of an NICU; for fear of using the wrong colors, too often practitioners avoid it altogether. Color must be handled very carefully if it is placed near infants because it will reflect on their skin and make observation of conditions such as cyanosis and jaundice difficult. For this reason, yellow should never be used in a nursery, and blue, although a calming and relaxing color, would also be unsuitable. Being able to detect subtle changes in the infant's skin color is important. Wallcovering borders or areas of color may be effectively used at a height where they are not apt to cause

10-32 *Custom-designed six-bassinet neonatal intensive care unit featuring central carousel for supplies, Schneider Children's Hospital, Long Island Jewish–Hillside Medical Center (New Hyde Park, NY) Architect: The Architects Collaborative*

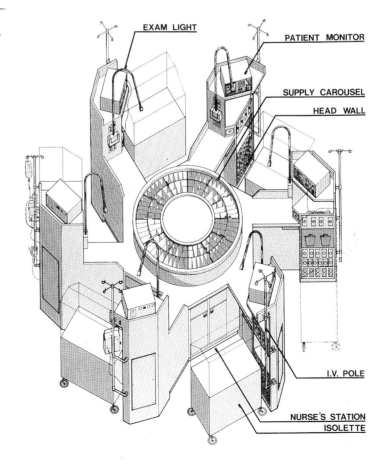

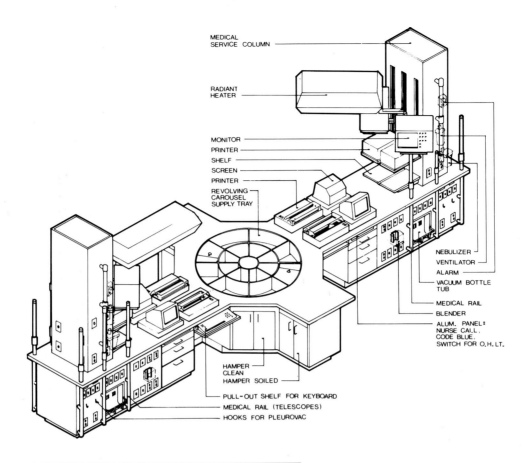

MEDICAL
SERVICE COLUMN

RADIANT
HEATER

MONITOR
PRINTER
SHELF
SCREEN
PRINTER
REVOLVING
CAROUSEL
SUPPLY TRAY

NEBULIZER
VENTILATOR
ALARM
VACUUM BOTTLE
TUB
MEDICAL RAIL
BLENDER
ALUM. PANEL:
NURSE CALL,
CODE BLUE,
SWITCH FOR O.H. LT.

HAMPER
CLEAN
HAMPER SOILED

PULL-OUT SHELF FOR KEYBOARD
MEDICAL RAIL (TELESCOPES)
HOOKS FOR PLEUROVAC

10-33 *Custom-designed case work for neonatal special care unit has lazy Susan feature for disposable supplies; Newark Beth Israel Medical Center (Newark, NJ)*
   Architect: Gonchor & Sput

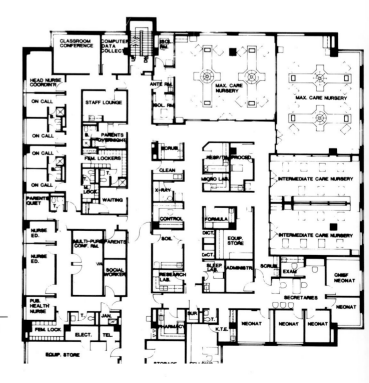

10-34 *Floor plan of neonatal special care unit, Newark Beth Israel Medical Center (Newark, NJ)*
   Architect: Gonchor & Sput

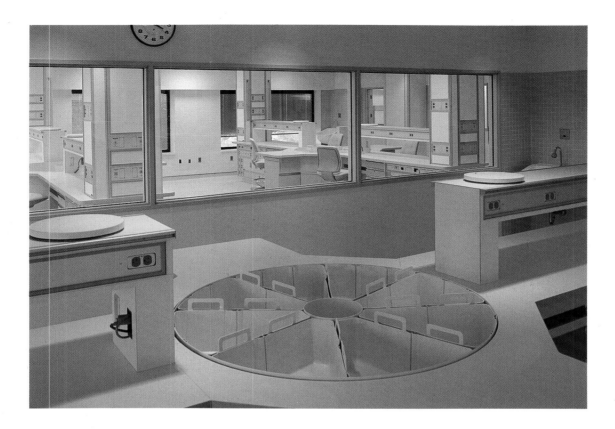

10-35 *Neonatal special care units provide maximum visibility and specially designed treatment islands; Newark Beth Israel Medical Center (Newark, NJ) Architect: Gonchor & Sput; Interior design: RHD Interior Design; Photographer: David Anderson*

a problem (Fig. 10-34). The combined effects of room colors, plus the color temperature of the fluorescent lamp and its reflection on the baby's skin, must be considered.

Two schools of thought have developed with respect to an appropriate color palette for an NICU. Some believe a relaxing, cool palette of blues and greens to be most appropriate in high-stress environments, but sometimes caregivers request a palette of stimulating warm colors in order to keep them pepped up and alert.

Aesthetics

An odd combination of starkness and clutter is often apparent in an NICU. Carts, wires, and tubes are everywhere, and color is often totally lacking. Wood trim can provide a nice contrast to high-tech equipment (Figs. 10-30 and 10-36). Patterns in flooring material can be effectively used, provided they do not offer a figure-ground reversal or visual rhythm that may be tiring on the eyes. Seamless flooring seems to be the

preferred material in an NICU, and several colors of a pattern can be combined with either heat-welded or chemically welded seams to produce an interesting design. A wallpaper border around the ceiling of the room would add color, as would curtains on windows. Adjustable-height stools should be provided so that parents can sit at the height of the isolette portholes. In intermediate and minimal care units, rocking chairs enable parents and nurses to cuddle infants. The height and type of arm on rocking chairs are critical for comfort in cuddling and feeding.

Note the excellent use of wood, carpet insets, variety of indirect lighting sources, sandblasted glass design, and coffered ceiling in the special care nursery in Figures 10-37 and 10-38.

Accommodation for Family

Parents want to be involved in caring for their babies. When they cannot be in the NICU, they need a lounge with phones, bathrooms, vending machines, a place to store a coat or handbag, and overnight sleeping accommodations either in guest bedrooms (Fig. 5-4) or perhaps in lounge chairs that convert to beds. Breastfeeding rooms off the nursery offer privacy. A

visiting room for siblings may be provided near the minimal risk area of the NICU, and a grieving room or meditation room may be provided near the high-risk or maximal care area.

Security

Security is a very important planning and design issue in nurseries because infant thefts continue to rise.

SUMMARY

Many benefits can be derived from reducing environmental hazards inherent in special care nurseries. Infants in quieter environments grow faster, have less hearing loss, and are able to sleep more soundly, which is thought to reduce the occurrence of apnea (temporary cessation of breathing). Under lower levels of lighting, babies are more likely to open their eyes and look around, spend more time in a stabilized state, experience quieter sleep, and have less risk of developing retinopathy.

10-36 *Elevated nurse station in special care nursery, Bethesda Oak Hospital (Cincinnati, OH)*
  Architecture and interior design: KZF Incorporated; Photographer: Gordon Morioka

10-37 *Nurse station and window frames feature cherry wood to create a hospitality ambience; Family Centered Maternity Care, Bethesda Oak Hospital (Cincinnati)*

Architecture and interior design: KZF Incorporated; Photographer: Gordon Morioka

10-38 Young Wings, *a commissioned work of etched art glass, highlights the entry to the special care nursery, as do the vaulted ceiling and special lighting; Family Centered Maternity Care, Bethesda Oak Hospital (Cincinnati, OH)*

Architecture and interior design: KZF Incorporated; Photographer: Gordon Morioka

REFERENCES

Alpern, Barbara. 1987. *Reaching Women: The Way to Go in Marketing Healthcare Services.* Chicago: Pluribus Press Inc.

Armstrong, Penny, and Sheryl Feldman. 1990. *A Wise Birth: Bringing Together the Best of Natural Childbirth with Modern Medicine.* New York: William Morrow.

Committee on Assessing Alternative Birth Settings, Institute of Medicine. 1982. *Research Issues in the Assessment of Birth Settings: Report of a Study.* Washington, DC: National Academy Press.

Committee on Environmental Hazards, American Academy of Pediatrics. 1974. Noise pollution: Neonatal aspects. *Pediatrics* 54(4):476–79.

Falk, S. A., and N. F. Woods. 1973. Hospital noise levels and potential health hazards. *New England Journal of Medicine* 289(15):774–81.

Flynn, J., A. Segil, and G. Steffy. 1988. *Architectural Interior Systems: Lighting/Acoustics/Air Conditioning,* ed. 2, New York: Van Nostrand Reinhold Co., Inc.

Glass, Penny. 1987. The effects of lighting on the premature infant. In *Perspectives in NICU Planning.* Columbus, OH: Ross Laboratories, pp. 50–55.

Glass, P., G. B. Avery, and others. 1985. The effect of bright light in the hospital nursery on the incidence of retinopathy of prematurity. *New England Journal of Medicine* 313(7):401–4.

Gottfried, A. W., P. Wallace-Lande, S. Sherman-Brown, and others. 1981. Physical and social environment of newborn infants in special care units. *Science* 214(4521):673–75.

Graven, Stanley. 1987. Impact of the environment on development. In *Perspectives in NICU Planning.* Columbus, OH: Ross Laboratories, pp. 9–15.

Jones, C. L. 1979. Criteria for evaluating infant environments in hospitals. *Journal of the Association for the Care of Children in Hospitals* 7(4):3–11.

League, R., J. Parker, and others. 1972. Acoustical environments in incubators and infant oxygen tents. *Preventive Medicine* 1(1–2):231–39.

Leveno, K., F. Cunningham, and others. 1986. A prospective comparison of selective and universal electronic fetal monitoring in 34,995 pregnancies. *New England Journal of Medicine* 315(10):615–19.

Littlefield, V. M., and B. N. Adams. 1987. Patient participation in alternative perinatal care: Impact on satisfaction and health locus of control. *Research in Nursing and Health* 10:139–48.

Malkin, J. 1987. The changing interior design of hospitals. *California Hospitals* 4:12–17.

———. 1987. Women's health centers: a sign of the times for gender-specific needs. *Designers West* June:144, 145, 200.

Olds, Anita, and Patricia Daniel. 1987. *Child Health Care Facilities: Design Guidelines and Literature Outline.* Bethesda, MD: Association for the Care of Children's Health.

Peterson, Kristine. 1988. *The Strategic Approach to Quality Service in Health Care.* Rockville, MD: Aspen Publishers, Inc.

Rooks, J., N. Weatherby, E. Ernst, and others. 1989. Outcomes of care in birth centers: The national birth center study. *New England Journal of Medicine* 321(26):1804–11.

Ross Planning Associates. 1988. *Planning and Design for Perinatal and Pediatric Facilities.* Columbus, OH: Ross Laboratories.

chapter 11

PSYCHIATRIC FACILITIES

Demand for mental health services has increased explosively in recent years. As the stigma associated with the treatment of mental disorders has declined, more individuals are seeking help to deal with problems associated with family, job, or the stresses of contemporary living. Looking at statistics, the growth in this market segment has been astonishing. Between 1971 and 1977, psychiatric bed capacity in general acute care hospitals increased by 23 percent. In the following three years, the rate doubled (Mills 1984). A survey of companies having more than 5000 employees found that the cost of mental health benefits rose 47 percent in 1989, causing experts to forecast that mental health coverage in 1990 accounted for a third or more of employee health insurance premiums (Williams 1990). Rapid growth seems to have created a state of chaos among health care providers who are struggling to develop effective treatment protocols within the parameters of unstable and poorly defined reimbursement policies.

This chapter acquaints readers with the historical events leading up to the current state of affairs, explains how design can support therapy goals, introduces research, and presents design guidelines. The treatment environment is important not only for the patient but also for optimum performance of staff, physicians, and allied health professionals. The interior design of the setting expresses to the general public, spouses, and parents of children and adolescents the attitude the mental health facility has toward their family member.

HISTORICAL CONTEXT

The Community Mental Health Centers Act of 1963 resulted in the deinstitutionalization of a large population of mentally ill patients. The concept that sparked a revolution in psychiatric care was the idea that psychiatric patients should be treated in their home communities rather than in large state institutions, where they developed "institutionalized" behaviors as a result of being isolated from family, friends, and the community. Although well intended, this act failed because funding never followed the patient back into the community. The federal government made available monies referred to as Hill-Burton funds to be used for building new psychiatric facilities. The loan was then repaid by providing free care to indigent patients who were being returned to the community. Unfortunately, care was never provided to the patient population that the act intended to serve. This system failure resulted in people with severe mental illness wandering the streets or living in substandard housing and subsisting at the lowest poverty levels. This situation remains with us today in our homeless population, which is said to consist of 30 to 50 percent mentally ill individuals who are unable to get adequate psychiatric treatment.

Deinstitutionalization (discharge of large numbers of mentally ill from state institutions) released into the community many individuals who require considerable aftercare as well as treatment for occasional acute psychotic episodes (Friedman 1981). For years the mentally ill were warehoused in state institutions where they received custodial care. The lack of humanity in the design of these buildings invited study and criticism by social scientists, behaviorists, and cultural anthropologists, most notably Robert Sommer, Erving Goffman (1961), and Edward T. Hall. Hideous descriptions of what Sommer refers to as "hard architecture" abound in this literature: "A Kafka-like atmosphere compounded of naked electric lights, echoing corridors, and walls encrusted with the paint of decades, and the stale air of rooms shut up too long" (Sykes as reported in Sommer 1974). Many of these studies were done in the 1960s and 1970s, during which time a condition called *institutionalization* was recognized. It is a process by which institutionalized individuals acquire a reduced capacity for independent thought and action as they succumb to the isolation and routine imposed by their custodial care. Instead of rehabilitating patients, the institution made them increasingly less able to survive on their own.

One of the most common problems noted by these researchers was stimulus deprivation, which was caused by the bleak, colorless environment surrounding patients. As further evidence of this condition, a study of color preferences of mental patients revealed that short-stay patients preferred long-wavelength colors (red and yellows), whereas short-wavelength colors (blues and greens) were more popular with long-stay patients; the senses seem to be deadened by prolonged stays in institutions (Katz as reported in Sommer 1974).

COMMUNITY-BASED CARE

One aspect of the 1963 act dealt with Medicaid funding. It stipulated that Medicaid funds would pay for treatment of psychiatric patients between the ages of 21 and 62 years, provided patients were treated in general acute care hospitals; Medicaid would not fund the care of these patients in freestanding psychiatric facilities. This funding mechanism was structured in this fashion to ensure that patients being pushed back into the community would be treated in a community setting. The problem, however, was inadequate funding to treat these severely ill patients. Because of the lack of funding, few general acute care hospitals created separate psychiatric units, and a portion of the returning patient population did not receive any treatment at all. No general acute care beds were available, and, ironically, these patients could not be treated in newly built freestanding psychiatric facilities.

In the late 1970s and early 1980s, with the advent of more direct competition in health care and increasing efforts to reduce health care costs, the emphasis shifted to outpatient treatment for all types of patients, thereby dramatically decreasing hospital occupancy rates. This decrease resulted in excess bed capacity. In the early 1980s the federal government's fixed fee reimbursement policies based on DRGs (diagnosis related groups) exempted distinct psychiatric units because, unlike medical diseases, mental disorders are much harder to define in terms of when a ''cure'' occurs. Administrators with excess bed capacity saw an opportunity to fill empty beds, circumvent the DRG system, and create a relatively favorable reimbursement status—thus the increase in community psychiatric beds. Between 1970 and 1986, the number of beds in state and county hospitals per 100,000 people dropped

from 207.4 to 49.7, according to the U.S. Department of Health and Human Services. Interestingly, the number of beds in private psychiatric hospitals rose by 75 percent during this period, from 7.2 to 12.6 per 100,000 people, and the number of beds in general acute care hospitals offering psychiatric services increased even more dramatically (Williams 1990).

SPECIALTY PSYCHIATRIC PROGRAMS

Continual deregulation of mental health care resulted in increased competition, which in turn led to for-profit providers having saturated the psychiatric services market. Consequently, a need arose to develop specialty psychiatric programs and create new markets. Competition and demands of third-party payers forced health care providers to develop a continuum of care that allows the patient to be treated in the most appropriate and least restrictive environment. Day treatment and outpatient programs are levels within this continuum that may be appropriate for certain patients.

Communities that had become saturated with general psychiatric and substance abuse programs provided the stimulus for health care providers to develop a number of specialty programs targeted to specific age groups (e.g., geriatrics or adolescents) or to individuals having specific disorders (e.g., obsessive-compulsive disorder, panic disorder, phobias, anorexia) as a means of carving out new market niches. Most of these programs can be handled appropriately in an outpatient setting.

Geriatric or geropsychiatric units have become increasingly common to accommodate the elderly suffering from depression, Alzheimer's disease, and other forms of dementia. Design for this patient population should incorporate guidelines from this chapter as well as those from chapter 14.

MEDICAL-BEHAVIORAL EXPLOSION

Industry analysts often speak of a medical-behavioral explosion when they refer to the great increase in demand for mental health care. The increasing awareness of the interaction between emotional and physical components of illnesses has led some to speculate that in the future a mental health clinician may be on 24-hour duty in the emergency room of many hospitals. Treatment may consist of both medical and psychobehavorial assessments. Individuals needing treatment for psychiatric or behavioral disorders are listed below:

Patients Most Likely to Need Psychiatric or Behavioral Assistance

1. Persons who have been hurt by others

   ▪ Victims of child abuse
   ▪ Persons injured by spouses or adult children
   ▪ Victims of crimes of passion; usually injured by relatives or acquaintances
   ▪ Victims of rape

2. Persons who hurt themselves

   ▪ Attempted suicides
   ▪ Drug overdosers
   ▪ Acute or chronic alcoholics

3. Persons with psychiatric disorders

   ▪ Acute: depressed patients, acting-out patients, patients with abrupt onset of bizarre or unusual behavior
   ▪ Chronic: manic-depressives, schizophrenics, patients with other recurring psychoses (usually these persons are brought to the emergency department by relatives, police or other authorities, or friends, when their bizarre, violent, or suicidal symptoms flare up)

4. Persons with stress-related illnesses

   ▪ Patients who have suffered heart attacks or other cardiac distresses
   ▪ Patients being treated for ulcers, colitis, hypertension, and so on (these persons need psychological or behavioral treatment to change habits and life-styles in order to reduce illness-provoking stress)

5. Patients vulnerable to stress due to the nature of their treatment for physical illnesses

   ▪ Amputees, recipients of organ transplants, patients on kidney dialysis, persons with terminal diseases, individuals facing major surgery

6. Persons who must modify their behavior to sustain health and prevent onset of illness

   ▪ Heavy smokers
   ▪ Obese persons
   ▪ Heavy drinkers
   ▪ Sedentary persons

7. Children in outpatient or inpatient care

   ▪ Children with emotional reactions to hospitalization
   ▪ Children with a diagnosable psychiatric disorder (As many as one in four children seen in outpatient clinics has a diagnosable psychiatric disorder. In half of these cases, the behavioral problem is the primary cause for bringing the child to the clinic. These percentages double among children admitted to inpatient care. From these figures, it is estimated that one in four hospitalized children is confined due to their behavioral disturbances.)[1]

IMAGE AND UTILIZATION

Apart from obvious benefits to patients, an attractive inpatient environment invites additional physician referrals. A psych unit in a general hospital can too easily become isolated and infrequently visited by primary care physicians. Hiding the unit in a remote area of the hospital reinforces negative images and stereotypes that limit utilization. Family members are less apprehensive about admitting a loved one to a mental health unit if the environment is residential, cheerful, and comfortable. Family and friends visit more frequently and experience less anxiety in that type of setting.

SPACE PLANNING IN SUPPORT OF THERAPY GOALS

A growing body of research supports the theory that the interior environment is richly coded with sensory cues that stimulate expected behaviors. For decades mental hospitals were designed with little regard for this concept. Typically, a program (list of rooms) was developed without a clear description of the types of behavior the room was expected to elicit. Large dayrooms offered ease of surveillance and multipurpose flexibility of use. Current thought, however, holds that large dayrooms have an inherent ambiguity that may be architecturally pathogenic for emotionally disturbed individuals who are unable to manipulate it to meet their needs.

Certainly the shift from the custodial care of state institutions to community-based programs has sparked more interest in environmental issues. Lengths of stay have been reduced, and multidisciplinary treatment—offering patients a comprehensive program of therapeutic activities provided by a team of mental health professionals including occupational therapists, social workers, and psychologists—has become the most common practice. Advances in antidepressant and antipsychotic medications, plus recent development of a myriad of other drugs, have made the management of patients considerably easier.

DEFINITION OF TERMS

Psychiatric units are often referred to as *closed* or *open*. A closed unit is locked, and patients are not able to leave. An open area is unlocked, and patients can, theoretically, leave if they wish. Swing areas are sometimes located between open and closed units. These patient rooms can add beds to either the open or closed unit, as needed, or be used for special care patients.

Electroconvulsive therapy (ECT), commonly known as *shock treatment*, has gained renewed credibility in psychiatry, "emerging as the treatment of choice for the most severe depression when drugs and other therapy fail to help" (Goleman 1990). A sign of renewed vitality is the amount of scientific research currently being conducted on this form of treatment. Patients for whom electroshock therapy is recommended, according to a 1990 report by the American Psychiatric Association, are those who are so severely depressed they do not eat, sleep very little, and are suicidal; many suffer from delusions. "But in about 80 percent of cases, electroshock therapy can lift their depression within a few weeks, restoring them to mental health" (Goleman 1990). Patients receiving shock therapy are given muscle relaxants and a short-acting general anesthetic. A brief pulse of electric current is passed through the brain, causing a convulsion or short seizure. In spite of renewed credibility, critics claim the increased use of ECT has resulted principally because insurance companies are anxious to get patients out of the hospital sooner.

An interior designer has an opportunity to be involved in the design of both treatment room and recovery room. Although the general appearance is that of a hospital operating room,

color, lighting, and space planning can positively influence staff and patients' attitudes.

ENVIRONMENTAL MESSAGES

Every room or space has a "personality" that makes a statement about its occupants or what the institution thinks of the occupants. Architectural detailing, style of furnishings, attention to housekeeping and maintenance, lighting, use of space (crowded or spacious), and color influence the viewer's perception of the occupants' status, societal worth, and prognosis for recovery. Hard architecture—bars on windows, concrete block walls, glossy paint, hard-surface floors, and indestructible, uncomfortable furniture—must destroy the patient's self-esteem "to learn that the staff of the treatment center holds such a low opinion of him and is so frightened of his actions. Patients . . . in this case, [are] told by their environment [how] to behave. Once a building has been constructed it . . . begins to flash out messages about that patient which are necessarily implicit in the design" (Spivack 1984, 88).

SPECIFICITY OF BEHAVIOR

Roger Barker uses the term *behavior setting* to describe "a physical environment with a high degree of specificity into which particular behavior patterns of groups or individuals fit with the precision of a key; . . . such behavior patterns may be observed repeatedly in this particular environment" (Spivack 1984). He favors designing a setting with the specific objective of accommodating desired activities, which in turn will encourage in the residents appropriate behaviors and discourage the inappropriate.

His term *standing behavior* refers to "behavior patterns in those settings in which the behavior pattern remains constant over an extended time, while the individual actors come and go" (Spivack 1984, 86). An example of this concept is a Boy Scout troop that retains its identity year after year, consistently repeating events and outings, while an ever-changing population of youngsters passes through the system. As the patient population in a mental health facility is constantly changing, spaces that could be relied upon to elicit specific behaviors would be highly desirable. Examples of this concept are noted in the discussion that follows. (The reader is also referred to chapter 5 for a discussion of environmental variables that act as behavioral cues.)

Dayrooms

Large dayrooms with little internal articulation evolved from the need for staff to have visibility of all patients in the space. Spivack refers to open-ended spaces as behavioral "catch-alls" (Spivack 1984). The multipurpose nature of such rooms no doubt holds some appeal for program directors, but the inability of a large space to support a wide range of behaviors has caused researchers to study how individual needs can be met without sacrificing the staff's ability to observe residents.

An individual's freedom of choice in a given physical setting depends on the design of that setting (size, shape, light, sound, and temperature) and the presence of other people. If the structure is such that it does not allow a resident to retreat to read, write a letter, or listen to music, then privacy is invaded and the number of behavioral options is reduced. Dayrooms and corridors are sometimes the only spaces available to patients for daytime activities. As social interaction is one of the prime goals of therapy, patients are encouraged to leave the security of their bedrooms; therefore, they must have appropriate rooms to go to.

In thinking about rooms as being able to elicit specific behaviors, the bed (with its inducement of escape through sleep) is a very specific behavior setting in an otherwise nonspecific environment, which makes it a tempting alternative for depressed or confused patients who do not know what to do with themselves (Spivack 1984).

People who are "normal" generally adapt an environment to suit their needs, whether it is a hospital waiting room or a hotel lobby. They rearrange furniture, perhaps move a lamp if they need better reading light, or complain to a clerk if something is bothersome. Mentally ill patients, by contrast, must adapt their behavior to the institutional environment in which they find themselves. They are usually not capable of manipulating the setting to meet their needs. When confronted with a large, ill-defined flexible space such as a dayroom, patients may "find themselves forced into random, relatively undirected behavior patterns" (Spivack 1984, 87). These ill effects are not limited to the interpersonal sphere, however: the physical environment and its organization of space can strongly affect social interaction as well. Space can be thought of as *sociopetal* (bringing people together) or *sociofugal* (keeping them apart [Osmund as reported in Spivack 1984]). This concept is discussed in greater detail later in this chapter.

The effects of space on residents' behavior have been demonstrated in a study by Spivack, Barton, and Mishkin (Spivack 1984). They examined behavior patterns of spatially differentiated areas of a psychiatric dayroom for a patient population with a three-month average length of stay and with clinical diagnoses varying from acute neurotic problems (daycare patients) to those with chronic psychosis. Eight major behavioral events were observed and recorded: talking, participating in games, passively watching others, reading, standing alone, lying on a sofa, sleeping in a sitting position, and sitting alone with no discernible focus of activity. Each observed behavior tended to be restricted to specified spatial areas of the room with very little overlap: researchers hypothesized that spaces may actually evoke particular modes of behavior. The conclusions of this study were:

1. Most socializing takes place at the perimeter of the room. In the center of the room, a person may feel unprotected and open to attack; the wall serves to reduce incoming stimuli and also may help to define personal space or territory. A wall is a tangible barrier; in the center of a room a person may feel overly conspicuous. Both socializing and nonsocializing behaviors gravitate to the perimeter of the room to cause an overload of patients in that area; a patient who comes to the dayroom to read or rest quietly is surrounded by talkers and game players and becomes uncomfortable. A large, open dayroom reinforces social rather than isolated behaviors because isolating oneself from those engaged in social interaction is difficult. The researchers point out that in this case patients may exhibit exaggerated expressions of their behavioral intentions or needs. Thus lack of alternatives may force a patient to feign sleep in order to avoid social contact.

2. Healthier patients tended to move chairs into an arc near the dayroom entrance, which meant their backs faced the less healthy patients and made entry into the circle difficult.

3. By introducing low partitions and rearranging furniture, feelings of safety and comfort could be increased without substantially decreasing opportunities for surveillance of patients. Dividing internal space into subareas where patients seeking quiet, as well as those seeking social interaction, could find fulfillment would support a wider range of behaviors. In effect, these low partitions create additional ''perimeters'' inside the room and make the room available to more people.

4. The most frequently occurring behaviors are talking and sitting alone.

Quiet Room

Much has been written of late about the real purpose of a quiet room, also known as a *seclusion* or *isolation room*. In fact, the current preference for the designation *quiet room* is an indication of the shift in viewpoint. As clinicians have begun to recognize the behavioral impact of physical settings, the notion of the quiet room as a barren, unyielding, punitive space has changed. The behavioral message of the space, coded in the way the room is designed and furnished, tells the patient he or she is ''expected to be destructive, to have no soft emotions requiring warmth and comfort, no gentleness'' (Spivack 1984, 207). Increasingly, this room is being thought of as a refuge for the out-of-control patient who is overwhelmed by sensory stimuli and needs a protective environment to keep self or others from being harmed.

The quiet room must be designed to be as suicide resistant as possible, with no exposed light switches, electrical outlets. operable windows, accessible light fixtures, or hardware that can be used to injure oneself. The room needs soothing colors and easily cleaned floor and wall finishes. Carpet, although desirable to ''soften'' the room, is almost impossible to maintain because of appearance, odor retention, and infection control. Often these rooms have a steel-framed ''bed'' bolted to the floor, with an exposed mattress (a sheet, being a loose object, may allow patients to choke or hang themselves). Sometimes a mattress, without a bed frame, is placed directly on the floor. Some feel that a built-in bench or platform, upholstered in carpet, might be more appropriate, but the problem of sanitation remains. Loose cushions with Velcro closures would allow some manipulation of the environment by the patient.

Quiet rooms are often located close to nurse stations and may have a Lexan window in the door so that the patient can be observed. Sometimes a camera is camouflaged and located where the patient cannot reach it to provide constant closed-circuit surveillance by nursing staff.

Some have speculated that views· of nature may help to calm or soothe an agitated patient. If the psychiatric unit is on an upper floor of the hospital, the view out the window may be nothing but sky, which can be disorienting. Perhaps a view of trees and flowers would be more effective in decreasing aggressive behavior. No doubt a significant variable would be the patient's reality orientation because an individual who is virtually unaware of the surroundings and who has withdrawn into a private world could be assumed to be unaffected by the view.

Harvard psychiatrist Martin Teicher has applied for a grant to explore the design of an optimally effective quiet room for children and adolescents. He plans to study the effects of installing one of Joey Fischer's Windows of Nature (see chapter 8), a computer-controlled Ektagraphic rear-projection image that changes gradually and continuously to simulate a 24-hour cycle. The hypothesis of the study is that children who require time in the quiet room will be less aggressive and demonstrate faster rates of remission in a specially designed quiet room, and that children will need fewer major interventions such as physical restraints or psychotropic drugs. (See chapter 5 for additional discussion of quiet room design options.)

Patient Bedroom

The patient room should be simple and comfortable but not so cozy as to tempt a patient to cling to it during the day. As the size of the patient bedroom increases, the quality of social interaction between patients changes from active to passive. The smaller the room, the greater the sense of privacy experienced by patients and the greater the freedom of choice for alternative behaviors (Ittelson as reported in Spivack 1984). The rooms in Figures 11-1 and 11-2 are fairly typical of patient bedrooms. Each provides a clearly defined territory or personal space with desk, night table, dormitory bed (often having storage in the base), and wardrobe or chest of drawers. Carpeting is desirable. Light-colored walls with a pastel accent

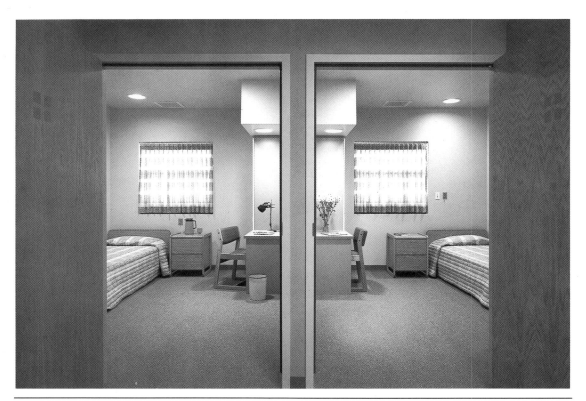

11-1 *Typical patient rooms, Psychiatric Facility, Deaconess Medical Center (Billings, MT)*

Architect: A & E Partnership; Interior Design: Ellerbe Becket; Photographer: © Peter Aaron/Esto

11-2 *Typical semiprivate patient room features built-in case work and a number of safety features; Adolescent Psychiatric Center, St. Luke's Methodist Hospital (Cedar Rapids, IA)*

Architecture and interior design: Ellerbe Becket; Photographer: Steve Greenway

color on the ceiling allow the room to appear bright but still have an accent of color.

Some feel that providing private patient rooms has a therapeutic basis. Studies have shown that institutionalized psychiatric patients interacted more frequently when given private rooms (Proshansky and others as reported in Zimring 1981). "When private space is missing, it encourages more aggressive boundary-control behavior in public and encourages withdrawal to limit interaction" (Zimring 1981, 153).

Furniture must be too heavy to throw or use as a weapon. Additionally, it must not have sharp corners, trim, or hardware that can easily be disassembled, and anything tall—such as a wardrobe—must be attached to the wall lest it be laid down and used to block entrance to the room. In a closed unit, where patients are sicker, furniture has to be placed away from doors or openings to rooms where a patient can stand on it and ambush an attendant who is entering the room.

Classrooms

Classrooms require tailored spaces (simple geometry) and cool colors to foster concentration and diminish distractions. Corridors or transition spaces leading to classrooms or therapy rooms may have more detail (skylights, clerestories, or trim) and stronger color. Patients often have trouble concentrating and paying attention; therefore, extraneous stimulation should be avoided in classroom settings.

DYSFUNCTIONAL ENVIRONMENTS

Some of the most interesting research in this area has been done by Mayer Spivack. His study of sensory distortions in tunnels and corridors has become a classic (Spivack 1967).

Optical Illusions

In his tunnel and corridor studies, Spivack documented optical illusions created by glare on floors and walls, reflections on glass, and lighting. These illusions relate to the way people walking down a corridor are viewed by patients at the other end. Sometimes sunlight, blindingly contrasted with dim artificial lighting, makes people appear to be blurred silhouettes as if their ankles, feet, wrists, and necks had been pinched off. This contrast makes bodies appear to float over the floor. According to Spivack

(1967) "tiny people preceded by grotesque elongated shadows performed an indiscernible ballet." These vastly elongated spaces (corridors) and hard surfaces reportedly created a strange cacophony of echoes due to the clicking of high heels, clanking of door latches, and scuffing of shoes. Faces were all but unrecognizable until they were very close to the patient, almost threateningly close.

One of the most interesting optical illusions illustrated in Spivack's photos results from corridors that have a change in elevation from one end to the other. Because the ceiling is constant and does not slope parallel with the floor, the ceiling height changes dramatically from one end of the corridor to the other, creating very bizarre optical illusions: a person descending the ramp would appear to be shrinking, and the doorway at the foot of the ramp into which he would disappear (from the upper vantage point) would look about the size of the rabbit hole through which Alice entered Wonderland. Speed is also misperceived in this setting; an illusion of faster or slower subjective time is perceived, depending on the direction of the viewer and the movement.

Paradoxical Images

One of the most dramatic of Spivack's photos illustrates what appears to be a man walking through a solid wood door. This illusion may occur at an entry foyer where a door has a glass sidelight. As the man approaches the door on the patients' side of the foyer, his reflection is seen in the glass as though he is coming from the opposite direction and walking through the solid wood door on the other side of the foyer (Fig. 11-3). Such a phenomenon would make anyone even moderately confused think that he or she were having a hallucination. To a "normal" person the optical illusion and distortion are understandable, but to a schizophrenic, who has difficulty defining reality, the discomfort and anxiety must be monumental.

Meretricious Materials

Spivack also talks about the deleterious effects of finishes or surfaces that camouflage an item. An example would be a wood-grain finish on a metal door. Metal doors have characteristics that are familiar (weight, thermal conductivity, and sound), but when they have a deceptive surface finish, a degree of perceptual confusion

11-3 *Reflection on glass creates the illusion of an individual walking through wall*
Photo courtesy Mayer Spivack

is bound to occur. A table, for example, that has claw feet resembling an animal, might represent a hallucination to a person whose visual world is already unstable and full of contradictions. To be therapeutic, the physical setting must help the patient to develop a clear and reliable perception of it.

ALTERNATIVE SOLUTIONS

The design of mental health facilities has evolved over the past 20 years, each project building on the successes and failures of previous efforts as architects tried to refine their solutions for a highly challenging patient population. For this reason a number of earlier projects are interesting, especially those designed by Kaplan/McLaughlin/Diaz, a firm noted for its expertise in this area.

Marin County Community Mental Health Center (Greenbrae, California, 1969)

Architects Kaplan/McLaughlin/Diaz implemented a concept referred to as *indeterminate* design, which translates as "loosely defined spaces with architectural variety." The floor plan of this building represents a village concept with a hierarchy of spaces symbolic of the community outside (Fig. 11-4). An architecture of irregularity emphasizes change and choice and allows patients the opportunity to try out different behaviors, which is a contradiction to current thought about providing highly structured spaces coded with behavioral cues. The challenge and stimulation of this environment were expected to make residents feel independent. Patient bedrooms were clustered around large communal spaces.

The architects did postoccupancy evaluations in 1969, shortly after opening, and five years later, in 1974. The staff reportedly felt that the design definitely increased socializing and decreased strong feelings of territoriality, both physically and psychologically. However, the large communal spaces (Fig. 11-5) and plan of the unit were overly challenging to severely disoriented "crisis" patients who needed control and supervision. For these patients small-

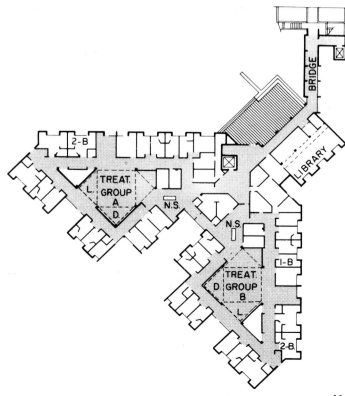

scale, simple spatial experiences, undemanding environmental details, and a homelike atmosphere with familiar and clearly defined spaces would have been more appropriate (McLaughlin 1975).

Elmcrest Psychiatric Institute (Portland, Connecticut, 1974)

Designed by the Environmental Design Group of New Haven, Connecticut, to which Herbert McLaughlin was a consultant, this 99-bed private hospital for adults and adolescents features an interesting space plan (Fig. 11-6). Eight-bed "family groups" are clustered in a large community space. Each cluster has an individual dining and kitchen area. Patients return from outside activities in other buildings on

---

11-4 *Floor plan, Marin County Community Mental Health Center (Greenbrae, CA)*
    Architect: Kaplin McLaughlin Diaz

11-5 *Large dayroom offers natural light and a variety of spaces to accommodate quiet activities or social interaction; Marin County Community Mental Health Center (Greenbrae, CA)*
    Architect: Kaplin McLaughlin Diaz; Interior design: Lenore Larsen & Associates; Photographer: Joshua Freiwald

campus through an entrance near the kitchen and snack bar and may help themselves to snacks. This arrangement certainly seems like a step in the right direction toward trying to normalize an institutional environment and create a residential setting. As is the trend today on campuses of psychiatric hospitals, a series of buildings, surrounded by lush landscaping, provides a more normal environment than a large monolithic structure with internal corridors. The architecture provides degrees of structured organization that respond to specific institute programs. Varied ceiling heights, the pitch of the roof, and architectural features define spatial transitions (McLaughlin 1975).

Vista Hill Hospital (Chula Vista, California, 1982)

Designed by Kaplan/McLaughlin/Diaz, this 58-bed acute care psychiatric facility for adolescents and adults is comprised of four buildings: nursing, administration, activities and dining, and treatment center, stepped into a hillside. Because of the campuslike arrangement of buildings, the site planning itself is therapeutic: patients who are unable to cope on the outside learn to go to and from "home" and "work," make choices, and meet schedules as they

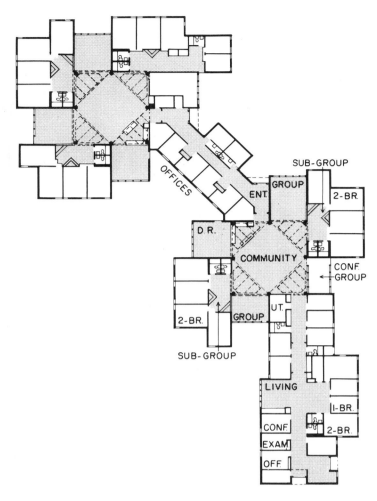

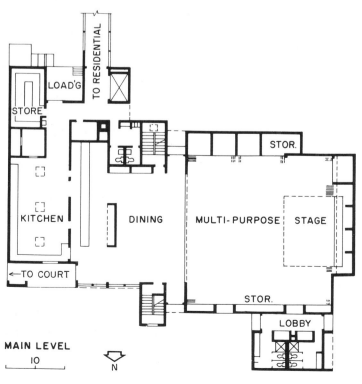

MAIN LEVEL

10

N

commute back and forth. An added advantage to this plan is reduction in construction costs because only the nursing/residential building must be designed to meet hospital codes.

The layout of the nursing building is innovative in that it totally eliminates corridors (Fig. 11-7). Mardelle Shepley's research for Camarillo State Hospital (chapter 5) indicated that many aggressive acts take place in transition spaces such as corridors. This design would tend to resolve that issue nicely, but it raises another question: Do the large, open dayrooms fail to provide areas of privacy for those who want to be alone or engage in quiet activities? In this plan, the patient is either secluded in a bedroom or totally exposed to social interaction. Nevertheless, in view of Spivack's studies about sensory distortions inherent in long corridors and other studies about the institutional character of the double-loaded corridor, this plan seems to be a successful alternative. Certainly the undulating curves of the building give the architecture a character not normally associated with psychiatric facilities.

In fact, something salubrious about the curves of this building—a fluidity—expresses optimism about the potential for recovery, in contrast to the ridigity of straight lines and 90-degree angles, which seem symbolically to circumscribe patients' alternatives. The stucco exterior carries strong red horizontal banding that has a "grounding" effect on patients, constantly returning the eye to plants and flowers visible through floor-to-ceiling expanses of glass.

The organization of space is such that patients progress from the closed or locked area to the open (unlocked) area, with a swing area between that allows rooms in that section to be open or closed (or used for chemical dependency patients), as the need dictates. Although not visible in the floor plan, behavioral cues to spaces are indicated by architectural elements such as soffits dropped over lounge areas and outlining the "imaginary" corridor. Color was used to further define space, and carpet bor-

11-6 *Floor plan, Elmcrest Psychiatric Institute (Portland, CT)*

Architect: Environmental Design Group in association with Kaplin McLaughlin Diaz

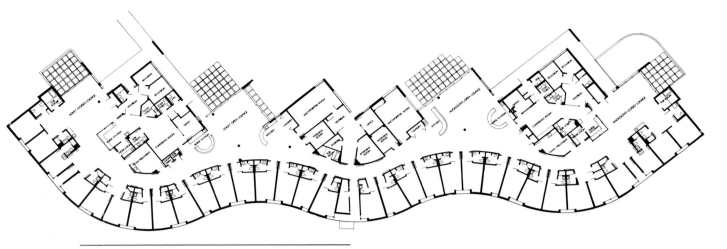

11-7 *Serpentine floor plan eliminates corridors in nursing unit; Vista Hill Psychiatric Hospital (Chula Vista, CA)*
   Architect: Kaplin McLaughlin Diaz

ders were occasionally used to visually separate areas.

Based on information provided by the medical director, color was also used to reinforce behavior. A soft, grayed blue with accents of burgundy was used in the closed area where sicker patients required a more subdued, soothing palette; patients progressed to the open area in which blue became a minor color and the dominant palette changed to rose, peach, and burgundy, colors thought to stimulate outward-directed activity and social interaction.

The Menninger Foundation
(Topeka, Kansas, 1982)

Designed by Skidmore, Owings and Merrill and the Kiene and Bradley Design Group, these 18 buildings added 260,000 square feet to the 332-acre Menninger campus, a pastoral hilltop overlooking Topeka. The Foundation is a center for treatment, research, and education in psychiatry—dedicated to treatment of the whole person in a caring and accepting environment. The architecture is a manifestation of that philosophy; it consolidates and integrates the museum, education, and research functions with the new diagnostic, treatment, and administrative facilities. The philosophy of treating patients in a community setting is reflected in the variety of indoor and outdoor spaces available for quiet reflection or group interaction.

The new buildings are approached diagonally, not frontally, along the oblique and curvilinear paths that reflect the site's natural contours.

This orientation provides a varied, three-dimensional perception of the buildings' form and mass. A wide range of structural shapes have been incorporated into the plan, including pitched roofs, flat roofs, one story, two-story arcades, porches, and garden walls (Fig. 11-8). Automobiles are barred from the campus. A series of courtyards binds together the new buildings with red brick older buildings. Covered walkways connect these sheltered courtyards, the residential quarters, related patient therapy and professional offices, and a gymnasium. Notice that the shed roofs give a residential scale to structures of institutional size.

Indoors, a slanted central atrium lights the main staircase linking the auditorium and classrooms of the conference center, which are often used for national and international mental health programs. Cafeteria and outdoor terrace seating are available in the 250-seat commons and dining facility where patients and staff dine together informally (Fig. 11-9). An advantage of family-style dining at large tables is the interaction it allows among staff members of the hospital, research buildings, outpatient departments, and tower building. Clerestory windows illuminate the library, manual arts studios, and patient classrooms, which are organized in a series of three buildings along a covered linear spine. Walkways to the small professional office buildings interspersed among living units are sheltered beneath projecting second stories. The existing tower building, a near replica of Philadelphia's Independence Hall, has become a museum, ad-

11-8 *Buildings clustered like a village, The Menninger Foundation (Topeka, KS)*

Architect: Skidmore, Owings, & Merrill in association with Kiene and Bradley Design Group; Photographer: Nick Merrick, Hedrich-Blessing

ministrative, and visitor center and is the focal point of the community.

In contradiction to recent trends in psychiatric care, the Menninger Hospital continues to focus on long-term treatment, which makes homelike residential living units mandatory. The 166 patients are housed in four L-shaped residence halls (Fig. 11-10), one of which is devoted to short-term treatment programs such as chemical dependency. This facility is successful for having created a dignified, high-quality aesthetic environment with handcrafted Scandinavian-style furnishings throughout, exposed wood ceilings, varied ceiling heights, clerestory glass, carefully designed lighting, textured tapestries, and varied wall surfaces (Fig. 11-11). The predominantly neutral palette of camel-colored carpet, white walls, and wood ceilings is accented by colorful earth-tone fabrics. Color is also used as a wayfinding device: entry walls and the nurse station of each living unit use an accent color that is repeated in the staff office building associated with that residence unit.

Patient rooms are uncommonly attractive and inviting for this kind of facility. Double rooms

11-9 *Patients and staff dine together in this facility; The Menninger Foundation (Topeka, KS)*

Architecture and interior design: Skidmore, Owings, & Merrill in association with Kiene and Bradley Design Group; Photographer: Nick Merrick, Hedrich-Blessing

11-10 *Floor plan, residential building, The Menninger Foundation (Topeka, KS)*

Architecture and interior design: Skidmore, Owings, & Merrill in association with Kiene and Bradley Design Group

11-11 *Small alcove seating areas interrupt residential corridors and provide opportunities for staff and patients to chat informally; The Menninger Foundation (Topeka, KS)*

Architecture and interior design: Skidmore, Owings, & Merrill in association with Kiene and Bradley Design Group; Photographer: Nick Merrick, Hedrich-Blessing

(Fig. 11-12) have almost as much privacy as single rooms (Fig. 11-13) by virtue of a cleverly designed full-height room divider that incorporates desk units and chests of drawers. Problems sometimes associated with sharing bathroom facilities are eased because the shower is separate from the toilet and vanity area. Much of the furniture is built in; however, the loose cushions on the sofa allow the resident to rearrange them for sitting on the floor, or they may be stacked in a corner to provide

11-12 *Divider wall affords each resident maximum privacy; The Menninger Foundation (Topeka, KS)*

   Architecture and interior design: Skidmore, Owings, & Merrill in association with Kiene and Bradley Design Group; Photographer: Nick Merrick, Hedrich-Blessing

11-13 *Private patient room is residential in character, uncluttered, and tastefully designed; The Menninger Foundation (Topeka, KS)*

   Architecture and interior design: Skidmore, Owings, & Merrill in association with Kiene and Bradley Design Group; Photographer: Nick Merrick, Hedrich-Blessing

space for a stereo on the sofa platform. One of the accent stripes in the bedspread is picked up on a bulletin board wall over the desk in each room. Patient rooms have individual thermostatic controls to allow residents to adjust the temperature to their own comfort level.

Mayer Spivack was a consultant for this project. His research on distortions caused by inappropriate lighting, the disorienting influence of long corridors, excessive use of glass, and the ways furniture can be arranged to manipulate communication patterns were carefully considered in planning this facility. Considerable thought was given to acoustics, as well, with sound readings taken in areas of the existing hospital to determine which activities produced excessive noise. Residential units include an in-

terview room that can be used for family visits, an exercise room, kitchen and activity room, lounge, and a staff work area separate from the nurse station. Rooms are arranged so that corridors are interrupted by small alcove seating areas where patients can chat informally with staff members (Fig. 11-11). The entire hospital complex is handicapped-accessible.

**Palo Verde Hospital
(Tucson, Arizona, 1984)**
This 62-bed (67,000 square feet) psychiatric hospital on the campus of the Tucson Medical Center was designed by The NBBJ Group. Designed around a number of courtyards and patios (Fig. 11-14), the architecture responds to a therapeutic model that accommodates needs

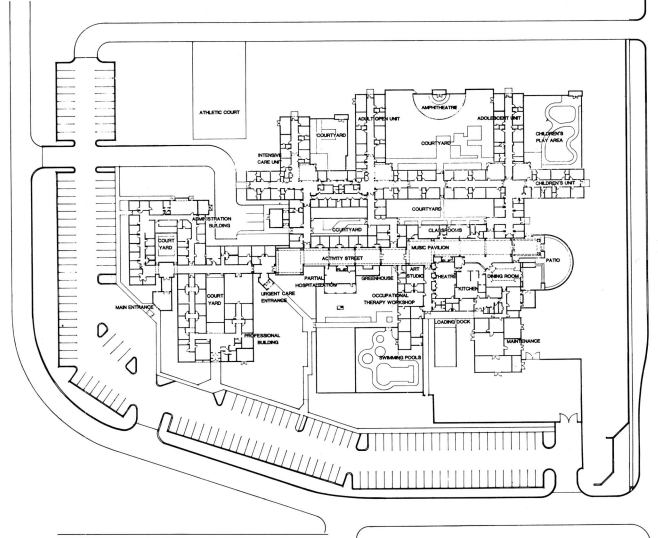

11-14 *Floor plan of sixty-two-bed psychiatric hospital on Tucson Medical Center campus, Palo Verde Hospital (Tucson, AZ)*
Architects: The NBBJ Group

11-15 *Central circulation spine is an indoor activity street for recreation, dining, and social interaction; Palo Verde Hospital (Tucson, AZ)*
Architecture and interior design: The NBBJ Group; Photographer: Douglas Kahn

for both privacy and community. The central circulation spine of the hospital is an indoor activity street of recreation, dining, and learning spaces that create a lively social atmosphere. This richly detailed architectural space features changes in ceiling height, indirect lighting, skylights, and wing walls that provide privacy for seating along the perimeter (Fig. 11-15). A varied palette of colors, artwork, live plants, and oak furniture with nubby upholstery fabric and soft cushions make this project unique. This facility seems remarkably successful in having achieved the kind of softness and residential qualities that are thought to be therapeutic. If a physical setting is encoded with behavioral cues, then this one says that its patients are very important people to be treated with respect and dignity; they are worthy of interesting architecture, carefully designed lighting, and soft, comfortable furniture upholstered in fabric, not vinyl.

**The Arbour Hospital
(Jamaica Plain, Massachusetts, 1984)**

In a suburb of Boston, this 118-bed (70,000 square feet) psychiatric facility designed by Graham/Meus Architects is remarkable for preservation of residential scale and its ability to blend stylistically into the neighborhood of Victorian homes. The architects did a superb job of blending interesting materials with a variety of stylistic details such as turrets, gabled roofs, shingled bays, and a circular porch (Fig. 11-16). After a protracted dialogue with local zoning officials and members of the community, replacement of the original mental hospital was finally approved. Although the facility had a low budget, the architecture is interesting and provides a number of high quality details in the interior space, such as circular glass block walls, built-in wooden benches, and a dropped ceiling in the corridor with bands of fluorescent lighting that outline the circulation corridor (Fig. 11-17). Each patient room contains a built-in desktop in front of a window, and patient room bathrooms have appropriately designed showers incorporating safety features.

11-16 *Renovation of original turn-of-the-century structure resulted in a new psychiatric facility designed to fit in with neighboring Victorian houses; The Arbour Hospital (Jamaica Plain, MA)*

Architecture and interior design: Graham/Meus Inc. Architects; Photographer: © Paul Ferrino, 1990

11-17 *Nurse station has good visibility of patient dayroom; The Arbour Hospital (Jamaica Plain, MA)*

Architecture and interior design: Graham/Meus Inc. Architects; Photographer: © Paul Ferrino, 1990

**Deaconess Medical Center
(Billings, Montana, 1988)**

This 57-bed (48,000 square feet) psychiatric facility designed by Ellerbe Becket has four quadrants that house a closed adult unit, open adult unit, a unit for children and adolescents, and an administration wing (Figs. 11-18 and 11-19).

A soothing palette of blue and gray and teal and gray, accented with oak trim, is carried throughout the facility. Nurse stations have clerestory windows and skylights. The group therapy room adds bright rose accents to the blue-gray palette. The occupational therapy room (Fig. 11-20) has a cool color palette and attractive, contemporary furniture.

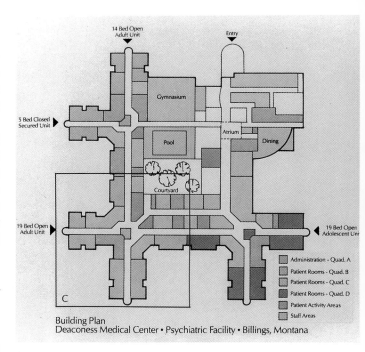

Building Plan
Deaconess Medical Center • Psychiatric Facility • Billings, Montana

11-18 *Building plan showing how the quadrants relate to commons area spaces; Psychiatric Facility, Deaconess Medical Center (Billings, MT)*
   Architect: A & E Partnership; Interior Design: Ellerbe Becket

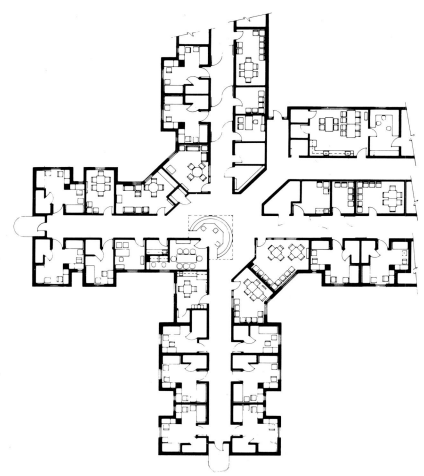

11-19 *Floor plan, quadrant C, Psychiatric Facility, Deaconess Medical Center (Billings, MT)*   *Architect: A & E Partnership; Interior Design: Ellerbe Becket*

11-20 *Occupational therapy room, Psychiatric Facility, Deaconess Medical Center (Billings, MT)*
Architect: A & E Partnership; Interior Design: Ellerbe Becket; Photographer: © Peter Aaron/Esto

St. Luke's Methodist Hospital, Adolescent Psychiatric Center (Cedar Rapids, Iowa, 1988)

The challenge in this 18-bed unit designed by Ellerbe Becket was to integrate patient bedrooms, games and activity rooms, exercise rooms, seclusion rooms, laundry, classrooms, family therapy, and staff office areas, all in 8500 square feet. A residential ambience conducive to the family-oriented treatment program was created with careful attention to risk-management and safety issues.

Upon entering the vestibule, patients are guided to the nurse station (Fig. 11-21). The two-sided station allows staff to observe residents in the large communal space, activity and game rooms, and in patient rooms. The community room, lined with built-in lockable case work and cooking appliances, was designed to encourage small group interaction and participation in planned activities. A folding partition makes the area more adaptable and flexible to the group's size and activity level. Heavy-duty

wallcoverings, vinyl upholstery, stain-resistant carpeting, and soft-edged, easily movable furniture are used to meet the continually changing program requirements of the space (Fig. 11-22). Design treatment around patient room doors uses four alternating colors keyed to the bedroom palette to help residents identify their rooms. The pastel colors of the commons area extend into patient rooms with a selection of muted peach, pink, green, and lavender finishes. Based on color preference and mood, patients may select the room of their choice, provided it is available. Dual-color case work units provide storage for personal items, clothing, and books, plus a desk for completing homework assignments (Fig. 11-2). The cabinet is locked and can be accessed only with an attendant.

Incorporated into the double-occupant rooms were such safety features as nonoperable windows, nonaccessible ceilings and light fixtures, radiant ceiling panels, recessed bulbs, sockets, and plumbing, breakaway hooks, and laminated glass mirrors to reduce the possibility of accidental or self-inflicted injuries. Notice that door hardware is flush, which makes hanging oneself from the doorknob impossible, and that hinges allow the door to swing in both directions, preventing a patient from barricading the door.

11-21 *Nurse station, Adolescent Psychiatric Center, St. Luke's Methodist Hospital (Cedar Rapids, IA)*

Architecture and interior design: Ellerbe Becket; Photographer: © Peter Aaron/Esto

11-22 *Multipurpose congregate space flanked by patient rooms, Adolescent Psychiatric Center, St. Luke's Methodist Hospital (Cedar Rapids, IA)*

Architecture and interior design: Ellerbe Becket; Photographer: © Steve Greenway

WARD GEOGRAPHY

Sommer's term *ward geography* is an engaging description of principles relating to furniture arrangement in mental hospitals. The studies reported in *Personal Space* (1969) were executed some twenty years ago in large state institutions, but vestiges of that type of thinking no doubt can be found today in some facilities. He noted that furniture in dayrooms was routinely arranged by custodians for ease of maintenance rather than to stimulate social intercourse. A chair was something to sweep around rather than a tool for encouraging social interaction. In Sommer's words, "Patients were being arranged by the furniture" (1969, 80). Oddly enough, when he rearranged furniture into different configurations in order to study potential benefits, patients as well as staff quickly moved it back to the "proper" place: they considered it their duty to correct any deviations from the way things "belonged."

He noted that foodservice and housekeeping staff with their large carts would often take shortcuts through dayrooms, in effect creating highways that forced patients' seating around the perimeter of the room. In spite of the deleterious effects, an "institutional sanctity" seemed to prevail; these rituals of furniture placement were always upheld. At that time staff did not realize the therapeutic potential of the physical setting for patients who were extraordinarily passive and dependent. "For the most part, they are not going to arrange . . . rooms to suit their needs; it is up to others to do it" (Sommer 1969, 80).

Today, some of these issues become moot points, however, because the average length of stay of less than two weeks mitigates the deleterious effects of certain environmental conditions.

FURNITURE PLACEMENT AND SOCIAL INTERACTION

An experimental hospital dayroom was designed to observe the effects of four types of seating arrangements on the social interactions of psychiatric patients. The experimental conditions were *sociofugal* (chairs arranged around the perimeter of the room), *sociopetal* (chairs arranged around two small tables in the center of the room), *mixed* (chairs arranged around the

perimeter as well as around a table in the center of the room), and *free* (patients told to arrange chairs any way they wished). The findings documented that seating arrangements indeed exert significant influence over patients' social behavior.

The sociopetal arrangement fostered a greater amount of socializing and conversation than did the sociofugal arrangement. Qualitatively, the sociopetal conversation was characterized by more energy and a willingness to discuss personal feelings and intimate topics. The conversation often involved more than two persons. The sociofugal conversation, in contrast, proceeded haltingly and lacked the intensity of the sociopetal one. Topics were rarely personal or intimate and most often could be characterized as small talk. The study showed that patients in the free setting had less social interaction than in sociopetal or mixed settings and just slightly more than in the sociofugal setting; researchers concluded that patients were unable to direct themselves without prior training. Patients' reluctance to manipulate the seating was also attributed to Sommer's concept of institutional sanctity, whereby psychiatric patients have been consistently trained to be directed by others and to perceive hospital environments as unalterable.

SPECIFIC DISORDERS

Any number of psychiatric disorders deserve special study and attention with respect to environmental accommodation, but schizophrenia and seasonal affective disorder figure most prominently in environmental research.

SCHIZOPHRENIA

One of the most devastating and disabling psychiatric disorders, schizophrenia affects approximately 1 percent of the population worldwide. It generally manifests itself between adolescence and early adulthood. In terms of numbers, it is the major mental illness affecting human beings and is thought to result from a combination of genetic determinants and nongenetic factors, which some hypothesize could be a specific stressful situation or life experience, inclusive of parental upbringing (Feierman 1982).

Behavioral Manifestations

Schizophrenia is characterized by a number of psychological manifestations, including delusions and hallucinations. (Hallucinations can be auditory, visual, tactile, or olfactory; they can be single or multiple simultaneous experiences.) Common objects may appear fixed and unalterable or charismatic and magical. A fabric pattern on a chair may take on symbolic meaning, and the patient may not sit down on the chair without performing a special ritual. Perceptual distortions of size and distance are common; as an example, a schizophrenic may perceive a large object seen at a great distance to be as small as it appears. Bizarre behavior such as talking to oneself, flailing one's arms, or a catatonic trance sometimes occur. Impaired thinking in which goal directedness and normal associations between ideas are distorted is also characteristic. Ritualistic behaviors and a passion for order or symmetry are not uncommon. As a general condition, schizophrenics suffer from too much sensory stimulation. They are unable to filter out and block what is irrelevant or unimportant. It has been described as analogous to hearing three radio stations simultaneously. Some speculate that schizophrenics withdraw and try to limit contact with other individuals in an attempt to reduce further sensory input.

Schizophrenia as a Phylogenetic Adaptation

One of the most thought-provoking theories to explain schizophrenia postulates that it is a phylogenetic adaptation[2] caused by genetically nocturnal individuals being forced to function actively during daylight (Feierman 1982). In this situation, such an individual would be processing information while awake but with a brain that is processing information as though asleep. To appreciate this theory, two facts should be noted: A diurnal individual's life is spent half in daylight (or artificial light) and half in darkness. A nocturnal individual, unless coerced to do otherwise, would spend all of his or her life in darkness. In nonschizophrenic individuals, the functional state of the brain during sleep would be operational, obviously, only during sleep. In schizophrenic individuals, however, the functional state of the brain during sleep would be operational both during sleep and during wakefulness, provided the individual were exposed to environmental light.

Fascinating as it is, this theory has not yet been proven; however, Feierman has cited an impressive number of studies to support his hypothesis. The following observations will be interesting to environmental designers because they demonstrate clearly the biological effects of light on the human organism (Feierman 1982).

1. Delusions (errors in logic) might be explained by an individual trying to understand his external reality while his brain is in the sleep mode. During sleep, the brain transfers information being held in short-term memory and stores it in long-term memory. To be awake during this process may make comprehending the present reality difficult, accounting for illogical conclusions.

2. Hallucinations (sensory misperceptions) might be explained by an individual being aware of the information transfer between short-term and long-term memory because the individual is awake while the brain is in the sleep mode. This state might account for the perception of sensory stimuli that do not actually exist externally.

3. Catatonia (simultaneous contraction of both flexor and extensor muscles to produce a rigid immobility) may be viewed as an adaptation to avoid predators during daytime. It is a deceptive pseudo rigor mortis.

4. A solitary style of living is considered one of the most obvious differences between schizophrenic and nonschizophrenic individuals. As most nocturnal species are normatively solitary, the fact that schizophrenics prefer solitude may be explainable by the nocturnal theory.

5. A statistically significant excess of schizophrenic births occur during winter months, as reported by the United States, England, Wales, Denmark, Norway, and Sweden (Torrey and others as reported in Feierman 1982). This pattern is thought to be related to photoperiod, which by its effect on testicular and ovarian functioning is the principal factor influencing the seasonal distribution of conception and birth. The pineal gland is the photoneuroendocrine transducer within the body capable of light and dark discrimination. It secretes melatonin and is known to be influenced strongly by the frequency, duration, and intensity of environmental light (Feierman 1982). The researcher notes that the connection between the clustering of schizophrenic births in winter and the mechanism of the pineal gland is not clear.

6. Schizophrenia is absent in blind persons. Re-

searchers postulate that a totally light-blind individual's brain would be in continuous darkness, and even if the blind person had a genetic determinant for schizophrenia the manifestations would not be activated because the brain's sleep mode would be operational only during sleep. The frequency of schizophrenia in deaf persons is the same as in the population at large.

7. One hypothesis suggests that if schizophrenic individuals were placed in a clinical research setting in which red lights were the only light source, many of the clinical manifestations of schizophrenia would disappear because the brain would be in the nonsleep mode during wakefulness. (In terms of melatonin synthesis, both red light and darkness affect the pineal gland similarly.) A deficiency in the theory, observed Feierman, is that schizophrenics would be expected to have a rod-dominated retina, as do most normatively nocturnal species. He indicates a need for research documenting this type of anatomical data.

Seasonal Affective Disorder (SAD)

Seasonal affective disorder (SAD) is a depression experienced by some people during winter months. It typically disappears in the spring. Other symptoms of SAD are decreased physical activity, lethargy, increased craving for carbohydrates, and irritability. Treatment for this disorder often consists of daily treatments of bright, full-spectrum light, which produces a marked antidepressant effect (Rosenthal, Sack, and others 1985).

RISK MANAGEMENT

Psychiatric risk management is an organized effort to identify, assess, and reduce risks to patients, visitors, and staff. Health care accrediting organizations require that risk management issues be reviewed according to established protocols. The present discussion is limited to those risk management issues that are relevant to the physical design of the environment. The principal goal of psychiatric risk management is to provide a safe environment for patients and staff. The following guidelines serve as a checklist for risk management features. I developed them over the years from personal experience, numerous articles, and conversations with unit supervisors and risk management consultants. In particular, Marion Gaudinski, a psychiatric risk management consultant, and administrator Donald Allen provided many insights and contributions to this list.

DESIGN GUIDELINES

The following checklist is helpful in assessing risk management issues.

General

These are general issues that apply to all patient care areas.

1. Nothing sharp, ingestible, or throwable.
2. Tamper-proof hardware.
3. No glass, including mirrors.
4. Tamper-proof grilles for heating, ventilating, and air-conditioning; locate in ceilings or high on walls.
5. Tamper-proof screws.
6. Closets must have poles that break away at 30 lb. to prevent hanging.
7. Baseboard must be glued and screwed securely to the wall to prevent razor blades, matches, and other harmful objects from being hidden there. Psychotic patients sometimes hoard bits of paper or food and may tuck them into available crevices such as baseboards or moldings. No base at all should be considered in closed areas or intensive care units. A wainscot of Kydex is indestructible in high-abuse areas.
8. Avoid design details that can easily be destroyed.
9. Suspended ceilings make concealing razor blades, needles, and weapons easy.
10. To prevent locking oneself in the room or hanging, patient rooms with private baths should be designed so that doorknobs of the room and bathroom cannot be tied together with a belt, pantyhose, or shoelaces.
11. Door hardware with flush handles and hinges that allow the door to swing in both directions is desirable.
12. Elevators should operate only with keys.
13. Fire doors should have alarm-released locks.

Bathrooms

Bathrooms pose special problems because patients cannot be observed, and these rooms contain numerous items that can cause injury.

1. Toilets with flush valves, not tanks.
2. Recessed shower heads and controls.
3. Locked temperature-control valves to prevent burns.
4. Breakaway shower and tub rods; shower curtain must slide over rod with Velcro attachment or other method not using hooks.
5. Standard glass mirror may not be used. Stainless steel is sometimes used but causes distortion. Reflective mirror types of plastic laminates can be used or other types of unbreakable reflective surfaces, such as ¼-inch-thick laminated safety glass.
6. Fiberglass tubs and showers provide easy-to-clean, indestructible surfaces.
7. An alarm system might be considered. It would ring at the nurse station if a patient tried to remove the shower rod, for example. Bathrooms always pose a security risk because the patient is in there alone and cannot be observed.
8. Unit flooding (plugging toilets, showers, and/or sinks so that they overflow) is a not uncommon occurrence.

Kitchens
Cooking or snacking is a 24-hour activity in some community settings; a kitchen is commonly accessible to patients but certain security measures must be heeded.

1. Cabinets should be safe and reachable without the use of stools or chairs.
2. Areas for locked sharps and knives are needed.
3. Appliances mounted under the cabinet (such as a microwave or can opener) leave countertops free and decrease the urge to remove items.
4. The microwave has replaced cooktops, stoves, and hot plates as it is considered safer for all with the exception of pacemaker-implanted patients.
5. Instant hot water taps should be avoided in acute admission, geriatric, and child psychiatric units.

Lighting
Lighting is a critically important issue.

1. Avoid shadows, which can be scary.
2. Fixtures must be vandal-proof, especially in bedrooms and bathrooms.

3. Light fixtures and exit signs must be recessed in ceilings or walls and have unbreakable covers.
4. Use full-spectrum fluorescents.

Windows
Windows are important for admitting views of nature and natural light, but if not designed properly they become a potential escape route.

1. Use shatter-proof glass or Lexan.
2. Use Velcro tabs on draperies or another attachment method that avoids drapery pins. Drapery rods must break away at 30 lb. to prevent hanging. Use manual pulls, not traverse cords.
3. Window treatment is required in most areas as psychotic patients are sometimes treated with phenothiazine medications (such as Thorazine) that make them light sensitive. Light hurts their eyes, and their skin sunburns quickly.

Finishes
Interior finishes help create a residential ambience, but their selection must be based on many functional parameters.

1. Painted walls are easier to repair than vinyl; residents often pick at seams of wallcovering.
2. Wooden doors work well because they can be sanded and repaired in-house.
3. Avoid mirrored reflections of faces on shiny surfaces.
4. Carpet should be directly glued to the floor without tack strips or pad. Shag carpet is not appropriate because residents can hide things in it.
5. Use nontoxic paint.
6. Patients are very aware of patterns and often experience visual distortions, especially geriatric patients, who have problems with depth perception. Subtle patterns may be used sparingly, provided the values of colors are fairly close to avoid figure-ground reversal.
7. Pattern in floors and walls of staff lounges, dining, or charting rooms is fine, provided patterns are not too busy.
8. Intensive care areas require passive colors (pale rose, apricot, pale yellow, pale blue) in very light tints and no intricate patterns or design details—nothing overly stimulating.
9. Solution-dyed, antimicrobial carpets with

synthetic backing are recommended: jute backing tends to rot as a result of constant cleaning and other sources of moisture.

10. All finishes must meet state and local codes for fire retardancy for hospitals and high-risk occupancies.

COLOR

In this environment the selection of color must be based on a solid understanding of the symbolic and psychological meanings it may have for individuals.

Use of Color
Equally important, selection must be based on the laws of perception that govern how colors work together when combined, and how they alter our perception of space.

1. Use stimulating colors on nondestructible surfaces and neutral colors on items that are easy to vandalize in order not to call attention to them.
2. Warm colors work well in rooms where social interaction is appropriate—lounges, therapy rooms, activity rooms. Cool colors are best for rooms where inner-directed thought or reflection is desired, such as quiet rooms. A combination of warm and cool colors is appropriate for patient bedrooms.
3. Doorframes of "staff only" rooms should be painted to match adjacent walls; doorframes of rooms accessible to patients may be painted accent colors.
4. Color may be used to assist disoriented residents in finding their rooms.
5. Red should be avoided for its association with blood. Research has shown that schizophrenics dislike yellow.

Color and Mental Disorders[3]

A variety of color tests—among them the Rorschach and the color pyramid test, the latter devised by Swiss psychologist Max Pfister in 1950—are used as diagnostic tools in determining normality/abnormality. Because so many tests involving color preference, response, and placement have been made on the mentally and emotionally ill, with such a plethora of conflicting results, it is clear that the data must be interpreted

cautiously and in conjunction with those from other tests. The most abused area here is probably preference, as some have not hesitated to link preference for specific colors to specific disorders, in irresponsible and unproven attribution. Eric P. Mosse, as quoted in Birren, reveals:

We generally found in hysterical patients, especially in psychoneuroses with anxiety states, a predilection for green as symbolizing the mentioned escape mechanism. . . . Red is the color of choice of the hypomanic patient giving the tumult of his emotions their "burning" and "bloody" expression. And we don't wonder that melancholia and depression reveal themselves through a complete "blackout." Finally, we see yellow as the color of schizophrenia. . . . This yellow is the proper and intrinsic color of the morbid mind. Whenever we observe its accumulative appearance, we may be sure we are dealing with a deep-lying psychotic disturbance. (1969, 30)

Birren, a noted color historian, disagrees: "Yellow may be looked upon as an intellectual color associated both with great intelligence and mental deficiency" (1969, 30). He claims that schizophrenics prefer blue. The contradictions are legion. A study done by Warner, in which 300 patients were tested including diagnosed anxiety neurotics, catatonic schizophrenics, manics, and depressives, found in most cases no significant correlation of preference with psychiatric disorders.

Rorschach Inkblot Test. How does the Rorschach contribute to clinical diagnosis? Rorschach's hypothesis was that color responses are measures of the affective, or emotional, state, and he noted that neurotics are subject to "color shock" (rejection), as manifested in a delayed reaction time when presented with a color blot. He also stated that red evoked the shock response in neurotics more often than did other colors. Schizophrenics also suffer color shock when presented with the chromatic or color cards (following the black and white cards) of the Rorschach. Birren postulates that color may represent an unwanted intrusion into their inner life.

In the realm of color research, however, nothing goes uncontested, and the Rorschach is no exception. Two major criticisms of it are the lack of work with normal subjects as a criterion against which pathological groups could be compared, and also the basic postulate that the way in which a person responds to color in ink-blots reflects his or her typical mode of dealing with, or integrating, affect. In fact, researchers Cerbus and Nichols, in trying to replicate Ror-schach's findings, found no correlation between color responsiveness and impulsivity, and no significant difference in use of color by neurot-ics, schizophrenics, and normals. Nevertheless, the weight of evidence still favors the Ror-schach color-affect theory.

Color and Depression. Almost unanimous agreement exists regarding the depressive's total lack of interest in color. However, some studies indicate that depressed people prefer dark colors of low saturation, and others claim they prefer bright, deeply saturated colors. Probably both conclusions are accurate be-cause color can be either a stimulant or com-pensation for dreariness and lack of excitement as well as a reflection of one's inner state. Seen in another manner, the depressive's attraction for bright colors may be an expression of homeostasis—the organism's subconscious striving for balance or equilibrium.

Compton Fabric Preference Test. Another test done with the mentally ill that deserves mention is the Compton fabric preference test. Sharpe (1974) reports that Compton tested the fabric and design preferences of a group of hos-pitalized psychotic women, in terms of the rela-tionship between concepts of body, image boundary, penetration of boundary, and clothing preference. People with mental and emotional problems were anticipated to be likely to suffer some aberrant form of body image, and those with weak body boundaries were found to tend to reinforce them with fabrics of strong figure-ground contrasts and brighter, more highly saturated colors that allowed them to feel less vulnerable to penetration—in a sense armored by the ''strength'' of the color and pattern.

Furniture
The selection of furniture for this patient popu-lation must be based on many functional consid-erations.

1. No sharp edges.

2. Beanbag chairs may be appropriate for some areas; if thrown, they cannot injure anyone.
3. Wooden furniture (if dark wood) can be a problem with respect to carved obscenities. Oak furniture works well because it is too heavy to throw and, if kept a natural color, it can easily be sanded and refinished in-house.
4. No tacks, pins, or clips may be used in bulletin boards or accessory items. Velcro fasteners are acceptable.
5. Mattresses without box springs are appropriate. Mattress should not have zippers or pockets and must have vinyl covers that, when punctured, will not rip and expose innersprings. Foam mattresses, of course, have no springs.
6. Casters, if provided, must be nonremovable. Casters can be risky, however, if they allow furniture to move when leaned upon.
7. Bedroom furniture should either be built in or affixed to floor or wall so that it is not movable; furniture in dayrooms should be movable as rearranging the furniture is a therapeutic activity enjoyed by some patients.
8. Furniture should have notched or recessed finger pulls, rather than surface-mounted handles.
9. Furniture construction should be evaluated in terms of joinery details of wood frames and composition of upholstery. Furnishings must withstand high abuse. Psychotic patients sometimes possess superhuman strength when agitated.
10. Avoid furniture that is too low or too soft, as these features make rising difficult for elderly patients once they are seated.
11. Stereos, televisions, VCRs, and the like should be housed in unbreakable containers and be out of reach.
12. In placing furniture, especially built-ins, consider its proximity to doors and hidden corners so that a staff member entering a room or turning a corner cannot be surprised by a patient's ambush (patient may stand on furniture and leap onto aide).
13. Artwork cannot be covered by glass and must be securely attached to a wall. California photographer Joey Fischer has printed his images on stainless steel panels (virtually indestructible) for use even in high-security areas of psychiatric facilities.
14. All mattresses and upholstered furniture should meet California Bulletin 133 (quickly

becoming the national standard for fire retardancy in hospitals and public buildings).

Quiet Rooms

The design of quiet rooms must, above all, consider issues of patient safety.

1. Install stripping on outside bottom door to prevent passage of razor blades, matches, or pills into room.
2. Locate light switches outside room.
3. Consider surveillance into room by camouflaged camera or window in door.
4. Keep locked when not in use.
5. Use mattresses without zippers or pockets.
6. No exposed electrical outlets, surface-mounted light fixtures, or hardware.
7. Eliminate blind corners and visual obstructions.
8. Refer to other items discussed previously in text.
9. A full bathroom with shower, or at least a sink and toilet, should be immediately adjacent to the seclusion room. A separate door may provide direct access from the seclusion room.

Utility and Medication Rooms, Treatment and Activity Areas

Here are a few suggestions for these areas:

1. Provide locked cabinets for storage of equipment and supplies.
2. Install emergency call buttons.
3. Must be able to secure (lock) room when not in use.
4. Medication rooms should be designed to give staff the privacy they need to pour medications without being distracted in order to decrease the margin of error. Many facilities request that patients come to a central medication area, which may be designed with a Dutch door to allow the room to be open during dispensing of medications and locked when not in use.

Psychiatric Emergency Service

The closing of state psychiatric hospitals also necessitated the development of the psychiatric emergency service (PES) or crisis unit. This area is most often used for individuals who are brought to the facility against their will, although voluntary admissions are also evaluated here. The patient may be in handcuffs or leather re-straints or on a stretcher. Many times they are a transfer from an acute care hospital emergency room after major or minor suicide attempts.

The PES may be located immediately near or next to the hospital emergency unit, or it may be located in a freestanding psychiatric facility. Children, as well as adults and the elderly, may be admitted for evaluation and transfer to another facility. Patients may remain in the physical area for as long as 72 hours. This unit, more than any other, requires special considerations.

1. Provide seclusion rooms with adjoining bathrooms and showers.
2. Wide doors to accommodate stretchers.
3. Panic alarms and door openers in each seclusion room and in the nurse station.
4. A recessed locked area for police guns when police arrive on the unit.
5. The layout of the unit should avoid long corridors and permit maximum observation of patients.
6. Provide private but secure rooms for searching patients for weapons upon admission.
7. Provide interview rooms that allow for observation of staff and patient; safety and soundproofing are important in these rooms.
8. Space for patient lockers or possessions—clothing and valuables.
9. A medication-pouring area that affords privacy and storage of medications and emergency equipment.
10. Provide an enclosed, but "open" nurse or secretarial station with countertop partitions high enough to prevent patients from jumping over them or assaulting staff with an extended fist.
11. The nurse station needs appropriate work surfaces for computers and printers and wall space for a four- by four-foot memo board to keep track of census and to keep patient information available and confidential.

Miscellaneous Considerations

The following are not risk management issues but are important design considerations.

1. Square rather than round tables should be used in dining facilities or activity rooms because they make defining boundaries easier. The indetermi-

nate nature of a round table can be troubling to patients.

2. Carpet or sheet vinyl border designs, in theory, can effectively be used to define areas, but careful consideration must be given to contrast or value (remember problems of depth perception of the elderly) and to compulsive behavior disorders that prevent people from stepping on a line or moving inside a space defined by a border.

3. Incontinence, whether voluntary or involuntary, is a very real problem in intensive care and, in "closed" areas, for patients of all ages. It will become an even greater concern as the patient population includes more elderly. Vinyl upholstery (now available in a number of soft textures and small printed patterns) is the only solution. In addition, seating should be selected with an opening between the seat and back so that urine cannot collect at that crevice. Welting or cording should be avoided for the same reason; fabric wrapped around the cushion in a continuous piece and secured under the seat is suitable.

4. The dayroom requires a reality orientation board listing the season, date, day of the week, location (city), special holidays, and daily activities.

5. Selection of art images must be handled with care. Abstract or amorphous images might look too much like a Rorschach test and suggest ominous things to some viewers.

In risk management, no one perfect design will ever guarantee to prevent suicide or injury. As a general guideline, "if objects beep, move, project, hang, sway, or shatter, they have the potential to be destroyed or cause injury" (Gaudinski 1982, 63). Furthermore, two peripheral issues impact risk management. The first is the trade-off between safety and privacy, addressed previously in the text. The second issue is aesthetics; architects and interior designers must be highly skilled to be able to build these risk management features into the facility and still maintain a residential ambience that does not call attention to the many vandal-proof safety features.

POSTOCCUPANCY EVALUATION

The postoccupancy evaluation of Quincy Mental Health Center (Welch and Epp 1988) is an example of a comprehensive study of a state-owned community mental health center. The scope of this POE makes it an excellent refer-

ence not only for data relating to design of mental health facilities but also for the format of other POEs.[4]

SUMMARY

The evolution of care for the mentally ill has progressed over the past 30 years from custodial care to the current therapeutic community with its focus on social interaction and an aggressive program of therapies and activities. Granted, the introduction of tranquilizers and antidepressant medications has made rehabilitation more viable for many individuals. Cuts in reimbursement for treatment will pose a continuing challenge to quality care in the 1990s. On the bright side, exciting research in neuropsychiatry is underway and expected to be unveiled before the year 2000, causing some to speculate that the 1990s may be called "the decade of the brain."

NOTES

1. *Source:* E. Friedman. 1981. Hospital psychiatric services begin a changing of the guard. *Hospitals,* May 1:52–55.

2. A phylogenetic adaptation is an evolved structure, physiological process, or behavior pattern that makes or made an individual more fit to survive and to reproduce in comparison with other members of the same species (Feierman 1982).

3. Reprinted with permission of Van Nostrand Reinhold from Jain Malkin, *Medical and Dental Space Planning for the 1990s,* 1990, pp. 411–13.

4. This study may be ordered from Welch and Epp, 7 Greenough Avenue, Boston, MA 02130.

REFERENCES

Birren, Faber. 1969. Light, Color and Environment. New York: Van Nostrand Reinhold.

Cotton, N., and R. Geraty. 1984. Therapeutic space design: Planning an inpatient children's unit. *American Journal of Orthopsychiatry* 54(4):624–36.

Craig, J. 1981. Goal of west campus planners: Achieve comfort, human dignity. *Menninger Perspective* 22(2):27–30.

Feierman, J. 1982. Nocturnalism: an ethological theory of schizophrenia. *Medical Hypotheses* 9(5):455–79.

Friedman, E. 1981. Hospital psychiatric services begin a changing of the guard. *Hospitals* May 1:52–55.

Gaudinski, M. 1982. Risk management in psychiatric care. *Perspectives in Hospital Risk Management* II(3):63–65.

Goffman, Erving. 1961. *Asylums: Essays on the Social Situations of Mental Patients and Other Inmates.* New York: Anchor Books.

Goleman, D. 1990. The quiet comeback of electroshock therapy. *New York Times* August 2:B7.

Holahan, Charles. 1978. *Environment and Behavior: A Dynamic Perspective.* New York: Plenum Press.

Ittleson, W., H. Proshansky, and L. Rivlin. 1970. The environmental psychology of the psychiatric ward. In *Environmental Psychology: Man and His Physical Setting,* ed. H. Proshansky, W. Ittleson, and L. Rivlin. New York: Holt, Rinehart and Winston.

Keeran. C., R. Pasnau, and M. Richardson. 1981. Medical-behavioral "explosion" affects hospital operation, policy. *Hospitals* May 1:56–59.

Lacy, M. 1981. Creating a safe and supportive treatment environment. *Hospital and Community Psychiatry* 32(1):44–49.

Malkin, Jain. 1990. *Medical and Dental Space Planning for the 1990s.* New York: Van Nostrand Reinhold.

McLaughlin, H. 1975. Evolution and evaluation of environment for mental health. *Architectural Record* July:105–10.

Mills, G. 1984. Planning for specialized mental health services. *Hospitals* May 1:88–91.

Moltzen, S., H. Gurevitz, and others. 1986. The psychiatric health facility: An alternative for acute inpatient treatment in a nonhospital setting. *Hospital and Community Psychiatry* 37(11):1131–35.

Rosenthal, N., D. Sack, and others. 1985. Antidepressant effects of light in seasonal affective disorder. *American Journal of Psychiatry* 142(2):163–70.

Sharpe, Deborah. 1974. *The Psychology of Color and Design.* Chicago: Nelson Hall Co.

Sommer, Robert. 1969. *Personal Space.* Englewood Cliffs, NJ: Prentice-Hall.

———. 1974. *Tight Spaces: Ward Architecture and How to Humanize It.* Englewood Cliffs, NJ: Prentice-Hall.

Spivack, Mayer. 1967. Sensory distortions in tunnels and corridors. Hospital & Community Psychiatry January:24–30.

———. 1984. *Institutional Settings.* New York: Human Sciences Press.

Welch & Epp Associates. 1988. *Post Occupancy Evaluation of the Quincy Mental Health Center.* Boston: Welch & Epp.

Williams, L. 1990. Getting therapy for the high cost of mental health. *Los Angeles Times* August 5:D1, D7.

Zimring, C. 1981. Stress and the designed environment. *Journal of Social Issues* 37(1):145–71.

..

AMBULATORY CARE

This chapter is limited to a discussion of clinics, ambulatory diagnostic and treatment centers, and ambulatory surgical centers. The focus is primarily hospital-based facilities, either located on a hospital campus or owned by a hospital. Physicians' and dentists' offices are not represented because they were the focus of my last book, *Medical and Dental Space Planning for the 1990s*. For this same reason, the intricacies of space planning, traffic flow, accommodation of equipment, and efficient design of specific treatment rooms are not dealt with in this chapter. This chapter instead outlines broader issues and illustrates, with photographs, the wide range of solutions pursued by design professionals to meet the needs of specific communities.

DEMAND FOR AMBULATORY CARE

So much has been written about what *Hospitals* magazine (1990) calls a "skyrocketing demand" for ambulatory care that a recital of events leading to this condition would belabor the point. All indicators suggest continued growth in ambulatory care. Economic pres-

sures, technology, and reimbursement policies of third-party payers are contributing to this trend. Declining hospital admissions indicate the patient base is steadily shifting to more economical settings. Consequently, hospitals have been aggressively pursuing outpatient treatment programs and financially committing themselves to large, new ambulatory services buildings and to satellite clinics. One of the most ambitious of these projects is presently under construction at the University of California at Los Angeles. A $175 million outpatient medical plaza is under way on campus, with phased openings starting in the fall of 1991 (photos could not be included in this book). It is a project many in the industry will watch and study as a barometer of success in dealing with health care's tough issues: financing, reimbursement, utilization, and patient-centered care. This project includes 380,000 square feet of clinics plus a medical office building and neuropsychiatric center. Projects of this type are sometimes referred to as "hospitals without beds."

STATISTICS

Hospital outpatient visits increased 32 percent between 1984 and 1989. Outpatient revenues increased from 14.4 percent in 1984 to 21.1 percent in 1989. Projections for 1991 are that total net hospital revenue from outpatient services will reach 31.6 percent (Eubanks 1990).

Ambulatory services include more than clinical care, in the traditional sense of patients presenting themselves to be cured of a physical illness. Cuts in reimbursement for patients under a managed care plan, for Medicare patients, or for treatment of indigents (hospitals receive no payment for the uninsured) have encouraged hospitals to capture new private-pay markets by meeting the demand for wellness services with physical fitness and sports medicine centers, education and resource centers, and mental health programs targeted at specific groups interested in stress management, eating disorders, weight management, or substance abuse, to name a few. Ambulatory care may also include specialty and subspecialty clinics where care is limited to one organ system or to a specific disease process, such as cardiovascular centers, dialysis centers, or cancer centers.

ISSUES

Ambulatory care depends, for its success, on a vastly different orientation than that associated with inpatient care. Because of this factor, hospitals often recruit administrators for outpatient services from outside the hospital rather than promote an individual who has been successful in an inpatient setting. This administrator might be a maverick from another hospital, someone from the hospitality industry, or a corporate executive with a background in business or finance.

The biggest differences between inpatient and ambulatory care are the consumer focus and the speed with which services must be delivered. In ambulatory care everything is stat (immediate) because the patient is not sitting in a bed, available to clinicians as needed; staff also do not know whether the ambulatory patient will return for a follow-up visit. Treatment protocols and clinical judgments must address these issues. Medical schools and teaching hospitals are becoming increasingly aware of the need for residents to gain experience in the ambulatory setting because it is so different than examining a horizontal patient (Eubanks 1990). Unlike inpatient care, ambulatory care is totally consumer oriented and market driven, making the following issues so critical to its success.

CONVENIENCE

Consumers are interested in convenience, which means proximity to home or office and extended hours to accommodate working parents. Child care services and availability of parking in a safe, well-illuminated structure are important features.

EASY ACCESS

The facility should be easy to access from freeways. Once inside the building, individual clinics should be within short walking distances from the main lobby. A prominent information or reception desk near the entry is important to advise first-time visitors of registration procedures and to direct others to specialty clinics. Decentralized waiting rooms in specialty clinics provide more intimate spaces than do large lobbies.

USER-FRIENDLINESS

This topic may encompass anything from signage and ease of wayfinding to accommodation for special ethnic groups to barrier-free design.

WAYFINDING

In ambulatory care facilities entrances, exits, and circulation routes, both outside the building and inside, must be clearly defined. The larger the complex, the more critical wayfinding becomes. It should be anticipated that ambulatory services will grow and buildings will be expanded. Thinking ahead is important when developing a graphics program to ensure that the system selected will be as appropriate for a large, multilevel facility as it is for a small one.

Careful space planning that avoids unnecessary jogs or turns in corridors or complicated building shapes is the start of good wayfinding design. A central atrium creates an excellent landmark reference as individuals make their way through the building. Views of courtyards or special works of art also serve as wayfinding landmarks. A building might be laid out with a north-south axis corridor and an east-west axis corridor, with all clinic destinations located on these two axial spines. Where they intersect would naturally be the hub of the lobby, admitting or registration services, cafeteria, or other public use areas (see also chapter 16).

ETHNIC AND CULTURAL ACCOMMODATION

Facilities serving communities with large ethnic populations should consider bilingual signs and patient representatives who speak those languages, and should make an effort to understand specific cultural taboos or preferences that may exist about the use of certain colors, design features, or art images. This order can indeed be a tall one for a facility in an urban setting that serves diverse ethnic populations. At the very least, prominent displays of art from those individual cultures can be prominently exhibited in the building. Architects designing hospitals that serve populations of North American Indians have often included an area where the local religious leader can conduct healing services and have incorporated Indian motifs into the form of the building as well as in decorative elements.

BARRIER-FREE DESIGN

Every individual has the right to have ease of access to any public building. As the population of elderly grows, barrier-free accessibility will be important to many people, not just the physically disabled.

FAMILY-CENTERED CARE

Buildings designed for ambulatory care must consider the needs of the entire family, from young children to the elderly. Appropriate seating for the aging body must be provided, as well as entertainment and diversions for children. Play areas (Figs. 12-1 and 12-2) let children know they are welcome and make the visit more pleasant for parents and others who are waiting for care.

SEPARATE FACILITIES FOR CHILDREN AND ADOLESCENTS

Children and adolescents should not be mixed with adults in the same clinic, or at least they should be seen at different times. Some clinics provide separate entrances for children and adolescents. Clinic decor should be geared to the various age groups; adolescents may respond negatively to designs that they may think of as too pediatric.

SEPARATION OF WELL AND SICK KIDS

In pediatric waiting rooms, separating sick children from those who are well is advisable. Well visits include those for inoculations, periodic checkups, examinations prior to starting school, and allergy shots; sick children may have communicable diseases. Often sick and well waiting rooms are separate rooms on opposite sides of the pediatric reception desk. The reception desk would have three sides, allowing clerks to greet people straight ahead as they initially enter the waiting room or to turn and check them in at the transaction counter on the sick side or the well side.

SEPARATION OF EMERGENCY/URGENT CARE

The emergency or urgent care entrance to the building should be screened from the view of patients. These entrances should be promi-

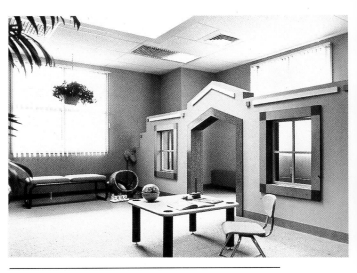

12-1 *Children's playhouse, St. Mary's Ambulatory Care Center, St. Mary's Hospital (Madison, WI)*
    Architecture and interior design: Cannon;
Photographer: William E. Mathis

12-2 *Children's entertainment center, Stateline Regional Emergency Center, Beloit Memorial Hospital (Beloit, WI)*
    Interior design: Watson Limited; Photographer: Steve Pitkin

nently marked and visible from a distance as one approaches the building. As managed care[1] and capitation[2] systems become more prevalent, ambulatory urgent care centers become more necessary because treating patients is far less expensive in this setting than in the hospital emergency room.

PATIENT-CENTERED CARE

Patient-centered care is consumer oriented and therefore sensitive to the vagaries of market demand. Consumers are fickle and easily influenced by public relations programs and advertising. Successful ambulatory care programs require an aggressive marketing plan that is continually refined to target patients for specific product lines and, on the flip side, to determine what new services and amenities consumers want.

Patient-centered care requires staff who are customer-service oriented and trained to view the patient as someone who has a choice among a number of provider organizations in what is, for many hospitals, a highly competitive market. This hospitality orientation is what hospitals seek to emulate from the hotel industry.

IMPORTANCE OF IMAGE

When consumers have a choice among health care providers, image becomes increasingly important. What constitutes an appropriate image is largely dependent upon the population served (age, education, socioeconomic level), architectural style and materials appropriate for that region, cultural or ethnic bias, and, last, budget. Today consumers (individual patients) are not the only ones who have to be marketed to; attracting and keeping top clinical staff is equally important. Wooing corporations and large employers has become a necessity. Market analysts observe that the health care setting (image) is especially important to young professionals and the elderly in making selections of health care providers.

Some provider organizations express their prominence with signature architecture, which was an objective for the Cleveland Clinic when they engaged Cesar Pelli to design their new 620,000-square-foot outpatient clinic complex described more fully later in this chapter.

The design of public space is most important in establishing a high-quality image for the facility; the lobby creates the first impression. The scale of the space (volume, ceiling height, massing of vertical or horizontal elements), relationship between indoor and outdoor space, use of materials, acoustics, lighting, and color all work together to create the image. In the lobby, gallery space may be allocated for patient education displays, including models, posters, photographs, and brochures. In clinic waiting rooms, carrels for watching videotapes on health topics may be provided. Large saltwater aquariums, built into a wall, fascinate most people and seem to provide better entertainment than television, which is noisy and can be offensive to those who wish to read (Fig. 12-3).

DESIGN CONSIDERATIONS

The projects presented in this chapter share a number of characteristics that make them outstanding. They show complete integration between architecture and interior design. The vocabulary of design elements introduced in the lobby generally carries through to individual clinics and is repeated in some form in waiting rooms and corridors. Surfaces are richly textured with a variety of materials including ceramic tile, stone, wood, fabric, metal, and glass. Patterns have been created by horizontal or vertical banding, the juxtaposition of honed and unhoned stone, and by natural light from windows, clerestories, and skylights. Nature is abundantly present through either interior landscaping or views of the outdoors. Color palettes are neither trendy nor anemic; interesting combinations of colors are used fearlessly. Scale is important: lobby spaces soar, elevating the spirit. Lighting is never incidental: it is carefully designed and varied. Main artery corridors are easy to differentiate because unique works of art and atria serve as reference landmarks for ease of wayfinding.

SIGNATURE ARCHITECTURE

Prominent institutions sometimes use architecture as a way of gaining attention and establishing a visual presence equal to their clinical and research reputations.

12-3 *Waiting room, orthopedic surgery suite, features 420-gallon saltwater aquarium (San Diego, CA)*
Architecture and interior design: Jain Malkin Inc.;
Photographer: Michael Denny

Cleveland Clinic

In the category of venerable institutions, the Cleveland Clinic is the second largest referral center in America, surpassed in volume only by the Mayo Clinic. The 620,000-square-foot building, completed in 1986, accommodates 22 separate clinics in a 14-story, stepped ziggurat of granite and glass. The surface of the building is rhythmically articulated by 34 separate stepped planes. An enclosed pedestrian bridge links the clinic, parking structure, hotel, and old and new hospital wings at the second level.

A significant aspect of this project is the Campus Green, designed to be the unifying core around which future additions will be built.

It is meant to be viewed from clinic waiting rooms and to be enjoyed as a landscaped park. Two paths, paved with granite and dotted with teak benches, travel the full length of the Green. Careful planning went into the selection of plant materials: the white oaks will become sculptural giants to anchor and frame the entire landscape 50 years hence, other trees offer fall color, and spring flowers abound. An interesting feature of the green is its perspective. Because it was designed to be viewed from clinic waiting rooms, centered on the building's main facade, telescoping lines of trees form an axial perspective, making the Green appear longer than it really is. At the far end, an oval of trees has

12-4 *View of the Campus Green, The Cleveland Clinic (Cleveland, OH)*
   Architect: Cesar Pelli & Associates; Photographer: Balthazar Korab Ltd.

12-5 *Lobby, The Cleveland Clinic (Cleveland, OH)*
   Architect: Cesar Pelli & Associates; Interior design: PHH Interspace; Photographer: Balthazar Korab Ltd.

been planted to end the perspective. Seen from the highest floors of the clinic, the oval becomes a perfect circle (Fig. 12-4).

Inside, the lobby is a stepped, three-story volume that recaps the overall mass of the building. The scale of the space and the richness of materials are reminiscent of a grand hotel (Fig. 12-5). Planters and appointment and reception desks are banded with oak half-rounds repeating the horizontality of the exterior window pattern (Fig. 12-6). Waiting rooms are stacked so that they share two-story-high atria and are differentiated by dramatic color palettes and works of art (Fig. 12-7).

12-5

12-6 *Elevator lobby, The Cleveland Clinic (Cleveland, OH)*

Architect: Cesar Pelli & Associates; Interior design: PHH Interspace; Photographer: Balthazar Korab Ltd.

12-7 *Clinic waiting area, The Cleveland Clinic (Cleveland, OH)*

Architect: Cesar Pelli & Associates; Interior design: PHH Interspace; Photographer: Jonathan Hillyer

Mayo Clinic, Scottsdale, Arizona

The quality of interior architecture in Mayo's second satellite facility (180,000 square feet, completed in 1987) is congruent with Mayo's reputation as the preeminent referral center in America. The Mayo tradition of innovation and quality in clinical care and research is expressed in the architecture and interior design of all their buildings. Each makes a unique design statement expressing strength, tradition, innovation, and hope. The Mayo Charlton Comprehensive Cancer Center is one of the most magnificent buildings ever designed for the practice of medicine. Spatial volumes, architectural detailing, wayfinding, selection of furniture, color and texture, and use of materials are deftly handled. Anyone who has an opportunity to visit this facility should do so.

Although responsive to its desert environment, Mayo Scottsdale has the same attention to detail in its interior architecture. Architectural forms of the building and color palette pay homage to the Arizona landscape. Two colors of

stone, a warm and a cool tone, contrast with each other and with the palette of soft greens, cream, rose, and amethyst. Similarly, two types of wood are used as counterpoints: bleached ash, reminiscent of the desert, is contrasted with the richness of mahogany on planters, reception desks, and in custom millwork.

Furniture is designed according to Mayo standards, incorporating ergonomic features as well as comfort. Seating is generally oversized and not what people expect in a medical clinic. The furniture seems to have been designed in concert with the building; pairs of armchairs fit between columns and give symmetry to the space (Fig. 12-8).

Although the alignment of chairs in the main waiting area (Fig. 12-9) may seem odd, Mayo has carefully studied seating preference patterns, which has caused it to align chairs in even rows, all facing the reception desk. They have found that most people, if given a choice, prefer to face the receptionist so that they are sure to see or hear when they are being called.

Author's note: Having recently attended a presentation by Robert Fontaine, director of environmental design of Mayo Clinics, I was astonished to learn of the Mayo brothers' early attention to environmental design features of their clinic. They systematically experimented

12-8 *Patient comfort is foremost in this waiting area, Mayo Clinic (Scottsdale, AZ)*

Architecture and interior design: Hammel Green and Abrahamson, Inc.; Photographer: Mark Boisclair

12-9 *Carefully detailed interior architecture complements a beautiful palette of desert colors and expresses quality in the Mayo Clinic (Scottsdale, AZ)*

Architecture and interior design: Hammel Green and Abrahamson, Inc.; Photographer: Mark Boisclair

with and refined the layout of clinical spaces (sizes and relationships of rooms) and continually modified examination rooms to achieve certain objectives. The Mayo Brothers are unique for their contributions to the field of medicine and also for their foresight in understanding the importance of the interior environment in patient care settings.

Ambulatory Services Building II, Brigham and Women's Hospital, Boston, Massachusetts

Brigham and Women's Hospital, a teaching and tertiary care institution, consolidated its ambulatory care services, which had formerly been scattered all over campus, into a new 108,000-square-foot building completed in 1987. Although high profile in image, the scale of the building is low profile; it blends in admirably with the neighborhood's Bostonian rowhouses (Fig. 12-10). To reduce the scale of the building, two of four treatment levels have been placed below grade. The lower two floors include an MRI facility, blood bank, rehabilitation, and radiology. The upper two floors house private physician groups including Brigham Medical Group, a large internal medicine practice.

The 300-foot atrium has become a signature for the building. It can be entered either from the vehicular drop-off or from the Main Pike (Fig. 12-11), an internal circulation corridor connecting buildings on the hospital campus. (Refer to Fig. 16-31 to reference the campus master plan.) A key element of the success of the atrium is the way it interfaces with the Main Pike; it allows natural light to spill over onto the Pike and provides interesting views of the Pike from the atrium. Wayfinding issues were carefully considered in the design of this building. The atrium serves as a reference landmark, and circulation corridors are straight and legible. Building entries are well marked, and elevators are prominently located, as is the reception and information desk. The patient's circulation path has been defined as starting at the garage elevator kiosk and continuing with prominent directories and well-coordinated, highly visible signage that guide visitors to all destinations. The wayfinding system is discussed in greater detail in chapter 16.

The atrium succeeds magnificently by all previously stated criteria for excellence in design. The scale of the space, with its focus on coffers and skylights, lifts the spirit. The complexity and

12-10 *Exterior design fits in with adjacent Bostonian rowhouses; Ambulatory Services Building II, Brigham and Women's Hospital (Boston, MA)*
Architect: Kaplan McLaughlin Diaz; Photographer: Steve Rosenthal

intricacy of forms and patterns and the layering of materials make the space visually stimulating. Every surface—whether floor, wall, or ceiling—was carefully considered in terms of proportion, texture, and color (Fig. 12-12). The horizontal banding of the exterior is repeated in the atrium, where it is broken every 20 feet by a pier (column) that carries the eye up to the ceiling and across the bottom of the coffer—reminiscent of beams—to the opposite side, where it meets an oak grille. Columns have an oak base and capital detail that serve as counterpoint for the wood grilles and furniture. Acoustical treatment includes Fabritrack panels at the north and south ends of the atrium as well as in ceiling coffers (Fig. 12-12).

Lighting is varied and interesting. Vertical piers and elevator lobbies feature wall sconces; carefully placed downlights highlight works of art, wood grilles in the atrium, and other features.

Interior design and architecture are so well integrated in this building that they cannot be viewed independently. A marriage this good is too rarely achieved. Semicircular bays of the exterior were repeated in the atrium and enhanced with railings, reveals created by a layering of gypsum board, and some (Fig. 12-13) have landscaped balconies. Flooring materials

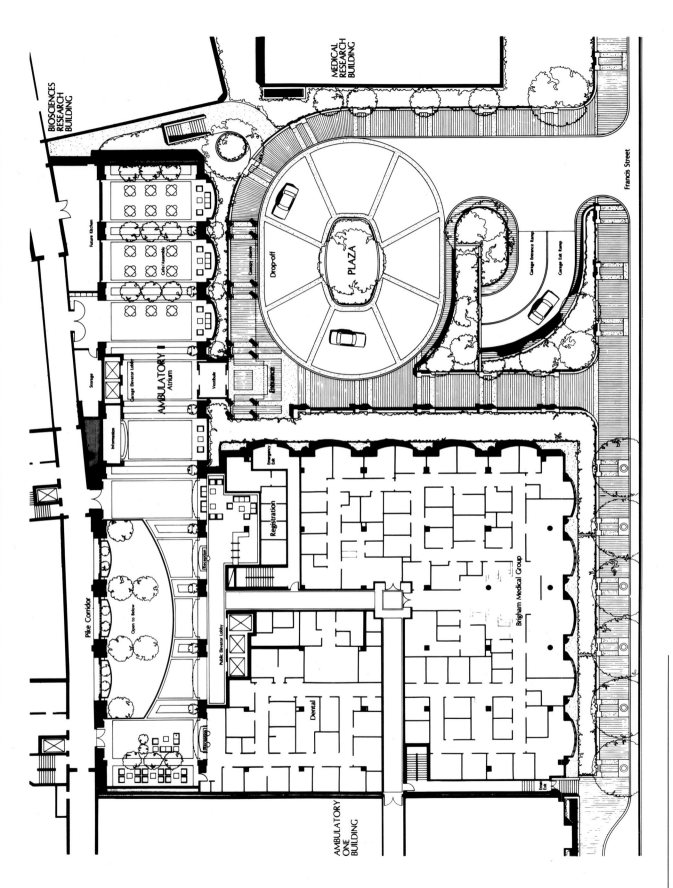

12-11 *Site plan, Ambulatory Services Building II,*
Brigham and Women's Hospital (Boston, MA)
* Architecture and interior design: Kaplan McLaughlin*
Diaz in collaboration with Tsoi/Kobus & Associates

The following labels appear within the site plan:

BIOSCIENCES RESEARCH BUILDING

MEDICAL RESEARCH BUILDING

Francis Street

Future Kitchen

Café/Assembly

Storage

Garage Elevator Lobby

AMBULATORY II
Atrium

Information

Vestibule

Entrance

PLAZA

Drop-off

Garage Entrance Ramp

Garage Exit Ramp

Pike Corridor

Open to Below

Emergency Exit

Registration

Reception

Public Elevator Lobby

Dental

Brigham Medical Group

AMBULATORY ONE BUILDING

Emergency Exit

12-12 *Level two lobby is filled with natural light and characterized by careful architectural detailing that expresses quality; Ambulatory Services Building II, Brigham and Women's Hospital (Boston, MA)*
Architecture and interior design: Kaplan McLaughlin Diaz in collaboration with Tsoi/Kobus & Associates; Photographer: Steve Rosenthal

12-13 *Level one lobby is flooded with natural light and features balcony bays that repeat the design of the building's exterior; Ambulatory Services Building II, Brigham and Women's Hospital (Boston, MA)*
Architecture and interior design: Kaplan McLaughlin Diaz in collaboration with Tsoi/Kobus & Associates; Photographer: Steve Rosenthal

identify three zones of the atrium: circulation, orientation, and waiting. A pairing of ceramic tile (in both slate and smooth finishes) with accents of marble provides a safe, nonslip surface at reasonable cost, complemented by the elegance of marble (Fig. 12-13). The changing geometries of this building as a visitor moves through it and appreciates it from different viewpoints give it vitality. Note that wall surfaces are treated differently in level one (Fig. 12-13) than

12-14 *Registration area, Ambulatory Services Building
II, Brigham and Women's Hospital (Boston, MA)
     Architecture and interior design: Kaplan McLaughlin
Diaz in collaboration with Tsoi/Kobus & Associates;
Photographer: Steve Rosenthal*

in level two (Fig. 12-12). The vocabulary of materials is the same, but the application is varied.
Furnishings have a timeless character and use
a restricted number of colors; the texture is allowed to become the dominant focus. Custom-
designed planters and directories feature inlaid
wood marquetry design.

Color is intensified in spaces away from the
atrium, such as the level two ambulatory services registration area (Fig. 12-14). Atrium detailing and flavor are carried into this space, yet
it has its own character. The balance among
color, texture, and shape and the addition of
fine art create an environment that is original
and visually stimulating. It tells patients that
they are very important people, and it sets up
perceptions of excellence in clinical care.

Individual medical suites within the building
have the same quality and originality of detailing
as the atrium, but each has a distinctive char-

acter. The typical public corridor and suite entry
destination incorporates oak doors and handrails. Radiology reception has a dramatic color
palette of amethyst, burgundy, and blue, complemented by original works of art (Fig. 12-15).
The reception desk and the soffit above have a
shape reminiscent of the semicircular bays of
the atrium. Note the consistency in signage
placement, style, and visibility throughout this
building. The rehabilitation waiting area features
seating that is appropriate for rehab patients,
ample circulation space for wheelchairs, and a
low divider to provide privacy (Fig. 12-16).

The orthopedics and rheumatology suite
(22,725 square feet) is located directly adjacent
to the parking structure to provide immediate
and convenient access for mobility-impaired patients. The main circulation spine of this clinic is
defined by a vocabulary of details that provide
wayfinding cues. These cues include arches at
intersections leading to various suites, a
change in wallcovering, windows providing
views into suite waiting areas, inset carpet accents, and an oak base that defines the main
artery but does not continue into spaces leading off of it (Fig. 12-17). Note the interesting
column detail at the outside corners of inter-
secting suite openings.

12-15 *Radiology reception area features beautifully designed reception desk; Ambulatory Services Building II, Brigham and Women's Hospital (Boston, MA)*

Architecture and interior design: Kaplan McLaughlin Diaz in collaboration with Tsoi/Kobus & Associates; Photographer: Steve Rosenthal

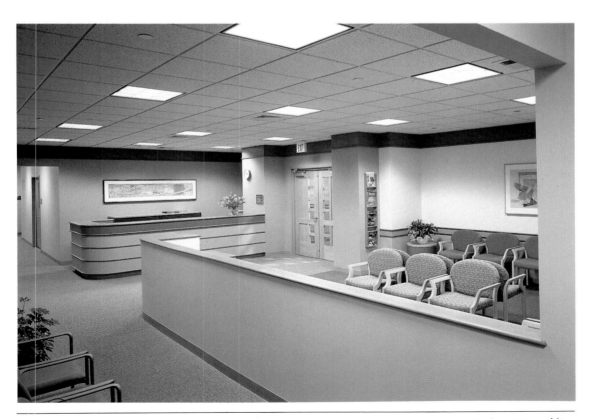

12-16 *Rehabilitation services waiting area, Ambulatory Services Building II, Brigham and Women's Hospital (Boston, MA)*

Architecture and interior design: Kaplan McLaughlin Diaz in collaboration with Tsoi/Kobus & Associates; Photographer: Steve Rosenthal

12-17 *Main artery corridor of a 22,725-square-foot orthopedic/rheumatology clinic features a number of visual cues to enhance wayfinding; Ambulatory Services Building II, Brigham and Women's Hospital (Boston, MA) Interior architecture: Tsoi/Kobus & Associates; Photographer: Steve Rosenthal*

PUBLIC SPACES

First impressions are created in the lobby. The soaring atrium of Kaiser Permanente's Kensington Medical Center (88,000 square feet) is a festive, celebratory space affirming optimism and good health (Fig. 12-18). A domed glass ceiling, cascading tiers of plants, a glass-paneled soffit that reflects the sky, and original artwork including colorful banners (Fig. 12-19) create a high-quality ambience that must make Kaiser members feel special. The lobby in Fig-

ure 12-20, although lacking the drama of an atrium space, uses texture and form to great advantage. Many of the refinements in architectural detailing are not visible in the photograph, but exquisite attention to the joining of materials and the composition of various architectural elements (proportions of windows, grids formed by window frames, spatial volumes, and selection of hardware) set an image of quality rarely seen in large clinic buildings. The building entrance (out of view) is at the far right of the photo. The direction of brick pavers leads visitors directly to the information desk and the optical dispensary, which figures prominently as a retail space in Kaiser facilities. The metal pan ceiling has been laid on a diagonal, leading the eye directly to the curved glass wall of the optical dispensary. Large columns are sheathed in a pale, iridescent green aluminum; walls feature acoustic fabric and have recessed bumper

12-18 *Clinic lobby is a festive celebratory space; Kaiser Permanente Kensington Medical Center (Kensington, MD)*

Architecture and interior design: Cannon; Photographer: Maxwell Mackenzie

12-19

12-19 *Upper level of atrium, Kaiser Permanente Kensington Medical Center (Kensington, MD)*
   Architecture and interior design: Cannon;
Photographer: Maxwell Mackenzie

12-20 *Clinic lobby features careful architectural detailing and a high-profile image; Kaiser Permanente Park Sierra Medical Office Building (Riverside, CA)*
   Architect: Langdon Wilson Architecture Planning; Interior design: HMC Architects, Inc.; Photographer: Milroy/McAleer

guards in the same aluminum material that covers columns.

Kaiser Vandever Clinic is a 115,000-square-foot ambulatory services building that is oriented to the outdoors. Visitors may wait in beautifully landscaped garden courtyards or in open waiting rooms that take advantage of full-height glazing and distant mountain views (Fig. 12-21). This feature is unusual in large clinics, which often have interior waiting rooms and a maze of internal corridors that create confusion in wayfinding. This building has a highly disciplined layout that makes wayfinding easy. All waiting rooms of various clinics open onto the main circulation spine, and a number of interior architectural details are consistently repeated

12-21 *Single-loaded corridor provides magnificent views for patients in waiting room; a consistent vocabulary of design details is carried throughout the clinic; Kaiser Permanente Vandever Medical Office Building (San Diego, CA)*

Architect: Neptune Thomas Davis; Interior design: Jain Malkin Inc.; Photographer: Sandra Williams

throughout each floor (Fig. 12-22). These details include the stairstepped soffit that defines each clinic waiting and reception room and carries the signature color associated with each floor. Other details include the stairstepped carpet design, light cove over the windows, design of the reception desk with inset reveals in the signature color, and details in elevator lobbies (Fig. 12-23). Elevator lobbies have a full-width, full-height window wall at one end and an easily remembered art element and bench at the other end that serve as landmark references. Ceilings

12-22 *Seating is arranged to take advantage of exterior views; Kaiser Permanente Vandever Medical Office Building (San Diego, CA)*

Architect: Neptune Thomas Davis; Interior design: Jain Malkin Inc.; Photographer: Sandra Williams

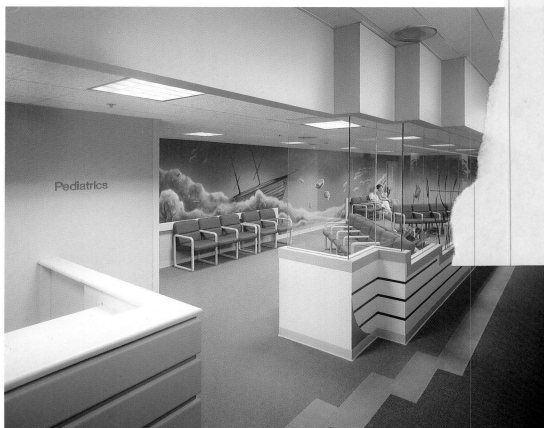

have indirect light coves and an upholstered wall with a horizontal banding of ceramic tile.

The pediatrics waiting room is semienclosed in glass and incorporates a sophisticated undersea theme that can be appreciated by children, adolescents, and adults. The rear wall has a realistic airbrushed mural of a shipwreck, and glass panels are painted with saltwater fish and kelp; the room appears to be a large aquarium or underwater space in which patients waiting appear to be colorful fish (Fig. 12-24).

REGIONAL CHARACTER

Some buildings are successful for their ability to embody the character of the region and the spirit of the community. Kaiser Permanente Rockwood in Portland, Oregon, is such a facility. Nestled in a grove of fir trees, the cedar and brick exterior and the gabled porte cochere, with its large fir beams and seamed sheet metal roof, convey the essence of Pacific Northwest architecture (Fig. 12-25). In fact, the building has the ambience of the mountain lodges on nearby Mount Hood. Inside, a vaulted ceiling of exposed trusses and beams carries the eye upward to focus on a magnificent 15- x 30-foot stained- and etched-glass window designed by Portland artist Ed Carpenter. At night, when illuminated from within, the building has the aura of a cathedral (Fig. 12-26). During the day, light filtering through the etched and colored glass creates lacy patterns on walls. Throughout the building is an expression of hand craftsmanship, not just in the stained glass but also in built-in seating, a wood grid ceiling (Fig. 12-27) spanning corridors and waiting rooms (to conceal

12-25 *Regional architecture of the Pacific Northwest is expressed in this building, Kaiser Permanente Rockwood Medical Clinic (Rockwood, OR)*
Architecture and interior design: BOOR/A; Photographer: Strode Eckert

12-23 *Elevator lobbies feature coved lighting treatment and upholstered wall with horizontal reveals of ceramic tile; Kaiser Permanente Vandever Medical Office Building (San Diego, CA)*
Architect: Neptune Thomas Davis; Interior design: Jain Malkin Inc.; Photographer: Sandra Williams

12-24 *Pediatric waiting room features a whimsical human aquarium; people waiting appear to be colorful fish; effect is enhanced by airbrushed mural of shipwreck on back wall; Kaiser Permanente Vandever Medical Office Building (San Diego, CA)*
Architect: Neptune Thomas Davis; Interior design: Jain Malkin Inc.; Photographer: Sandra Williams

fluorescent lighting), and the wood joinery of exposed structural elements (Fig. 12-28). This facility exemplifies patient-centered care. The 48,000-square-foot clinic, completed in 1985, has warmth, comfort, and the familiarity of a country doctor's office while it makes available high-tech treatment and equipment.

Architecture of the American Southwest houses the Center for Non-Invasive Diagnosis at the University of New Mexico in Albuquerque. Rather than design a high-tech structure to symbolize magnetic resonance imaging technology, the architect chose to pursue a style more familiar to the desert environs. Domestic in scale, a series of geometric stucco forms are beautifully articulated to produce an interesting yet different composition when viewed from each direction. Indentations, niches, and trellises create beautiful patterns of sun and

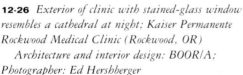

12-26 *Exterior of clinic with stained-glass window resembles a cathedral at night; Kaiser Permanente Rockwood Medical Clinic (Rockwood, OR)*
Architecture and interior design: BOOR/A; Photographer: Ed Hershberger

12-27 *Clinic public areas feature open wooden gridwork ceiling treatment; Kaiser Permanente Rockwood Medical Clinic (Rockwood, OR)*
Architecture and interior design: BOOR/A; Photographer: Ed Hershberger

shadow. The building's main entrance is through a courtyard (Fig. 12-29). The reception area has clerestory windows on four sides to admit natural light and a wood ceiling that contrasts with polished chrome tubular lights (Fig. 12-30). The stairstepped geometric forms in interior spaces continue the expression of southwestern architecture.

The magnet room is entered beside a glass block, sunlit curved wall. Magnet rooms are clad in copper-sheathed plywood to repel outside radio waves; nonferrous materials were used near the magnet rooms (glass fiber concrete reinforcing, aluminum flashing, and plastic pipes and ducts). The west side of the building has sweeping, curved walls that follow the curves of the magnetic field to keep automo-

biles (moving ferrous objects) and people wearing pacemakers a safe distance from the magnets.

In contrast, a nineteenth-century textile manufacturing center established the architectural style of the 20,000-square-foot ambulatory care center, completed in 1987, for St. Mary's Hospital in Cedarburg, Wisconsin. It is a satellite facility designed to provide the services of a traditional rural hospital. Situated in a historic community, the ambulatory care center is designed to incorporate architectural forms familiar to the area such as the gable ends that were used to symbolize the center's three-element nature: diagnostic facilities, outpatient clinics, and ambulatory surgery (Fig. 12-31). The interior, however, is quite sophisticated to reassure

12-28 *Exposed trusses and beams embody Pacific Northwest regional architecture and convey a feeling of handcraftsmanship; Kaiser Permanente Rockwood Medical Clinic (Rockwood, OR)*

Architecture and interior design: BOOR/A; Photographer: Ed Hershberger

patients that they are receiving high-quality medical care (Fig. 12-32). Warm colors, indirect lighting, residential-style furnishings, and high-quality architectural detailing make this facility unique in its rural setting.

12-29 *Indigenous architectural forms reflect light and shadow at Center for Non-Invasive Diagnosis, University of New Mexico (Albuquerque, NM)*

Architecture and interior design: Westwork Architects; Photographer: Kirk Gittings, Syntax

12-30 *Reception area for magnetic resonance imaging suite, Center for Non-Invasive Diagnosis, University of New Mexico (Albuquerque, NM)*

   Architecture and interior design: Westwork Architects; Photographer: Kirk Gittings, Syntax

12-31 *Architecture responds to community's history as a nineteenth-century textile manufacturing center; Ambulatory Care Center, St. Mary's Hospital Ozaukee (Cedarburg, WI)*

   Architecture and interior design: Flad & Associates; Photographer: Joe Paskus

12-32 *Clinic lobby has residential character; Ambulatory Care Center, St. Mary's Hospital Ozaukee (Cedarburg, WI)*
   Architecture and interior design: Flad & Associates; Photographer: Joe Paskus

ARCHITECTURAL DETAILING

The quality of a facility is often expressed in its architectural detailing. Attention to transitions between materials, details of joinery, juxtaposition of materials so that their respective textures complement or contrast with each other, and matching patterns of wood grain are refinements that are sometimes overshadowed by slim budgets. Nevertheless, a quest for excellence demands that these items not be overlooked. The composition of a wood-paneled wall and its alignment with the ceramic tile base and floor (Fig. 12-33), the design of an HVAC grille set into a wall (Fig. 12-34), and a coved cornice detail that adds interest to a corridor

(Fig. 12-35) are the kind of features that add character to an interior environment and make them memorable. Excellence is the difference between haphazardly adding molding or trim to a reception room and carefully detailing it to become a key element in the composition of the room (Fig. 12-36). It is the difference between providing areas of clear or opaque glass to enhance privacy in the reception office and creating a sandblasted design on the glass to make it support the design theme (Fig. 12-37).

Quality can also be expressed with subtlety and simplicity (Fig. 12-38). Sometimes all elements of the interior environment complement each other so harmoniously that a visitor cannot imagine any element being changed (Fig. 12-37). Harmony is expressed in the symmetry of the entry to the Missouri Bone & Joint Clinic in Bridgeton, Missouri (Fig. 12-39). Tiered planters and glazing enhance the entry to the clinic

12-33 *Careful attention to detail involves meticulously aligning grout joints of the stone floor with the stone base and wall paneling*
   Architecture and interior design: Ellerbe Becket; Photographer: © Peter Aaron/Esto

12-34 *Meticulous architectural detailing involves a custom-designed HVAC grille, perfectly aligned with joints of stone panel in Figure 12-33*
   Architecture and interior design: Ellerbe Becket;
Photographer: © Peter Aaron/Esto

12-35 *Beautiful architectural detailing sets an image of high quality; Connecticut Neurological Center, Bridgeport Hospital (affiliated with Yale University School of Medicine, Bridgeport, CT)*
   Architecture and interior design: Cannon;
Photographer: Richard Mandelkorn

12-36 *Sandblasted glass and tiers of wood molding provide design interest in this clinic, Providence Downtown (Seattle, WA)*
   Architecture and interior design: The NBBJ Group;
Photographer: Karl Bischoff

by making it visually accessible and by introducing live plants, a symbol of nature and healing.

Quality may be expressed in many ways, as can attention to detail. As an example, the interior design for the new entrance and main lobby of New England Medical Center, located in Boston's Chinatown, began with the interior architect's purchase of an antique Chinese wedding robe, from which he derived the color palette for the space (Fig. 12-40). Small groupings of seating surrounded by built-in planters and room dividers afford privacy and diminish the scale of the large lobby.

12-37 *Primary care clinic located in Seattle's business district was created in former drive-through bank space; 12,000-square-foot clinic features skylit entry and calming colors; Providence Downtown (Seattle, WA)*
   Architecture and interior design: The NBBJ Group; Photographer: Karl Bischoff

12-38 *Attractive corridor design includes recessed suite entries; Ambulatory Care Center, Fairgrounds Medical Center (Allentown, PA)*
   Architecture and interior design: BLM Group; Photographer: Tom Crane Photography © Maureen C. Wilkiera

12-39 *Imaginative design characterizes clinic entry; Missouri Bone & Joint Clinic, DePaul Health Center (Bridgeton, MO)*

Architecture and interior design: The Hoffman Partnership Inc.; Photographer: Alise O'Brien Architectural Photography

12-40 *Chinese wedding robe inspired design of hospital lobby, located in Chinatown, of New England Medical Center (Boston, MA)*

Architecture and interior design: Tsoi/Kobus & Associates; Photographer: Sam Sweezy

COLOR AND TEXTURE

Color and texture are components of every interior environment, but some designers use it far more successfully than others. The richness and drama of color and texture, when used to full advantage, are exemplified in Figure 12-41. Even the selection of plant species enhances the texture of the room. The corridor (Fig. 12-42) is equally dramatic, with the angled space frame, lush plantings, upholstered benches, and stone floors. One signature color can be equally dramatic (Fig. 12-43 and 12-44).

Evans Army Hospital is noteworthy because it incorporates all of these characteristics of excellence. The architecture and selection of materials express strength and substance and show a continuity of detailing carried throughout

12-41 *Residential furniture, rich colors, and texture characterize this medical facility, Pacific Cataract and Laser Institute (Chehalis, WA)*

Architect: The BJSS Group; Interior design: TRA Interior Design; Photographer: Robert Pisano

12-42 *Spaceframe adds interesting geometry to clinic waiting area at Pacific Cataract and Laser Institute (Chehalis, WA)*

Architect: The BJSS Group; Interior design: TRA Interior Design; Photographer: Robert Pisano

12-43 *This 230,000-square-foot medical office building includes two levels of retail space; Hartford Hospital (Hartford, CT)*

Architecture and interior design: RTKL Associates Inc.; Photographer: Nick Wheeler

12-44 *Atrium provides natural light and an interesting view from second floor spaces of Evans U.S. Army Community Hospital (Fort Carson, CO)*

Architecture and interior design: Smith, Hinchman & Grylls Associates, Inc.; Photographer: Balthazar Korab Ltd.

12-45 *The geometry of exposed structural elements creates a composition that is varied and interesting; Evans U.S. Army Community Hospital (Fort Carson, CO)*

Architecture and interior design: Smith, Hinchman & Grylls Associates, Inc.; Photographer: Balthazar Korab Ltd.

all areas. A conservative choice of materials (brick, concrete, and steel) seems appropriate for a government building, yet the overall ambience is anything but traditional. The design is highly disciplined, with exquisite attention to pattern and composition (Figs. 12-45 and 12-

46). Unusual wall-mounted light fixtures add just the right accent to the pedestrian mall. Note how signage has been integrated into the design. This project is all the more unique because it is for the military, yet it has somehow averted the no-frills, clonelike austerity that characterizes too many military facilities.

The facility in Figure 12-47 uses a primary accent color on horizontal banding carrying department names and on railings. Although all of the surfaces are hard, a textured feeling is achieved through the interplay of glass block grid, railings, diagonal stair, and ceramic tile.

12-46 *The composition created by structural elements, combined with the signature accent color, makes this building a sculptural work of art; Evans U.S. Army Community Hospital (Fort Carson, CO)*

Architecture and interior design: Smith, Hinchman & Grylls Associates, Inc.; Photographer: Balthazar Korab Ltd.

12-47 *Glass block, ceramic tile, and pipe railings, combined with strong accent colors on railings and signage bands, create a stimulating composition; Minot Air Force Base Composite Medical Facility (Minot, ND)*

Architecture and interior design: Flad & Associates; Photographer: Joe Paskus

EXAMINATION AND CLINICAL AREAS

Mayo Clinic's passions for efficiency and patient-centered care come together in the design of their telemedicine examination room (Fig. 12-48), used for video transmission between clinics. (The examination table is out of view.) Notice the detail lavished on building-in the viewbox illuminator so that it blends into the wood-paneled wall. By contrast, Kaiser Permanente's typical exam room is efficiently designed and devoid of frills (Fig. 12-49). An

12-48 *Telemedicine conference examination room, Mayo Clinic (Scottsdale, AZ)*

Architecture and interior design: Hammel Green and Abrahamson, Inc.; Photographer: Mark Bosclair

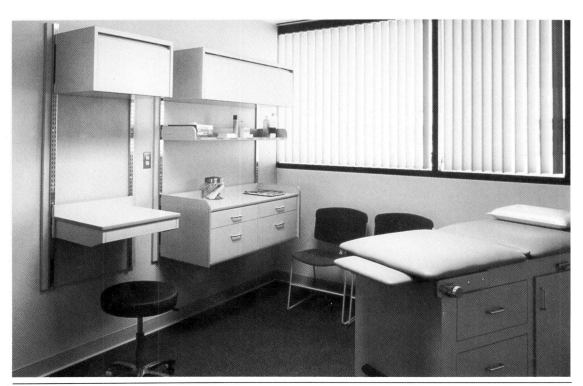

12-49 *Typical examination room, Kaiser Permanente Vandever Medical Clinic (San Diego, CA)*

Architect: Neptune Thomas Davis; Interior design: Jain Malkin Inc.; Photographer: Sandra Williams

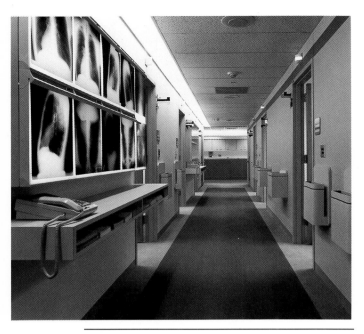

12-50 *Nurse station and examination room corridor, The Cleveland Clinic (Cleveland, OH)*
Architect: Cesar Pelli & Associates; Interior design: PHH Interspace; Photographer: Jonathan Hillyer

12-51 *Sloped windows of examination rooms capture light from internal corridor; Comprehensive Health Services of Detroit (Detroit, MI)*
Architecture and interior design: Smith, Hinchman & Grylls Associates, Inc.; Photographer: 1989 P. S. Bednarski

examination corridor in the Cleveland Clinic is functional, neat, and tidy in appearance (Fig. 12-50).

Most exam rooms benefit from natural light, even though it may not be a functional necessity for most specialties. Exam rooms in Figure 12-51 borrow light from the glass-enclosed corridor ceiling.

Much can be said about the layout and design of a patient examination room; however, these topics were discussed in detail in my last book, *Medical and Dental Space Planning for the 1990s* (1990). Issues of patient privacy, convenience (a place to dress), and the physician's ease of access to examine the patient must be considered. My intention here, however, is to present a typical exam room in one of the Kaiser, Mayo, or Cleveland Clinic facilities reviewed. Having seen their public spaces, a reader would naturally want to know how these large-scale providers of high-quality health care might design their exam rooms.

LOW-INCOME PROJECTS

The most challenging assignment is to create a clinic serving a low-income population. Typically the budget is meager and the need great to create a space that speaks of dignity and respect. The Columbia-Presbyterian Nagle Avenue Clinic, completed in 1988, serves a poor neighborhood in upper Manhattan. Yet this facility includes many amenities in both the interior design and functional layout of space. Patients register in a sit-down private alcove (Fig. 12-52) and wait in small-scale seating areas with wall sconce lighting and an interesting wall treatment (Fig. 12-53). To reinforce the private practice office model, the space plan decentralizes treatment areas into clusters (Fig. 12-54).

California Pediatric Center, completed in 1987, is an 18,000-square-foot nonprofit outpatient clinic providing medical and social services, physical therapy, and dentistry to children of low-income families living in the inner city of Los Angeles. The skylighted interior courtyard admits light into all rooms of the building (Fig. 12-55). Strong horizontal bands of color in pale yellow and pale blue encircle a stair tower that has a playful geometry. Inside the tower (Fig. 12-56), a bright yellow wall and windows make the stairs particularly inviting.

12-52 *This 10,000-square-foot clinic provides primary care to low-income residents in a dignified setting; Columbia-Presbyterian/Nagle Avenue Clinic, Washington Heights–Inwood Ambulatory Care Network (New York City)*

Architecture and interior design: Norman Rosenfeld, A.I.A., Architects; Photographer: © Norman McGrath ASMP

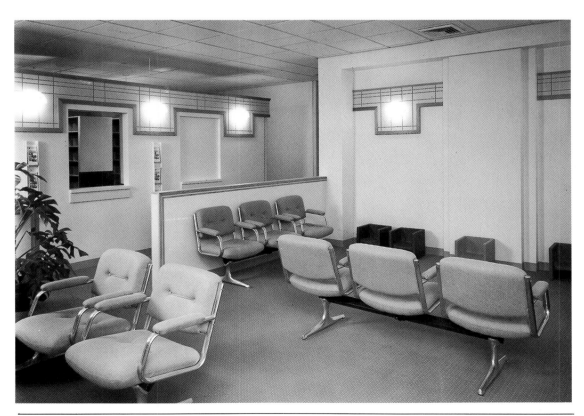

12-53 *Indirect cove lighting, wall sconces, and trim around reception/cashier windows enhance the quality image of the clinic; Columbia-Presbyterian/Nagle Avenue Clinic, Washington Heights–Inwood Ambulatory Care Network (New York City)*

Architecture and interior design: Norman Rosenfeld, A.I.A., Architects; Photographer: © Norman McGrath ASMP.

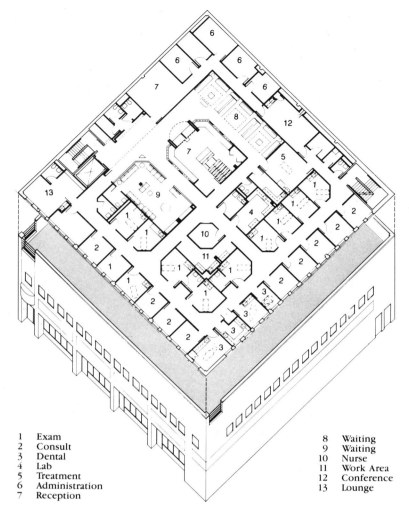

1	Exam	8	Waiting
2	Consult	9	Waiting
3	Dental	10	Nurse
4	Lab	11	Work Area
5	Treatment	12	Conference
6	Administration	13	Lounge
7	Reception		

12-54

12-55

12-56

AMBULATORY SURGICAL CENTERS

Ambulatory surgery refers to scheduled surgical procedures provided to patients who do not require overnight hospitalization. Ambulatory surgery may be provided in a physician's office —in which case it is called *office-based surgery*—or in a freestanding, independent facility specifically organized to provide scheduled ambulatory surgery.

The first successful freestanding ambulatory surgical center (FASC) is generally recognized to be the Phoenix Surgicenter, which began operations in February 1970. Anesthesiologists Wallace Reed and John Ford established the facility that has become the model for other non-hospital—based ambulatory surgical centers.

The freestanding ambulatory surgical center may be organized according to a variety of operational models that vary according to type of ownership and sponsorship, affiliation with hospitals, and types of services offered. The term *freestanding* may be used to refer to a facility that is physically separate from another, such as a hospital, or it may mean a facility whose program and ownership are independent and legally distinct from any other organization.

Ambulatory surgical centers may be located within a hospital, may be a separate building located on the hospital campus, or may be a satellite facility located off campus. Some ambulatory surgical centers are entrepreneurial enterprises owned and operated by a group of anesthesiologists or surgeons and have no affiliation with a hospital. These facilities are commonly located within a medical office building, or they may be physically freestanding in a single-tenant building.

ADVANTAGES OF AMBULATORY SURGERY

Ambulatory surgery has many advantages from both the patients' and the physicians' viewpoints. Some of these advantages follow.

1. Hospitals are geared to traditional inpatient surgery protocols, which are often inappropriate for ambulatory patients, whereas a facility organized for the sole purpose of ambulatory surgery has a staff trained to meet the specific needs of these patients. Hospitals sometimes find merging new protocols with existing systems difficult.

12-54 *Floor plan of Columbia-Presbyterian/Nagle Avenue Clinic (New York City) features continuous clerestory glazing along the corridor wall to permit natural light to pass from perimeter offices; circulation is clear and direct; Adult and pediatric waiting areas are separated by the reception/clerical island*
Courtesy Norman Rosenfeld, A.I.A., Architects

12-55 *Fanciful stair tower is focal point of clinic for children of low-income families; California Pediatrics Center (Los Angeles, CA)*
Architect: Bobrow/Thomas and Associates; Interior design: Kaneko Ford Design, Patricia Ford; Photographer: Annette Del Zoppo Photography

12-56 *View of stair tower from upper balcony, California Pediatrics Center (Los Angeles, CA)*
Architect: Bobrow/Thomas and Associates; Interior design: Kaneko Ford Design, Patricia Ford; Photographer: Annette Del Zoppo Photography

2. Ambulatory surgery patients are not sick; they are candidates for elective procedures. In a hospital, their families may have to share a common surgery waiting room with inpatients' families, which can have a devastating psychological effect. Imagine the stress of sitting next to someone whose husband is having open heart surgery.

3. Patients often experience psychological stress when entering a hospital. Fear of the unknown is heightened by unexpected sights, such as a view of a patient arriving in an ambulance or a patient on a gurney with an IV tube in the arm. Patients are generally less apprehensive when arriving for surgery in a facility located in a medical office building.

4. Physicians and staff often experience greater satisfaction in an FASC because they can tailor operational systems as they wish, with no bureaucratic red tape.

5. Scheduling of procedures is much more flexible in an FASC. In a hospital, ambulatory patients are bumped to open up the schedule for urgent or emergency patients. Both physicians and patients find ease of scheduling an advantage in an FASC.

6. Ambulatory surgery provides for better utilization of hospital beds and generally costs less than doing the same procedure in a hospital. The major saving is due to elimination of a hospital stay, and insurance providers often stipulate they will pay for certain procedures only if done within an ambulatory surgical center.

7. Ambulatory surgical patients receive less medication both preoperatively and postoperatively, and they often return to work sooner than inpatients who have those same procedures. The FASCs promote a wellness philosophy, treating patients as if they are healthy and allowing them to take responsibility for a large part of their own care.

MARKETING CONSIDERATIONS

Among the most attractive features of surgery in a freestanding facility is the element of choice. A physician may have privileges at several facilities and may offer the patient the opportunity to choose the preferred setting. Along with that choice comes the expectation of care delivered in a small-scale, nonclinical, friendly environment. Patient satisfaction is necessary for a facility's success, and many FASCs are keenly aware of guest relations.

The interior environment is a critical element of patient satisfaction. The entire facility should use color to relax and soothe patients, with texture introduced in carpets and wallcoverings, wherever appropriate (in terms of maintenance and infection control). Artwork and accessories should not be overlooked as a means of distracting patients and making the facility less threatening.

Patients and their families, however, are not the only ones who benefit from a well-designed environment. In order to attract top-quality physicians and nursing staff and to keep morale high, staff areas must be properly designed so that they are functional, and they should look as attractive as patient areas.

SURVEY OF SURGICAL PROCEDURES

Prior to designing a facility, understanding the types of procedures normally performed in an FASC is helpful. In a survey of 1221 facilities nationwide represented in Table 12-1, nearly 67 percent of procedures fall into four specialty categories.

Table 12-1. Specialty Surgical Procedures Performed in Freestanding Surgery Centers in 1989.

Type of Procedure	Percentage
Ophthalmology	28.2
Gynecological	18.9
Ear, nose, and throat	10.8
Orthopedic	9.5
General	8.7
Plastic	7.7
Podiatry	4.6
Urology	3.8
Gastroenterology	3.2
Dental and oral	1.7
Pain block	1.3
Neurology	0.3
Other	1.3
Total	100.0

Source: SMG Marketing Group Inc., Chicago, IL

FACILITY DESIGN

Careful planning precedes the development of an ambulatory surgical center. Feasibility studies analyze the demographics of the area and determine the demand for such a facility. In terms of codes and regulatory agency review, an FASC is certainly the most complicated of any outpatient facility.

The purpose of the current discussion is to present a general overview of the experience of ambulatory surgery from the patient's perspective and offer design guidelines for creating a supportive environment. A more technical discussion of planning issues appears in my book *Medical and Dental Space Planning for the 1990s* (1990).

Wellness Philosophy

Implementing a wellness philosophy means encouraging patients to be as independent as possible and to take responsibility for their own well-being; it involves teaching patients and their families what to expect from the ambulatory surgical experience. In this environment nurses are indoctrinated to repeatedly indicate to patients that they perceive them as well people, which in turn allows patients to participate in their own care. As an example, they may be allowed to shave or scrub the surgical site themselves, with the supervision of a nurse (McCartney, 1985).

In some facilities, patients are allowed to remain in street clothes until a few minutes prior to surgery so that they can meet most of the staff while wearing their own clothes. Studies have shown that giving up clothing may cause psychological stress because a person's identity and sense of control are threatened. Some facilities promoting a wellness philosophy are so concerned about patients feeling they have a sense of control that they allow patients to walk into the operating room unless, for some reason, they have had premedication.

An atmosphere of wellness can be communicated through a combination of physical layout, aesthetics, staff attitude, and attention to small details such as colored sheets, live plants, fresh flowers, and colorful attire for surgical staff. The facility in Figure 12-57 combines a warm, attractive color palette with indirect lighting and interesting ceiling and soffit detailing to create an environment that exudes wellness. Note the attention to detail in the cubicle curtain, which is notched to allow the wood valance to penetrate it.

Patient Flow

The seven stages of patient flow through a facility are preadmitting, arrival, patient prep, induction, recovery, postrecovery, and discharge. The patient's first encounter with the facility

may be a day or two prior to surgery to complete preadmission forms, have laboratory tests, and receive dietary instructions.

This visit may be the first time the patient has ever had surgery, or perhaps the first time the patient has had ambulatory surgery, and he or she may have no frame of reference upon which to rely to defeat fear and anxiety. Therefore, the preadmitting process gives the patient confidence about the experience. After all, a patient truly cannot evaluate the quality of clinical care or the surgeon's competence, but patients do make judgments nevertheless, based on interactions with staff and an assessment of the interior environment.

A patient's confidence can be bolstered by an understanding of exactly what to expect on the day of surgery. Nursing staff, anesthesiologists, and surgeons all play a significant role in educating and reassuring the patient. If the facility is designed well, circulation patterns will be predictable and convenient and allow easy access for patients, staff, and family. Good design should make doing things right easy for staff.

The patient arrives on the day of surgery between one and a half and three hours prior to the scheduled surgery time, accompanied by an escort. Some facilities do lab work on the day of surgery, which means patients may have to arrive a little earlier. The patient is next directed to a preparation area where street clothes are exchanged for surgical apparel. This exchange may be handled in a number of ways. Some facilities have dressing rooms and lockers for storage of the patient's belongings, whereas others have the patient undress in a private prep and exam room, and belongings are placed in a container that remains on the patient's gurney throughout the stay. In the postanesthesia recovery room, belongings are returned to the patient before dressing for discharge.

Some facilities do not have individual patient prep rooms and, instead, use a large room (called *pre-op holding*) similar to the recovery room, with gurneys separated by cubicle drapes for privacy. In this situation, patients sometimes change clothes within this enclosure, or they may use a dressing or locker room.

After the patient is undressed, the operative site is scrubbed, shaved, and prepped for surgery. The anesthesiologist generally talks to the patient in the prep area or in the preoperative

12-57 *Beautiful architectural detailing expresses high quality in this ambulatory surgical unit recovery room, Somerset Medical Center (Somerville, NJ)*
Architecture and interior design: The BLM Group;
Photographer: © Tom Crane

holding area, discusses the alternatives for anesthesia, and answers any questions the patient may have. Most FASCs do not use preoperative sedatives, which increase recovery time. Therefore, patients may read or chat with each other prior to being inducted into surgery. The patient may walk or may be wheeled into the operating room. Some facilities prefer to

have patients walk to enhance the patient's perception of himself or herself as a healthy individual.

Anesthetic induction almost always takes place in the operating room, although an intravenous fluid may be started in the preoperative holding area. Following surgery, patients are transferred to the postanesthesia recovery area until they are conscious and stabilized. Many facilities also have a second-stage recovery area that has recliner chairs and lounge seating. Patients remain here after they are dressed, have some juice or tea, and leave when they feel well enough for discharge or when their escort has arrived. Often, the escort is allowed to sit with the patient in the secondary recovery lounge. Instructions for postoperative care may be delivered here or in a private office adjacent to the discharge area.

Waiting and Reception Areas

The patient's first impression of the surgical center will be formed in the waiting room. The patient should be able to reach the receptionist easily and be able to speak with a certain amount of privacy. The registration area, where scheduling and financial arrangements are made, needs to be private, quiet, and comfortable. The registration area may be divided into privacy carrels. A public telephone should be provided for the convenience of patients and their families.

The design of the waiting room allows the surgical center to demonstrate visually to patients its concern for their comfort. Colors should be cheerful and furniture comfortable. Lighting must be appropriate for reading and relaxing (Fig. 12-58). Natural light and views of the outdoors may be exploited whenever pos-

sible. Figure 12-59 shows a dramatic entry foyer of an ambulatory surgical center.

Patient Examination and Prep Area

The patient examination and prep areas are generally close to the waiting room and have a direct path to the operating rooms. Patient prep areas usually have a nurse station nearby where patients are weighed and their vital signs recorded.

In many facilities, the patient prep corridor is clinical in appearance, with portable medical equipment and gurneys stored there, all of which may contribute to the patient's anxiety. A nonclinical ambience, devoid of medical equipment clutter and using textured vinyl wallcoverings, carpeting, and artwork (Fig. 12-60), is preferable.

A nice touch in prep and recovery areas is colored bed linens, accompanied by color-coordinated privacy curtains and wallcoverings. If natural light is not available, adding windows between the prep room and the corridor helps to expand the space visually (Fig. 12-60).

12-58 *Sophisticated elegance expresses high quality in reception area of ambulatory surgical center, Louis and Vivian Berry Health Center, Sinai Hospital of Detroit (Farmington Hills, MI)*

Architecture and interior design: Harley Ellington Pierce Yee; Photographer: © Beth Singer

12-59

12-59 *Entry to Ambulatory Surgical Center, Louis and Vivian Berry Health Center, Sinai Hospital of Detroit (Farmington Hills, MI)*
Architecture and interior design: Harley Ellington Pierce Yee; Photographer: © Beth Singer

12-60 *Patient prep corridor of ambulatory surgical center is nonclinical in ambience; Mercy Hospital and Medical Center (San Diego, CA)*
Architect: Hope Architects and Engineers; Interior design: Jain Malkin Inc.; Photographer: John Christian

Operating Room

Operating room (OR) design requires the consideration of many technical factors, all of which are designed to assure life safety. The present discussion, however, focuses only on interior design issues.

Interior Finishes. Finish materials used in the OR must be durable enough to be cleaned with strong, germicidal agents. Materials should be as free of seams as possible. Frequent, harsh cleanings tend to open seams, which then harbor microorganisms.

12-60

Floors. ORs often used to have terrazzo floors. This material is excellent, but in today's market it is expensive and not adaptable to remodeling. A high-quality cushioned sheet vinyl with heat-welded or chemically welded seams is ideal for ORs. Attractive products are available that can be cut and inlaid with contrasting borders. Sheet vinyl should be installed with a self-coved, six-inch-high base. Conductive flooring is not required unless flammable anesthetic gasses are used.

Walls. For years operating rooms had ceramic tile walls, usually in a surgical green color. Largely for cost considerations, epoxy paint and smooth, heavy-duty vinyl wallcoverings became more common in recent years. Today, ceramic tile is once again the material of choice for ORs using lasers because paint, with its shiny finish, is too reflective. The tile, however, must have a nonreflective matte finish and should be of medium color value rather than light. Grout joints must be flush, and latex grout should be considered because it is less porous and therefore less likely to harbor microorganisms. Smooth vinyl wallcovering may be used as well, but it must have a dull finish and medium color value.

Ceilings. Operating room ceilings must be smooth and washable. Gypsum board with a washable, nonreflective paint in a medium color tone is recommended for laser rooms.

Color. Operating rooms and surgical suites used to be predominantly green, and staff wore green surgical apparel. The reason for this preference is based on a law of perception. After concentrating on a red spot (in this case, blood) and then looking away, the eye produces an afterimage of the complementary color, in this case cyan (blue-green). If walls and garments were white, surgeons would see green spots before their eyes every time they looked away from the operative site. Thus blue-green walls and surgical apparel act as a background to neutralize these afterimages. In spite of this phenomenon, operating rooms today are rarely green, and in ambulatory surgical centers surgical attire may run the gamut from floral prints to bright fuchsia.

Recovery. The patient's destination from the OR is the postanesthesia recovery room. The level of asepsis control that must be applied in this area is based on licensing and accreditation guidelines. A sheet vinyl flooring is recommended for the high volume of wheeled traffic and also to facilitate cleanup if someone vomits. Indirect lighting is ideal, with light levels lower over recovery beds and higher at the nurse station (Fig. 12-61). The area should be colorful, but avoid busy patterns or bold colors that may disturb a patient who is nauseated. Cubicle drapes are probably the best vehicle for accent color, as they are easily changed (Fig. 12-57). The color of fluorescent lamps in this area is a critical factor because skin tone is an indicator of the patient's condition.

As the patient becomes more alert, and as soon as vital signs have stabilized and the level of nausea has subsided, the patient dresses and walks to the second-stage recovery lounge. This room accommodates the final stages of recovery in a more comfortable setting, where companions may sit with the patient. When staff observe that the patient has been stable for at least half an hour, discharge instructions are given and the patient is formally discharged. The recovery lounge, equipped with comfortable recliner chairs and lounge seating, should be immediately adjacent to postanesthesia recovery (Fig. 12-62). Patients undergoing ophthalmic surgery with a local anesthetic may proceed almost immediately from the OR to a recliner chair in second-stage recovery. The dressing area is immediately adjacent to secondary recovery.

Usually no restriction is made on types of interior finishes that may be used in second-stage recovery, other than what good sense would mandate with respect to flammability and maintenance. Carpet is an appropriate floor covering, and vinyl works well on walls. This area can be designed like a residential living room, with indirect lighting or table lamps. Natural light and views are highly desirable.

Pediatric Patients

If the facility serves a significant number of pediatric patients, a number of factors should be considered. The parent must be able to accompany the child through as much of the process as possible. Dedicated pre-op holding and recovery areas assure that parents will not be infringing upon the privacy of adult surgical pa-

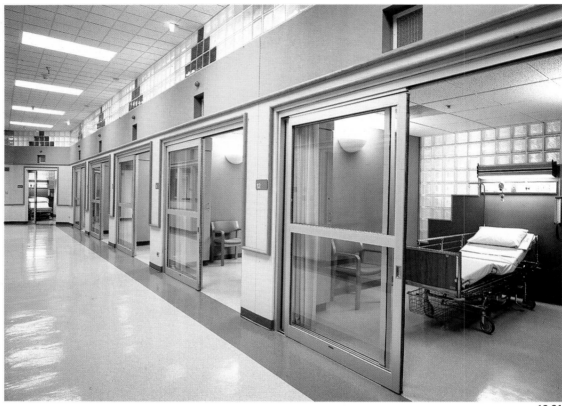

12-61

tients and that adult surgical patients will not be disturbed by the crying of children.

Pediatric recovery should receive the same interior finishes as the adult area but might have a pediatric wallpaper border to make the environment less clinical. Care should be taken to select a wallcovering image (avoid scary animals) that will not be frightening to young children.

Staff Areas

Although concern about patients' well-being is important, staff well-being is no less important. Staff members need a comfortable lounge for relaxing and dining, and interior design con-

12-61 *Ambulatory surgical center in office building features unique architectural detailing; 25 East Same Day Surgery Center (Chicago, IL)*

Architecture and interior design: Anderson Mikos Architects Ltd.; Photographer: Jay Wolke

12-62 *Second-stage recovery area, Somerset Medical Center (Somerville, NJ)*

Architecture and interior design: The BLM Group; Photographer: © Tom Crane

12-62

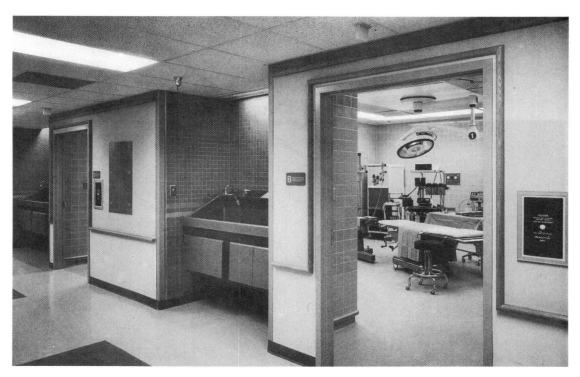

12-63 *Fine architectural detailing is carried into scrub and other staff areas; 25 East Same Day Surgery Center (Chicago, IL)*

Architecture and interior design: Anderson Mikos Architects Ltd.; Photographer: Jay Wolke

cepts should be carried through staff dressing areas, scrub, and sterile corridors (Fig. 12-63). Too often interior design is confined to patient areas, and operating rooms, staff dressing, and sterile corridors are (excuse the pun) aesthetically sterile. Many materials such as ceramic tile are colorful, attractive, and within the guidelines of materials that are easily cleaned. The facility in Figures 12-61 and 12-63 is unique for having consistently carried design detailing from patient care areas through the scrub area and into operating rooms. The use of color is excellent.

FRESNO RECOVERY CARE CENTER

Referred to as the nation's first "mini-hospital" by its owners, this 20-bed facility (classified as an I-1 skilled nursing facility) is part of a three-year experiment by the California legislature to evaluate the effectiveness of such facilities. Founded by orthopedic surgeon Alan Pierrot, the physician-owned facility is attached to an existing ambulatory surgical center that has five

operating rooms, two endoscopy rooms, and appropriate ancillary facilities. The 24,000-square-foot, three-story facility provides recovery care for patients who require up to 72 hours of postoperative care but who do not need the extensive care—and cost—of an acute care hospital (Figs. 12-64 and 12-65). More complicated procedures can be performed at the ambulatory surgical center because patients can stay overnight.

Consumer Appeal

An advertisement with the headline "Imagine recovering from surgery in a 5-star hotel . . . at far less cost than a hospital stay" promises "advanced surgical treatment" followed by the amenities of a fine hotel during recovery. The captivating ad lists other features: "a tastefully furnished private room where a loved one can live with the patient during recuperation; gourmet meals and a well-stocked refrigerator; an electronic entertainment center; a gracious environment where patient comfort comes first." It ends by stating that the facility is "founded on the simple but revolutionary concept that greater comfort hastens healing." This facility lives up to its promises.

Design Features

Celebrating the artistry of architect Charles Rennie Mackintosh (1862–1928), art nouveau

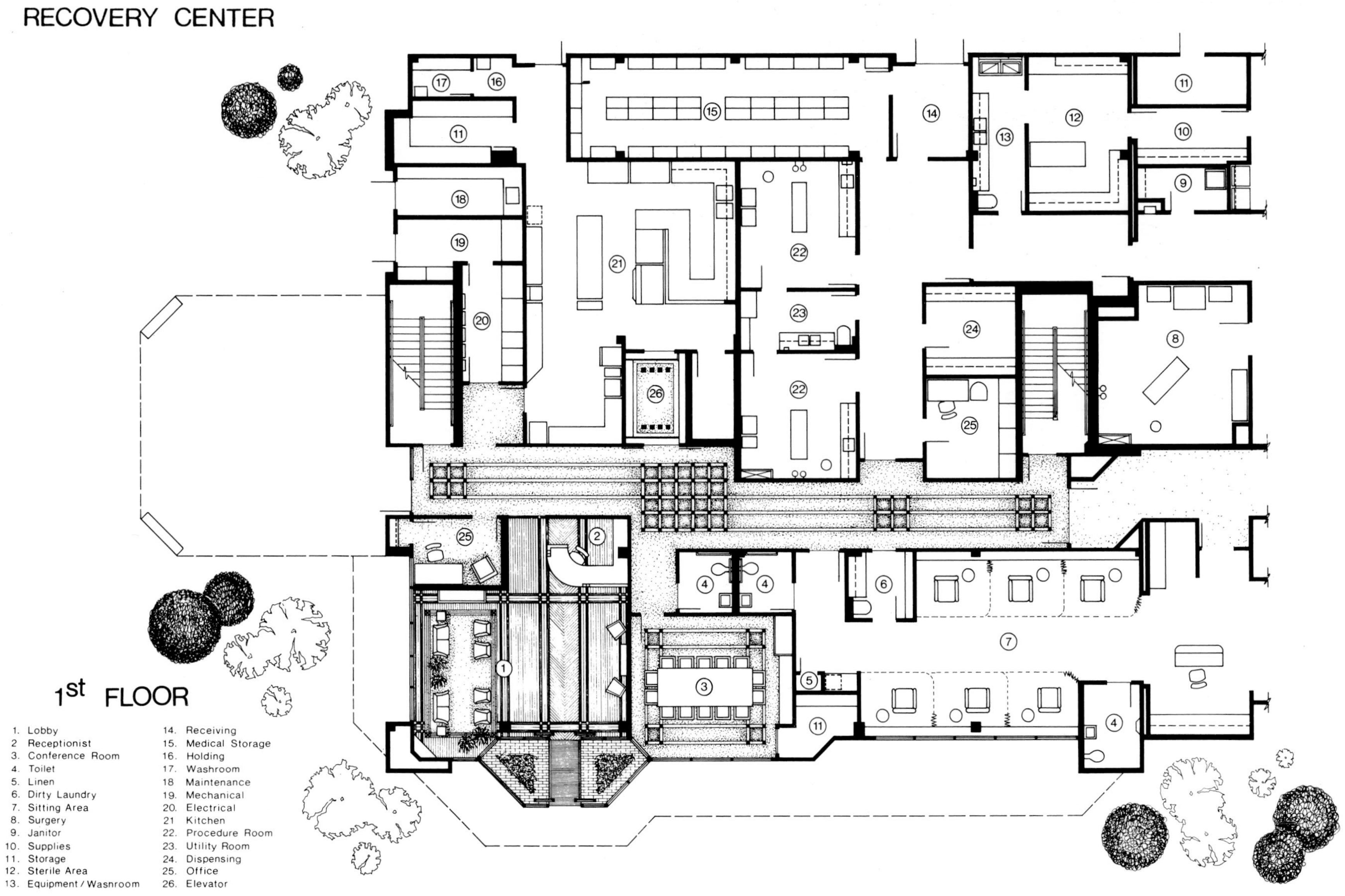
RECOVERY CENTER
1st FLOOR
1. Lobby
2 Receptionist
3. Conference Room
4. Toilet
5. Linen
6. Dirty Laundry
7. Sitting Area
8. Surgery
9. Janitor
10. Supplies
11. Storage
12. Sterile Area
13. Equipment / Wasnroom
14. Receiving
15. Medical Storage
16. Holding
17. Washroom
18 Maintenance
19. Mechanical
20. Electrical
21 Kitchen
22. Procedure Room
23. Utility Room
24. Dispensing
25. Office
26. Elevator

12-64 *Floor plan, Recovery Care Center (Fresno, CA) Architect: Wiens/Carlstrom Architects; Interior design: Struble-Chambers Design Associates*

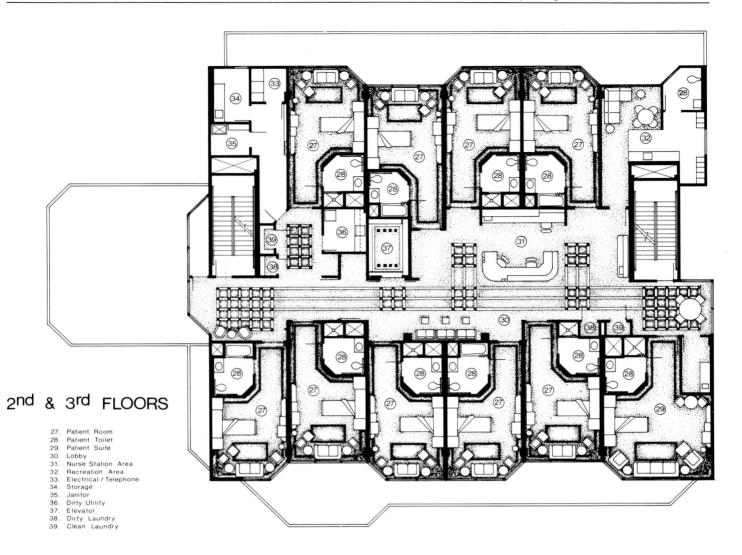

2nd & 3rd FLOORS

27. Patient Room
28. Patient Toilet
29. Patient Suite
30. Lobby
31. Nurse Station Area
32. Recreation Area
33. Electrical / Telephone
34. Storage
35. Janitor
36. Dirty Utility
37. Elevator
38. Dirty Laundry
39. Clean Laundry

12-65 *Floor plan, Recovery Care Center (Fresno, CA) Architect: Wiens/Carlstrom Architects; Interior design: Struble-Chambers Design Associates*

design motifs and exquisite craftsmanship combine to create an environment of rare beauty (Fig. 12-66). Etched-glass entry doors, walnut and maple inlaid floors, polished granite decorative elements, rhythmic reliefs in walls, and wood moldings are combined with furniture and fabrics designed by Josef Hoffmann and Eliel Saarinen. Contemporary adaptations of these styles are reflected in tables, beds, wardrobes, and patient room furnishings (Fig. 12-67). Design details are carried throughout the facility, including nurse stations (Fig. 12-68).

Patient rooms are especially beautiful. A local millwork shop fabricated the headboard and footboard, which were installed with Hill-Rom mounting clips (Fig. 12-67). Medical gasses

have been hidden behind the piece of art on the headwall, and sandblasted glass doors conceal storage of dressings and other supplies (Fig. 12-69). A reading light is mounted on the underside of the bridge unit connecting the two headwall storage cabinets. The decorative valance is painted wood with an inherently flame-retardant fabric draped through it. A fire-treated wooden blind controls privacy and light. Walls of patient rooms and other rooms throughout the facility have Zolatone paint. When questioned about potential acoustics problems from extensive gypsum board ceilings, the interior designer reported that staff have never complained about an echo, uncomfortable noise levels, or transmission of sound from room to room, although she does point out that the wooden floor can be noisy. A layer of sound board in the walls and carpeting on the floors of patients rooms assure comfort and privacy (Fig. 12-70).

12-66 *Beautiful architectural detailing and Art Nouveau furnishings evoke the ambience of an intimate, elegant hotel; Recovery Care Center (Fresno, CA)*

Architect: Wiens/Carlstrom Architects; Interior design: Struble-Chambers Design Associates; Photographer: © Kasparowitz Architectural Photography

12-67 *Patient room is sophisticated and tastefully designed; Recovery Care Center (Fresno, CA)*

Architect: Wiens/Carlstrom Architects; Interior design: Struble-Chambers Design Associates; Photographer: © Kasparowitz Architectural Photography

12-68 *Beautiful architectural detailing is carried through all staff areas, including this nurse station; Recovery Care Center (Fresno, CA)*

Architect: Wiens/Carlstrom Architects; Interior design: Struble-Chambers Design Associates; Photographer: © Kasparowitz Architectural Photography

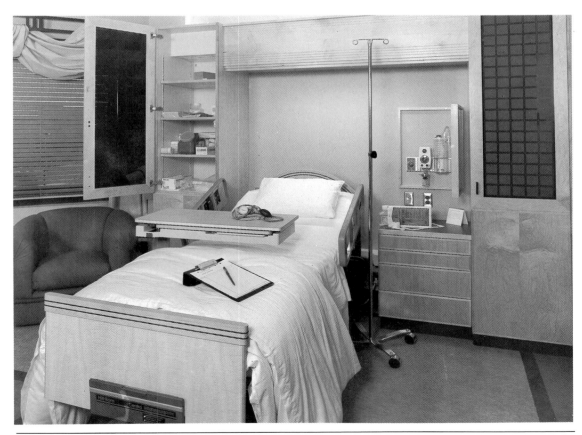

12-69 *Medical gasses are concealed behind artwork frame; Recovery Care Center (Fresno, CA)*

Architect: Wiens/Carlstrom Architects; Interior design: Struble-Chambers Design Associates; Photographer: © Kasparowitz Architectural Photography

12-70 *Patient room includes entertainment center and lounge area; Recovery Care Center (Fresno, CA)*

Architect: Wiens/Carlstrom Architects; Interior design: Struble-Chambers Design Associates; Photographer: © Kasparowitz Architectural Photography

Throughout public spaces and private patient suites, original art from the center's permanent collection of paintings, works on paper, and sculpture is displayed (Fig. 12-71). Fine and decorative arts have been combined with good architecture and exceptional craftsmanship to create a facility of rare quality and attention to detail.

NOTES

1. *Managed care:* a fee-for-service insurance plan in which physicians are reimbursed for services at prenegotiated discounted rates and access to services is controlled by someone other than the attending physician. As an example, the physician generally does not have the authority to decide if a patient requires surgery. Permission must be granted by an agent of the insurance company who administers the plan.

2. *Capitation:* a reimbursement system in which a health care provider receives a fixed monthly payment for every patient served, regardless of how many or how few services that patient requires. With this system physicians have great incentives to treat patients at the lowest possible cost. A large multispecialty group practice, operating as an HMO, would want to operate an urgent care clinic rather than have patients present themselves at a hospital emergency room, the payment for which would have to be borne by the HMO.

REFERENCES

Ayscue, D. 1986. Operating room design: Accommodating lasers. *AORN Journal* 43(6):1278–87.

Beck, W. C., and R. Meyer. 1982. *Health Care Environment: The User's Viewpoint.* Boca Raton, FL: CRC Press.

Belkin, N. 1986. Is your OR giving you the blues? It could be color. *AORN Journal* 43(4):792–96.

Bobrow, M., and J. Thomas. 1990. Targeting treatment. *Architectural Record* June:87–89.

Burns, L. 1984. *Ambulatory Surgery: Developing and Managing Successful Programs.* Rockville, MD: Aspen Publications.

Cramer, C., and V. Renz. 1987. Preoperative care unit. *AORN Journal* 45(2):464–72.

Eubanks, P. 1990. Outpatient care: A nationwide revolution. *Hospitals* 5:28–35.

Freidman, E. 1990. Medicare and Medicaid at 25. *Hospitals* 5:38, 42, 46, 48, 50, 54.

Laufman, H. 1981. *Hospital Special-Care Facilities: Planning for User Needs.* New York: Academic Press.

McCartney, D. 1985. Implementing wellness philosophy in an ambulatory surgery center. *Perioperative Nursing Quarterly* March: 63–67.

Malkin, Jain. 1990. *Medical and Dental Space Planning for the 1990s.* New York: Van Nostrand Reinhold.

O'Donovan, T. 1976. *Ambulatory Surgical Centers: Development and Management.* Germantown, MD: Aspen Systems Corp.

12-71 *Beautifully designed furniture, original works of art, and crafts express high quality and bolster confidence in the quality of clinical care; Recovery Care Center (Fresno, CA)*

Architect: Wiens/Carlstrom Architects; Interior design: Struble-Chambers Design Associates; Photographer: © Kasparowitz Architectural Photography

chapter 13

TEACHING AND RESEARCH FACILITIES

HEALTH SCIENCES EDUCATION CENTERS

facility components

- auditorium
- classrooms
- medical library
- conference rooms
- dining room
- catering kitchen
- lounges
- rest rooms
- gallery/exhibit space
- video production studio
- administrative offices
- registration/information desk
- bookstore

services

- teleconferencing
- large screen video replay in lecture rooms
- receptions/exhibits
- seminars/conferences
- audio/video taping of live events
- photo lab
- medical illustration/graphic design studio

special issues

- acoustics
- flexibility
- ability to accommodate future technology
- community access
- A-V equipment storage
- furniture storage
- art storage
- satellite uplink
- comfort
- display of announcements

Health sciences education centers are a relatively recent addition to hospital campuses (Fig. 13-1). These multifunctional facilities offer a variety of services and resources to the health professional and the community at large. For hospitals not associated with a school of medicine, an education building on campus provides a vital link between physicians and the information they need to meet the challenges of twenty-first century medicine.

OBJECTIVES

Medical education centers have five principal objectives.

1. To support the medical staff by providing access to a wide range of resources—electronic access to journals, teleconferencing, video production, and opportunities to share information with others across the nation and around the world.

2. To provide a resource center for patients and the community so that they can make educated judgments about treatment for themselves or their families and gain access to the latest medical information without the inconvenience associated with using a university medical school library.

3. To enhance the image of the hospital or medical center by providing a forum for the discussion of clinical and ethical issues facing the medical community in the twenty-first century.

4. To provide a bridge between the hospital and the community it serves by enhancing public awareness and understanding of major issues challenging today's physicians.

5. To generate revenue for the hospital by making the conference center available to outside groups to hold scientific meetings, corporate seminars, or corporate retreats. Depending on the hospital's locale and the presence of nearby hotels, restaurants, golf courses, and other attractions, the facility can be marketed as part of a destination resort to out-of-town groups of physicians, as an example, to hold medical meetings.

In addition to these planning and marketing objectives, the facility must offer state-of-the-art technology and comfort. However, state-of-the-art technology for sound recording and transmission and worldwide satellite communication can indeed be very expensive for a building of this type. The extent or level of

13-1 *Located adjacent to the historic 1928 Plummer Building, the new Education Building architecturally expresses both respect for tradition and a commitment to the future; Mayo Clinic (Rochester, MN)*

Architecture and interior design: Hammel Green and Abrahamson, Inc.; Photographer: Joel and Shin Koyama

audiovisual production facilities available within the building will be based on individual programming and financial decisions made by the hospital and its planning group.

Although patrons of the facility will expect the highest level of communications technology, they will appreciate it being delivered in a comfortable environment. The ambience is largely the province of the interior design consultant whose recommendations for color, texture, sizes of tables, appropriate seating, locations of clocks, drinking fountains, telephones, rest rooms, signage, lighting, coatracks, umbrella stands, and marker boards will determine the perceived level of satisfaction and comfort experienced by users.

SERVICES OFFERED

A wide variety of services may be offered, ranging from the obvious (conferences, lectures, exhibits, receptions) to a variety of support services such as a graphic design studio offering medical illustration, design of computer-generated slides for lectures, photo lab, and a competent audio and video engineering staff. Some facilities have laboratory classrooms with microscopes and individual video monitors at each station.

SPECIAL FEATURES

Education buildings often have a large atrium lobby or rotunda that can be used as a gallery and exhibit hall, as well as for registration of large conferences. This area should be sparsely furnished to allow for circulation of large numbers of people during registration, for special receptions, or as breakout space during day-long conferences. Interesting architectural features integrated with appropriately scaled plantscaping and artwork make these large gallery spaces especially pleasant. However, natural lighting from skylights or clerestories can quickly damage fine works of art. That issue notwithstanding, these spaces are ideal for display of antique surgical instruments, historical medical documents or case notes from famous clinicians (Figs. 13-2a, 13-2b, and 13-2c), or paintings depicting the history of medicine (Figs. 13-3 and 13-4). The building might house the medical center's permanent collection as well as display changing exhibits of art.

Display of the day's events must be planned for the lobby or gallery space. Video display monitors may be built into either the registration counter or the wall behind it to avoid having to position freestanding changeable letter boards elsewhere in the lobby. An attractive display case built into the wall, rather than planted on top of it, may be provided for display of posters announcing future events. If display cases are not planned in advance and integrated into the architecture at various key locations throughout the building, unsightly visual clutter will most likely appear here and there taped or tacked to walls.

In any building, refinement of small details enhances the users' appreciation of the space (Fig. 13-5). This response is especially likely in

an education building where people are seated and have to concentrate for long periods of time and where staff have to make rapid changes in equipment, lighting levels, and communication hookups between speakers. In this sense, comfort for the staff would mean having adequately sized storage areas for equipment immediately

13-2a *Donor recognition wall features clinical trial notes from the journals of Doctors Best and Banting, the discoverers of insulin; donor names are engraved alongside historical notes and photos; Joslin Diabetes Center (Boston, MA)*
Graphic design: Coco Raynes Graphics, Inc.; Photo courtesy Coco Raynes

13-2b *Close-up detail of clinical trial notes, Doctors Best and Banting, engraved into donor recognition panel, Joslin Diabetes Center (Boston, MA)*
Graphic design: Coco Raynes Graphics, Inc.; Photo courtesy Coco Raynes

13-2c *Close-up view of scientific journal, Doctors Best and Banting, from donor recognition wall, Joslin Diabetes Center (Boston, MA)*
Graphic design: Coco Raynes Graphics, Inc.; Photo courtesy Coco Raynes

5.00 PM dog in good condition. 47

Aug. 7th 12 midnight (Aug 6 - 7th,
1921 Blood sugar - .43

vol. urine from 2 P.M. till
12 midnight - 175 C.C.

the last 30 cc being catheter specimen
separate sugar testimation

10 hour total sugar - 3.36 g

" nitrogen - 1.20 g

G : N ratio 2.8

① 8 cc Isletin given

1. A.M. Blood sugar - .37

(marginal vertical handwritten note): and Best, giving a (volume of 2 cc .... this his columns .... It gives the date on .... in the ..... just time they ..... med the word

1

No.	FIRST VISIT Yr. Mo. Day	NAME	ADDRESS	ONSET AGE Yr. Mo.	ONSET DATE Yr. Mo.	DIAGNOSED DATE Yr. Mo.	DEATH DATE Yr. Mo.	DURATION Yr. Mo.				Heredity	Familial	Etiology	Pulse	B.P.	WEIGHT Max.	Onset	1st Visit	Height	Type of Onset	CLASSIFICATION	Hospital	CAUSE OF DEATH	DISTINCTIVE FEATURES
1	1873 VIII 2	Higgins Mary	257 Medford St Somerville, Mass.	26	1892 XII		D			F	S Irish	0			90		125	93		Grad.	D. m		Sudden death	
2	1897 VIII 29	Jorlin O.F.	Oxford Mass.	54	1896 III		1899 III 9		F	M Am	—	—		80		171	135		Grad.	D. m		Coma	Goitre
3	1898 IX 13	Lovell S.B.	156 Boylston St Jamaica Plain Mass.	63	1894 II		1899 II 2	11	F	W ?	+	—		100		132	144		Grad.	D. m		Coma	Infection just before coma
4	1898 VIII 16	Wilbur Alton		15	1897 VIII		1900 X 3	2	M	S Am	0						92		Acute	D. m		Coma	Acidosis
5	1898 IX 3	Sullivan	21 Norwich St Boston Mass	52	1896 VI		D Natural		E	y Irish	0					160	150		Acute	D. m			
6	1898 IX 17	Niele Otis	Ocean Spray Massachusetts	28	1863		1898	25	M	?	—			2y						D. m		Cerebral Hemorrhage	Duration
7	1898 X 25	Harmon Wm. F.	Somersworth New Hampshire	52 9	1898 II		1899 I	4	M	M Am	0					150	120	5'6	Acute	D. m		D. M. Coma Hemiplegia nephritis Pneumonia	
8	1899 III 31	Tozier Sarah P.	Oxford Mass	62	1899 VI		1913 VI	14	F	M Am	—					185	165			D. m			
9	1899 IV 6	Edwards	105 Mt Vernon St Boston Mass	63			1900 I		F	M Am	—									D. m		Cerebral Hemorrhage	
10	1899 X 9	Bliss Edward J.	9 Menlo St Brighton Mass	38 4			1900 X		M	M Am	+	+		102		200	160		Grad.	D. m		Pulmonary T.B.	
11	1899 XII 18	Cheney	264 Commonwealth Ave Boston Mass	56	1899		1901 IV		F	W Am	+	+		98		192			Grad.	D. m		Angina Pectoris	
12	1900 I 29	Kinsley Howard D.	68 Richard Sq Boston Mass	32	1898 I		1902 II	4	M	M Am	+			64		150	114		Grad.	D. m		Coma	
13	1900 III 20	Holt J.F.	65 Sudbury St Faneuil Boston	46	1899 X		1901 I	1 3	M	M Am	0			III+		240	184		Grad.	Unclas.		Cirrhosis of Liver	
14	1900 III 31	McFadden E.O.	140 Maples Road Brookline Mass	34	1898		1901 III	2 9	M	M Am	0			III		200			Grad.	D. M.		Coma	
15	1900 IV 18	Murphy	E. Dedham St Boston Mass	47	1897		D Natural		F	M						145				D. m		Arterio-sclerotic Condition	
16	1900 V 2	Swift Elijah	East Clare Wisconsin	65	1899		1906 VII	8 7	M	M Am	0					226	201		Grad.	D. m			
17	1900 VIII 8	Bancroft Dr. C.F.P.	Andover Academy Andover Mass	56	1898		1901 X	3	M	M Am	0			78		187	162		Grad.	D. m		Coma	Gall Stones
18	1900 VIII 9	Higgins James A.	130 State St Newburyport Mass	35			1921 VIII		F	M Am								5'3		D. m		Nephritis Cirrhosis	
19	1800 IX 9	Hastings Kate	517 Beacon St Boston Mass	47	1899		1907 II	9 7	F	S Am	+	+				220	162		Grad.	D. m		Coma	
20	1901 II 26	Rockwood Minnie	63 Auburn St Cor Everett	11	1900		1903 X	9	F	S Am										D. m		Coma	

1

13-3 *Lobby features large wood sculpture of heart and glass-enclosed historical display wall; Texas Heart Institute, St. Luke's Hospital (Houston, TX)*

Architecture and interior design: Morris Architects; Photographer: Rick Gardner

13-4 *Glass-encased educational exhibit of clinical photos and surgical instruments, Texas Heart Institute, St. Luke's Hospital (Houston, TX)*

Architecture and interior design: Morris Architects; Photographer: Rick Gardner

13-5 *Dark woods, traditional furnishings, and carefully designed lighting are carried through all areas of the Mayo Education Building, Mayo Clinic (Rochester, MN)*

Architecture and interior design: Hammel Green and Abrahamson, Inc.; Photographer: Joel and Shin Koyama

adjacent to where it might be needed, as well as lighting controls preprogrammed for various settings in a handy location.

Comfort for the participant or audience means comfortable seating that supports people's backs properly; enough space between rows of seating to accommodate those with long legs; excellent acoustics so that no "dead spots" occur anywhere in the auditorium; elimination of glare on marker boards, video display terminals, or other surfaces; and provision of an adequate number of telephones and rest rooms close to each conference space so that these needs can be met during a break without missing part of the next lecture. An all-day conference can be extremely tedious if the chair is

13-6 *Geometry of ceiling and walls create a striking architectural composition in this auditorium, Mayo Education Building, Mayo Clinic (Rochester, MN)*

Architecture and interior design: Hammel Green and Abrahamson, Inc.; Photographer: Joel and Shin Koyama

13-7 *Interesting ceiling, lighting, and comfortable seating characterize this auditorium at Mayo Clinic (Scottsdale, AZ)*

Architecture and interior design: Hammel Green and Abrahamson, Inc.; Photographer: Mark Bosclair

uncomfortable, one is straddling a table leg, or the room is too warm or too cool.

SPECIAL ISSUES

Although this section is not intended to be a complete checklist for this kind of building, a number of special issues must be considered.

Acoustics.   An acoustics consultant should be part of the design team for this type of facility. The auditorium is of special concern because every surface—walls, floors, drapery, and ceilings—has an impact on the room's acoustics (Figs. 13-6 and 13-7).

Flexibility.   Feasibility studies notwithstanding, no facility can accurately anticipate the utilization of various services or programs. Therefore, the facility must be flexible enough to accommodate both changing technology and users' needs. Flexibility is also important for individual rooms. Large spaces must be able to be divided into smaller areas, each of which has acoustical integrity. Rooms may be set up for lectures, theater-style seating, or seating around various configurations of tables (Fig. 13-8). A large multipurpose room, sometimes called a *great hall*, may be used as an auditorium and also set for dining (Fig. 13-9).

Accommodating Future Technology.   The sound studio and the communications network within the facility should be able to be upgraded as the state of the art evolves.

Community Access.   If community participation is desired, then the building should be located in a prominent position on the campus where it is immediately visible. Sometimes a clock tower or other unique feature is incorporated into the architecture to serve as a way-finding landmark. Convenient parking is essential.

13-8 *Well-appointed conference room features adjustable lighting and acoustic wall treatment; The University Hospital Atrium Pavilion (Boston, MA)*

Architect: Hoskins Scott Taylor and Partners Inc. in association with Hansen Lind Meyer; Interior design: Hoskins Scott Taylor and Partners Inc. in conjunction with University Hospital Design Services; Photographer: Paul Gobeil

13-9 *Meeting room has comfortable seating, good lighting, and attractive finishes; Mayo Education Building, Mayo Clinic (Rochester, MN)*
Architecture and interior design: Hammel Green and Abrahamson, Inc.; Photographer: Joel and Shin Koyama

Audiovisual Equipment Storage. This building type has a high ratio of storage to overall square footage. Items to be stored include projectors, easels, microphones, speakers, sound equipment, podiums, and often a grand piano that is moved into one room or another for receptions or recitals.

Furniture Storage. The amount of furniture to be stored to accommodate various arrangements of seating in each room can be mitigated somewhat by limiting the number of types of seating initially selected for the facility. In other words, if all classrooms and lecture rooms use the same chair, fewer chairs are needed in inventory because all rooms are unlikely to be set up for maximum capacity on any particular day. Color palettes in these rooms have to be compatible.

Art Storage. A secured area is necessary, with appropriately designed racks for storage of the facility's permanent collection when it is not being displayed, as well as for temporary storage of works belonging to others.

Satellite Uplink. Communications specialists should be part of the design team to make certain that the building is appropriately designed to incorporate satellite telecommunications equipment.

MEDICAL LIBRARY AND RESOURCE CENTER

facility components

- book stacks
- study carrels
- reference tables and chairs
- display of videotapes
- display of audio tapes
- display of medical journals
- display of consumer-oriented literature
- staff workroom
- electronic catalog of library's collections
- lounge seating/reading room
- reproduction area (fax, copy machines, coin changer)
- director's office
- volunteers' work area
- checkout/information desk

users

- physicians
- nursing staff
- patients
- community

special issues

- acoustics
- lighting
- electronic data access
- comfort

A medical library in a hospital might be a small area managed by one or two staff and accessible only to physicians, or it may be a large facility offering a broad range of resources to health care professionals, patients, and the community (Fig. 13-10). The Planetree model hospital project (see chapter 2) has raised the awareness of hospital administrators and physicians alike to the importance of making information available to patients and their families. Planetree's Resource Center has been a successful component of their program.

Massachusetts Eye and Ear Infirmary
Medical Library and Archives
Boston, Massachusetts

Legend

1	Microfiche	**8**	Index
2	Photo	**9**	Librarian
3	Journal Stack	**10**	Archivist
4	Circulation Desk	**11**	Rare Book Room
5	Reading	**12**	Stacks
6	Computer		
7	Book Stack		

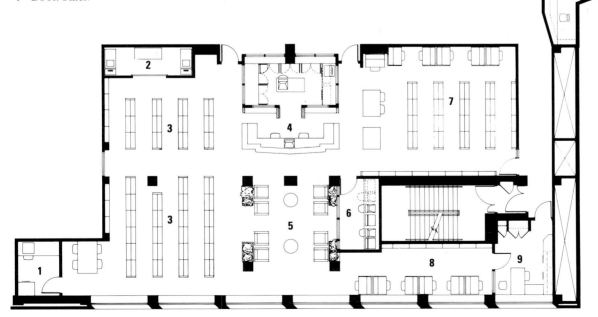

Archives

Library

13-10 *Floor plan, Medical Library and Archives, Massachusetts Eye and Ear Infirmary (Boston, MA) Architect: SBA/Steffian Bradley Associates Inc.*

In the near future all information storage and retrieval will probably be done electronically. The purpose of a hospital medical library is to provide ready access to the most frequently needed books and publications. Providing the full range of technical journals and international publications that would be available at a university medical school library is impossible, but quick access to those resources from the hospital's medical library should be possible. In fact, physicians should be able to review and access the library's collection from terminals in their homes or offices. A facsimile machine would allow a particular document to be transmitted immediately.

The medical library would house videotapes either purchased commercially or recorded by the engineering staff of the education building during the many lectures and symposia sponsored by the hospital. Carrels for viewing these videotapes must be provided. (Carrels should be four feet wide to accommodate equipment and allow for elbow room.)

A growing number of consumers are interested in prevention of disease or in the management of a current illness for themselves or a family member. Access to the latest health care information, including a variety of consumer-oriented publications, should be available. In some libraries, volunteer staff handle inquiries from the lay community, and professional librarians provide support to clinicians.

If the library is to be shared by physicians and the public, physicians should be provided a separate entrance and an area where they may work undisturbed without having to field questions from the public. Architectural detailing can make the space especially appealing for frequent users.

SPECIAL ISSUES

A number of special issues must be considered in designing a library. Chief among them are acoustics, lighting, electronic data access, and comfort.

Acoustics. All interior finish materials should be selected with acoustics in mind. Staff must be able to answer questions and take telephone calls in a normal tone of voice without disturbing others who are studying. Additional noise is generated by electronic printers, copy ma-

chines, and other equipment, some of which can be housed in acoustically shielded enclosures. Study carrels, of course, should have acoustic partitions.

Lighting. Lighting is a very important part of the library, both functionally and in terms of ambience. Given the number of video display screens, indirect lighting is most suitable. 30 to 40 maintained footcandles are required for overall illumination, with task lighting of 75 maintained footcandles for reading tables, lounge chairs, or study carrels. Book stacks require a minimum of 35 footcandles on the spines of books measured at 30 inches above the floor. Book stack lighting should avoid shadows (Fig. 13-11).

Electronic Data Access. Because of the great deal of electronic equipment in a modern library, a consultant should be used to coordinate and network the various units.

Comfort. Comfort in a library is a function of acoustics, lighting, color, and seating. Contrast must be minimized to avoid tiring the eyes. Soft, fairly light colors work best because books and displays add accent color. Studies have shown that cool colors (blues and greens) stimulate inward orientation and enhance concentration. Warm colors (reds and oranges) have the opposite effect and would not be as appropriate for a library. Comfortable lounge seating should be provided in the physicians' reading area (Fig. 13-12). Furnishings in this rare book room are complemented by a display of antique medical instruments (Fig. 13-13).

RESEARCH FACILITIES

facility components
- laboratories
- conference rooms
- storage
- computer equipment room
- classrooms
- administrative offices
- clean rooms
- vivarium
- receiving area
- lounge/lunchroom
- library

13-11 *Medical library features indirect lighting and attractive case work; Massachusetts Eye and Ear Infirmary (Boston, MA)*

Architecture and interior design: SBA/Steffian Bradley Associates Inc.; Photographer: Peter Lewitt

13-12 *The medical library is housed under a porcelain-enameled aluminum vault; main admission desk (left) sits under a massive skylight and ceramic wall sculpture; Detroit Receiving Hospital & Wayne State University Health Care Institute (Detroit, MI)*

Architecture and interior design (joint venture): William Kessler & Associates Inc., Zeidler Roberts Partnership, and Giffels Associates Inc.; Photographer: Balthazar Korab Ltd.

13-13 *Boardroom houses rare books in glass-enclosed case work, along with antique medical instruments; Massachusetts Eye and Ear Infirmary (Boston, MA)*
Architecture and interior design: SBA/Steffian Bradley Associates Inc.; Photographer: Peter Lewitt

special issues
- temperature
- humidity
- ventilation
- safety
- views of nature
- communication

Of all building types, research laboratories seem to be the least sensitive to the comfort of their users. Color, lighting, texture, and architectural detailing are handled in a most perfunctory way. Are scientists assumed to be so preoccupied unraveling life's great mysteries that they are unaffected by their environment? The focus seems to be entirely on the building's engineering systems to manage temperature, humidity, and ventilation and to provide utilities to the many pieces of expensive equipment. Budgets being what they are, anything that does not immediately support the research effort (color, upgrades in lighting, architectural va-riety, and interior detailing) is probably viewed as a needless frill. In spite of prevailing bias to the contrary, the facilities presented in this chapter are noteworthy for their use of color, selection of building materials, creation of intimate lounge areas to encourage conversation among scientists, and architectural features that give the buildings character.

The architecture of the Lewis Thomas molecular biology laboratory at Princeton University is an outstanding example of the merging of art and science. Well known for his eloquent and poetic writing style, Lewis Thomas's books *(The Medusa and the Snail, Lives of a Cell)* present the wonders of biology with humor and wit; he is the ultimate humanist. The building that houses his laboratory expresses the same measure of sophistication, wit, and humor. It is neither austere, high-tech, nor traditional in style (Fig. 13-14). The architect studied New England mills and Elizabethan manner houses for inspiration in patterning the ornamental brick bands and stonework that decorate the exte-

provides many opportunities for interaction with colleagues outside the confines of the laboratories. Lounges at the ends of each floor are equipped with chalkboards to facilitate informal conversations (Fig. 13-15). Looking at this room gives the feeling that it nurtures the occupants; great ideas ought to be discussed here. Natural light, color, and careful architectural detailing make this room and circulation corridors (Fig. 13-16) a textural contrast to the high-tech appearance of laboratory spaces.

Flexibility was a primary goal of the program in order to have labs that could accommodate a broad range of research activities and then be easily reassigned to meet new programs. The design solution incorporates those elements that are common to the research programs in a standardized, repetitive plan, divided by intermittent partitions. In response to strict safety guidelines, a corridor separates research labs from nontechnical spaces, which were organized around the two-story central atrium.

The Genetics Institute in Cambridge, Massachusetts is an exceedingly humane, people-oriented building designed for a privately owned research facility involved in molecular biology, plant biochemistry, and pilot lab production. A symmetrical floor plan arranges the labs, with adjacent support spaces, around the perimeter of the building in order to provide ample natural light and outdoor views (Figs. 13-17 and 13-18). A skylighted atrium serves as an orienting focus within the building and provides a space for informal conversations among researchers and staff. Opening onto the atrium are high-activity areas, including a seminar room, library, and cafeteria (Fig. 13-19). Note that the lecture room on the first level can be opened up with seating extended out into the atrium space. To encourage discussion, seating for coffee breaks and lunchtime are located on balconies overlooking the atrium (Fig. 13-20) that create the impression of shuttered houses surrounding a town square.

This building miraculously seems to incorporate most of the environmental features deemed necessary for good mental health and optimal intellectual functioning. This accomplishment is even more impressive because it has occurred in a research laboratory setting, understanding that the prevailing ethic is that such buildings are destined to be unattractive, noisy, dismal, and messy. This building, how-

13-14 *Whimsical facade expresses the wit of biologist Lewis Thomas; Lewis Thomas Laboratory, Princeton University (Princeton, NJ)*
  Architect: Payette Associates Inc., Architects in association with Venturi, Rauch, and Scott Brown; Photographer: © Paul Warchol

rior. In the words of Karen Stein (1986), "The polychromatic patchwork quilt of diaper and checkerboard patterns is, in fact, stitched together with the assidity of a seasoned couturier." Note the Gothic stone cutout above the main entrance, where richly textured wood doors introduce the palette of interior materials. Reputed to be one of the campus's most controversial buildings of the decade, the "complexity and contradiction" that make this building outstanding are the work of Venturi, Rauch, and Scott Brown and Payette Associates, Venturi being primarily responsible for the exterior and Payette for the interior of the building.

Although laboratory space planning and design are not within the scope of the present discussion, the layout of the research floors

13-15 *Informal classroom/lounge seems to nurture its occupants; one has the feeling great ideas will be discussed here. Lewis Thomas Laboratory, Princeton University (Princeton, NJ)*

Architecture and interior design: Payette Associates Inc., Architects in association with Venturi, Rauch, and Scott Brown; Photographer: © Paul Warchol

13-16 *Wooden doors and trim, as well as indirect lighting, make internal circulation spaces especially appealing; Lewis Thomas Laboratory, Princeton University (Princeton, NJ)*

Architecture and interior design: Payette Associates Inc., Architects in association with Venturi, Rauch, and Scott Brown; Photographer: Gregory Murphy

13-17 *Floor plan, Genetics Institute (Cambridge, MA) Courtesy Payette Associates Inc.*

13-18 *Floor plan, Genetics Institute (Cambridge, MA) Courtesy Payette Associates Inc.*

13-15

13-16

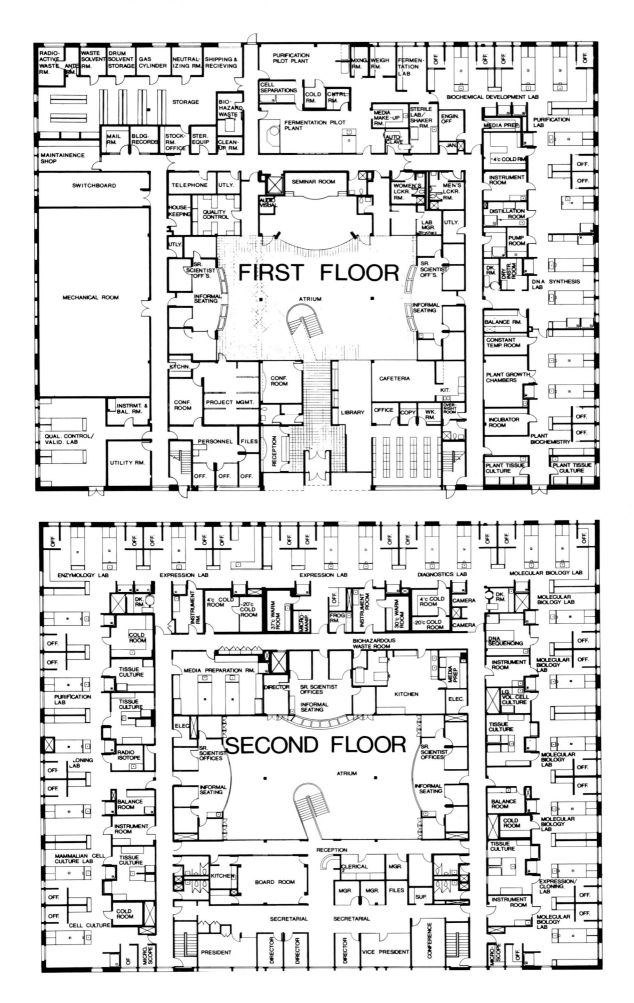

FIRST FLOOR

SECOND FLOOR

13-19 *Seminar room, lounges, cafeteria, and offices open to atrium space, giving the impression of shuttered homes around a town square; Genetics Institute (Cambridge, MA)*

Architecture and interior design: Payette Associates Inc.; Photographer: Paul Ferrino

13-20 *Wood-shuttered openings provide views of commons area below; Genetics Institute (Cambridge, MA)*

Architecture and interior design: Payette Associates Inc.; Photographer: Paul Ferrino

ever, is so visually stimulating with all the penetrations and attention to pattern that it says, *"This building is for creative people. They don't just come to work here. They live in this space; they talk, discuss ideas, and are intellectually stimulated by the space they are in."* Natural light and views are visible from every interior space in the core as well as on the perimeter of the building. Colors of burgundy and sea green used in fabrics, carpeting, and other finish materials add vitality to what must be one of the most pleasant, people-oriented workplaces a scientist may have the pleasure of using.

Some of the most successful laboratory environments have been designed by architect Kenneth Kornberg, whose parents and brothers are basic research scientists. In fact, the archi-

tect himself embarked upon a career in chemistry prior to switching to architecture. His intimate familiarity with scientists and their equipment and his understanding of their needs and ambitions allowed him to accommodate functional program requirements in buildings that are architecturally creative. Even interior spaces are flooded with natural light, laboratories all have views of the outdoors, and live plants are introduced, wherever possible, in interior spaces (Fig. 13-21). His lighting is varied and interesting, ceiling planes are at varied heights, and he is not timid about pattern or color (Fig. 13-22).

DNAX Research Institute in Palo Alto, California, applies advanced strategies of molecular and cellular biology toward understanding the immune system. One of the goals of their pro-

13-21 *Research laboratory features uncommon amenities: outstanding architectural design, excellent lighting, good use of color, and healthy live plants in low planters and cascading from plant soffits; DNAX Research Institute of Molecular and Cellular Biology (Palo Alto, CA)*
Architecture and interior design: Kornberg Associates; Photographer: Gerald Ratto

13-22 *Brightly colored gypsum-board baffles in skylight well add a playful quality to employee cafeteria, LTI/Liposome Technology Inc. (Menlo Park, CA)*
Architecture and interior design: Kornberg Associates; Photographer: Gerald Ratto

13-23 *Open space plan allows views of all laboratory spaces with labs requiring containment or isolation located behind walls; excellent use of lighting and color creates an upbeat, yet calming, environment for a high-volume, multi-state testing lab (30,600 square feet); International Clinical Laboratories (Seattle, WA)*
Architecture and interior design: The NBBJ Group; Photographer: Karl Bischoff

13-24 *View from corridor looking into conference center, Beckman Laser Institute (Irvine, CA)*
Architect: Bobrow/Thomas and Associates; Interior design: Kaneko Ford Design, Patricia Ford; Photographer: Pete Bleyer Studio

13-25 *Executive office, founder, Beckman Laser Institute (Irvine, CA)*
Architect: Bobrow/Thomas and Associates; Interior design: Kaneko Ford Design, Patricia Ford; Photographer: Pete Bleyer Studio

13-22

13-23

13-24

gram was to achieve an open atmosphere to encourage close interaction among colleagues. Informal conversation nooks (Fig. 13-21) encourage communication.

Research organizations in both the public and private sectors compete for the best personnel. An attractive, humane environment has many benefits. According to Kornberg (1988, 31), an architect who bridges the worlds of science and architecture, both fields emphasize a confluence of creativity and technology. "Imaginative, inspirational spaces . . . created by architects can excite scientists and challenge them to do their best work." Environments that use color (Fig. 13-23), natural light (Fig. 13-24), design (Fig. 13-25), and good architecture to achieve these goals will attract the brightest scientific minds.

REFERENCES

Kornberg, K. 1988. The scientific workplace. *Architecture California* 10(6):18–23, 31.

Stein, K. 1986. Back to the future. *Architectural Record* August:104–13.

13-25

LONG-TERM CARE

For years I had been conditioned by administrators of skilled nursing facilities (SNFs) to think that design decisions should be based on what would appeal to residents' families. After all, family members are the ones who decide when placing an individual in an institution is appropriate or necessary, and they decide which facility is chosen. Administrators must keep their facilities full and be responsive to boards of directors who set goals for economic viability and who, in fact, have their own ideas about what the facility should look like.

To further justify the notion of designing for patients' families, administrators often explain that the residents, especially those with dementia, are often unaware of color, style of furnishings, and other attributes of the interior environment. This view is consistent with the custodial mind-set of many SNFs, in which residents are expected to be dependent and to be acted upon, rather than encouraged to be as independent as their disabilities will allow.

GOOD FACILITIES ENABLE OPTIMUM FUNCTIONING

I now view long-term care facilities from a new perspective. When architects or interior designers ask me to refer them to a good facility, I ask them if "good" means aesthetically attractive or a facility that permits optimum functioning of the individual resident. In certain respects one cannot meet both criteria. Concealing functional items such as toilets, personal care products, or clothing is considered desirable in many contemporary environments in order to present an orderly, attractive appearance. Cognitively remembering where things are, even when they are out of sight, enables most of us to find things when we need them. Nursing home residents who suffer cognitive impairment, however, have trouble visualizing what they cannot physically see. Cognitive mapping is very difficult for these individuals. Therefore, placing toilet rooms in prominent locations and marking them with more than the perfunctory sign is extremely important. According to Margaret Calkins (1988), an awning sticking out into the corridor or arrows on the floor pointing to the toilet room can be quite effective in reducing the incidence of incontinence (Fig. 14-1). As the average incontinent person generates seventy pounds of laundry per day, any environmental

14-1. *Wayfinding cueing devices help residents locate toilet rooms, The Corinne Dolan Alzheimer Center at Heather Hill (Chardon, OH)*
Photo courtesy Margaret P. Calkins

adaptations that reduce the incidence of incontinence also reduce operating costs and benefit staff.

Glare constitutes a significant problem for the elderly. For this reason, unwaxed, matte-finish floors are best, but family members and other visitors tend to equate shiny with clean. They have to be educated to understand that shiny floors can decrease residents' mobility (for fear of falling) and even cause falls by reducing visibility.

With respect to color palette, individuals with reduced visual acuity see reds, oranges, and yellows most easily. Violets, blues, and greens are hard to see and should be avoided. However, many people would not consider red, orange, and yellow a particularly appealing color palette for a residential environment. A SNF presents any number of opportunities to color code and color cue interior spaces to enable residents to function at their highest levels; however, these prosthetic devices may appear odd or unattractive to family members or other visitors. In fact, even well-intentioned interior

designers may find themselves subconsciously resistant to employing these techniques, so deeply ingrained is the desire to make things appear aesthetically attractive by conventional standards. My personal approach to the design of long-term care facilities has forever been altered by exposure to the work of gerontologists and environmental psychologists such as Lorraine Hiatt and Margaret Calkins, whose persuasive and impassioned discourse opened my eyes to new possibilities. Designing environments for the elderly to maximize performance is more than a humanitarian gesture; it is the socially responsible thing to do.

DEFINING THE PROBLEM

This is in many ways the most difficult chapter in this book because there is no other patient population about whom so much has been written. Wading through hundreds of research studies, magazine articles, and books packed with useful information has been a herculean task. How can a few truths and practical design guidelines be distilled from such a vast amount of available material? I have decided, therefore, to take a personal approach to the material and present to readers those issues, studies, and conversations that were responsible for my enlightenment with the hope that doing so will increase their awareness of controversial issues and suggest new solutions to old problems.

LIMITATIONS OF DESIGN

The enormous complexity of issues that determine the physical and psychological well-being of the institutionalized elderly is discouraging. Although poor architecture and design can erode the quality of life for these individuals, an incompetent nursing staff is a far greater threat. Other critical environmental factors include administrative and professional leadership, philosophy of care, the psychosocial milieu, adequate staffing, good dietary practices, and organizational policies (Grant 1989). All of these factors, including architecture and interior design, influence the individual's ability to adapt to the environment. Other variables that significantly affect patients' well-being include organizational rules such as locked exits, forbidden areas, allowable eating times and locations, allowable behaviors in private and public spaces, and the quality and types of programs (Howell 1982).

Postoccupancy evaluations on this population, whose median age is 87, are difficult to carry out because of the enormous variability in competency levels and the difficulty of judging whether observed behaviors are due to dementia, sensory loss, or environmental factors. According to Howell (1982, 36–37), "inappropriate behaviors of older people are too often stereotypically misdiagnosed as organic brain diseases (dementias), however, confusion, depression, and disorientation can also result from drug therapy, malnutrition, social isolation, or sensory loss."

The multitude of health problems and sensory deficits, so individual in nature, makes auditing the effects of the built environment in explaining behaviors difficult. For example, incontinence is not always an involuntary medical problem; sometimes it results from not being able to locate the bathroom, because staff neglect to take the resident to the bathroom often enough, or because incontinence can be a way of expressing the need to be touched. Barbara Cooper (1986) explains that it can also result from the decline of sensory function (sight or hearing) in one area that causes a need to overcompensate in another area such as tactile sense. This illustration serves to point out that one cannot make hasty judgments to explain observed behaviors because of the difficulty of sorting out what is due to the natural process of aging, the patient's health status, the built environment, nursing care, nutrition, drug therapy, organizational policies, programs, and family support.

TYPES OF TREATMENT

Long-term care facilities are either custodial or rehabilitation oriented (Hiatt 1985). Treatment varies from medical-custodial through active rehabilitation to dominantly residential with available health and social service staff supports (Howell 1982). Skilled nursing facilities have evolved from a hospital model, which explains why making them seem like home is so difficult. Yet, they are indeed home to residents, 75 percent of whom stay from three to twelve years (Hiatt 1990). Although building codes often do not recognize a difference between an acute care hospital and a skilled nursing facility, in reality a SNF is a low-tech "quasi-medical" fa-

cility that is designed to accommodate the disabilities of residents in as homelike a setting as possible (Shield 1990).

The biggest problem with using the hospital model for an SNF is that it assumes a bedridden patient population, and thus the design of bedrooms, bathrooms, corridors, and doors are not always appropriate for the use. One can meet the code and not meet the need (Hiatt 1990). An example is handicapped-accessibility codes that mandate a five-foot circle for turning a wheelchair. These codes were based on the needs of Vietnam veterans who had considerable upper-body strength. The elderly do not have the range of motion to turn the wheel within a five-foot circle; they make a three-point turn (Hiatt 1990).

Custodial Versus Rehabilitative Orientation
Long-term care facilities with a custodial mindset focus on risk reduction through immobilization and control; an attempt is made to protect patients from harm. In some nursing homes dependency and lack of control are used to enhance patient manageability and treatability (Rodin 1986). The problems associated with custodial care are these: significantly more people attempt to leave and more actually do run away; nonwandering patients are more disoriented (Hiatt 1985); lack of mobility has psychological and physiological negative consequences (Hiatt 1988); and increased dependency lowers self-esteem and erodes residents' quality of life. This type of skilled nursing facility is bed based in design. Facilities with a rehabilitation orientation offer a richer set of programs and services to keep people more active and allow each individual to function at the highest level possible.

Mobility and Independence. Environmental gerontologist Lorraine Hiatt makes an impassioned plea to nursing homes to encourage and support patient mobility and independence. Positive outcomes of increased motor activity are increased cognitive facility, better digestion, and a lower rate of falls than experienced with restraints (Hiatt 1988). Wireless monitoring devices and cordless call systems may give residents more confidence in moving about. Rocking chairs also give increased mobility. The Rose chair by ADD Interior Systems (Los Angeles) is one of the best chairs on the market for safety, structural support, and a unique rocking motion that is remarkably soothing. The chair is designed to relieve pressure on the spine, regardless of the number of hours spent in the chair. The covering is mesh, which is cool and can be easily disinfected. Optional accessories include restraints and a tray that can be fastened to it for dining (chair is pictured in Fig. 7-1).

According to Hiatt (1988), 11 percent of residents in nursing homes wander; these individuals are on the move 39 percent of waking hours. Nonwanderers move only 4 percent of waking hours. Fear of falling, on the part of both the patient and staff, is the primary motivation for impeding motion, yet moving about should constitute a significant portion of a healthy individual's day. Hiatt recommends these solutions: provide walking paths and memory lanes, implement wayfinding cues (see the section on wayfinding later in this chapter), eliminate shiny finishes from floors, provide properly shaped grabrails (oval is best) on both sides of corridors, eliminate glare from overhead light fixtures to erase the appearance of slippery areas on the floor, and provide sufficient contrast where appropriate.

Mobility is not just an issue of exercising large muscle groups but also involves rehabilitation of manual dexterity through occupational therapy programs. Clothing with Velcro closures makes dressing easier. Implements with offset handles (silverware, toothbrushes, hairbrushes, garden or kitchen tools) are easier for arthritic hands or weak wrists to manipulate; an extensive array of well-designed, attractive prosthetic tools and implements are manufactured in Sweden (see chapter 7). A number of plumbing fixtures for bathing, as well as toilets, are illustrated and discussed in Valins (1988); they enable a frail individual to be reasonably independent and to enjoy the dignity of privacy while attending to these intimate functions. These toilets raise and lower themselves, and some wash and dry the individual for personal hygiene.

Sense of Control. Studies show that the health of the elderly is strongly affected by control-enhancing interventions and control-restricting life circumstances (Rodin 1986). As people age, many events occur over which they have little or no control, such as the death of a spouse, illnesses that restrict activity, loss of manual dexterity, and difficulty in generally fulfilling their wishes without the aid and support of others. A joint task force of the American medical and nursing associations concluded that "a sense of purpose and control over one's life is integral to the health of the aged" (Rodin 1986, 1271). Detrimental effects on individuals whose control of activities is restricted include increased blood pressure and heart rate, elevation of blood lipids, and ventricular arrhythmia.

An individual's perception about control affects stress by influencing coping behaviors. "To the extent that people believe that they can prevent, terminate, or lessen the severity of aversive events, they have less reason to be perturbed by them" (Rodin 1986, 1274). When people have some control over events such as time and place of eating, activities, privacy, and noise, their environment is more predictable, which has a strong positive effect on reduction of stress. Autonomic reactivity (blood pressure, gastric disturbance, hormonal secretion) is reduced. Rodin points out the need for options, however, as the exercise of control can result in negative psychological and physiological effects for some individuals.

Management of Agitation. The management of agitated behavior in the elderly represents a major challenge in geriatric care. Inappropriate verbal or motor activity (pacing, cursing, screaming, biting, repetitive motor activity, anxiety, irritability, and sleep disturbances) impair quality of life and burden caregivers (Thomas 1988). Agitated behavior, which is always inappropriate, includes abusiveness or aggressiveness toward self or others; appropriate behavior performed with inappropriate frequency, such as repeatedly asking questions; and inappropriate behavior according to social standards for the situation, such as putting on too many layers of clothing (Cohen-Mansfield and Billig 1986). Agitated behaviors may be caused by organic brain syndrome with symptoms that include regressive sexual behavior, tendency to hoard, exposing oneself, deterioration of personal appearance, or throwing food (Cohen-Mansfield and Billig 1986). According to Thomas (1988), pharmacological or physical restraints are only partially effective and have considerable risk profiles.

Patients with dementia may experience agitation because of frustration in not being able to do tasks that were once simple or because of inability to recall a name or event. Individuals with cognitive impairments often overreact to seemingly minor problems (called catastrophic reaction) is generally caused by feelings of being overwhelmed by an environment or experience, being frightened by strange people, or being lost or abandoned. One way of coping with catastrophic reaction is to move the person to a quiet room away from noise and activity (Calkins 1988).

Omnibus Reconciliation Act of 1987 (OBRA)

New requirements for nursing home participation in Medicare and Medicaid programs are outlined in the Omnibus Reconciliation Act of 1987, which became effective October 1, 1990. A copy of this act is available from the Health Care Financing Administration (Washington, DC) or from the American Association of Homes for the Aging (Washington, DC), which also publishes an OBRA audit document that helps to interpret and explain the act. Nursing home reforms incorporated into OBRA require many changes in the way skilled nursing facilities operate. Many of the protocols covered by the act have nothing to do with design issues, but designers should be familiar with the contents of this document, which helps to define residents' legal rights such as free choice, freedom from restraints, privacy, confidentiality, accommodation of needs, participation in resident and family groups, and participation in social, religious, and community activities. Sections of OBRA include the admissions process; resident records; staffing requirements; policies, procedures, and plans; notices; and in-service education.

AGE-RELATED CHANGES

Age-related changes deal principally with sensory decline, a change in the body's center of gravity, loss of manual dexterity, and lack of mobility due to a variety of causes including arthritis, congestive heart failure, poor circulation, osteoporosis, and muscle weakness. The following is a brief summary of these issues; however, the reader is referred to chapter 15 for a more thorough discussion and for design guidelines.

Sense of Loss

The many psychological and physical changes that occur in aging are associated with loss, whether the change is the death of a friend, loss of health, moving from the familiarity of the family home to a new location, or health-related restrictions such as favorite foods, pleasurable activities, or loss of visual acuity. Such changes require constant adjustment and may be a tremendous source of frustration, causing anxiety or depression.

Sensory Decline

Sensory deficits in vision, hearing, olfactory sense, and touch severely alter one's perception of the world and erode quality of life. These deficits are described in detail in chapter 15. Here the designer can have the greatest impact in adapting the environment to compensate for these losses. Good design enables the individual to feel more competent, have greater self-esteem, and function at the highest level.

Restricted Upgaze

In design for the elderly, the functional significance of restricted upgaze is important to understand. The normal limit of upgaze in young adults is 40 to 45 degrees. By age eighty it is reduced to an average of 16 degrees (Hutton, Shapiro, and Christians 1982). When limited upgaze is combined with restricted neck extension, seeing fire exit signs, room numbers, and other information mounted too high becomes difficult.

Structural Balance

Shifting weight is among the most difficult and challenging of skills demanded of the frail elderly. The body's center of gravity is pitched forward, making walking clumsy and apelike. Individual differences with respect to mobility and balance assure that no one placement of grab bars can be adequate (Hiatt 1988). This factor provides another example of how one can meet the code and not the need. Lorraine Hiatt, in her lectures, instructs her audience to place their bodies in certain postures that simulate the shift of center of gravity as well as restricted upgaze and then to try to walk in that position, attempt to sit down in a chair, or notice directional signage on a wall. This experiment is so effective a teaching device that it changes forever one's understanding of the difficulty of moving about with these structural limitations.

Although the frail elderly may not readily move about with ease, many adaptations can be made to the environment to reduce their fear of falling and address their concerns about getting lost. The goal should be to keep as many people as possible out of wheelchairs. In this regard, note that all wheelchairs are not alike. Some have more mobility, with front wheels that pivot to enable it to turn easily, This maneuverability makes the user less dependent on staff for assistance.

PSYCHOLOGICAL FACTORS

The environment or physical setting can often be a source of stress in a skilled nursing facility. Stress at any age is known to alter the release of hormones, elevate blood pressure, constrict blood vessels, cause muscle fatigue, and debilitate the immune system. For the elderly, stress may serve as a memory inhibitor, cause disorganized behavior, and even provoke wandering (Hiatt 1985). Noise and "traffic" are known to be major environmental stressors in a skilled nursing facility, especially in large dining rooms. According to Lorraine Hiatt, any noise beyond 30 decibels makes understanding conversation difficult. The noisier the environment, the higher the staff turnover. "Calling out" behavior ("Mama, mama, mama") decreases proportionately when noise decreases. The coping strategy that individuals adopt to deal with environmental stress is influenced by characteristics of the situation itself and by past experience. These reactions to stress may be expressed as denial, projection, confusion, or vulnerability to illness (Zimring 1981). Some of the psychological factors that may cause stress follow.

Loss
The elderly experience loss in many ways, including the death of loved ones, removal from the family home, sensory deficits, and failing health. Old age is a period of great adjustment.

Depression
The aggregate effect of losses and changes in one's life and daily rituals can lead to depression, which can also be caused by medications and restricted mobility.

Sense of Control
When people have some control over events, their environment is more predictable, which has a strong positive effect on stress reduction (Rodin 1986). A study was devised to test the hypothesis that the debilitated condition of many residents in institutional settings results, at least in part, from living in a virtually decision-free environment. An experimental group of SNF residents was told that they should be responsible for themselves; they were given the freedom to make choices and the responsibility of caring for a plant. The other group of residents was told that the staff would make decisions for them as well as take care of their plant. The results were remarkable: 71 percent of the second group became more debilitated over a three-week period, while 93 percent of the responsibility-induced group showed overall improvement, demonstrating that the condition is potentially reversible. In fact, this group reported greater feelings of happiness, showed significantly more activity, were rated to be more alert, and spent far more time visiting with other patients and engaging in social activity, rather than passively watching the staff. A follow-up study 18 months later indicated that the experimental group had sustained long-term beneficial effects (Langer and Rodin, as reported in Cohen and Weisman 1987).

Fear of Abandonment
Being institutionalized understandably carries with it the fear of abandonment by one's family and friends. Removal from the familiarity of one's home and neighborhood is traumatic for most people.

Loneliness and Isolation
Making friends is not easy at any age, and it is particularly difficult for elderly people who suddenly find themselves in a skilled nursing facility. Private rooms are not common because of third-party payer reimbursement policies; although they provide necessary privacy, they may not be the best solution for everyone regardless of cost. Some studies have indicated that residents show a preference for semiprivate rooms to foster companionship and reduce feelings of isolation. The semiprivate room that affords an appropriate level of privacy without compromising companionship might be a solution. In Figure 14-2, each individual has equal

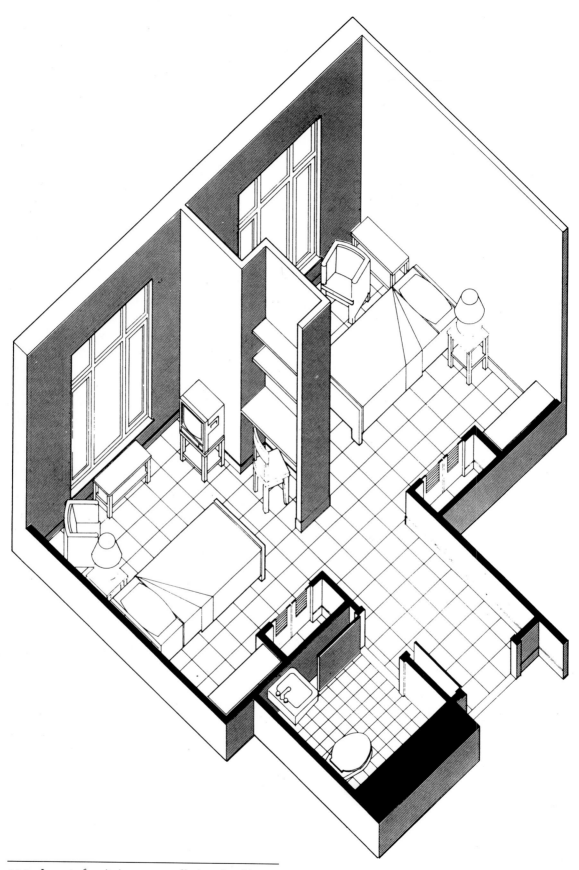

14-2. *Layout of semiprivate rooms affords each resident considerable privacy and equal access to windows and storage, Joseph L. Morse Geriatric Center (West Palm Beach, FL)*

Architect: Perkins Geddis Eastman

access to the window, privacy for visitors, and equal space for storage of personal possessions.

Sensory Deprivation

Sensory deprivation can occur in a bed-based nursing home where residents spend a great deal of time in their rooms with little visual stimulation. Consequences of sensory deprivation include confusion, hallucinations, and depression.

Independence

Skilled nursing facilities that foster independence enhance residents' quality of life. Promoting residents' independence requires a management attitude favoring rehabilitation and a design team who understands that the environment can support or thwart residents' efforts to achieve independence.

Dementia

Dementia is not a disease but a group of symptoms that includes memory loss, confusion, impaired judgment, and reduced capacity to reason (Calkins 1989). It may result in behavior changes and hinder individuals' attempts to dress themselves, follow instructions, and complete sentences or thoughts. Of the many forms of dementia, Alzheimer's disease is the most severe because it is progressive and degenerative, eventually leading to death. ARD is a commonly used term that refers to Alzheimer's disease and related dementias.

Trying to Go Home

Individuals with cognitive impairments often wander, frustrated by a need to go home that is often an attempt to return to a state of mind rather than to a physical place.

Fear of Falling

Fear of falling is one of the most significant inhibitors of mobility in the elderly population. A fall often results in broken bones and a descending spiral of events that can leave the individual with permanent impairment.

PRINCIPLES OF GERONTOLOGICAL RESEARCH

A great deal of research has been done on elderly populations, including those who live independently at home as well as those in sheltered settings such as assisted living units and skilled nursing facilities. In recent years many studies have been done on individuals with Alzheimer's disease. As of this writing, at least a dozen excellent books are available that deal with housing options and design for the elderly. Nevertheless, environmental psychologists and gerontologists caution that recipes or formulas cannot be uniformly applied. The characteristics of individual facilities and other factors demand highly personal solutions. At best, architects and interior designers can learn the principles and then determine where and how they apply to a specific facility.

Many studies reviewed for this chapter required a specialized academic background to interpret and really understand the practical application of the research. The following items, however, are fundamental tenets that underlie much gerontological research; understanding these principles leads to an appreciation of the impact of the environment on vulnerable individuals. The reader is also referred to chapter 15.

ENVIRONMENTAL DOCILITY HYPOTHESIS

The environmental docility hypothesis maintains that the environment has the greatest effect on the most vulnerable individuals or those of low competence (Lawton 1980). The corollary to this theory is the concept of environmental press postulated by Nahemow and Lawton (1976). Individuals are viewed in terms of various competencies (motor and perceptual abilities, intelligence) that enable them to adapt to the demand character of the physical environment. Environmental press refers to environmental stimuli. Even in the best-designed environments, some individuals are unable to behave in an adaptive manner, whereas even the most capable individuals may not behave in an adaptive manner in the most malign environments (Nahemow and Lawton 1976). Press has a greater demand quality as the competence of the individual decreases.

"The individual operates at his best when the environmental press is moderately challenging. If the environment offers too little challenge, the individual adapts by becoming lethargic and operates below his or her capacity" (Nahemow and Lawton 1976, 319). Nahemow and Lawton use the example of a widower who was accustomed to having his wife take care of him. Upon her death, he was overwhelmed by the unaccustomed demands of his new life and retreated psychologically, causing him to be placed in a nursing home. The simplified environment was at first appropriate to his psychologically weakened condition, but as he gained confidence in coping with this benign environment he was operating near the low-press borderline of his own positive adaptation zone and risked becoming dull and deteriorating. This example underscores the delicate balance between too much support, which causes dependency, and too much demand, which can overwhelm an individual of temporary or permanent low competence.

In dealing with highly vulnerable individuals such as the cognitively impaired or the frail elderly, small changes in the level of environmental press may evoke major changes in their quality of mood or behavior. Even with the most cognitively impaired individuals, evidence indicates that special attention to the physical and social environment can maintain or increase functional capacity, self-respect, and dignity (Lawton as reported in Calkins 1988). In summary, both support and demand are equally important in maintaining behavior; tension reduction and tension creation are both personally satisfying, depending on the individual and the situation (Nahemow and Lawton 1976).

INDIVIDUAL VARIABILITY

Almost all data in the area of gerontology—physiological and psychological—show increasing variability with aging. Characterizing the typical older person is extremely difficult (Rodin 1986), which is why designing for this population is so difficult. Interior designers often employ an overly simplified set of guidelines to any facility for the elderly. This uniform application of doctrine evidences a lack of understanding of the many behavioral variables that must be considered.

PHYSICAL AND ARCHITECTURAL FEATURES CHECKLIST (PAF)

The Physical and Architectural Features Checklist (Table 14-1) is an instrument that is often used to assess environmental features of sheltered care settings.

Table 14-1. Physical and Architectural Features Checklist

Subscale	Descriptions
Physical amenities	Measures the presence of physical features that add convenience, attractiveness, and special comfort
Social/recreational aids	Assesses the presence of features that foster social behavior and recreational activities
Prosthetic aids	Assesses the extent to which the facility provides a barrier-free environment as well as aids to physical independence and mobility
Orientation aids	Measures the extent to which the setting provides visual cues to orient the user
Safety features	Assesses the extent to which the facility provides features for monitoring communal areas and for preventing accidents
Architectural choice	Reflects the flexibility of the physical environment and the extent to which it allows residents options in performing necessary functions
Space availability	Measures the number and size of communal areas in relation to the number of residents, as well as size allowances for personal space
Staff facilities	Assesses the presence of facilities that aid the staff and make it pleasant to maintain and manage the setting

Source: Moos and Lemke, as reported in Cohen and Weisman 1987, p. 58.

ARCHITECTURAL AND DESIGN ISSUES

One of the most difficult challenges in an institutional setting is creating the feeling of home. Doing so is necessary because the institution truly is a home to its residents. "While it is a truism that nursing homes should reflect a homelike setting, relatively few have been successful in avoiding a hospital-like image" (Grant 1989, 121). According to Hiatt (1985), the topic of "homeyness," sometimes stated as a paragon of virtue, needs to be taken more seriously as an issue in orientation, at least for marginally impaired individuals. Studies have shown that familiarity, coziness, and comfort have special psychosocial significance, but how do efficient, modern institutions or those with utilitarian design accomplish these qualities?

Space planning and architectural design are the most significant determinants of domestic character. Resident bedrooms marching down a double-loaded, eight-foot, minimum-width corridor appear institutional regardless of superficial decorative effects. Beyond these factors, the many detailed features of the interior environment, including style of furnishings, bedspreads, window treatment, types of finishes, and lighting, contribute to the success of the project.

CREATING THE FEELING OF HOME

The nonverbal message of all residents' rooms being furnished and decorated alike is negative. It robs people of their individuality. The same bedspread on every bed, the same draperies, and identical furniture remind one of a dormitory or a hotel. By contrast, a highly personalized environment tells family members and staff that each resident is valued. Functional and clinical aspects of care often overshadow an image that says ''this is your home'' (Cormack 1990). The limited amount of research attention, the lack of published material, and the fact that the subject of environmental design is not included in the education of caregivers indicate the low status of the subject (Cormack 1990, 4). Although each of us has a different interpretation of what constitutes a homelike setting, a number of opportunities exist to domesticate the environment.

1. The resident's door may be personalized by color or design features that differentiate it from other residents' rooms. A frame may be placed on the door (at wheelchair height) to hold a photo of the resident or spouse. A glass-enclosed display cabinet may contain mementos of personal significance (Fig. 14-3). These displays have helped moderately confused individuals to locate their rooms at the Corinne Dolan Alzheimer's Center.

2. Furnish the dayroom or living room with an eclectic assortment of furniture rather than ''matching'' contemporary oak furniture such as that often found in institutions. Figure 14-4 shows a corridor alcove intended to be an informal spot for visiting, but it was seldom

14-3. *Glass display case at bedroom entrance, The Corinne Dolan Alzheimer Center at Heather Hill (Chardon, OH)*
      Architect: Taliesin Associated Architects; Photo courtesy Margaret P. Calkins

14-4. *''Before'' photo of corridor alcove, Northview Home (Waukesha, WI)*
      Photo courtesy Margaret P. Calkins

used because of its unattractive and institutional appearance. When changed to resemble a domestic dining area with a large oak table and defined by an oak railing, it became a popular spot for both staff and residents (Fig. 14-5). This setting no doubt triggers many pleasant memories for residents.

3. Avoid corridors cluttered with linen or utility carts by providing adequate storage throughout the facility so that staff have ready access to supplies without walking great distances. Corridors should be widened occasionally to provide seating alcoves and niches (Fig. 14-6). Handrails can be designed so that they enhance the environment instead of appearing to be prosthetic devices (Fig. 14-7). Also note in this photo that low partitions create privacy alcoves, built-in planters at wheelchair height add greenery, and nurse stations have a lowered section for communication with individuals in wheelchairs.

4. In residents' bathrooms, a sink set into a plastic laminate countertop with a ''banjo'' extension over the toilet diminishes the institutional character of the room and provides a place to display trinkets or store personal hygiene products.

14-5. *"After" photo of corridor alcove with residential design treatment, Northview Home (Waukesha, WI) Photo courtesy Margaret P. Calkins*

14-6. *Seating alcoves expand the corridor of an Alzheimer's Care Unit; note indirect lighting, tactile artwork, and the use of color contrast, Cokesbury Village (Hockessin, DE)*

Architect: Moeckel Carbonell Associates; Interior design: Mitchell Associates; Photographer: Tom Crane © 1986

14-7. *Alcove adjacent to nurse station provides a socialization area for residents in wheelchairs; Cokesbury Village (Hockessin, DE)*

Architect: Moeckel Carbonell Associates; Interior design: Mitchell Associates; Photographer: Tom Crane © 1986

14-8. *Semiprivate room has furniture and design detailing that create a residential ambience, Casa Palmera (Del Mar, CA)*

Interior design: Suzie King; Photographer: Kim Brun

5. Nursing units designed to accommodate a small number of residents in cluster groupings appear more residential.

6. Use a variety of styles and patterns for bedspreads, drapes, and accessories. Domestic beds (low, 16 inches off the floor) are preferable unless a hospital type of bed is functionally necessary (Fig. 14-8).

SPACE PLANNING

A poorly designed facility handicaps the staff's efforts to render care and frustrates residents' efforts to be independent. Owners should be encouraged to invest in design features that enhance the quality and function of the environment. Anything that can save staff time or result in more efficient staffing is worthwhile because capital costs represent a small portion of a facility's life-cycle costs; by far the largest portion of the pie goes to operating expenses. Some suggestions follow:

1. When residents have well-defined private space such as private bedrooms, they tend to socialize more and are less withdrawn (Zimring 1981).

2. Lounges on main circulation paths are used more frequently than remote lounges, which require greater social commitment. If, upon seeing who is in the lounge, the resident does not wish to enter, disengagement is easier in lounges on well-traveled circulation paths (Howell, Epp, Reizenstein and others as reported in Zimring 1981).

3. A number of small dining rooms are better than one large one because they are quieter and have a more domestic character (Figs. 14-9 and 14-10).

4. Decentralize residents' rooms into clusters based on staffing. The layout in Figure 14-11 provides a kitchen, dining room, and lounge area adjacent to the elevators, surrounded by three clusters of 15-bed units that can be operated in several combinations from a single

14-9. *Country kitchen has a homey feeling and provides a pleasant, familiar area in which residents may congregate, Alzheimer's Care Unit, Cokesbury Village (Hockessin, DE)*

Architect: Moeckel Carbonell Associates; Interior design: Mitchell Associates; Photographer: Tom Crane © 1986

14-10. *Small-scale dining room in Alzheimer's Care Unit is serene and offers views of nature, Cokesbury Village (Hockessin, DE)*

Architect: Moeckel Carbonell Associates; Interior design: Mitchell Associates; Photographer: Tom Crane © 1986

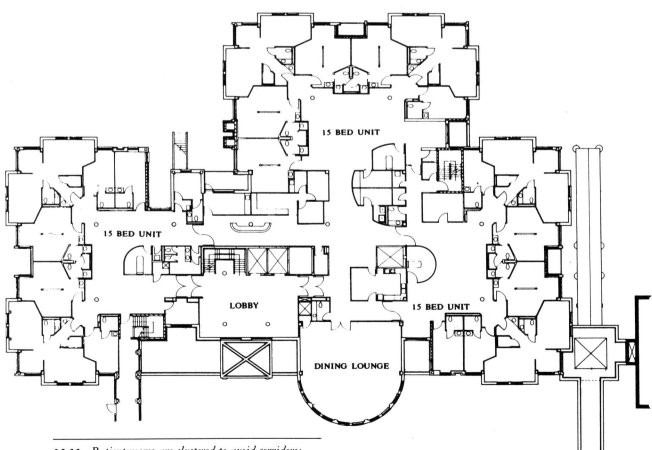

14-11. *Patient rooms are clustered to avoid corridors; each room has its own sunroom, Freeport Hospital (Kitchener, Ontario, Canada)*
   Architect: NORR Partnership Limited

nurse station. This arrangement of rooms
eliminates corridors, as circulation spaces are
wide and have the feeling of living rooms.
Another cluster design (Fig. 14-12) features a
group of rooms around a nurse station.

5. Provide several small dayrooms or lounges
rather than one or two large ones.

6. Sleeping areas should be as private as
possible, even though private rooms may not
be possible. Figures 14-13 and 14-14 show a
low partition placed as a divider between beds
to provide complete visual privacy, yet each
resident has access to a sunroom sitting area.
Note wooden window frames and sills. The
quad room in Figure 14-15 also has access to
a corner sunroom. Note that room layouts in
Figure 14-13 allow optional positioning of the
bed on the angled wall to give the resident a
measure of control over furniture
arrangements.

7. Consider building a number of suites for
residents who prefer and can afford a more
spacious environment (Fig. 14-16). In all
residents' rooms, allow enough space on all
sides of the bed for an elderly person in a

wheelchair to move about. Code-required
critical distances often are not adequate for
this population.

Freeport Hospital Health Care Village
This 350-bed chronic care nursing facility provides rehabilitation services primarily to geriatric patients. Funded jointly by the Ontario Ministry of Health and the general community of
Kitchener and Waterloo, the campus consists
of a number of brick buildings whose diverse
size and character have the image of a residential village. Nursing units are essentially corridor
free (Fig. 14-11).

The facility contains a number of well-
designed commons spaces including an auditorium with movable walls that allow the stage
to be opened to either the interior or the courtyard, which on summer evenings becomes the
equivalent of a drive-in theater for residents in
wheelchairs.

Interior spaces feature brick walls accented
by a teal signature color on ceilings, window
frames, and trim (Fig. 14-17), indoor plantscaping, and elaborately designed ceramic and vinyl

14-12. *Nurse station has a residential ambience, Casa
Palmera (Del Mar, CA)*
Interior design: Suzie King; Photographer: Kim Brun

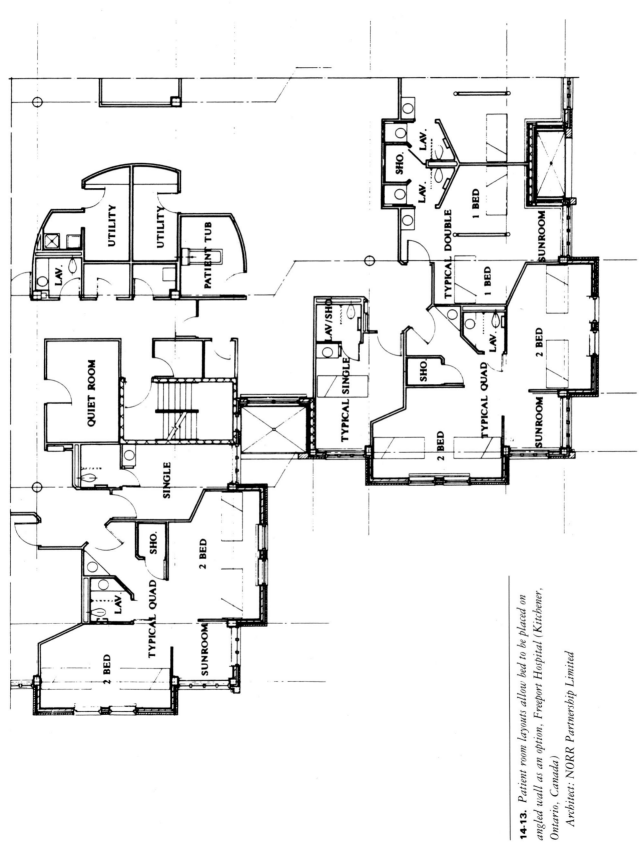

14-13. *Patient room layouts allow bed to be placed on angled wall as an option, Freeport Hospital (Kitchener, Ontario, Canada)*
Architect: NORR Partnership Limited

14-14. *Semiprivate room is cleverly divided with a privacy partition; each resident has equal access to the sunroom and views of nature, Freeport Hospital (Kitchener, Ontario, Canada)*

Architecture and interior design: NORR Partnership Limited; Photographer: Panda Associates

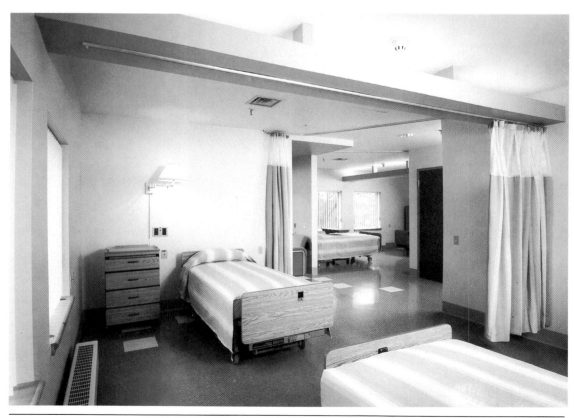

14-15. *View of quad rooms, Freeport Hospital (Kitchener, Ontario, Canada)*

Architecture and interior design: NORR Partnership Limited; Photographer: Panda Associates

14-16. *Parlor suite rooms, Miami Jewish Home & Hospital for the Aged (Miami, FL)*
Architecture: Perkins Geddis Eastman

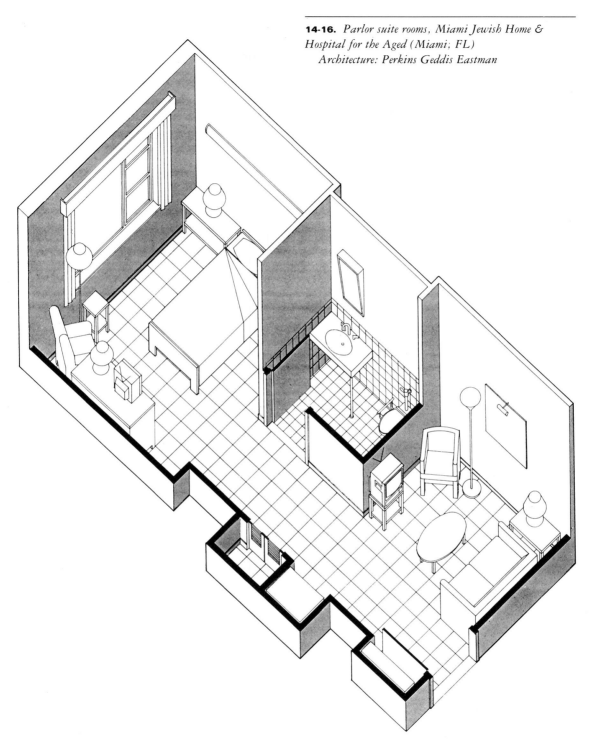

composition tile floor patterns (Fig. 14-18). A veranda space was designed for cognitively impaired residents who may wander freely in it without danger of elopement (Fig. 14-19).

LIGHTING

Lighting is one of the most significant aspects of the designed environment for the elderly. In-

adequate quantity of illumination, glare or shadows, and the spectral distribution of the light source can increase the risk of falling, decrease visual performance, impede mobility, and trigger undesirable physiological responses. Chapters 3 and 15 contain information on lighting and design guidelines that will not be repeated here. The following issues relate specifically to lighting long-term care facilities.

14-17. *Lobby features exterior brick, wood trim, and a strong signature accent color, Freeport Hospital (Kitchener, Ontario, Canada)*

Architecture and interior design: NORR Partnership Limited; Photographer: Panda Associates

14-18. *Semicircular lounge off of veranda corridor is adjacent to the cafe, library, and shops, and gives residents good views of activities outdoors while they remain in a protected environment, Freeport Hospital (Kitchener, Ontario, Canada)*

Architect and interior design: NORR Partnership Limited; Photographer: Panda Associates

14-19. *Veranda corridor is looped to provide cognitively impaired residents with a well-defined wandering route that is impossible to get lost in; as they meander they are exposed to stimulating activities, boutiques, and activity areas, Freeport Hospital (Kitchener, Ontario, Canada)*
Architecture and interior design: NORR Partnership Limited; Photographer: Panda Associates

Evolutionary Theory

Life evolved under the influence of sunlight; therefore, living organisms have developed an array of physiological responses to the spectral energy distribution characteristic of solar radiation. Many animal studies have documented these responses; for example, more dental caries, with ten times the severity of decay, have been observed in hamsters under fluorescent light lacking full-spectrum energy distribution. "These findings strongly suggest that the spectral quality of the illuminant is a major determinant of its effects on mammalian growth and development. Researchers are uncovering significant physiological and biochemical responses of the human body to solar radiation or its fluorescent equivalent" (Hughes and Neer 1981).

Psychobiological Effects

Indoor illumination plays an important role in regulating biochemical processes in the elderly, including neuroendocrine control, synthesis of vitamin D, cardiovascular regulation, and immunologic competency. Because institutionalized elderly often cannot get outside to experience the benefits of sunlight, high-quality indoor illumination can optimize their health. Lighting has a twofold impact on the individual: visual and photobiological, through the skin or photoreceptor (Hughes and Neer 1981).

Benefits of Ultraviolet Radiation. Russian research indicates that ultraviolet light promotes immunological responsiveness, as evidenced by reduced incidence of viral infections, colds, and functional disorders of the nervous system, and it also improves the individual's capacity to withstand stress (Hughes and Neer 1981). Furthermore, full-spectrum light affects the synthesis of melatonin in the pineal gland, which regulates the endocrine system (discussed in chapter 3). The relationship between ultraviolet radiation and vitamin D synthesis has created interest in the metabolic effects of long-term artificial lighting on individuals who spend most of their time indoors (Williams 1988). The elderly do not absorb dietary calcium normally and develop vitamin D deficiency, a serious condition leading to bone fragility and osteoporosis. Incandescent and conventional fluorescent lamps emit little or no ultraviolet radiation.

Enhanced Visual Performance. Aging involves progressive deterioration of the structures of the eye, and coping with the environment thus becomes increasingly difficult. Studies have shown visual performance can be vastly improved under full-spectrum illumination. In a study by Lange, Money, and Richards (Cooper et al. 1986), experiments were performed under Cool White, Ultralume, and Vitalite lamps. The poorest performance was observed under Cool White fluorescents. Furthermore, lighting with a high color-rendering index, such as broad spectrum, improves color discrimination in the elderly (Boyce and Simons as reported in Kolanowski 1990, 183).

The elderly require 3.5 times the contrast to see as well as a twenty- to thirty-year-old individual; the average time for performing tasks decreases significantly as illumination increases, at all age levels (Hughes and Neer 1981). Enhanced lighting should occur at locations where falls are most common, such as at the top of a stair landing where abrupt changes in illumination generally occur, in residents' bedrooms next to beds, and in bathrooms. Corridor intersections are areas where high contrast and adequate illumination can reduce injuries.

In summary, full-spectrum lamps are known to enhance visual clarity, give higher apparent brightness and perceptual satisfaction to an environment, cause less physiological fatigue, and shorten reaction time. If human skin is not exposed to solar radiation for long periods of time, disturbances will occur in the physiological equilibrium of the individual (Dantsig, Lazarev, and Sokolov as reported in Hughes and Neer 1981).

Visual Comfort Probability. Most problems affecting visual comfort are due to windows and light fixtures that lack adequate shielding. Low-brightness fixtures are extremely important in environments for the elderly. A visual comfort probability (VCP) rating of 70 or better generally assures comfort with respect to shielding and should be a minimum level employed. Parabolic louvers offer excellent brightness control

and a VCP in the nineties, whereas the standard prismatic lens generally has a VCP in the forties (Hughes and Neer 1981). Veiling reflections are a problem that can be minimized by avoiding placement of light sources in the offending zone and by the use of matte surfaces.

Restlessness. Restlessness is a condition observed in the institutionalized elderly that can be caused by the spectral distribution of artificial lighting. The symptoms of restlessness include inability to relax, insomnia, pacing, tapping fingers or feet, tossing in bed, or any type of uncontrolled motor activity of a repetitive nature. The purpose of restlessness is to prepare the organism to cope with challenge or threat; it is a disturbance of rhythmicity known to be related to environmental stimuli or changes perceived to be arousing (Norris 1975).

To create a more residential environment, facilities sometimes use Warm White lamps, which have energy concentrated at the red end of the spectrum (known to be highly arousing); full-spectrum lamps have energy evenly distributed across the spectrum, including the blue end, which is known to have a subduing effect. Autonomic nervous system arousal, as measured by heart rate and blood pressure, is less under broad-spectrum lamps than under Warm White fluorescents, and increased arousal causes greater motor activity (Barry as reported in Kolanowski 1990, 181). In summary, this research indicates that something as simple as the color of fluorescent lamps can have a substantial physiological effect on a vulnerable individual and erode his or her quality of life.

COLOR CUEING AND CODING

Color cueing and coding are recommended by environmental gerontologists to enhance function of the elderly. Barbara Cooper (1985; Cooper, Gowland, and McIntosh 1986; Cooper, Mohide, and Gilbert 1990) has conducted a number of studies to demonstrate that color cueing (color contrast applied to key objects in the environment) and increased lighting can enhance performance of the activities of daily living. She also evaluated these effects on various aspects of behavior such as an increase in functional independence. Finally, she studied whether improvement in the activities of daily living would correspondingly improve a resident's feelings of self-worth and well-being. She found that functional levels of the institutionalized elderly are favorably affected by enriching the environment with the specific use of color and light (Cooper, Gowland, and McIntosh 1986, 152).

The difference between color coding and cueing is important to understand. Cueing acts to isolate objects from their background field in order to make them more noticeable. If the environment contains multiple stimuli having equal value, one needs to camouflage those that are less important and selectively cue the important ones with color. Color cueing seems to enhance learning, especially in the activities of daily living such as grooming, eating, and finding the toilet. By contrast, color coding involves the consistent use of a color as an association device; for example, all bathroom doors may be painted red.

Guidelines for Applying Color

Color in the geriatric environment must not be applied haphazardly or inconsistently; one must understand the laws of perception (see chapter 3) and combine them with an understanding of vision changes in the aging eye.

1. Color selections should be based on the functional purpose of the space. Use warm colors (red, yellow, orange) to promote socialization, and cool colors (blue, green, violet) to promote relaxation and foster inward orientation or concentration.
2. Cue out (by camouflaging) doors, storage cabinets, and other items to minimize attention. Neutral colors with little contrast are recommended.
3. Bright color contrast should be used for coding and cueing. Itten's well-known seven rules of color contrast may serve as a reference.
4. Color coding and cueing should be used sparingly to avoid visual confusion or clutter (Cooper, Mohide, and Gilbert 1989).
5. Colors most easily seen by the elderly are red, orange, and yellow; blue, green, and violet are the first to fade. Blues and greens might be used, provided they are at least a number 8 on the Munsell saturation scale (conversation with Barbara Cooper).

Recommended Cueing for Activities of Daily Living

The aging eye has trouble isolating items of significance if their value (lightness or darkness) is similar to that of surrounding items or if their hue (color) is the same. Cooper's recommendations (1986) include painting an outline or silhouette around important items to make them stand out.

Patient's bathroom: Paint a highly contrasting silhouette behind the toilet and around the toilet tissue dispenser, mirror, and door jamb. The silhouette should be two to three inches larger than the object itself. Also paint grab bars a bright color.
Wheelchairs: Outline brakes, foot pedals, and the wheeling rim with colored tape, and apply brightly colored fabric on the back of the chair.
Bedroom: Apply bright color to grooming utensils and an area of wall behind the headboard; apply colored tape to the edges of night table drawers and light pulls, and accent the window frame. Apply color to the room number and the outside face of the door, but paint the inside face a color to match the interior wall color.

Changes in Behavior after Color Intervention

A study conducted by Cooper, Mohide, and Gilbert (1990) was undertaken to determine whether the specific use of color would discourage certain types of undesired behavior and encourage specific types of desirable behavior in the institutionalized elderly. The changes included the following: Doors leading into restricted areas and out of the ward were painted to match the adjacent wall; interiors of restricted areas were painted in pale colors to avoid attention; closet doors in bedrooms (formerly accent colors) were painted the same color as adjacent walls; bedroom doors and frames were painted in bright primary and secondary colors, with colors repeating as infrequently as possible; bathroom doors were accented with strong colors; walls behind toilets and sinks were painted the same color as bathroom doors; the door and adjacent walls leading into the activity area (also used for dining) were painted raspberry red; the interior of the activity area was painted a cream color on one wall, kelly green on another, and coral on a third.

The experiment showed that each type of un-desired behavior (with the exception of patients wandering into others' bedrooms) decreased; no change was noted in desired behaviors, ex-cept for longer stays in the activity area. Pa-tients appear to be attracted to strong color cues (as evidenced by increased wandering into other bedrooms); however, when cueing was coupled with coding, such as in the identifica-tion of the sunroom, patients seemed too dis-oriented to distinguish between colors or to associate specific colors with particular mean-ings. Staff noted that the less cognitively im-paired patients began to locate rest rooms more frequently after the color intervention. The authors of the study conclude that cueing out (minimizing attention by eliminating color cues) is an effective way of reducing undesired be-havior, and that color coding is an ineffective means of helping elderly patients function. They suggest that color coding may be more effec-tive when combined with other sensory cues, such as an accent color door combined with a photograph of the resident.

Other Suggestions

Environmental gerontologists often recommend redundant cueing, the use of cues that apply to more than one sense. Koncelik underscores the importance of tactile markers to identify a place through touch to aid those who are visually or hearing impaired. For example, handrails with a groove on the back can tell a traveler where they are, or texture on doorknobs can cue whether an entry is safe (Kalymun 1989). Simi-larly, corridor intersections can be cued by a change in flooring material. The following are a few additional suggestions:

1. A black toilet seat on a white bowl enhances depth perception.
2. Provide visual access to activity rooms and social spaces (Fig. 14-20).
3. Dementia is associated with a return to a preference for color over form (Goldstein and Oakley 1986). Using geometric symbols as a wayfinding aid would not be effective.
4. Avoid borders or decorative insets in carpet or hard-surface flooring; they may appear to be stairs, holes, or obstructions to an individual with impaired vision. However, do provide strong contrast to separate the floor from the wall, such as a colored baseboard.

Table 14-2. Changes in Behavior after Color Intervention

Behavior	Change noted	Comments
Undesired		
Hovering around exit	Partially eliminated	Patients walk to the door but do not linger
Straying into restricted areas	Almost totally eliminated	Dramatic change
Wandering into other patients' rooms	Increased	Patients are attracted by the brightly colored doors and cannot distinguish between rooms
Rummaging in other patients' closets	Almost totally eliminated	Dramatic change
Voiding in inappropriate areas	Partially eliminated	The more cognitively impaired patients no longer void in closets, but still do so in the corridor
Desired		
Finding own bedroom	None	Patients still cannot identify their own rooms
Finding a washroom	Minimal to none	Moderately cognitively impaired patients could find the washroom more easily if within sight of the door; no change noted for the severely demented
(a) locating (b) staying in activity area	(a) no change (b) substantial increase	Patients did not locate the activity area easily but, once there, stayed considerably longer

Source: Cooper, Mohide, and Gilbert 1990, p. 28.

Although color cueing has been shown to be effective in enhancing residents' ability to func-tion, these devices may compromise the con-ventional image of a residential setting.

INTERIOR FINISHES

The appropriateness of carpet versus hard-surface flooring in health care facilities, espe-

14-20. *French windows, starting at the floor, provide visual access to lounges for residents in wheelchairs, St. John's Mercy skilled nursing facility (St. Louis, MO) Architecture and interior design: The Hoffman Partnership, Inc.; Photographer: Alise O'Brien*

cially those for the elderly, has been the subject of endless debate. Ease of maintenance and life-cycle costs have to be the primary considerations, after safety issues have been resolved. Carpet lends a residential appearance, but even a short-napped carpet provides more resistance than a hard-surface floor for frail individuals maneuvering wheelchairs or walkers. Spills unattended to or improperly cleaned may stain carpet, although carpet tile is a good solution for high-traffic areas because an individual tile can be removed for cleaning without interrupting activity on the unit. The noise of vacuuming carpet is a negative factor, but the odor of cleaning agents and daily wet mopping is not appealing either. Furthermore, wet floors are slippery and cause falls.

Any type of flooring that is shiny is bad. Vinyl composition tile requires wet mopping and waxing, a two-step process, and the seams can harbor microorganisms and odors. Sheet vinyl is softer when an individual falls, requires only a one-step cleaning process, and is less slippery when wet. It seems to be preferred for corridors over vinyl composition tile because it is less expensive to clean, not shiny, and has few seams.

For those who prefer carpet, the concrete should be sealed because it expands and contracts with the weather and may harbor odors. A hospital type carpet with an antimicrobial agent and a waterproof barrier between the backing and the yarn will generally yield good results. If the yarn is solution dyed, it can be cleaned with bleach and not fade. Carpet mills have made great strides in the past five years with respect to high-performing hospital carpets; an institution should not rule out carpet without at least learning about what is currently available. Past experience with carpet that may have been improperly selected should not negatively bias options for a new facility. A combination of sheet vinyl and carpet, each selected for its appropriateness for an individual area, may be the best solution.

If the budget permits, wood floors with a clear vinyl protective layer are attractive, warm, residential in character, and easy to clean. In bathrooms, sheet vinyl is the recommended product because ceramic tile has grout joints that absorb urine.

Patterns

Great care should be exercised in the selection of patterns of carpet or wallcoverings in environments for the elderly. Patterns should be subtle and textural rather than bold. Figure-ground reversal and problems of depth perception increase the possibility of tripping on a boldly patterned carpet.

Wall Finishes

Wall finishes, whether paint or vinyl wallcovering, should have a matte finish. As with flooring, ease of maintenance is a critical factor. Bumper guards should be installed to protect walls from wheelchairs and carts.

FURNITURE

This topic is discussed more thoroughly in chapter 15, but the following are key points.

1. Avoid welting on seating as it provides a crevice in which urine can collect; a seat with a single piece of fabric that wraps around and is stapled under the seat makes cleaning easy.
2. An opening between the seat and back is desirable to avoid a crevice that makes cleaning difficult, especially with incontinent residents.
3. Make certain that seating and arms are adequately cushioned. The frail elderly bruise easily.
4. Select upholstery colors that contrast sufficiently with the floor so that the boundaries of the chair can easily be seen.
5. Do not select furniture to match; an eclectic grouping of styles would be more like home. Accessories such as birdcages also help to create a domestic character. If a particular style or element predominates in that locale, such as a fireplace in the Pacific Northwest, it should be used.
6. Dining tables should have a contrasting edge color and be wheelchair height. Make sure the padded armrests of wheelchairs fit under the tabletop or else the individual will not be able to get close enough to the table.
7. Vinyl upholstery fabrics are more practical than fabric on seating; manufacturers have introduced vinyls that have the texture and appearance of fabric.

WAYFINDING

Ease of wayfinding is especially important in a long-term care facility. Disorientation can result in inactivity as residents may not wish to risk the embarrassment or stress of getting lost; not being able to move about freely reduces one's sense of control. The three key issues are overall orientation, identification of specific rooms, and the cueing of restrictions. At a minimum,

residents should feel confident about being able to locate rest rooms, the water fountain, and a lounge or activity room and be able to identify their own bedrooms.

Spatial orientation necessitates knowing one's present location, knowing where one is going relative to the present location, and knowing how to get to the desired destination (Weisman, as reported in Cohen and Weisman 1987).

Orientation

A number of practical tips can be employed to enhance wayfinding, but a building with confusing circulation paths, little architectural differentiation from one area to another, and poor visual access to the outdoors will always be confusing and illegible.

1. Differentiate corridors with architectural features, colors, finishes, and landmarks so that they do not all look alike. Landmarks may include a unique treatment around the water fountain (Fig. 14-21) or old-fashioned barber poles adjacent to the barber shop or beauty salon. Naming corridors (Fig. 14-22) may also be effective. The name should have some significance to that locale or relate to prominent people and events from the past, such as well-known film stars. (Long-term memory is more potent than short-term; residents often find it easier to remember people and events from the distant past or from their childhood.) A corridor should not run more than 50 to 75 feet without introducing an element of differentiation (Olgyay 1988).
2. Contrast door frames with walls.
3. To help differentiate stairwells, paint yellow, eight-inch-high letters with the ward's name and apply a cutout design, such as a bouquet of daisies, to enable staff to reinforce wayfinding by saying to residents, "When you see the daisies, you know you're home" (Bertram 1989).
4. Apply yellow stripes on the floor to lead to rest rooms and red stripes to lead to "acceptable" exits. Solid lines, not dotted, are recommended to keep residents from trying to pick the dots off the floor. Fluorescent floor tiles can also be used to delineate exit routes (Bertram 1989).
5. For safety, mark the first and last steps in a

stairwell with a two-inch-wide fluorescent orange band across the entire width of the tread; intermediate steps may be edged only near the center of the tread (Bertram 1989).

6. To help residents locate their home "neighborhood," match the color of the corridor to the color of the resident's wristband (Shield 1990).

7. On destination signs, also use symbols keying function, such as a place setting on the dining room sign (Shield 1990).

8. Provide visual access (windows) to principal destinations such as dining, physical therapy, and lounges (Fig. 14-20).

14-21. *Attractive drinking fountain serves as a wayfinding landmark for residents; note interesting room signage, mounted low, with two parrots indicating a semi-private room, Casa Palmera (Del Mar, CA)*
Interior design: Suzie King; Photographer: Kim Brun

14-22. *Auburn Square nurse station is nonclinical in ambience; note the specific use of color, Peachwood Inn (Rochester Hills, MI)*
Concept: Arbor Corporation, Horace D'Angelo; Architecture and interior design: Hobbs & Black Associates, Inc.; Photographer: © Beth Singer

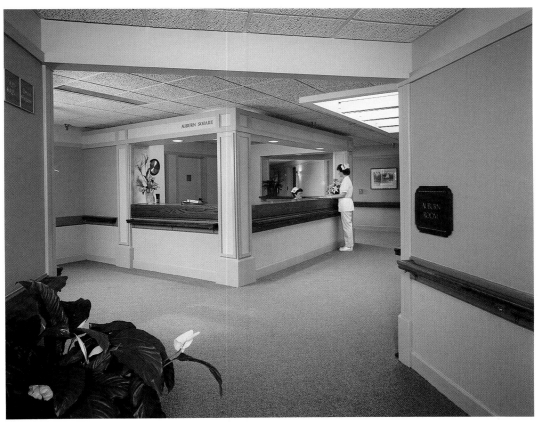

9. Provide uniform lighting.
10. Consider a wall stripe from the dining area to the bathroom (Shield 1990).
11. Provide redundant cueing at intersections (visual, tactile, auditory).

Identification

In addition to the previous color cueing suggestions, the following recommendations have been successful in enhancing identification:

1. Bedroom door: in addition to residents' names, include photographs of the individuals at the age they think of themselves as being (Olgyay 1988).
2. Signs: use uppercase and lowercase letters to improve legibility. Serif or sans serif are acceptable, but avoid excessive flourishes or variations in stroke width. Black signs with yellow letters are easiest for persons of low vision to read. Recommended mounting height is within the range of 3'6" to 5'; the average height of a woman over sixty-five is 5' 3"; with a cane or crutch and the slouch that occurs from compression of the disks between the vertebrae, the height drops to 4' 10", and 3' 10" in a wheelchair (Olgyay 1988).
3. Light switches for patient use should be replaced with brightly colored ones (Bertram 1989).
4. Use 10-inch-high raised numbers on bedroom doors; label the water fountain in 8-inch-high contrasting letters (Bertram 1989).

Restrictions

Residents may need to be protected from certain exits or stairways or from entry to rooms that might be hazardous.

1. Cue out restricted areas by painting the door a neutral color.
2. An elopement problem in an unlocked ward can be dealt with by camouflaging the exit doors with murals (Bertram 1989).

Staff Role in Wayfinding

In spite of the aforementioned suggestions for enhancement of wayfinding, the staff must explain to new residents that the orientation cues exist and that they are intended to help them be more independent. For established residents, periodic wayfinding orientation drills should occur. In-service education for all staff should acquaint them with the principles of wayfinding design so that they can continually reinforce the use of these devices to help residents be more independent.

A MODEL PROJECT

Peachwood Inn and Borden Court represent a new concept in long-term care facilities called a *Caretel.* The originator of this concept, Horace D'Angelo, Jr., set out to create a hybrid of an excellent nursing home and a European residential hotel. Nursing care units bear the names of English country manors: Devon, Auburn, and Picadilly. The building was designed in an **X**-shaped plan in order to incorporate a series of courtyards. Peachwood Inn, the health care component, is comprised of four 60-bed neighborhoods. Small, homelike dining facilities (Fig. 14-23) are shared between neighborhoods. Residents have a choice of large dining rooms or small intimate ones. Residents may join their families for a before-dinner drink in the Tavern on the Green (Fig. 14-24), followed by dinner in the elegant Bugatti Bar and Bistro (Fig. 15-14), both of which are located in Borden Court, an assisted living facility.

Residents' Rooms

Residents' rooms feature a variety of amenities to make them appealing and private. They have wallcovering, residential-style furniture (Fig. 14-25), and window seats for sitting or for displaying personal possessions. The facility has nine different room styles and configurations, offering residents variety and choice. Wing walls offer privacy to a resident lying in bed, cubicle curtains disappear into a pocket to make the room less institutional, and large windows offer a view of the courtyard. Two 14-inch-wide closet doors allow wheelchair-bound residents to open their own closets—a unique feature.

Wayfinding Cues

Nursing units are named (Fig. 14-22) and use color to cue different neighborhoods and locations of public spaces. The handrail appears to be a wainscot separating two colors. Great attention was devoted to the design of environmental features such as lighting and acoustics. Lighting is indirect and appropriate to the function of each area. Carpeted corridors make the

14-23. *Dining room in skilled nursing facility is small scale and has elegant appointments, Peachwood Inn (Rochester Hills, MI)*

Concept: Arbor Corporation, Horace D'Angelo; Architecture and interior design: Hobbs & Black Associates, Inc.; Photographer: © Beth Singer

14-24. *Tavern on the Green offers residents and guests a bit of nostalgia, Peachwood Inn/Borden Court (Rochester Hills, MI)*

Concept: Arbor Corporation, Horace D'Angelo; Architecture and interior design: Hobbs & Black Associates, Inc.; Photographer: © Beth Singer

14-25. *Residents' rooms are varied and interesting, offering nine different configurations, some with bay windows and other desirable features, Peachwood Inn/ Borden Court (Rochester Hills, MI)*

Concept: Arbor Corporation, Horace D'Angelo; Architecture and interior design: Hobbs & Black Associates, Inc.; Photographer: © Beth Singer

14-26. *Picadilly Lane offers residents a number of stimulating experiences for entertainment, shopping, or socializing, Peachwood Inn/Borden Court (Rochester Hills, MI)*

Concept: Arbor Corporation, Horace D'Angelo; Architecture and interior design: Hobbs & Black Associates, Inc.; Photographer: © Beth Singer

14-27. *View of gift shop, movie theater marquee, and at the terminus, Bugatti Bar & Bistro in Picadilly Lane, Peachwood Inn/Borden Court (Rochester Hills, MI)*

Concept: Arbor Corporation, Horace D'Angelo; Architecture and interior design: Hobbs & Black Associates, Inc.; Photographer: © Beth Singer

facility quieter and more residential in appearance.

Borden Court employs 16 colors of carpet and 30 wall colors in a subtle color transition from room to room.

Picadilly Lane is a popular destination for residents (Figs. 14-26 and 14-27). It includes Aunt Peach's Ice Cream Parlor, a gift shop, Shearlock's Holme Beauty Shop, and Bogie's movie theater. As residents approach Picadilly Lane, they pass the theater marquee with its display of old-time movie posters, surrounded by movie marquee lights, and they smell the aroma of fresh popcorn. Storefront facades and the highly textured combination of materials create a stimulating sensory experience. Picadilly Lane terminates at the Bugatti Bar and Bistro, where a replica of a vintage Bugatti is parked at the entrance to the dining room.

A Management Philosophy

According to Horace D'Angelo, Jr. (1990), the main difference between his facility and a typical nursing home is that living services, not nursing services, are his first priority. In addition to the high-quality design features that characterize this facility, careful selection of staff and the management philosophy have an impact on the residents' environment. A number of special features make it especially pleasant for family members to visit. "Cartoons and Clowns" programs staged for residents' grandchildren are an event children look forward to while visiting their grandparent. A laundry facility in Borden Court allows a resident's son or daughter to do the parent's laundry on-site (instead of carrying it home) while having lunch and visiting with the parent. A guest chef from a specialty restaurant provides a weekly dinner for residents and their guests. Courtyards offer a variety of options and experiences. Picadilly Park has a fountain and patio; Central Park features a shaded trellis and circular walk; the Garden Park is filled with flowers and a wide, European-style porch with awnings and chairs, whereas the Gazebo Park is quiet and small, with the gazebo as its focus. This project proves that a skilled nursing facility can be designed to offer pleasant surprises and endless variety with each room and every turn of a corner. Residents need not give up the refinements and amenities that make life enjoyable.

INNOVATIVE DESIGN FOR ALZHEIMER'S FACILITIES

Alzheimer's disease is a progressive, irreversible neurological disorder that presents great challenges to the victims' families and caregivers. Although the cause of Alzheimer's disease is not known, recent scientific investigation suggests a genetic predisposition and other causes such as a virus affecting brain cells, ingestion of aluminum from cooking utensils, and MSG (monosodium glutamate), a food additive known to affect the brain. The symptoms of Alzheimer's disease include memory loss, poor judgment, inability to perform routine tasks, confusion, impaired ability to reason, short attention span, an inability to plan, and difficulty completing a thought.

The planning and design of special care facilities for Alzheimer's patients require a thorough understanding of the disease and the behaviors manifested by its victims. The tremendous variability in cognitive impairment, stage of the disease, and individual personality characteristics of Alzheimer's victims preclude knowing the right answer or the best design solution for everyone or every facility. Nevertheless, many studies suggest that the environment is the most significant factor affecting the behavior and functional abilities of the Alzheimer's victim. Fortunately, a number of recent studies—and three books in particular—are available to guide architects and designers in planning facilities. Calkins's *Design for Dementia* (1988) and Cohen and Weisman's *Holding On to Home* (1991) contain a wealth of information and the most current research. Cohen and Weisman's annotated bibliography, *Environments for People with Dementia* (1987), is another excellent resource.

STAGES OF ALZHEIMER'S AND RELATED DEMENTIAS

The six commonly recognized psychosocial phases of the disease process each require appropriate care and design strategies (Calkins 1988). Starting with prediagnosis, a stage characterized by recognition of subtle cognitive problems, and proceeding to denial, and later anger, guilt, and sadness, the disease slowly becomes incorporated into the individual's daily life as coping strategies become established. Eventually the victim is unable to function independently, and at this point he or she may be placed in an institution because of problems associated with bowel and bladder incontinence, persistent wandering, and aggressive behavior. The final stage of the disease results in separation from self, a stage at which the individual is incapable of interacting meaningfully with people or the environment.

WANDERING BEHAVIOR

Geriatric wandering is a major patient-management problem for caregivers. Historically, the problem has been dealt with by chemical or physical restraints; however, codes usually require that patients be released and given exercise every two hours. Wandering behavior takes its toll in operating budgets because it requires more staff to keep retrieving patients. Thus, positive solutions to deal with the problem benefit the staff as well as the patient.

Individuals are known to wander for a variety of reasons including to get exercise, increase visual stimulation, or gain a sense of independence, all of which are positive reasons, or to look for home, search for their mothers, make dinner for the family, escape from an overly stimulating environment, or discharge energy. Problems associated with wandering include elopement, trespassing into others' bedrooms, safety risks, and the accompanying legal liability. Wandering disturbs ongoing activities and frustrates the individual who cannot, at will, return to a designated location. Some facilities lock their Alzheimer's units for purposes of security, but codes often forbid this practice and also forbid disguising fire doors. A number of wandering control products have been developed, such as wrist or ankle bracelets that trigger a visual or acoustic alarm at the nurse station. Some states allow electromagnetic door locks that use buttons or keypads to unlock doors for staff and visitor access and that are tied into a fire alarm system that causes doors to unlock automatically when necessary. The downside to this system is that it limits all residents, not just the cognitively impaired, from access and egress (Calkins 1989). A lock that involves a sequence of numbers is suggested by Calkins (1988), as are two buttons that must simultaneously be pushed, each located far enough apart that a cognitively impaired individual could not possibly complete the task.

Types of Wandering Patterns

As 50 to 60 percent of residents in nursing homes have some form of cognitive impairment, wandering is a significant problem. Individuals wander for a variety of reasons; therefore, control of the problem is not a simple process. It requires a comprehensive approach starting with space planning and incorporating wayfinding design features, activities programs, and in-service education. Many problem behaviors are the result of unskillful interactions of caregivers who have not been properly trained to deal with cognitively impaired persons (Rader 1987). With these individuals, repetition, structure, and predictability in the environment are critical elements in decreasing problem behaviors.

Hussian identifies four types of wandering patterns (Rader 1987, 756):

1. Exit seekers: want to leave
2. Akathesiacs: aimless pacing (perhaps due to effects of psychotropic medications)
3. Self-stimulators: may go to door and turn knob, but purpose is stimulation, rather than desire to escape
4. Modelers: follow others around

Control of Elopement

Individuals with dementia often perceive two-dimensional objects as three-dimensional (Hussian and Brown as reported in Chafetz 1990). Based on this, experiments were conducted to determine if a pattern of beige masking tape on a brown floor could create the perception of a barrier that would prevent patients from exiting. The results indicated that demented individuals will cross the grid if, as in this case, glass doors

14-28. *Entrance gates to Corinne Dolan Alzheimer Center at Heather Hill (Chardon, OH)*
Architect: Taliesin Associated Architects; Photo courtesy Margaret P. Calkins

offer a visually attractive view of physically unrestricted spaces that lie beyond (Chafetz 1990). At the Corinne Dolan Alzheimer's Center in Chardon, Ohio, staff learned that painting a pattern on the floor was unsuccessful in keeping patients from wandering out the door; the pattern attracted them to the door. They were successful, however, when they covered the panic hardware with a piece of cloth. According to Calkins (personal conversation), not giving visual access to areas patients do not, in reality, have access to is important. As an example, the attractive, open gates in Figure 14-28 proved to be frustrating to residents.

DESIGN SOLUTIONS

A number of recent projects are considered to be on the cutting edge of design for individuals with Alzheimer's disease. These facilities do not profess to have all the answers or to have resolved all problems, but their design has been based on research, and several have been designed to incorporate ongoing research projects.

Corinne Dolan Alzheimer's Center

Designed by Taliesin Associated Architects, this facility incorporates Frank Lloyd Wright's principles of organic architecture. The triangular layout of the floor plan eliminates dead-end corridors by creating a continuous walking track for wanderers (Fig. 14-29); dead-end corridors are

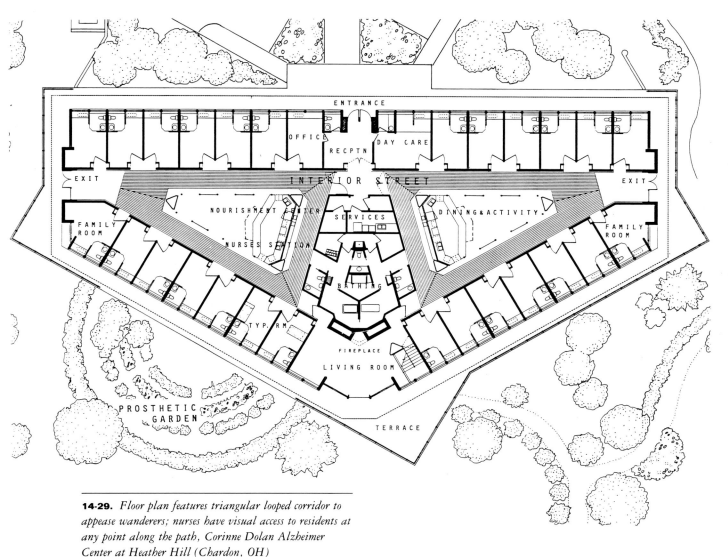

14-29. *Floor plan features triangular looped corridor to appease wanderers; nurses have visual access to residents at any point along the path, Corinne Dolan Alzheimer Center at Heather Hill (Chardon, OH)*
Architect: © 1990 Taliesin Associated Architects

known to frustrate and cause agitation in demented individuals. (In an older building where a racetrack corridor cannot be created, locating activity rooms at both ends of the corridor will decrease the feeling of reaching a dead end.) From the nurse stations, staff have unrestricted views of residents at any point in the wandering path. This facility has been designed in two equal halves in order to allow ongoing research with an experimental group on one side and a control group on the other. This facility has a full-time, on-site research staff, with which Margaret Calkins (1988) is associated.

A dining and activities area is located in the center of the space (Fig. 14-30). Different types of finish materials are used to delineate areas, such as the wooden flooring used in the corridor. A residential ambience has successfully

been created, with residents' bedrooms opening onto the space that functions as a living room. Natural materials such as brick and wood have been used extensively. A peach and terra cotta color palette predominates. Amish quilts are used as wayfinding cues, and various works of interactive art (Fig. 14-31) engage residents. This type of art consists of three-dimensional elements that can be manipulated by the viewer. For example, a painting might contain a tennis shoe that can be tied or untied. Tactile art is desirable because it engages more than one sense. The image of young children standing at a lace-curtained window (Fig. 14-31) may trigger long-term memories. (Studies have shown that items associated with the resident's childhood are the most successful in triggering memory.)

14-30. *Residential character of nursing unit is enhanced by architectural design features and the selection of finish materials, Corinne Dolan Alzheimer Center at Heather Hill (Chardon, OH)*
  Architecture and interior design: Taliesin Associated Architects; Photographer: Pete Guerrero

14-31. *Example of artwork for Alzheimer's Care Unit, Corinne Dolan Alzheimer Center at Heather Hill (Chardon, OH)*
  Photo courtesy Margaret P. Calkins

One prominent feature of this facility is the residential type of kitchen positioned close to residents' bedrooms. To enhance sensory experiences and to stimulate residents' appetites, staff and residents use a microwave or convection oven to heat quick-chilled food, fry onions or garlic, or bake bread at the nourishment center (Nemtin 1990). Normal activities like cooking, kneading bread, and washing and drying dishes establish a sense of normalcy on the unit and allow residents to participate in mealtime preparation. Poor appetite is a common problem among Alzheimer's patients; when food is prepared in a commercial kitchen and transported in a cart to another location for serving, residents are robbed of the wonderful aromas of food being prepared. Note in Figure 14-32 the countertop surfaces that pull out to enable residents to have an informal snack in a domestic setting. Appliances are colored to contrast sharply with surrounding case work. A number of safety features were built into the kitchen to allow residents the freedom to use it. A refrigerator is kept stocked with drinks and snacks available to residents as they wish.

Acoustics are a major concern in facilities for Alzheimer's patients because noise is known to

14-32. *Nourishment center is focal point of living unit; countertops pull out for informal snacking during the day, Corinne Dolan Alzheimer Center at Heather Hill (Chardon, OH)*

Architecture and interior design: Taliesin Associated Architects; Photographer: Pete Guerrero

cause agitation. Noise and too much visual stimulation often increase confusion and problem behaviors. Therefore, a number of small activity rooms increase attention span and help wanderers to join activities. The considerable use of wood in this facility, including high ceilings with nonparallel surfaces, helps to decrease noise. Carpet and large wallhangings also help in this regard.

Design of Resident's Bedroom

The design of the bedroom is especially interesting. An opening in the bathroom wall allows the resident to see the bathroom sink from the bed upon awakening (Fig. 14-33). The visual access is intended to remind the resident to use the bathroom. For the same reason, the room has no door, only a drapery that can be pulled. Dutch doors on bedrooms allow the lower half to be closed in order to control aimless wandering and rummaging around in other residents'

rooms. Bedrooms are carpeted, and bathrooms have matte-finish linoleum flooring. Residents are encouraged to bring their own furniture. Painted walls coated with Ronai Varichrome make them impervious to urine. All edges and corners of walls, case work, and furniture are rounded and soft.

Personalizing the Environment

One of the most interesting experiments conducted in this facility is the illuminated display cabinet outside each resident's bedroom (Fig. 14-3). It serves as a night-light and as a memory-cueing device to enable mildly confused residents to identify their rooms. The display contains mementos of personal significance from home. When researchers covered up the display boxes or put objects of no personal significance in them, mildly confused patients could not find their rooms, but there was no effect on high-functioning people who relied on other cues to identify their bedrooms (conversation with Margaret Calkins).

THE WASHINGTON HOME

Architects Oudens & Knoop devised a strategy of 12-bedroom clusters grouped around central

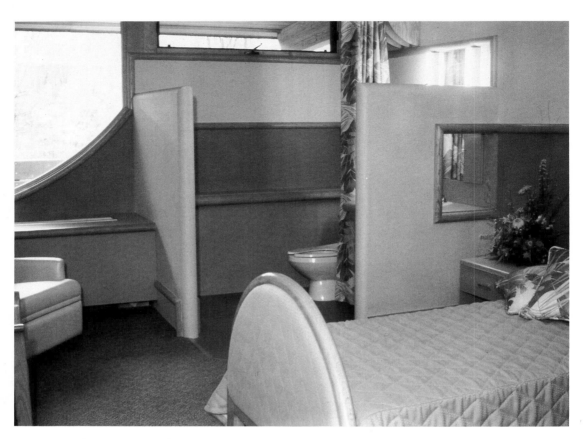

14-33. *Typical respite care room for Alzheimer's patient makes toilet and sink area highly visible, Corinne Dolan Alzheimer Center at Heather Hill (Chardon, OH)*
    Architecture and interior design: Taliesin Associated Architects; Photographer: Daniel Ruark

living areas (Fig. 14-34). This design gives a more residential appearance than the traditional nursing home organized around a double-loaded corridor. A front porch at each neighborhood cluster provides a secure transitional area between private and active spaces. As originally planned (Fig. 14-35), it truly resembled a front porch; however, due to budget constraints, it ended up as merely a 36-inch-high drywall partition with a wood cap. For the cognitively impaired, nursing support core elements are pushed to the side to open up the central activities area. An atrium provides accessible outdoor space for wanderers. In the units planned for the cognitively intact, nursing support elements are shifted to define separate activity areas.

REDUCED STIMULATION UNIT

Individuals with Alzheimer's disease often receive negative verbal feedback such as "You

can't come in here" from more alert patients, staff, and frustrated visitors. As an experiment, a special care unit was created that emphasized reduced stimulation to determine if patients' level of agitation might decrease, as well as their combative behavior. The physical aspects of the environment included neutral color and the absence of television, radios, and telephones. Patients were allowed to go anywhere, eat, and rest wherever or whenever they wished. Staff and visitor access were controlled. The results were positive. Patient weight loss was curtailed, agitation diminished, use of restraint was reduced, and wandering was no longer a concern of staff or other patients (Cleary et al. 1988). In addition, staff wasted much less time in retrieving patients and had fewer interruptions when giving care.

WOODSIDE PLACE

The Presbyterian Association on Aging developed Woodside Place as a model residential Alzheimer's facility patterned after a similar one in Birmingham, England. The building, designed by Perkins Geddis Eastman, is modeled after a Shaker or farm collective. Based on extensive research, the facility (currently under construc-

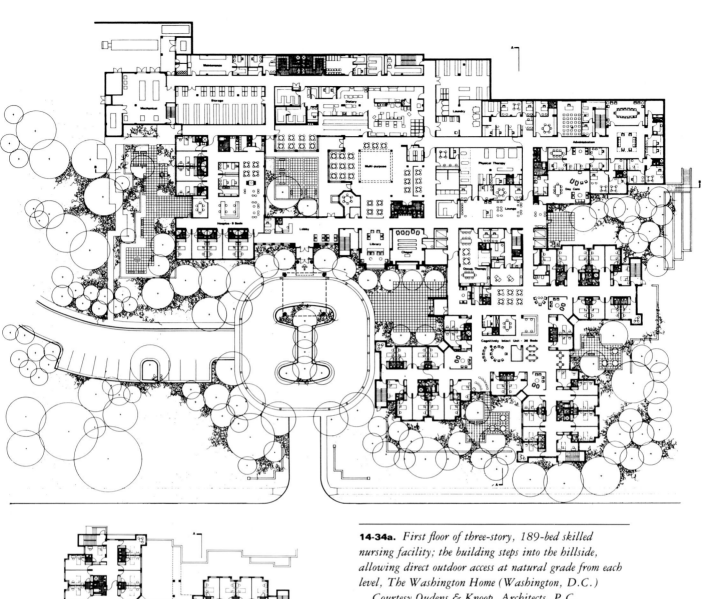

14-34a. *First floor of three-story, 189-bed skilled nursing facility; the building steps into the hillside, allowing direct outdoor access at natural grade from each level, The Washington Home (Washington, D.C.)*
Courtesy Oudens & Knoop, Architects, P.C.

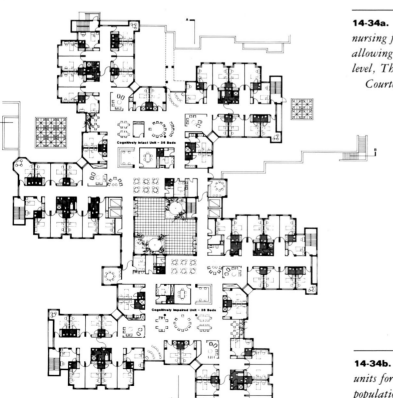

14-34b. *Typical layout of nursing floor showing separate units for the cognitively intact and cognitively impaired populations, with a central courtyard, The Washington Home (Washington, D.C.)*
Courtesy Oudens & Knoop, Architects, P.C.

14-35. *Architect's original concept of a front porch at entry to each 12-bed cluster of rooms to provide a transitional area between private and active spaces, The Washington Home (Washington, D.C.)*
Courtesy Oudens & Knoop, Architects, P.C.

tion) will incorporate the latest theories in the stabilization of dementia, including communications, signage, identifiable magnet spaces, and planned interior and exterior wandering spaces. The facility is comprised of three separate, distinct houses plus a commons area (Fig. 14-36). All rooms have views of gardens and nature, and individual spaces are distinctly different in character to create a feeling of home (Fig. 14-37). Scattered throughout the facility are trunks filled with things for rummaging.

PATHWAYS

The Pathways program, a joint project of the State of Florida Department of Health and Rehabilitative Services and the Miami Jewish Home and Hospital for the Aged, is designed to develop a continuum of residential environments and services for victims of Alzheimer's disease and their caregivers. It is intended to be a complete system of services that will work as a living laboratory for ways of caring for Alzheimer's victims in residential settings and is expected to serve as a local, regional, and national resource for information about this population (Williams 1988).

Pathways will be developed in a campus setting in order to provide a controlled research environment that has the feeling of a residential village. Developed on state land, Pathways and the Florida Alzheimer's Disease Initiative will provide the state with the housing and services research component needed to complement ongoing biomedical research. The Stein Gerontological Institute, associated with the Miami Jewish Home for the Aged, designed the project to forge a partnership between the caregiver (spouse, child, or other family member) and the formal care system to share the burden of caring for the Alzheimer's victim. This ambitious project, currently in the planning stages, is definitely one to watch.

HOLDING ON TO HOME

Holding On to Home (Cohen and Weisman 1991) is a remarkable book about people with dementia and the environments in which they live. It is the result of the combined research of many individuals and offers sensitive design solutions to frequently encountered problems. The authors kindly prepared for this chapter the following brief summary of design principles:

Selected Design Principles
Eliminating environmental barriers. Physical and cognitive impairments with dementia often make movement through and use of the environment difficult. Eliminating these barriers to

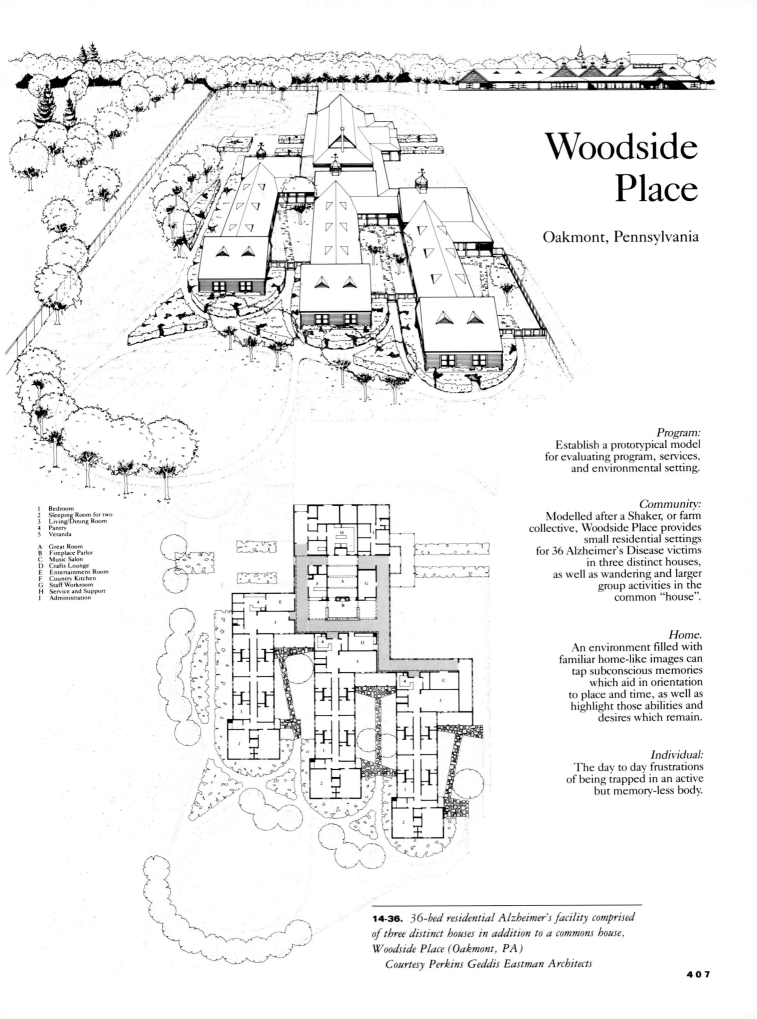

Woodside Place

Oakmont, Pennsylvania

1 Bedroom
2 Sleeping Room for two
3 Living/Dining Room
4 Pantry
5 Veranda

A Great Room
B Fireplace Parlor
C Music Salon
D Crafts Lounge
E Entertainment Room
F Country Kitchen
G Staff Workroom
H Service and Support
I Administration

Program:
Establish a prototypical model
for evaluating program, services,
and environmental setting.

Community:
Modelled after a Shaker, or farm
collective, Woodside Place provides
small residential settings
for 36 Alzheimer's Disease victims
in three distinct houses,
as well as wandering and larger
group activities in the
common "house".

Home.
An environment filled with
familiar home-like images can
tap subconscious memories
which aid in orientation
to place and time, as well as
highlight those abilities and
desires which remain.

Individual:
The day to day frustrations
of being trapped in an active
but memory-less body.

14-36. *36-bed residential Alzheimer's facility comprised
of three distinct houses in addition to a commons house,
Woodside Place (Oakmont, PA)
Courtesy Perkins Geddis Eastman Architects*

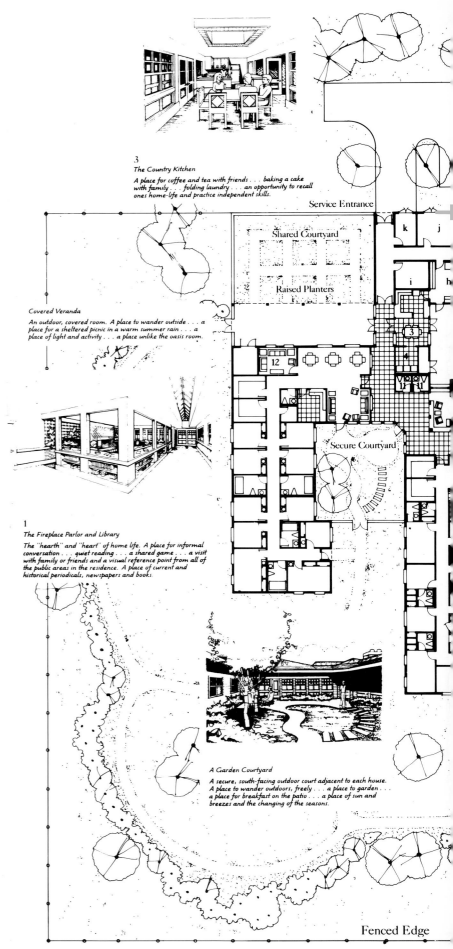

3

The Country Kitchen

A place for coffee and tea with friends . . . baking a cake with family . . . folding laundry . . . an opportunity to recall ones home-life and practice independent skills.

Service Entrance

Shared Courtyard

Raised Planters

Covered Veranda

An outdoor, covered room. A place to wander outside . . . . a place for a sheltered picnic in a warm summer rain . . . a place of light and activity . . . a place unlike the oasis room.

Secure Courtyard

1

The Fireplace Parlor and Library

The "hearth" and "heart" of home life. A place for informal conversation . . . quiet reading . . . a shared game . . . a visit with family or friends and a visual reference point from all of the public areas in the residence. A place of current and historical periodicals, newspapers and books.

A Garden Courtyard

A secure, south-facing outdoor court adjacent to each house. A place to wander outdoors, freely . . . a place to garden . . . a place for breakfast on the patio . . . a place of sun and breezes and the changing of the seasons.

Fenced Edge

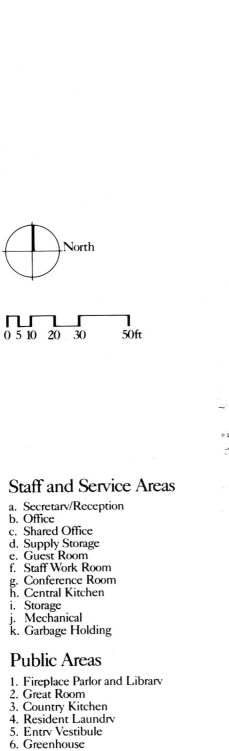

North

0 5 10 20 30 50ft

Staff and Service Areas

a. Secretary/Reception
b. Office
c. Shared Office
d. Supply Storage
e. Guest Room
f. Staff Work Room
g. Conference Room
h. Central Kitchen
i. Storage
j. Mechanical
k. Garbage Holding

Public Areas

1. Fireplace Parlor and Library
2. Great Room
3. Country Kitchen
4. Resident Laundry
5. Entry Vestibule
6. Greenhouse
7. Music Room
8. Crafts Lounge
9. Personal Hygiene
10. Oasis Room
11. Toilet
12. Den

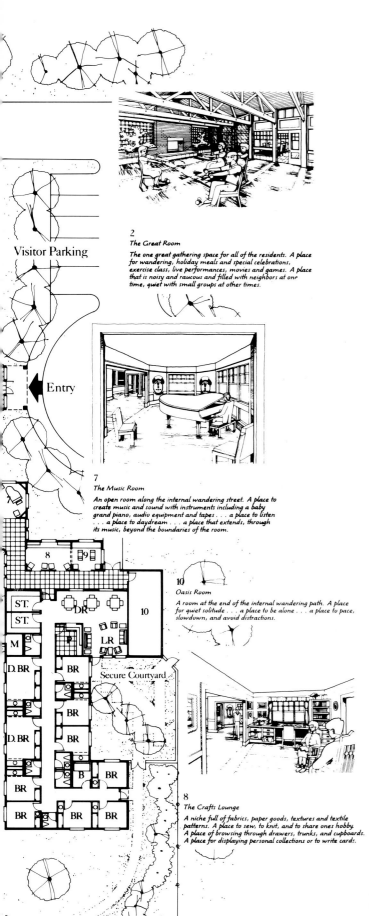

2

The Great Room

The one great gathering space for all of the residents. A place for wandering, holiday meals and special celebrations, exercise class, live performances, movies and games. A place that is noisy and raucous and filled with neighbors at one time, quiet with small groups at other times.

7

The Music Room

An open room along the internal wandering street. A place to create music and sound with instruments including a baby grand piano, audio equipment and tapes . . . a place to listen . . . a place to daydream . . . a place that extends, through its music, beyond the boundaries of the room.

10

Oasis Room

A room at the end of the internal wandering path. A place for quiet solitude . . . a place to be alone . . . a place to pace, slowdown, and avoid distractions.

8

The Crafts Lounge

A niche full of fabrics, paper goods, textures and textile patterns. A place to sew, to knit, and to share ones hobby. A place of browsing through drawers, trunks, and cupboards. A place for displaying personal collections or to write cards.

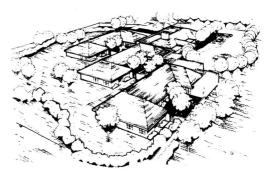

Wandering At Woodside Place

A series of residential cottages enclosing private, secure courtyards. The wandering paths inside the common areas of the residence lead into landscaped courts and then into a larger, safe wandering area enclosed by hedges. The variety of wandering paths outside allow for unrestricted movement. The paths purposely avoid physical and psychological "dead-ends" by bending the circulation, opening up vistas, and creating events, activities and opportunities.

14-37. *Room vignettes describe a number of special design features based on extensive research, Woodside Place (Oakmont, PA)*

Courtesy Perkins Geddis Eastman Architects

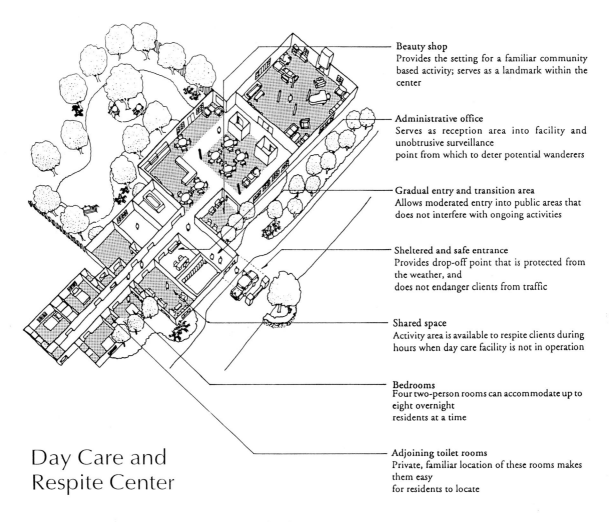

Beauty shop
Provides the setting for a familiar community based activity; serves as a landmark within the center

Administrative office
Serves as reception area into facility and unobtrusive surveillance
point from which to deter potential wanderers

Gradual entry and transition area
Allows moderated entry into public areas that does not interfere with ongoing activities

Sheltered and safe entrance
Provides drop-off point that is protected from the weather, and
does not endanger clients from traffic

Shared space
Activity area is available to respite clients during hours when day care facility is not in operation

Bedrooms
Four two-person rooms can accommodate up to eight overnight
residents at a time

Adjoining toilet rooms
Private, familiar location of these rooms makes them easy
for residents to locate

Day Care and Respite Center

The kitchen counter provides an unobstructed view of the dining area, the entry to the living room, and an outdoor activity area

The central space accommodates dining and informal activities, and provides opportunities for wandering at the periphery.

14-38. *Layout and special features of day care and respite center for individuals with dementia*
Courtesy Uriel Cohen and Gerald Weisman

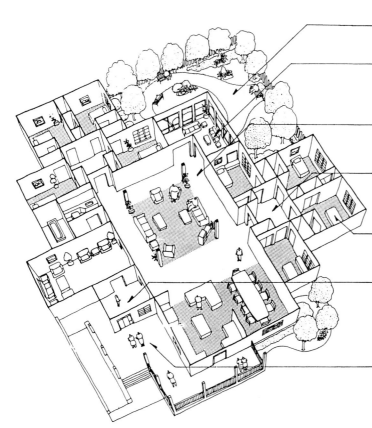

Positive outdoor spaces
Direct access to adjacent outdoor activity area

Places for visiting
Den and sun-room can be enclosed and separated from the more public core of the facility-could serve as places for visiting for family and friends.

Opportunities for meaningful wandering
Indoor walking path connecting different activity areas, and the key social spaces,

Clustering activities and spaces
Clusters of 4 resident rooms, around a semi-private core. Complete elimination of corridors. Public activities clustered around a public core.

Resident rooms
Private rooms with storage and baths to ensure maximum privacy

Public to private realms
Gradation of spaces from entry to living room, dining room, kitchen, to semi-public den, and sun-room, to semi-private zones adjacent to resident rooms, to the private core of individual resident rooms.

Non-institutional image
Residential scale with resident room clusters, no corridors, elimination of the nurses' station. Front porch and exterior residential imagery.

Group Home for Eight Residents

The living room can accommodate most communal activities of the home such as holiday meals. It is the central space of the house, connected to other functions and the clusters of residents' rooms, yet it has its own spatial boundaries. Columns and book cases define the living room and contribute to its residential character.

The den links the living room and its surrounding path to the outdoors. It can serve as an extension of the central activity area or, with the french doors closed, can become a private area for visiting or retreat.

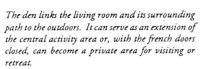

14-39. *Layout and special features of a group home for eight residents with dementia*
Courtesy Uriel Cohen and Gerald Weisman

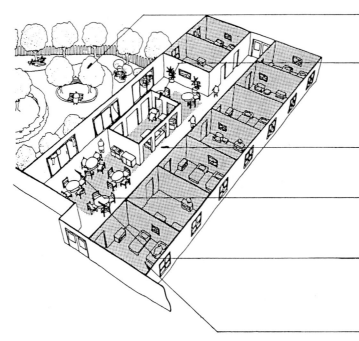

Links to the outside
Dining and activity areas have direct access to protected outdoor space.

Clustering activities and spaces
The corridor is interrupted to create social spaces that support familiar activities (dining, living, den) and to add to the home-like ambience. These spaces provide residents with opportunities for privacy or interaction.

Opportunities for meaningful wandering
A walking path extends to a secure outdoor area, and links key social spaces indoors.

Sensory stimulation without stress
Partial walls provide a sense of enclosure and security as well as views of activities in adjacent areas and corridor.

Intimate Dining
A clearly identifiable space is provided within the unit, for dining, as well as an adjoining kitchenette for food preparation and related activities.

Resident rooms
While two residents continue to share a room, newly created social spaces serve as places for privacy and reflection.

Renovation of a Long-Term Care Facility

The institutional corridor is interrupted by creating a social space including dining and living areas, on one side of the corridor, with resident rooms arranged in a regular grid on the other side.

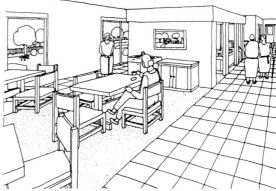

Living and dining areas constitute both the physical and functional center of the facility and the focus of activities.

14-40. *Layout and special features of a long-term care facility for residents with dementia*
Courtesy Uriel Cohen and Gerald Weisman

negotiability in environments for people with dementia is critically important. In addition to traditional solutions such as ramps or handrails, environmental interventions may include clear and consistent information and easy-to-operate handles and controls.

Things from the past. Familiar artifacts, activities, and environments can provide valuable associations with the past for people with dementia and can stimulate opportunities for social interaction and meaningful activity. Rather than being limited to a simple "rummage box," the total environment may potentially be used to trigger reminiscence.

Sensory stimulation without stress. Levels of sensory and social stimulation in environments for people with dementia should *not* differ dramatically from those encountered in domestic environments. Both sensory deprivation and overstimulation are conditions to be avoided. The physical and the organizational environments can be designed to regulate stimulation, providing interest and challenge without becoming overwhelming. Opportunities should be provided for increasing or reducing levels of stimulation to respond to changing needs and tolerance levels over the course of a day.

Opportunities for meaningful wandering. Wandering is a relatively common behavior among people with dementia. Too often in the past it has been viewed only as a problem and resulted in the use of chemical and physical restraints. A far more positive approach is to view wandering as an opportunity for meaningful activity. Both physical and organizational environments should be supportive of such activity and provide appropriate settings with secure and well-defined paths for wandering.

Public to private realms. People with dementia should be able to select from among a variety of spaces falling at distinct points along a continuum of public to private realms. Such a continuum, created through both architectural and administrative means, facilitates resident control of sensory and social stimulation and may reduce perceived intrusion of individual personal space.

Design Applications

The application of many design principles is shown in the context of a day care and respite center (Fig. 14-38), a community-based group home for eight residents (Fig. 14-39), and the renovation of a typical wing of a long-term care facility (Fig. 14-40).

SUMMARY

Agreement is limited regarding appropriate environmental design features to be incorporated into special care units for patients with dementia. A number of interesting and novel approaches to design have been suggested by a handful of new facilities, but they have not been operational long enough for substantive comparative analysis to have occurred. The ongoing research projects and recent books highlighted in this chapter offer great promise that, perhaps five years from now, more of a consensus will have been reached.

REFERENCES

Aranyi, Laszlo, and Larry Goldman. 1980. *Design of Long-Term Care Facilities.* New York: Van Nostrand Reinhold Co. Inc.

Ashmore, M. 1982. Reality orientation-boards: A new design. *Dimensions in Health Service* 59(11):15–16.

Bertram, M. 1989. The use of landmarks. *Journal of Gerontological Nursing* 15(2):6–8.

Breger, William, and William Pomeranz. 1985. *Nursing Home Development.* New York: Van Nostrand Reinhold Co. Inc.

Calkins, Margaret. 1988. *Design for Dementia.* Owings Mills, Md.: National Health Publishing.

———. 1989. Designing cues for wanderers. *Architecture* October:117–18.

Carstens, Diane. 1985. *Site Planning and Design for the Elderly: Issues, Guidelines, and Alternatives.* New York: Van Nostrand Reinhold Co. Inc.

Chafetz, P. 1990. Two-dimensional grid is ineffective against demented patients' exiting through glass doors. *Psychology and Aging* 5(1):146–47.

Cleary, T. A., C. Clamon, M. Price, et al. 1988. A reduced stimulation unit: effects on patients with Alzheimer's disease and related disorders. *Gerontologist* 28(4):511–14.

Cohen, Uriel, and Gerald Weisman (editors). 1987. *Environments for People with Dementia: Annotated*

Bibliography. The Health Facilities Research Program of the AIA/ACSA Council on Architectural Research.

Cohen, Uriel, and Gerald Weisman. 1991. *Holding On to Home.* Baltimore: Johns Hopkins University Press.

Cohen-Mansfield, J., and N. Billig. 1986. Agitated behaviors in the elderly. *Journal of American Geriatrics Society* 34 (10):711–21.

Cooper, B. 1985. A model for implementing color contrast in the environment of the elderly. *American Journal of Occupational Therapy* 39(4):253–58.

Cooper, B., C. Gowland, and M. McIntosh. 1986. The use of color in the environment of the elderly to enhance function. *Clinics in Geriatric Medicine* 2(1):151–62.

Cooper, B., A. Mohide, and S. Gilbert. 1990. Testing the use of colour in a long-term care setting. *World Hospitals* 27(1):25–29.

Cormack, D. 1990. The therapeutic influence of the environment: A *nursing* home or a nursing *home.* *Journal of Gerontological Nursing* 16(3):3–4.

D'Angelo, H. 1990. Skilled nursing facilities. *Journal of Health Care Interior Design.* Martinez, Calif.: National Symposium on Health Care Interior Design, Inc.

Design for Aging: An Architect's Guide. 1985. Washington, DC: AIA Press (AIA Foundation).

Goldstein, L., and D. Oakley. 1986. Colour versus orientation discrimination in severely brain-damaged and normal adults. *Cortex* 22: 261–66.

Grant, L. 1989. Environment and quality of life: A reaction from the perspective of social science and environmental design. NLN Publications. November:109–24.

Green, K. 1985. Design for aging. *Architectural Technology,* Summer:34–41.

Hiatt, L. 1985. *Wandering Behavior of Older People in Nursing Homes: A Study of Hyperactivity, Disorientation and the Spatial Environment.* Doctoral dissertation, City University of New York.

———. 1988. Mobility and independence in long-term care. In *Aging in a Technological Society,* ed. Gari Lesnoff-Caravaglia, pp. 58–64. New York: Human Sciences Press.

———. 1990. Long-term care facilities. *Journal of Health Care Interior Design.* Martinez, Calif.: National Symposium on Health Care Interior Design, Inc.

———. 1991. *Nursing Home Renovation Designed For Reform.* Boston: Butterworth Architecture.

Howell, Sandra. 1982. Built space, the mystery variable in health and aging. In *Advances in Environmental Psychology,* vol. 4: *Environment and Health,* ed. Baum and Singer, pp. 31–48. Hillsdale, N.J.: Lawrence Erlbaum Associates.

Hughes, P., and R. Neer. 1981. Lighting for the elderly: A psychobiological approach to lighting. *Human Factors* 23(1):65–85.

Hutton, J., I. Shapiro, and B. Christians. 1982. Functional significance of restricted upgaze. *Architectural Physical Medical Rehabilitation* 63:617–19.

Kalymun, M. 1989. Relationships between sensory decline among the elderly and the physical environment: Implications for health care. *Rhode Island Medical Journal* 72:161–67.

Kayser-Jones, J. 1989. The environment and quality of care in long-term care institutions. NLN Publications. November:87–107.

Kolanowski, A. 1990. Restlessness in the elderly: The effect of artificial lighting. *Nursing Research* 39(3):181–83.

Kolata, G. 1991. In a major advance, experts find a defect that causes Alzheimer's. *New York Times* February 16:1.

Laventhol & Horwath. 1986. *The Nursing Home Industry 1986: A Capsule View* (first annual report on the nursing home industry in the United States). Philadelphia: Laventhol & Horwath.

Lawton, M. Powell. 1980. *Environment and Aging.* Monterey, Calif.: Brooks Cole.

Lewin, T. 1990. Alzheimer's and architecture: A search for order. *New York Times* May 2:A9.

McKay, Donald. 1988. *Sanctuary.* Waterloo, Ontario: University of Waterloo Press.

Moeller, Tamerra. 1985. *The Sixth Sense.* Washington, DC: The National Council on the Aging, Inc.

Nahemow, L., and P. Lawton. 1973. Toward an ecological theory of adaptation and aging. In *Environmental Design Research,* Vol. 1, ed. Wolfgang

Preiser, pp. 315–21. Stroudsburg, PA: Dowden, Hutchinson & Ross.

Nemtin, S. 1990. Alzheimer's care centers. *Journal of Health Care Interior Design*. Martinez, Calif.: National Symposium on Health Care Interior Design, Inc.

Norris, C. 1975. Restlessness: A nursing phenomenon in search of meaning. *Nursing Outlook* 23(2):103–7.

OBRA Audit. 1987. Washington, DC: American Association of Homes for the Aging.

Olgyay, N. 1988. Wayfinding: Creating accessible environments. A report of a presentation by Gerald Weisman, "The Legible Environment: How Do We Get There from Here?" *Designer's West* December:122–26.

Rader, J. 1987. A comprehensive staff approach to problem wandering. *Gerontologist* 27(6):756–60

Raschko, Betty Ann. 1982. *Housing Interiors for the Disabled and Elderly*. New York: Van Nostrand Reinhold Co. Inc.

Regnier, Victor, and J. Pynoos (editors). 1987. *Housing the Aged: Design Directives and Policy Considerations*. New York: Elsevier.

Rodin, J. 1986. Aging and health: Effects of the sense of control. Science 233:1271–76.

Rubinstein, R. 1989. The home environments of older people: A description of the psychosocial processes linking person to place. *Journal of Gerontology: Social Sciences* 44(2):545–53.

Shield, R. 1990. Pathways and porches: A focus on corridors in nursing homes. *Rhode Island Medical Journal* 73(4):155–60.

Technology and Aging in America. 1985. Washington, DC: U.S. Congress, Office of Technology Assessment, OTA-BA-264, June 1985.

Thomas, D. 1988. Assessment and management of agitation in the elderly. *Geriatrics* 43(6):45–50.

Valins, Martin. 1988. *Elderly People*. London: The Architectural Press; New York: Van Nostrand Reinhold Co.

Williams, Judith K. 1989. *Pathways: Program Development Plan*, vol. 1. Miami: Miami Jewish Home and Hospital for the Aged.

Williams, M. 1988. The physical environment and patient care. *Annual Review of Nursing Research* 6:61–84.

Zimring, C. 1981. Stress and the designed environment. *Journal of Social Issues* 37(1):145–71.

Adult Day Care

Padula, Helen. 1986. *Developing Adult Day Care*. Washington, DC: The National Council on the Aging, Inc.

Standards for Adult Day Care. 1984. Washington, DC: The National Council on the Aging, Inc.

Von Behren, Ruth. 1986. *Adult Day Care in America: Summary of a National Survey*. Washington, DC: The National Council on the Aging, Inc., and National Institute on Adult Daycare.

CONGREGATE CARE

Housing an aging population is a task of monumental complexity and challenge. Known by a variety of names—the elderly, mature adult, or senior citizen—they constitute an increasingly large percentage of the population. Advertisers have been quick to realize the profit potential of targeting this new consumer group.

STATISTICS

Although often referred to as a homogeneous group, the aging population is actually comprised of three age segments. People age 55 to 64 comprise approximately half of this market, those age 65 to 74 constitute about a third, and individuals age 75 and older constitute the remainder. However, between 1987 and 1997, the number of persons age 75 and older is expected to grow an additional 29 percent, according to the Census Bureau (*American Demographics* as reported in Dispelling the Myths 1988). By the year 2050, a quarter of the U.S. population will be over the age of 65. The fastest-growing segment of the population is the over-85 group, which is expected to increase by 129 percent during the period 1980 to 2000. Despite the great interest in congregate housing, market analysts estimate that only about 20 percent of the nation's elderly will ever leave their homes. Only 8 percent of individuals age 75 to 85 live in a skilled nursing facility, although the number increases to 20 percent for individuals over the age of 85 (Bureau of the Census).

DEFINING THE MARKET

For the past 15 or 20 years, persons over the age of 65 were often lumped together under the classification "senior citizen" to refer to individuals who had reached the voluntary, or in some cases mandatory, retirement age. Today, people of age 65 seem young. The past ten years have focused attention on positive lifestyle habits including cessation of smoking and drinking, good nutrition, preventive health screening, and exercise. Advances in the treatment of disease and surgical intervention for life-threatening illnesses have extended the life span of many individuals. All of these factors have resulted in the phenomenon that has been referred to as the "graying of America."

In defining this market, the most important thing to realize is that it cannot be stereotyped. Individuals over the age of 65 are as varied and diverse in personality, needs, and wants as the under-65 population. People do not change because they become old; they do not suddenly become a homogeneous group that can be referred to as "the elderly" or "the mature adult." Only what the aging process does to people starts to define or segment the market. Starting approximately at the age of 65, a gradual loss of sensory acuity increases until, by the age of 85, multiple sensory deficits become significant and impair a person's ability to gather information and participate in social interaction.

In recognition of the size of this market, often referred to as the "senior living industry," developers have been striving to unlock the secret formula for providing housing that addresses the needs of this diverse group. About five years ago, many of the nation's largest developers, as well as consultants of all types who wish to service this industry, formed the National Association for Senior Living Industries (NASLI), headquartered in Annapolis, Maryland, for the purpose of researching and developing high-quality standards to meet the needs of this constituency. Through this organization, its newsletters, national conferences, and regional workshops, a great deal of pertinent information has been pooled and shared. Many of the initial studies focused on demographics in order to understand the size of the market and its component segments. The accounting firm Laventhol & Horwath (1985, 1986a, 1986b) targeted the senior living industry and produced excellent market research in the form of annual surveys. The information was useful to developers in devising strategies for market penetration, for insights into regional trends, and for planning new facilities. In fact, interest in senior living has spawned a sizable group of market research analysts who concentrate their efforts entirely on this industry.

HOUSING OPTIONS FOR THE ELDERLY

The variety of housing options available addresses the level of health, economic resources, and social preferences of individuals. At one end of the spectrum are the group referred to as "active retirement," and at the other are the frail elderly and those with some form of dementia who live in skilled nursing facilities. In between these two extremes are large groups of people who are, in varying degrees, self-sufficient but may not be able to prepare meals or who need assistance with bathing, grooming, medications, housekeeping, and transportation.

Active seniors seek independent living units, either rental or owned, in a congregate care or continuing care retirement community (CCRC). Other types of independent living might include granny flats, standard apartment complexes, or shared "cluster" housing; semi-independent persons may live in a retirement hotel, a board and care home, or in assisted living units (also called "personal care"). Dependent persons who require 24-hour nursing care and complete supervision live in an intermediate-level nursing unit or in a full-skilled nursing care environment.

This chapter focuses on congregate care facilities, but a number of excellent resources can acquaint readers with a wider scope of options. These references include Regnier and Pynoos (1987), Hoglund (1985), Carstens (1985), *Design for Aging: An Architect's Guide* (1985), and *Elderly Housing* (1988).

GLOSSARY

Understanding a few of the terms used in this industry is important.

SNF: Skilled nursing facility, a state-licensed health care facility that provides 24-hour, on-site nursing care that can be episodic or long term. It is also known as *convalescent hospital* or *nursing home.*

Congregate care: Rental or purchase living units that provide a package of services often including social activity programs, maid service, meals taken in a communal dining room, on-site health care, and transportation, to name just a few.

CCRC: The continuing care retirement community is similar to congregate care in services delivered except that a continuum of care, ranging from independent living to personal care and SNF, is always provided.

Personal care: Also known as *assisted living* or a *residential care unit*, it enables a person who needs assistance with the activities of daily living (bathing, grooming, meal preparation, and dressing) to receive a midpoint of care. In this manner, maximum independence is maintained.

Aging in place: The goal of this concept is to help the person remain in a familiar setting—his or her home—by offering various levels of care at the appropriate time, thereby helping the person to "age in place."

Lifecare: A congregate care facility that generally requires an entrance fee. An individual delivers to the management of the facility a predetermined sum of money that is invested, the interest from which helps to operate the facility. In return, the resident is cared for, at whatever level of care is required, until death or until he or she wishes to leave.

AGING IN PLACE

The senior living industry is in its infancy. In fact NASLI was founded only in 1985. With the impetuousness of youth a plethora of early projects in the 1980s, although well intentioned, isolated seniors in what have been described as "ghettos for the elderly." A developer might have found a beautiful piece of land in the country and built a congregate housing development on it, thereby removing residents from the fabric of urban life that they had known for the past 50 years. They interacted principally with other residents their age or with visitors. If a resident owned a car and was physically able to drive, the isolation was not as great. For many, however, being removed from familiar surroundings, from hearing schoolchildren playing outdoors on the sidewalk, walking to buy a newspaper, or visiting the baker, this life-style was the equivalent of being put out to pasture.

In recent years gerontologists, psychologists, and social anthropologists have favored the concept of aging in place. In the large sense, it means that the individual's living environment should be able to be adapted so that it can support the resident's deficits at various ages without the individual having to move to "special needs" housing. This change in perspective is due in large part to study of how European nations have provided for the elderly by integrating them into communities where they have an opportunity to interact with individuals of all ages (Hoglund 1985).

Advocates of universal design (see chapter 3) forecast that the housing industry may soon begin to address these issues in all new housing. Doing so would involve providing wheelchair access that does not look like a ramp appendage but rather is an integral part of the design whose purpose in assisting the disabled has been camouflaged. Other amenities would include wide doors, entries flush with the ground, and light switches, thermostats, fire alarms, bathroom towel bars, and drapery pulls mounted four feet off the floor. Bathroom walls may be reinforced for the installation of grab bars if they are needed at a later date. Bathroom vanity sinks and kitchen countertops and cabinets can be designed to be lowered, if necessary, by providing flexible plumbing connections. Books by Raschko (1982), Leibrock (1991), and Valins (1988) address these issues.

Aging in place also refers to CCRC communities that provide a continuum of care. One may start out living independently in an apartment and later require a personal care unit or be moved to a skilled nursing facility without having to surrender friends or a familiar environment. Similarly, if one spouse needs skilled nursing care after an illness or surgery, the trauma is lessened by the other spouse being nearby and able to visit frequently without having to arrange transportation. If all of these facilities are available on the retirement community campus, continuity with familiar people and comfortable surroundings can be maintained.

ASSISTED LIVING

Assisted living is also referred to as *personal care* or *residential care*, and it describes a semi-independent residential accommodation. Typically, assisted living units are studio apartments or one-bedroom units with a galley kitchen. Candidates for this type of living accommodation require some assistance with dressing, bathing, or medications. The principal chronic medical conditions of persons in assisted living settings are arthritis and rheumatism, high blood pressure, hearing and sigh-

deficits, and congestive heart failure (Kalymun and Seip 1990).

A residential care complex often includes a skilled nursing facility on the same site plus a full complement of congregate spaces such as dining room, coffee shop, beauty and barber salons, activity rooms, crafts room, card rooms, lounges, and administrative offices. Residential care facilities offer security, round-the-clock aid in case of an emergency, many planned activities and outings, and companionship. Market analysts speculate that this segment of the industry will experience the most rapid growth. In spite of this, Kalymun and Seip (1990, 29) lament (in their concluding remarks analyzing the results of a national survey) that "designers and developers . . . ignore the knowledge base in the area of environmental gerontology research, causing design mistakes to be repeated and strategies to be limited in optimizing and sustaining independence and control among residents over time."

THE HYBRID NATURE OF CONGREGATE CARE

Congregate care, in its simplest definition, is multifamily residential housing for the elderly. One of the most interesting aspects of congregate care is its hybrid nature. It might be said to be 50 percent residential, 25 percent hospitality, and 25 percent medical. Congregate care facilities may be very hospitality oriented both in the types of services and in ambience. Such facilities offer meals in an elegantly appointed dining room (Fig. 15-1), include a library/lounge (Figs. 15-2 and 15-3), card rooms, hobby rooms, an auditorium for concerts and performances, attractive gardens and outdoor spaces (Figs. 15-4 and 15-5), soda fountain, cocktail lounge, and a variety of retail shops. Living in this type of facility has been described as living in a country club environment. It is a catered experience that appeals to a certain segment of the mature adult population. It is especially appealing to active individuals who are in relatively good health and who like to entertain, participate in sports and social activities, and have a wide variety of conveniences and options readily available. Some view this type of living accommodation as their reward for a lifetime of hard work.

Researchers have learned, however, that a catered experience does not appeal to every-

15-1 *Penthouse multipurpose room has interesting ceiling and elegant appointments; Peninsula Regent (San Mateo, CA)*

Architect: Backen Arrigoni & Rossi, Inc.; Interior design: Project Associates; Photographer: Charles S. White

15-2 *The library is a warm, inviting space off the main lobby; Peninsula Regent (San Mateo, CA)*

Architect: Backen Arrigoni & Ross, Inc.; Interior design: Project Associates; Photographer: Charles S. White

15-3 *Beautifully accessorized library, Peninsula Regent (San Mateo, CA)*
   Architect: Backen Arrigoni & Ross, Inc.; Interior design: Project Associates; Photographer: Charles S. White

15-4 *Terrace at the croquet lawn features redwood furniture under a trellised colonnade; Peninsula Regent (San Mateo, CA)*
   Architect: Backen Arrigoni & Ross, Inc.; Interior design: Project Associates; Photographer: Charles S. White

one. Focus groups have shown that people of more modest means who have never been accustomed to having others do things for them may find a hospitality setting uncomfortable. The level of services offered and design ambience should be tailored to meet the needs of the individuals who are likely to be residents of that facility. The potential market depends on geographic location, cultural or ethnic characteristics of the population, and the economics of the project: what will the rental rates be or the condominium purchase costs and maintenance fees? Individuals for whom cost is a

15-5 *Cleverly designed pool has the benefits of both indoor and outdoor spaces; Peninsula Regent (San Mateo, CA)*
Architect: Backen Arrigoni & Ross, Inc.; Interior design: Project Associates; Photographer: Charles S. White

major determinant will not expect as many amenities, but they will still look forward to the security, organized social activities, and opportunities for companionship afforded by congregate living.

LOW-INCOME HOUSING

At the other end of the spectrum is congregate housing for low-income individuals. Across the nation architects have transformed buildings of historic significance, as well as dilapidated public housing projects, into sensitively designed homes that address residents' functional, psychological, and social needs. The Rosa Parks

Senior Apartments in San Francisco, by Marquis Associates, is such a project. Completed early in 1985, a vandalized, crime-ridden public housing project was transformed into an attractive, safe, enriched environment that admirably addresses physiological issues of aging. The design team included architects, interior designers, a social scientist, and a prominent color consultant. Some of the amenities provided include corridors that function like a pedestrian street with individual porch stoops and waist-high plant shelves outside windows. Spaces for gardening (waist-high vegetable beds) and areas for art classes and a library, plus an office for a public health nurse, were provided.

Bangor House is an historic landmark in Bangor, Maine. Originally built as a hotel in 1860, the structure fell into disrepair and had become a local eyesore. Architects Childs Bertman Tseckares & Casendino seized the opportunity to restore the structure and create a 121-unit government-subsidized housing development for the elderly. An original exterior court was enclosed to form a four-story atrium that is used as an indoor "outdoor" space during long Maine winters and serves as an orientation focus for people circulating through the building (Fig. 15-6). The local office on aging leases a portion of the ground floor and provides hot meals and other services to tenants and other local residents. In addition to a kitchen and dining room, the building includes a library, arts and crafts room, lounges and lobbies, a ballroom, and a room that serves as a museum for old hotel memorabilia. Restored to its former architectural elegance, the building is a landmark on the border of the central business district and is within walking distance of shopping, entertainment, religious, and medical facilities.

The architects did an extensive postoccupancy evaluation survey to determine if their original design expectations were compatible with residents' preferences and actual use of the facility. Questions included:

What do you like most about your apartment?

What is most annoying about your apartment?

Does your apartment accommodate your furniture needs?

Would you prefer larger windows even if wall space were reduced?

If you could make your bedroom larger by utilizing hall space, would you be willing to allow your guests to walk through your bedroom to use the bathroom?

Which of three types of kitchens would you prefer?

Would you rather have space for a small table in your kitchen or use that space to increase the size of the living room or bedroom?

Is there adequate storage within your apartment?

Do you have adequate privacy?

Are you bothered by noise from surrounding apartments?

Where would you prefer to live in the building relative to the main entrance?

Where would you like to live in the building relative to activities occurring outside?

Where would you most prefer to live in the building in relationship to the elevators?

Which of the following spaces do you use and what suggestions do you have for improving them?

15-6 *Atrium court provides natural light and lounge areas for residents in a safe, all-weather environment; Bangor House (Bangor, ME)*
Architect: Childs Bertman Tseckares & Casendino Inc.; Photographer: Steve Rosenthal

Residents' responses yielded a wealth of information that could be gained in no other manner. The architects are to be congratulated for pursuing such a well-designed, in-depth study of their project. It makes fascinating reading for design professionals who want to understand the sometimes very subtle psychological factors that can result in a successful project, compared with one that marginally meets residents' needs.

SUMMARY

In summary, congregate retirement communities demand the skills of a seasoned team of professionals who understand the complex nature of this type of housing In addition to accommodating comforts and conveniences we all desire in our dwellings, the building must be designed to encourage and foster a sense of community, as well as to environmentally support residents through various physiological changes caused by aging.

LIFE-STYLES AND VALUES OF MATURE ADULTS

The selection of living accommodation for the mature adult is either need driven or market driven. Individuals in failing health are driven by the necessity of requiring either skilled nursing or assisted living care, usually within a short time of the initial health failure. Active seniors, by contrast, are known to shop around and visit many retirement communities before selecting one. These individuals are likely to evaluate and compare the amenities of one facility versus another, creating tough competition among developers in many communities. Market analysts discovered that developers should be marketing life-style, rather than housing. For this reason interior design is one of the strongest marketing tools available for conveying a life-style image to prospective residents.

DISPELLING THE MYTHS

Mature adults or "senior citizens" are no more homogeneous a group than are adolescents or middle-aged individuals. In reality, they are a group of great diversity with needs, wants, and desires that vary widely depending on income, age, education, health status, and geographic location.

Younger persons often think mature adults want a life of leisure when they retire with maid service, catered meals, and no responsibilities. In reality, seniors worry about not leading productive lives after they cease to be active in the work force. David Wolfe, market analyst and founder of NASLI, explains:

> *At age 20–40:* People seek high possession experiences (first car, boat, home, wife/husband, baby) to achieve satisfaction.
> *At age 40–60:* People seek high catered experiences (great vacations, tickets to sporting events and the theater, great restaurants, fine hotels, and having others do one's laundry, cut the grass, or cater a party) to achieve satisfaction.

> *At age 60–80:* People seek high being experiences (learning something new, helping a friend, watching a sunset, contributing time and money to a cause) to achieve life satisfaction.

"Being" Experiences

Wolfe (1987) explains the need for life satisfaction among mature adults. He advocates segmenting markets according to behaviorally defined categories in order to promote products successfully in print and broadcast media advertising. Briefly, individuals are thought to fall into one of nine life-style types, which in turn are arranged into three umbrella categories called the *need-driven, outer-directed,* and *inner-directed.* Wolfe's study is based on considerable research and offers an opportunity to understand the psyche of mature adults, based on their individual personality characteristics and their drive toward acquiring more being experiences. This study is required reading for anyone associated with the design of congregate care communities.

Certain characteristics of the seniors market may be a surprise to younger individuals. For example, mature adults often feel 15 to 20 years younger than they are. They often look at individuals around them and think they look old, but they do not see themselves that way. This group is less conscious of cost than value. In fact, a study by the University of Pennsylvania found that America's 65 to 74 cohort (age group) had the highest net worth of any ten-year cohort in the population (Wolfe 1987). This affluence has afforded seniors the financial freedom to buy a wide variety of goods and services based on their desires to pursue a particular life-style.

People Buy What They Want to Be, Not What They Are

In summary, designers must remember that mature adults are a diverse group and that any attempt to stereotype their values will result in an unsuccessful project. Seniors are looking for life satisfaction, not sticks and bricks. Retirement communities that nurture self-esteem by providing many opportunities for residents to be productive and independent will give them a sense of empowerment and yield the maximum in life satisfaction. In terms of marketing, people buy what they want to be, not what they are. By appealing to seniors' aspirations for "being experiences," designers can help create a retirement community that unlocks the potential of its residents for life satisfaction.

Worman's Mill: A New Model

One of the most interesting retirement communities is based on a productivity model. Located in Frederick, Maryland, the development creates opportunities for residents to lead productive lives. Plans include a 30-acre working farm to be run by residents. Other components of the 224-acre community include a town square surrounded by townhouses with shops on the first floor, churches, cultural facilities, and a number of residential options such as attached and detached housing units in clusters of 8 to 12 units, congregate care apartments, a skilled nursing facility, and assisted living units.

The mill also includes a horticultural center with a plant nursery. Leisure is not the dominant culture. Worman's Mill's orchards and gardens provide the basis for a truck garden industry in the community that encourages people from nearby towns to visit and buy fresh produce. Cottage industries are expected to flourish, and neighborly events such as square dances, band concerts, and ice cream socials on the town square enhance and encourage small town friendliness.

The developers, Robert and Myra Wormald, set out to create a town as it was at the turn of the century, where everybody knew everybody else. To encourage interaction among residents, the development features a village green and gazebo anchoring its commercial square (Fig. 15-7). Encircling the town square, half of the shops have people living over them to assure that the town square is never unoccupied. The shops allow residents to convert hobbies or special interests to commercial ventures.

According to David Wolfe, a consultant on this development, seniors formed in their teens their image of what it means to be old. Based on this, Worman's Mill reflects basic human values of the rural and small-town America of the 1920s. Various services are available for residents of the community on an as-needed or pay-as-you-go basis. This community is anticipated to appeal to mature adults who are bored with the types of leisure activities that are the focus of many retirement communities. Creating such communities, however sound an idea, is easier said than done, according to developer Robert Wormald. He encountered major problems with lenders who do not generally embrace unusual projects and with zoning regulations that did not permit mixing retail structures with housing and farming. In fact, zoning laws had to be changed before the development could move forward.

Wolfe (1987) provides an in-depth discussion of the planning and sociological issues that form the basis for Worman's Mill. He concludes that seniors want to maintain and project to others a life-style that reflects their continuing value as members of society. Age segregation does not

15-7 *Model for town square, Worman's Mill (Frederick, MD)*

Architect: Smith and William; Photo courtesy Robert and Myra Wormald

keep them from moving into senior living communities, but rather what they perceive those retirement communities say about mature adults and their capabilities.

SENIORS AND TECHNOLOGY

Younger people sometimes wonder why mature adults are reluctant to use devices that may make their lives easier. Such devices may include closed-caption decoders for television sets, various types of alarms, voice-activated systems for controlling appliances, or the battery-powered carts available in some supermarkets. The reason, according to Bowe (1988), is that such devices are seen as a stigma of old age. Marketing such products requires emphasizing convenience, not necessity, in order to overcome the "difference" factor that makes the elderly feel stigmatized. In designing for this age group, convenience devices should be camouflaged so that they are inconspicuous.

Cost is another reason that accounts for seniors resisting available technology. A catch-22 situation exists in which, in order for seniors to want to use devices, advertising must emphasize convenience as opposed to need, but in order to be covered by insurance, these devices must be shown to meet a medical necessity. Bowe rightfully concludes that technology has progressed faster than psychology when he observes that many people are even reluctant to use available monitoring and alerting technology that makes home health care successful. The American Association of Retired Persons (AARP) in Washington, D.C., publishes *The Gadget Book*, which illustrates more than 325 ingenious devices for easier living.

NONVERBAL MESSAGES

Anticipated growth in the senior living market has stimulated the interest of four principal types of developers. Leaders in the hospitality industry see it as a way of diversifying their market; health care providers see it as an extension of their mission, a means of greater vertical integration, or a way to increase market penetration; and developers of mass-market housing view it as a new market to bolster sagging sales in other areas. Nonprofit religious-affiliated organizations have also entered the picture looking for investment opportunities and a means of expressing their mission. Sometimes collaboration by two or more of these developer types makes a better project. Projects developed by health care institutions often had too much of a clinical focus; those developed by hotel chains often suffered from a cosmetic approach to dealing with age-related issues necessitating specific design solutions; and developers of mass-market housing often focused too much on the bottom line and a stylebook of ornamental details thought to appeal to senior adults. Each of these groups seemed to be looking for the "magic formula" that could be refined as a prototype design, and used over and over, to assure success.

The saddest thing about some of these projects, apart from not really addressing in depth the sociological and psychological issues posed by consultants like David Wolfe, Victor Regnier (Regnier and Pynoos 1987), Diane Carstens (1985a, 1985b), or David Hoglund (1985), is the nonverbal messages communicated by the architecture and design. They include many false materials made to simulate something real such as extruded plastic moldings that pretend to be wood, windows with fake plastic mullions to simulate French doors, metal closet doors with raised panels and louvers to simulate wooden louver doors, sheet vinyl floors embossed to simulate ceramic tile and grout, and wood-grain plastic laminate. Such materials do not fool anyone and rob seniors of their dignity. On the exterior, these buildings sometimes resemble a pastiche or collage of reminders from the past, fragments of a life that was once rich and now has been reduced to a few symbolic or trivial remnants.

In the Midwest, for example, many people lived in homes that had front or back screened-in porches large enough to sit in—or sleep in—on warm summer evenings. Vestiges of these porches can be seen in certain senior living projects, but they are miniaturized and barely large enough for anything except a potted plant. Cruel though it may sound, the nonverbal message seems to be that the elderly are not worthy of a full porch, that at this stage of their lives they are entitled only to half a porch or a fragment of a balcony. The same could be said for fake colonial columns plastered onto facades of senior living communities in Georgia, and pastiches of brick veneer affixed to facades of colonial-looking buildings in New England.

Experience and Success

Nevertheless, across the nation is a vast array of sensitively designed senior living communities created by developers who were willing to take the time to understand the industry, hire the most experienced architects and consultants, and invest the time to develop and deliver a quality product. Mark Engelbrecht (1986) is an architect who has dedicated a 20-year career to retirement housing. His firm, Engelbrecht and Griffin Architects, has designed more than 60 retirement communities and long-term care facilities. He is a prolific writer and articulate spokesman for the senior living industry and brings a perspective shaped by experience with an extensive number of projects in geographically diverse regions. Recently this firm embarked on a postoccupancy evaluation survey of their retirement community designs created over a period of years. The study is being directed by environmental psychologist Jamie Horwitz, Ph.D., associated with the Department of Architecture at Iowa State University.

GERONTOLOGICAL RESEARCH

A great deal of research is available to inform decisions about design for the mature adult. Furthermore, gerontologists, social scientists, and psychologists rather consistently agree about the nature of age-related changes and the types of adaptations that would be appropriate to make the physical environment less stressful.

THEORETICAL PERSPECTIVES

Two of the most important theories in gerontological research are the environmental docility hypothesis generated by Lawton (1980) and the concept of environmental press developed by Lawton and Nahemow. In short, the environmental docility hypothesis maintains that the less competent the individual, the greater the impact of the environment on that person. The concept of environmental press deals with individual competencies and the demand character of the physical environment; the higher the level of competence, the greater the level of press tolerated without experiencing stress and discomfort. These concepts are explained more fully in chapters 3 and 14.

Person-environment fit in residential settings for the elderly is critically important in order to enhance well-being. Sensory abilities diminish with age. After a certain age, multiple sensory handicaps are the rule, rather than the exception, and they may occur either gradually or abruptly (Kalymun 1989). If the environment can be adapted to compensate for sensory losses, the individual's feelings of well-being can be maintained.

IMPORTANCE OF CONTROL

Aging is associated with biological changes and environmental experiences that affect both a person's perceived competence and the range of potentially controllable outcomes (Rodin 1986). Studies have shown that a sense of control is critically important for maintaining emotional and physical health. Failure to exercise control over one's own activities induces stress, causes hormonal changes, and affects immunologic competency (see chapter 2). As people age, many events happen over which they have little control, such as the death of a friend or spouse, retirement, and illness. Declining sensory abilities and lack of mobility may also affect their sense of competency and control. Therefore, a physical environment that compensates for disabilities without appearing to be a prosthetic environment will exert a strong positive effect on stress reduction.

SENSORY DECLINE

Loss is the word that describes many of the psychological and physical changes that occur in aging, whether it is the loss of a friend or spouse, loss of health, change in economic status (living on a fixed income), or loss of meaningful work and relationships. This period requires tremendous adjustment. In addition, numerous sensory deficits become more pronounced with time. Beyond age 85, multiple sensory deficits become so significant that they may impair the ability to gather information and to participate in social interaction (Kalymun 1989). Sensory deficits alter perception of the environment, which in turn decreases feelings of well-being. The quality of life can be enhanced, however, by enriching the environment to compensate for the deficits. The following information is principally from Kalymun (1989).

Vision

Changes in vision and hearing are the most common sensory impairments. The lens of the eye thickens and becomes opaque. The visual field narrows. Cataracts are common and cause fragmentation or blurring of the image. With cataracts, people have the sense of looking at an impressionist painting of an object. Eventually, recognizing objects or people becomes impossible; the effect is similar to smearing petroleum jelly on the lenses of eyeglasses. Fortunately, cataract surgery with the implantation of an artificial lens is a viable option for many individuals. Nevertheless, as a general rule, any type of signage needs to be large, with excellent contrast and wider spacing between letters.

Problems of Depth Perception. People with cataracts also suffer problems of depth perception that make difficult gauging which item is in the foreground and which is in the background. Floral or boldly patterned carpet should be avoided on stairs because it makes judging the height and the edge of a step more difficult.

Impaired Color Vision. Yellowing of the lens impairs color vision: violets, blues, and greens fade out of the color spectrum first, although the ability to see red, orange, and yellow is not much affected. This effect can be experienced by wearing a pair of eyeglasses with yellow lenses.

Importance of Color Contrast. Color contrast is extremely important to prevent accidents. When colors are closely related in hue or value (such as blue and green), an elderly person may not be able to distinguish them. A strong contrast between the wall and floor is always important; it can be accomplished with a contrasting baseboard.

Light Needs. Starting approximately at the age of 40, vision is gradually impaired. The pupil of the eye decreases in size, creating a need for more light. In fact, a 70- or 80-year-old individual requires three times as much light to see with the same clarity as someone 20 years old. Similarly, an elderly person's eyes need more time to adapt when moving from a space with a higher intensity of lighting to one that is darker. Once the transition has been made, the elderly person is able to see less than a younger person in the darkened room. A practical example of this effect would be moving from a lighted corridor into a lounge that has been darkened for a movie.

Evenness of Illumination. Evenness of illumination is especially important in order to decrease vulnerability to accidents. During the night when elderly people move from a dark area to a lighted one, their eyes may play tricks on them. Instead of understanding that the floor is level where the bedroom and hallway meet, it may be perceived as a step. In this case an inappropriate adjustment of body weight can precipitate a fall. The same situation can exist in commons areas when people move from a dimly lit corridor to an examination room or into a bright illuminated dining room. To ease the transition from a dimly lit room to one of higher illumination, intermediate lighting is required.

If light fixtures are spread far apart in corridors, they create a series of dark and light passages that cause considerable strain because of frequent adaptation from light to dark areas. Uniformity and evenness of lighting are extremely important to discourage accidents and make the environment easier to navigate.

Indirect Lighting and Glare. Indirect lighting should be used whenever possible to minimize the perception of strobing or flickering of fluorescent lamps and because a high level of illumination can be achieved without creating glare. Many studies have documented the benefits of full-spectrum lamps in terms of reducing stress levels, increasing visual acuity, reducing fatigue, and even increasing calcium absorption (see chapter 14).

Glare is one of the biggest problems associated with the aging eye. As the lens becomes more dense, light is scattered, producing sensations of uncomfortable brightness that interfere with vision. Light fixtures with clear glass bulbs (visible filaments) deteriorate the retina of elderly people. This type of lamp is common in wall sconces and chandeliers but should be avoided in favor of a frosted bulb. Continued exposure to glare elevates stress levels and places the body in a defensive mode that decreases attention span, increases loss of memory, and causes people to easily become irritated. Glare causes steps to blend together in bright sunlight and makes boundaries and edges difficult to perceive. To counteract the effects of glare, edges need to be emphasized by contrasting them with the color of the background surface.

In the interior environment, glare is pervasive. It may be either direct or reflective. Sunlight is an example of direct glare; reflective glare can be seen on tabletops, the glass covering a piece of artwork, hard-surface flooring, semi-gloss painted walls, or a myriad of other sources. Glare can be reduced by using carpeting, fabric upholstery as opposed to vinyl, shielded light fixtures, draperies or other window treatment, and roof overhangs.

Hearing

Fewer than 12 percent of those over 65 years of age have normal hearing, and between 30 to 50 percent have a hearing loss that significantly interferes with communication and relationships with others (Kalymun 1989). People tend to be less understanding and patient with individuals who suffer a hearing loss than with those who have poor vision. More men suffer hearing loss than women, presumably from the cumulative effects of environmental noise from past vocational settings.

Hearing is crucial to a sense of well-being, and an inability to hear leads to depression and causes greater social isolation than blindness (National Council on Aging as reported in Kalymun 1989). The inability to hear high-frequency sounds is the most common occurrence; therefore, for an item that chimes (doorbell, alarm, grandfather's clock), the lower the pitch of the chimes, the better. The other common hearing problem involves not being able to separate speech from background sounds. In a dining room, for example, the presence of music can make speech hard to understand. Similarly, loud mechanical sounds, noisy air conditioning, or appliances make understanding speech difficult. The inability to hear creates stress, leading to increased blood pressure, shortened attention span, headaches, and apparent loss of memory (Purdy as reported in Kalymun 1989).

The design of the environment can do much to lessen the debilitating aspects of auditory impairment. First, adequate lighting is needed to be able to see facial expressions and allow for lip reading. Next, in any rooms designed for conversation, acoustic treatments should block out background noise. Lounges should be separated from noisy areas such as the entry lobby, dining room, or crafts room. Draperies are effective in controlling high-frequency ranges. Dining rooms should not be large or have high ceilings, which compound the noise of numerous conversations and serving carts. A dining room broken into smaller, more intimate areas that can be acoustically treated would be more appropriate.

Background music creates a uniform dampening effect for the hearing impaired that blocks out characteristic sounds that identify a place such as a kitchen, card room, or lounge. Public telephones with amplification devices should be provided, and elevators should have distinctive auditory and visual cueing devices.

Tactile

Touch is an important nonverbal means of communication and is especially meaningful to individuals with visual and hearing impairments. Touching causes relaxation, decreases stress, and enhances feelings of well-being. Pet therapy, for example, has been shown to lower stress in patients recovering from heart attacks and to improve the well-being of nursing home residents. A varied and rich tactile environment is characteristic of residential settings and may help to compensate for other sensory losses.

Handrails and door pulls offer other opportunities to enhance texture. Tactile sensitivity also involves temperature. The elderly are sensitive to temperature changes and have difficulty maintaining a central body temperature (Hiatt as reported in Kalymun 1989). Care should be taken to design rooms that are free of drafts.

Taste and Olfaction

Ability to identify flavors and odors becomes less acute with increasing age. Two thirds of the capacity to taste depends upon the ability to smell (Kalymun 1989). Olfactory impairment also decreases appetite and may even make difficult detecting spoiled food or smoke.

SUMMARY

A person's perception of the world is drastically altered when multiple sensory deficits make it inaccessible. However, the quality of life and well-being of the mature adult can be enhanced by adapting the environment to compensate for these losses. Such changes will result in the individual feeling more competent and will similarly reinforce others' perception of their competence and abilities.

DESIGN GUIDELINES

In addition to the following list, refer to the suggestions in the section ''Sensory Decline'' in this chapter and *Design for Aging: An Architect's Guide* (1985).

1. Knowing what segment of the senior population is the target is critical. Market analysts can reveal the needs and desires of your market niche. The environment should be designed to accommodate aging in place.

2. Try to determine what special features are important to residents in your geographic area (e.g., front porch, view of a lake, cottages versus apartment-like entry off a common corridor, or patios).

3. The average age of residents moving into a congregate care development is 76. Although most are fairly healthy, they are comforted to know that on-site health care facilities are available. However, these facilities should be totally separate from independent living units.

4. In siting the building, the architect must consider the orientation of the building so that major public spaces such as the dining room do not receive a lot of glare. Vast expanses of glass and oddly shaped windows add character to the architecture but can be a source of glare if not covered. Such windows sometimes look absurd with draperies and blinds that camouflage their strength as architectural elements.

5. In developing the shape of the building, note that residents do not want to walk outdoors when traveling from their living units to reach commons areas. Cruciform and H-shaped buildings, with a commons area in the center, are possible solutions. Flat topography is best to avoid stairs and grade changes whenever possible. The number of stairs that have to be walked and distances between living units and commons areas are often a major deciding factor in the appeal of one development over another.

6. During site planning consider issues of security as well as residents' fears of falling. In many communities the elderly are a vulnerable population, constantly concerned about being attacked or robbed, even on the grounds of their retirement community.

7. Outdoor spaces require as much thought as indoor if they are to be enjoyed and used by residents. Benches and rest areas should be provided at regular intervals, but designed in such a way as to camouflage their real purpose; they can be located where they provide a view of a flower bed or fish pond, for example. Fountains and waterfalls may not be desirable because the sound of running water can exacerbate a weak bladder.

8. Space planning and architecture should provide variety and stimulation. For those whose mobility is limited, ''observation deck'' spaces that allow residents to view others who are more active provide vicarious pleasure.

COMMONS AREAS

The public or commons area of the facility is the shared communal space outside the residents' living units. It might be a totally separate building or connected to the residential units. The most desirable apartments tend to be those that are a short distance from the commons areas and even on the same floor. The importance of short walking distances and uncomplicated travel routes cannot be emphasized enough.

The commons area can be thought of metaphorically as the ''village square.'' Variety is important in the shapes of rooms, types of furnishings, and interior design features. The types of rooms typically found in the commons area lend themselves to unique design treatments: coffee shop, soda fountain, dining room, cocktail lounge, exercise room, game and card rooms, living room lounges, barber and beauty salon, crafts rooms, sewing room, music room, theater or auditorium, billiards room, library, lobby, convenience store, and men's and women's club rooms. Other rooms include a commercial kitchen, laundry, examination room, nurse's office, and offices for the social director, manager, director of foodservices, and perhaps the groundskeeper. Outdoor areas may feature tennis courts, pool or spa, putting green, and garden plots. Assisted living units and a skilled nursing facility may also be included.

1. Coaxing timid residents out of their apartments to enjoy the companionship of others is a challenge. Good space planning and the careful juxtaposition of rooms increase the possibility of chance meetings and social interaction.

15-8

15-8 *Corridor opens onto atrium courtyard; intermittent low wall functions as a bench for rest stops; Park Lane Retirement Suites (Salt Lake City, UT)*
Architect: Ron Mullin; Interior design: Life Designs; Photographer: Michael Schoenfeld

15-9 *Entry foyer opens onto brick-paved atrium courtyard; Park Lane Retirement Suites (Salt Lake City, UT)*
Architect: Ron Mullin; Interior design: Life Designs; Photographer: Michael Schoenfeld

15-10 *Balconies of residents' units* (right), *as well as corridors* (left) *open onto beautifully landscaped atrium courtyard; Park Lane Retirement Suites (Salt Lake City, UT)*
Architect: Ron Mullin; Interior design: Life Designs; Photographer: Michael Schoenfeld

15-11 *Atrium courtyard is a festive space with street lamps, park benches, fountain, Italian market umbrellas, and a restaurant with French doors that open onto it; Park Lane Retirement Suites (Salt Lake City, UT)*
Architect: Ron Mullin; Interior design: Life Designs; Photographer: Michael Schoenfeld

15-10

15-11

2. Emphasize things that residents can do well and do not focus on limitations. To accomplish this objective, incorporate design features that address the impairments associated with aging. The key here is that these items must appear to be decorative and not reflect their true prosthetic nature. Note in Figure 15-8 that the handrail (on both sides of the corridor) appears to be a decorative molding, the corridor features an even level of illumination, concrete stoops spanning arches act as benches where residents can rest, and openings in the corridor help residents orient themselves and enhance feelings of security because usually people are close by in the enclosed patio.

3. Corridors of living units and the commons area must provide intermittent rest stops and well-marked public rest rooms.

4. Careful thought must be given to the linking of various rooms. Picking up mail is one of the highlights of the day. The mailroom should be located in or near the lobby, adjacent to a coffee shop or soda fountain so that residents can pick up their mail and share it with a neighbor over a cup of coffee.

To encourage casual social interaction further, lounges on living units, as well as in the commons area, should have a glass wall or wide opening, so that a resident can see who is inside before making a commitment to enter the space. If these openings are located en route to key areas that are visited daily, such as the mailroom, convenience store, or dining room, they are more likely to be used. Note, in Figures 14-26 and 14-27, game tables opposite the gift shop. In Figure 14-26, the wall behind the popcorn machine features a movie marquee with a display of movie posters.

5. Some industry specialists suggest using design themes reminiscent of the period during which residents were in their adolescence or early adult years. This idea might be successful for a theme restaurant, cocktail lounge, or game room.

6. Residents especially like to congregate in the main lobby to await visitors, the mail carrier, or a ride, or just to watch the bustle of activity typical of this area (Fig. 15-9).

7. The retirement complex featured in Figures 15-8, 15-10, and 15-11 incorporates a number of excellent features: balconies of living units permit observation of activity in the courtyard below; the courtyard also serves as a wayfinding landmark for orientation; the courtyard is enclosed but filled with natural light and an abundance of trees and plants; brick pavers, park benches, fountain

streetlamps, and Italian market umbrellas convey a feeling of the outdoors and allow this space to be used even during winter; an elegantly designed restaurant with French doors (Fig. 15-10) opens onto the courtyard; large window boxes outside living units allow residents to tend a garden and see fresh flowers; residents can see who is in the courtyard from their apartments, and the courtyard provides natural light to residential corridors.

8. A small lounge or place for residents to sit should be provided just outside the dining room. Dining is one of the social highlights of the day; residents often arrive early and like to congregate in the foyer until they are seated (Fig. 15-12). The lounge may have small, decorative lockers (with open fretwork doors) recessed into a wall to provide a place for residents to store bottles of liquor and snacks. Glasses and ice would be available at a self-service bar.

9. Dining rooms should be broken into smaller units if possible in order to provide more intimacy and to avoid the acoustical problems inherent in large rooms (Fig. 15-13). Dining rooms designed with the ambience of a fine restaurant make dining more of a special event (Fig. 15-14).

10. Built-in buffets are sometimes used for self-serve breakfast and buffet meals (Fig. 15-15). Depending upon the age and overall health of the resident population, buffets may or may not be appropriate. Balancing a tray while walking to a table is difficult for some residents. The buffet could be an option for residents who feel comfortable using it as long as others may choose to be served at the table.

Wayfinding

Residents must be able to feel confident about finding their way around the building.

1. If all corridors look alike, residents will have trouble orienting themselves and may be timid about leaving their apartments. Landmarks or guideposts are necessary, such as a unique piece of art, an architectural element, a furniture grouping, or a view of the outdoors (Figs. 15-16 and 15-17). Elevator doors on different floors can be differentiated by a design that surrounds them. Each floor should have a large number (executed in an artistic manner) to designate it.

2. Signs are most readable if they have a dark background with white letters and use upper and lower case. Typefaces need to be large and have extra spacing between each letter in order to be

15-12 *Foyer to dining room provides an attractive space for residents to chat prior to meals; Peninsula Regent (San Mateo, CA)*

Architect: Backen Arrigoni & Ross, Inc.; Interior design: Project Associates; Photographer: Charles S. White

readable. Cataracts cause letters to blur and fragment, making them difficult to read. If the stroke of the letter is wide and the typeface is a style devoid of flourishes, with sufficient contrast, many more people will be able to read the signs.

3. Corridors can be thought of as neighborhood streets. They should not be too narrow and may be broken up with occasional niches that accommodate a bench or cluster of furniture for residents to rest.

4. At ends of residential corridors, natural light may be pleasant, as long as the window does not provide too much brightness or glare. If it does, walking toward it will be the equivalent of walking into a large searchlight.

15-13 *Formal dining room is divided into several intimate spaces and features indirect lighting, vaulted ceiling, and elegant furnishings; Peninsula Regent (San Mateo, CA)*

Architect: Backen Arrigoni & Ross, Inc.; Interior design: Project Associates; Photographer: Charles S. White

15-14

15-15

15-14 *Elegant dining room of Bugatti Bar and Bistro resembles a fine restaurant in decor; Peachwood Inn/ Borden Court (Rochester Hills, MI)*
Concept: Arbor Corporation, Horace D'Angelo; Architecture and interior design: Hobbs & Black Associates, Inc.; Photographer: © Beth Singer

15-15 *Main dining room has a casual elegance, carefully designed lighting, and a built-in buffet server; La Posada at Park Centre (Green Valley, Tucson, AZ)*
Architect: Englebrecht and Griffin; Interior design: Life Designs; Photographer: Edward Rosenberger

15-16 *Library reading room is set in a thicket of bamboo and other luxuriant foliage; The Gables at Old Farm Forest (Farmington, CT)*
Architect: Childs Bertman Tseckares & Casendino Inc.; Photographer: Hutchins Photography (Watertown, MA)

15-17 *Main lobby space features high ceiling, festive banners, and plants tucked into soffits; La Posada at Park Centre (Green Valley, Tucson, AZ)*
Architect: Englebrecht and Griffin; Interior design: Life Designs; Photographer: Michael Schoenfeld

15-16

15-17

Furniture

The selection of furniture is based more on functional considerations than aesthetics.

1. Furniture should contrast with the floor so that individuals with poor depth perception can separate the object (the chair) from the background (the floor). This goal can be accomplished by contrasting the furniture frame or the upholstery with the color of the floor. On dining tables, plates and glasses should contrast with the tablecloth color.

2. In lounges, furniture should be arranged to encourage socialization, which generally means placing seating at right angles. Groupings should not be oriented to large expanses of glass to avoid the discomfort caused by glare.

3. Furniture should be carefully selected to have high seats, extra-firm filling, and arms. Overstuffed sofas that are low and deep are inappropriate and hard for residents to get out of. Provide some seating that allows elevation of the feet.

4. In furnishing a dining room, allow more room than normal around tables for pushing chairs in and out and also for wheelchair accessibility.

Interior Finishes

The selection of finishes must be based on a thorough understanding of the aging person's sensory deficits.

1. Mark, with contrasting color, changes in plane such as stairs, doors, and ramps, both indoors and out. Consider the use of the recessed stair lights used in theaters.

2. Avoid indiscriminate contrast in floors purely for aesthetic purposes because such contrasts can appear to be steps.

3. Carpeting should be low pile and, if not directly glued to the floor, may have a thin, dense pad. The double-stick method of carpet installation, in which a thin, dense pad is glued to the floor and the carpet glued to the pad, would be appropriate.

4. Avoid height differences at transitions between materials such as ceramic tile and carpeting or carpeting and wood floors, or at door thresholds. Such problems can be avoided by feathering out the floor to equalize the difference gradually.

5. In selecting a color palette, think about the age segment of the consumer population and remember which colors are the first to fade as visual acuity deteriorates.

Lighting

Lighting design is particularly important to prevent injury resulting from falls.

1. Provide even illumination at the floor plane.

2. Increase illumination where corridors intersect.

3. Use indirect lighting wherever possible because it allows a high level of illumination without producing glare.

4. Consider the position or height of lighting, with respect to glare, for wheelchair users.

5. Maintain a 3-to-1 ratio between the brightness of walls, furniture, and other reflecting surfaces in a space. For example, the following recommended reflectance values provide this ratio for the tasks of writing on white paper or eating from white dinnerware (both with about 80 percent reflectance) and thereby reduce fatigue and eyestrain (*Design for Aging: An Architect's Guide* 1985):

- *Ceilings:* Reflectances should be as high as possible (70 to 90 percent) to bring the lightness of the ceiling close to the brightness of ceiling fixtures.
- *Walls:* Reflectances should range from 40 to 60 percent.
- *Floors:* The floor is within the range of vision of a person working at a desk or table. Therefore, the floor should be relatively light—about 30 to 50 percent reflectance.
- *Furniture:* Desktops and tabletops should have light, but nonglare, finishes with a reflectance range of 35 to 50 percent. Most light wood furniture falls within this range.

LIVING UNITS

Market research indicates a preference for two-bedroom, two-bath units. A variety of apartment layouts enables residents, in theory at least, to select what best suits their needs. Additionally, it will not look like every other neighbor's apartment. Apartments clustered in 8- to 12-unit groups define a neighborhood or subcommunity within a large building.

1. The apartment entry is important. It should be recessed in a niche with a light positioned over the keyhole. Door hardware should minimize the possibility of getting locked out. A concave key cylinder allows insertion of the key by an unsteady hand. Lever hardware is essential. A shelf for packages alongside the door is a nice amenity, although sometimes it is used to personalize or accessorize the apartment entry. An attractive door, perhaps with raised panels, a peephole, and a door knocker, are recommended.

2. Ample storage should be provided so that residents are not forced to part with memory-laden treasures.

3. Units should be designed to allow room for guests. Many buildings include a number of guest suites that may be reserved for visiting relatives or friends.

4. Window treatment must be of a type that can be controlled easily by arthritic hands and individuals with little grip strength.

5. Deep windowsills are appreciated for plants and displays of trinkets.

6. Glass should be insulated to prevent drafts.

7. Adjustable shelves should be provided in linen closets and elsewhere to accommodate individual needs.

8. Provide a full-length mirror on a door.

Kitchen

Kitchens need to be adaptable to the body's physiological changes as the person ages.

1. Market studies show that women 65 and over prefer a full-size kitchen with standard-size appliances, even though they probably will not use it much. Most of these women were homemakers, and their cooking ability was often a measure of their worth. Psychologically, they need to retain this identity.

2. The kitchen should be ergonomically designed to meet the needs of an aging body. One of the most important changes is that a person's center of gravity moves forward. Changes in the middle ear may also affect balance. Shelves should pull out, and the highest reach should be 65 inches. Faucets should be the single-lever type.

3. A pantry scores high marks in studies of residents' preferences.

4. A pass-through window with wooden shutters, between the kitchen and dining room, saves steps and provides a view of the living room from the kitchen.

5. Appliances should be selected to be easy to operate with large numbers that are easy to read and range controls located on the front rather than on top to eliminate having to reach over hot surfaces. The range should have a timer device that automatically turns it off after one hour. The oven

may be self-cleaning and recessed in the wall to avoid bending. Mount the microwave oven so that controls are at eye level.

6. Upper-wall cabinets should be mounted 18 inches over the countertop, rather than the standard 24 inches.

7. Countertops that are a light color produce better contrast when objects are set against them and make things easier to see. It is also easier to see when the counter is dirty.

8. Cushioned sheet vinyl is softer underfoot and warmer, which is important to people with poor circulation.

9. Kitchen cabinets should feature task lighting to reduce shadows.

10. The switch for the garbage disposal must be remote from the unit to prevent accidentally hitting it when hands are near the unit; some models are inoperable unless the safety plug is fastened into the drain opening.

11. Switches and outlets near the sink should have ground fault interrupters to prevent shocks.

Bathroom

Bathrooms must be ergonomically designed to support an aging body in order to prevent injury.

1. Bathrooms must be designed with human factors in mind. For people with impaired mobility (e.g., arthritis), provide a shower with an umbilical-type shower head that can be hand-held, plus a properly located seat. Instead of grab bars, which remind people of limitations, a decorative towel bar mounted at the proper location and secured so that it can be used as a grab bar is much more desirable.

2. The bathroom door should swing outward to provide more space inside the bathroom and make it easier to access in case of an emergency.

3. Provide a linen closet for towels inside the bathroom.

4. A recessed medicine chest is best placed on the side wall next to the sink.

5. Electrical switches and outlets near the sink require a ground fault interrupter to prevent shocks.

6. Provide a wall-mounted incandescent light fixture over the bathroom mirror to eliminate shadows in addition to an overhead fixture.

7. Provide a heat lamp in the ceiling with a timer switch.

8. Provide separate switches for the exhaust fan and overhead light so that they can be used independently.

9. Provide an emergency call switch at 24 inches above the floor, where it can be reached from the toilet or the bathtub.

10. A fiberglass tub and shower unit, with integral grab bars and a fold-down seat, is easiest to clean. It must have a slip-resistant finish. The shower control should be a single-lever type with antiscald control mounted at 48 inches off the floor.

11. The vanity counter should extend over the toilet tank to provide additional surface for toiletries.

Special Electrical Issues

Many of these issues relate to convenience; others relate to safety.

1. Electrical outlets must be a minimum of 24 inches above the floor to eliminate bending. Some prefer them at 48 inches, although they are aesthetically very noticeable at that height.

2. Provide a number of locations for television and cable in the living room and bedroom to allow options for furniture placement.

3. A wall switch at the apartment entry and at entrances to bedrooms should be connected to an electrical receptacle in order to be able to turn on a table lamp before entering the room.

4. Provide an outlet in the entry hall to allow for a lamp on a console table, if space permits.

5. Provide illuminated switches at bedrooms and bathrooms to make them easy to find at night.

6. Mount the smoke detector (wired, not battery-operated) on the ceiling outside the bedroom door. It is less likely to be tripped by kitchen smoke or false alarms in this location.

7. Think about the location of outlets to serve as night-lights between bedroom and bathroom.

8. Provide an emergency call switch close to the bed and also a switched outlet that can be used to turn off a reading lamp.

9. The bedroom telephone outlet should be on the bathroom side of the bedroom to avoid having to walk around the bed to reach it.

10. A thermostat with large numbers should be mounted at 48 inches off the floor, close to a door frame, in order to keep the wall clear for artwork and furniture.

11. Provide, for closets, overhead lights that are triggered by opening the door. Mount the rod at 60 inches for hanging long dresses.

Note: A portion of this information was adapted from Jeffrey Los (1988).

Space Planning

The most persistent flaw in congregate care living units is the lack of imagination in space planning. Even those developments that feature exquisitely designed commons areas often have the most mundane living units. By contrast, the floor plans in Figures 15-18 through 15-21, which are remarkable for their imaginative and innovative use of space, are but four of the many unique layouts offered residents of this congregate care complex.

Figure 15-18 provides a large walk-in closet off one bedroom, and the other bedroom has "shaped" walls and an open vanity and dressing area large enough to accommodate a makeup table. Figure 15-19 uses angles to great advantage to make a small apartment seem larger and more interesting. It gives the sense of a real entry hall, a good-sized kitchen with pass-through to the dining room, a deep linen closet next to the bedroom, and a den that can serve as a bedroom for overnight guests. Figure 15-20 has a large double-entry bathroom, a large walk-in closet, and a den with double doors that can be furnished as an extension of either the bedroom or the living room. The feeling of openness and "racetrack" circulation makes the apartment seem large and minimizes steps between rooms.

Figure 15-21 has an arched entry with recessed door and marble threshold. The entry hall is large enough for a console table. Note that the den has an optional wall. Without it, the den becomes part of the living room; with the half-wall (as shown in Fig. 15-22), the room is more defined but adds spaciousness to the living room and offers increased storage space in cabinets below. Note the large master bedroom. This apartment layout allows the resident a number of options for expressing individuality.

Bedrooms with built-in storage make good use of vertical space for books and display of collections (Fig. 15-23). Readers will be interested in viewing the layout of the first floor of this building (Fig. 15-24), as well as Figures 15-1 through 15-5, 15-12, and 15-13. This project is outstanding in its attention to design and detail and for its total integration of architecture and interior design.

Special Care Units

On-site health care facilities must be as beautifully designed as the commons area of residential buildings to provide a feeling of continuity (Fig. 15-25).

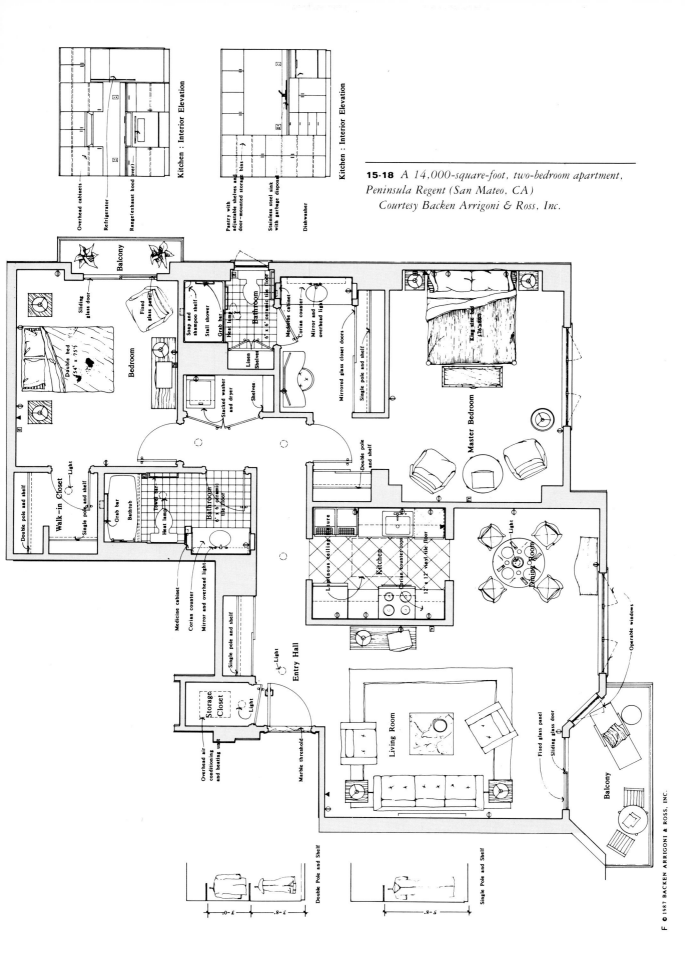

Kitchen : Interior Elevation

Overhead cabinets
Refrigerator
Range (exhaust hood over)

Kitchen : Interior Elevation

Pantry with adjustable shelves and door-mounted storage bins
Stainless steel sink with garbage disposal
Dishwasher

15-18 *A 14,000-square-foot, two-bedroom apartment,*
Peninsula Regent (San Mateo, CA)
Courtesy Backen Arrigoni & Ross, Inc.

Balcony

Sliding glass door

Fixed glass panel

Bedroom

Double bed
(54" x 75")

Soap and shampoo shelf
Grab bar
Heat lamp
Stall shower
Bathroom
6' x 6' ceramic tile floor

Linen Shelves
Shelves

Stacked washer and dryer

Medicine cabinet
Corian counter
Mirror and overhead light

Mirrored glass closet doors
Single pole and shelf

King size bed
(76" x 80")

Master Bedroom

Double pole and shelf

Walk-in Closet

Light
Double pole and shelf
Single pole and shelf

Grab bar
Bathtub
Towel bar
Heat lamp
Bathroom
6' x 6' ceramic tile floor

Medicine cabinet
Corian counter
Mirror and overhead light
Single pole and shelf

Double pole and shelf

Luminous ceiling fixture
Kitchen
Corian countertops
12" x 12" vinyl tile floor

Dining Room
Light

Operable windows

Entry Hall

Light
Light

Storage Closet

Overhead air conditioning and heating unit

Marble threshold

Living Room

Fixed glass panel
Sliding glass door

Balcony

Double Pole and Shelf
3'-0"
3'-8"

Single Pole and Shelf
5'-8"

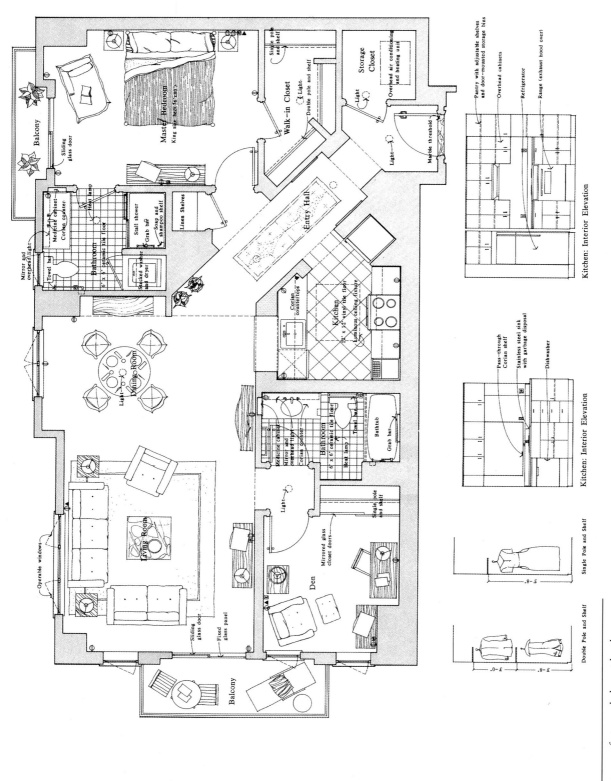

Balcony

Sliding glass door

Master Bedroom
King size bed 76x80

Single pole and shelf

Light

Walk-in Closet

Double pole and shelf

Light

Storage Closet

Overhead air conditioning and heating unit

Light

Marble threshold

Pantry with adjustable shelves and door-mounted storage bins

Overhead cabinets

Refrigerator

Range (exhaust hood over)

Kitchen: Interior Elevation

Medicine cabinet

Corian counter

Heat lamp

Mirror and overhead light

Towel bar

Bathroom

Stall shower

Grab bar

Soap and shampoo shelf

Linen Shelves

6' x 6' ceramic tile floor

Stacked washer and dryer

Entry Hall

Corian counter top

Kitchen

12" x 12" vinyl tile floor

Luminous ceiling fixture

Dining Room

Light

Pass-through Corian shelf

Stainless steel sink with garbage disposal

Dishwasher

Kitchen: Interior Elevation

Operable windows

Living Room

Sliding glass door

Fixed glass panel

Medicine cabinet

Mirror and overhead light

Corian counter

Bathroom

6' x 6' ceramic tile floor

Heat lamp

Towel bar

Bathtub

Grab bar

Light

Den

Mirrored glass closet doors

Single pole and shelf

Balcony

Single Pole and Shelf

5'-8"

Double Pole and Shelf

3'-0"

3'-8"

15-19 *A 1,020-square-foot, one-bedroom plus den apartment, Peninsula Regent (San Mateo, CA) Courtesy Backen Arrigoni & Ross, Inc.*

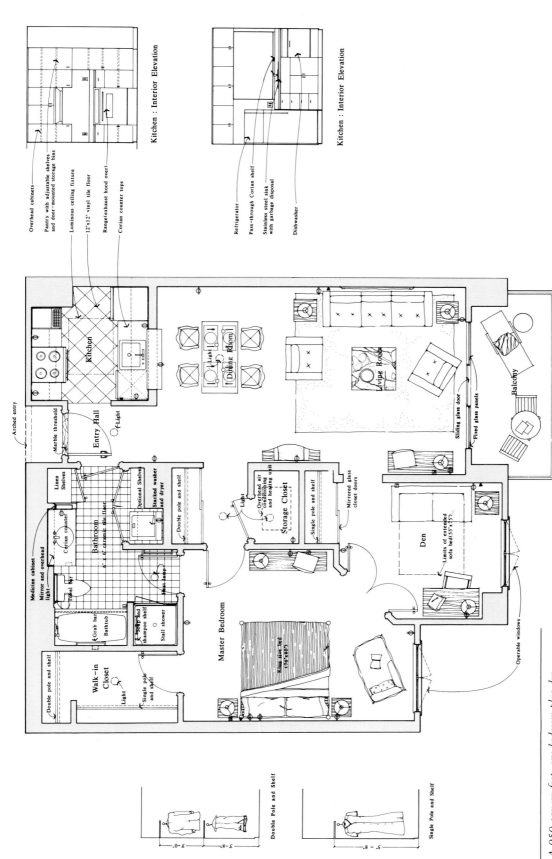

Kitchen : Interior Elevation

Kitchen : Interior Elevation

Overhead cabinets

Pantry with adjustable shelves
and door-mounted storage bins

Luminous ceiling fixture

12"x12" vinyl tile floor

Range(exhaust hood over)

Corian counter tops

Refrigerator

Pass-through Corian shelf

Stainless steel sink
with garbage disposal

Dishwasher

Arched entry

Marble threshold

Entry Hall

Light

Medicine cabinet

Mirror and overhead
light

Towel bar

Grab bar

Bathtub

Linen
Shelves

Corian counter

Bathroom
6' x 6' ceramic tile floor

Optional Shelves

Stacked washer
and dryer

Double pole and shelf

Soap and
shampoo shelf

Stall shower

Light

Overhead air
conditioning
and heating unit

Storage Closet

Single pole and shelf

Mirrored glass
closet doors

Floor lamp

Kitchen

Light

Dining Room

Living Room

Sliding glass door

Fixed glass panels

Balcony

Den

Limits of extended
sofa bed(55"x75")

Operable windows

Walk-in
Closet

Light

Single pole
and shelf

Double pole and shelf

Master Bedroom

King size bed
(76"x80")

Double Pole and Shelf

3'-0"

3'-8"

Single Pole and Shelf

5'-8"

15-20 *A 950-square-foot, one-bedroom plus den
apartment, Peninsula Regent (San Mateo, CA)
Courtesy Backen Arrigoni & Ross, Inc.*

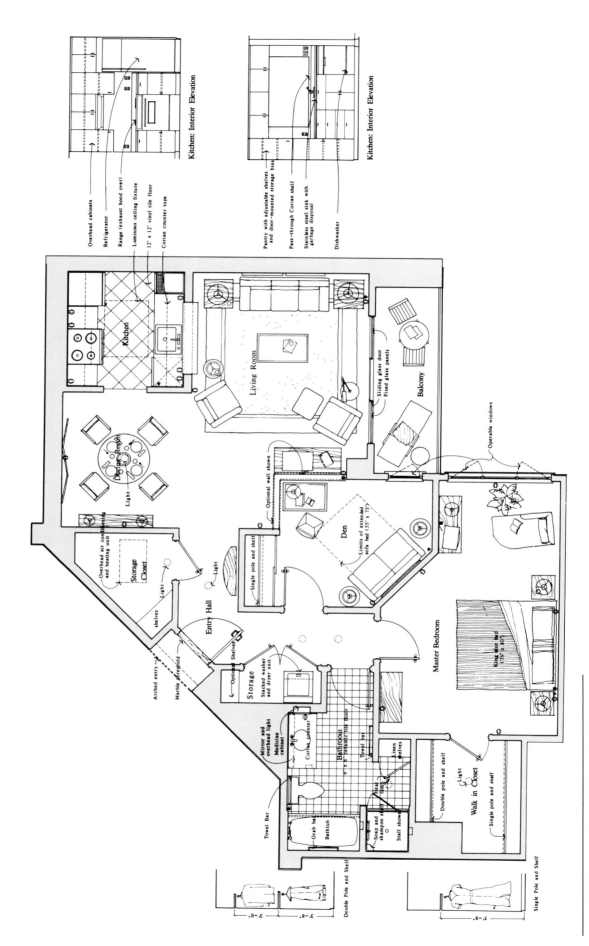

Overhead cabinets
Refrigerator
Range (exhaust hood over)
Luminous ceiling fixture
12" x 12" vinyl tile floor
Corian counter tops

Kitchen: Interior Elevation

Pantry with adjustable shelves and door-mounted storage bins
Pass-through Corian shelf
Stainless steel sink with garbage disposal
Dishwasher

Kitchen: Interior Elevation

Kitchen

Dining Region
Light
Light

Living Room

Balcony

Sliding glass door
Fixed glass panels

Optional wall shown

Operable windows

Den

Limits of extended sofa bed (55" x 75")

Overhead air conditioning and heating unit

Storage Closet
shelves
light
Light

Entry Hall

Single pole and shelf

Arched entry
Marble threshold

Optional Shelves

Storage
Stacked washer and dryer unit

Mirror and overhead light
Medicine cabinet

Corian counter

Bathroom
6 x 6 ceramic tile floor

Towel bar

Linen shelves

Master Bedroom

King size bed (75" x 80")

Double pole and shelf
Light
Walk in Closet
Single pole and shelf

Towel Bar

Grab bar
Bathtub

Heat lamp
Soap and shampoo shelf
Stall shower

Double Pole and Shelf
—3'-0"—
—3'-8"—

Single Pole and Shelf
—5'-8"—

15-21 *A 950-square-foot one-bedroom plus den apartment; note option for opening up den to view of living room; Peninsula Regent (San Mateo, CA) Courtesy Backen Arrigoni & Ross, Inc.*

15-22 *One-bedroom model unit showing den open to living area; Peninsula Regent (San Mateo, CA)*

Architecture and interior design: Backen Arrigoni & Ross, Inc.; Photographer: Dennis Anderson

15-23 *Bedroom of two-bedroom model unit, Peninsula Regent (San Mateo, CA)*

Architecture and interior design: Backen Arrigoni & Ross, Inc.; Photographer: Dennis Anderson

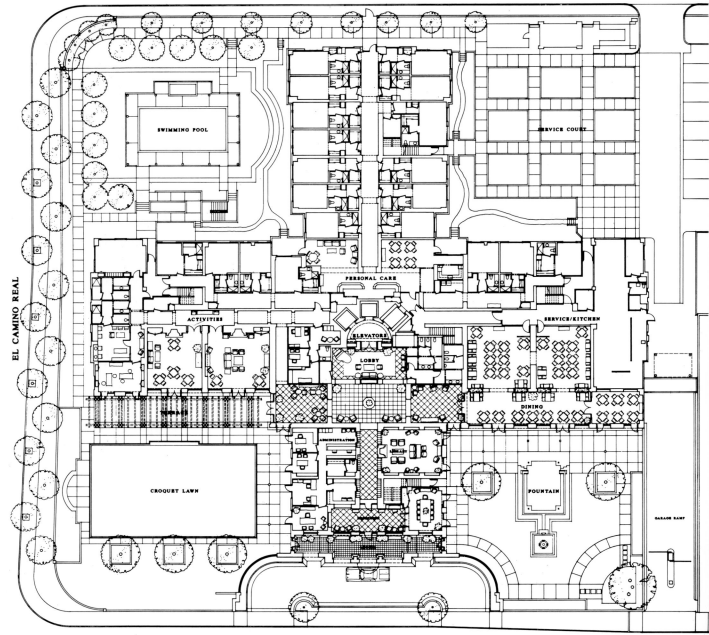

ST. MATHEWS AVENUE

EL CAMINO REAL

SWIMMING POOL

SERVICE COURT

PERSONAL CARE

ACTIVITIES

SERVICE/KITCHEN

ELEVATORS

LOBBY

DINING

TERRACE

ADMINISTRATION

LIBRARY

CROQUET LAWN

FOUNTAIN

GARAGE RAMP

BALDWIN AVENUE

15-24 *Building plan, Peninsula Regent (San Mateo,*
CA)

Architect: Backen Arrigoni & Ross, Inc.

SUMMARY

Successful design of housing for the elderly requires the combined talents of dedicated and experienced architects, developers, gerontologists, sociologists, and environmental psychologists. The need continues for a sharing of information, postoccupancy evaluations, information provided by focus groups, and surveys of what works and what does not. Those who design living environments for the elderly must, of necessity, make judgments about the pref-

15-25 *Patient room in skilled nursing facility, La Posada at Park Centre (Green Valley, Tucson, AZ) Architect: Englebrecht and Griffin; Interior design: Life Designs; Photographer: Michael Schoenfeld*

erences of those who will occupy the buildings they create, but these decisions must be based on research because the dignity and well-being of residents depend on it. People today have better health, a longer life, and greater affluence. They may spend as many years after retirement as they spent working. They are seeking an environment that provides the highest quality of life, supports them in being as independent as possible, and allows them to be productive citizens.

Author's note: Some readers may wonder why congregate care was included in a book on health care design. The reason is that this building type is very much influenced by research and an understanding of the process of aging. As such, this type of project is most often executed by health care architects and interior designers.

REFERENCES

American Association of Retired Persons. *The Gadget Book*. Washington, DC: AARP.

Bowe, F. 1988. Why seniors don't use technology. *Technology Review* August–September:35–40.

Carstens, Diane. 1985. *Site Planning and Design for the Elderly: Issues, Guidelines, and Alternatives*. New York: Van Nostrand Reinhold Co., Inc.

Design for Aging: An Architect's Guide. 1985. Washington, DC: AIA Press.

Displaying the myths. 1988. *NASLI News, III* (6), January–February:16.

Elderly housing. 1988. *Architecture California* 10(4):7–42.

Engelbrecht, M. 1986. An architect's reflections. *Contemporary Long-Term Care* August:22–28.

Franck, Karen, and Sherry Ahrentzen, editors. 1989. *New Households, New Housing.* New York: Van Nostrand Reinhold.

Grant, L. 1989. Environment and quality of life: A reaction from the perspective of social science and environmental design. *NLN Publications* November:109–24.

Hoglund, J. David. 1985. *Housing for the Elderly: Privacy and Independence in Environments for the Aging.* New York: Van Nostrand Reinhold Co., Inc.

Kalymun, M. 1989. Relationships between sensory decline among the elderly and the physical environment: Implications for health care. *Rhode Island Medical Journal* 72:163–67.

Kalymun, M., and D. Seip. 1990. Assisted living with residents in mind. *Contemporary Long-Term Care* January:25–29.

Laventhol & Horwath. 1985. *Lifecare Retirement Center Industry 1985.* Philadelphia: Laventhol & Horwath.

————. 1986a. *The Nursing Home Industry 1986: A Capsule View.* Philadelphia: Laventhol & Horwath.

————. 1986b. *The Senior Living Industry 1986.* Philadelphia: Laventhol & Horwath.

Lawton, M. Powell. 1980. *Environment and Aging.* Monterey, CA: Brooks Cole.

Lawton, M. P., and L. Nahemow. 1973. Ecology and the aging process. In C. Eisdorfer and M. P. Lawton (Eds.), *Psychology of Adult Development and Aging.* Washington, DC American Psychological Assn.

Leibrock, Cynthia. 1992. *Design* New York: Van Nostrand Reinhold.

Los, J. 1988. 50 design considerations. *Spectrum* July–August:12–15.

Moore, L. 1989. Active appeal. *Restaurant/Hotel Design* May:90–94.

National Association of Homebuilders. 1987. *Seniors Housing: A Development and Management Handbook.* Washington, DC: National Association of Homebuilders of the United States.

Newcomer, R., M. P. Lawton, and T. Byerts. 1986. Housing an Aging Society: Issues, Alternatives, and Policy. New York: Van Nostrand Reinhold Co., Inc.

Raschko, Betty Ann. 1982. *Housing Interiors for the Disabled and Elderly.* New York: Van Nostrand Reinhold Co., Inc.

Regnier, Victor, and J. Pynoos, editors. 1987. *Housing the Aged: Design Directives and Policy Considerations.* New York: Elsevier.

Rodin, J. 1986. Aging and health: Effects of the sense of control. *Science* 223:1271–76.

Senior housing. 1988. *Designers West* July:122–44.

Senior living. 1990. *Restaurant/Hotel Design* July (special issue).

Shashaty, A. 1987. 1300 unit community to offer seniors self-esteem. *Multi-Housing News* March:1.

Technology and Aging in America. 1985. Washington, DC: Office of Technology Assessment, U.S. Government.

Valins, Martin. 1988. *Elderly People.* New York: Architectural Press, Van Nostrand Reinhold Co., Inc.

Wolfe, David. 1987. *Life Satisfaction: The Missing Focus in Marketing to Seniors.* Annapolis: National Association for Senior Living Industries.

chapter 16

WAYFINDING DESIGN: A NEW LOOK AT AN OLD PROBLEM

Hospital corridors are often referred to as mazes. Traveling through them to reach a destination can be an exhausting, frustrating experience even for a hearty soul, let alone a patient or family member distressed by illness or worry. Under normal circumstances, getting lost is merely an annoyance. In a hospital context, getting lost might mean missing an appointment for diagnostic tests or not finding a child in the emergency room. Anxiety and stress can impair the ability to process information; for this reason, signs are often not read. In fact, some hospitals have so many signs that they become visual clutter rather than help to orient people.

Understanding why hospitals are so difficult to navigate is easy. Not only are they large and sprawling but also they are continually being remodeled and expanded. Each renovation seems to twist the circulation path awkwardly. Buildings whose initial geometry was symmetrical and easy to understand, after years of renovation, may have sprouted many complicated intersections. To make matters worse, hospital campuses often consist of numerous buildings linked by a series of underground tunnels, bridges, and parking structures, comprising an exceedingly complex route.

A medical center's growth often outstrips master plan projections, and buildings may be added or areas expanded without the kind of careful planning that would otherwise accompany them. New buildings, in keeping with hospital design guidelines, may have a homogeneous appearance that can be disastrous for wayfinding orientation. If buildings have little to differentiate them, visitors may have a difficult time developing significant references and a system of landmarks to help them thread their way through the hospital campus. Outdoor sculpture, a clock tower, a dramatic entrance or canopy over a building, and an accent color in window trim serve as quick points of reference for visitors.

For years major medical centers have grappled with the devastating effects of poor wayfinding, but realizing a problem exists does not make solving it any easier. Clearly, the answer was not more signage or different types of signage; each attempt to correct the problem with signage led to increased frustration. Within the last five years, however, behavioral scientists have focused their efforts on large buildings such as hospitals to explain why wayfinding is so difficult and to offer strategies for solving the problem. As with any number of great discoveries when viewed historically, the solutions often seem obvious. An understanding of the principles associated with making the environment legible changes forever a designer's approach to a project. It is a new way of seeing that informs decisions on space planning, color selection, and architectural detailing.

AN ORIENTATION SYSTEM FOR HOSPITALS

Wayfinding can be defined many ways; in this context it is an orientation or traffic management system for hospitals.

WHAT IS WAYFINDING?

Wayfinding is a general word for what people do whenever they walk or drive from one place to another. They guide themselves by points of reference called *landmarks*. They use visual cues to reinforce the path or route they are taking. They form a cognitive map or travel plan in their heads as they move along. When traveling a familiar route, they do these things subliminally without having to consciously think about them. When they are not familiar with the area, however, they consciously search for visual cues, landmarks, and signs to guide them. Wayfinding, in this sense, is an act of spatial problem solving.

A wayfinding design program consists of an integrated series of components that includes interior finishes, graphics and signage, color, artwork, lighting, and architectural detailing. Each of these components reinforces the others to form a language of visual cues that enables people to make navigational decisions at critical junctions en route to their destinations. Although these components are common to any interior design master plan, the systematic way these elements work together in main artery corridors is distinctly different.

COGNITIVE PROCESSES

Designers must understand the mental processes involved in wayfinding to be able to develop an effective program of visual cues. Travelers should be able to reach their destinations within reasonable limits of time and effort. As they progress through the space, at a number of junctures critical decisions must be made with respect to direction. Close attention must be focused on landmarks, signs, and architectural features that can be translated into a travel plan.

Wayfinding has been defined as a cognitive process comprised of three different abilities (Passini 1984b):

- *Cognitive mapping* (information gathering and imaging)
- *Decision making* (allows people to plan a strategy)
- *Decision executing* (transforms decisions into behavioral action)

The three abilities together constitute a spatial problem-solving process. People must be able to visualize the path they have to take to reach their destination and be able to formulate a travel plan in their mind's eye. As the environment becomes more familiar, people are able to recognize an increasing number of places, thereby reinforcing the path taken. First-time visitors experience the greatest difficulty. An added problem is that hospitals are visited infrequently by most people; although they may start to learn the route after frequent visits, if a long interval occurs prior to the next visit, much of this route learning may have been lost.

PARALLELS TO NAVIGATING URBAN ENVIRONMENTS

The mental processes involved in wayfinding are easy to understand if the experience of walking around the neighborhood is considered. Walking to lunch, for example, may involve proceeding three blocks straight ahead and then turning right for another two blocks to reach the restaurant. The decision to turn right is probably not precipitated by reading the name on the street sign but rather by seeing a visual cue such as a familiar shop, a large tree, or a house with a red roof that subliminally cues the traveler to turn right at the intersection. If the landmark or visual cue has been significantly altered (the red roof has been painted a different color, or the tree has been removed), the traveler perceives immediately that something is different and has to become consciously reoriented to the altered visual cue.

This phenomenon can be experienced more dramatically in neighborhoods visited infrequently. Navigation in this case depends more on remembered landmarks. For example, in a large city visited perhaps two or three times a year, the traveler may exit the freeway and search for a remembered cue, such as a bank on a street corner, in order to know where to turn. As long as the driver can carry the mental image of that bank, he or she can make a travel plan and be psychologically comfortable in the midst of traffic, noise, and many distractions. If the bank or familiar landmark has been razed and replaced by a parking lot, the traveler's wayfinding orientation is immediately disturbed, and he or she searches for a secondary landmark or reinforcement. Street signs are examples of reinforcements, but they are generally not what individuals use to orient themselves if landmarks and other significant points of reference are available.

Natural features such as mountains, city parks, and bodies of water are excellent landmarks that make outdoor navigation easy. In European cities, landmarks such as canals or rivers sometimes bisect a town into a left bank and a right bank, or a series of prominent features like bridges provide points of reference for wayfinding. Sometimes colorful paintings on the sides of buildings (Fig. 16-1) serve as a reference. Main traffic arteries are wider than

16-1 *Colorful graphic painted on exterior of building acts as a wayfinding landmark, Amsterdam, Holland*
Photographer: Jain Malkin

other streets and often have unique street lamps and other features that differentiate them. This type of visual cuing can be achieved within the main arteries of a hospital circulation system by creating landmarks and distinguishable architectural features so that where you are does not look like everywhere else. This cuing is the essence of making the building architecturally legible.

WAYFINDING FACILITATORS

Behavioral scientists generally agree on three major conditions that are prerequisites for ease of wayfinding (Garling 1984):

- *Degree of differentiation:* the degree of sameness or variation of interior spaces affects a person's ability to recognize it and use it as a landmark.
- *Visual access:* being able to see one part of the building from another or being able to see the lobby, an atrium, a bridge, or another architectural feature enables a person to maintain a point of reference (Fig. 16-2).
- *Complexity of spatial layout:* the number of possible routes to a destination and the frequency of intersections with jogs or odd angles.

Signage cannot overcome the negative effects of poor visual access, confusing space planning, and little differentiation between areas. The geometry and architecture of the building should facilitate wayfinding. As an example, separation of inpatient and outpatient circulation eliminates much confusion. Visitor elevators must be highly visible, but service elevators should be tucked away where visitors are not likely to find them. The reasons for this differentiation are that visitors are often ill at ease when they see patients on gurneys, and service elevators often carry people to "staff only" areas of the hospital that are remote from visitor destinations, leaving the visitor hopelessly lost. Instead of locating service elevators where they are highly visible and putting a sign on them cautioning "Staff Only," keeping them out of the visitor's path is more effective.

Assessment of Wayfinding

Assessment of wayfinding is a step that unfortunately is often overlooked in the design and master planning of buildings. Once the program is set and critical adjacencies have been established, planners should stand back and take a fresh look at the building from the perspective of a patient or visitor finding a way from the parking structure to the lobby and other destinations in the building.

16-2 *View from level two lobby looking down into level one; Ambulatory Services Building II, Brigham and Women's Hospital (Boston, MA)*

Architecture and interior design: Kaplan McLaughlin Diaz in collaboration with Tsoi/Kobus & Associates; Photographer: Steve Rosenthal

Successful Strategies for Linking Buildings

As a medical campus grows, orienting visitors and differentiating one building from another become increasingly difficult. Often a bridge or a tunnel is created to link these separate structures. The underground tunnel in Figure 16-3 connects new buildings to each other and to older parts of the medical center. Tunnels can be disorienting because of their length, monotonous character, and lack of reference to the horizon or the outdoors. This one, however, challenges the imagination with a futuristic design that hints at interplanetary travel. Giant mirrored periscopes pierce the ground with concrete wedges that provide unexpected views of the landscape above. The use of color is dramatic: red carpet insets cue transverse corridors, and gradations of blue on the ceiling and walls create a kind of internal horizon. Lighting has been superbly executed.

In Bishop Courtyard (Figs. 16-4 and 16-5), an atrium space has been created to link four major hospitals on the University Hospitals of Cleveland campus. Circulation between the hospitals previously involved a complicated labyrinth of corridors. In addition to simplifying circulation, the atrium provides overflow cafeteria seating, public waiting areas with views of gardens and a fountain, and a commons area for special events. The atrium courtyard has a spaceframe ceiling enclosed by multifaceted glass panels.

16-3 *Underground tunnel connects new buildings to each other and to older parts of the medical center; Detroit Receiving Hospital and Wayne State Clinics Building (Detroit, MI)*

Architecture and interior design: William Kessler & Associates, Inc., Zeidler Roberts Partnership, and Giffels Associates Inc.; Photographer: Balthazar Korab Ltd.

16-4 *New atrium courtyard connects several hospitals and provides additional commons area for dining, waiting, and special events; Bishop Courtyard, University Hospitals of Cleveland (Cleveland, OH)*

Architect: The DeWolff Partnership, Architects; Interior design: DeWolff Interiors; Photographer: William Schuemann

16-3

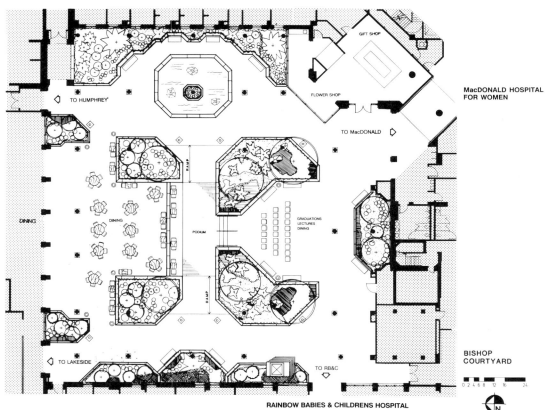

GIFT SHOP

MacDONALD HOSPITAL
FOR WOMEN

TO HUMPHREY

FLOWER SHOP

TO MacDONALD

DINING

DINING

GRADUATIONS
LECTURES
DINING

PODIUM

RAMP

RAMP

BISHOP
COURTYARD

TO LAKESIDE

TO RB&C

0 2 4 6 8   12   16   24

16-4   RAINBOW BABIES & CHILDRENS HOSPITAL

16-5 *Atrium courtyard is a light-filled, festive space with water elements and dense landscaping that can be enjoyed all year; Bishop Courtyard, University Hospitals of Cleveland (Cleveland, OH)*
    Architect: The DeWolff Partnership, Architects; Interior design: DeWolff Interiors; Photographer: William Schuemann

WHY PEOPLE GET LOST IN HOSPITALS

A number of reasons can explain why people get lost in hospitals.

Size

Hospitals are, by their very nature, large and complex buildings. Departing the hospital lobby, a network of corridors offers few landmarks. Every 40 or 50 feet a visitor is forced to make a decision to turn right, turn left, or proceed straight ahead. An incorrect turn leads deeper into the maze and results in considerable backtracking.

Incremental Expansion

Incremental expansion over a period of years often creates jogs or irregularities in corridors that were once neatly aligned, and sometimes departments that should be adjacent are not. Complex floor plans require too many choices during navigation.

Poor Space Planning

One of the most common problems, oddly enough, is that elevators are often hidden from view as in Figure 16-6. They are the hospital's main elevators, but they are not visible from the lobby. A visitor must travel down a long corridor and then enter a small doorway to reach them; every first-time visitor asks for help in finding the elevators. This situation was the aftermath of a remodeling project. The solution was to remove the non-load-bearing wall to provide visual access.

Poor space planning also creates circuitous routes with many alternative paths to a destination. No amount of signage can correct the problem (Figs. 16-7, 16-8, and 16-9). When signage fails, frustrated staff take matters into their own hands (Fig. 16-10). Sometimes the

16-6 *Elevators hidden from view cause patients and visitors to continually ask where the elevators are located*
    Photographer: Jain Malkin

16-7 *When conventional signage fails to direct people, a variety of graphic treatments, increasingly more prominent, are often employed*
    Photographer: Jain Malkin

16-6

16-8

16-7

16-8 *A series of arrows and signs directing people to the door on the left fails to accomplish the task because the destination entry lacks the prominence it should have to command attention*
        Photographer: Jain Malkin

16-9 *Main artery intersection has a variety of signs and arrows that lack consistency and create visual clutter*
        Photographer: Jain Malkin

16-9

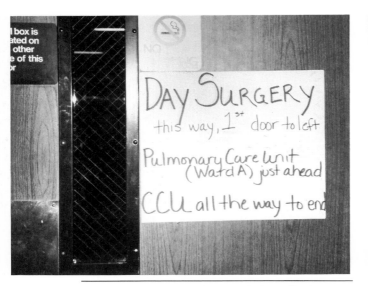

16-10 *When conventional signage fails, staff take matters into their own hands and post their own signs*
Photographer: Jain Malkin

16-11 *"Infinity" corridor has no distinguishing features or points of reference that can be remembered*
Photographer: Jain Malkin

only solution is to realign main artery corridors, even though it requires structural remodeling and moving departments.

Undifferentiated Architecture

A common problem, especially in older hospitals, is the lack of differentiation between areas. All corridors look alike in terms of architectural features and finishes, and many of them seem to go to infinity (Fig. 16-11). If corridors are devoid of any points of reference such as views of the outdoors, a garden, or a courtyard, they become disorienting. They have no landmarks, similar lighting levels, and identical finishes, and all doors look alike. Fortunately, newer hospitals often look like shopping malls with glass atria, escalators, gallery spaces, and unique architectural features that are excellent landmarks for wayfinding.

Inappropriate Nonverbal Cues

Nonverbal messages often communicate more effectively than signage. For example, a constricted opening says "keep out," even though it may be the gateway to a number of outpatient departments (Fig. 16-12). Despite the stack of signage and directional arrows, convincing patients and visitors to pass through this opening was virtually impossible because it did not look like a "destination." A similar situation is seen in Figure 16-8 where six arrows pointing to the door of Surgery Admitting failed to accomplish what a proper destination treatment could.

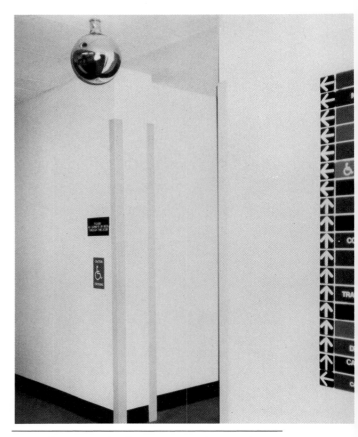

16-12 *Narrow opening is gateway to major outpatient destinations, but nonverbal cues say "keep out—staff only"; small sign on left says: "Please no gurneys or beds through this door"; in reality, pushing either of them through the opening would be impossible, but the sign is further indication that perhaps this is not a visitor destination*

Photographer: Jain Malkin

Lack of Consistency in Signage

Indiscriminate use of color or irregular sizes of signs is a common problem. In many hospitals, nonconforming signs spring up like mushrooms after a rain to cause confusion and visual clutter. Signage placement and wording is a science; engineering personnel, no matter how dedicated and well intentioned, cannot fulfill the role of a graphic designer in determining key decision points requiring signage and setting up a standards program. The signs in Fig. 16-13 have a number of colors, but whether the color has a function or is merely decorative is not clear to visitors. Impromptu signs, such as the one planted in concrete in a red-painted coffee can (Fig. 16-13), command attention but should be avoided.

Negative Effects Of Getting Lost

The negative effects of getting lost are physical, emotional, and practical. Physical effects include elevated blood pressure and irritation of a sore leg, for example, if a patient enters the wrong door and has to walk to the other side of the medical center to reach a destination. Emotional effects include anxiety, stress, and feelings of helplessness, often leading to frus-

tration and hostility. The practical aspects of getting lost include missing a doctor's appointment, having to reschedule, and taking time off from work, plus a considerable amount of staff time required to direct or lead people to their destinations.

Disorientation and stress are linked. Being spatially oriented is so important to many people that when they are lost they become anxious and panicky (Zimring 1981). Patients and visitors are not the only individuals who suffer stress when they cannot find their way; staff also have problems with wayfinding. Consider the possible casualties when a code blue response is delayed, a critical STAT lab specimen misses its destination, or the ambulance driver cannot find the emergency room.

COMPONENTS OF A WAYFINDING SYSTEM

Four principal elements help to guide people through a hospital. The function of each is to differentiate the space so that important features stand out and unimportant ones are camouflaged.

The two most obvious issues in hospital wayfinding problems are that all corridors are

16-13 *Employee suggestion boxes, bulletin boards for announcements, newspaper stands, or other accessory items Photographer: Jain Malkin*

should not be located adjacent to directional signage because they create visual clutter and are distracting

treated alike and all doors look alike. The designer needs to create a hierarchy of corridors that are differentiated by interior finishes, lighting, and color. Typically, a visitor searching for a destination must look at every door and read the name on it. In most hospitals the sign on the janitor's closet is exactly the same size as the sign marking a principal destination such as radiology. Reading the name on every door one passes is tiring. How much easier wayfinding would be if those few doors that are principal destinations were distinctly different from all other doors so that the visitor could see them from a distance.

DESTINATION

A destination is the entrance to an inpatient or outpatient department or to a waiting room, cafeteria, or other public space. It may be emphasized and differentiated from all other doors in a facility by recessing it, enhancing the lighting, adding windows for visibility, and insetting a design in the floor that can be seen from a distance (Fig. 16-14). By recessing the destination, adding planters and a bench, and stairstepping a soffit at the ceiling, an institutional hospital corridor is transformed into more of a pedestrian street.

Sometimes recessing a destination entry is not feasible because of cost or the inadvisability of structural remodeling. An effective destination treatment can be cosmetically created with applied layers of gypsum board, a wooden base, and moldings (Fig. 16-15). Remember that destinations should also have some sort of reinforcement marking the floor, as well as enhanced lighting.

MAIN ARTERY

The main artery corridor is the principal circulation spine connecting points of entry with various destinations and vertical circulation such as elevators or stairs. To define the main artery corridor, the designer needs to plot individual destinations on a floor plan. The line that connects them becomes the main artery corridor. Remaining corridors—typically two thirds of the total—"fall away" as secondary or tertiary corridors of lesser importance. In this process a complex network of corridors has become vastly simplified. Secondary or tertiary corridors

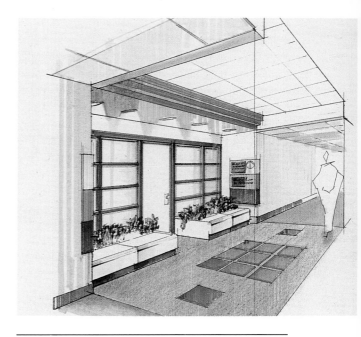

16-14 *An ideal destination entry incorporates a window, enhanced lighting, ceiling detail, prominent signage, widening of the corridor, and reinforcement set into the flooring*
Design: Jain Malkin Inc.; Rendering: Jain Malkin Inc., Greg Williams

are principally for staff, and they should be less prominent, in terms of finishes or design treatment, to discourage visitors from using them. This simplification can be accomplished by creating a "path" defined by color, finish materials, or architectural features that clearly delineates the main artery and keeps people moving almost subliminally on the "main road" (Fig. 16-16). In the H. Lee Moffitt Cancer Center (Fig. 6-11), a consistent vocabulary of design details, including a unique fabric ceiling, defines main artery corridors.

Why corridors such as the one in Figure 16-11 make wayfinding difficult may be easy to understand, but "attractive" corridors with carpeting, colorful wallcovering, and artwork can be equally problematic because color has been used indiscriminately for purposes of aesthetics and not for orientation. Typically color is introduced in finish materials, but signage, because of its intended longevity, is neutral, perhaps brown or gray. Understandably, then, the eye is drawn to color and not to the signage. Whether artwork, employee recognition boards, suggestion boxes, or signage (Fig. 16-13), simply too much is competing for the wayfinder's attention.

Anything placed in the main artery corridor should contribute to wayfinding. Art images that are purely aesthetic may be reserved for lobbies or lounges or perhaps used as landmarks, but they should not be mixed with wayfinding orientation devices. A neutral color palette in a main artery corridor allows accent colors to be used for signage, landmarks, or reinforcements in order to capture the viewer's attention (Figs. 16-16 and 16-17).

16-15 *Destination treatment consists of applied materials in order to make entry more prominent. Kaiser Permanente Medical Center·(San Diego, CA)*

Interior design and wayfinding design: Jain Malkin Inc.; Wayfinding images and signage: The Aesthetics Collection; Artist: Mario Uribe; Photographer: Sandra Williams

16-16 *Main artery corridor, University Hospital, The University of Michigan (Ann Arbor, MI)*

Architect: Albert Kahn Associates, Inc. Architects and Engineers; Wayfinding design consultant: Janet Carpman; Photographer: Balthazar Korab Ltd.

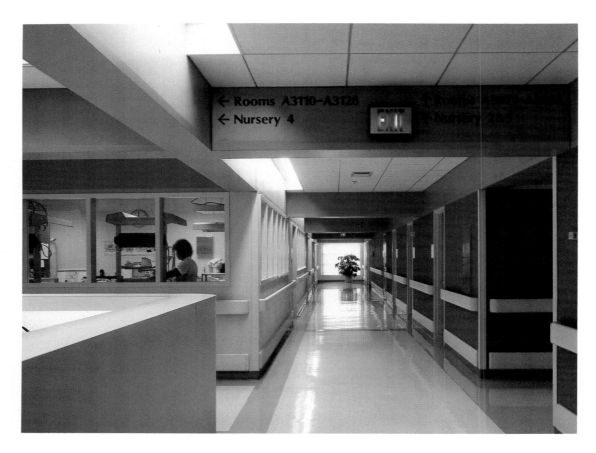

16-17 *Nursing unit has large, easy-to-read signage and identifiable accent stripe for ease of orientation; Methodist Hospital of Indiana (Indianapolis, IN)*
    Architecture and interior design: Smith, Hinchman & Grylls Associates, Inc.; Photographer: Balthazar Korab Ltd.

LANDMARK

A landmark is a highly memorable image that can be used as a point of reference when giving directions, and one that would be recalled by the exiting first-time user or the repeat visitor. Landmarks serve as organizers that are linked together through the establishment of a path; they play an important role in subdividing routes into separate segments of information (Golledge, Smith, and others 1985). A clock tower, for example, is a feature that makes identifying an individual building on the hospital campus easy (Fig. 16-18). Indoors, landmarks may be a set of elevators, a view of a courtyard or garden, a view of exterior sculpture, an atrium, another unique architectural feature (Fig. 16-19), or a highly memorable work of art that anyone would recognize, having once passed it. Passini

(1984a) observes that traveling on routes demands that people recognize, but not recall (remember), environmental features; recognition is easier than recall.

Mechanisms of Attention

Mechanisms of attention allow people to focus on what is pertinent in the environment. One mechanism of attention is based on interest, and the other, based on effort, is called into play when interest is lacking (James as reported in Kaplan and Kaplan 1983). Patterns of attention based on interest are called *involuntary attention*. A child drawn to a display in a candy store is an example. *Voluntary attention*, however, is defined as requiring effort, such as may be demanded in paying attention to traffic signals.

Following signs to a destination in a hospital requires voluntary attention and great mental effort. The more distraction in the environment (visual clutter, noise), the more effort is required to block it and focus on the tasks at hand, which causes mental fatigue. According to Kaplan and Kaplan (1983, 106), ''There is a sense of declining effectiveness and rising frustration as one's purposes are repeatedly shunted.'' The cumulative effect of this type of

16-18 *Clock tower is an excellent wayfinding landmark; Schaefer Hall, Miami Jewish Home and Hospital for the Aged at Douglas Gardens (Miami, FL)*
    Architect: Perkins Geddis Eastman; Photographer: Perkins Geddis Eastman

16-19 *A consistent vocabulary of architectural details are used in public circulation corridors for ease of wayfinding; Methodist Hospital of Indiana (Indianapolis, IN)*
    Architecture and interior design: Smith, Hinchman & Grylls Associates, Inc.; Photographer: Balthazar Korab Ltd.

fatigue, according to a number of studies, reveals itself in considerable irritability hours after the experience has occurred.

The implications of this information for wayfinding are:

- Principal circulation corridors should be free of irrelevant distractions and contain only visual cues necessary for wayfinding.
- Signage, when paired with art images, may be more effective in commanding attention by virtue of having combined it with an element interesting enough to be noticed involuntarily.

Selection of Art Images

The selection of art images to be used as wayfinding landmarks must be based on a thorough understanding of wayfinding principles. The criterion is that the image be conspicuous enough to be noticed and recognized by most people, regardless of stylistic preferences or ability to

appreciate art. According to Kaplan and Kaplan (1983), people are selective in what they perceive and in what information they attend to; some stimuli have such high salience that ignoring them requires considerable effort.

Appropriate themes might include regional landmarks that are immediately familiar to most visitors, photographic realism (Figs. 16-20 and 16-21), or any of a number of themes. The gymnasts used in the main artery of a large family practice clinic are a successful art image because anyone having passed it would clearly have noticed it and be able to use it as a wayfinding device when returning to the lobby (Fig. 16-22). Note the absence of visual clutter in the form of extraneous signage. Signs are placed overhead, where they are most noticeable; they have high contrast, large letters, and giant arrows. The signage is a reinforcement to other wayfinding elements such as the carpet border that delineates the main artery corridor. The boy

16-20 *Carefully selected photographs of people may be highly memorable and serve as excellent wayfinding landmarks when combined with directional signage; St. Joseph Mercy Hospital (Pontiac, MI)*
   Graphics: Quartus Photo Design Systems; Photographer: Margaret Peterson

16-21 *Landmark uses photograph image with perspective to draw visitors' attention to directional signage panel; The Good Samaritan Hospital of Santa Clara Valley (San Jose, CA)*
   Interior design and wayfinding design: Jain Malkin Inc.; Rendering: Jain Malkin Inc., Greg Williams; Photo image: Ron Christensen

16-22 *Highly memorable art images in corridor leading to family practice clinic, Kaiser Permanente Clinic (La Mesa, CA)*

Interior design and wayfinding design: Jain Malkin Inc.; Art images: The Aesthetics Collection; Photographer: John Christian

on the jungle gym is an example of a landmark image placed at a critical intersection (Fig. 16-23). It is an appropriate theme for a pediatrics clinic and a visually strong image that is easy to remember.

Landmark images, placed at critical intersections where people have to make decisions, can be directional in nature. For example, a color photograph of a boat dock might be used at the end of a long corridor to draw people straight ahead to a panel that contains directional information (Fig. 16-21). If most visitors are supposed to turn right, a photo image could be selected with a strong orientation to the right. Without even reading the signage, many people would turn right, especially if other visual cues reinforce a right turn. For example, the modular panels that comprise the landmark image can be arranged in a composition that stairsteps to the right; a carpet border can similarly stairstep

16-23 *Landmark image at critical intersection is highly memorable; signage is large and uncluttered; Kaiser Permanente Clinic (La Mesa, CA)*
    Interior design and wayfinding design: Jain Malkin Inc.; Art images: The Aesthetics Collection; Photographer: John Christian

16-24 *Art images can be directional in nature to subliminally lead people to a destination without resorting to signage and arrows; Kaiser Permanente Clinic (La Mesa, CA)*

Interior design and wayfinding design: Jain Malkin Inc.; Art images: The Aesthetics Collection; Photographer: John Christian

to the right. Note, in Fig. 16-24, how a series of images can lead people to a destination without relying on signage or arrows, in this case to a pediatrics department.

PAIRING DISSIMILAR OBJECTS

Research has shown that people tend to remember dissimilar things that are paired together or seen out of context. Such wayfinding images might include the theme of zoo animals and sports, as in Figures 16-25a and 16-25b. From a practical standpoint, landmark panels should be modular in order to accommodate a number of existing conditions and obstructions such as wet standpipes, and in order to be able to add additional signage panels as needed (Fig. 16-26).

REINFORCEMENTS

Reinforcements are additional supporting elements that reassure wayfinder that he or she is on the right path. The carpet inset in front of a destination, for example, is a reinforcement, as are signage, directories, lighting, and certain

16-25a Modular landmark panel incorporates signage; theme based on combining dissimilar objects, in this case, zoo animals and sports; Kaiser Permanente Medical Center (San Diego, CA)

Wayfinding design: Jain Malkin Inc.; Wayfinding images and signage: The Aesthetics Collection; Artist: Mario Uribe; Photographer: Sandra Williams

types of secondary artwork. Research has shown that directional signage is more effective when reinforced with a visual image (Fig. 16-26).

Signage

Less is definitely more when specifying signage. A mistake many hospitals make is listing every possible room and destination beyond that signage panel. Studies have shown that people generally do not read a directional sign panel with more than seven destinations listed. Thinking of wayfinding in terms of an airport traffic management system is helpful. The main

16-25b Landmark theme based on combining dissimilar objects, zoo animals and sports: Koala bear and golf clubs; Kaiser Permanente Medical Center (San Diego, CA)

16-26 *Modular landmark combines signage with imagery of local architectural landmarks. Kaiser Permanente Medical Center (San Diego, CA)*
    Interior design and wayfinding design: Jain Malkin Inc.; Wayfinding images and fabrication: The Aesthetics Collection; Photographer: Sandra Williams

artery corridor can be thought of as an airport concourse where travelers are dropped off at successive destinations along the way (Fig. 16-27). Destination listings are large and overhead; they carry people to the next drop-off point, where information for further destinations is listed. According to Passini (1980–81), a person deals with one problem or subtask at a time in a sequential fashion; information overload may result from presenting too much information at one time.

Destinations should be ranked in terms of volume of traffic in order to prioritize them; only the most important should be listed on major directional signage. Wayfinding design will never be effective for 100 percent of all visitors. If the system can enable just 60 or 70 percent of visitors to find their way to their destinations independently, a great benefit will have been achieved (Fig. 16-28). "Staff only" destinations should not be listed on major signage panels.

At busy artery intersections, directional signage should be uniform and consistent both in size and color and mounted to a background

panel to give it more prominence (Figs. 16-29 and 16-30). This type of treatment avoids the visual confusion seen in Figure 16-9. The vocabulary of design details that has been developed for wayfinding treatments should be scrupulously followed throughout the facility so that visitors can recognize it immediately.

INTEGRATION WITH THE MASTER PLAN

Interior design master plans do little to help people find their way. They assure that, over time, phased renovations will have a cohesive look, and they make it easier for facility managers to select finishes without having to engage a designer. Materials are selected on the basis of aesthetics, cost, and code requirements.

A wayfinding design system uses many of the same elements (color, finishes, and artwork) used in typical interior design master plans, but that is where the similarity ends. Color, texture, and compositions of line and form must be applied in a highly disciplined fashion in order to enhance wayfinding. Implementing wayfinding design in main artery corridors is all but impossible without redoing the finishes. One of the benefits of a wayfinding orientation system is that it provides a structure for implementing an interior design master plan, at least in the public areas of a facility.

16-27 *Main artery corridor is attractive and uncluttered, allowing wayfinders to focus on prominent signage overhead; University Hospital, The University of Michigan (Ann Arbor, MI)*

Architect: Albert Kahn Associates, Inc. Architects and Engineers; Wayfinding design consultant: Janet Carpman; Photographer: Balthazar Korab Ltd.

16-28 *Distinctive vocabulary of architectural details that announces destinations is combined with large, easy-to-read, uncluttered signage; Methodist Hospital of Indiana (Indianapolis, IN)*

Architecture and interior design: Smith, Hinchman & Grylls Associates, Inc.; Photographer: Balthazar Korab Ltd.

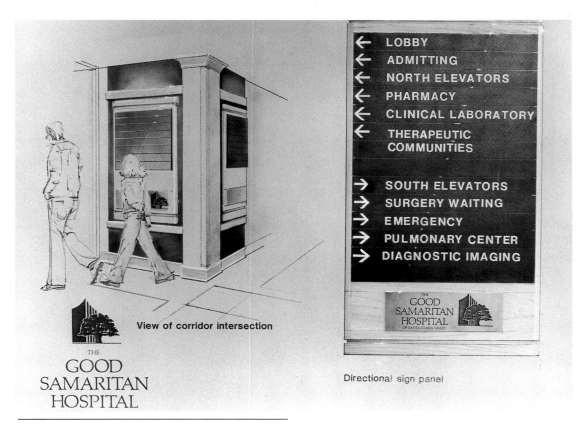

View of corridor intersection

THE
GOOD
SAMARITAN
HOSPITAL

← LOBBY
← ADMITTING
← NORTH ELEVATORS
← PHARMACY
← CLINICAL LABORATORY
← THERAPEUTIC COMMUNITIES

→ SOUTH ELEVATORS
→ SURGERY WAITING
→ EMERGENCY
→ PULMONARY CENTER
→ DIAGNOSTIC IMAGING

THE
GOOD
SAMARITAN
HOSPITAL
OF SANTA CLARA VALLEY

Directional sign panel

16-29 *Main artery intersection demands a well-defined area for placement of directional signage; The Good Samaritan Hospital of Santa Clara Valley (San Jose, CA)*
    Interior design and wayfinding design: Jain Malkin Inc.; Rendering: Jain Malkin Inc., Greg Williams; Photo image: Ron Christensen

16-30 *Main artery intersection demands a well-defined area for placement of directional signage*
    Wayfinding design concept: Jain Malkin Inc.; Rendering: Jain Malkin Inc., Greg Williams

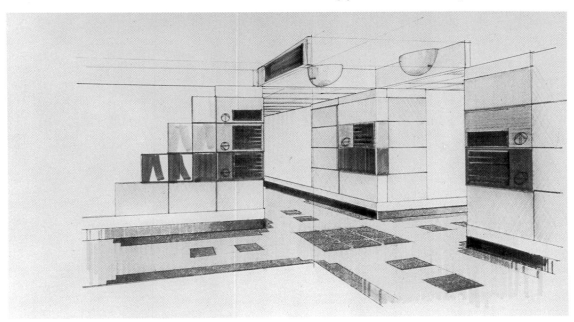

CASE STUDY

The main artery corridor in Figure 12-17 features a neutral background with color reserved for carpet insets and overhead signage that spans the corridor. Entries to destination waiting areas have glass to permit visual access, and destinations are announced by two open arch forms at the ceiling in addition to a "recessed" column detail. Note that the wooden baseboard and trim are carried throughout main artery corridors, but the baseboard changes to a different material when it leaves the main artery. These kinds of subliminal visual cues keep people moving in the main artery without being distracted by transverse corridors. Walls are uncluttered by signage or artwork; art may be viewed inside waiting rooms where it is not distracting to travelers trying to find their destinations. This corridor is part of the Brigham and Women's Hospital Ambulatory II building. Other

photos of this project are featured in chapter 12.

When this building was designed, the need to connect the various buildings on the medical center campus became apparent. A circulation spine called the Pike now connects all buildings on the Brigham and Women's Hospital campus (Fig. 16-31). The Ground Pike is one story below grade and gives access to the lower level of the Ambulatory II building (Fig. 12-13). The Main Pike, a quarter of a mile in length, is on grade and connects to the first floor of Ambulatory II (Figs. 12-11, 12-12, and 16-31). All destinations coming off the Pike have the same design vocabulary: a pair of wooden doors is recessed in a niche, and signage is highlighted by lighting. Note that the background is neutral (Fig. 16-32), and color is reserved to highlight key points of information. Nothing exists in the main artery (the Pike) that does not contribute to wayfinding orientation.

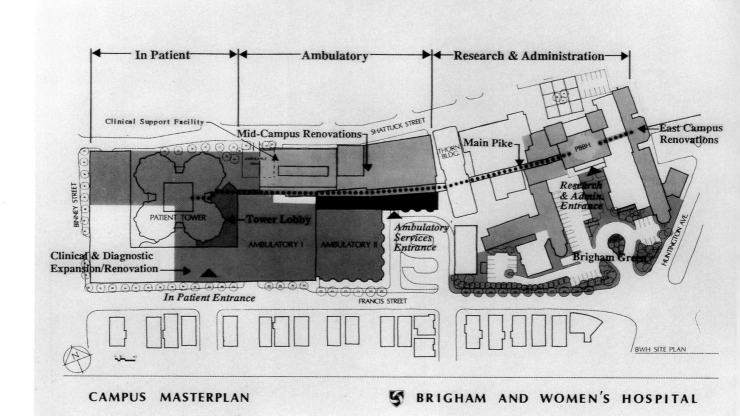

CAMPUS MASTERPLAN ⬩ **BRIGHAM AND WOMEN'S HOSPITAL**

16-31 *Master plan illustrating how Main Pike connects existing and new buildings; Brigham and Women's Hospital (Boston, MA)*

Courtesy Tsoi/Kobus & Associates, Inc.

16-32 *Main Pike corridor is easily recognized for purposes of wayfinding because of its consistent vocabulary of architectural details, neutral color palette, destination entry design, and clear, easy-to-read signage; Ambulatory Services Building II, Brigham and Women's Hospital (Boston, MA)*

Architecture and interior design: Kaplan McLaughlin Diaz in collaboration with Tsoi/Kobus & Associates, Inc.; Photographer: Sam Sweezy

THE DESIGN PROCESS

The steps in developing a wayfinding program are these:

- Site visits and photo survey of existing conditions
- Programming and interviews with key staff
- Review of architectural master plan

- Review of floor plans and plot destinations according to volume of traffic
- Development of vocabulary of design elements compatible with budget, regulatory codes, structural conditions, and maintenance objectives
- Coordination with architect and engineers (note existing obstructions, required lighting, and code issues)
- Engagement of art consultant (to develop landmark images)
- Engagement of graphics and signage consultant

The architectural floor plan of both new and existing buildings must be carefully analyzed as the first step in the wayfinding design process in order to determine if major wayfinding problems can be corrected by removing a wall, relocating a door, or eliminating a visual barrier. In some cases structural changes are the only way to solve a problem. Barnes Hospital in St. Louis had major wayfinding problems that, upon analysis, could be solved only by realigning the main artery corridor, which necessitated moving several large departments and involved considerable structural renovation. Additionally, Sverdrup Architects realized that 80 percent of visitor traffic was between the first and second floors, which choked the elevator. The solution was to add an escalator between those two floors to unburden the elevator and to move the lobby to the first floor. Wayfinding analysis begins with the space plan, and only after major issues have been resolved does it involve the creation of landmarks and reinforcements such as signage to help guide people. Major wayfinding problems have no quick-fix solutions.

SIGNIFICANT RESEARCH

One of the earliest studies in environmental cognition was done by Kevin Lynch (1960), who discovered that people tend to organize their cities in terms of five elements: memorable *landmarks, paths* people follow, *nodes* where paths cross, *edges* of neighborhoods, and socially or physically defined *districts*. Lynch and others have emphasized the importance of well-defined paths and distinctive landmarks to make the environment legible. Lynch's concepts are considered a milestone in environmental cognition theory. Whereas Lynch emphasized the importance of physical features

in his study of the city, another architect, David Appleyard (1969), emphasized environmental meaning as an important element in being able to recall an image.

Gerald Weisman (1981) suggests that wayfinding in buildings is affected by four design elements: perceptional access (visual access or being able to see where one is going), visual differentiation, signs, and architectural legibility.

Tommy Gärling (Gärling, Book, and Lindberg 1986) in Sweden has produced a great deal of research on the subject of spatial orientation and wayfinding. Romedi Passini (1984b), at the University of Montreal, did his doctoral dissertation on wayfinding in architecture. He equates wayfinding with spatial problem solving. His book is a comprehensive review of historical antecedents, recent research, and thought-provoking commentary on all aspects of wayfinding, from design of maps to analysis of wayfinding problems in well-known public buildings, including discussions of the efficacy of signage.

Although a number of environmental psychologists and planners had been researching and studying wayfinding for several years, not until Carpman, Grant, and Simmons published their landmark study in 1984 did wayfinding come to the attention of hospital planners and designers. This team of researchers was the first to study why people get lost in hospitals. In preparation for building the University of Michigan replacement hospital, they devised the Patient and Visitor Participation Project to test various hypotheses, such as appropriate spacing of signs, most effective type of you-are-here maps, terminology, and optimal floor and room numbering schemes. The results of their research were published in *No More Mazes* (1984) and in *Design That Cares* (1986), which also includes a number of helpful illustrations and wayfinding design guidelines.

SUGGESTIONS

These tips will make a wayfinding system more effective.

- Avoid jargon in signs. For example, most people know what radiology is, but may not understand "diagnostic imaging."
- Differentiate relevant signs from unimportant ones.
- Locate signs with consistency throughout the

facility; consistent placement allows the visitor to predict signage locations.

- Landmarks with written labels are more effectively remembered than landmarks without labels (Evans, Fellows, and others 1980).
- Elevator lobbies should be highlighted so that they can be seen from a distance. A large-scale carpet inset, unique lighting, and special wall treatments accomplish this goal.
- Place signs at every intersection or change in visual cues to reassure travelers that they are still on the correct path. When the route has no major decision points, studies have shown that signs should be placed every 150 to 200 feet (Carpman, Grant, and Simmons 1984).
- The designation of floors below grade level can cause confusion. Carpman's research showed that labels of *Sub 1* and *Sub 2* gave the user the clearest point of reference.
- The relationship among floors in different buildings can cause confusion. Avoid having the third floor of one building linking with the fifth floor of another (Carpman, Grant, and Simmons 1984).
- ''You-are-here'' maps at lobbies and critical points can help people understand the spatial layout of the building, provided certain guidelines are followed. Carpman, Grant, and Simmons (1984) found that a perspective bird's-eye view was preferred over a plan view map and that an inset that showed the hospital in the overall context of the medical center campus was helpful. You-are-here maps must be oriented to face the direction of the traveler.

RESEARCH INFLUENCING WAYFINDING DESIGN

Studies have demonstrated that people differ in the methods they employ to find their way around, based on their personal experiences, personality traits, and perceptional cues. One group relied heavily on signs, and the other relied on an understanding of the spatial properties of the setting. Designers must supply enough cues to satisfy both types of users (Passini 1984b).

A study executed to learn if certain stimuli (color and form) are remembered automatically proved that considerable effort is required to remember color, but that no effort is needed to remember position (whether an image occurs on the right or left, up or down, for example).

Pictures were more readily recalled than words. The implication is that the average person (as compared with designers, who are always aware of color) does not notice or remember color unless it is associated with form, such as a red apple (Park and Mason 1982). Therefore, color coding of various departments may not be as effective a wayfinding aid as establishing a ''form'' symbol.

In a study of a large institutional building, in which all the walls were monochromatic beige, a group of subjects had difficulty in wayfinding. After accent walls were painted, another group of subjects found understanding the building much easier. The implication is that monochromatic walls create an undifferentiated maze that can be disorienting. Accent walls serve as orientation aids as long as the colors are easy to distinguish from one another (Evans, Fellows, and others 1980).

Some of the most interesting wayfinding studies have been done on specific buildings such as the Dallas–Fort Worth airport and Boston City Hall (Zimring 1981). Both of these facilities have been associated with numerous incidents of psychiatric disturbance linked to spatial disorientation. This disorientation was shown to make people angry and hostile. Similarly, in an evaluation of the Arts and Architecture Building at the University of Illinois Chicago Circle campus, the circulation pattern is alleged to have upset the orientation of everybody who used the building. Many studies have reported that users actually became panicked when they were lost in large buildings, in subways, and in hospitals.

A study demonstrated that traumatically head-injured persons are impaired in discrimination learning and memory retention (Goldstein and Oakley 1986). They showed a preference for color over form dominance, which is a regression to a type of information processing typical of an earlier developmental stage. Dementia, in general, caused a preference for color dominance over form. The implication, in designing for special patient populations (rehabilitation units, skilled nursing facilities), is that wayfinding aids—perhaps—should emphasize color over form.

SUMMARY

Wayfinding is an enormously complex subject involving problem solving, cognition, percep-

16-33 *Landmark images are highly memorable and have enhanced lighting. Kaiser Permanente Medical Center (San Diego, CA)*
Interior design and wayfinding design: Jain Malkin Inc.; Wayfinding images and signage: The Aesthetics Collection; Artist: Mario Uribe; Photographer: Sandra Williams

tion, information processing, memory, and spatial cognition. Although I attempted in this chapter to simplify concepts and possible solutions, a million-square-foot medical center with linkage to several other buildings, plus several parking structures, involves a highly complex wayfinding system. At this scale additional techniques such as establishing ''color neighborhoods'' may be necessary to provide a sense of place.

To assure success, it must be understood that wayfinding is a dynamic process and that a wayfinding orientation system must be periodically updated. The program will be worthless unless staff ''buy into'' the concept, have a rudimentary understanding of why it works, and are trained to know how to give directions well. Staff should routinely be rotated through an in-service training program. Last, visitors must understand how to use the system by way of a brochure or guide handed out at the information desk.

Now that the negative effects of poor wayfinding have been well documented, it is the obligation of every socially responsible health care designer to address these issues. Certainly people prefer environments in which they can make sense of what they perceive (Fig. 16-33). If orientation aids are hard to understand they will be ignored or avoided; people are motivated to achieve clarity, and designers must facilitate this process.

REFERENCES

American Hospital Association. 1979. *Signs and Graphics for Health Care Facilities.* Chicago.

Appleyard, D. 1969. Why buildings are known. *Environment and Behavior* 1:131–56.

Carpman, Janet, Myron Grant, and Deborah Simmons. 1984. *No More Mazes: Research about Design for Wayfinding in Hospitals.* Ann Arbor: Patient and Visitor Participation Project, University of Michigan.

———. 1986. *Design That Cares.* Chicago: American Hospital Publishing.

———. 1990. Avoiding the hidden costs of ineffective wayfinding. *Health Facilities Management* April:28–37.

Evans, G., J. Fellows, and others. 1980. Cognitive mapping and architecture. *Journal of Applied Psychology* 65(4):474–78.

Follis, John, and Dave Hammer. 1979. *Architectural Signing and Graphics.* New York: Watson Guptill.

Gärling, Tommy. 1984. *Environmental Orientation during Locomotion.* Stockholm: Swedish Council of Building Research.

Gärling, T., A. Book, and E. Lindberg. 1986. Spatial orientation and wayfinding in the designed environment. *Journal of Architectural and Planning Research* 3(1):55–64.

Gärling, T., A. Book, and others. 1987. Memory for the spatial environment: empirical findings and their theoretical implications. *EDRA* 12:69–76.

Goldstein, L., and D. Oakley. 1986. Colour versus orientation discrimination in severely brain-damaged and normal adults. *Cortex* 22:261–66.

Golledge, R., T. Smith, and others. 1985. A conceptual model and empirical analysis of children's acquisition of spatial knowledge. *Journal of Environmental Psychology* 5:125–52.

Kaplan, Stephen, and Rachel Kaplan. 1983. *Cognition and Environment: Functioning in an Uncertain World.* Ann Arbor: Ulrich's Bookstore.

Lynch, Kevin. 1960. *The Image of the City.* Cambridge, MA: MIT Press.

Malkin, J. 1988. Knowing which way to turn. *Designers West* June: 132, 135, 136, 158.

———. 1989. Wayfinding: an orientation system for hospitals. *Progressive Architecture* November:107–8.

Park, D., and D. Mason. 1982. Is there evidence for automatic processing of spatial and color attributes present in pictures and words? *Memory and Cognition* 10(1):76–81.

Passini, Romedi. 1980. Wayfinding in complex buildings: An environmental analysis. *Man-Environment Systems* 10(1):31–40.

———. 1980–81. Wayfinding: A conceptual framework. *Urban Ecology* 5: 17–31.

———. 1984a. Spatial representations: A wayfinding perspective. *Journal of Environmental Psychology* 4:153–64.

———. 1984b. *Wayfinding in Architecture.* New York: Van Nostrand Reinhold Co., Inc.

Wayfinding: guiding the visitor through complex spaces. 1987. *Signs of the Times* October:57–76.

Weisman, G. 1981. Evaluating architectural legibility: wayfinding in the built environment. *Environment and Behavior* 13(2):189–204.

———. 1989. Designing to orient the user. *Architecture* October:113–14.

Zimring, C. 1981. Stress and the designed environment. *Journal of Social Issues* 37(1):145–71.

SUBJECT INDEX

FACILITIES INDEX